Power Programming...

Second Edition

Eric F. Johnson and
Kevin Reichard

MIS:
PRESS

A Subsidiary of
Henry Holt and Co., Inc.

Second Edition—1993

ISBN 1-55828-319-6

Printed in the United States of America.

10 9 8 7 6 5 4 3 2 1

MIS:Press books are available at special discounts for bulk purchases for sales promotions, premiums, fund-raising, or educational use. Special editions or book excerpts can also be created to specification.

For details contact: Special Sales Director
        MIS:Press
        a subsidiary of Henry Holt and Company, Inc.
        115 West 18th Street
        New York, New York 10011

Development Editor, Laura Lewin
Production Editor, Patricia Wallenburg
Copy Editor, Sara Black
Assistant Production Editor, Kevin Latham

Dedication

From Eric:

　　To Halloween, who certainly makes life more interesting.

From Kevin:

　　As always, to Penny, Sean, and Geisha.

TABLE OF CONTENTS

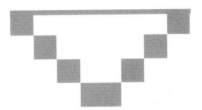

Introduction

Section I

Chapter I

Chapter 2

Chapter 3

Chapter 6

Chapter 7

Section 3

Chapter 10

Chapter 11

Chapter 12

Chapter 13

Chapter 16

Chapter 17

Section 4

Chapter 18

Chapter 19

Chapter 20

Chapter 21

Section 5

Chapter 22

Chapter 23

Chapter 24

Chapter 25

Section 6

Chapter 26

Chapter 27

Chapter 28

Chapter 29

Appendix A

Appendix B

Appendix C

Index

Introduction

This book introduces Motif programming and the Motif interface. After finishing this book, you should have a good working knowledge of the steps involved with programming Motif applications, and a good knowledge of how to put that information to practical use.

As with our previous programming books (*Professional Graphics Programming in the X Window System*, *X Window Applications Programming*, and *Advanced X Window Applications Programming*, as well as the first edition of *Power Programming Motif*), we've concentrated on the nuts and bolts of writing applications. This book is not a full reference work and will not describe in boring detail every obscure and rarely used Motif function call and data type. Instead, we hope to present the most important topics you'll need to get started writing Motif applications in the C programming language.

Almost every chapter has at least one sample Motif program; many provide two or three. We strongly believe that working source-code examples are a powerful tool in helping learn a new subject, especially one as complex as Motif. After reading this book, you should be ready to start writing

Motif applications. In fact, you'll develop a number of applications as you go through these pages.

The first edition of *Power Programming Motif* covered the transition from Motif 1.0 to 1.1. This second edition covers the move to Motif 1.2. We've updated all the example programs to work with both Motif 1.1 and 1.2. As we write this, a number of leading Motif vendors (such as Hewlett-Packard) have made the leap to Motif 1.2. Other vendors, such as Silicon Graphics, are just now making this transition. Usually these upgrades are part of a larger operating-system upgrade.

System administrators, however, tend to be a conservative bunch when it comes to upgrading operating-system versions. Because of this, many of you may still be working with Motif 1.1. Our goal is to help you write programs that are as portable as possible, to aid in your transition to Motif 1.2 and beyond. The Open Software Foundation is already working on the next release of Motif, but it will probably be a few years before this new version has been released by vendors and is widespread within the computer community. In other words, don't put off development plans because you're waiting for anything newer than Motif 1.2 to hit the streets.

WHAT IS MOTIF?

Motif was developed by the Open Software Foundation (OSF), an industry consortium that includes Digital Equipment Corp., Hewlett-Packard, and IBM. Actually, there's no such *thing* as Motif (much the same as there's no such *thing* as Open Look); instead, when someone refers to Motif, they can be referring to any one of the following:

■ A look-and-feel Style Guide for applications, based on IBM's Common User Access (CUA) guidelines, which are also implemented in OS/2 and Microsoft Windows.

■ A window manager, *mwm*, to help enforce the Style Guide.

■ A User Interface Language (UIL) interpreter, which places much of the user interface code into interpreted files.

■ A toolkit (C library) for building Style Guide-compliant applications, also called a widget set. This toolkit is based on the Xt Intrinsics, as are other toolkits like the Athena widgets and OLIT.

Motif allows you to create programs with a graphical-user interface that can run on a wide variety of computer platforms, including systems from Sun Microsystems, Hewlett-Packard, IBM, Silicon Graphics, DEC, and a slew of clone vendors who support UNIX on the 386/486/Pentium architectures.

Why Use Motif?

There are a number of reasons why you might want to use the Motif toolkit:

- Motif is one of the major interface standards in the UNIX world. In fact, the last major holdout, Sun Microsystems, finally bit the bullet and joined the Motif bandwagon.
- Motif was adopted as part of the Common Open Software Environment, or COSE, led by IBM, Hewlett-Packard, Sun, SCO, Univel, and UNIX System Laboratories.
- OSF/Motif compliance is needed for selling to many big firms and organizations.
- Using an X toolkit—any X toolkit—speeds programming.
- Motif provides nice-looking 3D effects.
- Motif fits in reasonably well with X standards with the use of window managers and resource files.

Motif and Event-Driven Programming

Motif also is part of some of the newer trends in software design and development. Included in this trend is the notion of event-driven programming.

If you're a UNIX hack venturing into the new realm of graphical computing, you're in for a major change in philosophy. (Or, as the computer pundits put it, a major *paradigm shift*, whatever the heck that means.) Traditional UNIX programming is *batch-oriented*: The user issues a command or series of commands, the program whirs along on its merry little way, and then the program generates output when the task is completed. This sequential form of computing dates back to the earliest days of computerdom, when interaction between person and computer was limited to punch cards and the like.

Today, however, most users expect more from their software. They like to be consulted about things as the tasks unwind. They like feedback if an operation takes a good amount of time. They like to feel *involved*.

Hence, the notion of event-driven programming. Instead of the batch determining the direction of the program, the user determines the direction of the program. Every Motif application is built around an event-loop, which patiently waits, looping endlessly, for the user's feedback in the form of keyboard entries, mouse movements, and so forth. These *events* direct the course of Motif applications, and your applications must be ready to accept events of all sorts.

Of course, this presents many challenges to the programmer, especially one not familiar with the structures of event-driven programming. This book will emphasize the role of event-driven programming—especially in the beginning chapters, since the notion of event-driven programming is so important to the innards of successful Motif applications—and illustrate when necessary the means needed to pull off true event-driven programming.

Why Should You Avoid Motif?

Motif is not the be-all and end-all of programming environments, and it's important that you walk in with your eyes open. Quite honestly, there are a number of trade-offs you face when you use the Motif toolkit. One of the biggest complaints about Motif is the size of even the smallest applications. Even though the size of the source code shown may be, the size of the executable program tends to the monstrous, usually in excess of 1 MB. Shared libraries help cut this size (if you're using more than one Motif program), but you still pay a hefty overhead for Motif. While RAM prices have declined for a number of years, you still should be concerned about the huge Motif overhead.

Motif and all Xt-based programs also tend to call `malloc` and other dynamic memory-allocation functions far too often. This tends to become a performance bottleneck. Xt-based programs, for example, allocate more than 50K of RAM at start-up time. For this and other reasons (mainly the high overhead), Motif programs tend to be slow.

Designed at a time when C++ or other object-oriented languages were not as widely available as today, the Xt Intrinsics include an odd object-oriented layer. Contrast this with other object-oriented toolkits like Fresco and OI, which were based on C++. Although Xt's object-oriented layer may seem like an advantage, programming with the Xt Intrinsics is a bear, especially if you want to create your own subclasses of existing widgets. So far there's no decent C++ interface to Motif or the Xt Intrinsics.

And finally, Motif and all Xt-based programs make extensive use of X resource files. X resources form a handy means to customize applications—without access to source code—but also tend to be impossible to debug. The X world has only recently moved in the direction of graphical resource editors, but it still hasn't moved far enough for our tastes.

Motif and the X Window System

Motif is based on the X Window System, a popular graphical environment. Therefore, for better or for worse, Motif has a lot in common with X.

The Motif toolkit sits on top of the Xt Intrinsics, a core part of the X Window System. Motif takes advantage of many Xt features and functions. In addition, Motif has a number of functions of its own, and Motif has its own widget set with its own look and feel. The Xt Intrinsics provide some basic mechanism for many widget sets to sit on top of (you'll find a lot of this mechanism stuff as you read the book). The Xt Intrinsics in turn sit on top of the X library, or Xlib, which is the low-level X Window application programmer's interface (API).

A higher-level toolkit like Motif does aid in the sometimes-torturous process of software development. However, the use of Motif doesn't *completely* hide all the details—which means that any serious Motif programmer should also have a good understanding of the basics of X Window programming. Luckily, there are several texts that do a good job of explaining X Window programming—and not so coincidentally, some were written by the authors of this tome. (See Appendix A for more details.)

What Is the X Window System?

The X Window System is a network-based graphical windowing system that runs on a wide variety of architectures and sits on top of virtually every operating system, including all major variants of UNIX as well as VMS, MS-DOS, Windows, Macintosh, and AmigaDOS.

X started life in MIT's legendary Project Athena, where the goal was to link a motley group of computers. Out of this project came some very important networking concepts, as well as the X Window System. Because a Project Athena goal was to provide graphical networking capabilities to a wide variety of computers, the original designers of X adopted a credo of *mechanism, not policy*. In short, this means that X provides the building blocks for the creation of graphical interfaces—it's up to others to use the blocks to provide an actual product. In the case of the Open Software Foundation, Motif became the actual product.

X is based on network technology, which means that you can run programs on one system—say, a Cray supercomputer—and display the output on the workstation or personal computer on your desk. X uses the concept of *client/server* but reverses the standard terminology (not the first time you'll see this kind of thing in a discussion of X Window and Motif). With X, the X server runs on the computer on your desk and communicates to another computer over the network, so long as that computer is also running an X server. The X server controls your physical monitor, mouse, and keyboard. In the case of our example, the X server on the Cray controls the output on your local workstation or personal computer.

However, you don't deal directly with the server, even if it's located on your local machine. Instead, you deal directly with *clients*—X speak for applications or programs. The client must communicate with X server software either running locally or over the network. Everything within X is a client—even the software that controls the windows and the general look and feel of the display, commonly known as the window manager. There are many different window managers available, but the Motif window manager (known as *mwm*) enforces the Motif look and feel.

The primary advantage of X is its near-universal adoption by all the major players in the computer industry. You can get an X implementation for just about any UNIX workstation or high-end PC.

Motif and COSE

As we were preparing this second edition, the UNIX giants got together and announced concrete plans to unite the UNIX world through the standardization of UNIX implementations. The Common Open Software Environment, or COSE, is made up of IBM, Hewlett-Packard, Sun Microsystems, Santa Cruz Operation, Univel, and UNIX System Laboratories.

Even though all specifications are not yet finalized, the group has already had a major impact on where Motif fits in the computer world. Motif was one of two primary X Window interfaces on the market; the other was Open Look, pushed by Sun Microsystems and AT&T. However, since the whole point of COSE is to enforce a certain conformity, the group decided to make Motif the primary X Window interface, as Sun Microsystems announced that development on Open Look and OpenWindows would be halted and Motif would be adopted immediately on Sun workstations. This is a major move: For many years Sun insisted that Open Look was the superior solution, and when the largest UNIX vendor makes such an argument, it's hard to fight that point of view.

However, we always maintained that the Motif/Open Look battle was totally silly, as the two were not mutually exclusive. You could always run Open Look applications on a Motif platform and vice versa, without much effort; the only difference would be that your applications could not take advantage of unique features found in the competing platform. For instance, if you want to run an Open Look application on a Motif platform, the application would not have access to pushpins, a distinguishing feature of the Open Look window manager.

For the purposes of this book, COSE has had an impact greater than the endorsement of Motif. In addition, COSE officially blessed PEX and PEXlib as the three-dimensional graphics of choice (which we'll discuss later) and the X Image Extension or XIE as the imaging standard of choice. (X was also officially anointed as the two-dimensional graphics standard of choice—a no-brainer, since every COSE member was already basing their graphical interfaces on the X Window System.) All these standards are closely tied to Motif—which is why they are receiving prominent emphasis in this second edition.

WHAT'S NEW IN THE SECOND EDITION

If you own the first edition of *Power Programming Motif*, you'll notice that the second edition is thicker. This is no accident: We kept most of that edition, updated the code, and included a slew of new material to keep the beginning Motif programmer as up to date as possible about the essentials of Motif programming. A good many of these additions were made at the behest of readers and their many helpful suggestions.

For example, we converted all the source code to ANSI/ISO standard C. In fact, we've upgraded just about every program and added twice as many new programs. If you love to read source code, this book is for you.

We now cover C++ programming with Motif, a very important trend as developers start working with object-oriented programming. We've added a chapter on the Motif clipboard. All example programs conform to the latest version of the *OSF/Motif Style Guide*. We added a chapter on internationalization, reflecting the ever-changing world of Motif applications. Few companies can afford to concentrate on just one market in our globally competitive world, and Motif 1.2 addresses that need. We added a chapter on PEXlib, covering 3D graphics with Motif. We also reorganized the book, and we think the new organization will better get you started in writing Motif applications.

Finally, we added a slew of new illustrations. How better to show the look and feel of a product than to actually show its look and feel in an illustration?

Motif 1.1 and 1.2

There have been enough changes to Motif between 1.0, 1.1, and 1.2 to raise red flags about compatibility between versions, but luckily the core changes between versions have been minimal—which means you should be able to run older code on newer systems. We've tested our example programs on a number of different platforms at a number of different release levels, both major and minor. Each new version of Motif adds major new features that you may want to take advantage of.

If you have not upgraded to Motif 1.2, we would urge that you do so. Motif 1.2 adds many essential features, such as support for internationalization and drag and drop.

As of this writing, the most widespread version of Motif is 1.1. A number of vendors, like Hewlett-Packard, IBM, and Silicon Graphics, have upgraded to Motif 1.2 with their most recent operating-system releases. Because of this, we provide example programs that should work fine (except where noted) on older Motif 1.1 systems as well as Motif 1.2 systems.

In general, you should avoid Motif 1.0, due to many problems both with Motif and the underlying Xt Intrinsics. Motif 1.1 and 1.2 are much more robust and workable for writing commercial-grade applications. Even so, each minor release of Motif, such as 1.1.4 and 1.2.2, fix a great number of bugs. Motif 1.2.2, for example, fixed over 250 bugs. Figuring out the exact minor version of Motif is virtually impossible, as each system vendor uses their own release-numbering scheme, and they usually do not tell you which minor version of Motif you're using.

ABOUT THIS BOOK

Each chapter follows the same format: a bulleted list of the chapter highlights, text, an example program, and a summary. In addition, each chapter features a shortcut at the beginning, which summarizes the chapter for those in a hurry, or for those who may already have some familiarity with Motif programming.

Section 1 introduces Motif programming, including the basic components of all Motif applications. We also cover the Motif window manager, or *mwm*. This application governs the specific Motif look and feel, and knowledge of this look and feel is vital to successful Motif applications.

Section 2 introduces the building blocks of a main application and covers such topics as the Motif main window, pull-down menus, container widgets, dialogs, strings, and text editing. These are components of virtually every Motif application, whether it be a simple file browser or a complicated electronic-publishing package.

Section 3 covers many of the nasty details under the hood of Motif applications. A large chunk of this section covers the Xt Intrinsics: Even though Motif is a higher-level toolkit, knowledge of the underlying low-level Intrinsics is also very important. This section also includes a new chapter on PEX and PEXlib—an important three-dimensional tool that will be an important part of Motif programming now and in the future.

Section 4 explains what is meant by *well-behaved* applications, and what you need to do to make your code coexist peacefully with other applications. This includes coverage of window managers (after all, *mwm* is merely another application), the Motif clipboard (which is a totally new chapter), and drag and drop (new in Motif 1.2). We also continue our coverage of the *OSF/Motif Style Guide*.

Section 5 includes translation tables, error handling, online help, and advanced menus.

Section 6 tackles the cutting-edge issues facing Motif programmers today: internationalization (a hot topic in the software-development world), C++ (another hot topic in the computer world), performance enhancements, and converting Open Look applications to Motif applications.

Finally, a series of appendices covers such topics as sources for further information.

Typographical Conventions

Important concepts are highlighted by *italic* type. File names and paths are identified by **bold face** type.

Program code and commands to be typed into the computer are highlighted by the `monospaced` type.

What You Should Know

To get the most out of this book, you should have a background in C programming, as all the sample programs are written in C. In addition, you should have a basic familiarity with the X Window System.

What You Will Need

You'll need a computer system that runs X Window and Motif programs. In addition, you'll need a developer's kit that is composed of C programming tools, X Window libraries, and Motif libraries. We recommended the purchase of the OSF reference documentation, if it did not ship with your system.

If you cannot run X or Motif, you won't get very far, unless your idea of a good time is skimming through source code.

HOW TO REACH THE AUTHORS

We welcome your comments on *Power Programming Motif*. Please send electronic mail to kreichard@mcimail.com.

SECTION I

Introducing Motif

This section introduces the basics of Motif programming and provides short Motif programs to get you going. You'll note that these introductory chapters stretch across a large number of pages. That's because the Motif learning curve is steep. We try to introduce Motif from the point of view of software developers and concentrate on the important material.

Chapter 1 begins with a short description of the Motif window manager, known as *mwm*. Your users will be interacting directly with mwm, and so it's important that you have at least a rudimentary understanding of mwm.

Chapter 2 introduces Motif programming, beginning with a discussion of where Motif fits in the X Window universe, the differing elements that make up Motif, and how Motif makes extensive use both of widgets—user-interface components in the Motif toolkit—and the model of event-driven programming.

The section ends with Chapter 3 and a discussion of resource files, which are used both by programmers and users to control various aspects of Motif client behavior. Resources control the color of a window, the text font of the window, and so on. There are many ways to set resources in Motif, and this chapter discusses them all.

CHAPTER 1

Using the Motif
Window Manager

WHAT YOU WILL LEARN IN THIS CHAPTER:

- Motif and IBM's CUA guidelines
- The distinctive look of the Motif window manager, *mwm*
- Working with multiple windows
- Using *mwm*'s window menu
- Pull-down and pop-up menus
- The Root Menu
- *Mwm* keyboard shortcuts
- Working with the mouse

MOTIF FROM THE USERS' POINT OF VIEW

If you're programming for a certain environment, you should be familiar with that environment. But we find this simple truism to be brutally ignored in the X Window and Motif worlds—leading, unfortunately, to some rather awkward programming efforts. It's too bad these efforts could have been remedied simply by spending some time using the target environment.

Circumstances certainly do play a role in the unfamiliarity, especially for the Motif programmer who must also find time to learn about a host of other X-related programming environments that are dissimilar enough to cause disruptions (Sun, Hewlett-Packard, Silicon Graphics). Still, with the overwhelming popularity of Motif in the marketplace (which is probably why you picked up this book in the first place), it would behoove you to spend a few minutes learning the basics of the Motif window manager, commonly known as *mwm*.

When people say they are using Motif, they really mean that they are using the Motif window manager. *Mwm* enforces the style guidelines set forth for all Motif-compliant applications: pull-down menus, window menus, mouse actions, and so forth. These Motif guidelines are set forth in the *OSF/Motif Style Guide* (see Appendix A for details), but they are actually part of a larger, more comprehensive set of guidelines, as set forth in IBM's Common User Access (CUA) style. After you start playing with the Motif window manager, you may feel a slight sense of déjà vu—as if you've already used software that conforms to the CUA guidelines. You probably have: In addition to *mwm*, IBM's OS/2 and Microsoft Windows conform to CUA guidelines.

In this beginning chapter we'll cover the basics of *mwm*, and we mean the *basics*. *Mwm* is close enough to other windows environments (thanks, mainly, to adherence to CUA guidelines) that if you've ever used OS/2, Windows, or even the Macintosh you should pick up on *mwm* and what it does rather quickly. If you're already familiar with *mwm*—or the X Window System, for that matter—you can skip this introduction and move on to Chapter 2, where we begin our discussion of Motif programming.

USING MWM

First and foremost, *mwm* is a *window manager* in a literal sense. Virtually everything in Motif involves window management of some sort: opening windows, closing windows, switching between multiple windows, resizing windows, and so on. A window manager controls these actions and is chiefly responsible for the look and feel of the interface by placing frames around a window, enforcing such conventions as pull-down menus, and managing how the mouse interacts with windows. In this sense, the window manager enforces a *style*, as defined by the creators of Motif. This style is shown in Figure 1.1.

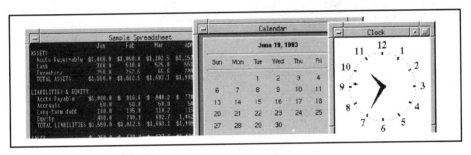

Figure 1.1   *The Motif window manager with multiple windows.*

Window managers are individualistic, and when you look at different window managers from different vendors, it's rather easy to tell the difference (as we show in Figure 1.2, an illustration of the Open Look window manager, and in Figure 1.3, an illustration of the Tab window manager). The Open Look window manager is commonly known as *olwm*, and the Tab (formerly Tom's) window manager is commonly known as *twm*.

Distinguishing Characteristics

To the user, *mwm* distinguishes itself by the *decorations* it places around the window. (As a programmer, you'll need to know about these decorations and plan accordingly.) A typical *mwm* window is shown in Figure 1.4.

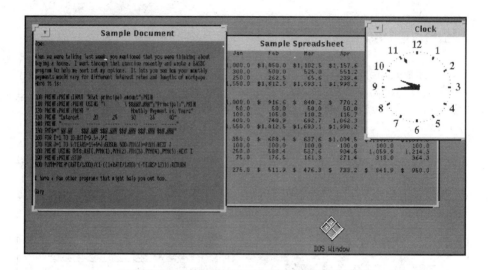

Figure 1.2 *The Open Look window manager.*

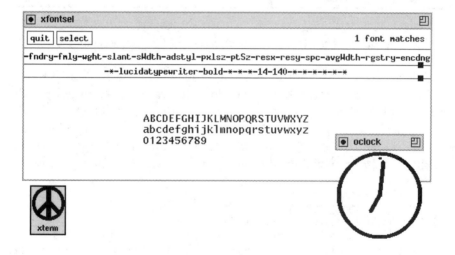

Figure 1.3 *The Tab window manager.*

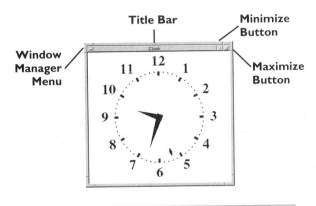

Figure 1.4 *The mwm window frame explained.*

Though they can appear to be rather subtle, there are many distinctive characteristics to a window managed by *mwm*. The top of the window is called the *title bar*, and it (not surprisingly) identifies the window by a text string called a *title*. Usually (but not always) this title is the name of the application, but this title is set up by programmers and can be changed by users who can change a resource file.

N O T E

Resource files are external files that specify much of the look and actions associated with a client—and since the window manager is itself a client, it has its own resource file. Since we're not dealing with advanced Motif usage options in this quick overview of *mwm* (and the manipulation of resource files is *definitely* an advanced option, which we cover in Chapter 3), we suggest that you consult your system documentation for more information on editing resource files or else check out our *Using X* (Johnson and Reichard, 1993, MIS:Press).

To the left of the title bar is the *Window Menu* button. All windows have a window menu, and the Motif style mandates that certain commands are always available in this menu, mostly relating to resizing and closing windows. (The Window Menu will be covered in the next section.) To the right of the title bar are two buttons. The small button, called the *Minimize* button, *iconifies* a window; that is, it replaces the current window with a small picture (or *icon* at the bottom of the screen). The large button, called the *Maximize* button, resizes the window to the largest size possible.

Projecting Three Dimensions in Two

Another noteworthy aspect of *mwm* is its three-dimensional look and feel. Windows are shaded so that they to appear to pop off the screen to trick users into thinking that they are pressing real buttons instead of using a mouse to click on an area of the screen. *Mwm* applies this three-dimensional look to all aspects of Motif: dialog boxes, command buttons, and the like, also sport 3D decorations.

MWM AND WINDOWS

As we mentioned before, the Motif window manager is first and foremost a tool for managing multiple windows.

Even though you may have multiple windows on your display, only one is *active* or has the *keyboard focus*; that is, only one accepts your direct keyboard input. This active window (also referred to as the *window with focus*) usually will be colored differently than other windows on the display (the exact color changes depend on your system configuration), and the cursor will usually change shape when placed over the active window. For instance, if you've opened up an *xterm* window (a popular X Window command-line terminal-emulation client) to perform some command-line processing on your own machine or another networked machine, the cursor will change to an I-beam cursor, indicating that text entry and editing occurs in that window.

The window with focus automatically receives all your keystrokes, no matter where the pointer is positioned. However, not every window accepts keystrokes. In the case of an application like *xeyes* or *xclock* made active for some reason or another (you might have moved or resized the window, for instance), your keystrokes will simply be ignored.

Motif follows the *click-to-type* model of window management: An active window stays active until the user explicitly clicks on another window, which then becomes the active window. (The converse of this model is *focus follows pointer*, where the active window is automatically the window underneath the mouse pointer. *Mwm* does support this option, and you can edit a resource file to implement it.)

Crowded Screens, Multiple Windows

As mentioned before, the average Motif user will probably have a multitude of windows on the screen. Accessories like *xclock* (which places a clock on the screen) are always popular; frills like *xeyes* (which opens a window containing a pair of eyes that follow the cursor movement across the screen), thanks to their novelty value, are frequently embraced by novices; and applications themselves frequently open up multiple windows on their own. Accordingly, *mwm* contains several tools for dealing with multiple windows.

The most direct tool for dealing with multiple windows has already been covered: making a window the active window. When you make a window active (as we detailed a short while ago), you will (in theory) place the active window above all other windows on the screen. (This is also true of icons, which we'll discuss a little later.) However, this rule isn't absolutely set in stone. An *mwm* resource called focusAutoRaise is usually set to automatically raise the active window to the top of the window hierarchy, and by editing a resource file you can disable this feature. We've run across at least one implementation of *mwm* where the default was *not* to raise the active window to the top of the heap—the DESQview/X implementation of *mwm*.

When you open multiple windows, you may find that they overlap a little too closely for your comfort.

In addition to the mouse, there are additional tools for manipulating windows. Some of these tools are found on the Window Menu. And while every aspect of the Window Menu isn't crucial to our discussion of *mwm*, it's still important as an example of how *mwm* handles pull-down menus.

The Window Menu

Every window under the Motif window manager features a Window Menu, as part of Motif's conformity to IBM's CUA guidelines. It can be accessed either by mouse pointer or keyboard, allowing you to manipulate a window without the use of a mouse. An explanation of how the Window menu, as shown in Figure 1.5, works will also illuminate how menus work under *mwm*.

N O T E

IBM's CUA guidelines provide only for the existence of a Window Menu, along with a few specific menu items. It is possible for a window manager (like the Microsoft Windows Program Manager, the OS/2 Presentation Manager, or *mwm*) to conform to CUA guidelines while not offering the same exact commands on the Window Menu. *Mwm*, for instance, features a Lower menu choice—a choice not found under the Microsoft Windows Program Manager.

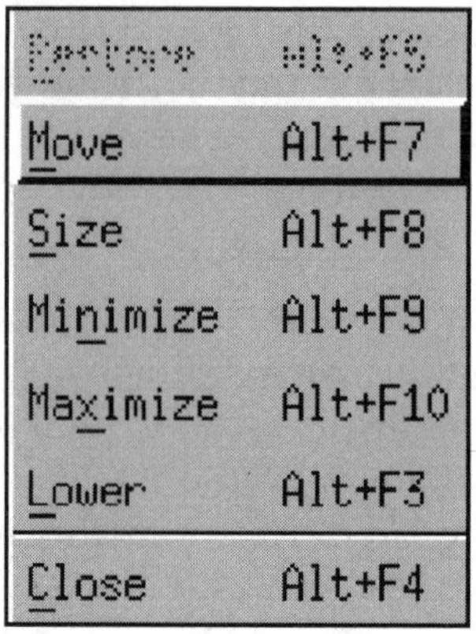

Figure 1.5 *The Window Menu.*

The Window Menu is an example of a *pull-down menu*. When you position the pointer over the button on the window frame, a menu is "pulled down" when you click on a mouse button. Pull-down menus are used throughout *mwm*—as items on a menu bar and as attachments to windows and icons. Their layout and style are proscribed by the *OSF/Motif Style Guide*, so even though you won't need to consciously create a Window Menu for your applications—the *mwm* client takes care of that—you can still learn a lot about how Motif expects you to handle windows and icons by taking a quick tour of the Window Menu.

There are seven choices on the default Window Menu:

- ■ **Restore**, which, after a window has been iconified, restores a window to its previous size.
- ■ **Move**, which turns the pointer into a cross cursor, indicating that the window can indeed be moved.
- ■ **Size**, which allows you to resize a window by dragging on the corners of the window.
- ■ **Minimize**, which replaces the window with an icon. We'll briefly discuss icons in the following section.
- ■ **Maximize**, which makes a window or icon as large as it can be.
- ■ **Lower**, which moves the active window to the bottom of the window hierarchy.

■ **Close**, which closes the window, usually quitting the program. Many X programs, like *xclock*, provide no means to quit. In cases like this, use the Close menu choice to stop the program.

You can customize these menu choices. Many vendors, such as Hewlett-Packard and Silicon Graphics, already do.

You don't need to use these menu commands to actually perform most of these actions, but the Window Menu does serve a valuable purpose as letting neophytes know exactly what can be done to windows at a given time.

Of more importance to us is the layout of the menu, particularly three things: shaded menu items, keyboard shortcuts, and the menu cursor.

You can use either the mouse pointer or the keyboard to move the menu cursor up and down the menu. Clicking the mouse button or pressing the **Enter** key activates the command highlighted under the menu cursor.

You'll notice in Figure 1.5 that the Window Menu contains shaded menu selections. When a menu selection is unavailable, it is shaded on the menu. (Some people use the term *ghosted* to indicate unavailable menu choices.)

Finally, we have *keyboard shortcuts*, or *mnemonics*, which allow you to perform routine actions from the keyboard. On our example Window Menu, for instance, there are two sets of keyboard shortcuts: Underscored letters in each command and **Alt**-*key* combinations. We'll use the Close command to illustrate each.

N O T E Specific **Alt**-*key* combinations fall under the rubric of the *OSF/Motif Style Guide*, in keeping with CUA guidelines. All CUA-compliant environments must use **Alt-F4** to close an application, for instance.

The *C* in *Close* is underscored. This tells us that if we were to press the *C* key with the Window Menu present, the Close command would be carried out.

Alternately, we have **Alt-***key* combinations, which work slightly differently. The Close command has **Alt-F4** next to it, which means that pressing first the **Alt** key and then the **F4** key will perform that command. The difference here is that the **Alt-F4** command will work in any active window *without* the Window Menu present, whereas the underscored *C* works *with* the Window Menu present.

You may be looking at the use of the **Alt** key with some wonderment, especially if your UNIX workstation lacks an **Alt** key. Despite what the menu says, the use of the **Alt** key doesn't *always* mean that the **Alt** key specifically should be used—in this case, **Alt** actually refers to the *Meta* key, which is different on each computer system.

NOTE

The Meta key is one of those wonderful abstractions in *mwm* that can be traced directly to X Window. The X Window System—and, by extension, Motif—relies heavily on hardware abstractions instead of specific physical configurations. X was designed to run on virtually any operating system and hardware configuration, and so the designers built in very few assumptions about the *exact* hardware configuration. Instead, the minimal assumption was made: That a *display* would encompass a screen (at least one screen, anyway), a keyboard, and a pointer (usually a mouse or a similar input device).

This was an especially wise policy, considering that X runs on such a wide range of operating systems, with various keyboard implementations on specific hardware platforms. No one has a key labeled *Meta* on their keyboard; instead, they have keys mapped to fill this role. On PC, SGI Indigo, and Data General Aviion keyboards, the Meta key is the **Alt** key. On Apple Macintoshes, the Meta key is the Apple key. On the Sun Type 4 keyboard, the Meta key is the diamond-shaped key next to the **Alt** key—*not* the **Alt** key itself. And finally, on Hewlett-Packard keyboards, the Meta key is the **Extend Char** key. We'll discuss the Meta key and keyboard shortcuts in more detail in Chapter 4.

Icons: Less-Than-Holy Symbols

Icons play a very important role in Motif, if only to allow you to organize the inevitable screen clutter when working in a multitasking graphical environment. If you're like us, you're going to be doing more than one task with your computer—which means opening multiple windows on your display. By iconifying a window, you replace it with a small symbol on the bottom of the screen. The application is still in your computer's memory, and depending on the application, it may or may not be actively working (for instance, some applications block input when the window is iconified). When you click on the icon, the window reverts to its full size. If you look closely at the icon in Figure 1.6, you'll see a text string on the bottom of the icon; this *label* (usually the name of the application) identifies the icon in the likely case you have multiple icons on the bottom of your display.

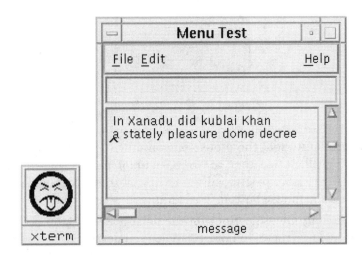

Figure 1.6   *A Motif display with a full window and an iconified window.*

The Root Menu

Pull-down menus are not the only menus supported by *mwm*. Indeed, if you've had any exposure to *mwm* whatsoever, you've already seen the other main type of *mwm* menu: the *pop-up menu*, in the form of the Root Menu.

The Root Menu serves as the focal point of most *mwm* usage. To bring up the Root Menu, press on the first mouse button (usually the left mouse button, unless you've changed your mouse-button configuration) and continue to hold it down as the menu appears, as shown in Figure 1.7.

Figure 1.7   *The Root Menu.*

As you continue to hold the mouse button down and move the mouse up and down, you'll notice that the menu cursor moves up and down the menu. When you have positioned the mouse button over the desired command, release the mouse button. The command is then enacted.

There are only five selections on the default Root Menu (as usual, you can reconfigure this menu to hold whatever you desire):

- **New Window**, which creates a new window usually running an *xterm* on the local machine. However, this isn't a universal action: With the DESQview/X version of *mwm*, New Window opens a DOS window on the local machine.
- **Shuffle Up**, which moves the bottom window in the window hierarchy to the top.
- **Shuffle Down**, which moves the top button in the window hierarchy to the bottom of the stack.
- **Refresh**, which refreshes the contents of the screen.
- **Restart...**, which quits the current *mwm* session and then immediately starts a new *mwm* session.

Again, you can customize this menu to your heart's content.

Of these commands, the only noteworthy command (for our purposes, anyway) is the **Restart...** command. The ellipses (...) tell us that there's more to this menu selection than a command: If you choose it, you'll be presented with a *dialog box*, which gives you a variety of options associated with the menu selection. A typical dialog box is shown in Figure 1.8.

Figure 1.8   *An mwm dialog box.*

MOUSING AROUND

Of course, to move around the multiple windows and icons, you need a pointing device of some sort—which *mwm* supports. Usually the pointing device is a mouse, and that's the assumption we'll make throughout this book, even though your pointing device might be a trackball, stylus, or graphics pad. As you move a mouse, a *cursor* moves around the screen. This cursor changes shape depending on its context:

■   The standard X cursor appears in the root window at all times.

■   An I-beam cursor is used in text-entry and text-editing situations. For instance, when working with *xterm*, a nongraphical X client, the Motif cursor will change into an I-beam cursor.

■   A cross cursor appears above the title bar and indicates that the window can be moved.

■   An hourglass shows that the client is performing a task and that you should sit and be patient while the task is completed.

■   Upper-left and lower-right arrows appear when the cursor is positioned over the corners of a Motif window, indicating that the window can be resized.

The cursor is actually a character in a font, which allows for better system performance. When using most Motif programs you don't need to worry about cursors, as the toolkit takes care of this for you.

Mouse Buttons

As with most graphical environments, the mouse is used for a variety of tasks. Motif supports up to five mouse buttons, although most users will be using three-button mice. Users can set mouse-button combinations by editing resource files (see the note earlier in this chapter about resource files), whereas programmers can designate specific mouse actions either through resource files or hard-coded designations—or rely on the defaults, as most programmers and users will more than likely do.

As mentioned before, X and *mwm* rely on abstractions instead of specific hardware configurations. This is also true of the pointer device, which may be a two-button mouse (many popular PC mice, such as the ubiquitous Microsoft Mouse, contain only two buttons), a three-button mouse, a multiple-buttoned mouse commonly found in the CAD world, a trackball, a pen, or a digitizing tablet. However, the assumption is that the mouse has three buttons. In the abstracted model, they are referred to as Button 1, Button 2, and Button 3. The default—since most people are right-handed—is that Button 1 maps to the left mouse button, Button 2 maps to the middle mouse button, and Button 3 maps to the right mouse button. Because of this setup, it's possible to change mouse-button mappings either through an X client called *xmodmap* or by editing a resource file (again, see the warning earlier this chapter regarding resource files).

Mouse Actions

Not all mouse buttons are created equally, of course. Most window manipulations involve the left mouse button—again, in deference to the many right-handed computer users.

The various mouse actions are as follows:

■ **Click.** Press a mouse button once and release it quickly. Various actions may call for single clicks, double clicks, or even triple clicks. This is the action that makes a window active, as discussed earlier in this section.

■ **Drag.** Press a mouse button down when the pointer cursor is positioned over an interface object (window, icon, dialog box) and continue to hold the button down while moving the mouse. This is how you move interface objects—by dragging their outlines around the screen. This is also how you resize window: by grabbing on the corner of a window and dragging accordingly.

■ **Press.** This painfully obvious option involves pressing a mouse button down and not releasing it.

■ **Release.** This painfully obvious option involves releasing the mouse button that has been pressed.

MWM VARIANTS

Many vendors, such as Silicon Graphics and Hewlett-Packard, customize *mwm* for their particular needs. These *mwm* variants, including SGI's *4Dwm* and HP's *vuewm*, generally look and act like *mwm*, but add new features, such as *vuewm*'s set of virtual desktops. Refer to your system documentation for more on these variants.

SUMMARY

Before you start programming in an unfamiliar computing environment, you should take the time to learn the basics about that environment. This chapter introduced the Motif user environment and concentrated on the Motif window manager, or *mwm*.

Mwm controls the way windows are laid out on the screen. With *mwm*, the user can move, resize, minimize, and maximize windows. Users can also quit applications using the Close menu choice from the Window Menu.

Mwm places a set of decorations around application windows. These decorations include a title bar showing the window's title, a Window Menu button, a Minimize button, a Maximize button, and a set of eight resize handles that allow you to resize the window in a number of directions.

Two types of menus dominate *mwm* usage: pull-down menus (where the user selects items from a pulled-down menu attached to a window) and pop-up menus (where the user selects items from a popped-up menu not attached to any window). The items on pull-down menus can be accessed at all times without the menu actually being pulled down, thanks to keyboard shortcuts.

Finally, we covered how *mwm* handles three mouse buttons even though there are several types of mice on the market.

CHAPTER 2

Motif Programming 101

This chapter introduces Motif programming, including:

- Introducing the X Toolkit Intrinsics
- Initializing the X toolkit
- Widget hierarchies
- Widget classes
- Creating widgets
- Setting up callback functions
- Creating an event-handling loop
- Managing widgets
- Realizing the widget hierarchy to create the windows on the display
- Starting the X Toolkit Intrinsics main event-handling loop
- Compiling and linking Motif programs

INTRODUCING MOTIF PROGRAMMING

This chapter lays out the basic structure of Motif programs. By the time you reach the end of this chapter, you will (technically) be a full-fledged Motif applications programmer. Before you go out and celebrate, though, be warned that programming Motif in the real world is much more complicated than the basics as presented here.

Quite honestly, it's not very easy to write Motif applications. This book is going to present Motif programming in as straightforward a manner as possible, but Motif and the underlying X Window System are very complex. Since we believe that the best way to learn something is to sit down and do it, we'll start out slowly with small Motif programs. Even though these programs are limited, the program code will introduce most of the basic Motif concepts you'll need.

Motif is many things. In this book, we'll treat it as a programmer's toolkit and a certain interface style (a *look and feel*, to use the popular terminology). As a toolkit, Motif builds upon the X Window System foundation that we discussed in the Introduction. Motif directly uses the Xt Intrinsics library from the X Window System—in this sense, Motif can be viewed as a widget set that sits on top of the Xt toolkit.

SHORTCUT

Quick and Dirty Motif Programming

To quickly get going with Motif programming, you first need to initialize the X Toolkit Intrinsics (also called Xt or just the Intrinsics) with XtAppInitialize. This sets up a connection between your program and the X server. Then create widgets—interface elements such as scroll bars, text-entry fields, and pushbuttons—with Motif widget creation functions like XmCreateLabel. Make the widgets visible by managing them with XtManageChild. Create the underlying X windows with XtRealizeWidget. Finally, enter the Xt main event-handling loop with XtAppMainLoop.

Putting this all together, we get a quick-and-dirty Motif "hello world" program:

```
#include <Xm/Xm.h>      /* Motif */
```

```
#include <Xm/Label.h>   /* XmLabel */

int main(int argc, char** argv)

{   /* main */
    Widget          parent;
    XtAppContext    app_context;
    Widget          label;
    Arg             args[20];
    Cardinal        n;

    /* Initialize the X toolkit. */
    n = 0;
    parent = XtAppInitialize(&app_context,
            "Ppm",                      /* app class */
            (XrmOptionDescList) NULL,/* options */
            0,                          /* num options */
            (Cardinal*) &argc,          /* num cmd-line */
            argv,                       /* cmd-line opts */
            (String*) NULL,             /* fallback res. */
            args, 0);

    /* Create a label widget. */
    n = 0;
    label = XmCreateLabel(parent, "hello", args, n);

    XtManageChild(label);

    /* make widgets real. */
    XtRealizeWidget(parent);

    /* Process events forever. */
    XtAppMainLoop(app_context);

    return 0;

}   /* main */
```

This program doesn't have a way to quit, but from it you should be able to get a good idea regarding what's in store with Motif programming. The rest of this chapter covers more about the X Toolkit Intrinsics and the basic format for all Motif programs. At the end, we'll create a slightly longer Motif program and cover how to compile and link with Motif.

The Xt Intrinsics and Motif

The Motif toolkit sits on top of the Xt Intrinsics library, which means that Motif uses many of the Xt features and functions. Motif does have a set of functions of its own, and Motif has its own widget set with its own look and feel. The Xt Intrinsics provide some basic mechanism for many widget sets (you'll find a lot of this mechanism stuff as you read about X). As such, the Xt Intrinsics provide no look and feel, so you can layer a number of X toolkits on top of Xt, as shown in Figure 2.1.

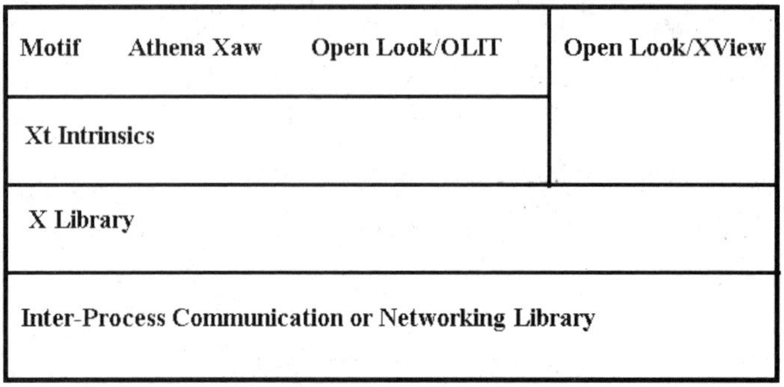

Motif Athena Xaw Open Look/OLIT	Open Look/XView
Xt Intrinsics	
X Library	
Inter-Process Communication or Networking Library	

Figure 2.1   *Xt-based toolkits.*

By layering on top of the Intrinsics, the Motif code has less work to do. This also means that all Motif applications pay for the added complexity and difficulty (and massive program size) of all Xt-based applications. You win some, and you lose some.

What Is an X Toolkit?

As we stated above, Motif is an *X toolkit*. An X toolkit is a software library of C functions aimed at speeding user-interface development under the X Window System. The whole idea is to avoid making tedious low-level calls to the X library and instead work at a higher level of abstraction. In this regard, the Motif toolkit works very well, except when you need to go beyond the toolkit—which you'll need to do for any complex application.

X Toolkit Intrinsics (Xt Intrinsics)

The Xt Intrinsics, as we discussed above, is an independent software layer that sits above the low-level X library. It provides a base for creating high-level X toolkits, like Motif, without imposing a specific look and feel. Xt presents an odd but reasonably consistent programming style.

The main concept introduced by Xt is the idea of a *widget*. Xt provides the basic concept of widgets and a set of functions for manipulating widgets but leaves it to the higher-level toolkit, also called a *widget set*, to layer on the actual look and feel. This is how both OLIT and Motif can provide different user interfaces and yet both be based on the Xt Intrinsics.

Other common widget sets include the free Athena widgets (Xaw) and the Motif/OLIT implementation, MoOLIT (available as part of UNIX System V Release 4.2). Of all the Xt-based toolkits, though, Motif is the clear winner in terms of use and software developer mindshare.

WHAT IS A WIDGET?

Since we've been bandying around the term *widget*, we should define it. A widget is a generic abstraction for user-interface components in the Motif toolkit. Widgets are used for scroll bars, pushbuttons, dialogs, and just about everything else in the toolkit. Most widgets have an associated window on the X display that holds the user-interface elements of the widget. This makes Motif programs create a great many windows on your X server.

Each widget has a C data structure that is dynamically allocated via `malloc` at creation time. This structure—which is supposed to be treated as an opaque data type—contains the widget's data attributes, called *resources*, and pointers to the functions, such as callbacks, that widgets may have. Each widget is of a certain class, and the class also defines a set of functions and resources that apply to every widget of that class.

If this looks suspiciously like object-oriented programming, you're catching on. There is a whole hierarchy of widget classes, so that a widget class like XmLabel inherits features of all ancestor classes. In this case, the label widget inherits from the Core and XmPrimitive class. Other classes, like XmPushButton, inherit in turn from the XmLabel widget class.

Normally, though, you really don't care which widgets inherit from what. What is really needed is a list of a widget's resources, including the resources inherited from ancestor widgets. You'll usually find these resource lists in the official *OSF/Motif Programmer's Reference* manual that should have come with your implementation of Motif. You'll use this manual a lot. We strongly advise you to pick up a copy of this manual if you don't yet have one. (See Appendix A, Where to Go From Here, for more information.)

Some widgets display graphics on the screen. Others serve as container widgets grouping other widgets, which are called *child widgets*.

Widget Hierarchies

There are two widget hierarchies, and they're quite different. First, the Motif widget *class* hierarchy is the tree of widget classes and how these classes are defined in terms of other widget classes. That is, the XmLabel widget class is a subclass of the primitive class (called XmPrimitive).

The second hierarchy is the hierarchy of widget *instances* you create when you program a Motif application. For example, in the program we call *first* (which we'll use as an example throughout the remainder of this chapter), we'll create a widget instance hierarchy that looks like (in an outline format):

```
* Top-level application shell, returned by XtAppInitialize.9 *
    XmPanedWindow
        * XmPushButton
        * XmLabel
```

This program-created hierarchy is a hierarchy of instances of widgets, not classes. The distinction is important.

Each widget instance in the hierarchy of instances has a parent widget, except for the top-level widget returned by XtAppInitialize. (You must start somewhere.)

This parent widget controls the layout (called the *geometry* in widget terminology) of its child widgets. Following this simple rule, there are a number of geometry-managing widgets that exist for the sole purpose of laying out child widgets. The XmPanedWindow widget, for example, lays out child widgets vertically, in panes. The XmForm widget, on the other hand, allows precise control over the placement of child widgets. (See Chapter 6 for more on these two widgets.)

Part of the key to Motif application development is understanding the top-down approach to creating interface elements. Not only are widgets arranged in a hierarchy, they must be created in the hierarchical order as well. When you're planning your applications, you'll need to choose what kind of widgets and how many you want to use. We've found it's best to start at the top and plan out the widget hierarchy, working from the top down. That makes it a lot easier to test and debug Motif applications.

Motif widgets are organized into widget classes or types from which you can choose when building your applications. (You can also write your own widgets, but this is an advanced topic.)

Throughout the rest of this book, we'll cover the most important widget classes and show you how to use Motif reference manuals to figure out the other Motif widget classes.

Widget Classes

Motif widgets fall into certain classes. The major widgets types are listed in Table 2.1 (some of the abstract classes and gadgets are skipped for clarity). The basic types of Motif widgets include managers, primitives, shells, and Xt-provided widgets.

Table 2.1 *Major types of Motif widgets.*

Widget	Function
Managers	Widgets that hold other widgets.
Primitives	Widgets that don't hold other widgets, such as a text label.
Shell Widgets	Manager widgets that interact with the window manager. This has nothing to do with UNIX shells like `csh` and `ksh`.
Xt Widgets	Provided in the base Xt Intrinsics.

Primitive Widgets

The primitive widgets are listed in Table 2.2.

Table 2.2 *The Motif primitive widgets.*

Widget	Function
`XmArrowButton`	Holds an arrow tip; used for the ends of scroll bars
`XmCascadeButton`	Used to pull down menus
`XmGadget`	Superclass for Motif gadgets (windowless widgets)
`XmLabel`	Displays a text message
	continued

XmList	Presents a list of choices
XmPushButton	Activates a callback when "pushed" with the mouse
XmScrollBar	Used for scroll bars
XmSeparator	Provides a horizontal line; used to separate menu items
XmText	Text-entry field; can be multiline or a single-line entry field
XmTextField	Single-line text-entry field
XmToggleButton	Pushbutton that holds a state (on or off); used for radio buttons

Manager Widgets

The manager widgets are listed in Table 2.3.

Table 2.3 *The Motif manager widgets.*

Widget	Function
XmBulletinBoard	Primitive manager widget; used for dialogs
XmCommand	Used to hold commands
XmDrawingArea	"Raw" window used for drawing
XmDrawnButton	Combination of XmPushButton and XmDrawingArea
XmFileSelectionBox	Used to ask the user to select a file name from a list of files
XmForm	Subclass of XmBulletinBoard with complex layout rules
XmFrame	Surrounds a widget with a 3D beveled frame
XmMainWindow	Used to hold elements of the application's main window such as the menu bar
XmPanedWindow	Lays out child widgets vertically in panes; may have sashes to separate
XmRowColumn	Lays out widgets in rows or columns, used to hold menus

continued

XmScale	A valuator widget
XmScrolledWindow	Presents a viewport onto a very large child widget

Shell Widgets

A *shell widget* is a top-level widget originally created as a child of a screen's root window. As such, the name *shell* is a bit of a misnomer. The shell provides functions to interact with window managers, which are special X programs that control the layout of top-level windows on the screen. For instance, it is the window manager that places the title bar on the top of shell windows.

The shell widgets are listed in Table 2.4.

Table 2.4   *The Motif shell widgets.*

Widget	Function
XmDialogShell	Used to hold dialogs; subclass of TransientShell
XmMenuShell	Used to hold menus; subclass of OverrideShell

Xt Classes

Motif also uses a number of Xt widgets directly, although you should note that Motif customizes these widgets. They are listed in Table 2.5.

Table 2.5   *The Xt classes.*

Class	Function
ApplicationShell	Shell returned by XtAppInitialize
OverrideShell	Holds menus
TransientShell	Used to hold transient windows, such as dialogs
TopLevelShell	Subclass of VendorShell, used for top-level windows
VendorShell	Subclass of WMShell with toolkit-specific features
WMShell	Superclass for shells that need to interact with the window manager.

Widget Standards

For each Motif widget class, there is a special function to create an instance of that class. Usually this function has the name of XmCreate*Type*, where *Type* is the type of widget you want to create. For example, XmCreatePushButton creates a pushbutton widget, an instance of an XmPushButton widget. Notice how most Motif functions and definitions start with *Xm*. (Xt functions usually begin with *Xt*.) Most widget classes have names, too, like XmPushButton for the pushbutton widget class.

There's also a global class pointer for each widget class. You need this class pointer if you use an alternate means for creating widgets, such as calling XtCreateManagedWidget (described in Chapter 4 under "Xt Widget Creation Functions"). If you call XtCreateManagedWidget, you'll need to pass the proper class pointer, which is usually something like xm*type*WidgetClass, again where *type* is the type of widget. Using the example above, the widget class pointer for XmPushButton widgets is xmPushButtonWidgetClass. (Note the lowercase *xm*.)

As you can tell, these Motif-style names can get quite long. The class pointer is usually defined in the widget's include file, in this case, <Xm/PushB.h>. In most cases, though, you won't need to worry about the widget class pointer.

Widget Include Files

For each widget, you'll normally include a widget header file, as well as <Xm/Xm.h>, the standard Motif header file. These Motif include files are normally stored in the /usr/include/Xm directory, but your system may place these files in some other location. On Hewlett-Packard systems, for example, you'll find Motif include files in /usr/include/Motif1.1/Xm or /usr/include/Motif1.2/Xm, depending on which version of Motif you're using. As of this writing, most vendors are migrating from Motif 1.1 to 1.2.

The name of the include file for a particular widget is usually the name of the widget class, except for classes with long names (as most seem to be). For example, the XmPushButton widget's include file is <Xm/PushB.h>.

Take a look at the files in /usr/include/Xm (or wherever the Motif include files are stored on your system). The listing from HP-UX 9.01, using Motif 1.2, follows:

ArrowB.h	FileSB.h	ScrollBar.h
ArrowBG.h	FileSBP.h	ScrollBarP.h
ArrowBGP.h	Form.h	ScrolledW.h
ArrowBP.h	FormP.h	ScrolledWP.h
AtomMgr.h	Frame.h	SelectioB.h
BaseClassP.h	FrameP.h	SelectioBP.h
BulletinB.h	GadgetP.h	SeparatoG.h
BulletinBP.h	Label.h	SeparatoGP.h
CacheP.h	LabelG.h	Separator.h
CascadeB.h	LabelGP.h	SeparatorP.h
CascadeBG.h	LabelP.h	ShellEP.h
CascadeBGP.h	List.h	TearOffBP.h
CascadeBP.h	ListP.h	TearOffP.h
Command.h	MainW.h	Text.h
CommandP.h	MainWP.h	TextF.h
CutPaste.h	ManagerP.h	TextFP.h
CutPasteP.h	MenuShell.h	TextFSelP.h
DesktopP.h	MenuShellP.h	TextInP.h
DialogS.h	MenuUtilP.h	TextOutP.h
DialogSEP.h	MessageB.h	TextP.h
DialogSP.h	MessageBP.h	TextSelP.h
Display.h	MwmUtil.h	TextStrSoP.h
DisplayP.h	PanedW.h	ToggleB.h
DragC.h	PanedWP.h	ToggleBG.h
DragCP.h	PrimitiveP.h	ToggleBGP.h
DragDrop.h	Protocols.h	ToggleBP.h
DragIcon.h	ProtocolsP.h	TransltnsP.h
DragIconP.h	PushB.h	VaSimpleP.h
DragOverS.h	PushBG.h	VendorS.h
DragOverSP.h	PushBGP.h	VendorSEP.h
DrawP.h	PushBP.h	VendorSP.h
DrawingA.h	RCUtilsP.h	VirtKeys.h
DrawingAP.h	RepType.h	VirtKeysP.h
DrawnB.h	RowColumn.h	WorldP.h
DrawnBP.h	RowColumnP.h	Xm.h
DropSMgr.h	SashP.h	XmAll.h
DropSMgrP.h	Scale.h	XmP.h
DropTrans.h	ScaleP.h	XmStrDefs.h
DropTransP.h	Screen.h	XmosP.h
ExtObjectP.h	ScreenP.h	

You'll notice a number of files, which we can divide into classifications, as shown in Table 2.6.

Table 2.6 Classifying Motif include files.

Include File	Use
whatever.h	Widget include file you use in your applications
whateverP.h	Private header file for widget *whatever*
whateverG.h	Gadget include you could use in your applications
whateverGP.h	Gadget private file

For example, the label-widget class, which we will introduce below, has four include files, as listed in Table 2.7.

Table 2.7 Motif label-widget and gadget include files.

Include File	Use
Label.h	The file we'll use in our applications
LabelP.h	The label-widget class's private header file
LabelG.h	The label-gadget class file
LabelGP.h	The label gadget's private header file

Unless you're writing your own widgets, you won't need to worry about the private include files. The *OSF/Motif Programmer's Reference* shows which include files are needed for each widget class and function. We'll also show which include files are needed for each of the example source files provided in this book and each of the widgets we use.

The Xt Intrinsics include files are normally located in /usr/include/X11, the location of all standard X include files. Except in a few cases, which we'll document later, you won't have to directly include Xt files. Instead, the Motif header files, notably <Xm/Xm.h>, will take care of this for you.

Gadgets or Windowless Widgets

Most Motif widgets create a window on your X display. A complex Motif application creates many windows, each of which uses up resources in the X Window server, as well as in your application.

As you might guess, creating these windows slows down Motif applications. To help these performance problems, the designers of Motif use a concept called *gadgets*, windowless widgets that serve to improve the performance of Motif applications, since they don't use as many system resources (both your application and the X server) as do widgets. Gadgets, if available, work much like widgets do. Unfortunately, not every widget class has a corresponding gadget class.

Each gadget class has a creation function. These functions have the same name as the corresponding widget-creation functions, but add the word *gadget*. For example, the function to create a pushbutton widget is `XmCreatePushButton`. The function to create a pushbutton gadget is `XmCreatePushButtonGadget`.

You may want to use gadgets in your applications if performance becomes an issue. Many gadgets use special gadget functions to get at their data, instead of the normal widget functions. This is something to watch out for. Since gadgets don't have their own windows, you'll have problems setting a gadget to use a different background color than its surrounding parent widget.

In addition, gadgets have received mixed reviews and may in fact be less efficient than using traditional widgets. The per-window overhead in the X server has dropped dramatically in the years since gadgets were first introduced. In fact, we usually advise software developers to stay away from gadgets, as they're more hassle than they're worth.

THE BASIC FORMAT OF MOTIF PROGRAMS

Diving right in, we're going to spend the rest of this chapter on the creation of a Motif client. Don't worry if you don't totally comprehend everything immediately, as we'll explain all these topics in more depth in later chapters. For now, we'll go over the basic format of all Motif programs and then show you a small program that follows this format.

Motif programs usually follow six basic steps:

■ Initialize the Xt Intrinsics (which also sets up the connection to the X server)

■ Create widgets

■ Set up any needed callback functions

■ Realize the widget hierarchy with `XtRealizeWidget`

■ Enter the event-handling loop

■ Loop forever—yes, forever

The *loop-forever* part is serious. Because of this, you'll need to set up at least one callback function to exit your program.

Motif Header Files

All Motif programs require the header file `<Xm/Xm.h>`. In addition, every Motif widget has its own header file, as covered in the previous section, "Widget Include Files". In the code examples throughout this book, we assume `<Xm/Xm.h>` is included.

XtAppInitialize

The first step in any Motif program is to initialize the Xt Intrinsics. The function `XtAppInitialize` does this:

```
Widget XtAppInitialize(
     XtAppContext* appcontext,  /* RETURN */
     String app_class_name,
     XrmOptionDescList xrm_options,
     Cardinal number_xrm_options,
     int* argc,       /* input/output */
     String* argv,    /* input/output */
     String* fallback_resources,
     ArgList args,    /* hard-coded resources */
     Cardinal number_args)
```

The application context is set up by `XtAppInitialize`. You use the application context, `appcontext`, in the call to `XtAppMainLoop`. The application-class name specifies a name used for looking up X resource values, which we describe in the next chapter. For this book, we use a class name of *Ppm* (short for Power Programming Motif).

For most of the parameters, you can safely pass NULL or zero. That's because XtAppInitialize offers many more options than most Motif programs need. In later chapters, we'll cover more of these options.

For now, we pass a 0 for the number_xrm_options and number_args, and NULL for xrm_options and fallback_resources. We pass no hard-coded resources in the args array.

N O T E
In X11 Release 4, the argc pointer was a Cardinal (unsigned int) pointer. In X11 Release 5, this is a normal int pointer. If you compile with both R4 and R5 and use ANSI/ISO C, you'll have to put in some code to cast to the proper type. We can finesse the problem by defining a macro for casting to the proper value, based on which release of X that we compile under. How can we tell which release of X we're using? In the include file <X11/Intrinsic.h>, the symbol XtSpecificationRelease holds this value. XtSpecificationRelease will be 4 for X11 Release 4, 5 for R5, and so on.

Even so, the following code sets up the macro ARGC_PTR to an int or Cardinal pointer as necessary:

```
#if XtSpecificationRelease > 4

#define ARGC_PTR    (int*)

#else   /* X11R4 */

#define ARGC_PTR    (Cardinal*)

#endif  /* X11R4 */
```

We can then cast the pointer argc, to the ARGC_PTR type, without worrying which version of the Xt library we're compiling under. If the compiler warnings don't bother you, you can skip this step.

XtAppInitialize In Real Use

In your code, you can call XtAppInitialize, passing mostly NULL values:

```
int main(int argc, char** argv)
```

```
{
Widget        parent;
XtAppContext  app_context;
Arg           args[20];
int           n;

n = 0;

parent = XtAppInitialize(&app_context,
         "Ppm",                     /* app class */
         (XrmOptionDescList) NULL,  /* options */
         0,                         /* num options */
         ARGC_PTR &argc, argv,      /* cmd line */
         (String*) NULL,            /* fallback res. */
         args, n);

/* ... */
}
```

SHORTCUT

Initializing Older Versions of Motif

Prior to X11 Release 4 and Motif 1.1, `XtAppInitialize` didn't exist. Since most systems now support at least these versions— or higher—of X and Motif, this normally isn't a problem.

If you are stuck with an old version of Motif, use `XtInitialize` instead of `XtAppInitialize`:

```
Widget XtInitialize(String shell_name,
     String application_classm
     XrmOptionDescRec* options,
     Cardinal number_options,
     Cardinal* argc,
     char** argv)
```

Motif 1.0 had quite a few problems, so we strongly suggest upgrading to Motif 1.1 or 1.2. If this is not possible, use `XtInitialize` and the corresponding `XtMainLoop` shown later.

Creating Widgets

There are two main ways to create Motif widgets. First, you can use the Xt-provided functions `XtCreateWidget` (and a host of variants, including `XtCreateManagedWidget` and `XtVaCreateManagedWidget`). Second, you can use the Motif-provided functions, one for each widget type, to create widgets. In most cases, this is all a matter of your preferred coding style.

There are a few exceptions, though, where it pays to use the Motif toolkit functions. Menus, dialogs, scrolled-text widgets, and other combinations have Motif front ends to a complex set of code hidden under the hood. If you use the Xt functions, you must mimic this code on your own. In those cases, we strongly urge you to use the Motif *Xm* convenience functions.

Among the built-in Motif functions is XmCreatePushButton.

XmCreatePushButton

XmCreatePushButton creates a pushbutton widget. You'll find all Motif XmCreate*Type* functions take the same parameters:

```
#include <Xm/PushB.h>

Widget XmCreatePushButton(Widget parent,
    char* widget_name,
    ArgList args
    Cardinal number_args)
```

When creating a pushbutton widget, you must pass the *parent* widget (remember that every widget—except for top-level widgets—must have a parent). The parent controls the size and location of the child widget, created by XmCreatePushButton. You also must pass the widget's name—every widget can be identified by its name. This name is important for resource-setting commands. The *args* and *number_args* parameters are the list of hard-coded resource values you want to set for the widget.

N O T E

The XmCreate*Something* functions create, but do not manage, widgets. Therefore, you must later call XtManageChild. An unmanaged widget does not appear in a window on the screen. When you manage a widget, the widget is then placed under control of its parent. Usually managed widgets are visible, but sometimes the parent sets the size and location of a managed child widget to something that you cannot see. In addition, if the parent widget isn't managed, then the child widget also won't be visible—even if the child widget is managed. Although this may seem odd, it's very useful for working with dialog windows.

The main purpose of a pushbutton widget is to call a function (a callback) when activated. A pushbutton is activated when the user presses and releases the leftmost mouse button (Button1 in X terminology) over the widget.

Xt Event Handling

Xt and Motif intercept and handle most X events, freeing your code from this responsibility. If you wish to be notified of an event, though, you can set up an event-handling *callback function* to handle an event. Motif makes heavy use of these callback functions to notify your application code when a high-level event occurs. For example, a pushbutton widget generates an *activate callback* when the user presses and releases the leftmost mouse button over it. When this happens, your function is "called back" (executed).

Setting Up Callback Functions

The Xt function XtAddCallback registers a function as a callback for a widget:

```
void XtAddCallback(Widget widget,
      String which_callback,
      XtCallbackProc callback_function,
      XtPointer client_data)
```

The *client_data* is a pointer to any extra data you want to pass to the callback function.

XtAddCallback adds your function to the list of callbacks for a particular widget. Every widget supports a number of callbacks, and each callback type is named. (Look in the *OSF/Motif Programmer's Reference* for a list of the callbacks supported for each widget type.) For the pushbutton widget, we use activateCallback:

```
Widget  widget;
void    callback();

XtAddCallback(widget,
    XmNactivateCallback,
    (XtCallbackProc) callback,
    (XtPointer) NULL);
```

XmNactivateCallback is defined as the text string "activateCallback". Each of the callbacks supported by a widget have a text name and a defined symbol that begins with *XmN*. These symbols are defined in the Motif include file <Xm/Xm.h>.

Callback-Function Parameters

All basic callback functions set up with XtAddCallback take the same parameters:

- The widget ID of the widget the callback was set up on.
- A pointer (normally XtPointer is an alias for caddr_t or void*) to your data, which is termed the *client data*. Xt keeps a copy of this pointer, so it's up to you to maintain the data that is pointed at. This data was originally passed to XtAddCallback. Passing data to a callback can be tricky. We'll show examples of it in later chapters.
- A pointer to a Motif structure that includes specific information about the callback. For example, a list-widget (XmList) callback structure includes the item that the user selected from the list. For the simple case of a pushbutton widget, though, you can normally ignore the *call_data* structure. You must cast the XtPointer *call_data* to the proper structure type. These are documented in the *OSF/Motif Programmer's Reference*, and we'll cover the important ones for each widget we introduce in this book. Most callbacks have no return value.

NOTE
Remember: *client_data* is your data, whereas *call_data* comes from the Motif or Xt toolkit. Many callbacks provide a specialized structure with information useful to your functions. Those structures are always in the *call_data* parameter. Any data you pass from XtAddCallback is passed as the *client_data* parameter. The easiest and most common mistake with callback functions is to reverse *client_data* and *call_data*. Usually you'll figure out that something is wrong right away. Exactly what is wrong, though, is often hard to determine.

If your callback doesn't seem to work properly, always check that the parameters are correct. This is a really easy error to make, and an even easier error to correct.

Here's an example callback function:

```
void CallbackFunction(Widget widget,
     XtPointer client_data,
     XtPointer call_data)

{    /* CallbackFunction */

     /* Your code goes here... */

}    /* CallbackFunction */
```

For each type of widget, *call_data* will contain a pointer to a Motif structure for that callback. A generic XmAnyCallbackStruct holds the data that are common to all Motif callbacks. This structure looks like the following:

```
typedef struct {
    int      reason;
    XEvent*  event;
} XmAnyCallbackStruct;
```

For the XmPushButton widget, the *call_data* will contain a pointer to an XmPushButtonCallbackStruct:

```
typedef struct {
    int      reason;
    XEvent*  event;
    int      click_count;
} XmPushButtonCallbackStruct;
```

This structure has a limited use to a pushbutton-choice callback, so we normally ignore the *call_data* parameter. (For other widgets, such as the XmList widget, the *call_data* is very important to callback functions.) In most cases, just acknowledging that the pushbutton was pushed is sufficient. We already know this—otherwise, the callback function wouldn't be called.

Most widgets support more than one callback, which we'll cover as we introduce the widgets, although you'll rarely use most types of widget callbacks.

Creating Pushbuttons

The following CreatePushbutton utility function creates an XmPushButton widget and sets up the activateCallback, returning the newly created widget. We find we code this task so often that it makes sense to have a utility function. To improve performance, we set up the callback function before managing the pushbutton. When the pushbutton gets managed, it may appear on the display, so we set up as much as we can *before* making the pushbutton widget visible. The code for CreatePushbutton follows:

```
#include   <Xm/Xm.h>
#include   <Xm/PushB.h>

Widget CreatePushbutton(Widget parent,
    char* name,
    XtCallbackProc callback,
    XtPointer client_data)

{   /* CreatePushbutton */

    Widget    push;
    Arg       args[20];
    Cardinal  n;

    n = 0;
    push = XmCreatePushButton(parent,
            name, args, n);

    /* Set up callback */
    XtAddCallback(push,         /* widget */
        XmNactivateCallback,  /* which callback */
        callback,             /* callback function */
        client_data);         /* extra data to pass */

    XtManageChild(push);
    return push;

}   /* CreatePushbutton */
```

CONTAINER WIDGETS AND COMPLEX PROGRAMS

Most Motif applications have a menu bar covering the top of the application's window, with pull-down menus on the menu bar. The main part of the application goes underneath the menu bar. The widget that controls the placement of the menu bar and your main data area is considered a *container widget*. Container widgets hold other (child) widgets and control the layout of these child widgets. Container widgets are used extensively in just about every Motif program.

Parent and Child Relationships

Every widget has a parent widget (except for the top-level shells, such as the one returned by XtAppInitialize). This parent widget is passed to XtCreateManagedWidget or XmCreate*Something* functions.

Only certain widgets, container and shell widgets, can be parent widgets. This parent widget controls the geometry (size and location) of child widgets. Examples of container widgets include `XmMainWindow`, `XmPanedWindow`, and `XmRowColumn`.

The common container widgets are listed in Table 2.8.

These widgets are subclasses of the `XmManager` widget (a meta-class widget that will never be created in your application programs). `XmManager` is important because it defines resources common to most container widgets. One such container widget is the paned window.

Table 2.8   Container widgets.

Widget Class Name	Created By	Covered In
XmBulletinBoard	XmCreateBulletinBoard	Chapter 6
XmDrawingArea	XmCreateDrawingArea	Chapter 11
XmFrame	XmCreateFrame	Chapter 6
XmForm	XmCreateForm	Chapter 6
XmMainWindow	XmCreateMainWindow	Chapter 4
XmPanedWindow	XmCreatePanedWindow	Chapter 6
XmRowColumn	XmCreateRowColumn	Chapters 4, 6
XmScale	XmCreateScale	Chapter 9
XmScrolledWindow	XmCreateScrolledWindow	Chapter 9

The paned-window widget places its child widgets from top to bottom in vertical *panes*—hence the name `XmPanedWindow`. Between each child, there is an optional *sash*—a line with a control box. The user can use the mouse pointer to move the sash up and down, controlling the size of each individual pane. You can also specify minimum and maximum sizes for panes, which the paned-window widget will enforce.

The include file for the paned-window class is `<Xm/PanedW.h>`. You can create one with `XmCreatePanedWindow`:

```
#include <Xm/PanedW.h>
```

```
Widget XmCreatePanedWindow(Widget parent,
            char* name,
            ArgList args,
            Cardinal number_args)
```

We'll use the paned-window widget returned by XmCreatePanedWindow as the parent widget for primitive widgets like XmPushButton and XmLabel.

Label Widgets

The label widget provides a static message, in text or a pixmap graphic, in a window. This doesn't sound very interesting, but most programs need to display some sort of text information to the user. Label widgets are also useful for displaying a company logo, if you want to get fancy. The label-widget class is also used as a parent for the pushbutton-widget class.

For now, we'll concentrate on label widgets that hold text strings. As we go along, we'll cover pixmap images. Create a label widget with XmCreateLabel:

```
#include <Xm/Label.h>

Widget XmCreateLabel(Widget parent,
            char* name,
            ArgList args,
            Cardinal number_args)
```

Managing Widgets

Managing a widget makes that widget visible. Technically, managing a widget places that widget under control of its parent's geometry management. If a widget is unmanaged, it will not be visible at all. If you manage a widget, then that widget will be made visible if the parent allows it. If you manage a child widget, but the child's parent is still unmanaged, then both widgets will remain invisible until you manage the parent.

Dialog widgets, for example, are usually left unmanaged. You do manage all the children of the dialog widgets, though. To show a dialog, you simply manage the dialog-shell widget. To hide a dialog, you unmanage the dialog-shell widget. See Chapter 7 for more on dialog widgets.

XtManageChild manages a widget. By default, all Motif-created widgets are created unmanaged, unless you use the XtCreateManagedWidget function. An unmanaged widget will not be made visible when your application calls `XtRealizeWidget`, so you must manage most widgets after you create them—that is, if you want those widgets to become visible in your application's interface, which you normally do.

`XtManageChild` takes one parameter, the widget to manage:

```
void XtManageChild(Widget widget)
```

For most widgets, call the `XmCreate`*Type* function to create the widget, set up any callbacks or customizations to the widget, and then call `XtManageChild` to manage the widget.

XtRealizeWidget

`XtRealizeWidget` realizes a widget and all its child widgets. Normally you must realize all top-level shell widgets, except for pop-up windows like dialogs and menus. For simple programs, you call `XtRealizeWidget` on the top-level shell widget returned by `XtAppInitialize`. `XtRealizeWidget` creates the actual window IDs used under the hood by Motif widgets. If you ever want to do advanced operations on the windows associated with Motif widgets, you must realize the widgets first. This forms a common stumbling block when programming Motif applications.

After you've set up all your widgets and managed them, then it is time to make them real. `XtRealizeWidget` takes care of all the initializations necessary for a widget and all its managed children. `XtRealizeWidget` takes one parameter, a high-level widget to be realized. Normally this is the widget returned from `XtAppInitialize`:

```
void XtRealizeWidget(Widget parent)
```

Sometimes `XtRealizeWidget` takes a long time to execute, since it must create a great many windows on the X display. Expect this.

After calling `XtRealizeWidget`, most applications let the Xt Intrinsics take over and loop awaiting events.

XtAppMainLoop

`XtAppMainLoop` executes the main event-handling loop of a Motif application. This function executes forever, so you must set up at least one callback function that will exit your program.

Looping forever doesn't seem very much fun, but it lets the Xt Intrinsics handle most of the work of an X application for you. With `XtAppMainLoop`, the Xt Intrinsics essentially take over your application. That's one of the prices you pay for using an Xt-based toolkit: The toolkit takes over. `XtAppMainLoop` loops checking for things the toolkit needs to do, including handling timeouts, work procedures, and input from the X server (including user input).

When an input event arrives, `XtAppMainLoop` determines which widget in your application should get the event and then passes the event on to the widget. The widget, then, determines whether to execute a callback function or to handle the event on its own. Usually, the more events that a widget can handle mean the less work your application code has to do.

We won't regain control until the user does something to execute a callback function, such as clicking a mouse button (usually Button 1, or the leftmost button) in pushbutton widget. When this happens, the widget executes its `activateCallback` function. At this point, your code regains control from Motif.

In your callback function, you can do what you want. Sometimes your callbacks will need to execute completely in a very short amount of time (such as in the millisecond range). For now, we can do what we want.

One of the things we want to do is create a callback function that will exit our program. To do so, we can call the C function `exit`, as we do in the `exitCB` callback function, in "A First Motif Program," below. Before any callbacks get called, though, your program must cede control to the Xt Intrinsics main event-handling loop by calling `XtAppMainLoop`:

```
void XtAppMainLoop(XtAppContext appcontext)
```

You pass `XtAppMainLoop` one parameter, the application context originally passed to `XtAppInitialize`.

N O T E   If you develop with Motif 1.0, you won't have an application context and you should use `XtMainLoop` instead of `XtAppMainLoop`. `XtMainLoop` takes no parameters and basically loops forever, like `XtAppMainLoop`.

```
void XtMainLoop()
```

XtMainLoop predates the later Xt functions that use application contexts. In general, you always want to use the *XtApp* functions unless you're working with an old system that doesn't have these functions.

A First Motif Program

We'll now put together all the lessons in this chapter and create our first full-fledged Motif program. This program creates a paned-window container widget with two children, a pushbutton, and a label. Our widget hierarchy for this program is as follows:

```
* Top-level application shell, returned by XtAppInitialize
    * XmPanedWindow
        *XmPushButton
        * XmLabel
```

The program code appears below:

```c
/* first -- first Motif program. */

/*  Xm.h is the basic Motif include file. */
#include <Xm/Xm.h>

/*
 *   Include a file for each widget
 *   type we use.
 */
#include <Xm/Label.h>   /* XmLabel */
#include <Xm/PushB.h>   /* XmPushButton */
#include <Xm/PanedW.h>  /* XmPanedWindow */

/*
 * exitCB() is a callback for the
 * pushbutton widget we create below.
 * exitCB() calls exit() to terminate
 * the program.
 */

void exitCB(Widget widget,
    XtPointer client_data,
    XtPointer call_data)

{   /* exitCB */

    exit(0);

}   /* exitCB */
```

```
int main(int argc, char** argv)

{    /* main */
    Widget          parent;
    XtAppContext    app_context;
    Widget          pane, push, label;
    Arg             args[20];
    Cardinal        n;

    /*
     * Initialize the X Toolkit
     * Intrinsics.
     */
    n = 0;
    parent = XtAppInitialize(&app_context,
            "Ppm",                        /* app class */
            (XrmOptionDescList) NULL,     /* options */
            0,                            /* num options */
            (Cardinal*) &argc,            /* num cmds */
            argv,                         /* cmd-line opts */
            (String*) NULL,               /* fallback res. */
            args, 0);

    /*
     * Create a paned-window
     * widget to contain all
     * the child widgets. Note that
     * the paned window is a child
     * of the top-level parent.
     */
    n = 0;
    pane = XmCreatePanedWindow(parent,
        "pane", args, n);

    /* We manage the pane later, below. */

    /*
     * Create a pushbutton widget,
     * as a child of the paned window.
     */
    n = 0;
    push = XmCreatePushButton(pane,
            "quit", args, n);

    /*
     * Set up a callback for the
     * pushbutton widget.
     */
    XtAddCallback(push,                   /* widget */
        XmNactivateCallback,              /* which callback */
        (XtCallbackProc) exitCB,          /* callback function */
        (XtPointer) NULL);                /* extra data to pass */
```

```
/* Manage the pushbutton widget. */
XtManageChild(push);

/*
 * Create a Label widget, as
 * a child of the paned window.
 */
n = 0;
label = XmCreateLabel(pane,
        "label", args, n);

XtManageChild(label);

/*
 * Note that we manage the paned-window
 * container *after* we fill in the
 * child widgets of the pane.
 */
XtManageChild(pane);

/*
 * Realize widget hierarchy, which
 * brings the top-level widget
 * (and all its children) to
 * reality. That is, create windows
 * for the widgets and then map
 * the windows.
 */
XtRealizeWidget(parent);

/* Process events forever. */
XtAppMainLoop(app_context);

return 0;

}   /* main */

/* end of file first.c */
```

COMPILING AND LINKING MOTIF PROGRAMS

Motif programs require the Motif library (libXm.a), the Xt Intrinsics library (libXt.a), and the low-level X library (libX11.a). To compile a C file named **foo.c**, you should use a command like:

```
cc -o foo foo.c -lXm -lXt -lX11
```

The first rule for compiling Motif programs is simple: *Read your system documentation.* Most vendor-supported versions of X and Motif come with manuals that describe how to compile X and Motif programs. We strongly advise you to use the settings recommended by your vendor. We've experienced some problems with a few systems, though, and would like to pass on our solutions and workarounds.

386/486 Systems

Some systems, particularly 386/486-based UNIX systems, require a number of other libraries, usually because networking is considered an option on those systems. SCO Open Desktop, for example, requires:

```
cc -Di386 -DLAI_TCP -DSYSV -o foo foo.c \
    -lXm -lXt -lX11 -ltlisock -lsocket -lnsl_s
```

Interactive (SunSoft) SVR3.2 requires:

```
cc -o foo foo.c -lXm -lXt -lX11 -lnsl_s
```

Hewlett-Packard Systems

Hewlett-Packard systems place the X include files in nonstandard locations. In addition, the libraries are also placed in nonstandard locations. HP-UX 8.0 uses X11 Release 4 (X11R4) and Motif 1.1:

```
cc -I/usr/include/X11R4 -I/usr/include/Motif1.1 \
    -o foo foo.c \
    -L/usr/lib/Motif1.1 -lXm  \
    -L/usr/lib/X11R4 -lXt -lX11
```

HP-UX 9.*x* upgrades to X11R5 and Motif 1.2 uses:

```
cc -I/usr/include/X11R5 -I/usr/include/Motif1.2 \
    -o foo foo.c \
    -L/usr/lib/Motif1.2 -lXm  \
    -L/usr/lib/X11R5 -lXt -lX11
```

Problems with C++ or ANSI C

C++ requires and ANSI/ISO standard C can use function prototypes. Depending on how your system is set up (and many configurations are not done properly), you may have problems compiling programs that use function prototypes. In such cases, the -DFUNCPROTO option should turn on function prototypes in the X and Motif header files, whereas -D_NO_PROTO should turn them off.

RUNNING THE FIRST MOTIF PROGRAM

After compiling and linking, you can run our example program, named *first*, without any command-line parameters.

```
first
```

The *first* program will display a pushbutton and a label, with a sash between, as shown in Figure 2.2.

Figure 2.2 *The first Motif program in action.*

You can resize the panes, using the sash, as shown in Figure 2.3.

Figure 2.3 *Resizing a pane.*

To quit the program, move the mouse pointer cursor on top of the Quit button and click button 1 (usually the leftmost mouse button, but if you're left-handed, you may have reversed that). The *first* program should quit. Pretty simple, huh?

The texts of the label and pushbutton widgets are simply the widget names we used when creating the widgets. That's the default behavior if you don't define any resources—data attributes—for the widgets. We'll cover these X resources in the next chapter and show how you can change the behavior of the first program without making any source code changes, nor even recompiling.

SUMMARY

This chapter introduced Motif programming and guided you through a sample client. Admittedly, there's not a whole lot to the client—essentially, the *first* program begins and ends—but it is still useful for explaining how Motif applications are structured under the hood.

The Motif toolkit sits on top of the Xt Intrinsics library. That means Motif uses many of the Xt features and functions. Motif does have a set of functions of its own, and Motif has its own widget set with its own look and feel. The Xt Intrinsics provide some basic mechanism for many widget sets (you'll find a lot of this mechanism stuff as you read about X). By layering on top of the Intrinsics, the Motif code has less work to do. This also means that all Motif applications pay for the added complexity and difficulty (and massive program size) of all Xt-based applications.

An important concept for any Motif programmer is the use of widgets, generic abstractions for user-interface components in the Motif toolkit. Widgets are used for scroll bars, pushbuttons, dialogs, and just about everything else in the toolkit. Most widgets have an associated window on the X display that holds the user-interface elements of the widget. Each widget has a C data structure that is dynamically allocated via `malloc` at creation time. This structure—which is supposed to be treated as an opaque data type—contains the widget's data attributes and pointers to the functions, such as callbacks, that widgets may have.

Some widgets display graphics on the screen. Others serve as container widgets grouping other widgets, which are called child widgets. There are two widget hierarchies, and they're quite different. First, the Motif widget class hierarchy is the tree of widget classes and how these classes are defined in terms of other widget classes. The second hierarchy is the hierarchy of widget instances you create when you program a Motif application.

Motif widgets fall into certain classes. The basic types of Motif widgets include managers, primitives, shells, and Xt-provided widgets.

For each Motif widget class, there is a special function to create an instance of that class. Usually this function has the name of XmCreate*Type*, where *Type* is the type of widget you want to create. For example, XmCreatePushButton creates a pushbutton widget, an instance of an XmPushButton widget. Most widget classes have names, too, like XmPushButton for the pushbutton widget class.

For each widget, you'll normally include a widget header file, as well as <Xm/Xm.h>, the standard Motif header file. These Motif include files are normally stored in the /usr/include/Xm directory, but your system may place these files in some other location.

Motif programs usually follow six basic steps:

■ Initialize the Xt Intrinsics (which also sets up connection to the X server)

■ Create widgets

■ Set up any needed callback functions

■ Realize the widget hierarchy with XtRealizeWidget

■ Enter the event-handling loop

■ Loop forever—yes, forever

Each of these steps is explained in detail.

Finally, we compile and link a simple program called *first*. This program merely places a window on the screen and gives the user the option of quitting the program through the Quit bushbutton. Compiling and linking procedures are then covered, including specific procedures for 386/486 UNIX systems and Hewlett-Packard UNIX implementations.

In the next chapter, we'll cover X resources and resource files—a means you can use to modify Motif programs without changing any source code.

Motif Functions and Macros Introduced in This Chapter

```
XmCreateLabel
XmCreatePanedWindow
XmCreatePushButton
```

X Toolkit Intrinsics Functions and Macros Introduced in This Chapter

```
XtAddCallback
XtAppInitialize
XtAppMainLoop
XtInitialize
XtMainLoop
XtManageChild
XtRealizeWidget
```

CHAPTER 3

Resources and Resource Files

In this chapter, we cover a tool for modifying Motif programs without access to the source code. X resources and resource files allow you to change widget data attributes like colors and fonts. This chapter introduces X resources and covers:

- Six ways to set X resource values
- Setting resource values
- Class vs. user resource files
- Setting resources with command-line parameters
- Fallback resources
- Hard-coding resources
- Resource file locations
- Resource environment variables

51

CUSTOMIZING A PROGRAM WITHOUT RECOMPILING

Resources are a generic means to customize X applications without modifying the application's source code. As such, resources form a powerful tool when building Motif programs. You can change colors, text fonts, and sizes of windows through *resource files*, text files with resource-setting commands.

Unfortunately, the designers of X must have liked the term *resources*, as it means a great many things in X documentation. In this chapter, we'll describe resources as a handy means to change the default settings of an X program. These resources apply to programs built with the X Toolkit (Xt) Intrinsics, such as *xterm*, *xclock*, and other Athena widget programs; Open Look applications built with OLIT (but not XView); and, of course, all Motif programs.

This chapter covers how you can set the values of resources outside of your Motif applications, an essential feature for building any sophisticated Motif program.

Setting resources externally has many advantages but gets really confusing when you try to figure out the dizzying array of resource options. (When your head starts to spin, don't say we didn't warn you.) Because of all the options, we consider setting resources external to a program to really be an advanced topic. Unfortunately, you really can't get much done in Motif without using resources.

SHORTCUT

Quick Resources

If you're impatient and want to get going quickly, type in the following resource file and name it **Ppm**.

```
! Set program background color.
*background:  lightgrey
! Set up quit message.
*quit.labelString: Push Here To Exit
```

Lines that start with a exclamation mark (!) are comments. These lines are ignored. All the other lines in the file are separate resource-setting commands. The first resource-setting command changes the background color for all widgets to light-grey by setting the background resource. The asterisk (*) indicates a wildcard. The asterisk without a widget name in front of the resource name (background) means that it applies to all widgets in the program.

The second resource-setting command sets the text message, the labelString resource, for the widget named quit to the text string *Push Here to Exit.*

Place this file in your home directory, then start up the program named *first* that was introduced in the last chapter. Note how the *first* program changes from what it displayed when you ran it for the last chapter. It will now look like Figure 3.1.

Figure 3.1 *Changing the first program with a resource file.*

You can set most Motif widget resources in a resource file. (There are a few exceptions, which we'll cover when we introduce the exceptional resources.)

Most of the discussion in this chapter applies to the X Toolkit Intrinsics in general and not necessarily specifically to Motif. Thus you can apply most of this chapter to X programs written with other Xt-based libraries (such as *xterm*, written using the Athena widget set) as well as to Motif applications.

N O T E

There is a portability problem with resources, though, that you'll quickly discover: X resource names are dependent on the toolkit used to build the program. *Xterm*, built with the Athena widgets, uses a resource named font to set the font. Motif programs, though, use a resource named fontList. Similarly, Athena programs use the label resource to specify the text displayed in a label widget. Motif uses the labelString resource.

While this may not seem like a big idea when you're creating software, it is a big problem for users, who often don't know which toolkit was used to build an application. Since this is a Motif book, we'll concentrate most on the Motif-specific names.

WHAT ARE RESOURCES?

Every Motif widget has a number of resources, or data attributes, that modify its behavior. These resources control whether scroll bars appear (and where they appear), how wide borders around objects are, what colors text is drawn in, and so on. You can set values to these resources in external resource files or hard-code them in your programs.

The primary advantage to setting resource values in external files is that it allows the end user to customize Motif applications without needing access to your source code. Also, the end user can change the customizations every time your applications are run.

Corporate readers should note that resources can be used to maintain systemwide consistency between applications. Perhaps your users want the foreground and background colors to be inverted. Or perhaps a vision-impaired user wants to use a very large font for better visibility. Different systems support different screen sizes and resolutions—what looks good on one system may be unreadable on another. Perhaps users want different colors instead if the default blue backgrounds. It's all possible.

There's a hitch, however. End users can customize your Motif applications for only those resources that you don't hard-code within your programs, as hard-coded resource values take precedence over all externally set resources values.

You set resource values for a widget using a resource-setting command. Each data value, such as the background color for a given widget, is set with a single resource-setting command. All in all, there are six ways to issue resource-setting commands.

SIX WAYS TO SET RESOURCE VALUES

There are six basic ways to set resource values, and four of them are external to your programs. You can set resource values:

1. *In a user resource file*. This is a text file that contains resource-setting commands. These files are called *user* resource files since they are usually set up by the user. These files can reside in a number of places, which we'll go into later, in the section entitled "Location of Resource Files," below. The resource-setting commands in these files can apply to all X and Motif applications.

2. In a *class resource file*. This is also a text file that contains resource-setting commands. However, these commands apply to just one application class. For example, *XTerm* is the class name for the *xterm* application. Thus the class resource file for *xterm* would be named *XTerm*. For our example applications, the resource class name is *Ppm*. Usually these class resource files set resources on an application-wide basis; that is, you many want to set up all *xterm* programs to act in a certain way. To do so, you could use a class resource file. System administrators may want to set up class resource files to establish systemwide standards and make life easier for the users.

3. In the *RESOURCE_MANAGER property* on the root window or the *SCREEN_RESOURCES property* for color information. These properties are created by the standard X Window program called *xrdb.* You can use *xrdb* to add resource values to this RESOURCE_MANAGER property. You may want to use *xrdb* if you're using an X terminal that doesn't have its own file system. (X uses the term *property* to refer to a named, typed collection of data stored with a window.)

4. In *fallback resources* passed to XtAppInitialize.

5. In *command-line parameters* passed to the program.

6. Inside a program, by hard-coding the resource values. Hard-coding resources prevents users from changing the resources using any of the five means above.

Hard-Coding Resource Values: The Good, the Bad, and the Ugly

There are some advantages to hard-coding resource values:

■ There's no problem with installing resource files in their particular locations.

■ There's no problem with conflicting UNIX environment variables.

■ There's no problem with file permissions.

■ Users don't need to learn the obscure, obtuse resource-setting syntax.

■ Users can't do any damage to your program. In the real world, it doesn't matter whether the user didn't install your resource file properly—if your program doesn't work right, you'll be blamed anyway. Think for a moment: How much of your program internals do you want end users to have access to? Changing font sizes is one thing, but you need to be careful what you allow in resource files. And why should users be forced to edit a separate file to change aspects of a program, when other operating systems place this power within the applications themselves? Resource-setting commands are rather obtuse, and there's a confusing plethora of options, especially for the location of resource files. If that's not enough, debugging resource files is almost impossible. Bottom line: You'll need to decide for yourself how much to hard-code and how much to place in resource files.

That's the good. The bad is that Motif allows you to create highly customizable applications. If you don't allow your users to take advantage of this feature, then you've defeated a major design goal of the Motif toolkit. You've already paid for the dynamic resource-setting code when you linked in the Motif and X libraries. It would be a shame if you added all this code to your application and never bothered to use it.

The ugly is that many users want their environment customized in a certain way. Perhaps they want to always use a particular font with every Motif application. If you hard-code the resources in your program, then you're defeating your own users. In addition, users in Germany, for example, just may want the text messages in your program to be in German. If you use hard-coded messages (such as labelString resources in your label widgets), then you've effectively prevented your applications from being internationalized in this way. (There's a lot more to internationalization, as you'll see in Chapter 27.)

Setting Resource Values

As mentioned, resource files are text (ASCII) files containing resource-setting commands. This process is simple, involving identifying the widget (or widgets) to be changed, specifying the resource to set (by name), and then providing the new value for that resource. A colon (:) separates the resource name from its new value. This will become clearer as you look at the line below.

```
widgets_to_apply.resourceName: value_to_set
```

For example, to set the labelString resource to *Hello* for a widget named fred, use the resource-setting command below:

```
*fred.labelString: Hello
```

All resource setting in resource files is done using text strings.

N O T E   If you make a mistake, the X toolkit just doesn't care. Most resource errors are silently ignored. If you make a mistake, you may have a very hard time figuring out what went wrong. This makes the already tough process of resource-setting tougher. Some relief is available in X11 Release 5, though, as covered later in the section "Stumbling to the Future: Editres."

The other difficult aspect of resources is naming exactly what you want to set. To help with this, we'll go through each of the three parts of a resource-setting command: identifying the widgets, naming the resource, and setting a new value for the resource.

Identifying the Widgets

When you use a resource-setting command, you're trying to change the behavior of a widget (or widgets, as the case may be). Remember that widgets are named data objects. It is by these names that you can modify widgets. Since we're writing the programs, we can name the widgets anything we want—so it shouldn't be too hard to come up with the name for a given widget. It's when you use programs written by others that you run into problems. In this case, the program author should have documented which widgets and which resources are available to set.

Widgets are created in a hierarchy. That is, we start out with a top-level shell and then we create a main-window (or a paned-window or a form or a RowColumn or whatever container) widget. After the container widget, we create a number of child widgets.

If we want to set a resource in a child widget, we have to specify the full widget path to that child, usually by widget names. Start with the name of the top-level shell (coincidentally, the application's class name, as passed to `XtAppInitialize`) then put a period and then put in the name of the next widget down and so on.

For example, let's just say we create a program with the widget hierarchy listed below. The widget names (the names we pass to the `XmCreateType` functions) are listed after the type of widget:

* Top-Level Shell—"Ppm"
    * `XmPanedWindow` Widget, to hold the other widgets—"pane"
        * `XmLabel` Widget—"label"
        * `XmPushButton` Widget—"quit"

Let's say that we want to set the text that the label widget above displays. The resource for the text message is the `labelString` resource (we show how to determine these resource names below in the section entitled "How Do You Find Out What Resources Can Be Set?"). We name this resource by going down the tree until we hit the widget's name, then we add the name of the actual resource to set:

```
Ppm.pane.label.labelString
```

This is the most specific means to name this widget. Specific resource-setting commands always take precedence over nonspecific commands (such as commands that use wildcards, as covered in the next section). To set the text label to display "This is a new label" on the label widget, we'd need a resource-setting command like:

```
Ppm.pane.label.labelString:    This is a new label
```

In this case, the period means that the resource specification is exactly as listed. This isn't so bad in a simple test program (as in the *first* program from the previous chapter), but this can get tedious, especially in a complex Motif application with a large widget hierarchy. It can get worse, too, if you decide to change the widget hierarchy. If you do so, your resource-setting commands may fail. Luckily, you can use wildcards in naming the resources.

Wildcards with Resources

An asterisk (*; often called a star) is used as a wildcard in naming resources. You can use a wildcard in place of a full resource path name, but be careful.

The above example can be written as:

```
Ppm*label.labelString:      This is a new label
```

This means that in all applications with a class name of *Ppm* (*Ppm* is also the name of the parent top-level widget), all widgets named *label* will have their `labelString` resource set. Beware: If you take the wildcards too far, you'll have problems. If you instead decided to use the following, you'll soon see what went wrong.

```
Ppm*labelString:      This is a new label
```

This states that *all* `labelString` resources in the application should be set to "This is a new label". We didn't really intend to set the `labelString` resource on the pushbutton, but we did it anyway by accident. Even worse would be:

```
*labelString:      This is a new label
```

This would set the `labelString` resource on every widget that had a `labelString`, in every application. The results would not be pretty. (There are some limitations, depending on the resource file in question, but in general this is what a wildcard can do.)

Using Class Names Instead of Widget Names

Instead of using each widget's name, you can also use its class name. The `XmLabel` widget above has a name (chosen by us and put into a C program) of *label* (the name could just as well be *foo*). Label widgets in Motif have a class name of `XmLabel`, so you could use the following resource-setting command:

```
Ppm*XmLabel.labelString:    This is our new label.
```

In a resource-setting command, names that begin with capital letters normally indicate widget classes. Names that begin with lowercase letters indicate widget and resource names. (The names of the actual resources also normally begin with a lowercase letter. If there is more than one word, like in `fontList`, the next words begin with a capital letter. There are no spaces in resource names.)

For another example, you could set the `labelString` resource in the pushbutton widget this time, using a class-based specification of:

```
Ppm*XmPushButton.labelString:  This is a push button
```

NOTE

When you use the widget-class names, watch out. All widgets of the same class will be modified. If you have three or more label widgets, you may not want all of them to have the same message. This leads us to a good rule: Be careful with wildcards in setting resource values.

Resource names themselves also have class names. The class names are usually the resource name with the first letter capitalized, such as Foreground, the class name for the foreground resource. For example:

```
Ppm*XmLabel.Foreground:  red
```

Specific names (lowercase) take precedence over the class names (which should start with an uppercase letter). If you try the two resource-setting commands listed below, you'll notice that this is true:

```
Ppm*fontList:           cursor
Ppm.pane.label.fontList:  variable
```

The above commands specify that all widgets in any application with a class name of *Ppm* will use the font named *cursor* (a font of cursor shapes, not alphabetic characters). The widget named *label* (which is a child of the widget named *pane*) overrides this, though. This widget will use a font named *variable*, which is a much better font for use with most applications.

Why use the *cursor* font, which makes for unintelligible labels, anyway? Since this font looks so odd, you'll be able to instantly tell if your X resource file is actually read in by your Motif program. Since the Xt Intrinsics ignores most errors, debugging can be difficult. By using odd colors and fonts, you're more likely to tell if you've placed the resource file in the proper location. We find this to be a good tip for debugging resource files.

How Do You Find Out What Resources Can Be Set?

You can find out the resources for a given Motif widget by looking up the widget class names in the *OSF/Motif Programmer's Reference*. The class name for a label widget, for example, is XmLabel. Look up XmLabel, and you'll see a host of resources. There will be both resources new to the given widget, such as XmLabel, and resources that the label widget inherits from other widgets, notably Core. You'll probably want the *OSF/Motif Programmer's Reference* constantly by your side when you write Motif programs.

Setting New Resource Values

After you've found the name of the resource you want to set, you then
need to find the acceptable values for that resource. Again, you can look in
the *OSF/Motif Programmer's Reference*. For each widget, you'll see a list
of resources and their types, along with the initial values. For example, the
XmLabel widget lists a number of resources, including those listed in
Table 3.1.

Table 3.1 *XmLabel resources.*

Resource Name	Type	Default Value
accelerator	String	NULL
acceleratorText	XmString	NULL
fontList	XmFontList	*dynamic*
labelString	XmString	*dynamic*
marginBottom	Dimension	0
marginHeight	Dimension	2
marginLeft	Dimension	0
marginRight	Dimension	0
marginTop	Dimension	0
marginWidth	Dimension	2

The default values listed as *dynamic* are determined at runtime.

In your C programs, you need to place an *XmN* prefix on all resource
names; that is, use the defined symbol XmNaccelerator for the
accelerator resource.

Most widgets inherit a common set of resources from the Core and
XmPrimitive widget classes, including those listed in Table 3.2.

Table 3.2 *Commonly set Core and XmPrimitive resources.*

Resource Name	Type	Default Value
background	Pixel	*dynamic*
borderColor	Pixel	XtDefaultForeground
borderWidth	Dimension	1
bottomShadowColor	Pixel	*dynamic*
foreground	Pixel	*dynamic*
height	Dimension	*dynamic*
shadowThickness	Dimension	2
topShadowColor	Pixel	*dynamic*
userData	XtPointer	NULL
width	Dimension	*dynamic*
x	Dimension	0
y	Dimension	0

When we introduce a new widget from this point on, we'll present a table like Tables 3.1 and 3.2 covering the most commonly used resources for that widget. This should help you create resource files or hard-code resource values inside your programs.

Resource Converters

In resource files, you set all values with text strings. Therefore, in order for resources files to work, you need some form of resource converter that converts values from strings to the proper types. It is these converters that change the text string "red" into the proper color index value (of type Pixel) for use inside your program.

Inside your programs, though, you must create the proper value in the proper data type. This can take a lot of work, especially for the Pixel (unsigned long colormap indices) and XmString types. Unless you use the proper converter, you cannot just use the string "red" to set a color inside your program. Instead, you must generate the proper Pixel value.

Now that we've explained the resource-setting commands, it's time to focus on resource files.

RESOURCE FILES

A *resource file* is an ASCII (ISO Latin-1, actually) text file containing resource-setting commands. When XtAppInitialize executes, it looks in a set of directories for resource files and automatically loads them. (This is one reason Motif applications take so long to start.) Common locations for resource files are in /usr/lib/X11/app-defaults and in your home directory.

Resource files are a very handy way to customize your applications. For example, you could place *all* text messages for an application in resource files. If you wanted to translate your application to run in French, for example, the majority of the work could be done by merely editing the resource file and translating the messages to French. Using resource files seems to be a great advantage, but it can also be a disadvantage: If the resource file isn't properly set up, the user may see a very confusing mess for the application.

To help you avoid a confusing mess, we've set up a number of resource-setting examples through resource files, command-line parameters, and hard-coding.

Class Resource Files

There are two basic types of resource files: class and user resource files. Class resource files pertain to applications of the same class. Usually this really means that class resource files pertain to separate applications, since most applications have their own class. For example, the *xterm* application that most X users use all the time has a class name of *XTerm* (note that most classes begin with a capital letter).

The class resource file is then given the class name, that is, *XTerm*. You can place this file in a number of locations that we cover below in the "Location of Resource Files" section. For now, place the class resource files in your home directory.

A class resource file for the *XTerm* class would pertain to the *xterm* application only. For example, say you wanted all *xterm* windows to have a black background and a white foreground (commonly called *reverse video*). If you set up these resource commands in the *XTerm* resource file, then the changes will apply only to applications with a class name of *XTerm*, which is most likely limited to the *xterm* program itself.

In the sample program below, we're going to use the program named *first* that we created in Chapter 2, which has a class name of *Ppm* (short for *Power Programming Motif*). This class name is passed to XtAppInitialize in the code in *first.c* (presented in Chapter 2 in the "A First Motif Program" section). Therefore, any class resource files for this application would have a file name of *Ppm*.

Every Xt-based application has a class name, such as *Ppm*, and an application name, such as *first*. Usually the application name is the program name or the contents of argv[0]. For resource-setting commands, you can normally start with either the class name or the application name, but most people use the class name.

In the examples below, we'll create three separate files and use each in turn. To use a resource file, copy it to your home directory and name it **Ppm**. Then, restart the *first* program.

Resource-Setting Examples

The following examples show resource-setting commands. By trying out a number of examples, we hope to show how resource-setting commands work and how they interrelate. This is a tough topic, so don't get too concerned if things don't work out the first time. Just keep trying and playing around. Eventually, it will all make sense.

Before you try these examples, though, run the *first* program from Chapter 2. Take a long look at the widgets displayed by the program. This will give you a rough idea of what the program is like without any external resources set. You'll be able to compare this and see the effects of each resource file in turn.

Then type in the file below. Name the file **Ppm** and place the file in your home directory (a default location for class resource files—you can look up more advanced locations in the "Location of Resource Files" section below). After you've placed the file in your home directory, restart the *first* program. You should see a marked difference. The **Ppm** resource file follows:

```
! Resource file #1 for Chapter 3 of
! Power Programming Motif.
!
! Copy this file to "Ppm" in your home directory.
```

```
!
! Global Resources
! Set font.
*fontList:  lucidasans-12

! Set program background color.
*background:  lightgrey

! Set up window title.
*title:  Res. 1

! Widget-Specific Resources
!
! Set up quit message.
*quit.labelString: Push here to exit

*label.labelString: Resource File Example 1

! end of resource file
```

All lines that begin with ! are comments.

The first resource-setting command in this file sets the fontList resource for all widgets to *lucidasans-12*. Note that since we're using a class resource file, the wildcarded resource (*fontList) applies only to all widgets in programs with a class of *Ppm*. If we had instead placed this resource-setting command in a user resource file such as .Xdefaults, this would apply to every X application.

The next resource-setting command sets the background color of the widgets to *lightgrey*. (You can use *grey* or *gray*, as X supports both spellings.) The normal Motif background color is blue.

The *title resource sets the window title for the application.

The last two resource commands set the labelString resources for the XmPushButton widget named *quit* and the XmLabel widget named *label*.

The second example of a class resource file introduces the backslash (\) character, which you can use to extend a resource command over more than one line. The fontList resource is set to a font name that is longer than a single line. In addition to the backslash to extend a resource value over more than one line, \n introduces a newline into an XmString value, as in the *label.labelString resource in the example file below. If you're setting a labelString resource, the \ does not add a newline into the string—only \n does this.

This example resource file also shows how more specific resource-setting commands override general commands. The *quit.background:white command sets the background color to white for the widget named quit. The general-purpose command *background:lightgrey sets the background color for all other widgets, except the one named quit.

Finally, this example introduces a number of resources for the paned-window widget (see Chapter 6 for more on the XmPanedWindow widget). The sash is the small control that sits between widgets inside a pane. You use the sash to change the size of a given pane in relation to the panes around it.

The text of the second resource file follows:

```
! Resource file #2 for Chapter 3 of
! Power Programming Motif.
!
! Copy this file to "Ppm" in your home directory.
!
! Global Resources

! Set font.
*fontList: \
    -*-helvetica-bold-r-normal--12-120-*-*-p-*-*-1

*background:     lightgrey

! Set up window title.
*title:  Res. 2

! Widget-Specific Resources

! Set up quit message.
*quit.labelString:  Push here to exit

! Set a different colors for the quit button.
*quit.background:  white
*quit.foreground:  black

*label.labelString:  This is a very long \
    labelString with a newline\n\
    that even continues \
    beyond one line\n\so you see.

! Paned window
*pane.sashHeight:  6
*pane.sashWidth:   12
*pane.sashIndent: -6
! Use -6 for sashIndent if you have scrollbars.
! end of resource file
```

The third example of a class resource file extends the first two lessons by adding a different font, a new background color, and more widget-specific colors. These colors should help show the precedence of resource-setting commands. The text for this resource file follows:

```
! Resource file #3 for Chapter 3 of
! Power Programming Motif.
!
! Copy this file to "Ppm" in your home directory.
!
! Global Resources

! Set font.
!
*fontList: \
 -*-helvetica-bold-r-normal--12-120-*-*-p-*-*-1

*background: sienna

! Set up window title.
*title: Res. 3
*geometry: 200x300+201+400

! Widget-Specific Resources

! Set up quit message.
*quit.labelString: Push here to exit

! Set different colors for the quit button.
*quit.background:    dimgray
*quit.foreground:    white

*label.labelString: Yet another label.
*label.foreground:    seagreen
*label.background:    bisque2
*pane.background:     maroon

! end of resource file
```

Setting the Window Geometry

One of the interesting new resources in the file above is the geometry resource. X uses the term *geometry* to mean a window's size and location. Therefore, the geometry command sets the window's size (width, height) and location (x,y):

```
*geometry: 200x300+201+400
```

In X, all coordinates are set from the upper left corner. That is, location 0,0 is the upper left corner of the screen. You can set the individual *width, height*, *x*, and *y* resources, or you can set the `geometry` resource, which allows you to set the whole thing through one resource. The `geometry` resource also allows you to specify locations in terms of the edges and corners of the screen, which is very handy if you're not sure what the pixel resolution of the screen is, or if you use a number of different X workstations from the same user account. The format for the geometry specification is *WidthxHeight+Xorigin+Yorigin*. You can omit either the size (*WidthxHeight*) or location (+*Xorigin*+*Yorigin*). For instance, you may not care how big the application's window is. Instead, you may just want to position the window.

The `geometry` resource above, then, sets the width to 200 pixels and the height to 300. The location is set to (201,400).

There are some special rules regarding the X and Y coordinates. A positive X coordinate means to position the *left* edge of the window *X* pixels from the *left* edge of the screen. A negative X coordinate of means to position the *right* edge of the window *x* pixels from the *right* edge of the screen. The Y coordinate is positioned using similar rules. A positive Y value means to position the *top* of the window *y* pixels from the top of the screen. A negative Y value means to position the *bottom* of the window *y* pixels above the bottom of the screen.

This leads to some odd contortions to specify the location of the corners of the screen, as seen in Table 3.3.

Table 3.3 *Specifying the corner of the display.*

Coordinate	Location
+0+0	Upper left corner
+0-0	Lower left corner
-0+0	Upper right corner
-0-0	Lower right corner

Putting this all together, when you run the *first* program with this resource file, you'll see something like Figure 3.2.

Figure 3.2   *The first program customized with our third resource file.*

User Resource Files

The examples so far have used a class resource file. In addition to these files, you can set up user resource files. The purpose of user resource files is to allow each user to customize and extend the application's defaults.

Even though there are a number of places and names for user resource files, the default grab-bag user resource file is named **.Xdefaults** and stored in your home directory.

The key thing to remember about user resource files is that the resource commands in these files apply to each and every X application you run. Therefore, you must be careful when using wildcards. For example, in a user resource file, the following command would set the font for every Motif application:

```
*fontList: lucidasans-12
```

In most cases, you don't want your resource-setting commands to have such a wide effect. We recommend that every command in a user resource file start with the application's class name, such as the *Ppm* class name we've been using so far.

Using the .Xdefaults File to Set Resources

Add the following resource-setting commands to your **.Xdefaults** file in your home directory. If you don't have a file named **.Xdefaults** in your home directory, then create one. These resource-setting commands are show below:

```
! Resources for the .Xdefaults file.
!
Ppm*fontList:-*-times-bold-i-normal--24-240-*-*-p-*-*
Ppm*background: red
```

After you've typed in these resource-setting commands, restart the *first* application. You should see something like Figure 3.3.

Figure 3.3   *The first program with a customized .Xdefaults file.*

If you don't see a difference, then your system is set up to ignore the **.Xdefaults** file.

Problems with .Xdefaults

There are a number of problems that can occur using the **.Xdefaults** file for resources. First, you may still have a file named **Ppm** in your home directory, and the resource-setting commands in this file may conflict with the commands in the **.Xdefaults** file. In addition, you may have one of a number of X environment variables that tell your application to look for X resources in some place other than the .**Xdefaults** file. To go even further, if you have a RESOURCE_MANAGER property, normally set up by the *xrdb* program (see "Using xrdb and the X Resource Manager Database," below), then the .**Xdefaults** file is ignored. In that case, try the following command:

```
xrdb -merge $HOME/.Xdefaults
```

This will load all the resource-setting commands in the file .**Xdefaults** and merge those commands with the resources already in the RESOURCE_MANAGER property. (Note that the designers of the Xt Intrinsics used the term *merge* in an odd manner, which we describe below.)

Setting Resources with Command-Line Parameters

You can set some common resources with standard X Window command-line parameters. For example, -fg stands for the foreground color. You can set the foreground color (usually the color the text is drawn in) to green with the command:

```
first -fg green
```

You can similarly set the background color with the -bg command-line parameter, as show below:

```
first -bg orange
```

Some common command-line parameters are listed in Table 3.4.

Table 3.4 *Common command-line parameters.*

Option	Data to Pass	Use
-bg	*background_color*	Sets background color
-display	*display_name*	Specifies X server to connect to
-fg	*foreground_color*	Sets foreground color
		continued

`-geometry`	*Width* x *Height* + *X origin* + *Y origin*	Sets window size and location
`-iconic`		Starts application as icon
`-name`	*application_name*	Sets instance (not class) name
`-title`	*window_title*	Sets window title for title bar
`-xnllanguage`	*language[_territory][.codeset]*	Sets locale for internationalization
`-xrm`	*X_resource_manager_string*	Used to set any other resources

In addition to the command-line parameters show in Table 3.4, you can add your own—if you're willing to set up the complex code to do it. We cover this topic in Chapter 14, "Initializing the Xt Intrinsics Revisited."

Of the standard command-line parameters, we covered the `-fg` and `-bg` options above. The `-geometry` option works just like the geometry resource also covered above. The `-display` option is needed to display your Motif program on another X server. The interesting one is the `-xrm` option.

Using the -xrm Command-Line Parameter

The *X_resource_manager_string* is a valid command to send to the X resource manager. The syntax of this command is basically the same as the syntax for a resource-setting command inside a resource file.

You can set resource options of an application from the command-line by sending the values to the X resource manager. The `-xrm` command-line parameter allows you to do this. For example, to set a value of the `fontList` resource (globally—but in this case only globally for the application), the syntax in a resource file would be:

```
*fontList:  lucidasans-12
```

The command line for the program *first* would then be:

```
first -xrm "*fontList: lucidasans-12"
```

The above command would run the *first* program and set its `fontList` resource (for all widgets in the *first* program) to the font lucidasans-12. The syntax *fontList:* usually means globally for all applications, but resources set with the -xrm option affect only the application specified in the command-line parameter.

You could also try:

```
first -xrm "Ppm*fontList: lucidasans-12"
```

(The lucidasans-12 font is not available on every X server. For a list of the fonts available on your server, use the *xlsfonts* program.)

With the -xrm command-line parameter, you can set basically any resource values that you can in a resource file, only you don't need to create a resource file to do it. Unfortunately, you do need to be a very good typist. If you have more than a few options, you'll probably want to create a resource file.

Setting Resources Application-wide with the -xrm Option

Try the following command to launch the *first* program:

```
first -xrm "Ppm*fontList: variable" \
      -xrm "Ppm*foreground: red"
```

This command uses wildcards (the *) to set resource values application-wide. You can also use -xrm options to set resource values for individual widgets.

Setting Resources for Individual Widgets with the -xrm Option

Try the following command:

```
first -xrm "Ppm*label.fontList: variable" \
      -xrm "Ppm*quit.fontList: cursor"     \
      -xrm "Ppm*quit.shadowThickness: 8"
```

You'll notice we use the cursor font for the **Quit** pushbutton. The cursor font normally contains X Window cursor shapes (like arrows and crosshairs), but it is still a full-fledged X Window font. You'll note that using the cursor font makes for a very visible outcome.

Fallback Resources

Fallback resources are a set of resource commands you pass to XtAppInitialize. These resources are used as a fallback mechanism in case the user didn't set up a resource file correctly. Fallback resources take effect only if the resource hasn't been set by any other means. Thus, fallback resources have the lowest priority of all resource-setting commands. Even so, fallback resources are very useful as a safety fallback strategy.

You can set up fallback resources as shown in the following code:

```
/* Set up fallback resources. */
static String fallback_resources[] = {
  "*fontList:  lucidasans-14",
  "*background: dimgray",
  "*foreground: white",
  NULL   /* end with a NULL */

}; /* fallback_resources */

    /* ... */
int main(int argc, char** argv)

{   /* main */

    /* ... */

    /* Initialize the X Toolkit Intrinsics. */
    n = 0;
    parent = XtAppInitialize(&app_context,
            "Ppm",
            (XrmOptionDescList) NULL,
            0,
            (Cardinal*) &argc,
            argv,
            fallback_resources, /* fallback resources */
            args, 0);

    /* ... */

} /* main */
```

See Chapter 14 for more on `XtAppInitialize` and fallback resources.

Hard-Coding Resource Commands

In addition to resource files and the `-xrm` command-line parameter, you can hard-code resource commands in your programs. The danger here is that hard-coded values *cannot* be overridden in resource files.

When you hard-code resource commands, you use resource-name/value pairs much as you would in resource files. You don't have to specify the widget names, though, because you use `Widget` pointers in your code. You do follow a very convoluted programming style, though. This style is unique to the X Window System.

There are two main steps to setting resource commands in your code. First, set the resource name and its new value into an element in an `Arg` array with `XtSetArg`. In resource files, you use resource names, such as *labelString*. In your C code, you use `XmN`*resourceName*, such as `XmNlabelString`. If you look in the Motif include files like `<Xm/Xm.h>`, you'll notice that `XmNlabelString` is really just a definition for the literal string *labelString*.

Resource names normally begin with a lowercase letter. Any words following start with an uppercase letter.

The XtSetArg Macro

To set a resource value into an `Arg` array element, use the following code:

```
Arg          args[20];
Cardinal     n;

n = 0;
XtSetArg(args[n], XmNwhich-resource,
     resource-value);
n++;
```

Note that we choose an arbitrary size of 20 for the `Arg` array. We find this size works with most Motif code. Each element in the `Arg` array, then, holds a resource name and a value:

```
typedef struct {
    String     name;
    XtArgVal   value;
} Arg, *ArgList;
```

Call `XtSetArg` for each resource you want to set in your code. For example:

```
n = 0;
XtSetArg(args[n], XmNsashWidth, 12);  n++;
XtSetArg(args[n], XmNsashHeight, 6);  n++;
XtSetArg(args[n], XmNsashIndent, -6); n++;
```

The above code sets up three paned-window resources: `sashWidth`, `sashHeight`, and `sashIndent`. C purists will have already noticed that n++ is placed on the same line as the call to `XtSetArg`, but this is a common usage in X. Why? So that you can comment out just one line to correctly remove a resource-setting command. Since the n++ is on the same line, you then ensure that your value for *n* is correct.

XtSetArg is a very complex macro. You really don't want to know what it does, but just in case, it follows:

```
#define XtSetArg(arg, n, d) \
    ((void)((arg).name = (n),(arg).value =(XtArgVal)(d)))
```

Note that the arg parameter to this macro is used more than once. This is why you cannot use the following shortcut:

```
XtSetArg(args[n++], XmNsashWidth, 12);  /* BAD code */
```

If you do use something like the above code, you'll find that *n* gets incremented twice, which is not the intended outcome.

Calling XtSetValues

We covered the first step to hard-coding resource values above. The second step is to pass this Arg array to a widget creation function or to XtSetValues:

```
void XtSetValues(Widget widget,
        ArgList args,
        Cardinal number_args)
```

XtSetValues is used to set resource values into a widget that is already created. In your code, you should call XtSetValues as follows:

```
Widget      widget;
Arg         args[20];
Cardinal    n;

n = 0;
XtSetArg(args[n], XmNwhich-resource,
        resource-value);
n++;

XtSetValues(widget, args, n);
```

For a more real example, the following code sets the labelString resource into an Arg array and passes this value on to XtSetValues:

```
Widget      widget;
XmString    motif_string;
```

```
Arg          args[20];
Cardinal     n;

n = 0;
XtSetArg(args[n], XmNlabelString, motif_string);
n++;

XtSetValues(widget, args, n);
```

You can also set resource values at the same time you create a widget. In fact, it's generally more efficient to do this at that time. The following code shows this:

```
Widget       widget, parent;
XmString     motif_string;
Arg          args[20];
Cardinal     n;

n = 0;
XtSetArg(args[n], XmNlabelString, motif_string);
n++;

widget = XmCreateLabel(parent, "hello", args, n);

XtManageChild(widget);
```

Both examples use the new data type XmString. We cover the complexities of XmString in Chapter 8.

Using a Variable Number of Parameters

Using the Arg arrays and XtSetArg may be a bit more tedious than you want. In that case, there's a set values function that takes a variable number of parameters, XtVaSetValues:

```
void XtVaSetValues(Widget widget, ...)
```

In your code, you can use XtVaSetValues as follows:

```
Widget       widget;
XmString     motif_string;

XtVaSetValues(widget,
    XmNlabelString, motif_string,
    NULL);
```

As you now understand, using XtVaSetValues is a lot easier than combining XtSetArg with XtSetValues.

When using any of the Xt variable-argument functions, be sure to terminate the function parameters with a NULL or you will definitely cause problems for your application.

NOTE

Retrieving Resource Values from Your Code

In addition to setting resource values, you can also get back the values of resources. This is especially useful in basing a new widget resource value on that of another widget. To extract a resource value from a widget, use XtGetValues:

```
void XtGetValues(Widget widget,
        ArgList args,
        Cardinal number_args)
```

Don't be deceived that XtGetValues and XtSetValues take the same parameters. The functions really are different both in their purpose and in the way you place data into the Arg array.

With XtSetValues you place in data values into the Arg array. With XtGetValues, you place in the address of variables into the Arg array, and XtGetValues then places the values into the addresses you provide.

The following code example extracts the value of the *width* and *height* resources for a given widget, which should be the widget's size in pixels:

```
Widget      widget;
Dimension   width, height;
Arg         args[10];

n = 0;
XtSetArg(args[n], XmNwidth,  &width);  n++;
XtSetArg(args[n], XmNheight, &height); n++;

XtGetValues(widget, args, n);
```

The calls to XtSetArg store the address of the *width* and *height* variables. The call to XtGetValues actually gets the values and stores the results in the values pointed at in the Arg array. The width and height resources should apply to every widget.

NOTE Before X11 Release 4, the `Dimension` data type was an unsigned short integer, often set to a 16-bit value. With Release 5 (which should correspond to Motif 1.2), `Dimension` became an unsigned int, which is normally a 32-bit value. Because of this, always use the proper data type, `Dimension`, for width and height values for Motif widgets. You can easily pass the wrong number of bytes on the stack and cause hard to track down problems in your applications. Don't assume `Dimension` is an int.

There's also a variable-number-of-arguments version of `XtGetValues`, called `XtVaGetValues`:

```
void XtVaGetValues(Widget widget, ...)
```

In your code, you can call `XtVaGetValues` as the following example shows:

```
Widget        widget;
Dimension     width, height;
XtVaGetValues(widget,
    XmNwidth,  &width,
    XmNheight, &height,
    NULL);
```

This code is equivalent to the code with `XtGetValues`, above.

Now that we've explained resource-setting commands, it's time to cover the locations of resource files.

LOCATION OF RESOURCE FILES

X resource files are loaded up by the Xt Intrinsics when you initialize Xt. Normally your code will call `XtAppInitialize` or `XtVaAppInitialize`, which in turn calls `XtDisplayInitialize`—the routine that handles loading in resource files under the hood.

Resource files may appear in many locations in your system. There's a number of common locations, such as `/usr/lib/X11/app-defaults` for class resource files. But, true to the X Window tradition, you can do a lot of customizing with resource files. Internationalization, for example, adds complexity to many of the standard resource file locations.

Resource definitions follow the order below. Hard-coded resource commands, at the top of Table 3.5, take precedence over all other resource settings. Command-line resources come next, going all the way down to fall-back resources, which you can pass to XtAppInitialize. In addition, resource commands that use direct names have precedence over class resource values.

This precedence is shown in Table 3.5.

Table 3.5 *Decoding X resource file locations.*

Resource Type	Locations
Hard-coded	Set into your code
Command-line	-xrm, -bg, -geometry, etc.
User host-based resources	XENVIRONMENT or $HOME/.Xdefaults-hostname
User server-based resources	RESOURCE_MANAGER/SCREEN_RESOURCES or $HOME/.Xdefaults
Application resources	XUSERFILESEARCHPATH, XAPPLRESDIR, or HOME
Application defaults	XFILESEARCHPATH or /usr/lib/X11/app-defaults
Fallback resources	Passed to XtAppInitialize

The list in Table 3.5 represents many different locations to remember. Because of this, we strongly advise you not to use the X environment variables unless you really need to. These environment variables often serve only to complicate matters. They become useful in very specialized circumstances. Unless you really need them, avoid them.

As you can tell, the rules for X resource files are exceedingly complex. We've already covered hard-coded, command-line, and fallback resources. In the text below, we'll cover each of the other options in depth.

User Host-Based Resources

The XENVIRONMENT environment variable can hold the name of a resource file. If set, this resource file is loaded by all Xt-based applications you run. XENVIRONMENT is the full, complete path name for a resource file.

For example, if you create a user resource file named **foo** in the /u/erc/resources directory, then you should set the XENVIRONMENT environment variable to /u/erc/resources/foo.

In the UNIX C shell, you can use the following command:

```
setenv XENVIRONMENT /u/erc/resources/foo
```

XENVIRONMENT points to a file, whereas XAPPLRESDIR points to a directory in which to look for files. The search-path variables, such as XUSERFILE-SEARCHPATH, point to a colon-delimited list of paths.

If the XENVIRONMENT environment variable is not set, then Xt will look for a file named .Xdefaults-*hostname* in your home directory. That is, Xt looks for $HOME/.Xdefaults-*hostname*, where *hostname* is the host (network) name for the machine the program is computing on. If you're running on a machine named *nokomis*, for example, the file loaded would be .Xdefaults-nokomis, located in your home directory.

Most users, though, don't set up host-based resources. Use host-based resources when you have a situation where you log into the same home directory from a number of machines and want to customize your X resources (particularly font sizes) on a per-machine basis.

User X Server-Based Resources

User resource files contain resource-setting commands for anything you care to set. Even though class resource files apply to just one application class, user resource files apply to just any application under X.

Inside one of these user resource files, though, you place the same resource-setting commands. The only difference is that these commands can apply to all application classes (that is, to all applications), so you need to be very specific on which application resources you choose to set. Use these files with care.

Maintain some discipline and be very careful with the use of wildcards. A good rule to follow: Never start an X resource-setting command with an asterisk.

The traditional grab-bag X resource file is a file named **.Xdefaults** in your home directory. This user resource file applies to all X programs. In fact, you probably already have a file named **.Xdefaults** in your home directory.

The RESOURCE_MANAGER and SCREEN_RESOURCES properties, if set, override the **$HOME/.Xdefaults** file. Many installations, though, use the *xrdb* program to load in the contents of the **.Xdefaults** file into the RESOURCE_MANAGER property, negating the difference.

Using xrdb and the X Resource Manager Database

The RESOURCE_MANAGER property is stored on the root window (of the first screen) of a display and contains, in text format, resource-setting commands that apply to all X clients on that display. This property (a named collection of data) then acts much like the **.Xdefaults** file described above. This may seem like yet another X Window attempt at complexity, but storing resource-setting commands only in files doesn't always work.

Two cases where resource files don't work are on X terminals (specialized displays with limited local computing power) and in cases where you run X programs on multiple machines and display them on your workstation. None of the resource files will pertain to programs running on another machine unless that machine and your user account on that machine share the same resource files and configuration.

You could, for example, set up similar resource files on every machine you log on, or you can use the RESOURCE_MANAGER property.

Normally, *xrdb* up loads a file called **.Xresources**, creating the RESOURCE_MANAGER property from this file.

With X11 Release 5, *xrdb* also manages the SCREEN_RESOURCES property. This property contains resource commands that pertain to a specific screen, such as color settings. (You could, for example, have a two-screen display, with one monochrome screen and one color.) If you have only one screen, just use RESOURCE_MANAGER and skip SCREEN_RESOURCES.

Many users configure their X systems to run *xrdb* at startup. *Xrdb* then creates the RESOURCE_MANAGER property from a resource file, using the -load command-line parameter.

The standard way to run *xrdb* follows:

```
xrdb [options] filename
```

To load in a file named **.Xresources** in a user's home directory and override any existing RESOURCE_MANAGER property, use the following command:

```
xrdb -load $HOME/.Xresources
```

If you run *xrdb* as part of your X startup, then you don't have to worry about overwriting preexisting commands in the `RESOURCE_MANAGER` property. Some systems, like Hewlett-Packard's VUE, do this automatically for you.

If you run *xrdb* later, you may want to preserve the resource commands that are already in the property. If so, use the `-merge` command-line parameter:

```
xrdb -merge my_resource_file
```

The term *merge* is a bit of a misnomer, as *xrdb* performs an odd "lexico-graphic sorted merge of the two inputs," according to the online manual.

When run, *xrdb* runs your resource file through `cpp`, the C compiler preprocessor, allowing you to use constructs like `#ifdef` and `#include` (which should be familiar to all C programmers). With X, you typically use `cpp` directives for separating monochrome and color resources. For example, you can use the following layout to define a set of resources for color and monochrome screens. *Xrdb* will define the symbol `COLOR` if you have a color screen:

```
#ifdef COLOR
!  ... color resources
Ppm*foreground:  white
Ppm*background:  lightgrey
#else
!  ... monochrome resources
Ppm*foreground:  black
Ppm*background:  white
#endif
```

The `#ifdef COLOR` directive is especially useful for Motif programs, because the three-dimensional effects of these two interfaces require special values on monochrome systems. Note that the normal X resource files are *not* run through `cpp`. Only *xrdb* does this.

Common *xrdb* command-line parameters are listed in Table 3.6.

Table 3.6 *Common xrdb command-line parameters.*

Parameter	Meaning
`-nocpp`	Don't run resource files through `cpp`, the C preprocessor, which is mainly used for include files and separating color from monochrome resources. *continued*

`-query`	Returns the contents of the `RESOURCE_MANAGER` property.
`-load`	Replaces the `RESOURCE_MANAGER` property with the new file's resource-setting commands.
`-merge`	Merges the resource-setting commands in the passed file with those already in the `RESOURCE_MANAGER` property.
`-remove`	Removes the `RESOURCE_MANAGER` property.
`-edit`	Works backwards. This option places the resource-setting commands in the `RESOURCE_MANAGER` property into the given file.

Application Resources

The Xt Intrinsics next search for application class resource files set up by the user. The default location for these application class resource files are the user's home directory. When we created resource file examples above, using the file named **Ppm** in the home directory, this is the type of resource file we set up.

The search for application resources checks the `XUSERFILE-SEARCHPATH` environment variable. If `XUSERFILESEARCHPATH` isn't set, the next directory checked is the one specified by `XAPPLRESDIR`. If neither `XUSERFILESEARCHPATH` or `XAPPLRESDIR` is set, the Intrinsics checks the user's home diretcory, stored in the `HOME` environment variable.

The XUSERFILESEARCHPATH Environment Variable

The `XUSERFILESEARCHPATH` environment variable holds a colon-delimited search path. Inside this search path, you can use a number of substitutions that are expanded at runtime. For example, `%N` in the search path is substituted with the application's class name, such as *Ppm*.

Most of the substitutions work for internationalizing X resource files, as shown in Table 3.7.

Table 3.7 *Path substitution in X search paths.*

Substitute	With
%C	Special customization, such as `-color` or `-mono`. New in R5.
%L	Full locale, such as `fr_CA.iso8859-1` for French in Canada or `ja_JP.EUC` for Japanese in Japan.
%l	Language part of locale, such as `fr`.
%t	Territory part of locale, such as `CA`.
%c	Codeset part of locale, such as `iso8859-1`.
%N	Application's class name.
%S	Suffix, such as `.bm` for bitmap files.
%T	File type, usually `app-defaults`.

These substitutions also apply to the `XFILESEARCHPATH` environment variable, which we cover below.

N O T E   `XUSERFILESEARCHPATH` ignores the %S and %T substitutions.

N O T E   X11 Release 5 introduced the customization substitution, %C. If your system has two monitors, one monochrome and one color, you may want to take advantage of this. Using this customization, you name your color class resource file `Ppm-color` and the monochrome file `Ppm-mono` and then set `XUSERFILE-SEARCHPATH` or `XFILESEARCHPATH` accordingly.

In X11 Release 5, the default `XUSERFILESEARCHPATH` is set to:

```
base/%L/%N%C: \
base/%l/%N%C: \
base/%N%C:    \
base/%L/%N: \
base/%l/%N: \
base/%N
```

The *base* is set to the value of the XAPPLRESDIR environment variable or the user's home directory, if XAPPLRESDIR isn't set.

If XUSERFILESEARCHPATH is set to anything other than the defaults listed above, then XAPPLRESDIR is ignored.

This seems confusing, but Table 3.8 should help. Assume the locale is set to fr_CA.iso8859-1, the class name to Ppm, the customization to -color, and the *base* to the user's home directory.

Table 3.8 *Expanding the XUSERFILESEARCHPATH.*

Base Value	Expands to
base/%L/%N%C:	$HOME/fr_CA.iso8859-1/Ppm-color
base/%l/%N%C:	$HOME/fr_CA.iso8859-1/Ppm-color
base/%N%C:	$HOME/Ppm-color
base/%L/%N:	$HOME/fr_CA.iso8859-1/Ppm
base/%l/%N:	$HOME/fr/Ppm
base/%N:	$HOME/Ppm

In the vast majority of cases, you'll place your class resource file in your home directory (or in /usr/lib/X11/app-defaults, the default for XFILESEARCHPATH).

The XAPPLRESDIR Environment Variable

If you're feeling particularly ambitious, you could use an environment variable, XAPPLRESDIR (which stands for X APPLication RESource file DIRectory). The XAPPLRESDIR environment variable provides another place (a directory) to find your class resource files.

Unfortunately, XAPPLRESDIR has changed over time. With X11 Release 3, you had to set XAPPLRESDIR to a directory and had to remember to end the directory name with a forward slash (/). Let's say that your class resource file is located in the directory /u/erc. In that case, the environment variable XAPPLRESDIR would be set to /u/erc/ (note the trailing slash character). In the UNIX C shell, you could use the following command:

```
setenv XAPPLRESDIR /u/erc/
```

With X11 Release 5, though, you can set XAPPLRESDIR to a simple directory name, such as using a period for the current directory (this is very useful for debugging):

```
setenv XAPPLRESDIN.
```

XAPPLRESDIR is associated with X11 Release 3. More modern systems should use the XFILESEARCHPATH environment variable.

Application Defaults

The application defaults resource files are simply class resource files but are stored in system locations such as /usr/lib/X11/app-defaults, the default location for these files. Normally, regular users don't have permission to change these files because they are meant to apply systemwide and are usually set up by system administrators.

The application defaults are looked for in the XFILESEARCHPATH search path or in /usr/lib/X11/app-defaults, if XFILESEARCHPATH isn't set. Note that some versions of X, notably on Sun systems, modify this default to be $OPENWINHOME/lib/app-defaults. For a class name of *Ppm*, the application defaults would search either the paths in the XFILESEARCHPATH environment variable or the traditional location of /usr/lib/X11/app-defaults.

The XFILESEARCHPATH Environment Variable

XFILESEARCHPATH holds a colon-separated list of directory paths. Each directory is searched in order to find the application defaults (class resource) file. For example, on a Sun OpenWindows system, you may want to set XFILESEARCHPATH to:

```
setenv XFILESEARCHPATH \
    /usr/lib/X11/%T/%N:$OPENWINHOME/lib/%T/%N
```

With X11 Release 5, the default for XFILESEARCHPATH is set to:

```
/usr/lib/X11/%L/%T/%N%C:\
/usr/lib/X11/%l/%T/%N%C:\
/usr/lib/X11/%T/%N%C:   \
/usr/lib/X11/%L/%T/%N:   \
/usr/lib/X11/%l/%T/%N:   \
/usr/lib/X11/%T/%N
```

The allowable substitutions are shown in Table 3.7. For a class name of *Ppm*, the last part of the default path expands to /usr/lib/X11/app-defaults/Ppm.

If you look in the default directory, /usr/lib/X11/app-defaults, you'll see a number of class resource files, as listed in Table 3.9.

Table 3.9 *Example class resource files.*

File	Application
XTerm	for the *xterm* application
XCalc	for the *xcalc* calculator application
XLoad	for the *xload* application
XClock	for the *xclock* clock application

None of these applications are Motif applications. If your system administrator has installed some Motif applications, though, this is the same directory where they would normally be placed.

Your system may have the app-defaults directory some other place if your X Window System isn't installed in the standard directories. If you suspect this (especially if you don't find a /usr/lib/X11/app-defaults directory), ask your system administrator.

To help wade through this confusing mess, Table 3.10 summarizes environment variables.

Table 3.10 *Resource file environment variables.*

Environment Variable	Example
XAPPLRESDIR	/u/erc/resources/
XENVIRONMENT	/u/erc/resources/foo
XFILESEARCHPATH	/usr/lib/X11/%L/%T/%N%C:/usr/lib/X11/%T/%N
XUSERFILESEARCHPATH	$HOME/%L/%N%C:$HOME/%N

Again, we urge you to stay away from the X environment variables unless you absolutely can't avoid it.

Now that we've tackled where resource files can go and all the millions of permutations, we can delve back into the formal syntax for resource-setting commands.

Formal Resource File Syntax

These resource-setting commands make a form of primitive programming language and follow a strict syntax. According to the online-manual page for X, the pseudo-language for resource-setting commands is formally defined by the syntax listed in Table 3.11.

Table 3.11 *Resource-setting commands.*

Component	Valid Values
ResourceLine	Comment | IncludeFile | ResourceSpec | <empty line>
Comment	"!" {<any character except null or new-line>}
IncludeFile	#" WhiteSpace "include" WhiteSpace FileName WhiteSpace
FileName	<valid filename for operating system>
ResourceSpec	WhiteSpace ResourceName WhiteSpace ":" WhiteSpace Value
ResourceName	[Binding] {Component Binding} ComponentName
Binding	"." | "*"
WhiteSpace	{" " | "\t" }
Component	"?" | ComponentName
ComponentName	NameChar {NameChar}
NameChar	"a"\-"z" | "A"\-"Z" | "0"\-"9" | "_" | "-"
Value	{<any character except null or unescaped newline>}

In Table 3.11, the vertical bar character (|), divides alternate values. The curly braces, { and }, surround zero or more repeated entries. Square brackets, [and], surround optional elements. Quotes, " and ", surround literal character strings.

You can include files in resource files, but only if a program supports the #include directive. The *xrdb* program, for example, does, but many X applications don't.

In a ResourceSpec, all whitespace characters that come before the name are ignored, as are all whitespace characters that come before the colon, or after the colon.

Special characters include:

- ■ \ for a leading space
- ■ \t for tab
- ■ \\ for a single backslash
- ■ \n for newline

To extend a resource command onto the next line, end the line with a single backslash (\). (Make sure a newline character comes right after the backslash to end the line.) You can encode special characters with their ISO Latin-1 (extended ASCII) values, using \nnn, where nnn is the character number—in octal.

A question mark (?) matches a single component name as a wildcard. That is, a question mark can replace a class name or other single component.

This syntax applies to all resource-setting commands in any resource file.

DEBUGGING RESOURCE COMMANDS

X handles resource-setting errors in the traditional X manner: Most errors are silently ignored. This makes debugging resource commands burdensome, especially if you define some of the many X environment variables.

Some resources, like fonts or colors, can generate error messages, but most don't. To help this, X11 Release 5 adds new support for debugging resource commands. You can set the StringConversionWarnings resource to on, which will print error messages if problems occur when trying to convert the text (strings) in a resource file into actual values. These messages, while somewhat cryptic, can help debug resource files.

```
*StringConversionWarnings:  on
```

LISTING THE RESOURCES FOR AN APPLICATION

In addition, you can use a program named *appres* to list the resources that an application is set up to load. This won't tell you all the resources available, but it will tell you how an application is customized. *Appres* looks in all the standard places for resource files (listed above in the section entitled "Location of Resource Files"), as well as the RESOURCE_MANAGER and SCREEN_RESOURCES properties, and then prints out what resources have been set in all those places. To get at class resource files, you need to pass the resource class name and an instance name.

We can use *appres*, for example, to determine what resources have been set for our *first* program. The command below tells *appres* that the class name for the *first* program is *Ppm*:

```
appres Ppm first
```

The output from *appres*, after using our third resource file example from above, looks like the following:

```
*fontList: -*-helvetica-bold-r-normal--12-120-*-*-p-*-*-1
*background:        sienna
*title:             Res. 3
*geometry:          200x300+201+400
*quit.background:   dimgray
*quit.labelString:  Push here to exit
*quit.foreground:   white
*label.background:  bisque2
*label.labelString: Yet another label.
*label.foreground:  seagreen
*pane.background:   maroon
```

We passed both the resource class name, *Ppm,* and the program name, *first,* to *appres,* so that we'd be sure to get any special resource customizations under either name.

Note that the output of *appres* tends toward the voluminous, even for a small program like *first*.

EDITORIAL: RESOURCE FILES ARE TERRIBLE ON THE USER

Although X resources and resource files provide a great deal of end-user configurability, resources are also one of the toughest aspects of X to master, especially for new users—as you've no doubt guessed by reading this long chapter.

Truly user-friendly applications wouldn't force users to memorize the complicated listing of possible resource file locations given in Table 3.5. Instead, a user-friendly application should provide a graphical means for the end user to configure the program. To do anything else defeats the whole point of providing a graphical interface in the first place. Just because X resource files are ASCII text, don't leave editing resource files to the user, as the resource syntax is decidedly not user friendly.

So far, you or your users have had to edit every resource file by hand with a text editor. With X11 Release 5, though, a new program named *editres* allows you to edit resource files with a graphical front end.

Stumbling to the Future: Editres

Editres queries an existing application for the set of resources and widgets it supports, as well as change an application's resources on the fly—but only if you compile the application with support for *editres*. In addition, *editres* can write out a set of resource commands to a file but is very likely to overwrite your existing resource files.

The *editres* application, as shown in Figure 3.4, is the first small step toward what the X Window System really needs: a graphical X resource editor. As such, *editres* provides a prototype to allow you to explore what could be done. In our minds, the whole purpose of *editres* is to spark discussion on graphical resource editors, because *editres* itself isn't that inspiring.

One thing that *editres* provides, though, is a semistandard protocol for exchanging X resource information between an Xt-based program (which includes Motif applications) and some other external entity, such as a resource editor. This protocol is what you can use to experiment with graphical resource editors.

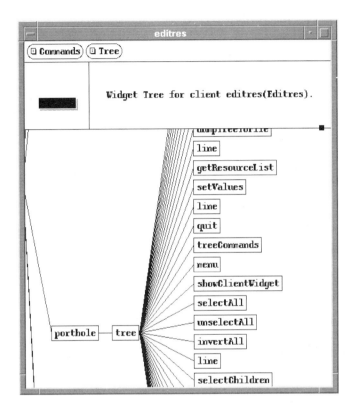

Figure 3.4   *The Editres program in action.*

Making Your Code Editres Compatible

There are just a few small steps you need to do to make your programs work with the *editres* protocol. First, you must ensure that you have X11 Release 5 or higher and the Xmu (X miscellaneous utilities) library. If you have an R5 or higher Xmu library, then add the following lines of code to your Motif applications:

```
#include <X11/Xmu/Editres.h>
```

```
Widget      shell_widget;
void        _XEditResCheckMessages();

XtAddEventHandler(shell_widget,
    (EventMask) 0,
    True,
    _XEditResCheckMessages,
    NULL);
```

You need to pass every shell widget you create to the `XtAddEventHandler` call, above. That is, replace `shell_widget` with the top-level shell widget returned by `XtAppInitialize` and any additional shell widgets you create.

When you link, you'll need to link in the Xmu library before the Xt library, as the following command shows:

```
cc -o foo foo.c -lXm -lXmu -lXt -lX11
```

We'll cover `XtAddEventHandler` in greater detail in Chapter 10 on events.

N O T E

Many Silicon Graphics systems, based on X11 Release 4, use an early version of *editres*. In this case, use `_EditResCheckMessages` (the initial X is missing) instead of `_XEditResCheckMessages`. You'll know if you need to do this if the linker cannot resolve `_XEditResCheckMessages`.

SUMMARY

Even though X resources are very handy, we find all the permutations exceedingly complex. Although resources will be covered throughout the remainder of this book, this chapter served as a basic introduction to resources. Instead of reviewing such a large chunk of this book in a pithy summary, we've compiled a Resource Quick Reference that you can refer to during the course of your programming sessions.

In the next few chapters, we'll show practical examples of using X resources in your programs, as well as flesh out Motif applications. We cover the first part of fleshing out an application—creating menus—in the next chapter.

N O T E

RESOURCE QUICK REFERENCE

!	starts a comment.
.(period)	separates widget names or classes, if you are specifying the widget hierarchy exactly.
*	is a wildcard. The wildcard can separate widget names or classes, without specifying the widget hierarchy exactly. We recommend using wildcards, but be careful, as it's easy to set the resources of too many widgets.

A resource-setting command looks like:

```
widgets_to_apply.resourceName: value_to_set
```

Some examples:

```
*push.labelString: This is a new label
*fontList:         *courier-bold-r-normal--*-140-*-*-*
```

X TOOLKIT INTRINSICS FUNCTIONS AND MACROS INTRODUCED IN THIS CHAPTER

```
XtSetArg
XtSetValues
XtGetValues
XtVaSetValues
XtVaGetValues
```

SECTION 2

Building the Base Application

This section expands on the Motif basics introduced in Chapters 1 to 3 and covers the creation of complete working Motif applications—the real reason most of you bought this book in the first place.

Chapter 4 introduces pull-down menus, menu bars, and the main-window widget. Menus are used for a variety of tasks in Motif, and their usage is proscribed by the *OSF/Motif Style Guide*—an important thing to know as you tackle your first Motif program.

Chapter 5 introduces the XmText and XmTextField widgets as a means to edit text. Also included is a discussion of scroll bars and scrolled-text editing.

Chapter 6 covers container widgets, which are used to control the layout of application windows. These widgets include row-container widgets, frame widgets, paned-window widgets, and more.

Chapter 7 explains dialogs from A to Z, including how to create them

97

and where to use them. Again, the *OSF/Motif Style* Guide provides a lot of detail about how dialogs should work—but a lot of flexibility is left to the programmer.

Chapter 8 introduces Motif's text format and `XmString` segments. In addition, this chapter discusses how Motif handles and imports fonts.

Finally, Chapter 9 discusses additional Motif widgets that you'll use frequently: `XmList`, `XmScale`, `XmArrowButton`, `XmScrolledWindow`, and `XmScrollbar`.

CHAPTER 4

Pull-Down Menus and the Main Window

This chapter introduces pull-down menus, menu bars, and the main-window widget. Topics include:

- Creating the main window and menu bar
- Customizing the main window
- Placing widgets in the main window
- Creating pull-down menus
- Filling in menus with menu choices
- Using gadgets and widgets
- Following the *OSF/Motif Style Guide* for menus
- Creating a help menu
- Keyboard accelerators
- Cascading, or pull-right, menus
- Motif's simple menu routines

99

MOTIF MENUS

Just about every graphical windowing environment specifies that a menu bar with menus should appear somewhere on the screen. The exact location depends on the specific environment: The Macintosh places a menu bar on the top of the screen, whiles Motif, Microsoft Windows, and OS/2 place a menu bar on each main window.

Most Motif applications have a menu bar at the top of the application's main window. Menus are pulled down from this menu bar and offer the user an easy-to-learn method of entering commands into an application. Using a menu bar at the top of the main window makes your applications consistent, so the user has an easier time learning your program. The menu bar also allows a user to browse the available menu choices, to see what commands are available.

Menus form one of the most important means users have to interact with your programs, and Motif offers quite a few variants for menus. This rather long chapter covers Motif's many menus. We'll also show how to set up your applications to conform with the *OSF/Motif Style Guide*.

According to the *OSF/Motif Style Guide*, your application should have a menu bar across its main window. Minimally, this menu bar should hold the File and Help menus, as shown in Figure 4.1.

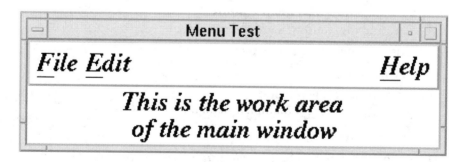

Figure 4.1   *A Motif menu bar.*

Most applications include more than the File and Help menus, however. The Style Guide has a whole set of rules for menus, which we cover starting in the section entitled "Following the OSF/Motif Style Guide for Menus," below.

Motif offers four types of menus:

- Pull-down menus
- Pull-right, or cascading, menus
- Option menus
- Pop-up menus

In this chapter, we cover pull-down and pull-right menus in depth. Later we'll cover option and pop-up menus, which are considered advanced topics.

SHORTCUT

Pull-Down Menus

The most common Motif menus are *pull-down menus*. As the name implies, the user "pulls" these menus down from a menu bar, by pressing the left mouse button. Despite the name *pull-right*, the same pull-down menu routines are used for pull-right menus. In Motif, all menus are XmRowColumn widgets, a specialized container widget that has a zillion options for each type of menu.

Building Pull-Down Menus

There are five steps to building pull-down menus:

1. Create a main-window widget, which holds the menu bar.
2. Create a menu bar, which holds the pull-down menus.
3. Create a pull-down menu.
4. Create a cascade button on the menu bar to display the menu when the user pulls down the menu. You must connect the cascade button to the pull-down menu via the subMenuId resource.
5. Create menu choices, which are usually XmPushButton widgets.

The code below briefly shows how to do this:

```
Widget    mainwindow, menubar, filemenu;
Widget    parent, cascade, exit_choice;
Cardinal  n;
Arg       args[20];

/* ... */

/* Create main window. */
n = 0;
mainwindow = XmCreateMainWindow(parent,
             "main", args, n);

/* Create menubar. */
n = 0;
menubar = XmCreateMenuBar(mainwindow,
          "menubar", args, n);

XtManageChild(menubar);

n = 0;
filemenu = XmCreatePulldownMenu(menubar,
           "filemenu", args, n);

/* Don't manage menu. */

/* Create cascade button and connect to menu. */
n = 0;
XtSetArg(args[n], XmNsubMenuId, filemenu);
n++;

cascade = XmCreateCascadeButton(menubar,
          name, args, n);

XtManageChild(cascade);

/* Create menu choice: pushbutton. */
n = 0;
exit_choice = XmCreatePushButton(filemenu,
              "quit", args, n);

/* Set up callback. */
XtAddCallback(exit_choice,
    XmNactivateCallback,
    (XtCallbackProc) callback,
    (XtPointer) NULL);

XtManageChild(exit_choice);

/* ... */
```

The Main-Window Widget

The first step in creating menus is to create a main window. The main-window widget exists as a handy convenience to manage the main window of an application. This widget manages up to six (depending on your version of Motif) specialized child widgets. These children are the menu bar, a work area (that is, an area where your application does its stuff), a command area (for the user to enter single-line commands), a message area (handy for status messages), and scroll bars (vertical and horizontal).

You don't have to set up *all* the children to use a main-window widget, and in fact, many applications use only a few children. The scroll bars, in particular, are often not needed, since it's usually more appropriate to place the scroll bars in the work area, with a scrolled-text or list widget.

The main purpose here for a main-window widget is to maintain the menu bar and other child widgets in their proper locations—proper as defined in the *OSF/Motif Style Guide*. The main-window widget fits the bill quite nicely and encourages your applications to use more of the standard features of Motif.

After calling XtAppInitialize, the first thing we need to do is to create a main-window widget. Table 4.1 summarizes the XmMainWindow class.

Table 4.1 *The XmMainWindow class.*

Widget class:	XmMainWindow
Class pointer:	xmMainWindowWidgetClass
Include file:	<Xm/MainW.h>
Create with:	XmCreateMainWindow

Create main-window widgets with XmCreateMainWindow:

```
#include <Xm/MainW.h>

Widget XmCreateMainWindow(Widget parent,
        char* widget_name,
        ArgList args,
        Cardinal number_args)
```

As usual with widgets created by Motif XmCreate*Type* functions, the main-window widget is created unmanaged. You must call XtManageChild after creating the widget. For best performance, wait until you set up all the main window's children before managing the main window.

Before we create the main-window widget, though, we may want to customize it a bit. We could add a 3D shadowing effect, using the shadowThickness resource (XmNshadowThickness in your C programs). In the code below, the number *4* is for a four-pixels-wide shadow.

```
Arg        args[10];
Cardinal   n;

n = 0;
XtSetArg(args[n], XmNshadowThickness, 4);
n++;

/* Create widget... */
```

Note the 3D effects of the shadow at the bottom of the window. You can try different values for the shadowThickness.

Main-Window Separators

We could also create separators, using the showSeparator resource (XmNshowSeparator in your C programs). This Boolean value specifies whether separator lines are to be created between the various children of the main window. The default is False, for no separators. Again, try this as True and False to see which you like better.

```
Arg        args[10];
Cardinal   n;

n = 0;
XtSetArg(args[n], XmNshowSeparator, True);
n++;

/* Create widget... */
```

These separators are widgets. If you ever need to get the widget values for these separators, there are two (or three, depending on your version of Motif) main-window functions to retrieve these values, XmMainWindowSep1 and XmMainWindowSep2:

```
#include <Xm/MainW.h>
```

```
Widget XmMainWindowSep1(Widget main_window)
```

```
Widget XmMainWindowSep2(Widget main_window)
```

Motif 1.2 adds in a third separator, which you can retrieve with XmMainWindowSep3:

```
Widget XmMainWindowSep3(Widget main_window)
```

These separators are visible only if the showSeparator resource is True.

What the Main Window Manages

In addition to the optional separators, the main-window widget manages five (or six) specialized (and optional) child widgets, identified in resources and listed in Table 4.2.

Table 4.2   *Main-window children.*

Resource Name	Name in C Programs	Typical Widget
commandWindow	XmNcommandWindow	XmText or XmCommand
horizontalScrollBar	XmNhorizontalScrollBar	XmScrollBar
menuBar	XmNmenuBar	XmRowColumn
messageWindow	XmNmessageWindow	XmLabel
verticalScrollBar	XmNverticalScrollBar	XmScrollBar
workWindow	XmNworkWindow	*anything*

These child widgets are placed as shown in Figure 4.2.

The commandWindow holds user-entered commands. This is often useful when porting older command-based software to Motif. We advise you to use a single-line XmText widget instead of an XmCommand widget for the commandWindow. Despite the name, the XmCommand widget is clunky and poorly laid out.

The menu bar and scroll bars are obvious. The workWindow is the main area of your application. For example, a text-editing program would place a scrolled-text widget as the workWindow. The messageWindow holds messages from the program for the user. (The `messageWindow` is new in Motif 1.2.) With most of your applications, you'll just use the `menuBar` and the `workWindow`. If there's a scrolled area, it will most likely be within the `workWindow`, so you won't want to create scroll bars for the entire main window.

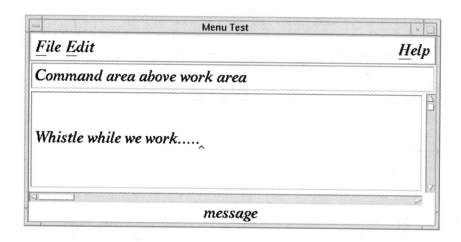

Figure 4.2 *The main window and its child widgets.*

There's a trick to using these resources, though. You cannot get or set these resources until the child widgets are created, but the main-window widget is the parent of these children. Therefore, you first create the main-window widget, then you create the children, all with a parent of the main-window widget. Finally, you tell the main window about the children you already created. It's weird, but it works.

You can either set each of the resources or call the `XmMainWindowSetAreas` convenience function:

```
#include  <Xm/MainW.h>

void XmMainWindowSetAreas(Widget main_window,
      Widget menu_bar,
      Widget command_widget,
      Widget horiz_scrollbar,
      Widget vert_scrollbar,
      Widget work_widget)
```

If you use a `messageWindow`, you must call `XmMainWindowSetAreas`.

You cannot call XmMainWindowSetAreas until you've created all the child widgets you plan to use. In the pull-down menu program, below (in the file **pullmenu.c**), we created only menu-bar and work-area children. Here's how you call XmMainWindowSetAreas with only two child widgets:

```
XmMainWindowSetAreas(main_window,    /* main window */
        menubar,                     /* menulbar */
        (Widget) NULL,               /* command area */
        (Widget) NULL,               /* horiz scroll */
        (Widget) NULL,               /* vert scroll */
        work area);                  /* work area */
```

Other handy main-window resources are listed in Table 4.3.

Table 4.3 *XmMainWindow resources.*

Resource Name	Type	Default Value
shadowThickness	Dimension	0
commandWindow	Widget	NULL
commandWindowLocation	unsigned char	*see below*
horizontalScrollBar	Widget	NULL
mainWindowMarginHeight	Dimension	0
mainWindowMarginWidth	Dimension	0
menuBar	Widget	NULL
messageWindow	Widget	NULL
scrollingPolicy	unsigned char	*application defined*
showSeparator	Boolean	False
verticalScrollBar	Widget	NULL
workWindow	Widget	NULL

Normally, the menu bar appears across the top of the main window. Just beneath the menu bar sits the command window, if you set the commandWindowLocation resource to XmCOMMAND_ABOVE_WORKSPACE. Then comes the (potentially scrolled) work area. If you set the commandWindowLocation resource to XmCOMMAND_BELOW_WORKSPACE, the command window appears just below the work area. In either case, the message window appears at the bottom of the main window. Figure 4.2 shows the `commandWindowLocation` set to `XmCOMMAND_ABOVE_WORKSPACE`. If you set the `commandWindowLocation` to `XmCOMMAND_BELOW_WORKSPACE`, then the main window will look like Figure 4.3.

Figure 4.3   *The main window with the command area below the workspace.*

How do you decide where to put the command area? According to the Style Guide, if you have a message window, set the `commandWindowLocation` to `XmCOMMAND_BELOW_WORKSPACE`. If you don't have a message window, set `commandWindowLocation` to `XmCOMMAND_ABOVE_WORKSPACE`.

The `scrollingPolicy` acts like that of the `XmScrolledWindow` widget, covered in Chapter 9. The default is application-defined scrolling, or `XmAPPLICATION_DEFINED`. Note that the `XmMainWindow` is derived from `XmScrolledWindow`.

MAKING A MENU BAR

After creating a main-window widget to manage the application's widgets, we next need to create a menu-bar widget to manage a menu bar. Menu bars help keep common functions like saving or loading files hidden until needed.

A menu bar is really a XmRowColumn widget, one of the set of container widgets, with the rowColumnType resource set to XmMENU_BAR. A convenience function, XmCreateMenuBar, takes care of all the work needed to create a XmRowColumn widget and configure that widget as a menu bar. This widget manages a bar across the application's main window that contains the names of pull-down menus. If you resize the window to be too small for a single line, the menu bar will try to make two or more lines to hold the menu names, as shown in Figure 4.4.

Figure 4.4 *A double-decker menu bar.*

The function XmCreateMenuBar creates a menu bar:

```
#include <Xm/RowColumn.h>

Widget XmCreateMenuBar(Widget parent,
        char* widget_name,
        ArgList args
        Cardinal number_args)
```

Call XtManageChild after creating the widget.

The menu-bar widget (which we know is really a `XmRowColumn` widget) should hold only one type of child widget: a cascade-button widget. Cascade buttons sit on the menu bar and display the names of the pull-down menus. Cascade buttons then perform the magic necessary to pull down pull-down menus.

Creating Pull-Down Menus

A pull-down menu is also based on a `XmRowColumn` widget, which manages all the child widgets (in this case, menu choices). There's more to a pull-down menu than that, but you can use a handy Motif convenience function, `XmCreatePulldownMenu`, to create a pull-down menu:

```
#include <Xm/RowColumn.h>

Widget XmCreatePulldownMenu(Widget parent,
    char* widget_name,
    ArgList args
    Cardinal number_args)
```

You should *not* call `XtManageChild` after creating the widget, since the cascade button will do that for you (more on that below).

The parent should be the menu-bar widget, not the cascade-button widget on the menu bar. You may want to set the `spacing` resource (`XmNspacing` in your C programs) to 0. This sets the vertical spacing between menu choices in the menu. Setting the spacing resource to 0 makes a better-looking pull-down menu:

```
Arg         args[20];
Cardinal    n;

n = 0;
XtSetArg(args[n], XmNspacing, 0); n++;

/* Create menu... */
```

That's all there is to creating a menu. Simple, isn't it? The only hitch is creating a cascade-button widget and connecting the cascade button to the pull-down menu. It is the cascade button that actually manages the menu.

Cascade Buttons

Cascade-button widgets display the names of any pull-down menus on a menu bar, such as File or Edit. The cascade-button widget is a lot like the pushbutton widget, only the cascade button is used to link a menu bar and a menu (or a menu with a submenu). Even so, a cascade button has an `activateCallback` function, just like a pushbutton, and you can really do what you want in the `activateCallback`. In virtually all cases, though, you ignore this `activateCallback` and just connect a cascade button to a pull-down menu with the `subMenuId` resource.

Table 4.4 summarizes the `XmCascadeButton` widget.

Table 4.4 *The XmCascadeButton class.*

Widget class:	XmCascadeButton
Class pointer:	xmCascadeButtonWidgetClass
Include file:	<Xm/CascadeB.h>
Create with:	XmCreateCascadeButton

To create a cascade button, use `XmCreateCascadeButton`:

```
#include <Xm/CascadeB.h>

Widget XmCreateCascadeButton(Widget parent,
    char* widget_name,
    ArgList args
    Cardinal number_args)
```

We assume the parent is a menu bar or pull-down menu.

Call `XtManageChild` to manage the widget after creating it.

Connecting a Pull-Down Menu to a Menu Bar

After we've created our menu, we still need to make it a pull-down menu by connecting the menu to the cascade button on the menu bar. To do this, we set the `subMenuId` resource (XmNsubMenuId in your C programs) on the cascade-button widget. The `subMenuId` resource needs a widget ID, which is the widget ID of the menu we created. We set this resource on the cascade-button widget, in effect telling the cascade button to call up our menu as needed:

```
#include <Xm/CascadeB.h>

/* ... */
```

```
Widget    cascade_widget; /* on menubar */
Widget    menubar;
Widget    menu_widget;    /* pull-down menu */
Arg       args[10];
Cardinal  n;

/* Set up button on menubar to pull down our menu. */
n = 0;
XtSetArg(args[n], XmNsubMenuId, menu_widget);
n++;

/* Create cascade button. */

cascade_widget = XmCreateCascadeButton(menubar,

                 "file", args, n);
```

We can put all this together into a utility function to create a pull-down
menu. The routine `CreatePulldownMenu`, below, cheats twice, but normally this is of no import. First, we use the same name for the pull-down
menu as the cascade button on the menu bar. Since you normally don't set
conflicting resources for these in a resource file, this should not create a
problem. The second cheat is that we return only the widget ID of the pull-
down menu and hide the widget ID of the cascade button. Again, chances
are you won't need the cascade button's widget ID. If you do, you'll obviously need to modify this function.

The code for `CreatePulldownMenu` follows:

```
Widget CreatePulldownMenu(Widget parent,
    char* name)

{   /* CreatePulldownMenu */
    Widget    menu;
    Widget    cascade;
    Arg       args[20];
    Cardinal  n;

    /* Create pull-down menu. */
    n = 0;

    menu = XmCreatePulldownMenu(parent,
            name, args, n);

    /* Don't manage menu. */

    /* Create cascade button and connect to menu. */
    n = 0;
    XtSetArg(args[n], XmNsubMenuId, menu); n++;

    cascade = XmCreateCascadeButton(parent,
```

```
                    name, args, n);

        XtManageChild(cascade);

        /*
         * We return the widget ID of
         * the menu, not the cascade.
         */
        return menu;

    }   /* CreatePulldownMenu */
```

Once we have the menu connected to the cascade button on the menu bar, the next step is to fill in the menu with, obviously enough, menu choices.

Filling Pull-Down Menus with Menu Choices

Filling in a pull-down menu (or Motif menus in general) is also easy. Each choice is a widget, normally a pushbutton widget (or a pushbutton gadget). That is, each menu choice needs a widget on the menu, which is different from many other windowing systems that treat menus as one combined unit. In fact, each widget on the menu is an independent unit that you create and adjust separately.

Pushbutton widgets, for example, have their own callback functions. In a menu, a pushbutton's activeCallback is called when the menu choice is selected by the user. To fill in a menu, create a widget (usually an XmPushButton) for each menu choice. The widget's activateCallback is the function that will be called when the user chooses that item in the menu. Add the menu items in the order, from top to bottom, that you want them to appear.

Appropriate widgets for menu choices are listed in Table 4.5.

Table 4.5 *Widgets for menu choices.*

Widget	Purpose
XmPushButton	General menu choice
XmPushButtonGadget	General menu choice
XmToggleButton	Choices that can be turned on or off
XmToggleButtonGadget	Choices that can be turned on or off
XmSeparator	Line between menu choices

continued

XmSeparatorGadget	Line between menu choices
XmLabel	Text label that user can't select
XmLabelGadget	Text label that user can't select
XmCascadeButton	For pull-right menus

Since Motif pull-down and pop-up menus are really row-column widgets, you can add all sorts of child widgets to a menu. In the sections below, we'll show how to add a menu title at the top of a menu, as well as separator lines between menu choices.

Most menu choices, though, are XmPushButton widgets. Creating a pushbutton widget should be old hat by now, as we've used pushbuttons since Chapter 2. To speed up the creation of menu choices, we present the following utility function. The CreatePushbutton function, below, creates a pushbutton widget, sets up the activateCallback, and then manages the widget to make it visible.

You pass a pointer to your callback function and another pointer to any *client_data*. This *client_data* will, in turn, be passed to your callback function.

N O T E   It's a common mistake to pass a pointer to a local variable or to reuse a global structure for the *client_data*. Don't do this. Motif just stores a *pointer* to your *client_data*. Motif does not copy this data. You must ensure that the data pointed at remains in a stable state when the callback gets executed.

The code for CreatePushbutton follows:

```
/* push.c */
#include   <Xm/Xm.h>
#include   <Xm/PushB.h>

Widget CreatePushbutton(Widget parent,
    char* name,
    XtCallbackProc callback,
    XtPointer client_data)

{   /* CreatePushbutton */
    Widget     push;
    Arg        args[20];
    Cardinal   n;
```

```
    n = 0;
    push = XmCreatePushButton(parent,
            name, args, n);

    /* Set up callback. */
    XtAddCallback(push,        /* widget */
        XmNactivateCallback, /* which callback */
        callback,            /* callback function */
        client_data);        /* extra data to pass */

    XtManageChild(push);

    return push;

}   /* CreatePushbutton */

/* end of file push.c */
```

Writing callback functions can be tedious, so you may be tempted to share the callbacks among a number of menu choices. To effectively do this, you'll need to pass some extra data to the callback so that the function can determine which menu choice called it. To do so, pass a number or a string or any other data you want as the *client_data*. With that information, you could share a callback function among all the choices in the menu. Or, you could specify a different callback for each menu choice, whichever best fits your needs.

Instead of pushbutton widgets, you may want to use pushbutton gadgets.

Pushbutton Gadgets

N O T E

Gadgets, or lightweight windowless widgets, were invented in an era when a window on an X display was an expensive prospect in terms of CPU resources—and Motif programs tend to create many windows on the X display. Thus, gadgets were intended to be lightweight widgets and save on memory use. In recent years, though, the overhead for a window has dropped dramatically. Windows are now cheaper in terms of CPU resources and performance. The perceived benefit of gadgets has decreased. In addition, for some versions of Motif, gadgets actually provide *worse* performance than widgets. We cover performance issues in Chapter 26. For now, we'll cover pushbutton gadgets in case you do decide that gadgets are worth the effort.

You can treat gadgets in general like widgets, except that sometimes gadgets need special gadget-based functions to access their internal values. Luckily, in our examples below, that isn't the case.

Table 4.6   *The XmPushButtonGadget class.*

Widget class:	XmPushButtonGadget
Class pointer:	xmPushButtonGadgetClass
Include file:	<Xm/PushBG.h>
Create with:	XmCreatePushButtonGadget

You can create a pushbutton gadget with XmCreatePushButtonGadget, as introduced in Table 4.6:

```
#include <Xm/PushBG.h>

Widget XmCreatePushButtonGadget(Widget parent,
        char* widget_name,
        ArgList args
        Cardinal number_args)
```

Note the G (for gadget) on the name of the include file, <Xm/PushBG.h>.

Drawing Lines Between Menu Choices with Separators

You can create a separator, or line, between menu choices. This separator is a Motif XmSeparator widget, summarized in Table 4.7.

Table 4.7   *The XmSeparator class.*

Widget class:	XmSeparator
Class pointer:	XmSeparatorWidgetClass
Include file:	<Xm/Separator.h>
Create with:	XmCreateSeparator

You can create an XmSeparator with XmCreateSeparator:

```
#include <Xm/Separator.h>
```

```
Widget XmCreateSeparator (Widget parent,
    char* widget_name,
    ArgList args
    Cardinal number_args)
```

Call XtManageChild to manage the XmSeparator widget.

Xt Widget Creation Functions

Instead of XmCreateSeparator, you may want to use one of the Xt Intrinsics functions to create a widget. These functions work best with simple widgets, like XmSeparator, and can cut out a lot of unnecessary code. The basic function to create a widget is XtCreateWidget:

```
Widget XtCreateWidget(const String name,
    WidgetClass widget_class,
    Widget parent,
    ArgList args,
    Cardinal number_args)
```

The name comes first and the parent widget later.

To use XtCreateWidget, you need the widget's class pointer. For the XmSeparator widget, this is xmSeparatorWidgetClass:

```
Widget     parent;
Widget     separator;
Arg        args[20];
Cardinal   n;

n = 0;
separator = XtCreateWidget("sep",
            xmSeparatorWidgetClass,
            parent, args, n);
```

XtCreateWidget doesn't gain you anything over XmCreateSeparator or any other Motif widget-creation function. XtCreateManagedWidget, which takes the same parameters as XtCreateWidget, does:

```
Widget XtCreateManagedWidget(const String name,
    WidgetClass widget_class,
    Widget parent,
    ArgList args,
    Cardinal number_args)
```

XtCreateManagedWidget both creates and manages the widget, saving you a call to XtManageChild. The Xt variable-argument create functions save you even more:

```
Widget XtVaCreateWidget(const String name,
    WidgetClass widget_class,
    Widget parent,
    ...)

Widget XtVaCreateManagedWidget(const String name,
    WidgetClass widget_class,
    Widget parent,
    ...)
```

With XtVaCreateManagedWidget, you can set X resource values without using the Arg array and the XtSetArg macro, which saves a lot of tedious coding on your part, in much the same way XtVaSetValues saves coding work over XtSetValues. As with XtVaSetValues, you must always terminate the list of resources with a NULL.

The following code creates and manages an XmSeparator widget, as well as setting the margin, shadowThickness, and orientation resources:

```
Widget    sep;
Widget    parent;

/* ... */

sep = XtVaCreateManagedWidget("sep",
        xmSeparatorWidgetClass,
        parent,
        XmNmargin, (Dimension) 4,
        XmNshadowThickness, 5,
        XmNorientation, XmHORIZONTAL,
        NULL);
```

As you can tell, XtVaCreateManagedWidget comes in handy at times. We advise you use this function only for simple widgets like XmPushButton, XmLabel, and XmSeparator. More complex Motif widgets actually include a number of subwidgets under the hood, so we find it better to use the Motif XmCreate*Type* functions for these widgets.

Separator Resources

After that digression, it's time to get back to the XmSeparator widget.

You'd be surprised at how many separator resources you can set to change the behavior of a simple line. Of these resources, there are four main separator resources that you may want to change (you may just want to experiment with this). These XmSeparator resources are listed in Table 4.8.

Table 4.8 *XmSeparator resources.*

Resource	Type	Default Value
`margin`	`Dimension`	`0`
`orientation`	`unsigned char`	`XmHORIZONTAL`
`separatorType`	`unsigned char`	`XmSHADOW_ETCHED_IN`
`shadowThickness`	`Dimension`	`2`

The `margin` resource specifies how many pixels sit between the edge of the menu and the start of the separator line, on both the right- and lefthand sides. The default for the `margin` resource (`XmNmargin` in your C programs) is 0 pixels. This normally looks the best. The `shadowThickness` resource (`XmNshadowThickness` in your C programs) controls the thickness of the horizontal or vertical shadow. For best results, set this to 2 pixels.

The `orientation` resource (`XmNorientation` in your C programs) determines whether the separator line is horizontal or vertical. A value of `XmHORIZONTAL` means—you guessed it—a horizontal line. `XmVERTICAL` specifies a vertical line.

The `separatorType` resource (`XmNseparatorType` in your C programs) can be one of the following:

- `XmSINGLE_LINE`
- `XmSINGLE_DASHED_LINE`
- `XmDOUBLE_LINE`
- `XmDOUBLE_DASHED_LINE`
- `XmNO_LINE`
- `XmSHADOW_ETCHED_IN`
- `XmSHADOW_ETCHED_OUT`
- `XmSHADOW_ETCHED_IN_DASH`
- `XmSHADOW_ETCHED_OUT_DASH`

`XmSHADOW_ETCHED_IN_DASH` and `XmSHADOW_ETCHED_OUT_DASH` are new in Motif 1.2. They are not defined in Motif 1.1.

The separator's shadow types are shown in Figure 4.5.

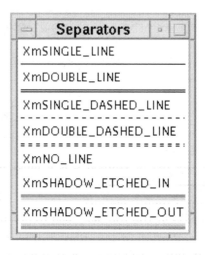

Figure 4.5 *XmSeparator types.*

The default is the 3D bevel of XmSHADOW_ETCHED_IN. This looks the best, so we advise you to stick with XmSHADOW_ETCHED_IN.

In addition, there are at least 33 other resources inherited by the separator widget that affect its behavior. All this for a simple line! Anyway, the *OSF/Motif Programmer's Reference* covers this in detail under the XmSeparator entry.

Separator Gadgets

Separator gadgets work basically like separator widgets. You can use XmCreateSeparatorGadget to create a separator gadget. Note the G (for gadget) on the name of the include file, <Xm/SeparatoG.h>:

```
#include  <Xm/SeparatoG.h>

Widget XmCreateSeparatorGadget(Widget parent,
    char* widget_name,
    ArgList args,
    Cardinal number_args)
```

Menu Titles

In addition to separators, you may want some menus to provide titles on the actual menu itself. This is different from the text for the cascade button that sits on the menu bar. You can make a menu title at the top of the menu by creating a label widget as the first child of the menu. You can also place a label anywhere within a menu, which creates a nonselectable menu choice. (If you just want to disable a menu choice, you should set a push-button menu choice to be insensitive to keyboard input, by setting the `sensitive` resource to `False`. This ghosts the menu choice—that is, it grays out the text of the menu choice. Use a label widget if you want a nonghosted, nonselectable item on the menu.)

To create a title for a menu, we just need to get the title at the top of the menu. To get the title at the top, we need to create it before any of the menu-choice pushbutton widgets are created. (We're not referring to the name on the menu bar, but a title on the actual pull-down menu itself.) To do so, we merely create a `XmLabel widget`, as we described in the "Label Widgets" section in Chapter 2.

Cascading Submenus

Cascaded or pull-right menus are just like the pull-down menus we've been using so far. You create these menus exactly the same as you create a pull-down menu, except that the parent widget isn't the menu bar, it's the pull-down menu that you want to cascade from. To make a menu choice that cascades to another submenu, you can call `XmCreatePulldownMenu` to create the choice that cascades to a new menu. You'll need to create a cascade-button widget in the original menu to pull the submenu at the appropriate time. In the first menu, this cascade button will sport a right-pointing triangle that indicates a pull-right menu. This is shown in Figure 4.6.

Since the code is the same, you can also use the utility function, `CreatePulldownMenu`, described above, to create a pull-right menu. `CreatePulldownMenu` will create a pull-down menu if you pass it a menu-bar widget as a parent. `CreatePulldownMenu` will create a pull-right menu if you pass it a pulldown menu widget as the parent.

Once created, a pull-right menu is filled with menu choices as we've shown for pull-down menus. This makes creating a pull-right menu down-right easy, which is a rarity with Motif.

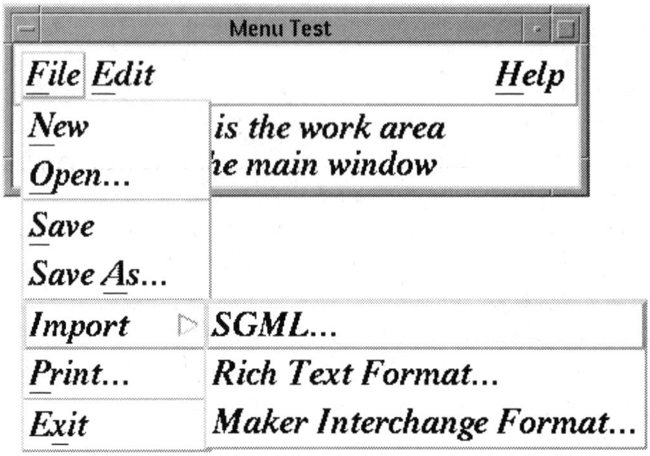

Figure 4.6 *A cascaded submenu.*

FOLLOWING THE OSF/MOTIF STYLE GUIDE FOR MENUS

The Motif toolkit should come with a document that defines the official look and feel for well-behaved Motif applications, the *OSF/Motif Style Guide*. The *Style Guide* is the official look-and-feel arbiter for Motif applications (until you go for certification from the Open Software Foundation), so it is a good idea to read this manual through and through. The *Style Guide* is exceedingly boring, though.

The *Style Guide* follows IBM's Common User Access (CUA) model of user interaction, so users familiar with Microsoft Windows or OS/2 Presentation Manager should be right at home using Motif programs—if you make your programs consistently follow the *Style Guide*. Therefore, the next sections cover Motif's rules for pull-down menus on the menu bar.

Standard Motif Menus and Menu Choices

In your menu bar at the top of your application's main window, you should plan for at least five menus: File, Edit, View, Options, and Help. (You can certainly add more). Only use the menus and menu choices that are appropriate for your application. The Motif style allows you a little leeway here, but we think that consistency is good. Unless you have a really good reason, you should use the naming conventions set up in the *OSF/Motif Style Guide*.

Menus on the menu bar should have mnemonics, as listed in Table 4.9.

Table 4.9 *Standard Motif menus.*

Menu Name	Mnemonic
File	F
Selected	S
Edit	E
View	V
Options	O
Help	H

Menu Mnemonics

In Figure 4.4, you may have noticed that the *H* in *Help* on the menu bar was underlined. This shows that *H* is a Motif *mnemonic*. You can press Meta-**H** on the keyboard, and the program will act the same as if you clicked in the Help cascade button. Mnemonic are also known as *keyboard shortcuts*.

Using Table 4.9, *F* (really Meta-F, which we'll get to below) is the mnemonic or shorthand for the File menu. As such, the mnemonic letter must be in the name of the menu, as *F* is in *File*. Mnemonics and other keyboard shortcuts called *accelerators* allow users to interact with a Motif program with minimal or no use of the mouse.

Mnemonics can help speed expert users who are well versed in the program. A lot of folks would rather keep their hands on the keyboard rather than interrupting their work to track down the mouse on their desk.

Mnemonics can also help users with disabilities who may have better dexterity with the keyboard than with the mouse, or who may have special keyboard input devices.

How you use a mnemonic is somewhat confusing, though. If the mnemonic is on the menu bar, then you press Meta-*letter* to engage the mnemonic. For example, you press Meta-**F** to pull down the File menu. Once a menu is pulled down, you can press Meta and another menu's mnemonic to pull down that menu.

The default for the choices in the actual menu is to press just the mnemonic key. That is, in the File menu mentioned above, the **Exit** choice has a mnemonic of *x* (*E* is used for the Edit menu). After the File menu is pulled down, you can press the **X** key (just the one letter *X*) to choose the **Exit** choice. Thus, the shortcut to quit most Motif programs is Meta-**F-X**. You don't use the Meta key for the mnemonics within the menu, just to pull down menus on the menu bar.

Since Motif applications are highly configurable, you could configure yourself in and out of this, but the basic (default) idea is to use the Meta key with the mnemonic key to pull down a menu, and just use the mnemonic key (without the Meta key) to choose a choice within that pulled-down menu.

In most Motif programs, you can press Meta-**F** to pull down the File menu and then press **X** to exit the program (actually, to choose the **Exit** choice). The mnemonic calls your `activateCallback` on the Exit menu choice, and so presumes that the Exit menu choice's callback function will indeed exit the program.

This takes a while to get used to, but really isn't all that confusing in practice.

N O T E

X uses the term *Meta* to reflect a key that unfortunately has a different symbol on just about every keyboard. On the Data General Aviion, for example, the Meta key is labeled **Alt**. **Alt** is also used on any PC keyboard when running SCO's OpenDesktop or SunSoft's Solaris. On a Sun SPARCStation, with a Type 4 keyboard, the Meta key is not the key labeled **Alt**, but instead the key with the diamond-shaped label that sits right next to the **Alt** key. On a Hewlett-Packard 700 workstation, the Meta key is labeled **Extend Char**. As you can see, this is why we use the generic term *Meta*. You'll have to experiment to find your Meta key, if you don't know it already. The *xev* program may help your experiments.

You can set up a mnemonic by setting the `mnemonic` resource (XmNmnemonic in C programs) with a value of type KeySym (a symbolic code for a given portable key on the keyboard):

```
Arg          args[10];
Cardinal     n;
KeySym       mnemonic;

n = 0;
XtSetArg(args[n], XmNmnemonic, mnemonic);
n++;

/* Create widget...*/
```

To set up *V* as a `mnemonic`, we could use the following code:

```
Arg          args[10];
Cardinal     n;

n = 0;
XtSetArg(args[n], XmNmnemonic, 'V');
n++;

/* Create widget...*/
```

 If you set the text (`labelString`) for a menu choice in a resource file, you should also set the `mnemonic` in the resource file. Because of this, you'll rarely hard-code the `mnemonic` resource.

N O T E

If you've ever used a Macintosh or run applications under Microsoft Windows, Presentation Manager, or DECwindows, the menu choices presented below will look very familiar. The basics are all here, starting with the File menu.

The File Menu

The File menu should always be the first menu on the menu bar. This menu has choices that, obviously, pertain to files, including loading, saving, and printing files. This assumes your application deals with files (which most do, including spreadsheets, word processors, and database managers).

The standard choices in the file menu are listed in Table 4.10.

Table 4.10 *File-menu choices.*

Menu Choice	Mnemonic	Purpose
New	N	Creates an empty new file for the user to act on
Open...	O	Opens a file that already exists
Save	S	Saves the current file to its current name
Save As...	A	Saves the current file to a different name
Print...	P	Prints the current file
Close	C	Closes window
Exit	x	Quits the application

Use common sense when building your menus. If your program has nothing to do with printing, for example, then skip the Print... menu choice.

A few of the choices include ellipses (...). The ellipses tell the user that this menu choice will call up a dialog window, requiring further action from the user to complete the menu choice. In the case of Open, a file-selection dialog will appear so that the user can choose a file.

For the File menu, if you use the Open... choice to open a file named foobar, the Save choice would save your work back to the file foobar.

For the Save As... menu choice, the ellipses implies a dialog will appear—again a file-selection dialog. This choice allows you to save the file under a different name.

The Print... menu choice can be Print or Print..., depending on whether a print dialog appears or not (to perhaps choose the printer, the print quality, and paper size).

Use the Close menu choice when your application has multiple independent top-level windows. The Close choice then closes one of these windows—the window from which the user makes the menu choice. If you don't use multiple top-level windows, skip the Close choice.

If the user exits a Motif program and work needs to be saved, your application should prompt the user to save the work.

Even if your application has nothing to do with files, you probably want to include a File menu with just one choice—the **Exit** choice, to maintain consistency. One of the primary advantages of Motif for your users is application consistency. It's nice to know that the last choice in the File menu is always an **Exit** choice. Users tend to feel safer using a program if they can easily quit that program.

The Selected Menu

The Selected menu is supposed to have menu choices that act on the currently selected data. The menu comes after the File menu and before the Edit menu. If you have a Selected menu, it should have a mnemonic of *S*. According to the *Style Guide*, the Selected menu looks a lot like the File menu, but the choices pertain to selected items. Even though **Open** in the File menu means to open a new file, **Open** in the Selected menu means to open the selected entity. Confusing? We agree.

In fact, we have yet to see a Motif application that uses a Selected menu. The concept seems confusing for the user, because it's hard to tell which menu to use: File, Selected, or Edit, to operate on a certain selection. We advise skipping the Selected menu.

The Edit Menu

The Edit menu essentially provides a menu-driven cut, copy, and paste mechanism. The Edit menu should come second on the menu bar (presuming you take our advice and skip the Selected menu) and is probably the hardest to actually implement, especially the **Undo** choice.

The standard Edit menu choices are listed in Table 4.11.

Table 4.11   *Edit menu choices.*

Menu Choice	Mnemonic	Purpose
Undo	U	Undoes the last thing the user did
Cut	t	Removes the selected material and puts it in the clipboard

continued

Copy	C	Copies selected material to clipboard
Paste	P	Pastes contents of clipboard to current location
Clear	I	Clears selected material
Delete	D	Wipes out the selected material
Select All	None	Selects everything
Deselect All	None	Deselects all selected items

There are few more possibilities described in the *OSF/Motif Style Guide*. The important choices are mentioned here.

Undo is normally the toughest menu choice to implement. Undo should undo the last thing the user did. The *OSF/Motif Style Guide* also recommends that the Undo text be changed to indicate what can be undone, such as *Undo Paste* to undo a paste operation and *Undo Typing* to undo the last text that was entered.

Cut removes the selected (highlighted) material and places that material (text, spreadsheet cells, whatever) into the Motif clipboard. (We cover the Motif clipboard in Chapter 19.)

Copy copies the selected material to the Motif clipboard but doesn't remove the material from where it was originally.

Paste pastes the contents of the clipboard at the current location (usually where an insertion cursor is). Everything after **Paste** is an optional choice.

Clear, an optional choice, removes the selected material but doesn't copy the material to the clipboard— potentially a dangerous operation. The **Clear** choice is supposed to leave a gap where the old material was. The **Delete** choice is also optional.

Keyboard Accelerators

Motif's menu *keyboard accelerators* are a lot like the mnemonics described above, except that keyboard accelerators are arbitrary key combinations. The keyboard accelerator can be any character, but is normally a **Control (Ctrl)**-*key* combination.

Standard Keyboard Accelerators

The *OSF/Motif Style Guide* lists a number of standard accelerators for the standard menus, as listed in Table 4.12.

Table 4.12 *Edit menu accelerators.*

Edit Menu Choice	Mnemonic	Accelerator
Undo	U	Alt+Backspace
Cut	t	Shift+Del
Copy	C	Ctrl+Ins
Paste	P	Shift+Ins
Select All	None	Ctrl+/
Deselect All	None	Ctrl+\

Macintosh Compatibility

The standard Motif mnemonics and keyboard accelerators are based on the IBM CUA model, which is also used in the Microsoft Windows Program Manager and the OS/2 Presentation Manager. Thus, the accelerator for **Copy** is **Ctrl+Ins**. On the Macintosh, though, the accelerators for the Edit menu are placed together on the bottom row of the keyboard. Because the Macintosh model has already been extended to other operating environments (applications running under both DECwindows and Microsoft Windows support the same set of keyboard shortcuts), Motif 1.2 introduced support of the Macintosh accelerators for the Edit menu, as listed in Table 4.13.

Table 4.13 *Alternate Edit menu accelerators.*

Edit Menu Choice	Accelerator
Undo	Ctrl+Z
Cut	Ctrl+X
Copy	Ctrl+C
Paste	Ctrl+V

You can use the keyboard accelerators from Table 4.12 or 4.13, whichever you prefer, for the **Undo**, **Cut**, **Copy**, and **Paste** choices.

N O T E

You cannot use both sets of accelerators (listed in Tables 4.12 and 4.13) simultaneously under Motif. This differs from the Microsoft Windows support of Macintosh mnemonics, which allows for simultaneous support; that is, selecting **Shift+Del** and **Ctrl+X** will accomplish the same thing—cutting a selection.

Syntax for Keyboard Accelerators

To set up keyboard accelerators, you need to set two Motif resources, as listed in Table 4.14.

Table 4.14 *Keyboard accelerator resources.*

Resource	Type	Usage
accelerator	String	Key combination
acceleratorText	XmString	Text to display in widget

The `accelerator` resource (XmNaccelerator in your programs) specifies which key combination will engage the accelerated function. For example, if the keyboard accelerator is holding down the **Control** key while pressing the **q** key, set the `accelerator` resource to `Ctrl<Key>q`.

The `acceleratorText` resource (XmNacceleratorText in your code) holds an extra text string to display, along with the value of a pushbutton's `labelString` resource. That is, both the `labelString` and `acceleratorText` will be displayed.

Why does Motif use two separate resources to build the text message displayed in the widget? This is to align all the text describing the keyboard accelerators. When you see a pull-down menu, all the accelerators will appear lined up, as shown in Figure 4.7.

For best results, don't hard-code the `accelerator` or `acceleratorText` resources. Instead, put these in a resource file. This will help your attempts to internationalize your code.

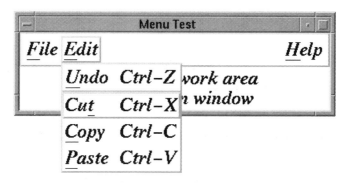

Figure 4.7 *The acceleratorText and labelString resources displayed in a menu.*

The View Menu

The View menu controls "views" of the data. That is, the View menu allows the user to adjust what is viewed in the main window of your application. Some examples of this include choosing how to sort the data, if the data should be sorted at all, and how much detail to show. An outlining application or example could use the View menu to control how many levels of the outline are visible at one time.

View menus are highly dependent on what your application actually does. A spreadsheet View menu will look a lot different than the View menu on an SQL query-by-forms application.

We've used the example View menu from the *OSF/Motif Style Guide* below to give you a flavor of what the View menu should look like, as shown in Figure 4.8.

The Options Menu

The Options menu is essentially a miscellaneous menu. Into this menu go various choices that allow the user to customize the application, such as choosing the colors (shown in Figure 4.9) that the application uses. As with the View menu, the Options menu is highly dependent on what your application actually does.

The Help Menu

Helping the user is an oft-neglected task, especially for UNIX-based software. But help is essential. After users see windows and pull-down menus, their expectations on user-friendliness go way up. Adding a good online-help system is an effective way to improve productivity with software you create.

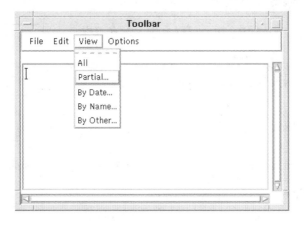

Figure 4.8   *A sample View menu.*

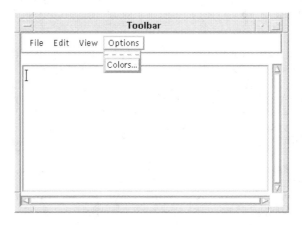

Figure 4.9   *A sample Options menu.*

The Help menu, obviously enough, provides help on the application. This is one area where most Motif applications fail miserably. Few provide really good help. Why? Because it's difficult. We discuss the basics of the Help menu below and delve into online help in Chapter 25.

The choices listed in Table 4.15 should be in the Help menu.

Table 4.15   *Help menu choices.*

Help Menu Choice	Mnemonic	Accelerator
On Context...	C	**Shift+Help**
On Help...	H	None
On Window...	W	None
On Keys...	K	None
Index...	I	None
Tutorial...	T	None
On Version...	V	None

If your application doesn't provide a certain type of help, such as an online tutorial, then you should skip that menu choice, obviously. (Few Motif programs provide an online tutorial, unfortunately.) Since every Help menu choice has an ellipses, each choice should bring up a help dialog.

The **On Context...** choice should provide help on the current context—that is, on what the user is currently trying to do. (Personally, we think the *On Context* name is wretched. The name here should change with the context of what the user is doing. For example, if the user is opening valves in a factory-automation package, the **On Context** choice should instead be an **On Opening Valves** choice.)

The **On Help...** choice shows how to use the help system. We really hope your help system isn't very tough to learn—otherwise, it won't be much help.

On Window...describes the window from which help was requested, including the standard ways to interact with that window.

On Keys... provides help on the special keys used in the application, especially on the mnemonics. Motif uses quite a few keyboard accelerators and allows the user to customize quite a bit more.

The **Index...** choice should provide an index to help topics.

You'll really be lucky if you ever see a **Tutorial...** choice in an application. If you create a quality online tutorial, your users will love you.

On Version... is a fun choice. Just look at Macintosh applications with their **About...** box equivalent. The **On Version...** choice should display information including the name of the application and any version numbers associated with the application. Usually copyright messages are part of this help choice. Macintosh applications especially have fun with this choice and include things like fireworks and animated dogs to liven up the display of boring version information.

In addition to the choices listed above, there's an alternate set of terms you can use for the Help menu choices, as shown in Table 4.16.

Table 4.16 *Alternate Help menu choices.*

Help Menu Choice	Mnemonic	Accelerator
Context-Sensitive Help	C	Shift+Help
Overview	O	None
Index	I	None
Keyboard	K	None
Tutorial	T	None
Using Help	H	None
Product Information	P	None

You can use the terminology from Table 4.15 or 4.16, but not both at once.

Creating a Help Menu

Not only is it a good idea to provide online help in an application, the *OSF/Motif Style Guide* demands it. In the Motif style, most menu bars have a Help menu as the last menu on the far right of the menu bar. (If the user is using Arabic, Hebrew, or another language where the direction of text is right to left as opposed to left to right, the Help menu may appear on the other side. In all cases, just let Motif place the Help menu and you'll do fine.)

This Help cascade button normally calls up a help menu. The only thing special about this Help cascade button is that we want the button to be on the far right, as the Motif Help menu is supposed to be. To do this, we have to set up the resource menuHelpWidget (XmNmenuHelpWidget in your C programs). This resource needs to be set on the parent menu bar (not on the Help cascade button) and needs to specify a widget—in this case, the help cascade-button widget.

For example, after you create the Help cascade button, you can call XtVaSetValues on the menu bar as follows:

```
Widget      menubar;
Widget      help_cascade;

/* ... */

XtVaSetValues(menubar,
    XmNmenuHelpWidget, help_cascade,
    NULL);
```

We can put all this together and modify our `CreatePulldownMenu` function to create a Help menu. The code for this new utility function, `CreateHelpMenu`, follows:

```
Widget CreateHelpMenu(Widget parent,
    char* name)

{   /* CreateHelpMenu */
    Widget      menu;
    Widget      cascade;
    Arg         args[20];
    Cardinal    n;

    /* Create pulldown menu. */
    n = 0;
    menu = XmCreatePulldownMenu(parent,
            name, args, n);

    /* Don't manage menu. */

    /* Create cascade button and connect to menu. */
    n = 0;
    XtSetArg(args[n], XmNsubMenuId, menu); n++;

    cascade = XmCreateCascadeButton(parent,
                name, args, n);

    XtManageChild(cascade);

    /*
     * We assume the parent is a menu bar.
     * Tell parent this is a help menu.
     */
    XtVaSetValues(parent,
        XmNmenuHelpWidget, cascade,
        NULL);
```

```
    /*
     * We return the widget ID of
     * the menu, not the cascade.
     */
    return menu;

}   /* CreateHelpMenu */
```

As a good tip, always create the Help menu last. If you make the Help menu last, then when the user uses the keyboard shortcuts to traverse the menu bar, the Help menu will be traversed in the proper order. Otherwise, all bets are off.

We go into more depth into online help in Chapter 25.

Tear-Off Menus

Motif 1.2 introduces a new option on menus: *tear-off menus*. Tear-off menus are Motif's answer to Open Look's highly popular *pushpins*, which pin a menu to the screen, making the menu stay visible. With a tear-off menu, the user can—you guessed it—tear a menu off the menu bar, making the menu into a small dialog window. This dialog remains on the screen until the user dismisses it.

For users, tear-off menus allow them to make menu choices more quickly from a frequently used menu. For the developer, tear-off menus are a neat feature that can be implemented with a minimum amount of work.

It's almost too easy. All you need to do is to set the `tearOffModel` resource (`XmNtearOffModel` in C programs) to `XmTEAR_OFF_ENABLED`. You must set this resource before creating the menu. That's it. When the menu appears, you'll see a small perforated line at the top of the menu, as shown in Figure 4.10.

You select the dashed line with the mouse and drag to tear off the menu. The torn-off menu gets a titlebar and window menu (dash icon), but no resize handles, as shown in Figure 4.11.

The following code snippet shows how to create a tear-off menu:

```
    /*
     * Create pulldown menu. Engage
     * tear-off menu if supported.
     */
    n = 0;
```

```
#ifdef XmNtearOffModel

XtSetArg(args[n], XmNtearOffModel,
    XmTEAR_OFF_ENABLED);
n++;

#endif  /* XmNtearOffModel */

menu = XmCreatePulldownMenu(parent,
        name, args, n);
```

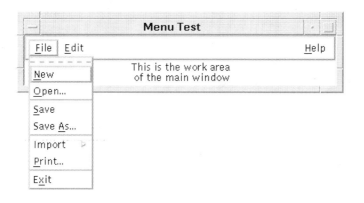

Figure 4.10   *A tear-off menu on the menu bar.*

Figure 4.11   *A tear-off menu torn off.*

NOTE We use #ifdef XmNtearOffModel to protect our code. The tearOffModel resource (and the corresponding ability to tear off menus) is new in Motif 1.2. All our programs, though, still need to work with Motif 1.1. We use #ifdef XmNtearOffModel to allow us to detect at compile time whether tear-off menus are supported by the Motif libraries.

Using the above code, we can extend our CreatePulldownMenu utility function to automatically configure a tear-off menu if this feature is supported. This new code appears below:

```
Widget CreatePulldownMenu(Widget parent,
    char* name)

{   /* CreatePulldownMenu */
    Widget    menu;
    Widget    cascade;
    Arg       args[20];
    Cardinal  n;

    /*
     * Create pulldown menu. Engage
     * tear-off menu if supported.
     */
    n = 0;

#ifdef XmNtearOffModel

    XtSetArg(args[n], XmNtearOffModel, XmTEAR_OFF_ENABLED);
    n++;

#endif  /* XmNtearOffModel */

    menu = XmCreatePulldownMenu(parent,
            name, args, n);

    /* Don't manage menu. */

    /* Create cascade button and connect to menu. */
    n = 0;
    XtSetArg(args[n], XmNsubMenuId, menu); n++;

    cascade = XmCreateCascadeButton(parent,
                name, args, n);

    XtManageChild(cascade);

    /*
     * We return the widget ID of
     * the menu, not the cascade.
     */
```

```
      return menu;

}     /* CreatePulldownMenu */
```

You may get the following warning if the user tries to tear off a menu that has already been torn off:

```
Warning: XtRemoveGrab asked to remove a widget not on the
         list
```

N O T E

You can ignore this warning, although it may be disconcerting for your users.

A PROGRAM TO TEST MOTIF MENUS

We've put together a program to show how pull-down and pull-right menus work. This program creates three pull-down menus: the File, Edit, and Help menus. It also uses a simple XmLabel for the main window's work area. In most programs, you'll probably use a container widget like an XmForm or XmPanedWindow for the work area.

We used accelerators in both the program code (hard-coded) and in the resource file that appears after the program. If tear-off menus are available, we set up those, too.

```
/* pullmenu.c */
#include <Xm/Xm.h>
#include <Xm/CascadeB.h>     /* Cascade button */
#include <Xm/Label.h>        /* Label */
#include <Xm/MainW.h>        /* Main window */
#include <Xm/PushB.h>        /* Push button */
#include <Xm/RowColumn.h>    /* Row column: menubar, menus */
#include <Xm/Separator.h>    /* Menu separator */

extern Widget CreatePushbutton(Widget parent,
    char* name,
    XtCallbackProc callback,
    XtPointer client_data);

    /* Callback to exit program. */

void exitCB(Widget widget,
    XtPointer client_data,
    XtPointer call_data)
```

p.3 (handwritten)

```
{   /* exitCB */

    exit(0);

}   /* exitCB */

/*
 * Generic callback, assumes
 * client_data has a text string.
 */

void genericCB(Widget widget,
    XtPointer client_data,
    XtPointer call_data)

{   /* genericCB */

    if (client_data != NULL) {
        printf("Menu callback for [%s]\n",
            (char*) client_data);
    }

}   /* genericCB */

Widget CreatePulldownMenu(Widget parent,
    char* name)

{   /* CreatePulldownMenu */
    Widget    menu;
    Widget    cascade;
    Arg       args[20];
    Cardinal  n;

    /*
     * Create pulldown menu. Engage
     * tear-off menu if supported.
     */
    n = 0;

#ifdef XmNtearOffModel

    XtSetArg(args[n], XmNtearOffModel,
        XmTEAR_OFF_ENABLED);
    n++;

#endif  /* XmNtearOffModel */

    menu = XmCreatePulldownMenu(parent,
            name, args, n);

    /* Don't manage menu. */

    /* Create cascade button and connect to menu. */
    n = 0;
```

```
    XtSetArg(args[n], XmNsubMenuId, menu); n++;

    cascade = XmCreateCascadeButton(parent,
                  name, args, n);

    XtManageChild(cascade);

    /*
     * We return the widget ID of
     * the menu, not the cascade.
     */
    return menu;

}   /* CreatePulldownMenu */

Widget CreateHelpMenu(Widget parent,
    char* name)

{   /* CreateHelpMenu */
    Widget    menu;
    Widget    cascade;
    Arg       args[20];
    Cardinal  n;

    /*
     * Create pulldown menu. Engage
     * tear-off menu if supported.
     */
    n = 0;

#ifdef XmNtearOffModel

    XtSetArg(args[n], XmNtearOffModel,
        XmTEAR_OFF_ENABLED);
    n++;

#endif  /* XmNtearOffModel */

    menu = XmCreatePulldownMenu(parent,
          name, args, n);

    /* Don't manage menu. */

    /* Create cascade button and connect to menu. */
    n = 0;
    XtSetArg(args[n], XmNsubMenuId, menu); n++;

    cascade = XmCreateCascadeButton(parent,
                  name, args, n);

    XtManageChild(cascade);

    /*
     * We assume the parent is a menu bar.
     * Tell parent this is a help menu.
```

```
    */
   XtVaSetValues(parent,
       XmNmenuHelpWidget, cascade,
       NULL);

   /*
    * We return the widget ID of
    * the menu, not the cascade.
    */
   return menu;

}   /* CreateHelpMenu */

int main(int argc, char** argv)

{   /* main */
   XtAppContext  app_context;
   Widget        parent;
   Widget        mainwindow;
   Widget        menubar;
   Widget        filemenu, editmenu, submenu;
   Widget        helpcascade, helpmenu;
   Widget        exitchoice;
   Widget        label, on_context;
   Arg           args[20];
   Cardinal      n;

   /* Initialize X toolkit */
   n = 0;
   XtSetArg(args[n], XmNallowResize, True); n++;

   parent = XtAppInitialize(&app_context,
           "Ppm",                   /* app class */
           (XrmOptionDescList) NULL,/* options */
           0,                       /* num options */
           (Cardinal*) &argc,       /* num on cmd-line */
           argv,                    /* cmd-line opts */
           (String*) NULL,          /* fallback res. */
           args, n);

   /* Create main window. */
   n = 0;
   mainwindow = XmCreateMainWindow(parent,
               "main", args, n);

   /* Create menubar. */
   n = 0;
   menubar = XmCreateMenuBar(mainwindow,
               "menubar", args, n);

   XtManageChild(menubar);

   /* Create File, Edit and Help menus. */
   filemenu = CreatePulldownMenu(menubar, "filemenu");
   editmenu = CreatePulldownMenu(menubar, "editmenu");
```

```
/* Set up menu choices for File menu. */
(void) CreatePushbutton(filemenu, "new",
        (XtCallbackProc) genericCB,
        (XtPointer) "New");

(void) CreatePushbutton(filemenu, "open",
        (XtCallbackProc) genericCB,
        (XtPointer) "Open...");

(void) XtVaCreateManagedWidget("sep",
        xmSeparatorWidgetClass, filemenu, NULL);

(void) CreatePushbutton(filemenu, "save",
        (XtCallbackProc) genericCB,
        (XtPointer) "Save");

(void) CreatePushbutton(filemenu, "saveas",
        (XtCallbackProc) genericCB,
        (XtPointer) "Save As...");

(void) XtVaCreateManagedWidget("sep",
        xmSeparatorWidgetClass, filemenu, NULL);

/* Create cascaded submenu as child of file menu. */
submenu = CreatePulldownMenu(filemenu, "submenu");

n = 0;
(void) XmCreateSeparator(filemenu, "sep", args, n);

(void) CreatePushbutton(filemenu, "print",
        (XtCallbackProc) genericCB,
        (XtPointer) "Print...");

(void) XtVaCreateManagedWidget("sep",
        xmSeparatorWidgetClass, filemenu, NULL);

(void) CreatePushbutton(filemenu, "exit",
        (XtCallbackProc) exitCB, /* Note callback! */
        (XtPointer) "Exit");

/* Set up menu choices for Edit menu. */
(void) CreatePushbutton(editmenu, "undo",
        (XtCallbackProc) genericCB,
        (XtPointer) "Undo");

(void) XtVaCreateManagedWidget("sep",
        xmSeparatorWidgetClass, editmenu, NULL);

(void) CreatePushbutton(editmenu, "cut",
        (XtCallbackProc) genericCB,
        (XtPointer) "Cut");

(void) CreatePushbutton(editmenu, "copy",
        (XtCallbackProc) genericCB,
```

```
                (XtPointer) "Copy");

        (void) CreatePushbutton(editmenu, "paste",
                (XtCallbackProc) genericCB,
                (XtPointer) "Paste");

        /* Set up menu choices for submenu. */
        (void) CreatePushbutton(submenu, "sgml",
                (XtCallbackProc) genericCB,
                (XtPointer) "SGML...");

        (void) CreatePushbutton(submenu, "rtf",
                (XtCallbackProc) genericCB,
                (XtPointer) "Rich Text Format...");

        (void) CreatePushbutton(submenu, "mif",
                (XtCallbackProc) genericCB,
                (XtPointer) "Maker Interchange Format...");

        /*
         * Create Help menu.
         * Note XmNmenuHelpWidget resource
         * and long method to create.
         */
        helpmenu = CreateHelpMenu(menubar, "helpmenu");

        /* Set up menu choices for Help menu. */
        on_context = CreatePushbutton(helpmenu, "context",
                (XtCallbackProc) genericCB,
                (XtPointer) "On Context");

        /*
         * Set an accelerator. Normally,
         * you should set this in an X
         * resource file.
         */
        XtVaSetValues(on_context,
                XmNaccelerator, "Ctrl<Key>q",
                NULL);

        (void) XtVaCreateManagedWidget("sep",
                xmSeparatorWidgetClass, helpmenu, NULL);

        (void) CreatePushbutton(helpmenu, "version",
                (XtCallbackProc) genericCB,
                (XtPointer) "On Version");

        /* Create label. */
        label = XtVaCreateManagedWidget("label",
                xmLabelWidgetClass, mainwindow, NULL);


        /* Set widgets into proper areas in main window. */
        XmMainWindowSetAreas(mainwindow,
            menubar,
```

```
            (Widget) NULL, /* command window */
            (Widget) NULL, /* horiz scroll */
            (Widget) NULL, /* vert scroll */
            label);        /* work area */

    XtManageChild(mainwindow);

    /* Realize widgets and enter event loop. */
    XtRealizeWidget(parent);
    XtAppMainLoop(app_context);

    return 0;

}   /* main */

/* end of file pullmenu.c */
```

In the code above, you'll note that we ignore the widget returned by
CreatePushbutton in most cases. These widget IDs are not important for
our example program. In most of your code, though, you'll want access to
every widget ID you can get your hands on.

A Resource File for the Pull-Down Menu Program

The resource file for the example program follows:

```
! Resource file for Chapter 4
! of Power Programming Motif.
!
*fontList:       lucidasans-12
*background:     lightgrey

*Ppm.width: 400

*title:      Menu Test

! File menu
*filemenu.labelString: File
*filemenu.mnemonic:      F

*new.labelString:    New
*new.mnemonic:       N

*open.labelString:   Open...
*open.mnemonic:      O

*save.labelString:   Save
*save.mnemonic:      S

*saveas.labelString: Save As...
*saveas.mnemonic:    A
```

```
*print.labelString:   Print...
*print.mnemonic:      P

*exit.labelString:    Exit
*exit.mnemonic:       x

! Submenu
*submenu.labelString:    Import
*sgml.labelString:       SGML...
*rtf.labelString:        Rich Text Format...
*mif.labelString:        Maker Interchange Format...

! Edit menu
*editmenu.labelString:   Edit
*editmenu.mnemonic:      E

*undo.labelString:       Undo
*undo.mnemonic:          U
*undo.accelerator:       Ctrl<Key>z
*undo.acceleratorText:   Ctrl-Z

*cut.labelString:        Cut
*cut.mnemonic:           t
*cut.accelerator:        Ctrl<Key>x
*cut.acceleratorText:    Ctrl-X

*copy.labelString:       Copy
*copy.mnemonic:          C
*copy.accelerator:       Ctrl<Key>c
*copy.acceleratorText:   Ctrl-C

*paste.labelString:      Paste
*paste.mnemonic:         P
*paste.accelerator:      Ctrl<Key>v
*paste.acceleratorText: Ctrl-V

! Help menu
*helpmenu.labelString:   Help
*helpmenu.mnemonic:      H

*context.labelString:    On Context...
*version.labelString:    On Version...

*label.labelString:      This is the work area\n of the main window
! end of resource file
```

Copy this file to your home directory and name it **Ppm**.

SIMPLE MENU FUNCTIONS

Motif provides a number of utility routines to create common components, such as a pull-down menu with all the menu choices or a radio box full of radio buttons. These convenience routines are called the *simple creation functions.*

XmCreateSimpleMenuBar, for example, creates a menu bar and all the cascade-button widgets on the menu bar. XmCreateSimplePulldownMenu creates a pull-down menu and all the menu choices. All these menu choices then call a special simple menu callback.

Unfortunately, these simple routines are not that simple, and we suggest you skip them. Motif also offers a set of variable-argument simple menu routines that are far easier to use.

For the variable-argument simple menu routines, you can create the following widgets within a menu, as listed in Table 4.17.

Table 4.17   Simple menu widgets.

Token	Widget Created
XmVaCASCADEBUTTON	Cascade button for a pull-right menu
XmVaCHECKBUTTON	Toggle button
XmVaDOUBLE_SEPARATOR	Double-line separator
XmVaPUSHBUTTON	Pushbutton
XmVaRADIOBUTTON	Toggle button set in radio mode
XmVaSEPARATOR	Separator
XmVaTITLE	Label widget
XmVaTOGGLEBUTTON	Toggle button

N O T E

There's also a definition of an XmVaSINGLE_SEPARATOR. Don't use this. We had problems with it in our test programs. Also, it is not documented in the *OSF/Motif Programmer's Reference* for Motif 1.2.

Creating a Simple Pull-Down Menu

The most illustrative menu function is XmVaCreateSimplePulldownMenu, which creates a simple pull-down menu:

```
Widget XmVaCreateSimplePulldownMenu(Widget parent,
        String name,
        int post_from_button,
        XtCallbackProc callback,
        ...)
```

The *post_from_button* parameter is the number of the cascade button in the parent menu bar that this menu should be called up from. Start counting with 0. A value of 0 means use the first cascade button in the menu bar, usually the File menu. A value of 1 means use the second cascade button, usually the Edit menu.

The *callback* function is a special form of the standard Motif callback. With the simple menu routines, you cannot pass a *client_data* parameter to the *callback*. Instead, Motif passes an integer value that tells you which menu choice was picked by the user. Again, start counting with 0.

After the callback, you set up each item in the menu using a variable number of parameters. Each item starts with a token, one of XmVaCASCADEBUTTON, XmVaCHECKBUTTON, XmVaDOUBLE_SEPARATOR, XmVaPUSHBUTTON, XmVaRADIOBUTTON, XmVaSEPARATOR, XmVaTITLE, or XmVaTOGGLEBUTTON. After the token comes a number of parameters, depending on the token, as listed in Table 4.18.

Table 4.18   Variable tokens for the simple menu functions.

Token	Parameters
XmVaCASCADEBUTTON	Label, mnemonic
XmVaCHECKBUTTON	Label, mnemonic, accelerator, accelerator text
XmVaDOUBLE_SEPARATOR	None
XmVaPUSHBUTTON	Label, mnemonic, accelerator, accelerator text
XmVaRADIOBUTTON	Label, mnemonic, accelerator, accelerator text
XmVaSEPARATOR	None
XmVaTITLE	Label
XmVaTOGGLEBUTTON	Label, mnemonic, accelerator, accelerator text

The labels are of type XmString, mnemonics of type KeySym, accelerators of type String (normally char*), and accelerator text of type XmString.

Make sure to use the proper number of parameters or you'll get into trouble.

If you make any mistakes with the simple menu routines, you will see odd output and have no other clue as to what went wrong.

N O T E

End this variable parameter list with a NULL.

This probably sounds confusing—and it is. To help clarify the situation, the following code creates a simple pull-down menu:

```
/* Create XmStrings for simple menus. */
open_xmstr = XmStringCreateSimple("Open...");
save_xmstr = XmStringCreateSimple("Save");
exit_xmstr = XmStringCreateSimple("Exit");

/* Create File menu. */
filemenu = XmVaCreateSimplePulldownMenu(menubar,
        "filemenu",
        0, /* cascade 0 in menubar */
        (XtCallbackProc) menuCB,
        XmVaPUSHBUTTON, open_xmstr, 'O', NULL, NULL,
        XmVaDOUBLE_SEPARATOR,
        XmVaPUSHBUTTON, save_xmstr, 'S', NULL, NULL,
        XmVaSEPARATOR,
        XmVaPUSHBUTTON, exit_xmstr, 'x', NULL, NULL,
        NULL); /* terminates list */

XmStringFree(open_xmstr);
XmStringFree(save_xmstr);
XmStringFree(exit_xmstr);
```

The above code creates a File menu with three choices: **Open...**, **Save**, and **Exit**. There's a separator between each choice. We pass NULL for the accelerators and accelerator text.

For now, you can ignore the XmStringCreateSimple function, which creates an XmString from a C string, and XmStringFree, which frees an XmString when done. We cover these functions in depth in Chapter 8. The XmStrings add some complexity to the simple menu functions, but they are easy to use.

We've had great problems under HP-UX 9.01 with the simple menu functions. It seems that using a separator causes these routines to fail.

N O T E

Simple Menu Callback Functions

The simple menu functions take over the *client_data* parameter from your callback functions and pass an integer value. This value is the number of the menu choice that the user picked. The choices start counting with zero. Also, separators aren't counted.

A sample simple menu callback follows:

```
void menuCB(Widget widget,
    int which_choice,
    XtPointer call_data)

{   /* menuCB */

    printf("Menu choice %d.\n", which_choice);

}   /* menuCB */
```

Simple Menu Bars

You can also create a simple menu bar. With this, you can create only cascade buttons, using the XmVaCASCADEBUTTON token from above. XmVaCreateSimpleMenuBar takes the following parameters:

```
Widget XmVaCreateSimpleMenuBar(Widget parent,
        String name,
        ...)
```

In your code, you can use XmVaCreateSimpleMenuBar as shown below:

```
/* Create menubar. */
casc_xmstr = XmStringCreateSimple("File");

menubar = XmVaCreateSimpleMenuBar(mainwindow,
        "menubar",
        XmVaCASCADEBUTTON, casc_xmstr, 'F',
        NULL);

XtManageChild(menubar);

XmStringFree(casc_xmstr);
```

The code for an example program using the Motif simple menu routines follows:

```c
/* smplmenu.c */
#include <Xm/Xm.h>
#include <Xm/CascadeB.h>
#include <Xm/Label.h>
#include <Xm/MainW.h>
#include <Xm/PushB.h>
#include <Xm/RowColumn.h>
#include <Xm/Separator.h>

void menuCB(Widget widget,
    int which_choice,
    XtPointer call_data)

{   /* menuCB */

    printf("Menu choice %d.\n", which_choice);

    /* Quit on choice 3. */
    if (which_choice == 3) {
        exit(0);
    }

}   /* menuCB */

    /* Callback to exit program. */

int main(int argc, char** argv)

{   /* main */
    XtAppContext    app_context;
    Widget          parent;
    Widget          mainwindow;
    Widget          menubar;
    Widget          filemenu, editmenu, submenu;
    Widget          helpcascade, helpmenu;
    Widget          exitchoice;
    Widget          label, on_context;
    Arg             args[20];
    Cardinal        n;
    XmString        open_xmstr, save_xmstr;
    XmString        togl_xmstr, exit_xmstr;
    XmString        casc_xmstr, labl_xmstr;

    n = 0;
    XtSetArg(args[n], XmNallowResize, True); n++;

    parent = XtAppInitialize(&app_context,
            "Ppm",                      /* app class */
            (XrmOptionDescList) NULL,/* options */
            0,                          /* num options */
            (Cardinal*) &argc,          /* num on cmd-line */
            argv,                       /* cmd-line opts */
            (String*) NULL,             /* fallback res. */
            args, n);
```

```
/* Create main window. */
n = 0;
mainwindow = XmCreateMainWindow(parent,
            "main", args, n);

/* Create menubar. */
casc_xmstr = XmStringCreateSimple("File");

menubar = XmVaCreateSimpleMenuBar(mainwindow,
        "menubar",
        XmVaCASCADEBUTTON, casc_xmstr, 'F',
        NULL);

XtManageChild(menubar);

XmStringFree(casc_xmstr);

/* Create XmStrings for simple menus. */
open_xmstr = XmStringCreateSimple("Open...");
save_xmstr = XmStringCreateSimple("Save");
togl_xmstr = XmStringCreateSimple("Toggle");
labl_xmstr = XmStringCreateSimple("Label Title");
exit_xmstr = XmStringCreateSimple("Exit");

/* Create File menu. */
filemenu = XmVaCreateSimplePulldownMenu(menubar,
        "filemenu",
        0, /* cascade 0 in menubar */
        (XtCallbackProc) menuCB,
        XmVaPUSHBUTTON, open_xmstr, 'O', NULL, NULL,
        XmVaDOUBLE_SEPARATOR,
        XmVaPUSHBUTTON, save_xmstr, 'S', NULL, NULL,
        XmVaDOUBLE_SEPARATOR,
        XmVaTOGGLEBUTTON, togl_xmstr, 'T', NULL, NULL,
        XmVaSEPARATOR,
        XmVaTITLE, labl_xmstr,
        XmVaSEPARATOR,
        XmVaPUSHBUTTON, exit_xmstr, 'x', NULL, NULL,
        NULL);

XmStringFree(open_xmstr);
XmStringFree(save_xmstr);
XmStringFree(togl_xmstr);
XmStringFree(labl_xmstr);
XmStringFree(exit_xmstr);

/* Create label. */
label = XtVaCreateManagedWidget("label",
        xmLabelWidgetClass, mainwindow, NULL);

/* Set widgets into proper areas in main window. */
XmMainWindowSetAreas(mainwindow,
    menubar,
    (Widget) NULL, /* command window */
```

```
        (Widget) NULL, /* horiz scroll */
        (Widget) NULL, /* vert scroll */
        label);        /* work area */

    XtManageChild(mainwindow);

    /* Realize widgets and enter event loop. */
    XtRealizeWidget(parent);
    XtAppMainLoop(app_context);

    return 0;

}   /* main */

/* end of file smplmenu.c */
```

When you run this program, you'll see a menu like the one shown in Figure 4.12.

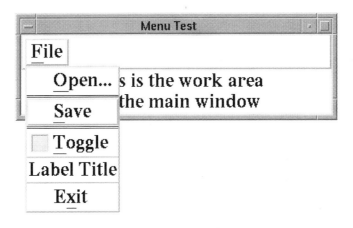

Figure 4.12 *A simple menu.*

Even though these routines are advertised as simple routines, we advise against using them for four reasons.

■ You need to hard-code too much of the menu's text. We strongly advise that you place the menu text, mnemonics, and keyboard accelerators in an external file, like an X resource file or in some form of message catalog file for internationalization.

▧ Motif creates a name for each of the widgets created by the simple menu routines. The problem is that the names the Motif toolkit uses for the widgets created by the simple menu routines are not consistent and may change in the future. This makes it even more difficult to set widget resources in a resource file.

▧ There are significant bugs in some versions of Motif regarding the simple menu routines. Under Hewlett-Packard's HP-UX 9.01, for example, separators cause the simple menu routines to fail.

▧ We dislike the fact that we lose the *client_data* parameter to the callback functions. This parameter gains importance as you use C++ with Motif and want to pass a C++ object pointer as the *client_data*.

SUMMARY

The *OSF/Motif Style Guide* describes the look and feel for well-behaved Motif programs. There is a lot of flexibility in the *Style Guide*, but your applications should start out with a menu bar and the five standard menus: File, Edit, View, Options, and Help. You really don't want to deviate too far from the *Style Guide* unless you have a good reason. One of the goals of a toolkit like Motif is to provide the users with a consistent, easy-to-use set of application software.

This chapter covered the mechanisms for creating menu bars, pull-down and pull-right menus, along with the proscribed menu choices for Motif menus, as well as acceptable keyboard shortcuts. It may seem like a lot more was covered in this chapter—but there's a lot involved in these procedures.

In the next chapter, we'll cover the core of virtually every application: text editing.

MOTIF FUNCTIONS AND MACROS INTRODUCED IN THIS CHAPTER

```
XmCreateMainWindow
XmCreatePopupMenu
XmCreatePulldownMenu
```

```
XmCreatePushButtonGadget
XmCreateSeparator
XmCreateSeparatorGadget
XmVaCreateSimpleMenuBar
XmVaCreateSimplePulldownMenu
XmMainWindowSep1
XmMainWindowSep2
XmMainWindowSep3
XmMainWindowSetAreas
```

X TOOLKIT INTRINSICS FUNCTIONS AND MACROS INTRODUCED IN THIS CHAPTER

```
XtCreateManagedWidget
XtCreateWidget
XtVaCreateManagedWidget
XtVaCreateWidget
```

CHAPTER 5

Text Editing

This chapter introduces text editing in Motif, including:

- ◾ XmText and XmTextField widgets
- ◾ Creating and placing scroll bars
- ◾ Scrolled-text editing
- ◾ Controlling text widgets
- ◾ Working with text files
- ◾ Text-widget resources
- ◾ Inserting text
- ◾ Text-widget callbacks
- ◾ Search and replace
- ◾ Data validation via widget callbacks
- ◾ Selecting between XmTextField or XmText widgets

TEXT WIDGETS

To this point we've covered the basics of creating the top part of an application—its menu bars and menus. With this chapter, we'll start concentrating on what goes below the menu bar, where the meat of most applications lie.

Text editing forms a central part of virtually every application, be it a single-line prompt or a full-fledged text editor. In Motif, the handy XmText widget covers both needs. Because of this, the text widget's options get rather complex. The text widget can be an all-purpose text editor or a single-line prompt. The best part about the text widget, though, is that it abstracts a very common application task into one widget class, saving you, the application writer, a lot of work.

A related widget, XmTextField, concentrates on single-line text entry fields, such as prompts. In this chapter, we'll cover the generic XmText first, then tackle XmTextField.

SHORTCUT

Working With Text Widgets

Table 5.1 summarizes the XmText and XmTextField widgets.

Table 5.1 *Text widget information in brief.*

	XmText	**XmTextField**
Widget class:	XmText	XmTextField
Class pointer:	XmTextWidgetClass	xmTextFieldWidgetClass
Include file:	<Xm/Text.h>	<Xm/TextF.h>
Create with:	XmCreateText	XmCreateTextField

Call XmCreateScrolledText to create a scrolled-text widget. Set the *rows* and *columns* resources to control the size of the widget, in character cells.

To set text into a text widget, call XmTextSetString or XmTextFieldSetString:

```
void XmTextSetString(Widget widget, char* text)
void XmTextFieldSetString(Widget widget, char* text)
```

To extract text from a text widget, call XmTextGetString or XmTextFieldGetString:

```
char* XmTextGetString(Widget widget)
char* XmTextFieldGetString(Widget widget)
```

Call XtFree to free the memory of the returned string.

Creating Text Widgets

You can create an XmText widget with the function XmCreateText:

```
#include  <Xm/Text.h>
Widget XmCreateText(Widget parent,
        String name,
        ArgList args,
        Cardinal number_args)
```

Be sure to call XtManageChild after creating the widget.

Single- and Multiline Text Widgets

You can configure a text widget as a single-line prompt, or you can make the text widget span a number of lines with scroll bars. The editMode resource controls whether an XmText widget spans multiple lines or is locked into a single line. The editMode resource can be one of:

▪ XmSINGLE_LINE_EDIT

▪ XmMULTI_LINE_EDIT

XmSINGLE_LINE_EDIT means that only one line of text is allowed in the widget. This is basically a prompt. XmMULTI_LINE_EDIT means that the text in the text widget can span many lines, and the user effectively has a built-in Motif text editor.

To set the editMode resource, use:

```
#include <Xm/Text.h>

Cardinal   n;
Arg        args[20];
```

```
n = 0;
XtSetArg(args[n], XmNeditMode,
    XmMULTI_LINE_EDIT);
n++;

/* Create widget... */
```

When you set the editMode resource to XmSINGLE_LINE_EDIT, an XmText widget acts essentially like an XmTextField widget. The XmTextField widget, though, uses a separate set of functions that begin with *XmTextField* instead of just *XmText*. Most of these functions act the same, but you must use the proper functions for the type of widget you create. We cover these functions when we introduce the XmTextField widget, below.

Scrolled-Text Widgets

XmCreateScrolledText creates a text widget as a child of a scrolled-window widget, whereas XmCreateText just creates a text widget:

```
#include  <Xm/Text.h>

Widget XmCreateScrolledText(Widget parent,
        String name,
        ArgList args,
        Cardinal number_args)
```

Scroll Bars

Scroll bars are used in most graphical interfaces as a means of showing only a portion of something too large to fit into a window. Scroll bars are controls that allow the user to browse through the larger text (or graphics), while using a much smaller portion of the screen's real estate. The concept of scroll bars is simple and intuitive—and scroll bars are used in just about every graphical interface.

Motif's scroll bars have a nice 3D shadowed effect, as shown in Figure 5.1.

The Text Widget with Scroll Bars

When you create a text widget with the XmCreateScrolledText function, a hidden scrolled-window widget is first created, and then a text widget is created as a child of the scrolled window. Normally, if you don't have enough data to warrant a scroll bar (either horizontally or vertically), then the scroll bar won't be visible. If, however, you always want a scroll bar visible, you can set the values of the scrollVertical (XmNscrollVertical in C programs) and scrollHorizontal (XmNscrollHorizontal in C programs) resources.

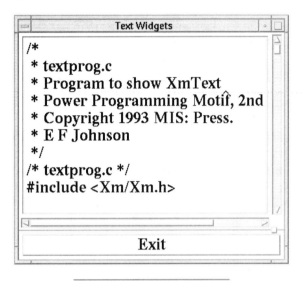

Figure 5.1 *Motif scroll bars.*

For each resource, if you set the resource to True, you'll always have a scroll bar. If you set the resource to False, you will not have the scroll bar in the particular direction.

The following code will turn on both horizontal and vertical scroll bars permanently:

```
#include <Xm/Text.h>

Widget      widget, parent;
Arg         args[10];
Cardinal    n;

n = 0;
XtSetArg(args[n], XmNscrollVertical,   True); n++;
XtSetArg(args[n], XmNscrollHorizontal, True); n++;
/* Create text widget. */
widget = XmCreateScrolledText(parent,
        "text", args, n);
```

Normally a vertical scroll bar will appear on the right side of the widget. You can change that, however, with the scrollLeftSide resource

(XmNscrollLeftSide in C programs). If the scrollLeftSide resource is False, then the scroll bar should be on the right side, which is the normal default for Western European languages like English. If the default language or the stringDirection resource is set to right-to-left processing, the default for scrollLeftSide may be True. If it is set to True, then the scroll bar, if there is a scroll bar, will appear on the left side of the window. This really doesn't seem to fit in with the *OSF/Motif Style Guide's* look-and-feel requirements, so most applications won't set this resource.

The scrollTopSide resource (XmNscrollTopSide in C programs) does the same thing for the horizontal scroll bar. If set to True, the scroll bar will appear at the top of the widget. If set to the default False, the scroll bar will appear at the bottom of the widget. Again, this isn't in the spirit of the Motif style, so you're advised to stay away from this resource, unless you just want to experiment. To experiment, you can play with these values in the resource file at the end of this chapter in the *textprog* example program (see the section entitled "A Program Using Scrolled Text," below).

Scrolled-Text Widget Resources

Table 5.2 summarizes the scrolled-text resources.

Table 5.2 *Scrolled-text resources.*

Resource	Type	Default Value
scrollHorizontal	Boolean	True
scrollLeftSide	Boolean	*dynamic*
scrollTopSide	Boolean	False
scrollVertical	Boolean	True

CHANGING THE TEXT IN A TEXT WIDGET

The most important operation you'll want to perform on a text widget is to set the text inside the widget. Three functions allow you to modify the text in an XmText widget: XmTextSetString, XmTextReplace, and XmTextInsert.

XmTextSetString sets the text inside a text widget to a C string. Unlike most other Motif widgets, the XmText and XmTextField widgets use normal C strings instead of XmStrings. With Motif 1.2, the XmText and XmTextField widgets also support multibyte and wide character data. (See Chapter 27 for a discussion of international text in multibyte and wide character formats.)

You pass the text widget you want to set and a character pointer to XmTextSetString:

```
void XmTextSetString(Widget widget, char* new_text)
```

 On some versions of Motif, XmTextSetString is known to leak memory. If you face memory problems with XmText widgets, chances are this is the case. If so, use XmTextReplace instead.

N O T E

To replace portions of the text within a text widget, use XmTextReplace. XmTextReplace replaces the text starting and ending at given positions with new text you pass as a parameter to XmTextReplace:

```
void XmTextReplace(Widget widget,
      XmTextPosition start_position,
      XmTextPosition end_position,
      char* new_text)
```

XmTextPosition is defined as a long integer in the file <Xm/Text.h>:

```
typedef long XmTextPosition;
```

The position counting is in bytes and starts with the first position being position zero (0). If both the *start_position* and *end_position* are the same, the *new_text* is inserted after the *start_position*.

Because of the memory problems with XmTextSetString, mentioned above, you can use XmTextReplace to replace XmTextSetString. The following code replaces the entire text in a text widget, using XmTextReplace:

```
Widget    widget;
char*     new_text;
```

```
XmTextReplace(widget,
    (XmTextPosition) 0,
    XmTextGetLastPosition(widget),
    new_text);
```

The code above used the function `XmTextGetLastPosition` to get the last position of the existing text in the text widget. `XmTextGetLastPosition` is defined as:

```
XmTextPosition
    XmTextGetLastPosition(Widget widget)
```

Search and Replace

You can use `XmTextReplace` to support a search-and-replace mechanism in the text widget. To do so, though, you need a means to find text within a text widget. `XmTextFindString` does this:

```
Boolean XmTextFindString(Widget widget,
        XmTextPosition start_position,
        char* search_string,
        XmTextDirection direction,
        XmTextPosition* position)  /* RETURN */
```

`XmTextFindString` starts at the given *start_position* and looks for the *search_string* in the given *direction*. The *direction* can be one of `XmTEXT_FORWARD` or `XmTEXT_BACKWARD`.

`XmTextFindString` returns `True` if the text was found. In that case, the *position* is set to the place in the text widget where the *search_string* was located. Positions start counting with 0. `XmTextFindString` returns `False` if the *search_string* was not found.

Inserting Text

You can insert new text into an `XmText` widget with `XmTextInsert`:

```
void XmTextInsert(Widget widget,
        XmTextPosition position,
        char* new_text)
```

`XmTextInsert` inserts text at the given position. Start counting positions at 0.

As a last means to change the text within a text widget, the actual text itself is stored in the `value` resource. Thus you can get and set this resource with `XtVaGetValues` and `XtVaSetValues`. Normally, though, using a function like XmTextGetString is easier and clearer in your code. Plus, different versions of Motif may treat the memory used by the value resource differently. Currently, you need to free the memory after you call XtVaGetValues to get the value resource—but this is not supposed to happen this way, as getting the value resource is supposed to result in a read-only string. Because of this ambiguity, we urge you to use XmTextGetString, which is clearly defined to make a copy of the string, instead of interacting with the value resource directly.

N O T E

The XmText widget can hold only a certain amount of text. You can determine the maximum length of the text you can store by calling XmTextGetMaxLength:

```
int XmTextGetMaxLength(Widget widget)
```

This length is often the maximum integer value on your system, usually 2,147,483,647. In many cases the allowable window size will only hold much less text than the maximum the text widget can theoretically contain. Of course, you may also come across virtual-memory limits in a highly loaded system.

You can set this length with XmTextSetMaxLength:

```
void XmTextSetMaxLength(Widget widget,
        int max_length)
```

The maximum length will be enforced for user-entered text. You can make an end-run around this limit by calling XmTextSetString or setting the value resource directly.

There's also a limit on window sizes in the X Window System. Because of this, a very long line of text may force a window to be too wide, resulting in an error. Too much text can make the window too high, scroll bars notwithstanding.

We just mention this as a word of warning. Be careful placing large amounts of text into an XmText widget.

Loading ASCII Text Files into Multiline Text Widgets

The function LoadFile, which we develop below, loads an ASCII text file into a text widget. The function opens the given text file for reading, checks how large the file is, allocates a buffer for the file's bytes, reads in the file's bytes, and then calls `XmTextSetString` to place the text into the text widget. You could also use `XmTextReplace` from above instead of `XmTextSetString`.

To allocate the memory, we use `XtMalloc`, an Xt front end to `malloc`:

```
char* XtMalloc(Cardinal number_of_bytes)
```

`XtFree` frees memory allocated with `XtMalloc`:

```
XtFree(char* pointer)
```

The code below loads in an ASCII text file into a `XmText` widget:

```
/* loadtext.c */
#include  <Xm/Xm.h>
#include  <Xm/Text.h>
#include  <stdio.h>
#include  <sys/types.h>
#include  <sys/stat.h>

/* Function to load a text file into an XmText widget. */

Boolean LoadFile(Widget widget,
    char* filename)

{   /* LoadFile */
    FILE*         fp;
    struct stat   file_info;
    char*         buffer;
    long          bytes_read;

    /* Open file. */
    fp = fopen(filename, "r");

    if (fp == NULL) {
        return False;
    }
    /* Get file size. */
    if (stat(filename, &file_info)  != 0) {

        fclose(fp);

        return False;
    }

    buffer = (char *) XtMalloc(file_info.st_size + 5);

    if (buffer == (char*) NULL) {

        fclose(fp);
```

```
        return False;
    }

    /* Read in file. */
    bytes_read = fread(buffer, 1, file_info.st_size, fp);

    fclose(fp);

    buffer[file_info.st_size -1] = '\0'; /* truncate */

    if (bytes_read <  file_info.st_size) {

        XtFree(buffer);
        return False;
    }
    /* Place text into XmText widget. */
    XmTextSetString(widget, buffer);

    /* Free memory for buffer. */
    XtFree(buffer);

    return True;

}   /* LoadFile */

/* end of loadtext.c */
```

We use the UNIX stat function to determine how large the file is. If you are using another operating system, like VMS or MS-DOS, you may have to convert LoadFile to your system.

 You may have problems compiling **loadtext.c**, especially on Hewlett-Packard systems. We had to define the symbol _POSIX_SOURCE under HP-UX 9.01.

N O T E

Now that we've covered how to put text into a text widget, the next task is how to retrieve text from a text widget.

Retrieving the Text

You can retrieve text from a text widget with XmTextGetString:

```
    char* XmTextGetString(Widget widget)
```

When you're done with the returned text, free the memory it uses with XtFree.

NOTE

With a multiline text widget, you could be dealing with megabytes of text data. Just think how much text a text widget used in a CD-ROM-based application could hold.

You can retrieve a portion of the text in a text widget with XmTextGetSubstring:

```
int XmTextGetSubstring(Widget widget,
       XmTextPosition start_position,
       int number_chars,
       int buffer_size,
       char* buffer)
```

XmTextGetSubstring copies a portion of the text into a *buffer* provided by your program. You must allocate the memory for the *buffer*, and it must be big enough to hold the text as well as a terminating NULL character. For international text, you can use the following formula to determine the buffer size:

```
buffer_size = (number_chars * MB_CUR_MAX) +1;
```

MB_CUR_MAX is a macro defined in <stdlib.h> that returns the current maximum character size, in bytes, under the current locale. XmTextGetSubstring returns XmCOPY_SUCCEEDED if all goes well, or XmCOPY_TRUNCATED if fewer than number_chars characters were copied (due to a too-small buffer), or XmCOPY_FAILED in the case of general failure.

In addition to reading in a text file into an XmText widget, which we discussed above, a common need is to take the text in an XmText widget and save it to a file.

Saving the Text in a Widget to a File

The following code uses XmTextGetString and shows how to save the text from an XmText widget to a file:

```
/* savetext.c */
#include <Xm/Xm.h>
#include <Xm/Text.h>    /* XmText */
#include <stdio.h>

/* Function to save XmText contents to a file. */

Boolean SaveFile(Widget widget,
```

```
            char* filename)

{   /* SaveFile */
    FILE*   fp;
    char*   text;

    /* Open file. */
    fp = fopen(filename, "w");

    if (fp == NULL) {
       return False;
    }

    /* Extract text from widget. */
    text = XmTextGetString(widget);

    if (text != (char*) NULL) {
       /* Write to file. */
       fprintf(fp, "%s\n", text);

       /* Free memory when done. */
       XtFree(text);
    }
    fclose(fp);
    return True;

}   /* SaveFile */
```

Controlling Text Widgets

The XmText widget supports a number of resources and functions that allow you greater control over how the widget works.

The editable resource (XmNeditable in C programs) determines whether the user can modify the text in the text widget. The default value is True, so that the user can edit the text. If you set this resource to False, you can only view the text in the widget, not modify the text. You can set this resource directly, as we show in the code below:

```
#include <Xm/Text.h>

Widget widget;

/* ... */

XtVaSetValues(widget,
    XmNeditable, False,
    NULL);
```

Motif also provides functions you can use with the text widget to get and set the editable resource. XmTextGetEditable returns the value of the editable resource: `True` or `False`. `False` means that the user cannot modify the text. `True` means the user can:

```
Boolean XmTextGetEditable(Widget widget)
```

`XmTextSetEditable` sets the value of the `editable` resource:

```
void XmTextSetEditable(Widget widget,
        Boolean status)
```

The wordWrap resource (`XmNwordWrap` in C programs) controls whether the text widget should break lines at word boundaries. When set to `True`, a multiline text widget will wrap words onto the next line if they would extend beyond the current number of visible columns. The default value for this resource is `False`. Turning on the `wordWrap` resource severely degrades the `XmText` widget's performance.

The columns (`XmNcolumns` in C programs) and rows (`XmNrows` in C programs) resources control the number of visible columns and rows of text. The default number of `columns` is 20 and the default number of `rows` is 1 (for the default single-line text widget). If you set either resource, you must set both the `columns` and `rows` resources to a value greater than 0.

N O T E

Since the text widget will be the child of another widget, any requests to change the size of the text widget may be ignored or modified by the text widget's parent widget.

Text-Widget Resources

Table 5.3 shows some useful resources supported by the `XmText` widget. The text widget inherits some of these resources from `Core`, `Primitive`, and, for scrolled-text widgets, `XmScrolledWindow` widgets.

Table 5.3 *Useful XmText resources.*

Resource	Type	Default Value
autoShowCursorPosition	Boolean	True
columns	short	Width of text area in columns

continued

cursorPosition	XmTextPosition	0
cursorPositionVisible	Boolean	True
editable	Boolean	True
editMode	int	XmSINGLE_LINE_EDIT
fontList	XmFontList	*dynamic*
marginHeight	Dimension	5
marginWidth	Dimension	5
maxLength	int	MAXINT
resizeHeight	Boolean	False
resizeWidth	Boolean	False
rows	short	Height of text area in rows
source	XmTextSource	Default is new source
topCharacter	XmTextPostion	0
value	String	0
valueWcs	wchar_t*	0
verifyBell	Boolean	*dynamic*
wordWrap	Boolean	False

The value resource holds the text string. If set, the valueWcs resource holds the text string in wide character format. This is especially useful for storing Asian language text. The valueWcs resource is new in Motif 1.2.

The resizeWidth and resizeHeight resources determine whether the XmText widget should try to resize to fit any new text. Normally you want the window size to remain constant unless the user changes it. Instead, use scroll bars to handle larger amounts of text.

The verifyBell resource, if True, rings a bell whenever changes to the XmText widget are vetoed by a modifyVerifyCallback. If False, the bell won't ring.

Controlling Text-Widget Scrolling

Motif provides a number of functions to help control scrolling in the XmText widget.

To make the text widget show the text at a given position, call `XmTextShowPosition`:

```
void XmTextShowPosition(Widget widget,
        XmTextPosition position)
```

The `XmText` widget will realign itself so that the given position is made visible. If you add text to the end of a text widget and want to display it, you can call `XmTextShowPosition` as follows:

```
Widget widget;

XmTextShowPosition(widget,
        XmTextGetLastPosition(widget) );
```

To set the top visible character, use `XmTextSetTopCharacter`:

```
void XmTextSetTopCharacter(Widget widget,
        XmTextPosition top_character)
```

`XmTextSetTopCharacter` makes the line that holds the given *top_character* be the top line visible in the window. You can also set the `topCharacter` resource (`XmNtopCharacter` in C programs). This function does not effect the text—it just controls what part of the text is made visible.

To scroll the text widget a number of lines, call `XmTextScroll`:

```
void XmTextScroll(Widget widget,
        int number_lines)
```

Passing a positive *number_lines* means to scroll upward. Passing a negative *number_lines* means to scroll downward.

Controlling the Insertion Position

You can also control where text will be inserted into a text widget. For example, if you place a default value into a text widget, you may want to place the text-insertion cursor at the end of the text. To do so, call `XmTextSetInsertionPosition`:

```
void XmTextSetInsertionPosition(Widget widget,
        XmTextPosition position)
```

Starting counting text positions with 0. This function sets the `cursorPosition` resource (`XmNcursorPosition` in C programs).

Don't call the older `XmTextSetCursorPosition`, which acts the same as `XmTextSetInsertionPosition`, but is not officially supported anymore.

WARNING

You can retrieve the insertion cursor position with `XmTextGetInsertionPosition`:

```
XmTextPosition XmTextGetInsertionPosition(Widget widget)
```

This function acts like the older `XmTextGetCursorPosition`.

If you create a scrolled-text widget, remember that `XmCreateScrolledText` creates *two* widgets, a scrolled window and then a text widget. `XmCreateScrolledText`, though, just returns the `XmText` widget. Because of this, when you place a scrolled-text widget inside a container widget and control its position (see the next chapter for more on this), you must place the *parent* of the scrolled `XmText` widget, not the text widget itself.

N O T E

You can call `XtParent` to get the parent widget for a given widget:

```
Widget XtParent(Widget widget)
```

A PROGRAM USING SCROLLED TEXT

We've created a program to show how the scrolled `XmText` widget works. This program loads an ASCII text file into a scrolled-text widget, places scroll bars, and allows the user to edit the text.

An Exit pushbutton quits the program. The `activateCallback` for this pushbutton saves the text out to a file and prints it to the screen.

The code for **textprog.c** follows:

```
/* textprog.c */
#include <Xm/Xm.h>
#include <Xm/PushB.h>
#include <Xm/PanedW.h>
#include <Xm/Text.h>
#include <stdio.h>
```

```
/* Callback to extract XmText data and then exit program. */

void exitCB(Widget widget,
    XtPointer client_data,
    XtPointer call_data)

{   /* exitCB */
    Widget  text_widget;
    char*   text;

    /* Note: We passed widget ID as client_data. */
    text_widget = (Widget) client_data;

    if (text_widget != (Widget) NULL) {

        /* Extract text from widget. */
        text = XmTextGetString(text_widget);

        if (text != (char*) NULL) {
            printf("XmText held:\n%s\n", text);

            /* Free memory when done. */
            XtFree(text);
        }
        /* Save text to file. */
        if (SaveFile(text_widget, "foo.txt") == False) {
            fprintf(stderr, "Error saving to file.\n");
        }
    }

    exit(0);

}   /* exitCB */
int main(int argc, char** argv)
{   /* main */
    Widget          parent;
    XtAppContext    app_context;
    Widget          pane, push, scrolled_text;
    Arg             args[20];
    Cardinal        n;
    int             max_length;

    /* Initialize the X Toolkit. */
    n = 0;
    parent = XtAppInitialize(&app_context,

            "Ppm",                  /* app class */
            (XrmOptionDescList) NULL,/* options */
            0,                      /* num options */
            (Cardinal*) &argc,      /* num on cmd-line */
            argv,                   /* cmd-line opts */
            (String*) NULL,         /* fallback res. */
            args, 0);

    /* Create a paned window to hold child widgets. */
```

```
    n = 0;
    pane = XmCreatePanedWindow(parent,
            "pane", args, n);

    /* We manage the pane later, below. */

    /* Create a scrolled multiline text widget. */
    n = 0;
    XtSetArg(args[n], XmNeditMode, XmMULTI_LINE_EDIT); n++;

    scrolled_text = XmCreateScrolledText(pane,
                        "text", args, n);

    /* Load in a text file. */
    if (LoadFile(scrolled_text, "textprog.c") == False) {
        fprintf(stderr, "Error in loading file.\n");
    }

    XtManageChild(scrolled_text);

    /* Get max size for scrolled text. */
    max_length = XmTextGetMaxLength(scrolled_text);
    printf("Max length of text in widget: %d\n",
        max_length);

    /*
     * Create pushbutton after scrolled text,
     * so we pass the widget pointer for the client_data.
     */
    n = 0;
    push = XmCreatePushButton(pane,
            "quit", args, n);

    /* Set up a callback for the pushbutton widget. */
    XtAddCallback(push,                 /* widget */
        XmNactivateCallback,            /* which callback */
        (XtCallbackProc) exitCB,        /* callback function */
        (XtPointer) scrolled_text); /* extra data to pass */

    XtManageChild(push);

    /* Manage paned window, since children are created. */
    XtManageChild(pane);

    XtRealizeWidget(parent);
    XtAppMainLoop(app_context);

    return 0;

}   /* main */

/* end of file textprog.c */
```

The *textprog* program, like most Motif programs, needs a resource file to be most effective. This resource file for the *textprog* program (and all other programs in this chapter) follows:

```
! Resource file for textprog.c, textfld.c and password.c
! in Chapter 5 of Power Programming Motif.
!
*fontList:       lucidasans-12
*background:     lightgrey

*title:   Text Widgets

*quit.labelString: Exit

! Set size of text widget to 80x25 chars.
*text.columns:   80
*text.rows:      25

*text.scrollLeftSide: True
*text.scrollTopSide:  True

! Change font for text widget to be a fixed-width font.
*text.fontList: \
  -*-courier-medium-r-normal--12-120-*-*-m-*-*-1

! password.c label
*label.labelString:  Enter password:
! end of resource file
```

When you run this program, you'll see a text-editing area like the one shown in Figure 5.2.

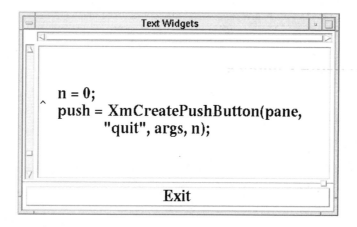

Figure 5.2   *The textprog program.*

Try changing the `scrollLeftSide` and `scrollTopSide` resources.

TEXT-WIDGET CALLBACKS

Aside from providing a general-purpose text editor, text widgets alone aren't worth much. That's why Motif supports a number of text-widget callback functions, as listed in Table 5.4.

Table 5.4 *XmText callback resources.*

Callback Resource	Called When
`activateCallback`	Called on **Enter** key in a single-line text widget
`focusCallback`	Widget gains keyboard focus
`losingFocusCallback`	Widget is losing keyboard focus
`modifyVerifyCallback`	Allows control over text changes
`modifyVerifyCallbackWcs`	Allows control over wide-character text changes
`motionVerifyCallback`	Allows control over changes in insert position
`valueChangedCallback`	Text in widget has changed

The Activate Callback

Like the `XmPushButton` widget described in Chapter 2, the `XmText` widget provides an `activateCallback` (`XmNactivateCallback` in C programs). This `activateCallback` gets executed when the user presses the `Enter` key in a single-line `XmText` widget. The `activateCallback` doesn't make any sense for a multiline text widget—in fact, it won't even be called in multiline mode.

If you set up an `activateCallback` with `XtAddCallback`, your callback function's *call_data* parameter will be in the form of a pointer to an `XmAnyCallbackStruct`:

```
typedef struct {
    int       reason;
    XEvent*   event;
} XmAnyCallbackStruct;
```

The *reason* field will be set XmCR_ACTIVATE. For an activateCallback, though, the data in the structure is normally not very useful. For other XmText callbacks though, such as modifyVerifyCallback, the data passed to the callback function is a lot more useful.

The Modify-Verify Callback

The modifyVerifyCallback gets a pointer to an XmTextVerifyCallbackStruct structure as its *call_data* parameter:

```
typedef struct {
    int           reason;
    XEvent*       event;
    Boolean       doit;
    long          currInsert, newInsert;
    long          startPos, endPos;
    XmTextBlock   text;
} XmTextVerifyCallbackStruct, *XmTextVerifyPtr;
```

The modifyVerifyCallback is called to determine whether to allow a modification to the text in the widget. That is, your application can control what to allow for data entry. This is very useful for both data validation and to create hidden data-entry fields, such as a password-entry widget, where you don't want to echo the user's password back to the screen. In the XmTextVerifyCallbackStruct structure, the *doit* field is the most important field. If you set the *doit* field to False, then the change will not occur. If set to True, the change will be allowed. This is how you can intercept changes to a text widget and perform data validation.

The *reason* field is set to XmCR_MODIFYING_TEXT_VALUE. The *currInsert* and *newInsert* fields hold the current insertion point. If you insert text into an XmText widget, the text will be inserted at currInsert. The *startPos* and *endPos* hold the positions spanning where new text will be inserted. For most single-character entries like those made on the keyboard, *currInsert*, *newInsert*, *startPos*, and *endPos* will all be the same. If the program calls XmTextInsert, there probably will be more than one character inserted, so all four values won't be the same.

The XmTextBlock structure holds the text:

```
typedef struct {
    char*           ptr;        /* data */
    int             length;     /* number data bytes */
    XmTextFormat    format;     /* which format */
} XmTextBlockRec, *XmTextBlock;
```

The *ptr* field holds the actual text. In most cases, this will be simply a normal C string. To be sure, you should check the *format* field. This field should be XmFMT_8_BIT for 8-bit text and XmFMT_16_BIT for 16-bit text. Even so, we find that the *format* field is often set to 0 and so cannot be depended on.

In older versions of Motif, such as version 1.1, these values are FMT8BIT for 8-bit text and FMT16BIT for 16-bit text.

N O T E

The XmTextFormat value is normally defined as an Atom, which is, in turn, a numeric-integer value:

```
typedef Atom    XmTextFormat;
```

There's no easy way to tell if the user pressed the **Delete** key instead of adding new text. The best way is to check if the *ptr* field is NULL or the *length* is 0.

Data Validation Using Callbacks

You can use the modifyVerifyCallback to perform data validation on a text widget. For example, you could force the user to enter in a numeric value. In such a case, your modifyVerifyCallback would need to check the XmTextBlock's *ptr* field to ensure that the new characters entered are numeric (or a decimal point, or a minus sign, and so on).

If the newly entered value is not valid, then set the *doit* field to False. This prevents the new change from occurring.

It is often normal for a partially completed field to look invalid just because the user isn't finished. For example, if the user must enter in a number between 1000 and 2000, the very first digit, 1, say, would represent an invalid number. Why? Because the user hasn't had enough time to type in 1001, a valid num-

N O T E

ber. When checking for data validation, you may want to delay some tests until the entire entry is complete by using the activate or losing-focus callbacks.

You can perform other tests character by character using the modifyVerifyCallback, though. For example, if the data must be numeric, you know that the letter *A* is invalid data.

Password Entry with Text Widgets

In a password-entry system, you want to take in characters that the user types, but you *don't want to display these characters. Instead, you want to display nothing or some innocuous character like an asterisk (*)*.

To do so, you need to keep a *shadow text string*. This shadow string contains the text that the user entered. You set the XmText widget, then, to hold only asterisks. The hardest part of doing this is that you have to mimic the text changes in your shadow text string.

The following code takes care of this problem. The modifyVerifyCB function acts as a modifyVerifyCallback for an XmText widget. We assume the code that sets up the XmText widget passes a pointer to the shadow text string as the *client_data* for the modifyVerifyCallback. The delete_at and insert_at functions handle deleting and inserting text.

The code for **password.c** follows:

```
/* password.c */
#include <Xm/Xm.h>
#include <Xm/Label.h>
#include <Xm/RowColumn.h>
#include <Xm/Text.h>
#include <stdio.h>
#include <string.h>

/* Global to hold password. */
#define MAX_PASSWORD    1024    /* Big password. */

char  password[MAX_PASSWORD+1];

/*
 * You should be able to come up
 * with better string algorithms.
 */
static void delete_at(int position,/* where to delete */
    char* string)                  /* delete from string */
```

```
{   /* delete_at */
    int     i, length;

    length = strlen(string);

    for (i = position; i < length; i++) {
        string[i] = string[i+1];
    }

    string[length-1] = '\0';

}   /* delete_at */

static void insert_at(int position,/* where to insert */
    int ch,                         /* what to insert */
    char* string)                   /* insert into string */

{   /* insert_at */
    int     i, length;
    char    string2[1024];

    length = strlen(string);\

    if (position >= length) {

        string[position] = ch;
        string[position +1] = '\0';
    } else {
        /* position < length. */
        for (i = 0; i < position; i++) {
            string2[i] = string[i];
        }

        string2[position] = ch;

        for (i = position; i < length; i++) {
            string2[i+1] = string[i];
        }

        string2[i+1] = '\0'; /* terminate */

        strcpy(string, string2);
    }

}   /* insert_at */

    /* Callback to control text changes. */
void modifyVerifyCB(Widget widget,
    XtPointer client_data,          /* holds string */
    XtPointer call_data)

{   /* modifyVerifyCB */
    XmTextVerifyCallbackStruct* ptr;
    char*                       string;
```

```
        ptr = (XmTextVerifyCallbackStruct*) call_data;

        if (ptr == NULL) {
            return;
        }

        /*
         * Assumes current password
         * is passed as client_data.
         */
        string = (char*) client_data;

        if (string == (char*) NULL) {
            return;
        }

        /* This function doesn't handle Asian languages. */
#ifdef XmFMT_16_BIT
        if (ptr->text->format == XmFMT_16_BIT) {
            return;
        }
#else   /* FMT16BIT */
        if (ptr->text->format == FMT16BIT) {
            return;
        }
#endif /* !XmFMT_16_BIT */
        /* If the text length is 0, we assume a delete. */
        if (ptr->text->length == 0) {

            /* Delete character at startPos. */
            delete_at(ptr->startPos, string);
        } else {
            if (ptr->text->length > 0) {
                /* Insert character at currInsert. */
                insert_at(ptr->currInsert,
                    ptr->text->ptr[0],
                    string);

                /* Modify data to only display stars. */
                ptr->text->ptr[0] = '*';
            }
        }

        /* Allow change to text. */
        ptr->doit = True;

    }   /* modifyVerifyCB */

        /* Callback when user presses Enter key. */

void activateCB(Widget widget,
    XtPointer client_data,
    XtPointer call_data)
```

```
{   /* activateCB */

    printf("Password is [%s]\n", password);

    exit(0);

}   /* activateCB */

int main(int argc, char** argv)

{   /* main */
    Widget          parent;
    XtAppContext    app_context;
    Widget          row, label, text;
    Arg             args[20];
    Cardinal        n;

    /* Initialize the X Toolkit. */
    n = 0;
    parent = XtAppInitialize(&app_context,
            "Ppm",
            (XrmOptionDescList) NULL,
            0,
            (Cardinal*) &argc,
            argv,
            (String*) NULL,
            args, 0);

    row = XtVaCreateManagedWidget("row",
            xmRowColumnWidgetClass, parent,
            XmNorientation, XmHORIZONTAL,
            NULL);

    label = XtVaCreateManagedWidget("label",
            xmLabelWidgetClass, row,
            NULL);

    /* Create a text widget. */
    text = XtVaCreateManagedWidget("pass_text",
            xmTextWidgetClass, row,
            XmNeditMode, XmSINGLE_LINE_EDIT,
            NULL);

    /* Set up text callbacks. */
    XtAddCallback(text, XmNactivateCallback,
        (XtCallbackProc) activateCB, (XtPointer) NULL);

    XtAddCallback(text, XmNmodifyVerifyCallback,
        (XtCallbackProc) modifyVerifyCB,
        (XtPointer) password);
    /* Initialize password. */
    password[0] = '\0';

    XtRealizeWidget(parent);
```

```
    XtAppMainLoop(app_context);

    return 0;

}   /* main */

/* end of file password.c */
```

When you run this program, you'll be prompted to enter a password, as shown in Figure 5.3.

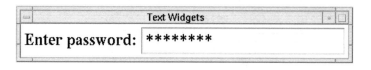

Figure 5.3 *The password program.*

Text appears as asterisks (*), yet the program maintains the actual text entered, as the user discovers when the **Enter** key is pressed.

ADVANCED TOPICS FOR TEXT WIDGETS

To improve performance of the XmText widget, you can temporarily disable updates to the widget. For example, if you need to make multiple changes to the text within the widget or to its controlling resources (wordWrap, topCharacter, etc.), then you may want to stop the text widget from updating itself after each change. Only when you're through do you want the text widget to update reflecting *all* the changes. To control this, call XmTextDisableRedisplay and XmTextEnableRedisplay. XmText-DisableRedisplay temporarily disables the redisplay of the text widget:

```
    void XmTextDisableRedisplay(Widget widget)
```

XmTextEnableRedisplay turns the redisplay back on, ending the temporary disabling of the redisplay code:

```
    void XmTextEnableRedisplay(Widget widget)
```

If you call XmTextDisableRedisplay, be sure to call XmTextEnableRedisplay.

Retrieving the Selected Text

Using the left mouse button, you can select a range of text in the text widget. Typically, users may want to copy this text to the Motif clipboard, paste it in the current program, or paste it to another program. To get the selected text, call `XmTextGetSelection`:

```
char* XmTextGetSelection(Widget widget)
```

Working with the selected text is an advanced topic. For more on this topic, look in Chapter 19 on the Motif clipboard for cut, copy, and paste operations and Chapter 20 on X Window selections.

Single-Line Text-Entry Fields

In addition to the `XmText` widget, Motif provides a widget tuned for single-line text entry, the `XmTextField` widget. You can generally assume that an `XmTextField` widget will act the same as an `XmText` widget with its `editMode` resource set to `XmSINGLE_LINE_EDIT`.

WARNING

There is a separate set of functions beginning with *XmTextField* (instead of *XmText*) that interact with `XmTextField` widgets. You should use these separate `XmTextField` functions with `XmTextField` widgets.

The functions listed in Table 5.5 take the same parameters and act similarly for the `XmText` and `XmTextField` widgets.

Table 5.5 *Similar functions for XmText and XmTextField.*

XmText	XmTextField
XmTextSetHighlight	XmTextFieldSetHighlight
XmTextGetSubstring	XmTextFieldGetSubstring
XmTextGetString	XmTextFieldGetString
XmTextGetLastPosition	XmTextFieldGetLastPosition
XmTextSetString	XmTextFieldSetString

continued

XmTextReplace	XmTextFieldReplace
XmTextInsert	XmTextFieldInsert
XmTextSetAddMode	XmTextFieldSetAddMode
XmTextGetAddMode	XmTextFieldGetAddMode
XmTextGetEditable	XmTextFieldGetEditable
XmTextSetEditable	XmTextFieldSetEditable
XmTextGetMaxLength	XmTextFieldGetMaxLength
XmTextSetMaxLength	XmTextFieldSetMaxLength
XmTextGetCursorPosition	XmTextFieldGetCursorPosition
XmTextGetInsertionPosition	XmTextFieldGetInsertionPosition
XmTextSetCursorPosition	XmTextFieldSetCursorPosition
XmTextSetInsertionPosition	XmTextFieldSetInsertionPosition
XmTextGetSelectionPosition	XmTextFieldGetSelectionPosition
XmTextGetSelection	XmTextFieldGetSelection
XmTextRemove	XmTextFieldRemove
XmTextCopy	XmTextFieldCopy
XmTextCut	XmTextFieldCut
XmTextPaste	XmTextFieldPaste
XmTextGetSelection	XmTextFieldGetSelection
XmTextSetSelection	XmTextFieldSetSelection
XmTextClearSelection	XmTextFieldClearSelection
XmTextGetSelectionPosition	XmTextFieldGetSelectionPosition
XmTextXYToPos	XmTextFieldXYToPos
XmTextPosToXY	XmTextFieldPosToXY
XmTextShowPosition	XmTextFieldShowPosition
XmTextGetBaseline	XmTextFieldGetBaseline

The XmTextField widget supports an activateCallback just like the
XmText widget. The XmTextField also supports the focusCallback,
losingFocusCallback, modifyVerifyCallback, and valueChanged-
Callback. Note that the focusCallback is not supported until Motif 1.2.

A Program to Show Text-Entry Fields

The following file, **textfld.c**, shows how the XmTextField callbacks interact:

```
/* textfld.c */
#include <Xm/Xm.h>
#include <Xm/PushB.h>
#include <Xm/PanedW.h>
#include <Xm/TextF.h>
#include <stdio.h>

    /* Callback to exit program. */

void exitCB(Widget widget,
    XtPointer client_data,
    XtPointer call_data)

{   /* exitCB */

    exit(0);

}   /* exitCB */

    /* Callback tracks keyboard focus. */

void focusCB(Widget widget,
    XtPointer client_data,
    XtPointer call_data)
{   /* focusCB */
    XmAnyCallbackStruct*     ptr;

    ptr = (XmAnyCallbackStruct*) call_data;

    if (ptr != NULL) {
        switch(ptr->reason) {
            case XmCR_FOCUS:
                printf("Gaining focus.\n");
                break;
            case XmCR_LOSING_FOCUS:
                printf("Losing focus.\n");
                break;
        }
    }

}   /* focusCB */

    /* Callback to control text changes. */

void modifyVerifyCB(Widget widget,
    XtPointer client_data,
    XtPointer call_data)
```

```
{    /* modifyVerifyCB */
    XmTextVerifyCallbackStruct* ptr;
    printf("Modify Verify CB.\n");

    ptr = (XmTextVerifyCallbackStruct*) call_data;

    if (ptr != NULL) {

        /* Print info on modification. */
        printf("\t currInsert: %d \t newInsert: %d\n",
            ptr->currInsert, ptr->newInsert);

        printf("\t startPos: %d   \t endPos: %d\n",
            ptr->startPos, ptr->endPos);

        printf("\t text length: %d \t new text: [%s]\n",
            ptr->text->length, ptr->text->ptr);

        /*
         * Note that we're not handling
         * Asian 16-bit text.
         */

        /* Assume we have a delete if we get 0 length. */
        if (ptr->text->length == 0) {

            /* Delete character at startPos. */
            printf("Delete char %d\n", ptr->startPos);
        }

        if (ptr->text->length > 0) {

            /* Insert character at currInsert. */
            printf("Insert [%s] at %d\n",
                ptr->text->ptr, ptr->currInsert);
        }

        /*
         * Allow change to text. Set doit
         * to False to prevent change.
         */
        ptr->doit = True;
    }

}    /* modifyVerifyCB */

    /* Callback when value changes. */

void valueChangedCB(Widget widget,
    XtPointer client_data,
    XtPointer call_data)

{    /* valueChangedCB */

    printf("Value Changed CB.\n");
```

```
}   /* valueChangedCB */

    /* Callback when user presses Enter key. */

void activateCB(Widget widget,
    XtPointer client_data,
    XtPointer call_data)

{   /* activateCB */
    char*   text;

    text = XmTextFieldGetString(widget);

    if (text != NULL) {
        printf("Activate CB with [%s].\n", text);

        XtFree(text);
    }

}   /* activateCB */

int main(int argc, char** argv)

{   /* main */
    Widget          parent;
    XtAppContext    app_context;
    Widget          pane, push, text_field;
    Arg             args[20];
    Cardinal        n;

    /* Initialize the X Toolkit. */
    n = 0;
    parent = XtAppInitialize(&app_context,
            "Ppm",
            (XrmOptionDescList) NULL,
            0,
            (Cardinal*) &argc,
            argv,
            (String*) NULL,
            args, 0);

    /* Create a paned window to hold child widgets. */
    n = 0;
    pane = XmCreatePanedWindow(parent,
            "pane", args, n);

    /* We manage the pane later, below. */

    /* Create a text field widget. */
    n = 0;

    text_field = XmCreateTextField(pane,
            "text", args, n);
    /* Set up text field callbacks. */
    XtAddCallback(text_field, XmNactivateCallback,
```

```
                    (XtCallbackProc) activateCB, (XtPointer) NULL);

        /*
         * Note: the XmNfocusCallback is not
         * supported in Motif 1.1 for XmTextField.
         */
        XtAddCallback(text_field, XmNfocusCallback,
            (XtCallbackProc) focusCB, (XtPointer) NULL);

        XtAddCallback(text_field, XmNlosingFocusCallback,
            (XtCallbackProc) focusCB, (XtPointer) NULL);

        XtAddCallback(text_field, XmNmodifyVerifyCallback,
            (XtCallbackProc) modifyVerifyCB, (XtPointer) NULL);

        XtAddCallback(text_field, XmNvalueChangedCallback,
            (XtCallbackProc) valueChangedCB, (XtPointer) NULL);

        XtManageChild(text_field);

        /* Create pushbutton to exit program. */
        n = 0;
        push = XmCreatePushButton(pane,
                    "quit", args, n);
        /* Set up a callback for the pushbutton widget. */
        XtAddCallback(push,
            XmNactivateCallback,
            (XtCallbackProc) exitCB,
            (XtPointer) NULL);

        XtManageChild(push);

        /* Manage paned window, since children are created. */
        XtManageChild(pane);

        XtRealizeWidget(parent);
        XtAppMainLoop(app_context);
        return 0;

    }    /* main */

/* end of file textfld.c */
```

As you enter text into the *textfld* program, you'll see various messages
printed to the screen. These messages show the order in which the various
callbacks get executed and provide a lot of information in particular on the
modifyVerifyCallback. The process is illustrated in Figure 5.4.

N O T E   The focusCallback for XmTextField widgets is not supported in many versions of Motif 1.1. The focusCallback is supported for XmText widgets, though. If you want to use
XmTextField widgets, upgrade to Motif 1.2.

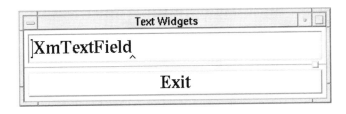

Figure 5.4 *Text entry with an XmTextField widget.*

Should You Use XmTextField or XmText Widgets?

The differences between XmText in single-line mode and XmTextField widgets are minimal. XmTextField widgets are tuned to single-line text editing, as opposed to all the baggage that is required for multiline scrolled-text editing. Even so, we recommend using XmText widgets for the following two reasons.

First, in Motif 1.1, there are many problems associated with XmTextField widgets. Most of these problems were solved in Motif 1.2. If you must support older platforms using Motif 1.1 libraries, stick to XmText widgets.

Second, we find that most applications already require a multiline text-editing widget, such as XmText. If you already link in all the XmText code, why link in extra XmTextField code to do the same thing? If you already use XmText widgets, you might as well stick to XmText and skip XmTextField.

UPCOMING CHANGES TO TEXT WIDGETS

The XmText widget currently is the primary means for entering text into Motif widgets. As such, it doesn't really work well for international text. To help solve these problems, the OSF plans to replace the XmText widget with a compound-string text widget.

This compound string text widget will support multiple fonts, multiple colors in the text, and right-to-left text (for Arabic and Hebrew). For now, keep using the XmText widget. When future versions of Motif arrive, you can then determine when to migrate over to the compound-string text widget.

SUMMARY

In this chapter, we introduced the text widget, a widget you will use over and over again in your applications. The complex text widget handles most text entry in Motif. It can be either a single-line prompt or a multiline text editor. You can add scroll bars to a multiline text widget, especially if you want to edit a large amount of text, such as a text file.

The function `XmCreateText` creates a text widget. `XmCreateScrolledText` creates a text widget as a child of a scrolled window widget—making a text widget with scroll bars. When you create a text widget with the `XmCreateScrolledText` function, a hidden scrolled-window widget is first created, and then a text widget is created as a child of the scrolled window. Normally, if you don't have enough data to warrant a scroll bar (either horizontally or vertically), then the scroll bar won't be visible. If, however, you always want a scroll bar visible, you can set the values of the `scrollVertical` (`XmNscrollVertical` in C programs) and `scrollHorizontal` (`XmNscrollHorizontal` in C programs) resources. For each resource, if you set the resource to `True`, you'll always have a scroll bar. If you set the resource to `False`, you will not have the scroll bar in the particular direction.

You can configure a text widget as a single-line prompt, or you can make the text widget span a number of lines with scroll bars. The `editMode` resource controls whether an `XmText` widget spans multiple lines or is locked into a single line.

You can use the `modifyVerifyCallback` to perform data validation on a text widget. For example, you could force the user to enter in a numeric value. In such a case, your `modifyVerifyCallback` would need to check the `XmTextBlock`'s *ptr* field to ensure that the new characters entered are numeric (or a decimal point, or a minus sign, and so on). In a password-entry system, you want to take in characters that the user types, but you *don't* want to display these characters. Instead, you want to display nothing or some innocuous character like an asterisk (*). To do so, you need to keep a shadow text string. This shadow string contains the text that the user entered. You set the `XmText` widget, then, to hold only asterisks. The hardest part of doing this is that you have to mimic the text changes in your shadow text string.

To improve performance of the XmText widget, you can temporarily disable updates to the widget. For example, if you need to make multiple changes to the text within the widget or to its controlling resources (wordWrap, topCharacter, etc.), then you may want to stop the text widget from updating itself after each change. Only when you're through do you want the text widget to update reflecting *all* the changes. To control this, call XmTextDisableRedisplay and XmTextEnableRedisplay. XmText-DisableRedisplay temporarily disables the redisplay of the text widget.

In addition to the XmText widget, Motif provides a widget tuned for single-line text entry, the XmTextField widget. You can generally assume that an XmTextField widget will act the same as an XmText widget with its editMode resource set to XmSINGLE_LINE_EDIT.

The XmText widget currently is the primary means for entering text into Motif widgets. As such, it doesn't really work well for international text. To help solve these problems, the OSF plans to replace the XmText widget with a compound-string text widget.

While we've just covered most text widget common options, there are a host of other options available. You should look up the XmText section in the *OSF/Motif Programmer's Reference* for more information on these options.

MOTIF FUNCTIONS AND MACROS INTRODUCED IN THIS CHAPTER

```
XmCreateScrolledText
XmCreateText
XmCreateTextField
XmTextDisableRedisplay
XmTextEnableRedisplay
XmTextFieldGetString
XmTextFieldSetString
XmTextFindString
XmTextGetEditable
XmTextGetInsertionPosition
XmTextGetLastPosition
XmTextGetMaxLength
XmTextGetSelection
XmTextGetString
XmTextGetSubstring
XmTextInsert
XmTextReplace
XmTextScroll
```

```
XmTextSetEditable
XmTextSetInsertionPosition
XmTextSetMaxLength
XmTextSetString
XmTextSetTopCharacter
XmTextShowPosition
```

X TOOLKIT INTRINSICS FUNCTIONS AND MACROS INTRODUCED IN THIS CHAPTER

```
XtFree
XtMalloc
XtParent
```

Organizing Applications with Container Widgets

This chapter introduces container widgets, which are used to control the layout of your application windows. We cover:

- Row-column widgets
- Toggle and radio buttons
- Creating more readable indicators
- Toggle callbacks
- Frame widgets
- Frame titles
- The form widget
- Paned-window widgets
- Making good-looking sashes on paned windows
- The bulletin-board primitive container
- Accessing children of a container widget

195

CONTAINER WIDGETS AND COMPLEX PROGRAMS

Motif offers many means to control the layout of your applications. A business data-entry form application, for example, needs all its widgets to line up like they appear in the real paper form that the computer application emulates. To get widgets to line up in this way requires that you use Motif's container widgets.

We've already introduced some of these widgets, including the XmRowColumn used by menus and XmPanedWindow in Chapter 2. But the programs presented so far haven't been all that interesting, because we've used very few widgets and have not concentrated on any layouts. This chapter extends our introduction of Motif's container widgets, including:

- XmRowColumn
- XmFrame
- XmForm
- XmPanedWindow
- XmBulletinBoard

CONTAINER WIDGETS

Container widgets are used extensively in just about every Motif program. The common container widgets are listed in Table 6.1.

Table 6.1   *Container widgets.*

Widget Class Name	Created By	Covered In
XmBulletinBoard	XmCreateBulletinBoard	Chapter 6
XmDrawingArea	XmCreateDrawingArea	Chapter 11
XmFrame	XmCreateFrame	Chapter 6
XmForm	XmCreateForm	Chapter 6
XmMainWindow	XmCreateMainWindow	Chapter 4

continued

XmPanedWindow	XmCreatePanedWindow	Chapter 6
XmRowColumn	XmCreateRowColumn	Chapters 4, 6
XmScale	XmCreateScale	Chapter 9
XmScrolledWindow	XmCreateScrolledWindow	Chapter 9

These widgets are subclasses of the XmManager widget, a meta-class widget that will never be created in your application programs. XmManager is in turn a subclass of Core, Composite, and Constraint (Core is the parent of all widgets). XmManager is important only because it defines resources common to most container widgets.

In every Motif program you'll create special widgets, like row-column widgets, to control the layout of child widgets—the widgets you're really interested in. All Motif programs share this top-down hierarchical design.

SHORTCUT

Form and Row-Column Widgets

The two most common container widgets are the XmRowColumn and XmForm widgets. With row-column widgets, you need to do nothing to place the child widgets inside the container: You merely create the child widgets using the row-column widget as a parent. Create a row-column widget with XmCreateRowColumn:

```
#include <Xm/RowColumn.h>

Widget XmCreateRowColumn(Widget parent,
    char* widget_name,
    ArgList args,
    Cardinal number_args)
```

You can configure the orientation resource to XmHORIZONTAL or XmVERTICAL to make, respectively, a horizontal or vertical row column.

Unfortunately, for all its simplicity, the row column doesn't offer much in the way of flexibility for controlling how the child widgets are laid out. If you need greater flexibility, try the XmForm widget. Create a form widget with XmCreateForm:

```
#include <Xm/Form.h>
```

```
Widget XmCreateForm(Widget parent,
      char* widget_name,
      ArgList args
      Cardinal number_args)
```

The form widget requires a lot more work to align the child widgets, but you do get a lot more control. Typically, you place attachment resources on the child widget. The parent XmForm then reads these child resources and lines up the child widgets accordingly.

THE ROW-COLUMN WIDGET

The row-column widget provides a handy way to simply lay out rows or columns of child widgets. To provide this simplicity, though, the row column skimps on flexibility. It seems that the row-column widget (as summarized in Table 6.2) was really designed as a means for laying out menu choices in a menu and evolved from there.

Table 6.2 *The XmRowColumn widget class.*

Widget class:	XmRowColumn
Class pointer:	xmRowColumnWidgetClass
Include file:	<Xm/RowColumn.h>
Create with:	XmCreateRowColumn

We've seen the XmRowColumn widget before, especially in menus and menu bars. So far, however, we haven't explicitly created one. Create a row-column widget with XmCreateRowColumn:

```
#include <Xm/RowColumn.h>

Widget XmCreateRowColumn(Widget parent,
      char* widget_name,
      ArgList args
      Cardinal number_args)
```

Call XtManageChild to manage a row column after creation.

The row-column widget is a *container widget*: it holds child widgets. Row-column widgets don't provide a lot of flexibility for attachments and so on. But the row column makes up for this lack of control with a simple means to add children.

Row-Column Resources

When you look up `XmRowColumn` in the *OSF/Motif Programmer's Reference*, prepare to be confused. Since the row-column widget is used for so many things (menu bars, pop-up menus, pull-down menus, holding radio buttons), there are a host of confusing resources. Most of them won't apply at any one time, unless you are using the `XmRowColumn` widget for a special purpose, like a menu. For instance, the common row-column resources are listed in Table 6.3.

Table 6.3   *XmRowColumn resources.*

Resource	Type	Default Value
adjustLast	Boolean	True
adjustMargin	Boolean	True
entryAlignment	unsigned char	XmALIGNMENT_BEGINNING
isAligned	Boolean	True
numColumns	short	1
orientation	unsigned char	*dynamic*
packing	unsigned char	*dynamic*
radioAlwaysOne	Boolean	True
radioBehavior	Boolean	False
spacing	Dimension	*dynamic*

The `adjustLast` resource (`XmNadjustLast` in C programs), if `True`, extends the last child widget to the far border if the column is laid out nonsymetrically.

The adjustMargin resource (XmNadjustMargin in C programs) if True, forces all the margins of child widgets to be the same.

Set the entryAlignment resource (XmNentryAlignment in C programs) to one of the following:

- XmALIGNMENT_BEGINNING
- XmALIGNMENT_CENTER
- XmALIGNMENT_END

This controls how label, pushbutton, or toggle-button widgets are placed inside a row column. The entryAlignment resource does not apply unless you also set the isAligned resource to True.

The orientation resource (XmNorientation in C programs) can have a value of XmVERTICAL or XmHORIZONTAL. The following code sets up the row column to align its children horizontally:

```
Arg        args[10];
Cardinal   n;

n = 0;
XtSetArg(args[n], XmNorientation, XmHORIZONTAL);
n++;

/* Create widget... */
```

The packing resource (XmNpacking in C programs) controls how close the widgets are placed in the rows and columns. This can be one of:

- XmPACK_COLUMN
- XmPACK_NONE
- XmPACK_TIGHT

With the packing resource set to XmPACK_COLUMN, all child widgets are placed as if they were the same size—each child widget is placed in a bounding box, with the bounding box the size of the largest child widget.

The child widgets are placed in the XmRowColumn widget in the direction of the orientation resource (that is, horizontally or vertically). The value of the numColumns resource determines how many columns (horizontal) or rows (vertical) there are.

With the packing resource set to XmPACK_TIGHT, child widgets are placed one after the other in the direction as set in the orientation resource. If there are too many child widgets, the XmRowColumn will wrap around and start a new column or row.

The numColumns resource (XmNnumColumns in C programs) specifies how many columns (or rows, depending on the orientation) you want the row-column widget to try to create. The numColumns resource applies only if the packing resource is set to XmPACK_COLUMN.

NOTE In some versions of Motif 1.1, you'll get a core dump if you add more than 256 child widgets to a row-column widget.

Radio Buttons and Radio Boxes

There are times when you must provide the user a single choice from a set of choices. These choices are called *radio buttons*. The name radio button comes from older car radios that sport a set of buttons of which only one can be pushed in at a time. Radio buttons appear in a radio box, which is really a specially configured XmRowColumn widget. A radio box appears in Figure 6.1.

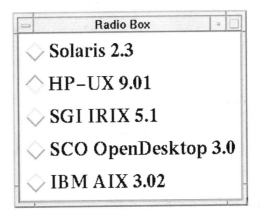

Figure 6.1 *A radio box.*

To create a radio-box row-column widget, you need to set two resources to True: radioBehavior (XmNradioBehavior in C programs) and radioAlwaysOne (XmNradioAlwaysOne in C programs).

The radioBehavior resource tells the XmRowColumn that of all its toggle-button (and toggle-button-gadget) children, only one can be set to True at a time.

The radioAlwaysOne makes sure that one of the toggle buttons (or toggle-button gadgets) is always set to True, after one of the toggles is originally set to True.

Together with the row-column widget, these two resources are all you need to set:

```
Widget   row, parent;

row = XtVaCreateManagedWidget("row",
         xmRowColumnWidgetClass, parent,
         XmNradioBehavior, True,
         XmNradioAlwaysOne, True,
         NULL);
```

Now that we know how to make a row-column widget enforce the policy for radio buttons, it's time to actually create some radio buttons.

Radio Buttons and Toggles

A toggle button is a Boolean selector: it can be either in or out (on or off, True or False). When the user clicks the mouse Button 1 in a toggle, the toggle changes state, from True to False, or False to True. A radio button is a special toggle button that appears in a mutually exclusive group. Only one radio button in the group can be on (with a state of True) at a time, while any number of toggle buttons can be on at any time. Usually radio buttons appear inside a row-column widget, described above, inside a 3D frame.

The XmToggleButton widget class, as summarized in Table 6.4, handles both toggle and radio buttons.

Table 6.4 *The XmToggleButton widget class.*

Widget class:	XmToggleButton
Class pointer:	xmToggleButtonWidgetClass
Include file:	<Xm/ToggleB.h>
Create with:	XmCreateToggleButton

Create a toggle widget with `XmCreateToggleButton`:

```
#include <Xm/ToggleB.h>

Widget XmCreateToggleButton(Widget parent,
    char* widget_name,
    ArgList args
    Cardinal number_args)
```

Call `XtManageChild` to manage a toggle button after creation.

Each toggle button can have a box or diamond that clicks in and out, as well as a text label. You can omit the box or diamond if you want, using the `indicatorOn` resource (`XmNindicatorOn` in C programs). Set `indicatorOn` to `True`, and the box or diamond will appear. Set `indicatorOn` to `False`, and the box or diamond will not appear. If you plan on following the Motif style, you should turn on the indicators. (Actually, you need to do nothing—just don't turn them off.)

Other interesting toggle resources are listed in Table 6.5.

Table 6.5 *XmToggleButton resources.*

Resource	Type	Default Value
fillOnSelect	Boolean	*dynamic*
indicatorOn	Boolean	True
indicatorSize	Dimension	*dynamic*
indicatorType	unsigned char	*dynamic*
labelString	XmString	*dynamic*
selectColor	Pixel	*dynamic*
set	Boolean	False
visibleWhenOff	Boolean	*dynamic*

The toggle button inherits from the Motif `XmLabel` widget, which means the toggle button displays a text message (or a pixmap) using the same `labelString` resource (`XmNlabelString` in C programs) as do pushbuttons and labels.

The shape displayed with the toggle button widget can be a box or a diamond, called an `XmN_OF_MANY` (box) and `XmONE_OF_MANY` (diamond). In the

OSF/Motif Style Guide, the diamond shape (XmONE_OF_MANY) is reserved for radio buttons of which only one in a group can be chosen at a time.

You can control the shape with the indicatorType resource (XmNindicatorType in C programs). The following code sets up the indicatorType to be a box:

```
Arg        args[10];
Cardinal   n;
n = 0;
XtSetArg(args[n], XmNindicatorType, XmN_OF_MANY);
n++;
/* Create the toggle widget... */
```

Both button shapes are shown in Figure 6.2.

Figure 6.2 *XmN_OF_MANY (left) and XmONE_OF_MANY (right) indicators.*

Normally you use a toggle button with an indicator. You can turn this off by setting the indicatorOn resource (XmNindicatorOn in C programs) to False. If you do this, it's a good idea to turn on the fillOnSelect resource (XmNfillOnSelect in C programs):

```
Widget   toggle;

/* Create widget... */

XtVaSetValues(toggle,
    XmNindicatorOn,   False,
    XmNfillOnSelect,  True,
    NULL);
```

This is makes a new form of toggle display, as shown in Figure 6.3.

Making More Readable Indicators

Many users complain that the indicator on the toggle button is confusing, as it's hard to discern whether the indicator is on or off. Since this is the key function of the toggle button, we need some way to make the state of the toggle clearer to the user. One way to do this is to make the indicator bigger.

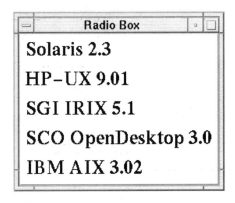

Figure 6.3 *Toggle buttons with indicators off.*

The indicatorSize resource (XmNindicatorSize in C programs) controls the size of the indicator, as you probably guessed. If you want a really large indicator, you can set this resource to a larger value. The value you provide is used for both the width and the height of the indicator, as the indicator is generally square. For example, if you make the indicatorSize 100 pixels, you'll see massive toggle widgets, as we somewhat facetiously show in Figure 6.4.

Unfortunately, when you set the indicator size directly, you're competing with Motif's logic for choosing an indicator size that best matches the current font size. You may think you're making a big indicator, but once your application is used around the world—especially in places like China, where larger fonts are the norm—you may actually shrink the indicator from Motif's desired size. In addition, the *Style Guide* frowns on changing the indicatorSize. We advise you not to do it—but you still need to find a way to make the indicator more readable. Our experience says that changing the toggle's selected color works the best.

The selectColor resource (XmNselectColor in C programs) controls the color of the indicator—when it's pushed in. If you set the selectColor to a color that contrasts highly with the rest of the widget's colors, the user has no trouble discerning if the toggle is on or off. For selection colors, we suggest yellow or white.

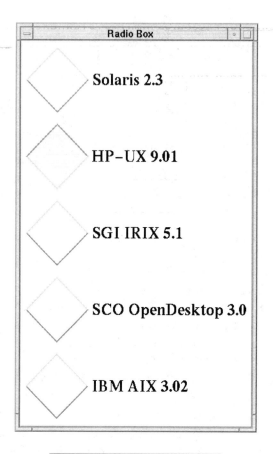

Figure 6.4 *Massive indicators.*

N O T E

The selectColor resource requires a data value of type Pixel. We cover X colors and Pixels in Chapter 15. For now, the easiest means to set the selectColor resource is to use a resource file. Inside the resource file, you can use English color names like *yellow* or *white* instead of going through the hassle of converting the color name to a Pixel value.

To set the selectColor resource, add the following line to your resource file:

```
*selectColor: yellow
```

If the visibleWhenOff resource (XmNvisibleWhenOff in C programs) is set to True, then the indicator is visible even when the toggle is turned off. This is the default case for all but menus. If a toggle button is a menu choice in a menu, then the default for the visibleWhenOff resource is True. The opposite setting, False, is shown in Figure 6.5.

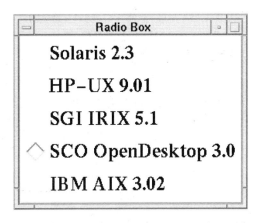

Figure 6.5 *Setting the visibleWhenOff resource to False.*

Toggle Callbacks

The toggle widget allows you to set up a function to be called back whenever the toggle's value changes (from True to False or False to True). This callback is the valueChangedCallback (XmNvalueChangedCallback in C programs). ValueChangedCallback sets up your callback function to receive a pointer to an XmToggleButtonCallbackStruct structure as the call data. This XmToggleButtonCallbackStruct structure looks like:

```
typedef struct {
    int      reason;
    XEvent*  event;
    Boolean  set;
} XmToggleButtonCallbackStruct;
```

The *set* field indicates the new (changed) state of the callback, True or False. The *reason* field should be equal to XmCR_VALUE_CHANGED. Here's a sample toggle callback function:

```
                /* Toggle button callback function. */
    void toggleCB(Widget widget,
        XtPointer client_data,
        XtPointer call_data)
    {   /* toggleCB */
        XmToggleButtonCallbackStruct* ptr;

        ptr = (XmToggleButtonCallbackStruct*) call_data;

        if (ptr != NULL) {

            /*
             * We passed a text string
             * as the client_data.
             */
            if (ptr->set == True) {
                printf("Toggle %s turned ON.\n",
                    (char*) client_data);
            } else {
                printf("Toggle %s turned OFF.\n",
                    (char*) client_data);
            }
        }

    }   /* toggleCB */
```

A group of toggle-button widgets can all be set independently, to `True` or `False`, as the user desires. Sometimes, though, choices are mutually exclusive. With radio buttons, as discussed earlier, you'll want to allow only one toggle of a group to be set to `True`, with the rest of the toggle buttons set to `False`, no matter what. To do this, what you need to do is to group the toggle buttons together into a radio box, which we described above under the `XmRowColumn` widget.

Getting and Setting the State in a Toggle-Button Widget

We've been going on a lot about the state of a toggle-button widget, so we'd better show how to set it. The state value of a toggle-button widget is kept in the `set` resource (`XmNset` in C programs), and we're sure you've already guessed how to set the state:

```
    Widget    toggle;

    XtVaSetValues(toggle,
        XmNset, True,
        NULL);
```

Motif also includes two functions for dealing with the set resource in toggle-button widgets (there are corresponding gadget functions, too). XmToggleButtonGetState returns the value of the set resource—the "state" of the toggle button:

```
Boolean XmToggleButtonGetState(Widget widget)
```

XmToggleButtonSetState sets the state of a toggle-button widget:

```
void XmToggleButtonSetState(Widget widget,
        Boolean state,   /* True or False */
        Boolean notify)  /* Generate callback? */
```

Set the *notify* parameter to True if you want to generate a callback—that is, if you want the valueChangedCallback to be called. Set the *notify* parameter to False if you don't want the valueChangedCallback function called. You can guess that a radio box row column uses XmToggleButtonSetState under the hood to force the state of the toggle button.

FRAME WIDGETS

The lowly XmFrame widget summarized in Table 6.6, places a 3D beveled frame around *one* child widget. Usually, this child widget is a container widget and, in turn, holds other widgets. And that's about it. This is very useful for those widgets, such as XmDrawingArea, that don't provide their own 3D highlighting. In addition, you'll often see an XmFrame surrounding an XmRowColumn to make a box of radio buttons. The XmRowColumn manages the XmToggleButton widgets (configured as radio buttons), whereas the XmFrame adds a visual separator to make the radio buttons appear as a group.

Table 6.6   *The XmFrame class.*

Widget class:	XmFrame
Class pointer:	xmFrameWidgetClass
Include file:	<Xm/Frame.h>
Create with:	XmCreateFrame

You can create a frame widget with the XmCreateFrame function:

```
#include <Xm/Frame.h>

Widget XmCreateFrame(Widget parent,
    char* widget_name,
    ArgList args
    Cardinal number_args)
```

Call XtManageChild to manage the frame after creation.

There are a few resources you'll want to set with the frame widget. The shadowThickness resource (XmNshadowThickness in C programs) controls how many pixels wide the 3D shadow is. In the code below, we set the shadowThickness to four (4) pixels wide:

```
#include <Xm/Frame.h>

Widget   frame;

/* Create widget... */

XtVaSetValues(frame,
    XmNshadowThickness, 4,
    NULL);
```

The other resource you may want to set is the shadowType resource (XmNshadowType in C programs). The available types of shadowing include:

- XmSHADOW_IN
- XmSHADOW_OUT
- XmSHADOW_ETCHED_IN
- XmSHADOW_ETCHED_OUT

XmSHADOW_ETCHED_IN is the default, which makes an inward-looking 3D line by drawing a double line with the proper colors to make it look 3D going inward. XmSHADOW_ETCHED_OUT makes a 3D double line that is outward looking. XmSHADOW_IN and XmSHADOW_OUT operate much the same, only these options don't create the 3D double line. The best way to understand these shadow options is to try each setting, as shown in Figure 6.6.

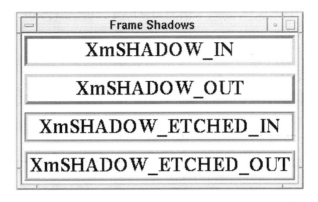

Figure 6.6 *XmFrame shadow types.*

Frame Titles

In Motif 1.0 and 1.1, XmFrame widgets supported only one child widget, the widget that is framed. Many other windowing systems that provide for frames also provide for frame titles, which is a text display that names the group you frame. With Motif 1.2, the XmFrame widget now supports a title—in this case, an XmLabel widget. This title is implemented as a second child widget for the XmFrame.

To create a title for a frame, you need to create an extra XmLabel widget for the frame's title. (You could actually use other widgets as the title, but a label makes the most sense.) On this *child* widget, you need to set the childType resource (XmNchildType in C programs) to XmFRAME_TITLE_CHILD.

Be sure to set this resource on the child (XmLabel) widget and not on the parent XmFrame. (Motif sports a whole number of resources that you place on child widgets to be interpreted by a parent container widget. The childType resource is just one of these. When we get to the XmForm widget, below, you'll see a whole lot more of these constraint widgets.)

The childType resource can have a value of XmFRAME_TITLE_CHILD, meaning this widget should be treated as a title for a frame; XmFRAME_WORKAREA_CHILD, meaning that this is the normal child widget that should go inside the frame; or XmFRAME_GENERIC_CHILD, meaning that the child widget should be ignored when the frame lays out its children. The default value is XmFRAME_WORKAREA_CHILD. Your old code, which doesn't set any of these values, will still work. The widgets you previously placed inside frames will still appear inside frames.

You can also set the position of the frame's title widget. The childHorizontalAlignment resource (XmNchildHorizontalAlignment in C programs) specifies how the title should be justified: to the left, to the right, or centered. You can set the childHorizontalAlignment resource to one of:

- XmALIGNMENT_BEGINNING
- XmALIGNMENT_CENTER
- XmALIGNMENT_END

These positions are all on the top edge of the frame. You can't place the title in the bottom of the frame's 3D box, for example.

You can also adjust where on the frame's top line to place the title widget. You can set the childVerticalAlignment resource (XmNchildVerticalAlignment in C programs) to one of:

- XmALIGNMENT_BASELINE_TOP
- XmALIGNMENT_BASELINE_BOTTOM
- XmALIGNMENT_CENTER
- XmALIGNMENT_WIDGET_BOTTOM
- XmALIGNMENT_WIDGET_TOP

XmALIGNMENT_CENTER is the default. In our trials, the rest of the settings led to relatively minor changes. XmALIGNMENT_WIDGET_BOTTOM, though, seemed to blank out the entire top edge of the frame. Remember that this vertical alignment is working with a very small area—no matter what, your title is going on the top part of the frame.

Finally, you can set the childHorizontalSpacing resource (XmNchildHorizontalSpacing in C programs) to the number of pixels to use for spacing.

Putting this all together, a frame widget with a title looks like Figure 6.7.

Figure 6.7   *An XmFrame with a title widget.*

Without a title, the frame looks more like Figure 6.8.

Figure 6.8   *An XmFrame without a title.*

We used the following program to create the pictures above. This should show you how to create XmFrames with titles, should your version of Motif support them:

```
/* framettl.c */
#include <Xm/Xm.h>
#include <Xm/Frame.h>
#include <Xm/Label.h>
#include <Xm/RowColumn.h>

int main(int argc, char** argv)

{   /* main */
    Widget          parent;
    XtAppContext    app_context;
```

```
Widget          label, title;
Widget          frame;
Arg             args[20];
Cardinal        n;

/* Initialize the X Toolkit. */
n = 0;
XtSetArg(args[n], XmNtitle, "Frame Title"); n++;

parent = XtAppInitialize(&app_context,
        "Ppm",
        (XrmOptionDescList) NULL,
        0,
        (Cardinal*) &argc,
        argv,
        (String*) NULL,
        args, n);

frame = XtVaCreateManagedWidget("frame",
        xmFrameWidgetClass, parent,
        NULL);

    /* Create frame title. */
#if (XmVersion > 1001)

title = XtVaCreateManagedWidget("frame_title",
        xmLabelWidgetClass, frame,
        XmNchildType, XmFRAME_TITLE_CHILD,
        XmNchildHorizontalAlignment,
            XmALIGNMENT_BEGINNING,
        XmNchildVerticalAlignment,
            XmALIGNMENT_BASELINE_BOTTOM,
        NULL);

#endif  /* Motif 1.2 or higher. */

    /* Create child INSIDE frame. */
label = XtVaCreateManagedWidget("label",
        xmLabelWidgetClass, frame,
        NULL);

XtRealizeWidget(parent);
XtAppMainLoop(app_context);

return 0;

}    /* main */

/* end of file framettl.c */
```

Problems with Differing Motif Versions

We have a problem with the **framettl.c** program, above. The `childType`
and other child resources are defined only in Motif 1.2 and will generate
compile errors under Motif 1.1. To get around this, we use the `XmVersion`

macro from <Xm/Xm.h>. The version macros from <Xm/Xm.h> (under
Hewlett-Packard's HP-UX 9.01) follow:

```
#define XmVERSION        1
#define XmREVISION       2
#define XmUPDATE_LEVEL   0
#define XmVersion (XmVERSION * 1000 + XmREVISION)
#define XmVERSION_STRING "@(#)OSF/Motif Version 1.2.0"
```

The XmVERSION_STRING macro is also new in Motif 1.2, but the
XmVersion exists in Motif 1.1. XmVersion will be 1001 for Motif 1.1 and
1002 for Motif 1.2. (There's no reliable way to determine the minor revision
numbers, such as Motif 1.1.4. Ironically, these minor numbers are very
important when dealing with bugs in the Motif toolkit.)

If your version of Motif does not support frame-widget titles, then the
above program should still work fine. Our goal is to create Motif programs
that work on the widest variety of systems.

A PROGRAM TO TEST FRAMES AND RADIO BOXES

The following program shows how to use row-column widgets as radio
boxes, fill in a row column with toggle buttons, and surround the whole
thing with a 3D frame:

```
/* radio.c */
#include <Xm/Xm.h>
#include <Xm/Frame.h>
#include <Xm/Label.h>
#include <Xm/RowColumn.h>
#include <Xm/ToggleB.h>
#include <stdio.h>

    /* Toggle button callback function. */

void toggleCB(Widget widget,
    XtPointer client_data,
    XtPointer call_data)

{   /* toggleCB */
    XmToggleButtonCallbackStruct* ptr;

    ptr = (XmToggleButtonCallbackStruct*) call_data;

    if (ptr != NULL) {

        /*
```

```
                    * We passed a text string
                    * as the client_data.
                    */
                   if (ptr->set == True) {
                      printf("Toggle %s turned ON.\n",
                          (char*) client_data);
                   } else {
                      printf("Toggle %s turned OFF.\n",
                          (char*) client_data);
                   }
                }

}    /* toggleCB */

        /* Creates XmToggleButton as a radio button. */

Widget CreateRadioButton(Widget parent,
        char* name,
        XtCallbackProc callback,
        XtPointer client_data)

{    /* CreateRadioButton */
     Widget  toggle;

     toggle = XtVaCreateManagedWidget(name,
             xmToggleButtonWidgetClass, parent,
             XmNindicatorType, XmONE_OF_MANY,
             NULL);

     XtAddCallback(toggle,
         XmNvalueChangedCallback,
         callback,
         client_data);

     /*
      * Uncomment the following two resources to
      * see a toggle without the indicator.
      */
     /*
     XtVaSetValues(toggle,
         XmNindicatorOn,   False,
         XmNfillOnSelect,  True,
         NULL);
     */

     return toggle;

}    /* CreateRadioButton */

int main(int argc, char** argv)

{    /* main */
     Widget           parent;
     XtAppContext     app_context;
     Widget           row;
     Widget           frame, title;
```

```
Arg             args[20];
Cardinal        n;
char            name[40];

/* Initialize the X Toolkit. */
n = 0;
XtSetArg(args[n], XmNtitle, "Radio Box"); n++;

parent = XtAppInitialize(&app_context,
        "Ppm",
        (XrmOptionDescList) NULL,
        0,
        (Cardinal*) &argc,
        argv,
        (String*) NULL,
        args, n);

frame = XtVaCreateManagedWidget("frame",
        xmFrameWidgetClass, parent,
        NULL);

/* Create frame title. */
#if (XmVersion > 1001)

title = XtVaCreateManagedWidget("frame_title",
        xmLabelWidgetClass, frame,
        XmNchildType, XmFRAME_TITLE_CHILD,
        XmNchildHorizontalAlignment,
            XmALIGNMENT_BEGINNING,
        XmNchildVerticalAlignment,
            XmALIGNMENT_BASELINE_BOTTOM,
        NULL);

#endif  /* Motif 1.2 or higher. */

/* Create child INSIDE frame. */
row = XtVaCreateManagedWidget("row",
        xmRowColumnWidgetClass, frame,
        XmNradioBehavior,  True,
        XmNradioAlwaysOne, True,
        NULL);

/*
 * Create radio buttons.
 * Note: we pass text as client_data.
 */

(void) CreateRadioButton(row, "toggle_0",
    (XtCallbackProc) toggleCB, (XtPointer) "Solaris");

(void) CreateRadioButton(row, "toggle_1",
    (XtCallbackProc) toggleCB, (XtPointer) "HP-UX");

(void) CreateRadioButton(row, "toggle_2",
    (XtCallbackProc) toggleCB, (XtPointer) "IRIX");
```

```
        (void) CreateRadioButton(row, "toggle_3",
            (XtCallbackProc) toggleCB, (XtPointer) "SCO");

        (void) CreateRadioButton(row, "toggle_4",
            (XtCallbackProc) toggleCB, (XtPointer) "AIX");

        XtRealizeWidget(parent);
        XtAppMainLoop(app_context);

        return 0;

}   /* main */

/* end of file radio.c */
```

To test out toggle buttons without indicators, you can uncomment the XtVaSetValues call in the CreateRadioButton function. You can also play with the resource file, below:

```
! Resource file for radio.c
! in Chapter 6 of Power Programming Motif.
!
*fontList:      lucidasans-12
*background:    lightgrey

! radio.c toggle labels.
*toggle_0.labelString:  Solaris 2.3
*toggle_1.labelString:  HP-UX 9.01
*toggle_2.labelString:  SGI IRIX 5.1
*toggle_3.labelString:  SCO OpenDesktop 3.0
*toggle_4.labelString:  IBM AIX 3.02

! Show selected toggles better.
*selectColor:  yellow

*frame_title.labelString: Operating System

! Uncomment the next line to see a large indicator.
!*indicatorSize:  100
! end of resource file
```

Name this file **Ppm** and place it in your home directory. Uncomment the *indicatorSize:100 line to see very large indicators.

THE FORM WIDGET

The form widget, XmForm, is one of the most versatile, but confusing, of Motif's container widgets. You'll find the form useful for aligning data-entry forms or creating toolbars so commonly found beneath menu bars in modern software.

The XmForm widget, as summarized in Table 6.7, is descended from XmManager through XmBulletinBoard.

There's a number of ways you can use a form widget. You can create a form as a dialog with XmCreateFormDialog or just create a form with XmCreateForm or XtCreateWidget, which we'll use in the source-code examples below. (We cover dialogs, including the form dialog, in the next chapter.)

Table 6.7 *The XmForm widget class.*

Widget class:	XmForm
Class pointer:	xmFormWidgetClass
Include file:	<Xm/Form.h>
Create with:	XmCreateForm

Create a form widget with XmCreateForm:

```
#include <Xm/Form.h>

Widget XmCreateForm(Widget parent,
    char* widget_name,
    ArgList args
    Cardinal number_args)
```

Call XtManageChild to manage a form after creation.

Form widgets are very complex, but they allow a host of ways to attach child widgets. For example, you can attach a label widget to the top of a form, to its left or right side, or to the bottom of the form. You could actually attach it to all sides of a form, but that would be boring.

The basic idea is that a form widget holds other widgets as children. You can control the placement of these children and what happens to the size of the children when the parent form changes size. Does every child grow when a form grows larger, or should only some children grow? With the XmForm widget, you can control these answers.

A form widget is useful, though, only when you attach child widgets.

Attaching Child Widgets to Forms

Follow these rules for creating a form and its children and then attaching the children to the form.

1. Create the form widget. This will be the parent widget for the children widgets. Don't manage the form widget just yet.
2. Create the child widget as a child of a form widget.
3. Use `XtSetValues` or `XtVaSetValues` to add the proper form-attachment resources to the child widget, or pass these resources when creating the child widget.
4. Manage the form widget.

The hardest part is getting the child widgets to appear in the form the way you want them to. The basic idea is that you attach edges of the child widgets to something. With the proper set of attachments (no easy feat, unfortunately), the child widgets line up the way you want. To set up the attachments, you set resources on the *child* widgets, not the parent `XmForm`.

Motif allows four basic styles of attaching child widgets to a form:

■ Attaching an edge of the child widget to an edge of the form

■ Attaching an edge of the child widget to a proportional position within the form

■ Attaching an edge of the child widget to itself

■ Attaching an edge of the child widget to the edge of another widget

The Motif resource values for these four types are listed in Table 6.8.

Table 6.8 *Form-attachment styles.*

Resource Value	Attachment Style
`XmATTACH_FORM`	Attach edge of child to edge of form
`XmATTACH_OPPOSITE_FORM`	Attach edge of child to edge of form
	continued

`XmATTACH_POSITION`	Attach edge of child to a proportional position
`XmATTACH_SELF`	Attach edge of child to itself
`XmATTACH_WIDGET`	Attach edge of child to edge of another widget
`XmATTACH_OPPOSITE_WIDGET`	Attach edge of child to edge of another widget

These attachments aren't easy to figure out, so expect to spend some time experimenting with the `XmForm` widget. When in doubt, try out a test program.

You can set an attachment resource for each of the four edges of a child widget: top, bottom, left, and right. Use the resources listed in Table 6.9 to identify which edge you're trying to constrain.

Table 6.9 *Form-edge-attachment resources.*

Resource	In C Programs
`topAttachment`	`XmNtopAttachment`
`bottomAttachment`	`XmNbottomAttachment`
`leftAttachment`	`XmNleftAttachment`
`rightAttachment`	`XmNrightAttachment`

Normally you'll want to do something to control the width and height of each child widget in a form, as the insane form defaults are generally *not* what you want. In most cases, you need to set at least one of the vertical attachments (top or bottom) and one of the horizontal attachments (left or right). In many of these cases, you'll attach all sides of the child widgets. One thing you will find with the form widget is that the attachments are not intuitive. Expect to spend some time experimenting with the form to get things right.

The XmATTACH_FORM Attachment

The `XmATTACH_FORM` attachment allows you to attach an edge of the child widget to a particular side of the parent `XmForm` itself. You can also attach a child to a number of sides of the form. For example, if you attached a child widget to both the right and left sides of a form, as the form grew or shrunk, the child widget would maintain contact with both the left and right sides of the form, meaning the child would grow and shrink horizontally as the form does.

To set up a child to attach to the left and right sides of a parent form, you'll need to code something like this:

```
Widget  child;

XtVaSetValues(child,
    XmNleftAttachment,  XmATTACH_FORM,
    XmNrightAttachment, XmATTACH_FORM,
  NULL);
```

To attach to all the sides of the form (generally not a good idea, since this would obscure other children in the form), you would use:

```
Widget  child;

XtVaSetValues(child,
    XmNtopAttachment,    XmATTACH_FORM,
    XmNbottomAttachment, XmATTACH_FORM,
    XmNleftAttachment,   XmATTACH_FORM,
    XmNrightAttachment,  XmATTACH_FORM,
    NULL);
```

XmATTACH_FORM is the easiest method of attachment.

The XmATTACH_OPPOSITE_FORM Attachment

The XmATTACH_OPPOSITE_FORM attachment is just like XmATTACH_FORM, only XmATTACH_OPPOSITE_FORM attaches to the opposite side. That is, the following code attaches a widget's *top* side to the *bottom* of the form. If this seems odd to you (and it should), you'll want to experiment with the *formtest* program below. Try out different types of attachments and see what they really do. Experimenting will make this text a lot clearer.

```
Widget  child;

XtVaSetValues(child,
    XmNtopAttachment, XmATTACH_OPPOSITE_FORM,
    NULL);
```

We find that XmATTACH_OPPOSITE_FORM is rarely, if ever, used.

The XmATTACH_POSITION Attachment

The XmATTACH_POSITION attachment attaches a side of the child to a relative position in the form. This relative position is contained in the corresponding position resource and based on the fractionBase resource (XmNfractionBase in C programs). The fractionBase is normally 100, which means your positions are percents; that is, a position of 50 means 50 percent into the widget.

The following code maintains a position in the middle of a form, at about one-half the horizontal widget of the form, assuming the fractionBase is 100:

```
Widget  child;

XtVaSetValues(child,
    XmNleftAttachment,  XmATTACH_POSITION,
    XmNleftPosition,    25,
    XmNrightAttachment, XmATTACH_POSITION,
    XmNrightPosition,   75,
    NULL);
```

We lock the left edge of the widget at 25 percent of the form (horizontally) and the right edge at 75 percent.

XmATTACH_POSITION is one of the most useful attachments. You can set up a form to have two or more columns of data-entry widgets, using a position of 50, for example. You can use XmATTACH_POSITION to set up widgets that all maintain their sizes relative to one another (such as four child widgets, each one-quarter the width of the parent form).

Each time you use XmATTACH_POSITION, you must specify a position for the side, using one of the form position resources listed in Table 6.10.

Table 6.10   *XmForm position resources.*

Resource	In C Programs
topPosition	XmNtopPosition
bottomPosition	XmNbottomPosition
leftPosition	XmNleftPosition
rightPosition	XmNrightPosition

You'll use a two-part resource command. The first command tells that you're using a positioned attachment. The second specifies what the desired position is.

The XmATTACH_SELF Attachment

The XmATTACH_SELF attachment makes the given side attach to its initial position and stay there. That is, after the initial placement is made, the side (or sides) with XmATTACH_SELF will remain where they are.

This code would make the bottom side of the child stay put:

```
Widget  child;

XtVaSetValues(child,
     XmNbottomAttachment, XmATTACH_SELF,
     NULL);
```

The XmATTACH_WIDGET Attachment

In most forms, you'll only use three types of attachment: XmATTACH_FORM, XmATTACH_WIDGET, and XmATTACH_OPPOSITE_WIDGET. XmATTACH_WIDGET is used to make one edge of a child widget attach to an edge of another widget. You may want the first widget to attach to the top of the form, the next child widget in line to attach right below the first child, and so on. When you use XmATTACH_WIDGET, you must specify which widget to attach to, using one of the widget-attachment resources listed in Table 6.11.

Table 6.11 *XmForm widget-attachment resources.*

Resource	In C Programs
topWidget	XmNtopWidget
bottomWidget	XmNbottomWidget
leftWidget	XmNleftWidget
rightWidget	XmNrightWidget

We use these resources in the following code:

```
Widget   first_child;
Widget   second_child;

XtVaSetValues(second_child,
```

```
    XmNtopAttachment, XmATTACH_WIDGET,
    XmNtopWidget,     first_child,
    NULL);
```

The code above specified that the *second_child*'s top side should attach to the bottom side of the *first_child*.

The code below will attach the *first_child* widget to the top of the form, and to the right and left sides. The *second_child* widget will attach to the bottom of the *first_child*, and also to the left and right sides of the form:

```
Widget  first_child;
Widget  second_child;

/*
 * Attach first child to the top,
 * left and right of the form.
 */
XtVaSetValues(first_child,
    XmNtopAttachment,   XmATTACH_FORM,
    XmNleftAttachment,  XmATTACH_FORM,
    XmNrightAttachment, XmATTACH_FORM,
    NULL);

/*
 * Attach the top of the second_child
 * to the bottom of the first_child.
 */
XtVaSetValues(second_child,
    XmNtopAttachment,   XmATTACH_WIDGET,
    XmNtopWidget,       first_child,
    XmNleftAttachment,  XmATTACH_FORM,
    XmNrightAttachment, XmATTACH_FORM
    NULL);
```

The XmATTACH_OPPOSITE_WIDGET Attachment

XmATTACH_OPPOSITE_WIDGET attaches a side of a child widget to the same side of another child widget:

```
Widget  first_child;
Widget  second_child;

XtVaSetValues(second_child,
    XmNtopAttachment, XmATTACH_OPPOSITE_WIDGET,
    XmNtopWidget,     first_child,
    NULL);
```

The code above attaches the top side of the *second_child* widget to the top side of the *first_child* widget. In this case, we assume both widgets, *first_child* and *second_child*, are on the same row in the form.

We want both widgets to share the same top position. In this case, we choose the *first_child* widget as the leader: The *second_child* widget's dimensioning will be controlled by *first_child*, the driving widget.

This may seem to make even less sense than the XmATTACH_OPPO-SITE_FORM, but try it out and it will make more sense. In real life, XmATTACH_OPPOSITE_FORM is *very* useful, if confusing, when aligning data-entry forms.

The XmATTACH_NONE Attachment

This unattachment is the default for all sides not attached any other way. Generally, it's a good idea to specify all the proper attachments you want in a form and not use XmATTACH_NONE.

N O T E Don't use `XtCreateManagedWidget` or `XtVaCreateManagedWidget` (or other functions that create and manage a widget in one call) to create XmForm widgets. Why? Because you want to delay managing the XmForm until all you create of its child widgets and then set the proper attachment resources on the children. This will make your layouts work better. `XtVaCreateWidget` is fine, though, because it does not manage the widget.

In addition to the attachments, the XmForm widget provides for offsets.

Form Offsets

The form widget provides four offset resources (listed in Table 6.12), which you can use to add additional space between the widgets.

Table 6.12 *Form-offset resources.*

Resource	Type	Default Value
bottomOffset	int	0
leftOffset	int	0
rightOffset	int	0
topOffset	int	0

The default value for all these offsets is 0 pixels. You can increase this if you desire.

ALIGNING DATA-ENTRY FORMS

Data-entry forms are used in just about every application. Just about every Motif program presents a set of widgets that you'd like to line up. To help show how the XmForm widget works, we'll provide an example of a simple data-entry form. This requires more sophisticated uses of the above attachment styles.

Before we get into the gory details of our example, here's some tips when aligning data-entry forms:

1. Always draw out the layout by hand first, then determine the best way to set up the resources. This will save you a lot of trouble with the form.

2. Different widget types make layouts tougher because they often have different default heights. For example, a common need is to pair an XmLabel with a single-line XmText, yet both have different default heights, even when using the same font.

3. Always constrain at least one horizontal and one vertical attachment. Generally, you'll want to constrain all four edges of every widget.

4. When choosing widget leaders for attachments, choose the widest or the tallest widget, depending on the dimension you're trying to control.

5. Avoid circular dependencies with the form-attachment resources. You generally won't like the result.

N O T E

If you make a mistake with the form layout, you may get an error like the following:

```
Warning:
    Name: form
    Class: XmForm
    Bailed out of edge synchronization after 10,000 itera-
    tions.
    Check for contradictory constraints on the children of
    this form.
```

```
X Error of failed request:  BadAlloc (insufficient
resources for operation)
   Major opcode of failed request:  1 (X_CreateWindow)
   Serial number of failed request:  398
```

This is generated if you have a grossly incorrect layout or circular references in the attachments.

In the program below, we choose our first label widget, *label1*, to be the leader. We constrain its top edge by the top of the form and the widget's bottom edge to 25 percent of the form's height. We have four rows, so we chose 25 percent for each.

Next, we need to constrain this widget's width. We attach the left edge to the edge of the form. The right edge gets locked to a position 50 percent across the form.

We have two columns, which is why we chose 50 percent.

The code to constrain the *label1* widget follows:

```
Widget  label1, form;

label1 = XtVaCreateManagedWidget("label1",
        xmLabelWidgetClass, form,
        XmNtopAttachment,     XmATTACH_FORM,
        XmNbottomAttachment,  XmATTACH_POSITION,
        XmNbottomPosition,    25,
        XmNleftAttachment,    XmATTACH_FORM,
        XmNrightAttachment,   XmATTACH_POSITION,
        XmNrightPosition,     50,
        NULL);
```

Horizontally across from the *label1* widget lies an XmText widget. The label is the prompt, and the text widget accepts the user's input. This widget attaches to the top and right edges of the form. The code for this follows:

```
Widget  text1, form;

text1 = XtVaCreateManagedWidget("text1",
        xmTextWidgetClass, form,
        XmNeditMode, XmSINGLE_LINE_EDIT,
        XmNtopAttachment,     XmATTACH_FORM,
        XmNbottomAttachment,  XmATTACH_POSITION,
        XmNbottomPosition,    25,
        XmNleftAttachment,    XmATTACH_POSITION,
        XmNleftPosition,      50,
        XmNrightAttachment,   XmATTACH_FORM,
        NULL);
```

This isn't very interesting, except that we use the text widget's taller height as the leader for attaching the next row of widgets. Normally, text widgets will be taller than label widgets. Here's how we attach the first widget in the second row:

```
Widget  toggle, form;

/* Second row. */
toggle1 = XtVaCreateManagedWidget("toggle1",
        xmToggleButtonWidgetClass, form,
        XmNindicatorType,     XmN_OF_MANY,
        XmNtopAttachment,     XmATTACH_WIDGET,
        XmNtopWidget          text1,
        XmNbottomAttachment,  XmATTACH_POSITION,
        XmNbottomPosition     50,
        XmNleftAttachment,    XmATTACH_FORM,
        XmNrightAttachment,   XmATTACH_OPPOSITE_WIDGET,
        XmNrightWidget,       label1,
        NULL);
```

Note that we attach the top edge to the *text1* widget, even though this widget is not adjacent to the *toggle1* widget! The *toggle1* widget sits on the left side of the form, whereas *text1* sits on the right side. We also use the `XmATTACH_OPPOSITE_WIDGET` attachment to line up the right edge of this widget with the *label1* widget's right edge. The *label1* widget then becomes the leader for horizontal positioning.

The end result is shown in Figure 6.9.

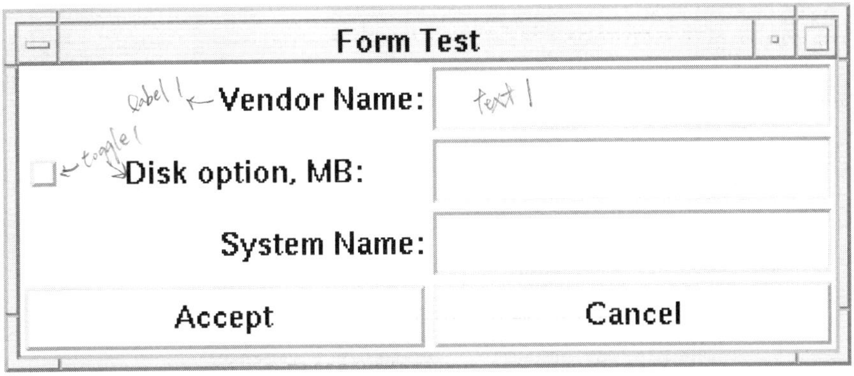

Figure 6.9   *Our desired layout implemented.*

The **formtest.c** code to implement this follows:

```c
/* formtest.c */
#include <Xm/Xm.h>
#include <Xm/Form.h>
#include <Xm/Label.h>
#include <Xm/PushB.h>
#include <Xm/Text.h>
#include <Xm/ToggleB.h>
#include <stdio.h>

int main(int argc, char** argv)

{   /* main */
    Widget              parent;
    XtAppContext        app_context;
    Widget              form;
    Arg                 args[20];
    Cardinal            n;
    Widget              label1, label2;
    Widget              text1, text2, text3;
    Widget              push1, push2;
    Widget              toggle1;

    /* Initialize the X Toolkit. */
    n = 0;
    parent = XtAppInitialize(&app_context,
            "Ppm",
            (XrmOptionDescList) NULL,
            0,
            (Cardinal*) &argc,
            argv,
            (String*) NULL,
            args, n);

    /* Note: not managed! */
    form = XtVaCreateWidget("form",
        xmFormWidgetClass, parent,
        NULL);

    /* Create data-entry area to left side. */


    /* Top row. */
    /*
     * We set up a lot of options on
     * this first widget because it's a leader.
     */
    label1 = XtVaCreateManagedWidget("label1",
            xmLabelWidgetClass, form,
            XmNtopAttachment,    XmATTACH_FORM,
            XmNbottomAttachment, XmATTACH_POSITION,
            XmNbottomPosition,   25,
            XmNleftAttachment,   XmATTACH_FORM,
            XmNrightAttachment,  XmATTACH_POSITION,
```

```
                    XmNrightPosition,     50,
                    NULL);

       text1 = XtVaCreateManagedWidget("text1",
                    xmTextWidgetClass, form,
                    XmNeditMode, XmSINGLE_LINE_EDIT,
                    XmNtopAttachment,      XmATTACH_FORM,
                    XmNbottomAttachment,  XmATTACH_POSITION,
                    XmNbottomPosition,     25,
                    XmNleftAttachment,     XmATTACH_POSITION,
                    XmNleftPosition,       50,
                    XmNrightAttachment,    XmATTACH_FORM,
                    NULL);

       /* Second row. */
       toggle1 = XtVaCreateManagedWidget("toggle1",
                    xmToggleButtonWidgetClass, form,
                    XmNindicatorType,      XmN_OF_MANY,
                    XmNtopAttachment,      XmATTACH_WIDGET,
                    XmNtopWidget,          text1,
                    XmNbottomAttachment,  XmATTACH_POSITION,
                    XmNbottomPosition,     50,
                    XmNleftAttachment,     XmATTACH_FORM,
                    XmNrightAttachment,    XmATTACH_OPPOSITE_WIDGET,
                    XmNrightWidget,        label1,
                    NULL);

       text2 = XtVaCreateManagedWidget("text2",
                    xmTextWidgetClass, form,
                    XmNeditMode, XmSINGLE_LINE_EDIT,
                    XmNtopAttachment,      XmATTACH_WIDGET,
                    XmNtopWidget,          text1,
                    XmNbottomAttachment,  XmATTACH_POSITION,
                    XmNbottomPosition,     50,
                    XmNleftAttachment,     XmATTACH_WIDGET,
                    XmNleftWidget,         label1,
                    XmNrightAttachment,    XmATTACH_FORM,
                    NULL);

       /* Third row */
       label2 = XtVaCreateManagedWidget("label2",
                    xmLabelWidgetClass, form,
                    XmNtopAttachment,      XmATTACH_WIDGET,
                    XmNtopWidget,          text2,
                    XmNbottomAttachment,  XmATTACH_POSITION,
                    XmNbottomPosition,     75,
                    XmNleftAttachment,     XmATTACH_FORM,
                    XmNrightAttachment,    XmATTACH_OPPOSITE_WIDGET,
                    XmNrightWidget,        label1,
                    NULL);
       text3 = XtVaCreateManagedWidget("text3",
                    xmTextWidgetClass, form,
                    XmNeditMode, XmSINGLE_LINE_EDIT,
                    XmNtopAttachment,      XmATTACH_WIDGET,
                    XmNtopWidget,          text2,
```

```
                    XmNbottomAttachment, XmATTACH_POSITION,
                    XmNbottomPosition,   75,
                    XmNleftAttachment,   XmATTACH_WIDGET,
                    XmNleftWidget,       label1,
                    XmNrightAttachment,  XmATTACH_FORM,
                    NULL);

        /* Bottom row */
        push1 = XtVaCreateManagedWidget("push1",
                xmPushButtonWidgetClass, form,
                XmNtopAttachment,    XmATTACH_WIDGET,
                XmNtopWidget,        text3,
                XmNbottomAttachment, XmATTACH_FORM,
                XmNleftAttachment,   XmATTACH_FORM,
                XmNrightAttachment,  XmATTACH_OPPOSITE_WIDGET,
                XmNrightWidget,      label1,
                NULL);

        push2 = XtVaCreateManagedWidget("push2",
                xmPushButtonWidgetClass, form,
                XmNtopAttachment,    XmATTACH_WIDGET,
                XmNtopWidget,        text3,
                XmNbottomAttachment, XmATTACH_FORM,
                XmNleftAttachment,   XmATTACH_WIDGET,
                XmNleftWidget,       label1,
                XmNrightAttachment,  XmATTACH_FORM,
                NULL);

        /* Manage manager widget. */
        XtManageChild(form);

        XtRealizeWidget(parent);
        XtAppMainLoop(app_context);
        return 0;

    }   /* main */


    /* end of file formtest.c */
```

You'll also need a resource file for this program:

```
! Resource file for formtest.c in
! Chapter 6 of Power Programming Motif.
!
*fontList:      lucidasans-12
*background:    lightgrey
*title: Form Test
*selectColor: yellow
*label1.labelString:  Vendor Name:
*toggle1.labelString: Disk option, MB:
*label2.labelString:  System Name:
*push1.labelString:   Accept
*push2.labelString:   Cancel
! Note how we set alignments.
```

```
*XmLabel.alignment:    alignment_end
! end of resource file
```

Name this file **Ppm** and place it in your home directory.

If all else fails when attempting to line up your data-entry forms, you may want to create some separator widgets and force the other child widgets to line up with these.

N O T E

Building a Toolbar with an XmForm Widget

A form widget is also very useful for building a toolbar, a horizontal row of bitmap pushbuttons that stretches across your main window just underneath the menu bar, as shown in Figure 6.10.

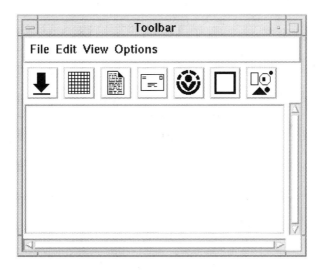

Figure 6.10 *A toolbar.*

Treat a toolbar as a data-entry form with just one row. Depending on how you want the toolbar to resize, you may just want to attach the widgets to the previous widget in the toolbar.

MORE ON THE PANED-WINDOW WIDGET

We first introduced the paned-window widget in Chapter 2. In this section, we'll go into some paned-window resources that we only briefly touched upon in Chapter 2.

The paned-window widget, as summarized in Table 6.13, places its child widgets from top to bottom in vertical panes—hence the name XmPanedWindow. Normally, each child widget is placed in order (but see the positionIndex resource, below).

Between each child, there is an optional sash—a line with a control box. The user can use the mouse pointer to move the sash up and down, controlling the size of each individual pane. You can also specify minimum and maximum sizes for panes, which the paned window widget will enforce.

Table 6.13 *The XmPanedWindow widget class.*

Widget class:	XmPanedWindow
Class pointer:	xmPanedWindowWidgetClass
Include file:	<Xm/PanedW.h>
Create with:	XmCreatePanedWindow

Create a paned window with XmCreatePanedWindow:

```
#include <Xm/PanedW.h>

Widget XmCreatePanedWindow(Widget parent,
    char* widget_name,
    ArgList args
    Cardinal number_args)
```

Call XtManageChild to manage a paned window after creation.

The paned-window widget will size itself horizontally to the width of its widest child.

Pane Resources

A number of resources that apply to the paned-window widget are listed in Table 6.14.

Table 6.14 *XmPanedWindow resources.*

Resource	Type	Default Value
marginHeight	Dimension	3
marginWidth	Dimension	3
sashHeight	Dimension	10
sashIndent	Dimension	-10
sashWidth	Dimension	10
separatorOn	Boolean	True
spacing	Dimension	8

Using the Paned-Window Sash to Resize a Pane

Users can adjust the sizes of the panes in a paned-window widget by adjusting the control sash that separates the panes. This control sash is optional. To use it, you'll need to set the separatorOn resource for the paned-window widget:

```
Widget pane;

XtVaSetValues(pane,
    XmNseparatorOn, True,
    NULL);
```

The separatorOn resource (XmNseparatorOn in C programs) turns on the separating line between panes. The default is True.

Controlling the Sash

The default sash provided between panes in the paned window isn't an optimal design. You can use the sash-related resources to configure better-looking panes, though.

The sashHeight determines the height of the sash. It defaults to 10 pixels, but 6 looks better. The sashWidth resource determines the width of the sash. Try 12 pixels instead of the default of 10.

The sashIndent resource, if set to a positive value, places the sash a number of pixels from the left side of the paned window. If the value is negative, such as the –10 pixel default, the sash is placed from the right of the paned window, in this case 10 pixels from the right edge. Try a value of –4 (–6 if you have a scrollbar) instead. Put together, we find a better-looking sash shown in Figure 6.11.

Figure 6.11   *A better-looking sash.*

The above size recommendations are found in an excellent book on designing user interfaces with Motif, *Visual Design With OSF/Motif* (Shiz Kobara, 1991, Addison-Wesley).

Paned-Constraint Resources

Like the form widget, the paned-window widget supports a number of constraint resources you can place on child widgets. Paned-constraint resources are listed in Table 6.15.

The `allowResize` resource (`XmNallowResize` in C programs) allows the individual pane to be resized. The `paneMinimum` and `paneMaximum` (`XmNpaneMinimum` and `XmNpaneMaximum` in C programs) control the minimum and maximum sizes for a particular pane.

Table 6.15 *XmPanedWindow constraint resources to place on child widgets.*

Resource	Type	Default Value
allowResize	Boolean	True
paneMaximum	Dimension	1000
paneMinimum	Dimension	1
positionIndex	short	XmLAST_POSITION
skipAdjust	Boolean	True

If you set the skipAdjust resource (XmNskipAdjust in C programs) to True, then the paned window won't automatically resize the pane.

The positionIndex resource (XmNpositionIndex in C programs), new in Motif 1.2, is tricky. You can place a widget within a paned window at a given position (start counting with 0). The default value of XmLAST_POSITION means that new widgets will be placed in the bottom pane (at the end of the list). There's some odd quirks with the positionIndex resource, so it's best to try it out, as we do in the following program:

```
/* panetest.c */
#include <Xm/Xm.h>
#include <Xm/Label.h>
#include <Xm/PanedW.h>
#include <Xm/PushB.h>

    /* Callback, adds a new child to the pane. */
void addCB(Widget widget,
    XtPointer client_data,
    XtPointer call_data)
{   /* addCB */
    Widget*   pane;

    /* Pass parent widget as client_data. */
    pane = (Widget*) client_data;

    (void) XtVaCreateManagedWidget("middle",
        xmPushButtonWidgetClass, *pane,
        XmNallowResize, True,
#ifdef XmNpositionIndex
        XmNpositionIndex, 1,
#endif /* XmNpositionIndex */
        NULL);
```

```
}   /* addCB */

int main(int argc, char** argv)

{   /* main */
    Widget          parent;
    XtAppContext    app_context;
    Widget          pane;
    Arg             args[20];
    Cardinal        n;
    Widget          add, top, bottom;
    /* Initialize the X Toolkit. */
    n = 0;
    XtSetArg(args[n], XmNtitle, "Pane Test"); n++;

    parent = XtAppInitialize(&app_context,
            "Ppm",
            (XrmOptionDescList) NULL,
            0,
            (Cardinal*) &argc,
            argv,
            (String*) NULL,
            args, n);

    pane = XtVaCreateManagedWidget("pane",
            xmPanedWindowWidgetClass, parent,
            NULL);

    /*
     * Create three child widgets normally.
     * These widgets should appear in order.
     */
    top = XtVaCreateManagedWidget("top",
            xmLabelWidgetClass, pane,
            XmNallowResize, True,
            NULL);

    add = XtVaCreateManagedWidget("add",
            xmPushButtonWidgetClass, pane,
            XmNallowResize, True,
            NULL);

    /*
     * Set up callback to add widget.
     * Paned widget is client data.
     */
    XtAddCallback(add, XmNactivateCallback,
        (XtCallbackProc) addCB,
        (XtPointer) &pane);

    bottom = XtVaCreateManagedWidget("bottom",
            xmLabelWidgetClass, pane,
            XmNallowResize, True,
            NULL);
```

```
    XtRealizeWidget(parent);
    XtAppMainLoop(app_context);

    return 0;

}    /* main */

/* end of file panetest.c */
```

Press the *Add* button and see where the new widget goes. If you don't have Motif 1.2, the new widget will appear at the end of the paned window (in the last pane).

THE BULLETIN-BOARD CONTAINER WIDGET

The bulletin-board widget, as summarized in Table 16.6, is one of the most primitive Motif container widgets. Basically, the XmBulletinBoard imposes no control over the layout of its child widgets. As such, an XmBulletinBoard widget is often used to build up dialogs—which just happens to be the topic of the next chapter.

Table 6.16   *The XmBulletinBoard widget class.*

Widget class:	XmBulletinBoard
Class pointer:	xmBulletinBoardWidgetClass
Include file:	<Xm/BulletinB.h>
Create with:	XmCreateBulletinBoard

Create an XmBulletinBoard with XmCreateBulletinBoard:

```
#include <Xm/BulletinB.h>

Widget XmCreateBulletinBoard(Widget parent,
    char* widget_name,
    ArgList args
    Cardinal number_args)
```

Call XtManageChild to manage a bulletin board after creation.

About the only thing you can control with the XmBulletinBoard is to disallow any resize requests from child widgets that would allow the widgets to overlap. Do this by setting the `allowOverlap` resource (`XmNallowOverlap` in C programs) to `False`. (It defaults to `True`.)

Other than that, you'll need to set the `x` and `y` resources (`XmNx` and `XmNy` in C programs) for child widgets of a bulletin board.

You generally won't use the bulletin-board widget on its own, unless you need to build a custom dialog and this widget fits. In most cases, you'll use bulletin-board widgets without even knowing it, as they are commonly used under the hood for Motif's standard dialogs.

GENERAL TECHNIQUES WITH CONTAINER WIDGETS

Before we finish our discussion of Motif's container widgets, we thought we'd cover two useful techniques that apply to all containers: We'll show how to get at the children of a container and then mention a word of warning when it comes to using scrolled widgets with containers.

Getting at the Children

All container widgets that are derived from the `Composite` widget class support two read-only resources, as listed in Table 6.17.

Table 6.17 *Composite constraint resources.*

Resource	Type	Default Value
children	WidgetList	NULL
numChildren	Cardinal	0

You can query these resources to get a list of the widgets that are children of a given container widget. With this information, you can list out these widgets or do whatever you need (we've found this information handy at various times). Note that some child widgets may bypass these resources.

The following program creates a paned-window widget and three child label widgets. After they are created, the widget names are printed:

```
/* children.c */
```

```
#include <Xm/Xm.h>
#include <Xm/Label.h>
#include <Xm/PanedW.h>
#include <stdio.h>

void PrintChildren(Widget widget)

{   /* PrintChildren */
    Cardinal    number_children;
    Widget*     ptr;
    char*       name;
    int         i;

    printf("Children of %s:\n", XtName(widget) );

    XtVaGetValues(widget,
        XmNnumChildren, &number_children,
        XmNchildren,    &ptr,
        NULL);

    for (i = 0; i < number_children; i++) {

        name = XtName( ptr[i] );

        printf("Child %d [%s]\n", i, name);
    }

}   /* PrintChildren */

int main(int argc, char** argv)

{   /* main */
    Widget          parent;
    XtAppContext    app_context;
    Widget          pane;
    Arg             args[20];
    Cardinal        n;
    Widget          top, middle, bottom;

    /* Initialize the X Toolkit. */
    n = 0;
    XtSetArg(args[n], XmNtitle, "Child Test"); n++;

    parent = XtAppInitialize(&app_context,
            "Ppm",
            (XrmOptionDescList) NULL,
            0,
            (Cardinal*) &argc,
            argv,
            (String*) NULL,
            args, n);

    pane = XtVaCreateManagedWidget("pane",
            xmPanedWindowWidgetClass, parent,
            NULL);
```

```
    top = XtVaCreateManagedWidget("top",
            xmLabelWidgetClass, pane,
            NULL);

    middle = XtVaCreateManagedWidget("middle",
            xmLabelWidgetClass, pane,
            NULL);

    bottom = XtVaCreateManagedWidget("bottom",
            xmLabelWidgetClass, pane,
            NULL);

    XtRealizeWidget(parent);

    /* Now get widget children. */
    PrintChildren(pane);

    XtAppMainLoop(app_context);

    return 0;

}   /* main */

/* end of file children.c */
```

Running the *children* program yields what is shown in Figure 6.12.

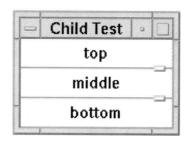

Figure 6.12   *The children program.*

We also see the following output:

```
Children of pane:
Child 0 [top]
Child 1 [middle]
Child 2 [bottom]
Child 3 [sash]
Child 4 [separator]
Child 5 [sash]
Child 6 [separator]
```

```
Child 7 [sash]
Child 8 [separator]
```

Note that we only created the first three widgets explicitly. The paned window created the rest.

To print out meaningful information about the widgets, we need to get the widget names from the widget data. To do so, we call `XtName`:

```
String XtName(Widget widget)
```

`XtName` returns a widget's name.

Do *not* free the returned string when done. The memory is owned by the X Toolkit.

N O T E

Parenting Scrolled Text and List Widgets

If you create a scrolled `XmText` widget with `XmCreateScrolledText`, Motif really creates a scrolled-window widget as a parent and then a text widget as a child of the scrolled window. The widget returned by `XmCreateScrolledText`, though, is the text widget. Because of this, if you place a scrolled-text widget inside a form, you'll need to really place the parent widget, the scrolled window. Any form-constraint resources, such as `topAttachment`, need to be placed on the *parent* of the `XmText` widget, and *not* on the `XmText` widget itself. Use `XtParent` to get the parent of a widget:

```
Widget XtParent(Widget widget)
```

Then set the resources onto this widget:

```
Widget    scrolled_text;
Widget    parent;

parent = XtParent(scrolled_text);

XtVaSetValues(parent,
    XmNtopAttachment, XmATTACH_FORM,
    NULL);
```

SUMMARY

Motif offers many means to control the layout of your applications. A business data-entry form application, for example, needs all its widgets to line up like they appear in the real paper form that the computer application emulates. To get widgets to line up in this way requires that you use Motif's container widgets.

The row-column widget provides a handy way to simply lay out rows or columns of child widgets. To provide this simplicity, though, the row column skimps on flexibility. It seems that the row-column widget was really designed as a means for laying out menu choices in a menu and evolved from there.

When you look up XmRowColumn in the *OSF/Motif Programmer's Reference*, prepare to be confused. Since the row-column widget is used for so many things (menu bars, pop-up menus, pull-down menus, holding radio buttons), there are a host of confusing resources. Most of them won't apply at any one time, unless you are using the XmRowColumn widget for a special purpose, like a menu.

There are times when you must provide the user a single choice from a set of choices. These choices are called radio buttons. The name radio buttons comes from older car radios that sport a set of buttons of which only one can be pushed in at a time. Radio buttons appear in a radio box, which is really a specially configured XmRowColumn widget.

A toggle button is a Boolean selector: It can either be in or out (on or off, True or False). When the user clicks the mouse Button 1 in a toggle, the toggle changes state, from True to False, or False to True. A radio button is a special toggle button that appears in a mutually exclusive group. Only one radio button in the group can be on (with a state of True) at a time, whereas any number of toggle buttons can be on at any time. Usually radio buttons appear inside a row-column widget, described above, inside a 3D frame.

Many users complain that the indicator on the toggle button is confusing, as it's hard to discern whether the indicator is on or off. Since this is the key function of the toggle button, we need some way to make the state of the toggle clearer to the user. One way to do this is to make the indicator bigger. Another method—and the one preferred by the authors—is to change the colors of the indicator when selected.

The toggle widget allows you to set up a function to be called back whenever the toggle's value changes (from `True` to `False` or `False` to `True`). This callback is the `valueChangedCallback` (`XmNvalueChangedCallback` in C programs). `ValueChangedCallback` sets up your callback function to receive a pointer to an `XmToggleButtonCallbackStruct` structure as the call data.

We also introduced the Motif 3D frame widget, a widget that does nothing but enhance the look of your user interface. `XmCreateFrame` creates a frame widget. The lowly `XmFrame` widget places a 3D beveled frame around *one* child widget. Usually, this child widget is a container widget and, in turn, holds other widgets. And that's about it. This is very useful for those widgets, such as `XmDrawingArea`, that don't provide their own 3D highlighting. In addition, you'll often see an `XmFrame` surrounding an `XmRowColumn` to make a box of radio buttons. The `XmRowColumn` manages the `XmToggleButton` widgets (configured as radio buttons), where the `XmFrame` adds a visual separator to make the radio buttons appear as a group.

The bulletin-board widget is one of the most primitive Motif container widgets. Basically, the `XmBulletinBoard` imposes no control over the layout of its child widgets. As such, an `XmBulletinBoard` widget is often used to build up dialogs—which just happens to be the topic of the next chapter.

If you create a scrolled `XmText` widget with `XmCreateScrolledText`, Motif really creates a scrolled-window widget as a parent and then a text widget as a child of the scrolled window. The widget returned by `XmCreateScrolledText`, though, is the text widget. Because of this, if you place a scrolled-text widget inside a form, you'll need to really place the parent widget, the scrolled window. Any form-constraint resources, such as `topAttachment`, need to be placed on the *parent* of the `XmText` widget, and *not* on the `XmText` widget itself.

In the next chapter, we'll introduce Motif dialogs and build a custom dialog using the `XmForm` widget.

MOTIF FUNCTIONS AND MACROS INTRODUCED IN THIS CHAPTER

```
XmCreateBulletinBoard
XmCreateForm
```

```
XmCreateFrame
XmCreatePanedWindow
XmCreateRowColumn
XmCreateToggleButton
XmToggleButtonGetState
XmToggleButtonSetState
```

X Toolkit Intrinsics Functions and Macros Introduced in This Chapter

```
XtName
```

CHAPTER 7

Designing Dialogs

This chapter introduces Motif's dialogs and covers:

- Motif's built-in convenience dialogs
- Dialog resources
- Dialog callbacks
- Getting input from dialogs
- Extending the convenience dialogs
- Creating custom dialogs
- Bulletin-board and form dialogs
- Dialog shell widgets
- The *OSF/Motif Style Guide* and dialogs
- Managing and unmanaging dialogs
- Modal dialogs

247

Motif Dialogs

Motif—and by default, the underlying X Window System—follows the model of *event-driven programming*. Instead of working on tasks in a sequential order (much like the old batch processing associated with the early days of computing), Motif waits for events to come in and then acts upon them.

Central to event-driven programming is the notion that the user controls the action. Tools like menu bars, pull-down menus, and the like allow the user to exert this power. Similarly, dialogs are used in Motif to have the user reply to a question or to a situation. If the user asks for help, for example, you may present a help message in a dialog, such as an information dialog. You'll want the help message to remain on the screen until the user is done with the message. This may be a long time and the question arises: How do you know when the user is done with the help message?

In Motif, most dialogs remain on the screen until the user clicks a mouse button in a pushbutton widget or presses the **Return** key.

There are many instances where you'll want to prompt the user for input. For instance, you may want the user to respond to a warning posted before the point of no return, such as warning the user that deleting a file will permanently remove the file. These dialog widgets ask the user whether to go ahead with a task that cannot be undone, such as the dialog used in Figure 7.1 that asks the user, Are you sure?.

Figure 7.1 *An Are you sure? dialog.*

Motif provides a number of standard dialogs, including the simple-question dialog. These standard Motif dialogs range in complexity from simple dialogs to the most complex, the file-selection dialog, which is shown in Figure 7.2.

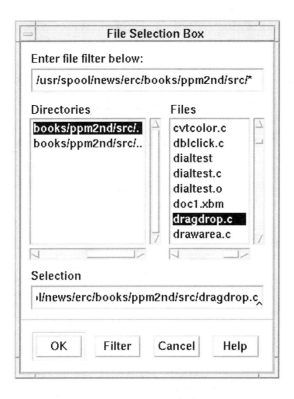

Figure 7.2   *The file-selection dialog.*

This dialog allows the user to choose a file from a list of file names that match some pattern. This is a complex dialog in practice, but an easy one to create. Since selecting files is a common occurrence, it's nice to have this widget built into the toolkit. For the user, it's nice to have this common task standardized.

SHORTCUT

Motif Convenience Dialogs

Motif has a number of raw dialog widgets, but you normally won't use the basic dialog widgets. Instead, you'll most often use a compound dialog built up from the base classes above, wrapped together with a convenience function to create the whole conglomeration. These dialogs are listed in Table 7.1.

Table 7.1 *Motif convenience dialogs.*

Dialog	Create With
Bulletin board	`XmCreateBulletinBoardDialog`
Error	`XmCreateErrorDialog`
Field selection	`XmCreateFileSelectionDialog`
Form	`XmCreateFormDialog`
Information	`XmCreateInformationDialog`
Prompt	`XmCreatePromptDialog`
Question	`XmCreateQuestionDialog`
Selection	`XmCreateSelectionDialog`
Warning	`XmCreateWarningDialog`
Working	`XmCreateWorkingDialog`

These dialogs have all necessary features built in, and the convenience functions that create these dialogs take care of all the messy work.

Most of these dialogs have **OK**, **Cancel**, and **Help** pushbuttons that allow the user to confirm the choice (**OK**), cancel the operation, or get help on the dialog. You'll usually need to set up an `okCallback` and a `cancelCallback` for each of the dialogs you create.

To make a dialog appear or pop up, manage the dialog widget with `XtManageChild`. To make a dialog disappear or pop down, unmanage it with `XtUnmanageChild`.

How Dialogs Work

A Motif dialog is usually contained within a separate top-level window, at the same level as the top-level application shell widget. A dialog, therefore, often has a window-manager title bar (placed by the Motif window manager, *mwm*), and you can move it about the screen. These windows are called *transient windows* in X Window terminology.

Dialogs are widgets—usually a shell widget with a container child. Most dialogs contain some text and at least three configurable pushbutton child widgets, normally labeled **OK**, **Cancel**, and **Help**. Widgets associated with a dialog are created together when you call one of the dialog convenience functions listed above.

When the user selects something in the dialog or clicks on a pushbutton, you may have a function called back if you previously set up a callback. This is how your programs know what the user choose in the dialog. Usually these callback functions are simply `XmText` or `XmPushButton` callbacks, although the Motif dialog convenience routines often obscure this fact.

There are seven basic steps for using dialogs:

1. Include the proper include files for the dialog.

2. Convert your dialog message to an `XmString` or place it in a resource file.

3. Create the dialog using the dialog convenience functions.

4. Call `XtUnmanageChild` to get rid of any pushbuttons you don't want.

5. Call `XtAddCallback` to set up your callback functions for the dialog.

6. Call `XtManageChild` with the dialog widget to make the dialog pop up. The trick is to create the dialog once and then manage it or unmanage it when necessary.

7. Call `XtUnmanageChild` with the dialog widget to make the dialog pop down. (Note that this is for dialogs you want to repeatedly pop up and down.)

We'll cover the most common Motif dialogs in the sections below. A test program, called *dialtest*, will display different types of dialogs to show how they work.

MOTIF'S BUILT-IN DIALOGS

One of the simplest forms of Motif compound dialogs has three pushbuttons, a text message (an XmString), and an icon shape that looks like an exclamation mark, a question mark, or an hourglass. The icon shows what kind of dialog it is, and the text should clarify the reason for putting up the icon in the first place. These simple dialogs are all based on the XmMessageBox widget. Among these simple dialogs is the question dialog.

The Question Dialog

With the information dialog, the user doesn't really have much of a chance to interact. The user confirms the dialog and sends it away; usually both operations are done by pressing **OK**. The question dialog requires more interaction from the user.

The question dialog asks a question of the user, such as *Save file before exiting?* or *Are you really really sure you want to delete all the files on the disk?* The user either presses **OK** or cancels the operation by pressing **Cancel**. Confused users can press **Help** to get more information.

Create a question dialog by calling XmCreateQuestionDialog:

```
#include <Xm/MessageB.h>

Widget XmCreateQuestionDialog(Widget parent,
        char* widget_name,
        ArgList args
        Cardinal number_args)
```

Most of Motif's built-in dialogs are descended from the XmMessageBox widget class. These MessageBox-descended dialogs require the include file <Xm/MessageB.h>. All Motif dialog convenience functions create an XmDialogShell widget and then a manager widget, such as an XmMessageBox widget as a child. The creation function then returns this child widget. Because of this, if you ever need to access the dialog shell directly, you'll need to call XtParent on the widget returned by XmCreateQuestionDialog or one of the other creation functions.

The icon shape for the question dialog is a question mark, as shown in Figure 7.3.

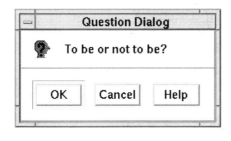

Figure 7.3   *A question dialog.*

You can customize this and any other dialog by manipulating the dialog's resources either through an X resource file or right in your C code.

Dialog Resources

The following resources, shown in Table 7.2, apply to all the dialogs based on the XmMessageBox widget. We'll cover the resources you're most likely to change in the next few sections.

Table 7.2   *Message box resources.*

Resource	Type	Default Value
cancelLabelString	XmString	*dynamic*, usually *Cancel*
defaultButtonType	unsigned char	XmDIALOG_OK_BUTTON
dialogTitle	XmString	NULL
helpLabelString	XmString	*dynamic*, usually *Help*
messageAlignment	unsigned char	XmALIGNMENT_BEGINNING
messageString	XmString	*dynamic*
minimizeButtons	Boolean	False
okLabelString	XmString	*dynamic*, usually *OK*
symbolPixmap	Pixmap	*dynamic*

First set the text message for the dialog by setting the messageString resource (XmNmessageString in C programs). This is the actual text to be displayed, such as *Are you sure you want to delete all files?*.

The dialogTitle (XmNdialogTitle in C programs) is the title of the dialog window. This is inherited from the XmBulletinBoard widget, which is one of the parent types for the XmMessageBox widget. Even though the default value is NULL, Motif will come up with a title for your dialogs—usually a title you don't want. Obviously you'll want to set this resource.

If the minimizeButtons resource (XmNminimizeButtons in C programs) is True, then the buttons (**OK**, **Cancel**, and **Help**) are set to their preferred sizes. If False (the default), then all the buttons are set to the same size—the width of the widest and the height of the tallest.

The symbolPixmap resource (XmNsymbolPixmap in C programs) is the bitmap picture to display. Normally, this is set up by Motif, and you don't need to mess with it.

Setting the Default Pushbutton

In Motif toolkit programs, the user often presses the **Return** key to accept a default choice. With these dialogs, the **OK** button is usually that default choice, but you can certainly change the default choice. The default button usually has an extra-wide border around it, signifying that it's the default.

The defaultButtonType resource specifies which button is the default—or rather, which button will be acted upon if the user presses the **Return** key. In C programs, use the defined symbol XmNdefaultButtonType.

The choices for which button is the default are shown in Table 7.3.

Table 7.3 *Default button choices.*

Motif Symbol	Button
XmDIALOG_CANCEL_BUTTON	Cancel
XmDIALOG_OK_BUTTON	OK
XmDIALOG_HELP_BUTTON	Help

The default is `XmDIALOG_OK_BUTTON`.

To set the default button to the **Help** button, use:

```
#include <Xm/MessageB.h>

Widget dialog;

XtVaSetValues(dialog,
    XmNdefaultButtonType, XmDIALOG_HELP_BUTTON,
    NULL);
```

`XmDIALOG_NONE` turns it off. You normally don't want to mess with the button defaults, though.

Changing the Pushbutton Text

The **OK**, **Cancel**, and **Help** pushbuttons have default messages. You can change any of the messages or lose the buttons altogether. The text of each button's message is an `XmString`, just like the pushbuttons used in the previous chapters. The resources are listed in Table 7.4.

Table 7.4   *Dialog pushbutton text resources.*

Button	Resource Name	Defined Name in C Programs
Cancel	`cancelLabelString`	`XmNCancelLabelString`
Help	`helpLabelString`	`XmNhelpLabelString`
OK	`okLabelString`	`XmNokLabelString`

You can set the **OK** button to display *You Bet!* rather than **OK**, but this wouldn't follow the Motif style. (Too bad.) Normally, you'll leave these resources alone, too.

Basic Message Dialog Callbacks

One thing you normally *do* want to set is a callback on the dialog. You may actually want to set a callback on more than one button, but normally this is not necessary, since the **Cancel** choice means don't do the operation. If you change the `autoUnmanage` resource, though, you'll want to set up both callbacks. Dialog-button callbacks are listed in Table 7.5.

In the callback for the **OK** button, you want to perform the operation that the dialog was asking about, such as print a file, format a disk, or back up data files to tape. For simple dialogs like the information or error dialogs, the callback for the **OK** button doesn't do much at all, except unmanage the dialog.

Similarly, the callback on the **Cancel** button usually unmanages the dialog. Be sure to unset any state variables, to cancel whatever operation was in place.

Table 7.5 *Dialog-button callbacks.*

Button	Resource Name	Defined Name in C Programs
Cancel	cancelCallback	XmNcancelCallback
OK	okCallback	XmNokCallback
Help	helpCallback	XmNhelpCallback

You set up these callbacks with XtAddCallback.

In your callback function, if the **OK** button was pushed, the *reason* field of the XmPushButtonCallbackStruct will be XmCR_OK. If the user pushed the **Cancel** button, the *reason* field holds XmCR_CANCEL.

The Warning Dialog

The warning dialog warns the user of the consequences of an action. For example, you can warn the user that a certain operation cannot be undone.

You can create a warning dialog with XmCreateWarningDialog:

```
#include <Xm/MessageB.h>

Widget XmCreateWarningDialog(Widget parent,
        char* widget_name,
        ArgList args,
        Cardinal number_args)
```

The icon shape for the warning dialog shows an exclamation mark, as illustrated in Figure 7.4.

Figure 7.4   *A warning dialog.*

The Error Dialog

An error dialog is used to let the user know that something went wrong. You can create an error dialog with <u>XmCreateErrorDialog</u>:

```
#include <Xm/MessageB.h>

Widget XmCreateErrorDialog(Widget parent,
        char* widget_name,
        ArgList args
        Cardinal number_args)
```

The icon shape is an error symbol (a circle with a line through it), as shown in Figure 7.5.

Figure 7.5   *An error dialog.*

In a perfect world, errors would never occur in a program. If an error does occur, your program may want to provide some means to try an operation again or attempt a workaround. The more sophisticated error handling you can provide, the better for the user.

The Working Dialog

Working (or progress) dialogs tell the user that your program is busy doing some time-consuming operation, like recalculating a large spreadsheet or printing a document. In Motif toolkit programs, you should allow the user a chance to cancel a lengthy operation. Hence the working dialog.

In Figure 7.6, we haven't changed the default labels on the pushbuttons. You will probably want to replace the **OK** label with **Close**, or perhaps you will have other means of allowing the user to interact regarding a lengthy operation. You may also want to add **Pause** and **Resume** buttons to the dialog to let the user temporarily stop and then restart the lengthy task.

You may even want to put in a scale widget (see Chapter 9) to show the user how far the operation has gone and how far it has to go. If you can provide a progress indicator, do so. A progress indicator of any sort—even a text display of the time left until completion—is especially helpful when the task is *very* long and measured in hours or days.

The working dialog displays an hourglass icon to show that your program is busy, as shown in Figure 7.6.

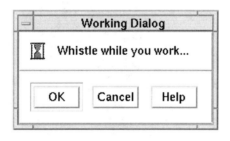

Figure 7.6 *A working dialog.*

Create a working dialog with XmCreateWorkingDialog:

```
#include <Xm/MessageB.h>

Widget XmCreateWorkingDialog(Widget parent,
        char* widget_name,
```

```
ArgList args
Cardinal number_args)
```

The `cancelCallback` for a working dialog should stop the lengthy task. In order for this to work, you must continue to check for events while processing the lengthy task.

The `okCallback` should merely send the dialog away.

The Information Dialog

Information dialogs are used to present information to the user, such as a notice that electronic mail has arrived, as shown in Figure 7.7.

***Figure* 7.7**   *An information dialog.*

The icon shape for the information dialog is a stylized *i*. Create an information dialog with the function `XmCreateInformationDialog`:

```
#include <Xm/MessageB.h>

Widget XmCreateInformationDialog(Widget parent,
        char* widget_name,
        ArgList args,
        Cardinal number_args)
```

An information dialog should have **OK** and **Help** buttons, or else only an **OK** button. You should remove the **Cancel** button.

Removing Unused Buttons from a Dialog

Ridding yourself of a dialog button takes two steps. First, you need to get the widget for the actual button. Second, call `XtUnmanageChild` on the pushbutton widget. Unmanaging the widget makes it invisible.

`XmMessageBoxGetChild` returns the child widget of an XmMessageBox-based dialog:

```
#include <Xm/MessageB.h>

Widget XmMessageBoxGetChild(Widget widget,
        unsigned char which_child)
```

You need to pass a widget and an unsigned char ID that specifies which child you want. The *which_child* parameter can be one of:

- XmDIALOG_CANCEL_BUTTON
- XmDIALOG_DEFAULT_BUTTON
- XmDIALOG_HELP_BUTTON
- XmDIALOG_MESSAGE_LABEL
- XmDIALOG_OK_BUTTON
- XmDIALOG_SEPARATOR
- XmDIALOG_SYMBOL_LABEL

After you have the widget, you can remove it with XtUnmanageChild:

```
void XtUnmanageChild(Widget widget)
```

For example, to get rid of the **Cancel** button in an information dialog, you first need to get that button's widget value.

```
Widget  dialog_widget;        /* parent */
Widget  child_button_widget;  /* RETURN */
child_button_widget =
    XmMessageBoxGetChild(dialog_widget,
        XmDIALOG_CANCEL_BUTTON);
```

Sometimes you don't want to totally remove the button. Instead, you just want to disable it to show that the button is not available. For example, if your application doesn't provide help on some dialogs, you could disable the **Help** button.

To disable a widget, you make it insensitive to user input. That is, you make it ignore any mouse buttons clicked or keys typed into the widget. To do so, call XtSetSensitive:

```
void XtSetSensitive(Widget widget,
        Boolean flag)
```

Set the *flag* to False to disable it from receiving input. Set the *flag* to True to reenable input. If you make a widget insensitive, it usually appears to be grayed out or provides some other visual cue that it is not available.

GETTING INPUT FROM DIALOGS

Most of the dialogs support only a very limited interaction with the user. The user can press **OK**, **Cancel**, or **Help** only, which does not provide for a lot of input. Motif offers a set of more complex convenience dialogs that allow for greater user input. The simplest one of these is the prompt dialog.

Prompt Dialogs

The prompt dialog asks the user to fill in a value, as shown in Figure 7.8.

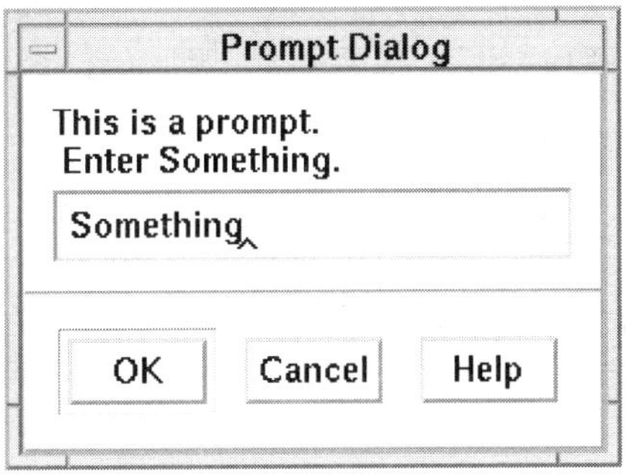

Figure 7.8   *A prompt dialog.*

The prompt dialog is based on the XmSelectionBox widget and not on the XmMessageBox widget. Create a prompt dialog with XmCreatePromptDialog:

```
#include <Xm/SelectioB.h>

Widget XmCreatePromptDialog(Widget parent,
        char* widget_name,
        ArgList args,
        Cardinal number_args)
```

The include file is different: `<Xm/SelectioB.h>` (with no *n*).

So far, it's pretty much the same. There are two new resources to change, though: `selectionLabelString`, which is the text to place above the user's response (the prompt) and `textString`, into which you can put a default response.

The `selectionLabelString` resource, or `XmNselectionLabel-String` in your Motif program, contains a prompting string. It usually defaults to something dumb like *Selection*. To make a clear, understandable dialog for your users, you should change this.

You can put in a default response by changing the `textString` resource. Remember that all these strings are of the Motif type `XmString`, and you'll need to convert your normal C program strings to type `XmString`, a topic covered in the next chapter.

The Prompt Callback Function

The prompt dialog is also different than the rest in that it sends different data to its callback function. The call data in your callback receives a pointer to an `XmSelectionBoxCallbackStruct` structure. The structure looks like:

```
typedef struct {
    int       reason;
    XEvent*   event;
    XmString  value;
    int       length;
} XmSelectionBoxCallbackStruct;
```

The key part here is the *value* field, since this field contains the string the user entered into the prompt dialog. If you want to prompt the user, you can pop up a prompt dialog, then set up a callback on the **OK** pushbutton. This callback should extract the text entered from the *value* field of the `XmSelectionBoxCallbackStruct`. This string is, of course, stored XmString format.

Here's a sample callback function for a selection box or a prompt dialog:

```
/* Callback for OK button for prompt. */
```

```
void promptCB(Widget widget,
    XtPointer client_data,
    XtPointer call_data)
{   /* promptCB */
    XmSelectionBoxCallbackStruct*  ptr;
    char*                          string;

    ptr =
      (XmSelectionBoxCallbackStruct*) call_data;

    XmStringGetLtoR(ptr->value,
        XmSTRING_DEFAULT_CHARSET,
        &string);

    printf("Selected [%s]\n", string);

    XtFree(string);

}   /* promptCB */
```

We call XmStringGetLtoR to extract a C string from an XmString. We'll cover this function in depth in the next chapter. We also call XtFree to free the C string when done with it.

Getting Child Widgets in a Prompt Dialog

Just as XmMessageBox dialogs have a special function to access child widgets in the dialog, so do dialogs like the prompt dialog, which are based on the XmSelectionBox widget. Call XmSelectionBoxGetChild to access a child widget in a prompt dialog:

```
Widget XmSelectionBoxGetChild(Widget dialog,
        unsigned char which_child)
```

The *which_child* parameter should be one of:

- ▥ XmDIALOG_APPLY_BUTTON
- ▥ XmDIALOG_CANCEL_BUTTON
- ▥ XmDIALOG_DEFAULT_BUTTON
- ▥ XmDIALOG_HELP_BUTTON
- ▥ XmDIALOG_LIST
- ▥ XmDIALOG_LIST_LABEL
- ▥ XmDIALOG_OK_BUTTON
- ▥ XmDIALOG_SELECTION_LABEL
- ▥ XmDIALOG_SEPARATOR

■ XmDIALOG_TEXT

■ XmDIALOG_WORK_AREA

The File-Selection Dialog

In just about any editor-based application, such as drawing editors, text editors, electronic-publishing packages, and the like, users pick files to load, save, merge, and so on. Motif provides the file-selection dialog to help automate this task. With this dialog, users can browse through directories until they find the file they are looking for. The file-selection dialog also has a filtering capability to, for example, view only the files that end in .c (C program files), as shown in Figure 7.9.

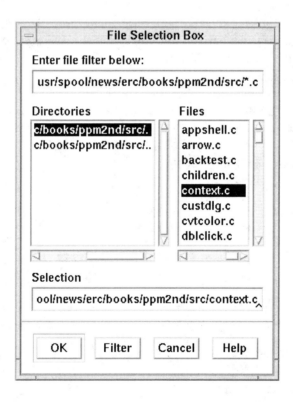

Figure 7.9 *A file-selection box.*

From the looks of the figure, this is obviously a complex dialog, the most complex of the compound Motif dialogs available. We find it rather handy that the Motif toolkit includes a widget like this.

The file-selection dialog contains two scrolled lists, one of directories and one of files. The user can jump up or down directories and then select a file.

You create a file selection dialog with XmCreateFileSelection-Dialog:

```
#include <Xm/FileSB.h>

Widget XmCreateFileSelectionDialog(Widget parent,
        char* widget_name,
        ArgList args,
        Cardinal number_args)
```

The include file is <Xm/FileSB.h>.

N O T E

File-Selection-Box Resources

Common resources you may want to change in the file-selection box are listed in Table 7.6.

Table 7.6   *File-selection-box resources.*

Resource	Type	Default Value
directory	XmString	*dynamic*
dirListLabelString	XmString	*dynamic*
dirMask	XmString	*dynamic*
dirSpec	XmString	*dynamic*
fileListLabelString	XmString	*dynamic*
fileTypeMask	unsigned char	XmFILE_REGULAR
filterLabelString	XmString	*dynamic*

The `directory` resource (`XmNdirectory` in C programs) specifies the directory to use. The directory is also influenced by the search patterns and search procedures. The `dirListLabelString` resource (`XmNdirListLabelString` in C programs) holds the text to display above the directory window. Usually, the default value is *Directories*.

The `dirMask` resource (`XmNdirMask` in C programs) is the filtering mask used to choose file names. The default is `*`—that is, display all files in the given directory. You could change that to `*.c` to display only the files ending in *.c*. The user can also change this value interactively. The `dirMask` requires an `XmString` type, as does the `dirSpec` resource.

The `dirSpec` resource (`XmNdirSpec` in C programs) is the name of the last file chosen by the user. It should contain the complete path and file name for the file. (With a file-selection dialog, users can normally choose more than one file.) By setting this resource, you can specify a default file name.

The `fileListLabelString` resource (`XmNfileListLabelString` in C programs) holds the text displayed above the scrolled list of files. Usually, this defaults to *Files*.

The `fileTypeMask` resource (`XmNfileTypeMask` in C programs) specifies what type of files to look for in the scrolled list of files. The possible values are:

- `XmFILE_REGULAR`
- `XmFILE_DIRECTORY`
- `XmFILE_ANY_TYPE`

The `filterLabelString` resource (`XmNfilterLabelString` in C programs) contains the text string to display as a prompt to the user above the area where the user enters a filter string. The default is *Filter*.

In most cases, you can get away with changing few of these resources. The `filterLabelString` is a prime candidate for replacement, though. If you need much more control over the file-selection box, look up the search procedures for this widget in the Motif programmer's reference. You can actually change the functions called to search through directories, should you need to.

The File-Selection Callback

Unlike most of the other dialogs, the **OK** pushbutton on the file-selection dialog leaves the dialog on the display. All the other dialogs go away when the **OK** pushbutton is clicked, except for the file-selection dialog. (Your callback should unmanage the widget if you want the dialog to go away.) The **Cancel** pushbutton unmanages the dialog, making it appear to pop down.

The file-selection callback function gets a pointer to an XmFileSelectionBoxCallbackStruct structure:

```
typedef struct {
    int        reason;
    XEvent*    event;
    XmString   value;
    int        length;
    XmString   mask;
    int        mask_length;
    XmString   dir;
    int        dir_length;
    XmString   pattern;
    int        pattern_length;
} XmFileSelectionBoxCallbackStruct;
```

The most important field of this structure is the *value* field, which contains the full path name of the selected file.

The following is a sample callback function for the file-selection dialog:

```
void filesbCB(Widget widget,
    XtPointer client_data,
    XtPointer call_data)

{   /* filesbCB */
    XmFileSelectionBoxCallbackStruct* ptr;
    char*    string;

    ptr =
        (XmFileSelectionBoxCallbackStruct*) call_data;

    XmStringGetLtoR(ptr->value,
        XmSTRING_DEFAULT_CHARSET,
        &string);

    printf("Selected file named [%s]\n", string);
    XtFree(string);

}   /* filesbCB */
```

We again call XmStringGetLtoR to extract a C string from an XmString and XtFree to free the C string when done with it. Both are covered in depth in the next chapter.

Getting the Child Widgets of a File-Selection Dialog

The dialogs descended from the XmMessageBox widget class provided a function, XmMessageBoxGetChild, to get at the individual widgets inside the dialog. The file-selection box also provides such a function, XmFileSelectionBoxGetChild. XmFileSelectionBoxGetChild returns one of the child widgets in a file-selection dialog:

```
#include <Xm/FileSB.h>

Widget XmFileSelectionBoxGetChild(Widget widget,
    unsigned char which_child)
```

The *which_child* parameter should be one of:

- XmDIALOG_APPLY_BUTTON
- XmDIALOG_CANCEL_BUTTON
- XmDIALOG_DEFAULT_BUTTON
- XmDIALOG_DIR_LIST
- XmDIALOG_DIR_LIST_LABEL
- XmDIALOG_FILTER_LABEL
- XmDIALOG_FILTER_TEXT
- XmDIALOG_HELP_BUTTON
- XmDIALOG_LIST
- XmDIALOG_LIST_LABEL
- XmDIALOG_OK_BUTTON
- XmDIALOG_SELECTION_LABEL
- XmDIALOG_SEPARATOR
- XmDIALOG_TEXT
- XmDIALOG_WORK_AREA

The XmDIALOG_APPLY_BUTTON is actually the **Filter** button, which causes the file-selection box to perform a filtering operation.

To find the widget of the **OK** pushbutton in a file-selection dialog, use `XmFileSelectionBoxGetChild` as follows:

```
Widget          child_widget;
Widget          dialog_parent;

child_widget =
    .XmFileSelectionBoxGetChild(dialog_parent,
        XmDIALOG_OK_BUTTON);
```

Initiating a File and Directory Search

You can force the file-selection box dialog to initiate another search of directories and files by calling the `XmFileSelectionDoSearch` function:

```
#include <Xm/FileSB.h>

void XmFileSelectionDoSearch(Widget widget,
    XmString directory_mask)
```

The *directory_mask* acts like the `dirMask` resource.

Compiling and Linking with the File-Selection Dialog

The file-selection box uses the `regcmp` and `regex` string comparison routines that are stored in **libPW.a** on many systems, such as those from Hewlett-Packard, Silicon Graphics, and SunSoft/Interactive. When linking, you may need to add a `-lPW` at the end of your `cc` command, as in the following example:

```
cc -o foo foo.c  -lXm -lXt -lX11 -lPW
```

EXTENDING MOTIF DIALOGS

If you need more than what Motif offers in the form of standard dialogs, you're left with two choices: either find some way to extend the existing dialogs or create your own from scratch. Ideally, all you'd have to do is extend an existing dialog and avoid all the work it would take to create your own dialog from scratch. After all, most of the dialogs use Motif container widgets under the hood, so why not just add in a new widget?

In fact, you can extend the standard Motif dialogs by adding a single widget to each one. Be careful to add only one new widget. That's the theory. We've found in practice that this technique usually fails miserably.

We first tried to add a scrolled-text widget to an information dialog, which is based on the XmMessageBox widget. This resulted in a complete mess under Motif 1.1. We next attempted to change a prompt dialog, which is based on the XmSelectionBox widget, and we experienced much better luck.

We switched to the prompt dialog because the XmSelectionBox widget supports the childPlacement resource (XmNchildPlacement in C programs). The childPlacement resource allows you to specify where a new widget would be placed. You can use one of the following:

- XmPLACE_ABOVE_SELECTION
- XmPLACE_BELOW_SELECTION
- XmPLACE_TOP

Thus we were able to add a widget to this dialog. The results are shown in Figure 7.10.

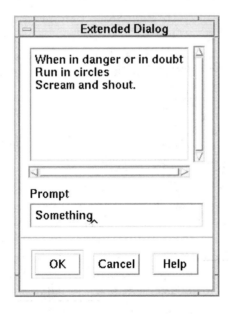

Figure 7.10 *Extending a prompt dialog.*

The code to do this is simple: Simply create one widget as a child of the dialog widget and manage this new widget. That's it. If you have complex needs, create a container widget so you can stick in new children. The restriction is that only one new widget can be a direct child of the dialog widget. In our *dialtest* program, below, we extend a prompt dialog with the following code:

```
Widget    parent, extenddlg, scrtext;
Arg       args[20];
Cardinal  n;
/* ... */

/* Create an extended prompt dialog. */
n = 0;
XtSetArg(args[n], XmNallowOverlap, False); n++;
extenddlg = XmCreatePromptDialog(parent,
             "extenddlg", args, n);

    /* Note different OK callback. */
XtAddCallback(extenddlg, XmNokCallback,
    (XtCallbackProc) promptCB,
    (XtPointer) "extenddlg");

XtAddCallback(extenddlg, XmNcancelCallback,
    (XtCallbackProc) cancelCB,
    (XtPointer) "extenddlg");

XtAddCallback(extenddlg, XmNhelpCallback,
    (XtCallbackProc) helpCB,
    (XtPointer) "extenddlg");

/* Create scrolled text for extended dialog. */
n = 0;
XtSetArg(args[n], XmNeditable, False); n++;
XtSetArg(args[n], XmNeditMode,
        XmMULTI_LINE_EDIT); n++;
XtSetArg(args[n], XmNrows, 8); n++;
scrtext = XmCreateScrolledText(extenddlg,
            "scrtext", args, n);

XmTextSetString(scrtext, EXT_MESSAGE);
XtManageChild(scrtext);
```

We had many problems performing this seemingly simple task, so we advise you to try this out on as many systems as possible. We had terrible luck with the dialogs based on the XmMessageBox widget.

If this isn't sufficient, you'll need to either create a custom dialog or, if you have Motif 1.2, use the template dialog.

The Template Dialog

Motif 1.2 adds a new template dialog as an aid to building your own dialogs. Create a template dialog with XmCreateTemplateDialog:

```
#include <Xm/MessageB.h>

Widget XmCreateTemplateDialog(Widget parent,
        String name,
        ArgList args,
        Cardinal number_args)
```

XmCreateTemplateDialog creates a template that is used for the Motif convenience dialogs. You get the separator automatically. If you set up the okCallback and okLabelString, you then get the **OK** button. You can similarly set up the **Cancel** and other buttons. You can set the symbolPixmap and messageString resources to get the image and text that appears in most Motif dialogs.

We generally stay away from XmCreateTemplateDialog because it's new in Motif 1.2 and all our systems are not yet upgraded.

CUSTOM DIALOGS

If extending a dialog doesn't work, you'll need to create your own dialog from scratch. This is actually more common than you'd think, because just about every Motif application needs some form of complex dialog, that goes beyond the simple features that Motif offers. For example, you'll probably need to create a help dialog, a printer dialog if your application supports printing, a search-and-replace dialog if your application edits text, and so on.

To build a custom dialog, you can create an XmDialogShell widget on your own or use some of the Motif convenience functions. For the bare-bones convenience dialogs, the main choices are creating a message box, a bulletin-board, or a form dialog. We've had the best luck creating a form or bulletin-board dialog for our custom dialogs. Both of these dialogs provide a flexible area in which to create and place your own widgets.

The Bulletin-Board Dialog

The bulletin-board widget is like a real bulletin board: You can place things in it and stick these things to certain locations. This widget is a container widget that manages any number of child widgets but does not provide as complex placement control as the form widget. In fact, most of the time you use a bulletin-board widget, you'll place your child widgets by hand and then keep the child widgets locked in place. This may not seem like it offers enough, but the bulletin-board widget, as the parent class of other dialog widgets, provides a number of services that aid in creating your own dialogs.

Creating the Bulletin-Board Dialog

You can create a bulletin-board dialog with `XmCreateBulletinBoard-Dialog`:

```
#include <Xm/BulletinB.h>

Widget XmCreateBulletinBoardDialog(Widget parent,
        String name,
        ArgList args,
        Cardinal number_args)
```

`XmCreateBulletinBoardDialog` creates an `XmBulletinBoard` widget as a child of an `XmDialogShell` widget and does everything else that is necessary to have a simple dialog. The function returns the bulletin board's widget ID.

Placing Widgets in a Bulletin-Board Dialog

As with last chapter's discussion of the bulletin-board widget, we place child widgets in a bulletin-board dialog by setting the x (`XmNx` in C programs) and y (`XmNy` in C programs) resources on the child widgets. This tells the bulletin-board widget (the parent) where we'd like the child widgets to go. This is a tedious process at best, but it allows you to make a dialog that looks exactly like you want it to. The bulletin-board widget does not support attachments like the form widget, but we think you'll find the ability to place items works well enough for creating dialogs.

Controlling Resizing of a Bulletin-Board Dialog

If you place child widgets at a given *x,y* location within a bulletin-board dialog, you probably don't want your placements messed up. One way to avoid getting your placements messed up is to control the ability of the user to resize your dialog. If the user cannot change the size of your dialog, then all your items will always remain visible. (Of course, that's assuming your users have screens large enough to show your whole dialog.)

The noResize resource (XmNnoResize in C programs) controls whether the bulletin-board dialog will allow itself to be resized.

If you set the noResize resource to True, then the user will not be able to resize your dialog, provided the window manager cooperates. If you are running the Motif window manager, *mwm*, you won't see the resize handles on the window's border.

Creating a Form Dialog

You can also create a form dialog: an XmDialogShell parent with an XmForm child. XmCreateFormDialog creates such a dialog and returns the form widget's ID:

```
#include <Xm/Form.h>

Widget XmCreateFormDialog(Widget parent,
        String name,
        ArgList args,
        Cardinal number_args)
```

We generally find that the form dialog is easier than the bulletin-board dialog because the form widget provides more versatile layout policies.

After you create one of these dialogs, you can fill in any child widgets you want, making for all sorts of custom dialogs. The following code creates a custom form dialog:

```
/* custdlg.c */
#include  <Xm/Xm.h>
#include  <Xm/Form.h>

Widget CreateCustomDialog(Widget parent,
    char* name)

{   /* CreateCustomDialog */
    Widget      dialog;
    Arg         args[20];
    Cardinal    n;

    /* Note: not managed. */
    n = 0;
    XtSetArg(args[n], XmNallowResize, True); n++;

    dialog = XmCreateFormDialog(parent,
            name, args, n);

    return dialog;
```

```
}    /* CreateCustomDialog */

/* end of file custdlg.c */
```

We covered the form widget in Chapter 6, and most of that material applies to a form dialog as well.

Following the Motif Style with Custom Dialogs

One thing you may want to do when you create your own dialogs, though, is provide for the pushbutton area at the bottom, with the standard **OK**, **Cancel**, and **Help** buttons. On top of this button area should be a separator.

To place this separator, you can use the XmForm attachments that we outlined in the last chapter. The *dialtest* example program, which we present in the "A Program to Test Dialogs" section, below, creates a custom dialog this way. You'll need to play with the resource settings, particularly the margins and offsets, to come up with an optimum custom dialog.

The Message-Box Dialog

In addition to the form and bulletin-board dialogs, you may want to create a raw message-box dialog. Remember that the basic Motif dialogs, such as the warning and error dialogs, are built on top of the XmMessageBox widget. The message-box dialog gives us a message area and the three standard dialog pushbuttons: **OK**, **Cancel**, and **Help**.

You can create a message-box dialog with XmCreateMessageDialog:

```
#include <Xm/MessageB.h>
Widget XmCreateMessageDialog(Widget parent,
        char* widget_name,
        ArgList args,
        Cardinal number_args)
```

Dialog-Shell Widgets

All the dialog routines so far created an XmDialogShell widget. The XmDialogShell widget class inherits from the Core, Composite, Shell, WMShell, VendorShell, and TransientShell widget classes, as listed in Table 7.7.

Table 7.7   The XmDialogShell widget class.

Widget class:	XmDialogShell
Class pointer:	xmDialogShellWidgetClass
Include file:	<Xm/DialogS.h>
Create with:	XmCreateDialogShell

The main resource you need to set for a dialog shell is the transientFor resource (XmNtransientFor in C programs), as listed in Table 7.8.

Table 7.8   Dialog shell resources.

Resource	Type	Default Value
allowResize	Boolean	False
transientFor	Widget	NULL

Set the transientFor resource to a widget ID for the main widget of your application, which is usually the widget returned by XtAppInitialize. This widget ID is used by the Motif window manager to iconify all the dialogs for a given application at the same time the application's main window is iconified. Other window managers may treat transient windows differently.

In your code, though, you'll rarely create an XmDialogShell directly. Instead, create a raw dialog using XmCreateBulletinBoardDialog or XmCreateFormDialog. These functions create an XmDialogShell and a bulletin board or form child, respectively.

The OSF/Motif Style Guide and Dialogs

We've already covered the *OSF/Motif Style Guide* rules on menus. Now we extend that discussion by going into the Motif style guidelines for dialogs, especially the customized, complex dialogs that you are likely to need in any real application.

Again, we're going to start with the *OSF/Motif Style* Guide. And again, we expect that you'll have your copy handy. Even thought the official references are expensive, any serious Motif development efforts require that you have the official information. We won't cover everything in the style guide on dialogs. Instead, we'll focus on the basic rules for dialogs.

Common Pushbuttons in Dialogs

In the standard Motif dialogs we've used up to now, we've seen only **OK**, **Cancel**, and **Help** pushbuttons. Motif, though, allows for a number of standard pushbuttons beyond these three.

In Table 7.9, we list the pushbutton's label, what action should be taken, and whether the dialog should remain on the screen after the action is performed.

Table 7.9 *Dialog pushbuttons.*

Pushbutton	Action	Remains on Screen
Apply	Applies the changes the user made in the dialog	Yes
Cancel	Combines the **Reset** and **Close** operations	No
Close	Makes the dialog go away	No
Help	Presents help on the dialog	Yes
No	Answers no to the given question	No
OK	Combines the **Apply** and **Close** operations	No
Pause	Pauses task in working dialog	Yes
Reset	Resets the values displayed in the dialog	Yes
Resume	Resumes paused task in working dialog	Yes
Retry	Attempt to perform a task again	Depends
Stop	Ends whatever task is in progress	Depends
Yes	Answers yes to the given question	No

To clarify some of the items in Table 7.9, we'll mention a few notes.

If you use a standard name, like **Apply**, then you should implement the **Apply** button like the definition above. Otherwise, you'll mess up the consistency of Motif applications.

Help should always be the rightmost pushbutton, just as a Help menu is always the rightmost menu. It's a good idea to offer help on dialogs, especially complex dialogs.

It is very easy to confuse yes and no in certain questions, so be *very* careful when using **Yes** and **No** pushbuttons. *Are you sure you don't want to continue?* is an example of a bad yes/no question.

Reset should set the values in the dialog to what the values were when the dialog first appeared.

Retry could be used to retry to print after encountering a printer error (such as out of paper). If a serial communications program gets a busy signal, **Retry** would attempt to make the connection again.

With the **Stop** choice, your application may wait until a convenient stopping point to actually stop the operation.

Ordering the Buttons

You should choose one of the following sets of buttons for your dialogs:

- **OK**, **Cancel**, **Help**
- **OK**, **Apply**, **Cancel**
- **OK**, **Apply**, **Cancel**, **Help**
- **OK**, **Apply**, **Reset**, **Cancel**, **Help**
- **Yes**, **No**, **Help**
- **Yes**, **No**, **Cancel**, **Help**

Use these buttons in the order given above.

Defining Your Own Buttons

You are free to define your own buttons if they make sense, such as **Log Out** or **Format Disk**. In general, the more specific the pushbutton titles the better.

The pushbuttons should generally go at the bottom of the dialog, just like in the standard Motif dialogs. Do not use too many pushbuttons in a dialog.

When creating your own dialogs, you should group like components so the user doesn't have to search for all the available choices. Often, it is a good idea to place a frame widget around a set of controls in a dialog to group them.

Which Dialog to Use?

We've presented a host of different types of Motif dialogs and their convenience functions. We've tried to describe situations where you'd want to use one dialog type over another. But if you're not sure which dialog is appropriate for what you want to display, a good source of help is the *OSF/Motif Style Guide*.

Once you decide which dialog to use, there are a few more techniques needed when working with dialogs.

MANAGING AND UNMANAGING DIALOGS

Motif's built-in dialogs will generally unmanage themselves when the user presses on the **OK** or **Cancel** buttons. We often find such automatic behavior undesirable, so we turn it off. If you do turn this off, though, you are responsible for managing and unmanaging the dialog yourself. If you do decide to manage and unmanage dialogs on your own, you'll need to set the autoUnmanage resource (XmNautoUnmanage in C programs) to False:

```
Arg        args[10];
Cardinal   n;

n = 0;
XtSetArg(args[n], XmNautoUnmanage, False);
n++;

/* Create widget... */
```

Setting the autoUnmanage resource to False tells the dialog to keep its hands off and allow your program to explicitly manage and unmanage the dialog with XtManageChild and XtUnmanageChild, respectively.

You can tell if a widget is managed by calling XtIsManaged:

```
Boolean XtIsManaged(Widget widget)
```

In your code, you can unmanage a dialog widget, but you should do so only if it is already managed:

```
if (XtIsManaged(widget) ) {
    XtUnmanageChild(widget);
}
```

The function `manageCB`, in the **dialtest.c** program, below, calls `XtIsManaged` to check if a dialog widget is managed or not.

Do not use `XtPopup` to make a Motif dialog appear. Instead, use `XtManageChild`. Do not use `XtPopdown`, either. Use `XtUnmanageChild` instead.

N O T E

MODAL DIALOGS

Up to now, all our dialogs were *modeless*—no dialog forced the user to respond before doing anything else. The Motif toolkit offers you the possibility, though, of creating *modal* dialogs, which require user interaction (either accepting or canceling) before going on.

The `dialogStyle` resource (`XmNdialogStyle` in C programs) controls the user-interaction model for dialogs based on the bulletin-board widget. You can set this resource to one of the following:

■ `XmDIALOG_SYSTEM_MODAL`

■ `XmDIALOG_PRIMARY_APPLICATION_MODAL`

■ `XmDIALOG_FULL_APPLICATION_MODAL`

■ `XmDIALOG_MODELESS`

You can set this resource only if the bulletin board is unmanaged.

If you set the `dialogStyle` resource to `XmDIALOG_SYSTEM_MODAL`, the user must respond to your dialog before doing anything with any other application or window. This can quickly lock up a system, especially if there are any problems with the software. Use `XmDIALOG_SYSTEM_MODAL` only if you're sure you know what you're doing.

This mode depends on help from the Motif window manager. If *mwm* isn't the window manager in use, then `XmDIALOG_SYSTEM_MODAL` won't work.

XmDIALOG_FULL_APPLICATION_MODAL means that the user must respond to the dialog before doing anything else in the application.

XmDIALOG_PRIMARY_APPLICATION_MODAL means that the user must respond to the dialog before interacting with the ancestor of the dialog widget, that is, the parent widget used to create the dialog.

XmDIALOG_MODELESS, of course, means that your dialogs place no such restrictions.

When to Use Modal Dialogs

To answer the basic question of when to use modal dialogs, we generally answer: never.

Modal dialogs seem very useful and can ease your task as a programmer, but they severely restrict the user. In fact, every modal dialog that we've ever come across—on any windowing system—has proven problematic. You simply cannot conceive of all the legitimate reasons a user has to bypass a modal dialog. For example, in safety-critical applications, such as software to control medical systems or a nuclear-power plant, the user should always have a means to deal with emergencies. A *file not found* modal dialog is simply not acceptable in those circumstances.

In many more mundane applications, modal dialogs can interfere with the user's desired way of interacting with the program. For example, a user may legitimately not remember the file name used to store January's project reports. In such a case, the user may need to run another application to check which file to load. In this case, an XmDIALOG_SYSTEM_MODAL dialog would prevent this.

And, quite honestly, modal dialogs really aren't needed. To get around a perceived need for modal dialogs, put Motif's callback functions to good use. For example, if you have a dialog that asks the user, *Are you sure you want to delete the file?*, then have that dialog's **OK** button callback actually delete the files in question. If you never get to the program state where you're performing the action until the proper confirmed callback is called, then you simply won't have a problem with modeless dialogs.

Enough sermonizing. The next step is to try all these new techniques out with an example program.

A Program to Test Dialogs

To pull together all the lessons in this chapter, we've built a dialog test program. This program creates a set of pushbuttons from which you can manage and unmanage many of the dialogs we covered in this chapter.

We also share many of the callback functions. For example, the **OK** and **Cancel** button callbacks use similar functions.

For the prompt and file-selection dialogs, we show how to extract the data entered by the user. We also show how to extend a prompt dialog and create your own custom dialog.

Since there are many intricacies when working with Motif's dialogs, we urge you to try out this program and experiment. The code to **dialtest.c** follows:

```
/* dialtest.c */
#include <Xm/Xm.h>
#include <Xm/FileSB.h>
#include <Xm/Label.h>
#include <Xm/MessageB.h>
#include <Xm/PushB.h>
#include <Xm/RowColumn.h>
#include <Xm/SelectioB.h>   /* Note: no "n". */
#include <Xm/Separator.h>
#include <Xm/Text.h>
#include <stdio.h>

/*
 * Extended message.
 */
#define EXT_MESSAGE \
"When in danger or in doubt\n\
Run in circles\n\
Scream and shout."

extern Widget
CreatePushbutton(Widget parent, char* name,
    XtCallbackProc callback,
    XtPointer client_data);

extern Widget
CreateCustomDialog(Widget parent, char* name);

    /* Callback to exit. */
void exitCB(Widget widget,
    XtPointer client_data,
    XtPointer call_data)
```

```
{    /* exitCB */

    exit(0);

}    /* exitCB */

    /* Callback to manage dialogs. */
void manageCB(Widget widget,
    XtPointer client_data,
    XtPointer call_data)

{    /* manageCB */
    Widget* ptr;

    /*
     * We assume dialog widget was
     * passed with client_data.
     */
    ptr = (Widget*) client_data;

    /*
     * Manage if unmanaged.
     * Unmanage if managed.
     */
    if (XtIsManaged( *ptr ) ) {
        XtUnmanageChild( *ptr );
    } else {
        XtManageChild( *ptr );
    }
}    /* manageCB */

    /* Callback for cancel button. */
void cancelCB(Widget widget,
    XtPointer client_data,
    XtPointer call_data)

{    /* cancelCB */
    char*    ptr;

    /* Assumes name is passed via client_data. */
    ptr = (char*) client_data;

    printf("Cancel callback for %s.\n", ptr);

}    /* cancelCB */

    /* Callback for OK button. */
void okCB(Widget widget,
    XtPointer client_data,
    XtPointer call_data)
{    /* okCB */
    char*    ptr;

    /* Assumes name is passed via client_data. */
```

```
        ptr = (char*) client_data;

        printf("OK callback for %s.\n", ptr);

}    /* okCB */

        /* Callback for Help button. */
void helpCB(Widget widget,
        XtPointer client_data,
        XtPointer call_data)

{    /* helpCB */
        char*    ptr;

        /* Assumes name is passed via client_data. */
        ptr = (char*) client_data;

        printf("Help callback for %s.\n", ptr);

}    /* helpCB */

        /* Callback for OK button for prompt. */
void promptCB(Widget widget,
        XtPointer client_data,
        XtPointer call_data)

{    /* promptCB */
        XmSelectionBoxCallbackStruct*  ptr;
        char*                          string;

        ptr =
          (XmSelectionBoxCallbackStruct*) call_data;

        XmStringGetLtoR(ptr->value,
            XmSTRING_DEFAULT_CHARSET,
            &string);

        printf("Selected [%s]\n", string);

        XtFree(string);

}    /* promptCB */

void filesbCB(Widget widget,
        XtPointer client_data,
        XtPointer call_data)

{    /* filesbCB */
        XmFileSelectionBoxCallbackStruct* ptr;
        char*    string;
        ptr =
            (XmFileSelectionBoxCallbackStruct*) call_data;

        XmStringGetLtoR(ptr->value,
            XmSTRING_DEFAULT_CHARSET,
```

```
            &string);

    printf("Selected file named [%s]\n", string);

    XtFree(string);

}   /* filesbCB */

    /* Test Function to create a custom dialog. */

Widget CreateCustDlg(Widget parent)

{   /* CreateCustDlg */
    Widget  cust;
    Widget  ok, cancel, help;
    Widget  sep, label1, label2;

    cust = CreateCustomDialog(parent, "cust");

    /* Fill in custom dialog. */
    label1 = XtVaCreateManagedWidget("label1",
        xmLabelWidgetClass, cust,
        XmNtopAttachment,   XmATTACH_FORM,
        XmNleftAttachment,  XmATTACH_FORM,
        XmNrightAttachment, XmATTACH_FORM,
        NULL);

    label2 = XtVaCreateManagedWidget("label2",
        xmLabelWidgetClass, cust,
        XmNtopAttachment,   XmATTACH_WIDGET,
        XmNtopWidget,       label1,
        XmNleftAttachment,  XmATTACH_FORM,
        XmNrightAttachment, XmATTACH_FORM,
        NULL);

    sep = XtVaCreateManagedWidget("sep",
        xmSeparatorWidgetClass, cust,
        XmNtopAttachment,   XmATTACH_WIDGET,
        XmNtopWidget,       label2,
        XmNleftAttachment,  XmATTACH_FORM,
        XmNrightAttachment, XmATTACH_FORM,
        NULL);

    ok = XtVaCreateManagedWidget("ok",
        xmPushButtonWidgetClass, cust,
        XmNtopAttachment,   XmATTACH_WIDGET,
        XmNtopWidget,       sep,
        XmNbottomAttachment,XmATTACH_FORM,
        XmNleftAttachment,  XmATTACH_FORM,
        XmNrightAttachment, XmATTACH_POSITION,
        XmNrightPosition,   30,
        NULL);

    cancel = XtVaCreateManagedWidget("cancel",
        xmPushButtonWidgetClass, cust,
```

```
            XmNtopAttachment,    XmATTACH_WIDGET,
            XmNtopWidget,        sep,
            XmNbottomAttachment,XmATTACH_FORM,
            XmNleftAttachment,   XmATTACH_POSITION,
            XmNleftPosition,     35,
            XmNrightAttachment,  XmATTACH_POSITION,
            XmNrightPosition,    64,
            NULL);

    help = XtVaCreateManagedWidget("help",
        xmPushButtonWidgetClass, cust,
        XmNtopAttachment,    XmATTACH_WIDGET,
        XmNtopWidget,        sep,
        XmNbottomAttachment,XmATTACH_FORM,
        XmNleftAttachment,   XmATTACH_POSITION,
        XmNleftPosition,     68,
        XmNrightAttachment,  XmATTACH_FORM,
        NULL);

    return cust;
}    /* CreateCustDlg */

/*
 * This routine adds the OK, Cancel,
 * and Help callbacks for a given
 * dialog widget, passing the
 * widget name as the client_data.
 * Your programs would obviously
 * do something different.
 */
void AddStdCallbacks(Widget widget,
    char* name)

{    /* AddStdCallbacks */

    XtAddCallback(widget, XmNokCallback,
        (XtCallbackProc) okCB,
        (XtPointer) name);

    XtAddCallback(widget, XmNcancelCallback,
        (XtCallbackProc) cancelCB,
        (XtPointer) name);

    XtAddCallback(widget, XmNhelpCallback,
        (XtCallbackProc) helpCB,
        (XtPointer) name);

}    /* AddStdCallbacks */

Widget CreateInfoDialog(Widget parent,
    char* name)

{    /* CreateInfoDialog */
    Widget       info, cancel;
    Arg          args[20];
```

```
        Cardinal    n;

        n = 0;
        info = XmCreateInformationDialog(parent,
                name, args, n);

        AddStdCallbacks(info, name);

        /* Remove Cancel button from info dialog. */
        cancel = XmMessageBoxGetChild(info,
                    XmDIALOG_CANCEL_BUTTON);

        XtUnmanageChild(cancel);

        return info;

}   /* CreateInfoDialog */

int main(int argc, char** argv)

{   /* main */
    Widget          parent;
    XtAppContext    app_context;
    Widget          row;
    Widget          working, error, prompt, cancel;
    Widget          filesb, question, info, warning;
    Widget          cust, extenddlg, scrtext;
    Arg             args[20];
    Cardinal        n;

    /* Initialize the X Toolkit. */
    n = 0;
    XtSetArg(args[n], XmNallowResize, True); n++;

    parent = XtAppInitialize(&app_context,
            "Ppm",
            (XrmOptionDescList) NULL,
            0,
            (Cardinal*) &argc,
            argv,
            (String*) NULL,
            args, n);

    /* Create question dialog. */
    n = 0;

    question = XmCreateQuestionDialog(parent,
                "question", args, n);

    AddStdCallbacks(question, "question");

    /* Create information dialog. */
    info = CreateInfoDialog(parent, "info");

    /* Remove Cancel button from info dialog. */
```

```
cancel = XmMessageBoxGetChild(info,
            XmDIALOG_CANCEL_BUTTON);

XtUnmanageChild(cancel);

/* Create working dialog. */
n = 0;
working = XmCreateWorkingDialog(parent,
            "working", args, n);

AddStdCallbacks(working, "working");

/* Create warning dialog. */
n = 0;
warning = XmCreateWarningDialog(parent,
            "warning", args, n);

AddStdCallbacks(warning, "warning");
/* Create error dialog. */
n = 0;
error = XmCreateErrorDialog(parent,
            "error", args, n);

AddStdCallbacks(error, "error");

/* Remove Cancel button from error dialog. */
cancel = XmMessageBoxGetChild(error,
            XmDIALOG_CANCEL_BUTTON);

XtUnmanageChild(cancel);

/* Create prompt dialog. */
n = 0;
prompt = XmCreatePromptDialog(parent,
            "prompt", args, n);

    /* Note different OK callback. */
XtAddCallback(prompt, XmNokCallback,
    (XtCallbackProc) promptCB,
    (XtPointer) "prompt");

XtAddCallback(prompt, XmNcancelCallback,
    (XtCallbackProc) cancelCB,
    (XtPointer) "prompt");
XtAddCallback(prompt, XmNhelpCallback,
    (XtCallbackProc) helpCB,
    (XtPointer) "prompt");

/* Create file selection dialog. */
n = 0;
filesb = XmCreateFileSelectionDialog(parent,
            "filesb", args, n);

    /* Note different OK callback. */
XtAddCallback(filesb, XmNokCallback,
```

```
        (XtCallbackProc) filesbCB,
        (XtPointer) "filesb");

XtAddCallback(filesb, XmNcancelCallback,
    (XtCallbackProc) cancelCB,
    (XtPointer) "filesb");

/* Create an extended prompt dialog. */
n = 0;
XtSetArg(args[n], XmNallowOverlap, False); n++;
extenddlg = XmCreatePromptDialog(parent,
            "extenddlg", args, n);

    /* Note different OK callback. */
XtAddCallback(extenddlg, XmNokCallback,
    (XtCallbackProc) promptCB,
    (XtPointer) "extenddlg");

XtAddCallback(extenddlg, XmNcancelCallback,
    (XtCallbackProc) cancelCB,
    (XtPointer) "extenddlg");

XtAddCallback(extenddlg, XmNhelpCallback,
    (XtCallbackProc) helpCB,
    (XtPointer) "extenddlg");

/* Create scrolled text for extended dialog. */
n = 0;
XtSetArg(args[n], XmNeditable, False); n++;
XtSetArg(args[n], XmNeditMode,
    XmMULTI_LINE_EDIT); n++;
XtSetArg(args[n], XmNrows, 8); n++;

scrtext = XmCreateScrolledText(extenddlg,
        "scrtext", args, n);

XmTextSetString(scrtext, EXT_MESSAGE);
XtManageChild(scrtext);

/* Create custom dialog. */
cust = CreateCustDlg(parent);
/* Create main interface. */
row = XtVaCreateManagedWidget("row",
        xmRowColumnWidgetClass, parent,
        NULL);

/* Create pushbuttons inside row. */
(void) CreatePushbutton(row, "working_btn",
    (XtCallbackProc) manageCB,
    (XtPointer) &working);

(void) CreatePushbutton(row, "error_btn",
    (XtCallbackProc) manageCB,
    (XtPointer) &error);
```

```
(void) CreatePushbutton(row, "question_btn",
    (XtCallbackProc) manageCB,
    (XtPointer) &question);

(void) CreatePushbutton(row, "info_btn",
    (XtCallbackProc) manageCB,
    (XtPointer) &info);

(void) CreatePushbutton(row, "warning_btn",
    (XtCallbackProc) manageCB,
    (XtPointer) &warning);

(void) CreatePushbutton(row, "prompt_btn",
    (XtCallbackProc) manageCB,
    (XtPointer) &prompt);

(void) CreatePushbutton(row, "filesb_btn",
    (XtCallbackProc) manageCB,
    (XtPointer) &filesb);

(void) CreatePushbutton(row, "ext_btn",
    (XtCallbackProc) manageCB,
    (XtPointer) &extenddlg);

(void) CreatePushbutton(row, "cust_btn",
    (XtCallbackProc) manageCB,
    (XtPointer) &cust);

(void) CreatePushbutton(row, "exit",
    (XtCallbackProc) exitCB,
    (XtPointer) NULL);

XtRealizeWidget(parent);
XtAppMainLoop(app_context);

return 0;

}   /* main */

/* end of file dialtest.c */
```

Our test program uses the following resource file:

```
! Resource file for dialtest.c in
! Chapter 7 of Power Programming Motif.
!
*fontList:       lucidasans-12
*background:     lightgrey

*Ppm*title: Dialog Test

*warning.messageString: This is a warning dialog.
*warning.dialogTitle:   Warning Dialog

*working.messageString: Whistle while you work...
```

```
*working.dialogTitle:      Working Dialog

*error.dialogTitle:        Error Dialog
*error.messageString:      When in danger\n\
 or in doubt,\n\
 run in circles,\n\
 scream and shout.

*info.dialogTitle:         Information Dialog
*info.messageString:       Elm:\n New electronic mail\
 has arrived\n\
from kreichard@mcimail.com.
*question.dialogTitle:     Question Dialog
*question.messageString:   Are you sure you want to\
\n\n Delete all files on disk?

*prompt.selectionLabelString:  This is a prompt.\n\
Enter Something.
*prompt.dialogTitle:               Prompt Dialog

*filesb.filterLabelString: Enter file filter below:
*filesb.dialogTitle:       File Selection Box

*extenddlg.dialogTitle:            Extended Dialog
*extenddlg.selectionLabelString: Prompt

! Pushbuttons
*working_btn.labelString:  Create Working Dialog...
*error_btn.labelString:    Create Error Dialog...
*prompt_btn.labelString:   Create Prompt Dialog...
*question_btn.labelString: Create Question Dialog...
*info_btn.labelString:     Create Information Dialog...
*warning_btn.labelString:  Create Warning Dialog...
*filesb_btn.labelString:   Create File Selection Dialog...
*ext_btn.labelString:      Create Extended Dialog...
*cust_btn.labelString:     Create a Custom Dialog...
*exit.labelString:         Exit
! Custom dialog
*cust.title:          Custom Dialog
*label1.labelString: Label 1 in custom dialog
*label2.labelString: Label 2 in custom dialog
*ok.labelString:      OK
*cancel.labelString: Cancel
*help.labelString:   Help
! end of resource file
```

As usual, name this file **Ppm** and place it in your home directory.

Running the Dialog Test Program

When you run this program, you'll see a window full of pushbuttons, as shown in Figure 7.11.

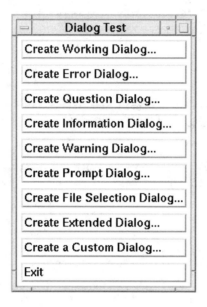

Figure 7.11 *The main dialtest window.*

Each pushbutton calls up (manages) a separate dialog. Pushing again unmanages the dialog. We've already shown these dialogs in the text of this chapter.

SUMMARY

In this chapter, we introduced Motif's dialog widgets and showed how to create some of the more common dialogs, including the prompt dialog and the file-selection box. These dialogs are created using Motif's convenience routines.

This chapter covered the basic rules for Motif dialogs and introduced the bulletin-board and form dialogs—commonly used to create custom dialogs.

Creating a dialog by hand is a tough task, but most Motif applications will need to do this at one time or another. The code in **dialtest.c** can be used as an example whenever you want to roll your own dialogs.

In the next chapter, we'll tackle one of the most confusing aspects of Motif programming: dealing with Motif's proprietary string format, `XmString`.

MOTIF FUNCTIONS AND MACROS INTRODUCED IN THIS CHAPTER

```
XmCreateBulletinBoardDialog
XmCreateErrorDialog
XmCreateFileSelectionDialog
XmCreateFormDialog
XmCreateInformationDialog
XmCreateMessageDialog
XmCreatePromptDialog
XmCreateQuestionDialog
XmCreateTemplateDialog
XmCreateWarningDialog
XmCreateWorkingDialog
XmFileSelectionBoxGetChild
XmFileSelectionDoSearch
XmMessageBoxGetChild
XmSelectionBoxGetChild
```

X TOOLKIT INTRINSICS FUNCTIONS AND MACROS INTRODUCED IN THIS CHAPTER

```
XtIsManaged
XtSetSensitive
XtUnmanageChild
```

CHAPTER 8

Motif Text Strings and Fonts

This chapter introduces:

- Motif's text format
- Fonts under the X Window System
- How Motif `XmStrings` relate to fonts
- Font lists
- Working with multifont text
- Building strings with font tags
- `XmString` segments
- Extracting data from font-list entries
- Extracting a C string from an `XmString`
- Fonts and resource files
- Listing available fonts with *xlsfonts*

295

MOTIF'S TEXT FORMAT

Motif uses its own text string format, XmString. An XmString is a specially formatted string that Motif uses to allow for international character sets and text that goes left-to-right and right-to-left. XmStrings may also cross multiple lines and use multiple fonts. Just about every Motif widget that uses text (except for XmText and XmTextField) uses XmStrings for the text it displays. Thus, we find knowledge of the XmString format essential for developing Motif applications.

SHORTCUT

Converting Strings

Since most of the text in your applications is probably stored in the traditional C string format (a NULL-terminated array of type char), you'll need routines to convert C strings back and forth to the XmString format.

Create an XmString from a C string with XmStringCreateSimple:

```
XmString XmStringCreateSimple(char* string)
```

When you're done with an XmString, free the memory with XmStringFree:

```
void XmStringFree(XmString motif_string)
```

Extract a C string from an XmString with XmStringGetLtoR:

```
Boolean XmStringGetLtoR(XmString xmstring,
            XmStringCharSet charset,
            char** string)  /* RETURN */
```

Free the returned *string* with XtFree when done. Note that XmStringGetLtoR works only for left-to-right text and may fail with Arabic or Hebrew.

XmStrings in Resource Files

Up to now we've used X resource files to convert C strings to XmStrings. For example, a label widget (XmLabel) supports a labelString resource of type XmString. Yet, in a resource file, you can place a normal string, such as the following:

```
*exitchoice.labelString:    Exit
```

In the above example, Motif will translate the text string *Exit* into an XmString.

In this short chapter, though, we go into the methods you can use in your C programs to create, extract, compare, and modify XmStrings. We also cover fonts and how you build multifont text strings.

CREATING XMSTRINGS

The main functions used to create XmStrings include:

- XmStringCreateSimple
- XmStringCreateLocalized
- XmStringCreateLtoR
- XmStringCreate

You create an XmString from a traditional NULL-terminated C string. With Motif 1.2, the preferred method to create an XmString is to call XmStringCreateLocalized:

```
XmString XmStringCreateLocalized(char* string)
```

XmStringCreateLocalized creates an XmString in the current locale. (We cover locales in Chapter 27 on internationalization.)

Unfortunately, since XmStringCreateLocalized is new in Motif 1.2, much of your code won't be able to use the function. If that's the case, then try XmStringCreateSimple:

```
XmString XmStringCreateSimple(char* string)
```

XmStringCreateSimple creates an XmString using the default locale. This is usually what you want anyway.

The old method for creating XmStrings was to use XmStringCreateLtoR. XmStringCreateLtoR creates an XmString that goes from left to right, the direction of text used by most Western languages:

```
XmString XmStringCreateLtoR(char* string,
                char* tag)
```

XmStringCreateLtoR creates a left-to-right XmString. It adds a neat property in that every new line, \n, in the string is converted to an XmString *separator* (one of the possible components in an XmString). You should use XmStringCreateLocalized instead of XmStringCreateLtoR with Motif 1.2.

N O T E

Prior to Motif 1.2, XmStringCreateLtoR took the following parameters:

```
XmString XmStringCreateLtoR(char* string,
                XmStringCharSet charset)
```

In Motif 1.2, the *charset* becomes a *font-list tag*. The default tag is XmFONTLIST_DEFAULT_TAG. Before, the default charset was XmSTRING_DEFAULT_CHARSET. Some Motif 1.2 header files still show the old XmStringCharSet parameter.

XmStringCreate creates a Motif string from a regular NULL-terminated C string with the given font-list tag:

```
XmString XmStringCreate(char* string,
                char* tag)
```

In most cases, you'll use the default tag. XmStringCreate is useful when you want to create multifont text, which we cover below in the "Displaying Multifont Text" section.

N O T E

All the functions that create XmStrings allocate memory dynamically with malloc. This may become a performance problem.

Freeing XmStrings

When you're done with an XmString, free the memory with XmStringFree:

```
void XmStringFree(XmString motif_string)
```

Using XmStrings to Set Resources

With this information, we can now set the labelString resource for XmLabel, XmPushButton, and XmToggleButton widgets. The labelString resource, as we covered in Chapter 2, is of type XmString.

In your code, you can use the following SetLabel function to set the labelString resource from a NULL-terminated C string:

```
void SetLabel(Widget widget, char* string)

{   /* SetLabel */
    XmString    xmstring;

    xmstring = XmStringCreateSimple(string);

    XtVaSetValues(widget,
        XmNlabelString, xmstring,
        NULL);

    XmStringFree(xmstring);

}   /* SetLabel */
```

The SetLabel function takes any widget that supports the labelString resource and a C string as parameters. The C string contains the new text for the label widget.

Extracting a C String from an XmString

After you've created an XmString, the next step is to extract a traditional C string back from the XmString. We do this to extract the user-entered data from a prompt dialog, a file-selection dialog (covered in the last chapter), or from the XmList widget (covered in the next chapter). In fact, you'll find that a lot of your Motif code does exactly that: converts C strings to XmStrings and then later converts them back again.

XmStringGetLtoR pulls a plain old C string from an XmString:

```
Boolean XmStringGetLtoR(XmString xmstring,
        XmStringCharSet charset,
        char** string)  /* RETURN */
```

The *LtoR* in XmStringGetLtoR stands for left-to-right, the direction of most Western text. Free the returned *string* with XtFree when done.

In your code, you can call XmStringGetLtoR as follows:

```
XmString    xmstring;
char*       string;

XmStringGetLtoR(xmstring,
                XmSTRING_DEFAULT_CHARSET,
                &string);

printf("The string is %s\n", string);

XtFree(string);
```

`XmStringGetLtoR` returns *True* if `XmStringGetLtoR` found a string with the proper charset inside the `XmString`; it returns `False` otherwise. If you use `XmSTRING_DEFAULT_CHARSET`, you should always match.

Copying and Appending XmStrings

You can copy an `XmString` with `XmStringCopy`:

```
XmString XmStringCopy(XmString xmstring)
```

`XmStringConcat` appends *xmstring2* onto the end of *xmstring1*. The end of *xmstring1* depends on the string order (left-to-right or right-to-left) and how many lines are in *xmstring1*:

```
XmString XmStringConcat(XmString xmstring1,
            XmString xmstring2)
```

Comparing XmStrings

Motif supports a number of functions to compare `XmStrings`, including:

- `XmStringByteCompare`
- `XmStringCompare`
- `XmStringEmpty`

You can compare two `XmStrings` with `XmStringCompare`:

```
Boolean XmStringCompare(XmString xmstring1,
            XmString xmstring2)
```

`XmStringCompare` returns True if both strings are equivalent. In your code, you can call `XmStringCompare` as follows:

```
XmString    xmstring1, xmstring2;
```

```
if (XmStringCompare(xmstring1, xmstring2) == True) {

    /* Both XmStrings are equivalent... */
}
```

If XmStringCompare is not sufficient, you can compare XmStrings byte-by-byte with XmStringByteCompare:

```
Boolean XmStringByteCompare(XmString xmstring1,
        XmString xmstring2)
```

NOTE XmStringByteCompare assumes that both XmStrings have the same font tag and direction. In addition, many widgets may change the internal data of an XmString to make it more efficient. Consequently, you should use XmStringCompare instead of XmStringByteCompare where possible.

To determine if an XmString is empty, use XmStringEmpty:

```
Boolean XmStringEmpty(XmString xmstring)
```

Determining the Size of XmStrings

There's a number of routines you can call to get a handle on how large a given XmString is, including:

- ◼ XmStringBaseLine
- ◼ XmStringExtent
- ◼ XmStringHeight
- ◼ XmStringLength
- ◼ XmStringLineCount
- ◼ XmStringWidth

Many of these routines require font-list parameters, which we introduce below in the "Font Lists" section. This is natural; the size of the text in pixels will always depend on the size of the font used to draw the text.

XmStringBaseline returns the *baseline*, the distance between the text baseline of the first line of text in *xmstring* and the top of the character box:

```
Dimension XmStringBaseline(XmFontList fontlist,
               XmString xmstring)
```

XmStringExtent determines the size of the smallest rectangle that can enclose the given *xmstring* using the given *fontlist*:

```
void XmStringExtent(XmFontList fontlist,
         XmString xmstring,
         Dimension* width,     /* RETURN */
         Dimension* height)    /* RETURN */
```

To get the length in bytes of an **XmString**, use **XmStringLength**:

```
int XmStringLength(XmString xmstring)
```

XmStringLength includes the text, the font tags, and any separators in the **XmString**.

XmStringLineCount returns the number of separators—plus 1—in the given **XmString**:

```
int XmStringLineCount(XmString xmstring)
```

You can determine the height and width of an **XmString**, using a given *fontlist*, with **XmStringHeight** and **XmStringWidth**:

```
Dimension XmStringHeight(XmFontList fontlist,
               XmString xmstring)

Dimension XmStringWidth(XmFontList fontlist,
               XmString xmstring)
```

Both routines check all the lines within the given *xmstring*. **XmStringHeight** totals the height of every line. **XmStringWidth** returns the widest width.

X WINDOW FONTS

Motif gets its font capabilities directly from the X Window System. Fonts are necessary because all the text in the **XmString** format is drawn to the screen using X fonts. We'll introduce fonts and font lists and then show how to use multiple fonts with one **XmString**.

You gain access to these different typefaces by loading fonts into the X server. A complete set of characters of one size of one typeface—including upper- and lowercase letters, punctuation marks and numerals—is called a *font*. All fonts in X are bitmaps; each character has a specific bitpattern within the font. Each face, style, and size correspond to at least one font—Times at 25 pixels high and Times at 12 pixels high are two different fonts in X terminology. The X11 Release 5 font server offers the ability to scale fonts, and many font servers support outline, scalable fonts. This font server serves fonts to the X server. Your X applications, though, still treat these fonts as bitmaps, once scaled to the proper size. Some typical fonts are shown in Figure 8.1

Times Roman	Helvetica	Courier
Times Roman Italic	*Helvetica Italic*	*Courier Italic*
Times Roman Bold	**Helvetica Bold**	Courier Bold

Figure 8.1 *Some typical fonts.*

However, there are a few tricks to dealing with X fonts. For instance, not all X servers support all fonts. You have to carefully design your applications to have a set of fallback fonts, in case the desired fonts are not available. Sun's OpenWindows, for example, provides a set of Open Look fonts that are not commonly available on other platforms.

In addition, a font is either single-byte (8-bit) or two-byte (16-bit). Single-byte fonts can handle up to 256 characters, whereas the two-byte fonts can handle up to 65,536 characters. Text in Japanese, Chinese, or Korean, for example, requires many more than 256 characters.

Tracking Down What Fonts Are Available

A standard X application program called *xlsfonts* lists the available fonts on a workstation. Using this program will tell you what fonts are available to the system. Running *xlsfonts* on a Release 4 or higher X server will result in pages and pages of text output. Release 5 adds a font server, which adds even more fonts to the mix.

Here's some sample output from *xlsfonts*:

```
-adobe-courier-medium-o-normal--8-80-75-75-m-50-iso8859-1
-adobe-courier-medium-r-normal--10-100-75-75-m-60-iso8859-1
-adobe-courier-medium-r-normal--11-80-100-100-m-60-iso8859-1
-adobe-courier-medium-r-normal--12-120-75-75-m-70-iso8859-1
-adobe-times-medium-r-normal--24-240-75-75-p-124-iso8859-1
9x15
8x13
fixed
cursor
```

You can abbreviate the long names using an asterisk as a wildcard.

For more information on X fonts, including how to determine the size of a given font, you may want to look up *Professional Graphics Programming in the X Window System* and *X Window Applications Programming* (Johnson and Reichard, MIS: Press).

X Window Fonts and Motif

Motif complicates text and fonts with the concept of Motif's compound strings and font lists. The complications added by Motif consist mainly of a new format for font sets called a *font list* and the Motif string format, XmString, which we covered above.

In Motif terminology, a *font* is a collection of glyphs or bitmap images associated with a given character set. A *font set* is the collection of fonts needed to display text in a given language. English, for example, needs a font set with only one font. Japanese, though, needs at least three fonts in a font set. A *font list* is then a collection of font sets or fonts, each of which is in a font-list entry. Most of the font-list code was added in Motif 1.2 to support X11 Release 5's internationalization. Each element in a font list has a *font-list tag*, an arbitrary name used to identify a font. We'll use font-list tags to display multifont text in an XmString. Finally, a *font-list entry* holds either a font or a font set.

A Motif font list may support a number of font names. For example, Japanese text may require a font for Kanji, another for Kana, and a third for Latin (that's ASCII to the rest of us). For example, you could place a number of font names in a Motif *fontList* resource:

```
*fontList:\
  -JIS-fixed-medium-r-normal--26-180-100-100-c-240,\
  -GB-fixed-medium-r-normal--26-180-100-100-c-240,\
  -adobe-courier-medium-r-normal--25-180-100-100-m-150
```

You can also provide arbitrary font-list tags:

```
*fontList:\
  -*-courier-medium-r-normal--25-180-100-100-m-150=ROMAN,
  -*-courier-bold-r-normal--25-180-100-100-m-150=BOLD
```

In this case, *ROMAN* and *BOLD* are purely arbitrary tags. We could use them, for example, to draw text using normal (Roman) and bold fonts.

N O T E   The documentation for Motif is unclear regarding the use of a colon (:) rather than an equal sign (=) as a font-tag delimiter. The basic idea is to associate a tag with a whole set of fonts or just a single font. The actual syntax is rather complex and poorly described in the official literature. To specify a single font associated with a tag in a font list, use:

> *font_name = tag*

To tie a whole font set to a *single* tag, use:

> *font_name ; font_name ; font_name : tag*

We found, though, that anything with colons (:) fails miserably with Motif 1.1.

You can use as many font names as necessary. In both of the above examples, the spaces are added for clarity.

Character Sets

Much of the added complexity of font lists comes from internationalization concerns. Computing around the world requires multiple character sets, some of which, such as Chinese, tend to be very large. In X, a character set is a mapping between byte-codes and characters. For example, the ISO 8859-1 character set, often called Latin-1 (a superset of US ASCII that covers most languages in Western Europe) uses the value 65 for an uppercase letter *A*. Most Asian languages require multiple bytes per character. Some common character sets include are listed in Table 8.1.

Most fonts in X are then created to a single character set. For example, most of the X fonts use the ISO 8859-1 character set.

The Motif routines that convert resources from the strings in resource files to actual data types and values handle the onerous chore of converting the above to an XmFontList structure. In fact, you may want to avoid this problem entirely and let the user specify all fonts in resource files.

Table 8.1 *Common character sets.*

Language	Character Set
Cyrillic Russian	ISO 8859-5
Japanese	UJIS, Shift JIS
U.S. English	ASCII, ISO 8859-1

FONT LISTS

The basic data structure for a font list is the XmFontList structure. The XmFontList structure is considered opaque and hidden by the Motif toolkit in the include file <Xm/Xm.h>:

```
/* opaque to outside */
typedef struct _XmFontListRec  *XmFontList;
```

Note that the font-list code gets complicated right away. If you don't think you'll need to use font lists, you can skip ahead to the section on "Displaying Multifont Text."

Creating Font Lists

Up to now, we've used X resource files to take care of all the hassles of creating font lists. In your code, the first thing you need to do with font lists is create one. XmFontListCreate creates a new font list, starting with a single font using the given *charset*:

```
XmFontList XmFontListCreate(XFontStruct* font_struct,
        XmStringCharSet charset)
```

You can pass XmSTRING_DEFAULT_CHARSET for the *charset*.

The XFontStruct is a low-level X library structure that identifies a single X font. See one of our other books, *Professional Graphics Programming in the X Window System* (MIS: Press, 1993), for more information on the XFontStruct structure.

To add a font to a font list, use XmFontListAdd:

```
XmFontList XmFontListAdd(XmFontList old_fontlist,
            XFontStruct* font_struct,
            XmStringCharSet charset)
```

XmFontListAdd returns a new font list built from the old and the new font.

When you're done with a font list, free it with XmFontListFree:

```
void XmFontListFree(XmFontList fontlist)
```

Font-List Entries in Motif 1.2

With Motif 1.2, you're supposed to make a font list from a set of font-list entries instead of calling XmFontListCreate.

Before you can call the new function XmFontListAppendEntry, you need to create an XmFontListEntry. To create a font list entry, use XmFontListEntryCreate:

```
XmFontListEntry XmFontListEntryCreate(char* tag,
            XmFontType type,
            XtPointer font)
```

XmFontListEntryCreate creates an XmFontListEntry from a *tag* and either a font or a font set. You can use either an XFontStruct pointer or an XFontSet. In each case, you cast the XtPointer *font* parameter to the proper type. In addition, you have to tell XmFontListEntryCreate which *type* of data you're passing. The *type* parameter does this, as listed in Table 8.2.

Table 8.2   *XmFontListEntryCreate parameters.*

Font Parameter	Type Parameter
XFontStruct*	XmFONT_IS_FONT
XFontSet	XmFONT_IS_FONTSET

The XmFontType data type holds one of XmFONT_IS_FONT or XmFONT_IS_FONTSET. The XmFontListEntry structure is another opaque data type.

If you haven't already loaded the font, or created the font set as the case may be, you can call XmFontListEntryLoad to both load the font and create an XmFontListEntry out of it:

```
XmFontListEntry XmFontListEntryLoad(Display* display,
                    char* fontname,
                    XmFontType type,
                    char* tag)
```

Again, the *type* parameter tells whether you want a font set (XmFONT_IS_FONTSET) and have a font-set name in the *fontname* parameter, or you just have a simple font name in the *fontname* parameter (with *type* set to XmFONT_IS_FONT).

You can append a font list entry to a full-blown font list using XmFontListAppendEntry:

```
XmFontList XmFontListAppendEntry(XmFontList old_fontlist,
                    XmFontListEntry entry)
```

XmFontListAppendEntry returns the new combined font list. If you don't have a font list already, you can pass NULL for *old_fontlist* and XmFontListAppendEntry will create a new font list from your XmFontListEntry.

When you're done with a font list entry, free it with XmFontListEntryFree:

```
void XmFontListEntryFree(XmFontListEntry* entry)
```

This frees the font-list *entry*, not the font list.

Extracting Data from Font-List Entries

To extract the XFontStruct pointer or XFontSet from a font-list entry, use XmFontListEntryGetFont:

```
XtPointer XmFontListEntryGetFont(XmFontListEntry entry,
        XmFontType* type)  /* RETURN */
```

The *type* parameter is set to XmFONT_IS_FONT if XmFontListEntryGet-Font returns an XFontStruct pointer. The *type* parameter is set to XmFONT_IS_FONTSET if the function returns an XFontSet.

DISPLAYING MULTIFONT TEXT

Now that we've covered font lists, we can use arbitrary font tags to display text in different fonts. A common use for this is to provide bold, roman, and italic fonts for text. We can then display our text using any or all of these fonts.

One way to do this, is to create XmStrings using arbitrary font tags, in our case *ROMAN*, *BOLD*, and *ITALIC*.

Before we can create a program, we need to build an XmString that contains segments of text with different font tags.

XmString Segments

To delve into the internals of the XmString format, a Motif compound string, stored in an XmString, holds one or more *segments*. Each segment may hold:

- text
- a font list tag (which used to be called a charset)
- a direction
- a separator (used in place of the newline character)

The font-list tag is an arbitrary name that you can use to make a text string use a particular font. For example, we make *ROMAN* and *BOLD* tags later on in this chapter to create a string that uses multiple fonts. In addition, there are conventions for font-list tags in countries such as Japan, which needs Kanji, Kana, and Latin fonts for everyday use. A default font list tag is XmFONTLIST_DEFAULT_TAG.

Building Strings with Font Tags

To build a string with arbitrary font tags, we can call XmStringCreate to create new XmStrings using the given tags. Then we concatenate the strings together, one at a time, using XmStringConcat. This builds a combined XmString where each segment in the string can potentially use a different font. The utility function, CombineStrings, below, handles this:

```
XmString CombineStrings(XmString old_xmstring,
    char* string,
    char* tag)

{   /* CombineStrings */
    XmString    new_xmstring;
    XmString    combined_xmstring;

    /* Create new string. */
    new_xmstring = XmStringCreate(string, tag);

    /* Now, combine. */
    if (old_xmstring != NULL) {

        /* Combine XmStrings. */
        combined_xmstring = XmStringConcat(old_xmstring,
            new_xmstring);

        /* Free memory. */
        XmStringFree(new_xmstring);

    } else {
        combined_xmstring = new_xmstring;
    }

    return combined_xmstring;

}   /* CombineStrings */
```

After we build together an XmString with multiple font tags, we need to then associate the XmString with a *fontList* resource. This *fontList* resource will then force our text to be displayed using the fonts from the font list.

In our case, we want to use *ROMAN* as a tag for roman or normal text, *BOLD* for bold text, and *ITALIC* for italic text. To do so, we set up a font list in a resource file as follows:

```
*font_test.fontList:\
  -*-helvetica-medium-r-normal--*-180-75-75-*-*=ROMAN,\
  -*-helvetica-bold-r-normal--*-180-75-75-*-*=BOLD, \
  -*-helvetica-medium-o-normal--*-180-75-75-*-*=ITALIC
```

All the fonts are the same size and all are the same family, Helvetica, so that the text looks fine together. We use a resource file because it's a lot simpler than programming our own font list, as you now understand after reading the font list section, above.

A PROGRAM TO DISPLAY MULTIFONT TEXT

A sample program that creates a Motif `XmLabel` widget and places text with multiple fonts into that widget appears below. Note the three calls to `CombineStrings` to combine strings with font tags.

```
/* multfont.c */
#include  <Xm/Xm.h>
#include  <Xm/Label.h>

/*
 * Creates a new XmString from an old XmString
 * and a new text string. The tag can be used to
 * determine the font.
 */

XmString CombineStrings(XmString old_xmstring,
    char* string,
    char* tag)

{   /* CombineStrings */
    XmString    new_xmstring;
    XmString    combined_xmstring;

    /* Create new string. */
    new_xmstring = XmStringCreate(string, tag);

    /* Now, combine. */
    if (old_xmstring != NULL) {

        /* Combine XmStrings. */
        combined_xmstring = XmStringConcat(old_xmstring,
            new_xmstring);

        /* Free memory. */
        XmStringFree(new_xmstring);

    } else {
        combined_xmstring = new_xmstring;
    }

    return combined_xmstring;

}   /* CombineStrings */
int main(int argc, char** argv)

{   /* main */
    XtAppContext    appcontext;
    Widget          parent;
    Widget          label;
    Arg             args[20];
```

```
Cardinal      n;
XmString      xmstring1, xmstring2, xmstring3;

/* Initialize X toolkit */
n = 0;
parent = XtAppInitialize(&appcontext,
        "Ppm",
        (XrmOptionDescList) NULL,
        0,
        &argc, argv,
        (String*) NULL,
        args, n);

/*
 * Create XmString components for
 * the various fonts.
 */
xmstring1 = CombineStrings( (XmString) NULL,
            "This is bold text, ",
            "BOLD");

xmstring2 = CombineStrings(xmstring1,
            " this is italic text, ",
            "ITALIC");

xmstring3 = CombineStrings(xmstring2,
            "and this is normal text.",
            "ROMAN");

/* Create a label widget to display the text. */
label = XtVaCreateManagedWidget("label",
        xmLabelWidgetClass, parent,
        XmNlabelString, xmstring3,
        NULL);

XtManageChild(label);

/* Free XmStrings. */
XmStringFree(xmstring1);
XmStringFree(xmstring2);
XmStringFree(xmstring3);

/* Create the windows. */
XtRealizeWidget(parent);
XtAppMainLoop(appcontext);

return 0;

}    /* main */

/* end of file multfont.c */
```

The resource file, which is necessary to specify more than one font, follows:

```
! Resource file for multfont.c in
! Chapter 8 of Power Programming Motif.
!
*fontList:        lucidasans-12
*background:      lightgrey

*Ppm*title: Multiple Font XmString

! Note how use use the font list tags
! ROMAN, BOLD and ITALIC.
*label.fontList:\
 -*-helvetica-medium-r-normal--*-180-75-75-*-*=ROMAN,\
 -*-helvetica-bold-r-normal--*-180-75-75-*-*=BOLD, \
 -*-helvetica-medium-o-normal--*-180-75-75-*-*=ITALIC
! end of resource file
```

Name this file **Ppm** and store it in your home directory.

The results of this program are shown in Figure 8.2.

Figure 8.2   *Multiple font text with Motif.*

Note the three fonts used for the text.

SUMMARY

Motif uses its own text string format, `XmString`. An `XmString` is a specially formatted string that Motif uses to allow for international character sets and text that goes left-to-right and right-to-left. `XmStrings` may also cross multiple lines and use multiple fonts. Just about every Motif widget that uses text (except for `XmText` and `XmTextField`) uses `XmStrings` for the text it displays. Thus we find knowledge of the `XmString` format essential for developing Motif applications. This chapter covered the ins and outs of `XmString` performance.

In addition, fonts and font management were introduced through our explanation of the X Window System's treatment of fonts.

MOTIF FUNCTIONS AND MACROS INTRODUCED IN THIS CHAPTER

```
XmStringBaseline
XmStringByteCompare
XmStringCompare
XmStringConcat
XmStringCopy
XmStringCreate
XmStringCreateLocalized
XmStringCreateLtoR
XmStringCreateSimple
XmStringEmpty
XmStringExtent
XmStringFree
XmStringGetLtoR
XmStringLength
XmStringLineCount
XmStringHeight
XmStringWidth
XmFontListAdd
XmFontListAppendEntry
XmFontListCreate
XmFontListEntryCreate
XmFontListEntryLoad
XmFontListEntryFree
XmFontListFree
XmFontListEntryGetFont
XmFontListEntryGetTag
```

CHAPTER 9

More Motif Widgets

This chapter introduces a number of handy Motif widgets, including:

- XmList
- XmScale
- XmArrowButton
- XmScrolledWindow
- XmScrollBar

WORKING WITH MOTIF WIDGETS

This chapter extends our set of Motif widgets for building user interfaces. With this chapter, we've rounded out our discussion of what you need to start building Motif applications. The widgets we cover here provide useful features we've needed in most of our Motif programs. These widgets include:

■ The list widget, which displays a list of choices to the user, with optional scroll bars

■ The scale widget, a valuator that allows users to set analog values

■ The arrow-button widget, often used to increment values

■ The scrolled-window widget, used to scroll other widgets

■ The scroll-bar widget, which holds an individual scroll bar

SHORTCUT

Fast Track to Scrolled Lists

To quickly get up to speed with the list widget, create a scrolled list with XmCreateScrolledList:

```
#include <Xm/List.h>

Widget          list, parent;
Arg             args[10];
Cardinal        n;
XtCallbackProc  callback;
XtPointer       client_data;

/* ... */

n = 0;
XtSetArg(args[n], XmNselectionPolicy,
    XmSINGLE_SELECT); n++;
XtSetArg(args[n], XmNscrollBarDisplayPolicy,
    XmSTATIC); n++;

list = XmCreateScrolledList(parent,
        "list", args, n);

XtAddCallback(list,
    XmNsingleSelectionCallback,
    callback, client_data);

XtManageChild(list);
```

Add items to the list with `XmListAddItemUnselected`:

```
XmString    xmstring;

XmListAddItemUnselected(list,
    xmstring,
    0); /* position 0 means append. */
```

This should get you going with the list widget. We cover the rest below.

LIST WIDGETS

The `XmList` widget allows the user to select one (or more) choices from a list. You can add scroll bars, much like the `XmText` widget. We show a list widget in Figure 9.1, and summarize it in Table 9.1.

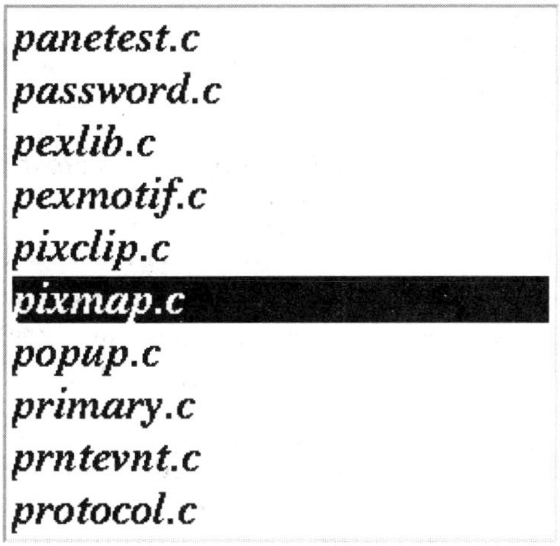

panetest.c
password.c
pexlib.c
pexmotif.c
pixclip.c
pixmap.c
popup.c
primary.c
prntevnt.c
protocol.c

Figure 9.1   *A list widget.*

The list widget manages a number of items and allows the user to scroll through those items (with optional scroll bars). The user can then choose items from the list. With every choice, the list widget calls an optional callback function.

We've already seen a list widget in the file-selection box in Chapter 7. In this chapter, though, we're going to delve in far more depth into the list widget.

Table 9.1 *The XmList widget class.*

Widget class:	`XmList`
Class pointer:	`xmListWidgetClass`
Include file:	`<Xm/List.h>`
Create with:	`XmCreateList`

There are two main functions to create a list widget, `XmCreateList` and `XmCreateScrolledList`:

```
#include <Xm/List.h>

Widget XmCreateList(Widget parent,
     char* widget_name,
     ArgList args
     Cardinal number_args)

Widget XmCreateScrolledList(Widget parent,
     char* widget_name,
     ArgList args
     Cardinal number_args)
```

Call `XtManageChild` to manage a list widget after creation.

`XmCreateList` creates a list widget, obviously, while `XmCreateScrolledList` creates a scrolled-window widget and then a list widget as a child of the scrolled-window widget. We saw this scrolled-window widget in the previous chapter. You can view `XmCreateList` as an analog to `XmCreateText` and `XmCreateScrolledList` as an analog to `XmCreateScrolledText`.

To get the widget ID of the parent scrolled-window widget or to get the widget ID of the parent of any widget, use the X toolkit function `XtParent`, introduced in Chapter 5.

The two most common list operations are adding items into a list and selecting items from a list. Selecting items from a list is an incredibly complex operation.

Selecting Items in a List

There are four selection polices that govern how the user selects items in a list. These four polices are:

- XmBROWSE_SELECT
- XmEXTENDED_SELECT
- XmMULTIPLE_SELECT
- XmSINGLE_SELECT

Each of these policies acts differently, and each policy has its own callback type. You'll probably want to modify the *listtest* program, below, to try out all four of these selection types, so you'll get a better understanding of how they all work.

Single Selection

The single-selection policy is the easiest to use and understand. When the user clicks (using mouse button 1, in the default case at least) on an item, that item becomes selected. Any previously selected item becomes unselected, which means that only one single item may be selected at a time—hence the term *single selection*. To set the selection policy, you place a value in the selectionPolicy resource (XmNselectionPolicy in C programs). To set the selection policy to single selection, set the selectionPolicy resource to XmSINGLE_SELECT:

```
Arg       args[10];
Cardinal  n;

n = 0;
XtSetArg(args[n], XmNselectionPolicy,
    XmSINGLE_SELECT);
n++;

/* Create widget... */
```

Browse Selection

With browse selection, the user can move the mouse pointer over a number of items while the mouse button is pressed. Each item is selected when the mouse pointer moves on top of the item and unselected when the mouse pointer moves away from the item. When the mouse button is released, the item underneath the mouse pointer, if there is one, is selected. Only one item can still be selected at a time, like the single-selection policy.

Multiple Selection

With multiple selection, the user clicks on any item, and it becomes selected. If other items were already selected, then those other items remain selected (thus multiple items can be selected). If the user clicks on an item that is already selected, then that item becomes unselected. This allows for noncontiguous selections in the list.

Extended Selection

With extended selection, the user can drag the mouse over a number of items while holding down mouse button 1. All these items then become selected. Unfortunately, any noncontiguous selected items are deselected by this feature. This limits the usefulness of the extended selection policy.

If you intend to use any selection policy other than single select, we strongly advise you to read and reread the *OSF/Motif Programmer's Reference* entry on XmList. (We also advise you to play with all four selection policies to get the hang of them. The nuances here can be tricky.) Of the selection policies, we find the single and multiple polices are the most useful.

List Callbacks

Each of the four selection policies has its own callback, as listed in Table 9.2.

Table 9.2   *List-callback resources.*

Resource Name	Name in C Programs
browseSelectionCallback	XmNbrowseSelectionCallback
defaultActionCallback	XmNdefaultActionCallback
extendedSelectionCallback	XmNextendedSelectionCallback
multipleSelectionCallback	XmNmultipleSelectionCallback
singleSelectionCallback	XmNsingleSelectionCallback

Set up the selection callbacks with XtAddCallback. You'll use only one of these selection policies at a time. You can also set up the defaultActionCallback along with one of the selection callbacks. This is the callback that is called on double-click events. That is, if the user double-clicks the mouse button over a list item, the list widget will first call the selection callback (for the policy in use) and then call the defaultActionCallback.

All the different list callbacks send the same data structure as the call-backs' *call_data*, an XmListCallbackStruct structure:

```
typedef struct {
    int      reason;
    XEvent*  event;
    XmString item;
    int      item_length;
    int      item_position;
    XmString* selected_items;
    int      selected_item_count;
    int*     selected_item_positions;
    char     selection_type;
} XmListCallbackStruct;
```

The *item* field is the most important field in the XmListCallbackStruct structure, as this field contains the actual item selected (in Motif XmString format). The *item_position* field holds the position of the selected item.

The *reason* field is one of the constants listed in Table 9.3.

Table 9.3   *The list callback reason field.*

Constant	Meaning
XmCR_BROWSE_SELECT	Browse-selection callback
XmCR_DEFAULT_ACTION	Default action (double-click) callback
XmCR_EXTENDED_SELECT	Extended-selection callback
XmCR_MULTIPLE_SELECT	Multiple-selection callback
XmCR_SINGLE_SELECT	Single-selection callback

For the multiple- and extended-selection policies, the *selected_items* field points to an array of XmStrings, one for each selected item. The *selected_item_count* field tells how many total items are selected. The *selected_item_positions* is an array of integers that holds the position of each selected item.

The *selection_type* field applies only to the extended-selection policy. This field will have a value of XmINITIAL if the selection is the initial item. The value will be XmMODIFICATION if the selection extends a contiguous selection (usually with a **Shift**-mouse click) or XmADDITION if the selection added a noncontiguous item (usually with a **Ctrl**-mouse click).

Don't confuse XmEXTENDED_SELECT with XmCR_EXTENDED_SELECT. The former is the selectionPolicy value, and the latter is a possible value for the XmListCallbackStruct *reason* field. The two values are very similar, so watch out.

Here's a sample callback function for a single-selection policy list widget:

```
    /* List widget callback. */
void listCB(Widget widget,
    XtPointer client_data,
    XtPointer call_data)

{   /* listCb */
    XmListCallbackStruct*  ptr;
    char*                  string;

    ptr = (XmListCallbackStruct*) call_data;

    XmStringGetLtoR(ptr->item,
        XmSTRING_DEFAULT_CHARSET,
        &string);

    printf("Last selected item is [%s]",
        string);

    printf(" at position %d.\n",
        ptr->item_position);

    /* Free text string. */
    XtFree(string);

}   /* listCb */
```

Detecting Deselection

In addition to selecting items in a list, the user can undo the selection by deselecting an item. Usually clicking on an item toggles the state from deselected to selected or selected to deselected.

The problem comes with the multiple- and extended-selection policies. In this case, you don't know whether the item field of the XmListCallbackStruct holds the newly selected item or the item that was just deselected. Motif doesn't really help in this regard, so the workaround we came up with searches the list of selected item positions and sees if the value of the *item_position* field is in that list. If so, then you have a selection. If not, then the item was deselected.

The following code takes a pointer to an XmListCallbackStruct, which is passed to your callback function, and returns True if the list callback is for a selected item. The routine returns False if the list callback is for a deselected item. The code for the IsSelected function follows:

```
          /* Determine if selection or deselection. */
   Boolean IsSelected(XmListCallbackStruct* ptr)

   {    /* IsSelected */
       int     i;

       for (i = 0; i < ptr->selected_item_count; i++) {

           if (ptr->selected_item_positions[i] ==
               ptr->item_position) {

               return True;
           }
       }

       return False;

   }    /* IsSelected */
```

Note that the *selected_item_positions* and *selected_item_count* fields of the XmListCallbackStruct are valid only for the extended- and multiple-selection policies. If you try to access these fields from the single- selection callback, you'll likely get a core dump.

List Resources

In addition to the selectionPolicy, the list widget supports a number of other useful resources, as listed in Table 9.4.

Table 9.4 *XmList resources.*

Resource	Type	Default Value
itemCount	int	0
items	XmStringTable	NULL
listSizePolicy	unsigned char	XmVARIABLE
scrollBarDisplayPolicy	unsigned char	XmAS_NEEDED
selectedItemCount	int	0

continued

selectedItems	XmStringTable	NULL
selectionPolicy	unsigned char	XmBROWSE_SELECT
topPosition	int	1
visibleItemCount	int	*dynamic*

Specifying the Height of the List Widget

You can set the height of the list widget by setting the number of visible items. This list widget will then try to size itself to be tall enough to hold that many items. The visibleItemCount resource (XmNvisibleItemCount in C programs) holds this value.

Setting the visibleItemCount resource is a request. The list widget or the list's parent are all free to refuse the resize request.

Controlling List Scroll Bars

The scrollBarDisplayPolicy resource (XmNscrollBarDisplayPolicy in C programs) specifies the policy used for displaying the vertical scroll bar. This policy can be XmAS_NEEDED or XmSTATIC. The default is XmAS_NEEDED. With this value, the vertical scroll bar will be displayed only if there are more items in the list than there are visible items. With a scrollBarDisplayPolicy of XmSTATIC, the vertical scroll bar will always be visible.

The horizontal scroll bar depends on the value of another resource, the listSizePolicy resource (XmNlistSizePolicy in C programs). The listSizePolicy resource can have one of the following values:

■ XmCONSTANT

■ XmRESIZE_IF_POSSIBLE

■ XmVARIABLE

The default is XmVARIABLE. XmVARIABLE means that the list widget will try to grow to the width of the widest item—thus no horizontal scroll bar will be visible. With a value of XmCONSTANT, a horizontal scroll bar is added when necessary, and the list is not made wider. With a value of XmRESIZE_IF_POSSIBLE, the list will first try to resize itself so that it fits the widest item within the list. If the list cannot grow that wide, then a horizontal scroll bar is added.

Getting the Number of Items in a List

The itemCount resource (XmNitemCount in C programs) keeps a count of the number of items in the list. This resource is automatically updated when you add or delete items in the list.

The number of items should reflect the actual number of items in the list. You are asking for problems if you set the number of items to reflect a value that is not accurate. Normally you'll treat this as a read-only value.

The items resource (XmNitems in C programs) is the current list. This resource is an array of XmStrings. We've found it easier to use the function XmListAddItem or XmListAddItemUnselected to add an item to the list than it is to mess with the items resource.

Adding Items to a List

To add an item to a list, you can use XmListAddItem or XmListAddItemUnselected. Both functions take the same parameters:

```
#include <Xm/List.h>

void XmListAddItem(Widget widget,
        XmString item,
        int position)

void XmListAddItemUnselected(Widget widget,
        XmString item,
        int position)
```

The difference between XmListAddItem and XmListAddItemUnselected is minor. XmListAddItemUnselected makes sure the new item is not added to the list being already selected. If you add an item to a list between two selected items, your new item may become selected depending on the selection policy in use. To avoid any problems in this area, we always use XmListAddItemUnselected.

The position parameter specifies where in the list you want to add the new item. The first position in the list has position 1. Since much of C programming assumes you start counting at zero, this is a common "gotcha" in Motif programming. Remember that the first position in the list is position 1. Position zero (0) is used to specify the last position in the list. If you want to append an item to the end of a list, pass a *position* of 0.

NOTE

If you add more than 1,000 or so items to a list, you may experience severe performance problems.

The function `AppendToList`, below, adds an item, in a regular C string, to the given position in a list. `AppendToList` first converts the new item to an `XmString` type and then calls `XmListAddItemUnselected`. The code follows:

```
void AppendToList(Widget list, char* item)

{   /* AppendToList */
    XmString    xmstring;

    xmstring = XmStringCreateSimple(item);

    XmListAddItemUnselected(list,
        xmstring,
        0); /* position 0 means append. */

    XmStringFree(xmstring);

}   /* AppendToList */
```

To add a number of items at once, use `XmListAddItems` or `XmListAddItemsUnselected`:

```
void XmListAddItems(Widget widget,
        XmString* items,
        int number_items,
        int position)

void XmListAddItemsUnselected(Widget widget,
        XmString* items,
        int number_items,
        int position)
```

Determining How Many Items Are in a List

Since the `itemCount` resource is automatically updated when we add an item to the list using `XmListAddItem` or `XmListAddItemUnselected`, we can read the value of this resource to determine how many items are presently in the list.

The function `NumberListItems`, below, does just that and returns the number of items in the list:

```
/* Return number of items in list. */
```

```
    int NumberListItems(Widget list)

{   /* NumberListItems */
    int number_items;

    XtVaGetValues(list,
        XmNitemCount, &number_items,
        NULL);

    return number_items;

}   /* NumberListItems */
```

Removing Items From a List

There are a number of functions to delete an item or a number of items from a list. The function to clear out all items from a list is XmListDeleteAllItems:

```
    void XmListDeleteAllItems(Widget widget)
```

This function is really useful when you have a list widget that you want to clear out and then fill with a new set of items.

Before deleting all the items in a list, it's a good idea to deselect them all, so the list's pointers to the selected items don't become invalid. Call XmListDeselectAllItems to deselect all the items in a list:

```
    void XmListDeselectAllItems(Widget widget)
```

We always call XmListDeselectAllItems before clearing out a list.

XmListDeleteItem deletes a single item from a list. Unfortunately, it is only useful when you know exactly what you want to delete. To use XmListDeleteItem, first create a Motif XmString and fill it with the item you want removed from the list. Then call XmListDeleteItem:

```
    void XmListDeleteItem(Widget widget,
        XmString item)
```

To delete a number of items, use:

```
    void XmListDeleteItems(Widget widget,
        XmString* items,
        int number_items)
```

Unless you know exactly what you want to delete, XmListDeleteItem won't help. More often than not you'll know the position of what you want to delete, but not the actual contents of the list at that position. In that case, use XmListDeletePos:

```
void XmListDeletePos(Widget widget,
    int position)
```

To delete a number of items starting at a given position, use XmListDeleteItemsPos:

```
void XmListDeleteItemsPos(Widget widget,
    int number_items,
    int position)
```

As above, position 1 is the first item in the list. If you use a position of zero (0), calling XmListDeletePos means to delete the last item in the list.

Selecting and Deselecting Items

To select an item, use XmListSelectItem:

```
void XmListSelectItem(Widget widget,
    XmString item,
    Boolean notify)
```

The *notify* parameter specifies whether (True) or not (False) to call the current selection callback.

To select by position, call XmListSelectPos:

```
void XmListSelectPos(Widget widget,
    int position,
    Boolean notify)
```

You can also deselect individual items in a list with XmListDeselectItem and XmListDeselectPos:

```
void XmListDeselectItem(Widget widget,
    XmString item)
```

```
void XmListDeselectPos(Widget widget,
    int position)
```

Moving to a Given Position in the List

In your applications, you may have a particular item in a list that you want the user to see. For example, you may want to start out at the last choice a user made. Or maybe the list is the result of some query and you want a particular item to be at the top of the list display.

XmListSetItem jumps a list to the given item. That item will be shown as the top item in the list widget's window:

```
void XmListSetItem(Widget widget,
        XmString item)
```

This function will not change the ordering in the list, just what is currently displayed, as the user can still use the scroll bars to move the list display to any position desired.

Before using XmListSetItem, you must create and fill a Motif XmString with the item you are looking for. This usually isn't very efficient, which is why Motif provides XmListSetPos.

XmListSetPos works like XmListSetItem, but XmListSetPos sets the top of the visible list display to a given item number:

```
void XmListSetPos(Widget widget,
        int position)
```

Remember that position 1 is the first item in the list. Position 2 is the second item in the list, while position zero (0) is the last item in the list.

A Program to Show How the List Widget Works

The *listtest* program creates a simple scrolled-list widget and fills it with eight items. When you click on an item, the function listCB will print out the item you clicked on.

The function CreateScrolledList creates a scrolled list with a given selection policy and shows how to set up the proper callback functions. The *listtest* program defaults to the single-selection policy (the easiest), but we suggest you try all four policies. In our programs, we tend to stick to the single- and multiple-selection policies.

Pushbuttons allow you to clear the list, append an item onto the list, and quit the program. For appending, the appendCB function appends a new item onto the list and then sets that item to be the top position, using XmListSetPos. This makes the list scroll to the newest entry.

We've made this program as simple as possible to concentrate just on the list widget, since you'll no doubt use lists in just about every application you write. You'll learn the most if you experiment around with all the list resources described above. The code follows:

```
/* listtest.c */
#include <Xm/Xm.h>
#include <Xm/List.h>
#include <Xm/PanedW.h>
#include <Xm/RowColumn.h>
#include <stdio.h>

extern Widget
CreatePushbutton(Widget parent, char* name,
    XtCallbackProc callback,
    XtPointer client_data);

    /* Callback to exit. */
void exitCB(Widget widget,
    XtPointer client_data,
    XtPointer call_data)

{   /* exitCB */

    exit(0);

}   /* exitCB */

    /* List widget callback. */
void listCB(Widget widget,
    XtPointer client_data,
    XtPointer call_data)

{   /* listCb */
    XmListCallbackStruct*  ptr;
    char*                  string;

    ptr = (XmListCallbackStruct*) call_data;

    XmStringGetLtoR(ptr->item,
        XmSTRING_DEFAULT_CHARSET,
        &string);

    printf("Last selected item is [%s]",
        string);

    printf(" at position %d.\n",
        ptr->item_position);

    printf("Callback type is ");

    switch(ptr->reason) {
        case XmCR_DEFAULT_ACTION:
            printf("Default action callback.\n");
            break;
        case XmCR_BROWSE_SELECT:
            printf("Browse select.\n");
            break;
        case XmCR_EXTENDED_SELECT:
            printf("Extended select.\n");
```

```
                break;
            case XmCR_MULTIPLE_SELECT:
                printf("Multiple select.\n");
                break;
            case XmCR_SINGLE_SELECT:
                printf("Single select.\n");
                break;
            default: ;
        }

        switch(ptr->selection_type) {
            case XmINITIAL:
                printf("\t Initial selection.\n");
                break;
            case XmMODIFICATION:
                printf("\t Modification to selection.\n");
                break;
            case XmADDITION:
                printf("\t Addition to selection.\n");
                break;
            default: ;
        }

        /* Free text string. */
        XtFree(string);

    }    /* listCb */

        /* Return number of items in list. */
    int NumberListItems(Widget list)

    {    /* NumberListItems */
        int number_items;

        XtVaGetValues(list,
            XmNitemCount, &number_items,
            NULL);

        return number_items;

    }    /* NumberListItems */

    void AppendToList(Widget list, char* item)

    {    /* AppendToList */
        XmString    xmstring;

        xmstring = XmStringCreateSimple(item);

        XmListAddItemUnselected(list,
            xmstring,
            0); /* position 0 means append. */

        XmStringFree(xmstring);
```

```
}    /* AppendToList */

    /* Callback to clear list. */
void clearCB(Widget widget,
    XtPointer client_data,
    XtPointer call_data)

{    /* clearCB */
    Widget*    list;

    /* List widget is passed as client data. */
    list = (Widget*) client_data;

    /* Make sure nothing is selected. */
    XmListDeselectAllItems( *list);

    /* Delete all list items. */
    XmListDeleteAllItems( *list);

}    /* clearCB */

    /* Callback to append item to list. */
void appendCB(Widget widget,
    XtPointer client_data,
    XtPointer call_data)

{    /* appendCB */
    Widget*    list;
    char       string[100];
    int        number_items;

    /* List widget is passed as client data. */
    list = (Widget*) client_data;

    /* Get number items. */
    number_items = NumberListItems( *list );

    /* Build string to append. */
    sprintf(string, "append_%d", number_items);

    AppendToList( *list, string);

    /*
     * Show the last position.
     * Try this like below and then
     * try commenting it out.
     */
    XmListSetPos( *list, 0);

}    /* appendCB */

Widget CreateScrolledList(Widget parent,
    char* name,
    int list_type,  /* e.g., XmCR_SINGLE_SELECT */
    XtCallbackProc callback,
```

```
    XtPointer client_data)

{   /* CreateScrolledList */
    Widget      list;
    Arg         args[20];
    Cardinal    n;

    n = 0;
    XtSetArg(args[n], XmNselectionPolicy,
        (unsigned char) list_type);
    n++;

    /* We always want a vertical scroll bar. */
    XtSetArg(args[n], XmNscrollBarDisplayPolicy,
        XmSTATIC);
    n++;

    list = XmCreateScrolledList(parent,
            name, args, n);

    /* Set up proper callback. */
    switch(list_type) {
        case XmBROWSE_SELECT:
            XtAddCallback(list,
                XmNbrowseSelectionCallback,
                callback, client_data);
            break;
        case XmEXTENDED_SELECT:
            XtAddCallback(list,
                XmNextendedSelectionCallback,
                callback, client_data);
            break;
        case XmMULTIPLE_SELECT:
            XtAddCallback(list,
                XmNmultipleSelectionCallback,
                callback, client_data);
            break;
        case XmSINGLE_SELECT:
            XtAddCallback(list,
                XmNsingleSelectionCallback,
                callback, client_data);
            break;
        default: ;
    }

    /* Set up double-click callback. */
    XtAddCallback(list,
        XmNdefaultActionCallback,
        callback, client_data);

    XtManageChild(list);

    return list;

}   /* CreateScrolledList */
```

```c
int main(int argc, char** argv)

{   /* main */
    Widget          parent;
    XtAppContext    app_context;
    Widget          pane;
    Widget          row;
    Widget          list;
    Widget          quit, clear, append;
    Arg             args[20];
    Cardinal        n;

    /* Initialize the X Toolkit. */
    n = 0;
    parent = XtAppInitialize(&app_context,
            "Ppm",
            (XrmOptionDescList) NULL,
            0,
            (Cardinal*) &argc,
            argv,
            (String*) NULL,
            args, n);

    /* Create paned window container. */
    n = 0;
    pane = XmCreatePanedWindow(parent,
            "pane", args, n);

    /* Create scrolled list. */
    list = CreateScrolledList(pane, "list",
            XmSINGLE_SELECT,
            /* XmMULTIPLE_SELECT,  */
            /* XmEXTENDED_SELECT,  */
            /* XmBROWSE_SELECT,  */
            (XtCallbackProc) listCB,
            (XtPointer) NULL);

    XtVaSetValues(list,
        XmNvisibleItemCount, 10,
        NULL);

    /* Add command-line parameters to list. */
    for (n = 0; n < argc; n++) {
        AppendToList(list, argv[n]);
    }

    /* Create button area at bottom. */
    n = 0;
    XtSetArg(args[n], XmNorientation,
        XmHORIZONTAL);
    n++;

    row = XmCreateRowColumn(pane,
        "row", args, n);
```

```
clear = CreatePushbutton(row,
            "clear",
            (XtCallbackProc) clearCB,
            (XtPointer) &list);

append = CreatePushbutton(row,
            "append",
            (XtCallbackProc) appendCB,
            (XtPointer) &list);

quit = CreatePushbutton(row,
            "quit",
            (XtCallbackProc) exitCB,
            (XtPointer) NULL);

XtManageChild(row);

XtManageChild(pane);

XtRealizeWidget(parent);
XtAppMainLoop(app_context);

return 0;

}    /* main */

/* end of file listtest.c */
```

The resource file for the *listtest* program follows:

```
! Resource file for listtest.c in
! Chapter 9 of Power Programming Motif.
!
*fontList:      lucidasans-12
*background:    lightgrey

*Ppm*title: List Test

*append.labelString:   Append Item
*clear.labelString:    Clear List
*quit.labelString:     Exit
! end of resource file
```

Name this file **Ppm** and store it in your home directory.

Running the Listtest Program

When you run the *listtest* program, you'll see a list like the one shown in Figure 9.2.

Figure 9.2   *The listtest program in action.*

Try selecting and unselecting items to see what happens.

SCALE WIDGETS

The scale widget allows users to adjust values using an analog scale or slide. Often called a *valuator* or *slider*, the scale widget provides a nice means to have the user select a value within a prespecified range. We show a scale widget in Figure 9.3 and describe the class in Table 9.5.

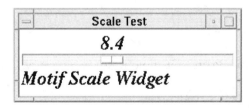

Figure 9.3   *A scale widget.*

Table 9.5   *The XmScale widget class.*

Widget class:	XmScale
Class pointer:	xmScaleWidgetClass
Include file:	<Xm/Scale.h>
Create with:	XmCreateScale

Use XmCreateScale to create a scale widget:

```
#include <Xm/Scale.h>

Widget XmCreateScale(Widget parent,
     char* widget_name,
     ArgList args
     Cardinal number_args)
```

As usual, call XtManageChild to manage the widget.

Scale widgets can go up, down, left, or right, all by setting resource values, including those listed in Table 9.6.

Table 9.6   *Scale resources.*

Resource	Type	Default Value
decimalPoints	short	0
maximum	int	100
minimum	int	0
orientation	unsigned char	XmVERTICAL
processingDirection	unsigned char	*dynamic*
showValue	Boolean	False
titleString	XmString	NULL
value	int	*dynamic*

Horizontal Scales

Horizontal scales are created by setting the orientation resource (XmNorientation in C programs). This value can be set to either

XmHORIZONTAL or XmVERTICAL. You can guess which one creates a horizontal scale.

With a horizontal scale, the high value on the scale (the maximum) can be on the right side or the left side. The processingDirection resource (XmNprocessingDirection in C programs) controls this. For horizontal scales, the choices are XmMAX_ON_RIGHT or XmMAX_ON_LEFT.

Vertical Scales

Vertical scales are also created by setting the orientation resource. This value should be set to XmVERTICAL for a vertical scale.

After the scale is set to go up and down, you need to decide where the maximum value is—on the top or on the bottom. Again, the processingDirection resource controls this. For vertical scales, the choices are XmMAX_ON_TOP or XmMAX_ON_BOTTOM. Figure 9.4 shows a vertical scale with XmMAX_ON_TOP.

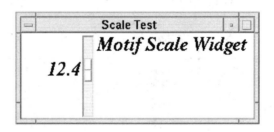

Figure 9.4 *A vertical scale with the max on top.*

Scale Values

So far we've mentioned maximum (and by assumption) minimum values. The scale widget allows the user to select a value between the maximum and minimum. You can, of course, set both of these, as the defaults and 100 and 0, respectively. The maximum (XmNmaximum in C programs) and minimum (XmNminimum in C programs) resources are both int types.

With the maximum and minimum (as well as the value), the scale widget just deals in integers. Yet the scale widget can display fixed-point decimal values, as you've seen in all the screen dumps in this chapter so far. What gives?

Well, the scale widget allows you to specify how many decimal points to shift over the value—for display purposes only. The real value under the hood is always kept as an integer. This is very important when you set up a value changed callback function—you'll get an int, not a float value.

The `decimalPoints` resource (`XmNdecimalPoints` in C programs) controls how many decimal points to shift the number over. The default is zero (0).

For a simple example, if `decimalPoints` is set to 1, a value of 100 will be displayed as 10.0. If `decimalPoints` is set to 2, the value displayed would be 1.00. The value under the hood would be 100 in both cases. Just the value displayed in the scale is different.

You can get or set the `value` of the scale widget using the `value` resource (`XmNvalue` in C programs). In addition to using the `value` resource directly, Motif has two functions for getting and setting the scale widget's value. `XmScaleGetValue` returns the `value` resource:

```
void XmScaleGetValue(Widget widget,
        int* value)
```

Of course, the scale widget must already be created before calling `XmScaleGetValue`.

`XmScaleSetValue` does the opposite of `XmScaleGetValue`, as we're sure you can figure out from the function name:

```
void XmScaleSetValue(Widget widget,
        int value)
```

Remember, the *value* parameter is an integer—the integer before the `decimalPoints` are applied.

Showing the Value Textually, Too

In all the screen dumps so far, the scale widget—an analog selector—had a digital value right next to the scale (like digital and analog watches side-by-side). This value represents the value of the scale (as modified by the `decimalPoints` resource). This digital value follows the scale's slider around (play with this a bit—it's fun). You can elect to display the digital value or not by setting the showValue resource (XmNshowValue in C programs) to True or False.

A value of True means that the digital value will be shown. A value of False (the default) means that the digital value will not be shown.

Scale Titles

Each scale widget can also have a title associated with the scale. This title, like most strings in Motif, is of the XmString type, so you must convert your C strings. The titleString resource (XmNtitleString in C programs), if you set it, holds the title for the scale widget. This title will be displayed alongside the scale.

Scale Callbacks

The scale widget supports two useful callbacks, as shown in Table 9.7.

Table 9.7 *Scale callbacks.*

Callbacks	Name in C Programs
dragCallback	XmNdragCallback
valueChangedCallback	XmNvalueChangedCallback

The most useful callback is the valueChangedCallback. This function is called whenever the scale's value changes, obviously. The odd thing about valueChangedCallback is that the value isn't considered changed until the user releases the mouse button. If the user drags the scale back and forth, valueChangedCallback won't be called until the user releases the mouse button. The scale then holds the new value.

Sometimes, though, you need to get at the scale's value while the slider is in motion. In this case, set up a dragCallback. The dragCallback is called while the slider is being dragged about. This callback is useful when you need to display continuously changing values. For example, a color editor would need a dragCallback to show how moving the slider affects the color displayed. With the dragCallback, you could dynamically change the color value while the sliders move.

Having a dragCallback, however, severely drains performance, so only set up a dragCallback if you really need it.

Both callbacks pass an XmScaleCallbackStruct as the *call_data* to your callback function:

```
typedef struct {
    int      reason;
    XEvent*  event;
    int      value;
} XmScaleCallbackStruct;
```

With the valueChangedCallback, the *reason* field should be XmCR_VALUE_CHANGED. For the drag callback, the *reason* field will be XmCR_DRAG. The *value* field is the new value of the scale. This is an integer, even if the decimalPoints resource is greater than zero (0).

If so, you'll have to divide the value by 10 raised to the decimalPoints power. If the decimalPoints resource is set to 3, you'll have to divide the returned value by 10 raised to the third power (1000) to get the proper value. With a value field of 12345 and a decimalPoints of 3, the real value (the value displayed on the scale widget) would be 12.345.

The *value* field is the only important element of this callback. The following code shows a very simple callback function for the scale widget:

```
    /* Scale widget callback. */
void scaleCB(Widget widget,
    XtPointer client_data,
    XtPointer call_data)

{   /* scaleCB */
    XmScaleCallbackStruct*  ptr;
    short                   decimal;
    float                   value;

    ptr = (XmScaleCallbackStruct*) call_data;

    if (ptr->reason == XmCR_DRAG) {
        printf("Drag callback.\n");
    }

    if (ptr->reason == XmCR_VALUE_CHANGED) {

        XtVaGetValues(widget,
            XmNdecimalPoints, &decimal,
            NULL);

        value = (float) ptr->value;

        /* Divide for decimal point, if needed. */
```

```
        while (decimal > 0) {
            value   = value / (float) 10.0;
            decimal = decimal - 1;
        }

        printf("New scale value is: %f\n", value);
    }

}   /* scaleCB */
```

If you want a read-only scale widget, call `XtSetSensitive`, as discussed in Chapter 7.

NOTE

The Scale Program

We've created a very simple program, called *scale,* to demonstrate how the scale widget works. The meat of this program is in the file **scale.c**:

```
/* scale.c */
#include <Xm/Xm.h>
#include <Xm/Scale.h>
#include <stdio.h>

    /* Scale widget callback. */
void scaleCB(Widget widget,
    XtPointer client_data,
    XtPointer call_data)

{   /* scaleCB */
    XmScaleCallbackStruct*  ptr;
    short                   decimal;
    float                   value;

    ptr = (XmScaleCallbackStruct*) call_data;

    if (ptr->reason == XmCR_DRAG) {
        printf("Drag callback.\n");
    }

    if (ptr->reason == XmCR_VALUE_CHANGED) {

        XtVaGetValues(widget,
            XmNdecimalPoints, &decimal,
            NULL);

        value = (float) ptr->value;

        /* Divide for decimal point, if needed. */
        while (decimal > 0) {
```

```
                    value   = value / (float) 10.0;
                    decimal = decimal - 1;
            }

            printf("New scale value is: %f\n", value);
    }

}   /* scaleCB */

int main(int argc, char** argv)

{   /* main */
    Widget          parent;
    XtAppContext    app_context;
    Widget          scale;
    Arg             args[20];
    Cardinal        n;

    /* Initialize the X Toolkit. */
    n = 0;
    parent = XtAppInitialize(&app_context,
            "Ppm",
            (XrmOptionDescList) NULL,
            0,
            (Cardinal*) &argc,
            argv,
            (String*) NULL,
            args, n);

    /* Create scale. */
    n = 0;
    XtSetArg(args[n], XmNshowValue, True); n++;

    XtSetArg(args[n], XmNorientation,
        XmHORIZONTAL); n++;
    XtSetArg(args[n], XmNprocessingDirection,
        XmMAX_ON_RIGHT); n++;

    /* Try a vertical scale as well. */
    /*
    XtSetArg(args[n], XmNprocessingDirection,
        XmMAX_ON_TOP); n++;
    XtSetArg(args[n], XmNorientation,
        XmVERTICAL); n++;
    */

    scale = XmCreateScale(parent,
            "scale", args, n);

    XtAddCallback(scale,
        XmNvalueChangedCallback,
        (XtCallbackProc) scaleCB,
        (XtPointer) NULL);

    XtAddCallback(scale,
```

```
        XmNdragCallback,
        (XtCallbackProc) scaleCB,
        (XtPointer) NULL);

    XtManageChild(scale);

    XtRealizeWidget(parent);
    XtAppMainLoop(app_context);

    return 0;

}   /* main */

/* end of file scale.c */
```

Try this program with the scale's `orientation` set to `XmVERTICAL` and `XmHORIZONTAL`, with the `processingDirection` set to `XmMAX_ON_TOP`, `XmMAX_ON_RIGHT`, and so on.

The *scale* program uses the following resource file:

```
! Resource file for scale.c in
! Chapter 9 of Power Programming Motif.
!
*fontList:      lucidasans-12
*background:    lightgrey

*Ppm*title: Scale Test

*scale.titleString:    Motif Scale Widget
*scale.maximum:    200
*scale.minimum:      0
*scale.decimalPoints: 1

! end of resource file
```

Name this file **Ppm** and place it in your home directory.

ARROW BUTTONS

The arrow-button widget, as summarized in Table 9.8, is a simple widget that basically just presents an arrowhead, much like what you see at the end of a scroll bar, as shown in Figure 9.5.

Many programs use arrow buttons to increment values up and down. Normally you'd place two arrow buttons (up and down) right on top of each other. If the user pressed on the up arrow, the value would move up. The down arrow acts similarly. You'll often find widgets like this in calendar programs, used to jump to the next month, for example.

Figure 9.5   *An arrow-button widget.*

Table 9.8   *The arrow-button widget class.*

Widget class:	XmArrowButton
Class pointer:	xmArrowButtonWidgetClass
Include file:	<Xm/ArrowB.h>
Create with:	XmCreateArrowButton

Create an arrow button with `XmCreateArrowButton`:

```
#include <Xm/ArrowB.h>

Widget XmCreateArrowButton(Widget parent,
    char* widget_name,
    ArgList args
    Cardinal number_args)
```

Call `XtManageChild` to manage the widget.

The `arrowDirection` resource (`XmNarrowDirection` in C programs) tells the arrow button which way to point. The possible values include:

■ `XmARROW_UP`

■ `XmARROW_DOWN`

■ `XmARROW_LEFT`

■ `XmARROW_RIGHT`

The `arrowDirection` resource defaults to `XmARROW_UP`. The arrow-button callbacks are listed in Table 9.9

Table 9.9 *Arrow-button callbacks.*

Callback	Name in C Programs
activateCallback	XmNactivateCallback
armCallback	XmNarmCallback
disarmCallback	XmNdisarmCallback

Each callback passes an `XmArrowButtonCallbackStruct` as the *call_data*. This structure looks like:

```
typedef struct {
    int     reason;
    XEvent* event;
    int     click_count;
} XmArrowButtonCallbackStruct;
```

The *reason* field holds the values listed in Table 9.10, depending on the callback.

Table 9.10 *Values for the XmArrowButtonCallbackStruct reason field.*

Callback	Reason Field
activateCallback	XmCR_ACTIVATE
armCallback	XmCR_ARM
disarmCallback	XmCR_DISARM

A widget is *armed* when the mouse button (usually button 1, the leftmost button) is pressed inside the widget. When the mouse button is released, the disarm callback is called (along with the activate callback, if the mouse was both pressed and released inside the widget).

The following program allows you to test out the arrow button:

```
/* arrow.c */
#include <Xm/Xm.h>
#include <Xm/ArrowB.h>
```

```c
#include <Xm/RowColumn.h>
#include <stdio.h>

    /* Widget callback. */
void arrowCB(Widget widget,
    XtPointer client_data,
    XtPointer call_data)

{   /* arrowCB */
    XmArrowButtonCallbackStruct*  ptr;

    ptr =
        (XmArrowButtonCallbackStruct*) call_data;

    switch(ptr->reason) {
        case XmCR_ACTIVATE:
            printf("Activate %s.\n", (char*) client_data);
            break;
        case XmCR_ARM:
            printf("Arm %s.\n", (char*) client_data);
            break;
        case XmCR_DISARM:
            printf("Disarm %s.\n", (char*) client_data);
            break;
        default : ;
    }

}   /* arrowCB */

    /* Adds three callbacks to each widget. */
void AddArrowCallbacks(Widget arrow,
    char* client_data)

{   /* AddArrowCallbacks */
    XtAddCallback(arrow,
        XmNactivateCallback,
        (XtCallbackProc) arrowCB,
        (XtPointer) client_data);

    XtAddCallback(arrow,
        XmNdisarmCallback,
        (XtCallbackProc) arrowCB,
        (XtPointer) client_data);

    XtAddCallback(arrow,
        XmNarmCallback,
        (XtCallbackProc) arrowCB,
        (XtPointer) client_data);

}   /* AddArrowCallbacks */

int main(int argc, char** argv)

{   /* main */
    Widget          parent;
```

```
XtAppContext      app_context;
Widget            row;
Widget            arrow1, arrow2, arrow3, arrow4;
Arg               args[20];
Cardinal          n;

/* Initialize the X Toolkit. */
n = 0;
XtSetArg(args[n], XmNtitle, "Arrow"); n++;

parent = XtAppInitialize(&app_context,
        "Ppm",
        (XrmOptionDescList) NULL,
        0,
        (Cardinal*) &argc,
        argv,
        (String*) NULL,
        args, n);

row = XtVaCreateManagedWidget("row",
        xmRowColumnWidgetClass, parent,
        XmNnumColumns,  1,
        XmNpacking,     XmPACK_COLUMN,
        XmNorientation, XmHORIZONTAL,
        NULL);

arrow1 = XtVaCreateManagedWidget("arrow1",
            xmArrowButtonWidgetClass, row,
            XmNarrowDirection, XmARROW_UP,
            NULL);

AddArrowCallbacks(arrow1, "Up");

arrow2 = XtVaCreateManagedWidget("arrow2",
            xmArrowButtonWidgetClass, row,
            XmNarrowDirection, XmARROW_DOWN,
            NULL);

AddArrowCallbacks(arrow2, "Down");

arrow3 = XtVaCreateManagedWidget("arrow3",
            xmArrowButtonWidgetClass, row,
            XmNarrowDirection, XmARROW_LEFT,
            NULL);

AddArrowCallbacks(arrow3, "Left");

arrow4 = XtVaCreateManagedWidget("arrow4",
            xmArrowButtonWidgetClass, row,
            XmNarrowDirection, XmARROW_RIGHT,
            NULL);

AddArrowCallbacks(arrow4, "Right");

XtRealizeWidget(parent);
XtAppMainLoop(app_context);
```

```
    return 0;

}   /* main */

/* end of file arrow.c */
```

When you run this program, watch how the arm and disarm callbacks work.

SCROLLED WINDOWS

Many times you'll need a very large set of data—too much data to fit into a window. In some cases, the XmList or XmText widgets, in their scrolling incarnations, can take care of this problem. If those widgets aren't appropriate, though, you can set up a container widget like the XmForm or XmRowColumn to scroll.

What you're basically doing is creating a really, really big form widget (populated with many child widgets) and then placing the XmForm widget into a scrolled window. The scrolled window then shows only part of the XmForm at a time. Those parts get drawn and can interact with the user. The rest of the form is hidden, as the data is clipped by the borders of the scrolled window's clipping window.

The scroll bars then allow the user to modify the visible area, as shown in Figure 9.6.

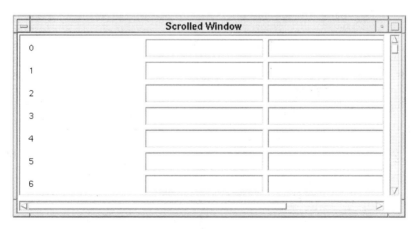

Figure 9.6 *A scrolled window.*

To do all this, you need to use the `XmScrolledWindow` widget class, as listed in Table 9.11.

Table 9.11   *The XmScrolledWindow widget class.*

Widget class:	`XmScrolledWindow`
Class pointer:	`xmScrolledWindowWidgetClass`
Include file:	`<Xm/ScrolledW.h>`
Create with:	`XmCreateScrolledWindow`

Create a scrolled window widget with `XmCreateScrolledWindow`:

```
#include <Xm/ScrolledW.h>

Widget XmCreateScrolledWindow(Widget parent,
    char* widget_name,
    ArgList args
    Cardinal number_args)
```

Call `XtManageChild` to manage the widget.

Scrolled-Window Resources

The scrolled window provides a number of useful resources, as listed in Table 9.12.

Table 9.12   *Scrolled-window resources.*

Resource	Type	Default Value
`horizontalScrollBar`	Widget	*dynamic*
`scrollBarDisplayPolicy`	unsigned char	*dynamic*
`scrollBarPlacement`	unsigned char	`XmBOTTOM_RIGHT`
`scrollingPolicy`	unsigned char	see below
`verticalScrollBar`	Widget	*dynamic*
`visualPolicy`	unsigned char	*dynamic*
`workWindow`	Widget	`NULL`

The workWindow (XmNworkWindow in C programs) is the window you want to be scrolled. Normally this is a container widget, like an XmForm, or a raw drawing widget.

The most important scrolled-window resource is the scrollingPolicy (XmNscrollingPolicy in C programs). This resource determines whether the scrolled window should act fully automated or whether it should kick you into manual mode.

In automatic mode (XmAUTOMATIC), the scrolled window will automatically create child horizontal and vertical scroll bars, set up the scrolling callbacks, and handle all the chores necessary to scroll your workWindow when the user moves the scroll bars. Obviously, this is the easiest mode to work in.

Sometimes, though, you have far too much data to place into one window or need to perform some special processing to get at more data. For example, a database query program may need to communicate with the database program to get each page or window-full of data. In such a case, set the scrollingPolicy resource to XmAPPLICATION_DEFINED. When you do this, you must create the scroll bars (XmScrollBar widgets) and take care of all scrolling yourself. If you do use the XmAPPLICATION_DEFINED method of scrolling, then you'll call the XmScrolledWindowSetAreas function to set up the proper child widgets (much like the call to XmMainWindowSetAreas sets up the main window's child widgets). The XmScrolledWindowSetAreas function takes the following parameters:

```
#include <Xm/ScrolledW.h>

void XmScrolledWindowSetAreas(Widget scrolled_window,
        Widget horz_scroll,
        Widget vert_scroll,
        Widget work_window)
```

As with XmMainWindowSetAreas, you can pass NULL for any of the child widgets.

The Scroll-Bar Display Policy

You can set the scrollBarDisplayPolicy (XmNscrollBarDisplayPolicy in C programs) to XmAS_NEEDED (scroll bars appear when necessary) or XmSTATIC (scroll bars always appear). If the scrollingPolicy resource is set to XmAPPLICATION_DEFINED, the scrollBarDisplayPolicy resource *must* be set to XmSTATIC. This usually looks better. It also helps you to lay out your widgets because adding a scroll bar to the widget on the fly changes the layout, but usually the widget won't gain any size. This makes a once-nice layout turn sour. So we advise you to turn on the scroll bars with XmSTATIC.

Of course, there are a lot of complaints about scrolled windows in general. Why? If you place a number of widgets inside a scrolled window, the resulting program doesn't look as good as a well-designed (unscrolled) layout. In addition, users may not know about the hidden widgets (and these widgets may be very important to the program).

In general, we find that scroll bars work well on single objects, such as a scrolled list, scrolled text, or scrolled drawing-area widget. But if you scroll multiple widgets, this isn't very attractive. An exception, though, is a scrolled spreadsheet, which may contain multiple widgets but still looks like it was well-designed, mainly because each row in the spreadsheet contains the same set of widgets.

A Scrolled-Window Test Program

We've put together a program to test out the scrolled-window widget in its automated mode of XmAUTOMATIC. The code for **scrollw.c** follows:

```
/* scrollw.c */
#include <Xm/Xm.h>
#include <Xm/Label.h>
#include <Xm/RowColumn.h>
#include <Xm/ScrolledW.h>
#include <Xm/Text.h>
#include <stdio.h>

    /* Create a single-line text widget. */
Widget CreateTextEntry(Widget parent,
    char* name)

{   /* CreateTextEntry */
    Widget      widget;

    widget = XtVaCreateManagedWidget(name,
            xmTextWidgetClass, parent,
            XmNeditMode, XmSINGLE_LINE_EDIT,
            XmNcolumns, 24,
            NULL);

    return widget;

}   /* CreateTextEntry */
```

```
        /* Create label and hard-code labelString. */
Widget CreateLabel(Widget parent,
    char* name,
    char* text) /* text to display as labelString */

{   /* CreateLabel */
    Widget      widget;
    XmString    xmstring;

    xmstring = XmStringCreateSimple(text);

    widget = XtVaCreateManagedWidget(name,
                xmLabelWidgetClass, parent,
                XmNlabelString, xmstring,
                NULL);

    XmStringFree(xmstring);

    return widget;

}   /* CreateLabel */

    /*
     * Creates a row of widgets for the
     * scrolled window. For this test
     * program, we're going to create a
     * lot of rows, hence this function.
     */
void CreateRow(Widget parent,
    int row)

{   /* CreateRow */
    Widget  label, text1, text2, text3;
    char    string[100];

    sprintf(string, "%3d", row);

    label = CreateLabel(parent, "label", string);

    text1 = CreateTextEntry(parent, "text1");
    text2 = CreateTextEntry(parent, "text2");
    text3 = CreateTextEntry(parent, "text3");

}   /* CreateRow */

int main(int argc, char** argv)

{   /* main */
    Widget          parent;
    XtAppContext    app_context;
    Widget          row;
    Widget          scrolled_window;
    Arg             args[20];
    Cardinal        n;
    int             i;
```

```
    /* Initialize the X Toolkit. */
    n = 0;
    XtSetArg(args[n], XmNtitle, "Scrolled Window"); n++;

    parent = XtAppInitialize(&app_context,
            "Ppm",
            (XrmOptionDescList) NULL,
            0,
            (Cardinal*) &argc,
            argv,
            (String*) NULL,
            args, n);

    /* Create scrolled window. */
    n = 0;
    XtSetArg(args[n], XmNscrollingPolicy,
        XmAUTOMATIC); n++;
    XtSetArg(args[n], XmNscrollBarDisplayPolicy,
        XmSTATIC); n++;

    scrolled_window = XmCreateScrolledWindow(parent,
            "scrollw", args, n);

    /* Number rows in scrolled window */
#define NUMBER_COLUMNS  100

    row = XtVaCreateManagedWidget("row",
            xmRowColumnWidgetClass, scrolled_window,
            XmNnumColumns,   NUMBER_COLUMNS,
            XmNpacking,      XmPACK_COLUMN,
            XmNorientation, XmHORIZONTAL,
            NULL);

    XmScrolledWindowSetAreas(scrolled_window,
        (Widget) NULL,
        (Widget) NULL,
        row);  /* work area */

    /* Fill in lots of widgets. */
    for (i = 0; i < NUMBER_COLUMNS; i++) {
        CreateRow(row, i);
    }

    XtManageChild(row);

    XtManageChild(scrolled_window);

    XtRealizeWidget(parent);
    XtAppMainLoop(app_context);

    return 0;

}   /* main */

/* end of file scrollw.c */
```

Our scrolled-window program uses a constant (NUMBER_COLUMNS) to determine how many rows of a primitive spreadsheet to create. Each row is then made up of a label widget and three text widgets in single-line mode. We did this to create a lot of widgets quickly and to show a layout that can look good inside a scrolled window.

Watch out for performance problems, though, if you create hundreds of widgets inside the scrolled window.

Making Areas Visible

You can control the scrolling in a scrolled window if you use an XmAPPLICATION_DEFINED scrollingPolicy. You do this by controlling the scroll bars. If you choose the automatic mode, though, you can still capture some control over scrolling. To make a given widget visible within a scrolled window, use XmScrollVisible:

```
#include <Xm/ScrolledW.h>

void XmScrollVisible(Widget scrolled_window,
        Widget  widget_to_make_visible,
        Dimension horizontal_margin,
        Dimension vertical_margin)
```

XmScrollVisible makes the given widget (*widget_to_make_visible*) visible, by scrolling the window the proper amount. You have an even finer control by using the *horizontal_margin* and *vertical_margin*. The *horizontal_margin* is a margin that the scrolled window will set up between the *widget_to_make_visible* and the horizontal edge (left or right) of the scrolled window (whichever edge the window was moved from). This takes effect only if the scrolled window must move horizontally. The *vertical_margin* applies the same way in the vertical direction.

Creating Scroll Bars

If you use the manual mode (XmAPPLICATION_DEFINED) in the scrolled window, then you must create the scroll bars yourself. Do so by using an XmScrollBar widget, as listed in Table 9.13.

Table 9.13 *The XmScrollBar widget class.*

Widget class:	XmScrollBar
Class pointer:	xmScrollBarWidgetClass
Include file:	<Xm/ScrollBar.h>
Create with:	XmCreateScrollBar

For a scrolled window, you'll need to create two scroll bars: one horizontal and one vertical. Create a scrol-bar widget with XmCreateScrollBar:

```
#include <Xm/ScrollBar.h>

Widget XmCreateScrollBar(Widget parent,
    char* widget_name,
    ArgList args
    Cardinal number_args)
```

Call XtManageChild to manage the widget.

Scroll bars are a lot like scale widgets in that they have a value that represents a position between a minimum and a maximum. The scroll bar basically maintains an integer value for the current location of the scroll bar. When displayed, the scroll bar has a thumb, which the user can drag forward or backward. The thumb is placed at the position of the scroll bar's value. At each end of the scroll bar lie arrows. The user can click the mouse over an arrow to move the thumb one position with each click. Between the thumb and the arrows lies a trough. There can be a trough both before and after the thumb. Clicking the mouse in the trough increments the thumb by a page increment. Clicking the mouse over an arrow or a trough with the **Control** key held down jumps to that end of the scroll bar.

Scroll-Bar Resources

The scroll bar provides a number of useful resources, as listed in Table 9.14.

Table 9.14 *Scroll-bar resources.*

Resource	Type	Default Value
increment	int	1
maximum	int	*dynamic*
minimum	int	0
orientation	unsigned char	XmVERTICAL
pageIncrement	int	10
processingDirection	unsigned char	*dynamic*
showArrows	Boolean	True
sliderSize	int	*dynamic*
value	int	*dynamic*

Most of these resources are old hat. We'll cover the new ones.

The increment is the value that the slider's value will change if the user clicks the mouse over one of the arrows at each end. The pageIncrement is the amount that the slider's value will change if the user goes up or down a page. Usually, clicking the mouse in the trough area before or after the thumb will result in a jump of one page.

The showArrows resource allows you to turn off the arrows if you set it to False. The default is to show the arrows (True).

The sliderSize controls the size of the slider's thumb. Generally, the size of the thumb should indicate how much of the data are actually visible. If all the data is visible, then the slider thumb should extend all the way across the slider, since there's no sense in scrolling if everything is visible. If only half of the data is visible, then the thumb should cover half the area of the slider.

The value is the current position of the slider, between the minimum and the maximum.

Making a Progress Indicator

In many programs, you need to tell the user to wait for a time while a time-consuming task completes. In such cases, it's a good idea to display a working dialog, as explained in Chapter 7. If you have extra information about this time-consuming task, such as how much of the task is complete, then it's a good idea to also provide this information to the user. In general, the more you can tell a user about a long task, the better. This also helps the user feel confident your program hasn't crashed while in a tight loop.

If you know how much of the time-consuming task is complete, you should display some form of progress indicator. You can display a simple label widget with the percent done, such as *Task is 55% complete*, but this isn't as visually satisfying as a graphical indicator.

You can create a graphical progress indicator with the scroll-bar widget by customizing a few resources:

1. Create a horizontal scroll bar.

2. Turn off the arrows by setting the showArrows resource to False.

3. Set the maximum resource to the final value, such as 100 for 100 percent.

4. Set the minimum resource to 0.

5. Set the scroll bar's value resource to the minimum (0).

6. Set the sliderSize resource (the thumb size) to 1.

7. Normally, you set the scroll bar's value resource to indicate a position. With a progress indicator, though, you leave the value locked in place and instead increase the sliderSize. What this does is gradually fill the scroll bar with the thumb, which looks a lot like a bar chart gradually approaching the far end of the scroll bar. Each time you increase the percentage of the job (the percentage of the job that's been completed, that is), increase the sliderSize resource. Make sure, though, that the sliderSize does not exceed the value of the maximum resource.

Scroll-Bar Callbacks

The scroll bar provides a number of callbacks, as listed in Table 9.15.

Table 9.15 *Scroll bar callbacks.*

Callback	Name in C Programs
decrementCallback	XmNdecrementCallback
dragCallback	XmNdragCallback
incrementCallback	XmNincrementCallback
pageDecrementCallback	XmNpageDecrementCallback
pageIncrementCallback	XmNpageIncrementCallback
toBottomCallback	XmNtoBottomCallback
toTopCallback	XmNtoTopCallback
valueChangedCallback	XmNvalueChangedCallbac

Setting up a dragCallback, as you can expect, slows down the scroll bar's performance.

All the callbacks pass an XmScrollBarCallbackStruct pointer as the *call_data*:

```
typedef struct {
    int      reason;
    XEvent*  event;
    int      value;
    int      pixel;
} XmScrollBarCallbackStruct;
```

The most important field is the *value*, which holds the new position of the slider.

Adjusting the Scroll Bar

The user can move the scroll bar, and you can also adjust its value from within your programs. You can set the scroll bar's resources directly or set a number of values with one call to XmScrollBarSetValues:

```
#include <Xm/ScrollBar.h>

void XmScrollBarSetValues(Widget widget,
    int value,
```

```
        int slider_size,
        int increment,
        int page_increment,
        Boolean notify)
```

The *notify* flag specifies whether (True) or not (False) to call the valueChangedCallback.

To retrieve the same values, call XmScrollBarGetValues:

```
#include <Xm/ScrollBar.h>

void XmScrollBarGetValues(Widget widget,
        int* value,             /* RETURN */
        int* slider_size,       /* RETURN */
        int* increment,         /* RETURN */
        int* page_increment)    /* RETURN */
```

A Program to Test Scroll Bars

We've put together a program to help decipher the scroll-bar callback functions. The code for **scrollb.c** follows:

```
/* scrollb.c */
#include <Xm/Xm.h>
#include <Xm/ScrollBar.h>
#include <stdio.h>

    /* Widget callback. */
void scrollbCB(Widget widget,
    XtPointer client_data,
    XtPointer call_data)

{   /* scrollbCB */
    XmScrollBarCallbackStruct*  ptr;

    ptr =
        (XmScrollBarCallbackStruct*) call_data;

    switch(ptr->reason) {
        case XmCR_DECREMENT:
            printf("XmCR_DECREMENT");
            break;
        case XmCR_INCREMENT:
            printf("XmCR_INCREMENT");
            break;
        case XmCR_PAGE_INCREMENT:
            printf("XmCR_PAGE_INCREMENT");
            break;
        case XmCR_TO_TOP:
            printf("XmCR_TO_TOP");
            break;
```

```
            case XmCR_TO_BOTTOM:
                printf("XmCR_TO_BOTTOM");
                break;
            case XmCR_PAGE_DECREMENT:
                printf("XmCR_PAGE_DECREMENT");
                break;
            case XmCR_VALUE_CHANGED:
                printf("XmCR_VALUE_CHANGED");
                break;
            case XmCR_DRAG:
                printf("XmCR_DRAG");
                break;
            default : ;
    }

    printf(" value is %d\n", ptr->value);

}   /* scrollbCB */

int main(int argc, char** argv)

{   /* main */
    Widget          parent;
    XtAppContext    app_context;
    Widget          scrollbar;
    Arg             args[20];
    Cardinal        n;

    /* Initialize the X Toolkit. */
    n = 0;
    XtSetArg(args[n], XmNtitle, "Scrollbar"); n++;

    parent = XtAppInitialize(&app_context,
            "Ppm",
            (XrmOptionDescList) NULL,
            0,
            (Cardinal*) &argc,
            argv,
            (String*) NULL,
            args, n);

    scrollbar = XtVaCreateManagedWidget("scrollbar",
                xmScrollBarWidgetClass, parent,
                XmNorientation, XmHORIZONTAL,
                XmNmaximum,     100,
                XmNsliderSize,  24,
                NULL);

    /* Add the zillions of callbacks. */
    XtAddCallback(scrollbar,
        XmNdecrementCallback,
        (XtCallbackProc) scrollbCB,
        (XtPointer) NULL);

    XtAddCallback(scrollbar,
```

```
        XmNincrementCallback,
        (XtCallbackProc) scrollbCB,
        (XtPointer) NULL);

    XtAddCallback(scrollbar,
        XmNpageDecrementCallback,
        (XtCallbackProc) scrollbCB,
        (XtPointer) NULL);

    XtAddCallback(scrollbar,
        XmNpageIncrementCallback,
        (XtCallbackProc) scrollbCB,
        (XtPointer) NULL);

    XtAddCallback(scrollbar,
        XmNdragCallback,
        (XtCallbackProc) scrollbCB,
        (XtPointer) NULL);

    XtAddCallback(scrollbar,
        XmNtoBottomCallback,
        (XtCallbackProc) scrollbCB,
        (XtPointer) NULL);

    XtAddCallback(scrollbar,
        XmNtoTopCallback,
        (XtCallbackProc) scrollbCB,
        (XtPointer) NULL);

    XtAddCallback(scrollbar,
        XmNvalueChangedCallback,
        (XtCallbackProc) scrollbCB,
        (XtPointer) NULL);

    XtRealizeWidget(parent);
    XtAppMainLoop(app_context);

    return 0;

}   /* main */

/* end of file scrollb.c */
```

When you run this program, you'll see a scroll bar like the one shown in Figure 9.7.

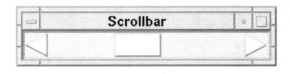

Figure 9.7 *A scroll bar.*

SUMMARY

This chapter introduced a number of new widgets that are useful for fleshing out Motif applications:

■ The list widget, which displays a list of choices to the user, with optional scroll bars.

■ The scale widget, a valuator that allows users to set analog values.

■ The arrow-button widget, often used to increment values.

■ The scrolled-window widget, used to scroll other widgets.

■ The scroll-bar widget, which holds an individual scroll bar.

MOTIF FUNCTIONS AND MACROS INTRODUCED IN THIS CHAPTER

```
XmCreateList
XmCreateScrollBar
XmCreateScrolledList
XmCreateScrolledWindow
XmCreateScale
XmListAddItem
XmListAddItemUnselected
XmListDeleteAllItems
XmListDeleteItem
XmListDeletePos
XmListDeselectItem
XmListDeselectPos
XmListSelectItem
XmListSelectPos
XmListSetItem
XmScaleGetValue
XmScaleSetValue
XmScrollBarGetValues
XmScrollBarSetValues
XmScrollVisible
XmScrolledWindowSetAreas
```

SECTION 3

Getting Down and Dirty with Motif, Xt, and the X Library

The Motif toolkit provides a lot of handy functions and really speeds the creation of user interfaces, as opposed to coding all this manually with the low-level X library. As such, Motif does a good job for what it's built for—creating user interfaces. But just about every application we've ever built requires a lot more than Motif offers. In fact, every sophisticated application we've done requires access to the rest of the X Toolkit Intrinsics and the low-level X library.

This section concentrates on those cases where you need to go beyond what Motif offers and delve down into lower layers of the X Window System. Most applications need to retrieve X Window events and customize how Motif handles incoming events. In addition, if you're porting an older application to Motif, chances are your event-handling doesn't

365

mesh well with the Motif event look in `XtAppMainLoop`. Chapter 10 covers X events and how you can get at them.

We tackle drawing with the X library inside an `XmDrawingArea` widget, which is very useful especially when porting graphical applications to Motif, in Chapter 11.

Most modern applications present some form of bitmap pictures in the interface, such as a toolbar that sits underneath the menu bar and presents quick access to commonly used functions. And every Motif application should set up its own icon. We introduce bitmaps, pixmaps, and icons in Chapter 12.

Spreadsheet applications need to recalculate the spreadsheet cells in the background. Other applications have time-consuming tasks and also require background processing. Xt timers help provide evenly spaced, smooth animations. We show how to do all this in Chapter 13 on Xt background processing and timers.

Up to now, we've used `XtAppIntialize` to perform all the tasks necessary to get going with Motif. More complex applications, though, require greater control over this process. So Chapter 14 revists initializing the Xt Intrinsics.

Every application works with color, which happens to be one of the most complicated areas of X. Chapter 15 introduces color and shows you how to allocate color cells and find the best visual on a 24-bit display.

Chapter 16 melds 3D graphics using the PEX library, or PEXlib, with Motif and the drawing-area widget.

Chapter 17 shows you how to create multiple independent top-level windows. You'll often need a second top-level window for presenting online help, for example.

All in all, this section shows you how to go beyond Motif to get real work done.

CHAPTER 10

X Events and the Xt Event-Handling Loop

This chapter covers:

- The X Window event model
- Keyboard traversal in Motif
- An overview of X Window events
- Xt event-handling callback functions
- The Motif event loop itself
- KeySyms and osfKeySyms
- Creating your own event-handling functions
- Event masks
- Adding other inputs to the event loop
- Creating your own main event loop
- Updating displays

367

MOTIF AND EVENT-DRIVEN PROGRAMMING

Motif programs, like all programs that sit on top of the X Window System, are driven by events arriving from the X server. These events include notification of keys pressed on the keyboard, mouse motions, and window movement. Motif handles these events in a central loop that reads the event and then dispatches it to the proper widget. In this way, Motif takes care of all X events coming from the server.

This central event loop, XtAppMainLoop, forever loops awaiting events. When an event arrives, XtAppMainLoop dispatches the event to the proper widget. Each widget then chooses how to best deal with the event. For example, an XmText widget takes incoming keys pressed on the keyboard as new text for the widget, while an XmPushButton looks for mouse button events or a keystroke that represents a mnemonic.

Event-driven applications are powerful because the program essentially cedes control to the user. It's the user who drives the program by generating the majority of the events. The program is really still in control, but it gives the user the feeling that the user is running the show. This is very important if your applications support users who are new to computing. The big difference with event-driven programming is that events can come in at any time and in any order.

Luckily, Motif again takes care of most of this for us. With a few exceptions, Motif manages the events for all the windows created with the toolkit. This frees you, the application writer, from having to write code to handle all these event types, which is, of course, one of the reasons to use an X toolkit. XtAppMainLoop saves you from the tedium of writing a giant switch statement on each type of event that is required by other windowing systems like Microsoft Windows and the Macintosh. Even so, there are a number of occasions where you need more control over the way the Motif toolkit handles events. That's why this chapter provides an overview of a number of ways in which you can intercept Motif events, including:

- Setting up Motif widget callbacks
- Writing Xt event-handler callbacks
- Creating your own main event loop

SHORTCUT

Gaining More Control Over Incoming Events

To gain more control over X events, you can set up a widget callback (as we've done in just about every chapter so far), set up an event-handling callback function, or create your own main event loop.

If you want to track a certain X event on a widget, you can set up an event-handling callback function with XtAddEventHandler:

```
void XtAddEventHandler(Widget widget,
     EventMask eventmask,
     Boolean nonmaskable,
     XtEventHandler callback,
     XtPointer client_data)
```

The best way to set up your own main event loop is to copy the sources for XtAppMainLoop and then customize:

```
void XtAppMainLoop(XtAppContext app_context)

{
     XEvent      event;

     for (;;) {
          XtAppNextEvent(app_context, &event);

          /* You may want to intercept keys here... */

          XtDispatchEvent(&event);
     }
}
```

XtAppMainLoop loops forever, blocking until the next event arrives from the X server (or another input source, such as a timer, generates an event).

In order to handle incoming events in more detail, you need a thorough understanding of the X Window event model. This discussion covers events in the X Window System in general but, of course, focuses on how Motif applications deal with these events.

X WINDOW EVENTS

X events are messages generated by the X server and sent to your program. Sometimes other programs generate these events and then send them to your program through the X server. The user may create events by pressing keyboard keys, clicking mouse buttons, or moving the mouse pointer about the screen. Technically, the X server generates these events by monitoring the physical devices such as the keyboard, mouse, trackball, or box of dials. X even goes a step further than most windowing systems: A KeyPress is one event; the corresponding KeyRelease is another. Your applications can track mouse ButtonPress and ButtonRelease events as well.

An event occurs when a window-manager program works with the user to change the size of a window on the screen. And an event happens when one program sends an event to another program. Events tell your application programs exactly what is happening on the display screen.

More technically, an event is a fixed-size packet of information sent to your program by the X server. X provides many different types of events, and each one interprets the contents of the data packet differently. Your application sees this event in the form of an XEvent structure. In fact, the event Motif widget callback function so far provides an XEvent pointer as part of the callback's *call_data* structure. We've ignored this structure so far, but in this chapter we rectify the situation.

The X Event Model

The X server generates events on windows. For example, a mouse button press occurs within a given window. The X server then forwards that event on to the application that owns the window. Actually, to get into more technical detail, the X server forwards the event to the application that asked for ButtonPress events on the given window. In virtually all cases, though, this is the application that created the window in the first place.

To get an event of a particular type, such as a ButtonPress, your application must ask the X server. The X server, then, delivers only the event types that were asked for on a given window. (There are a few exceptions, though.) Luckily, Motif again takes care of this for us, unless we want to set up an event-handling callback for a particular type of event that the toolkit isn't already asking for.

Each Motif program sets up a connection to the X server with XtAppInitialize. The X server in turn provides each connection an event queue. This event queue is a first-in, first-out list of all events generated for the program's windows. XtAppMainLoop reads events from this queue and responds to them by dispatching the events to the proper widgets. Normally, this is the widget holding the window on which the event was generated. The X server, of course, has no concept of widgets. It just knows about the underlying windows.

Keyboard Focus

There are some exceptions to this window orientation. Keys pressed on the keyboard go to whatever window currently has the *keyboard focus*. This focus window is normally whatever window the mouse pointer is in. Motif, though, supports a complex means for changing which window has the keyboard focus. In Motif terminology, this is called *keyboard traversal*.

You can gain limited control over which widget has the keyboard focus by calling XmProcessTraversal:

```
Boolean XmProcessTraversal(Widget widget,
    XmTraversalDirection direction)
```

XmProcessTraversal returns True if it succeeded and False otherwise.

You can pass a *direction* of one of the flags listed in Table 10.1.

Table 10.1 *Motif traversal directions.*

Flag	Meaning
XmTRAVERSE_CURRENT	Makes widget have keyboard focus
XmTRAVERSE_DOWN	Go to next widget down
XmTRAVERSE_HOME	Makes first widget in current group active
XmTRAVERSE_LEFT	Go to next widget to left
XmTRAVERSE_NEXT	Go to next item in group
XmTRAVERSE_NEXT_TAB_GROUP	Jump to next tab group
XmTRAVERSE_PREV	Go to previous item in group

continued

XmTRAVERSE_PREV_TAB_GROUP	Jump to previous tab group
XmTRAVERSE_RIGHT	Go to next widget to right
XmTRAVERSE_UP	Go to next widget above

If you call `XmProcessTraversal` from inside a `focusCallback` or a `losingFocusCallback`, you may get a segmentation fault.

WARNING

Much of the keyboard traversal depends on the concept of a *tab group*. Each widget is assumed to be within a tab group. A tab group is a group of widgets you can tab through with the **Tab** key. Usually a tab group is all the widgets that accept input that are children of a given container widget, like an `XmForm`. In Motif applications, the **Tab** key moves the keyboard focus to the next active widget in the current tab group. If more than one tab group is visible, you can jump between them.

In most situations, though, tab groups leave a lot to be desired, and `XmProcessTraversal` doesn't act the way you thought it should. The `XmTRAVERSE_CURRENT` flag, for example, often requires you to call `XmProcessTraversal` twice to make the given *widget* hold the keyboard focus. In addition, different versions of Motif sport differing implementations and different bugs related to keyboard traversal.

N O T E

In general, if you can avoid messing with the keyboard focus, you'll be better off. If not, try experimenting with `XmProcessTraversal` to see how it works.

Setting the Initial Focus

You can also set which widget gets the initial keyboard focus for a container widget by setting the `initialFocus` resource and then place the value of the widget that you want to receive the initial keyboard focus. This widget must be a child of the container widget. You set this resource on the container widget, such as an `XmForm` or `XmRowColumn` widget.

You can also change the `traversalOn` resource, which controls whether the child widgets of a container will allow keyboard traversal as we documented above. Set the `traversalOn` resource to `False` to turn off traversal for all children of the container widget. Set the `traversalOn` resource to `True` to allow traversal.

We summarize these resources in Table 10.2.

Table 10.2 *Traversal resources on container widgets.*

Resource	Type	Default Value
initialFocus	Widget	NULL
traversalOn	Boolean	True

TYPES OF X EVENTS

Up to now we've used the callback structures and pointedly ignored the `XEvent` field of most Motif callback structures. We've ignored it so far because the *event* field really hasn't been all that useful—yet. In your programs, however, you may need everything the *event* field can give. The X Window `XEvent` structure is a union of many types of event structures. The basic union is rather long and looks like:

```
typedef union _XEvent {
    int                 type;
    XAnyEvent           xany;
    XKeyEvent           xkey;
    XButtonEvent        xbutton;
    XMotionEvent        xmotion;
    XCrossingEvent      xcrossing;
    XFocusChangeEvent   xfocus;
    XExposeEvent        xexpose;
    XGraphicsExposeEvent xgraphicsexpose;
    XNoExposeEvent      xnoexpose;
    XVisibilityEvent    xvisibility;
    XCreateWindowEvent  xcreatewindow;
    XDestroyWindowEvent xdestroywindow;
    XUnmapEvent         xunmap;
    XMapEvent           xmap;
    XMapRequestEvent    xmaprequest;
    XReparentEvent      xreparent;
    XConfigureEvent     xconfigure;
```

```
XGravityEvent          xgravity;
XResizeRequestEvent    xresizerequest;
XConfigureRequestEvent xconfigurerequest;
XCirculateEvent        xcirculate;
XCirculateRequestEvent xcirculaterequest;
XPropertyEvent         xproperty;
XSelectionClearEvent   xselectionclear;
XSelectionRequestEvent xselectionrequest;
XSelectionEvent        xselection;
XColormapEvent         xcolormap;
XClientMessageEvent    xclient;
XMappingEvent          xmapping;
XErrorEvent            xerror;
XKeymapEvent           xkeymap;
long                   pad[24];
} XEvent;
```

The first element of the XEvent union is the *type*. The *type* field tells, surprisingly enough, what type of event has been received. The include file <X11/X.h>, which is automatically included by <Xm/Xm.h>, defines a set of constants, one for each X event. These constants include Expose and KeyPress.

Each type of event has its own structure—its own interpretation of the XEvent data, layered on top of the XEvent union. All structures share a common part, which includes the following fields:

```
int            type;
unsigned long  serial;
Bool           send_event;
Display*       display;
Window         window;
```

The *serial* field is a serial number generated by the X server. The *send_event* flag is True if the event was generated by another X application and sent via the XSendEvent function. The *display* field indicates which display connection the event came from (any X program may connect to multiple X servers, although the vast majority of X programs connect to just one X server). Finally, the *window* field indicates on which window the event was generated. This window field is sometimes named *event* or *parent*.

The X events are listed in Table 10.3.

Table 10.3 *X events.*

Event	Meaning
ButtonPress	Mouse button is pressed
ButtonRelease	Pressed button is released
CirculateNotify	Window stacking order changes
CirculateRequest	Request to change a window's stacking order
ClientMessage	Arbitrary data sent to the application
ColormapNotify	Changes which colormap is active for a given window
ConfigureNotify	Window's size, location, border, or stacking order changes
ConfigureRequest	Request to change a window's configuration
CreateNotify	Notifies when a window is created
DestroyNotify	Notifies when a window is destroyed
EnterNotify	Mouse cursor enters window
Expose	Part of a window needs to be redrawn
FocusIn	Window gains keyboard focus
FocusOut	Window loses keyboard focus
GraphicsExpose	Source for a copy operation wasn't available
GravityNotify	Notifies when a window is moved due to parent's size change
KeymapNotify	Keyboard or mouse focus is now in window
KeyPress	Key is pressed on keyboard
KeyRelease	Pressed key is released
LeaveNotify	Mouse cursor leaves window
MapNotify	Window is mapped to screen
MappingNotify	Keyboard mapping has changed
MapRequest	Request to map a window
MotionNotify	For any of the motion masks

continued

`NoExpose`	No `GraphicsExpose` event was generated
`PropertyNotify`	Window's property has changed
`ReparentNotify`	A window was reparented, done by window managers
`ResizeRequest`	Requests to resize window
`SelectionClear`	Owner of selection lost ownership
`SelectionNotify`	Selection owner tells client status of selection request
`SelectionRequest`	Client requests data from selection owner
`UnmapNotify`	Window is unmapped
`VisibilityNotify`	Window's visibility changed

In the next section, we go into a number of these event types in detail.

Individual Event Types

An event in X is generated whenever the user presses a key on the keyboard—and whenever the user releases the key, too. Events are also generated by mouse-button clicks (press and release both generate events). In addition, the X server also generates events on its own. When a window changes size, the X server sends a `ConfigureNotify` event. When part of the window needs to be redrawn due to other windows moving out of the way, the X server sends an `Expose` event (or more likely, a number of `Expose` events).

Expose Events

The X Window System makes no guarantees that what you draw to a window will stay there. The user could very well place another window on top of yours. (Even though we know that your application windows are better than anyone else's, the user is still free to cover up your windows.)

Some window systems maintain in memory the pixels that were in your window, but are now covered up, with a *backing store*. When necessary, the window system uses this backing store to refresh the formerly obscured parts of windows.

In X, you can request that the X server maintain a backing store for your windows, but this is just a request. The X server can ignore you entirely, or the server can run out of memory. In any case, you cannot depend on the X server to maintain the contents of your windows for you. (And, to be fair, the X documentation clearly points this out, so you're forewarned.)

When your window becomes uncovered (either partially or fully), the X server sends your application an Expose event. You'll also get Expose events when your window first appears on the screen. In most cases the Motif toolkit automatically handles these Expose events. In fact, you can watch as a slow Motif program refreshes each window, one at a time, as the windows first appear on the screen. Under the hood, Motif is reacting to incoming Expose events. Expose events are interesting in your Motif programs when you use the XmDrawingArea and XmDrawnButton widgets, which we describe in the next chapter.

Inside the event structure that comes with each Expose event are the coordinates of a rectangle that was exposed (and needs to be redrawn). The first Expose event you get generally is for the whole window and comes down the pike about the time your window is first created. Other Expose events come in batches as the user moves windows about the screen and new windows appear and disappear.

The Expose event part of the XEvent union looks like:

```
typedef struct {
    int             type;        /* Expose */
    unsigned long   serial;
    Bool            send_event;
    Display*        display;
    Window          window;
    int             x, y;
    int             width, height;
    int             count;
} XExposeEvent;
```

For Expose events, the important fields are:

- *type*
- *window*
- *x, y*
- *width*
- *height*
- *count*

The *type* field is set to Expose. The *window* field contains the ID of the window in which the event occurred. The *x, y, width,* and *height* fields contain the rectangular area that needs to be redrawn. Finally, the *count* field indicates how many more Expose events are expected to arrive. When the *count* field is 0, the last Expose event in a given sequence has arrived. All Expose events arrive in batches.

Expose events are guaranteed to be generated in a sequence. That is, if a window moves about on the screen and this movement uncovers part of your application's window, all the Expose events for that movement will arrive as part of one group. The *count* field counts down the events in the batch, until the *count* is 0, the last event in the group.

This helps your application efficiently update the display. If you wait until all Expose events in a batch have arrived, you could, for example, then update the smallest rectangle that encloses *all* the damaged area. Lazy applications could just redraw the entire window when the *count* field becomes 0.

ButtonPress Events

X provides a number of mouse-tracking events. X mouse-button events are generated when the user:

- ▩ presses down a particular mouse button
- ▩ releases the button
- ▩ moves the mouse pointer
- ▩ moves the mouse pointer while holding down a mouse button within an active window or within the child of an active window

A ButtonPress event occurs when the user presses a button on the mouse. A ButtonRelease event occurs when the user releases that same button. (Yes, it's up to your application to deal with the fact that users can press a mouse button in one of your application windows and then move the mouse outside of your windows, releasing the button there.)

The ButtonPress and ButtonRelease structures look the same:

```
typedef struct {
    int          type;
    unsigned long serial;
    Bool         send_event;
```

```
        Display*        display;
        Window          window;
        Window          root;
        Window          subwindow;
        Time            time;
        int             x, y;
        int             x_root, y_root;
        unsigned int    state;
        unsigned int    button;
        Bool            same_screen;
    } XButtonEvent;

    typedef XButtonEvent        XButtonPressedEvent;
    typedef XButtonEvent        XButtonReleasedEvent;
```

The *type* field is set to `ButtonPress` or `ButtonRelease`. The important field here is the *button* field, which contains a bitmask that shows which button was pressed or released. The X Window System defines constants for five mouse pointer buttons (although most mice have one, two, or three buttons). These constants are, not surprisingly, `Button1`, `Button2`, `Button3`, `Button4`, and `Button5`.

Generally, `Button1` is the leftmost mouse button, followed by `Button2` (middle on a three-button mouse) and then by `Button3` (right on a three-button mouse). In Motif, `Button1` is used to select items on the display, such as choosing a menu choice. `Button2` is used for drag and drop (starting with Motif 1.2), and `Button3` pops up a pop-up menu, if one is available.

The *x* and *y* fields are also useful, in that these fields show where (the coordinates) the mouse was in relation to your drawing-area window when the mouse button was pressed or released.

Modifier Keys

The *state* field indicates which mouse buttons and modifier keys, such as the **Shift**, **Caps Lock**, **Control**, or *Meta* (**Alt**, **Extend Char**, or strange-pretzel-like character, depending on your keyboard) keys, were held down at the time the event was generated. For a `ButtonRelease` event, the event is assumed to be the moment *before* the user released a mouse button—otherwise you'd never know for sure which button was released. The *state* field is set to the inclusive OR of the following bit masks listed in Table 10.4.

Table 10.4   *The state field.*

Mask	Meaning
Button1Mask	The first mouse button was down.
Button2Mask	The second mouse button was down.
Button3Mask	The third mouse button was down.
Button4Mask	The fourth mouse button was down (usually not available).
Button5Mask	The fifth mouse button was down (usually not available).
ShiftMask	A shift key was down.
ControlMask	Control key was down.
LockMask	Caps lock was down.
Mod1Mask	Typical Meta key was down.
Mod2Mask	Second Meta key was down.
Mod3Mask	Another Meta key, often not found on the keyboard, was down.
Mod4Mask	Another Meta key, often not found on the keyboard, was down.
Mod5Mask	Another Meta key, often not found on the keyboard, was down.

Printing Button-Event Information

To help decode these events, the following code will print out some of the information on a ButtonPress or ButtonRelease event:

```
    /* Print info on button event. */
void PrintButtonEvent(XButtonEvent* event)

{   /* PrintButtonEvent */

    if (event->type == ButtonPress) {
        printf("ButtonPress   ");
    } else {
        printf("ButtonRelease ");
```

```
        }

        printf("at %d, %d time %ld with ",
            event->x, event->y, event->time);

        /*
         * X defines up to five mouse buttons,
         * but most mice have only three.
         */
        switch(event->button) {
            case Button1:
                printf("Button1.\n");
                break;
            case Button2:
                printf("Button2.\n");
                break;
            case Button3:
                printf("Button3.\n");
                break;
            default: ;
        }

        if (DetectDoubleClick(event) == True) {
            printf("Double-click.\n");
        }

    }   /* PrintButtonEvent */
```

Detecting Double-Clicks of the Mouse

The code above calls the utility function `DetectDoubleClick`, which we use to detect a double-click event on the mouse. Unlike other windowing systems, X provides almost no support for detecting double clicks of the mouse buttons. Even so, users generally expect windowed software to provide some form of double-click events.

What is a double-click event? You're looking for a `ButtonPress`, `ButtonRelease`, and `ButtonPress` event that occurs within a short period of time at about the same location. No, we're not using fuzzy logic when we mention *about the same location* and *short period of time*. We say about the same location because users cannot be expected to keep the mouse steady. We expect the user to jostle the mouse a few pixels when clicking the buttons. We also expect that the user is not lightning-fast with the mouse.

The following code can help tell if a mouse event was really the second click of a double-click:

```
/* dblclick.c */
#include <Xm/Xm.h>
#include <stdio.h>

/* Globals for double-click detection. */
int global_x      = (-10);
int global_y      = (-10);
Time global_time  = (Time) 0;
int global_button = (-1);

    /* Number of pixels allowed for double-click. */
#define PIXEL_RANGE 5

    /*
     * Amount of time differential.
     * You may need to adjust this.
     */
#define TIME_RANGE   200

    /* Detect mouse double-click. */
Boolean DetectDoubleClick(XButtonEvent* event)

{   /* DetectDoubleClick */

    /* We only track ButtonPress events. */
    if (event->type != ButtonPress) {
        return False;
    }

    /* Check on double-click. */
    /* Press, release, press all in same area, at same time. */
    if ((global_button == event->button) &&
        (event->x < (global_x + PIXEL_RANGE)) &&
        (event->x > (global_x - PIXEL_RANGE)) &&
        (event->y < (global_y + PIXEL_RANGE)) &&
        (event->y > (global_y - PIXEL_RANGE)) &&
        (event->time < (global_time + TIME_RANGE)) &&
        (event->time > (global_time - TIME_RANGE)) ) {

        /* Zero out values for next check. */
        global_x      = (-10);
        global_y      = (-10);
        global_time   = (Time) 0;
        global_button = (-1);

        return True;
    } else {
        /* Save current values for next time. */
        global_x      = event->x;
        global_y      = event->y;
        global_time   = event->time;
        global_button = event->button;

        return False;
    }
```

```
}    /* DetectDoubleClick */

/* end of file dblclick.c */
```

DetectDoubleClick returns True if we have the second click of a double-click composite pseudo-event; False otherwise.

We use a few global variables to hold the last ButtonPress event for comparison. We also provide for two definitions to control the laxness or tightness of our definition of a double-click event: TIME_RANGE and PIXEL_RANGE.

There are a few limitations of this method for detecting double-click events, though. The main limitation is that since the second click may never arrive (if the user just clicked once on the mouse button), we must always perform the single-click action first and then add in the double-click action if the second click arrives. This, of course, assumes these actions are additive. This may not be the case, however. If so, you should look up timers in Chapter 13.

Mouse Movement Events

You can ask for mouse motion events to be generated only while the user holds down a mouse button, or all the time the mouse moves. Obviously, if you ask for all mouse motion, regardless of button presses, you'll see a *lot* of mouse motion events.

All these events arrive in the XMotionEvent structure:

```
typedef struct {
    int            type;
    unsigned long  serial;
    Bool           send_event;
    Display*       display;
    Window         window;
    Window         root;
    Window         subwindow;
    Time           time;
    int            x, y;
    int            x_root, y_root;
    unsigned int   state;
    char           is_hint;
    Bool           same_screen;
} XMotionEvent;

typedef XMotionEvent     XPointerMovedEvent;
```

The *type* field is set to MotionNotify. The rest of the structure generally mimics the XButtonEvent structure presented above.

Mouse Event Masks

To ask for the various kinds of mouse-motion events, there are a number of event masks, as listed in Table 10.5. Use these event bit masks to ask for events in functions like XtAddEventHandler.

Table 10.5   *Mouse pointer event masks.*

Mask	Meaning
ButtonMotionMask	The mouse is moved while a button is pressed.
Button1MotionMask	The mouse is moved while Button 1 is pressed.
Button2MotionMask	The mouse is moved while Button 2 is pressed.
Button3MotionMask	The mouse is moved while Button 3 is pressed.
Button4MotionMask	The mouse is moved while Button 4 is pressed.
Button5MotionMask	The mouse is moved while Button 5 is pressed.
ButtonPressMask	A mouse pointer button is pressed down.
ButtonReleaseMask	A mouse pointer button that was pressed down was released.
PointerMotionMask	The mouse pointer was moved (which happens very often).
PointerMotionHintMask	Special mask that asks X to compress a number of mouse movements into one event.

KeyPress Events

A KeyPress event is generated when the user presses a key on the keyboard. A KeyRelease event is generated when the user releases the pressed key. Both events arrive with an XKeyEvent structure.

```
typedef struct {
    int           type;
    unsigned long serial;
    Bool          send_event;
    Display*      display;
    Window        window;
    Window        root;
    Window        subwindow;
    Time          time;
    int           x, y;
```

```
   int          x_root, y_root;
   unsigned int state;
   unsigned int keycode;
   Bool         same_screen;
} XKeyEvent;

typedef XKeyEvent XKeyPressedEvent;
typedef XKeyEvent XKeyReleasedEvent;
```

The *keycode* tells which key was pressed or released. Unfortunately, these keycodes are vendor-specific and inherently nonportable. A keycode is the code returned by the keyboard in use for a particular key. To make use of the keycode, you really need to translate it into a more portable KeySym or a plain old ASCII string, such as *A* for when the user presses the **A** key.

A KeySym is a portable number, used across every X server, to identify a key with a given engraving. For example, the same KeySym (XK_Escape) indicates the **Esc** key on every keyboard, no matter what the key's location or underlying vendor-specific keycode is.

Looking Up KeyPress Events

The Xlib function XLookupString converts a KeyPress event into both a KeySym (a portable key encoding scheme) and an ASCII string (really an ISO Latin-1, but close enough to ASCII):

```
int XLookupString(XKeyEvent* event,
     char* string,                      /* RETURN */
     int max_length,
     KeySym* keysym,                    /* RETURN */
     XComposeStatus* compose_status) /* in/out */
```

XLookupString comes from the low-level X library, which sits underneath the Xt Intrinsics.

Usually the XComposeStatus is not handled at all. X still provides only primitive support for international applications and keyboards.

The *event* parameter is the event structure that the X server (or in this case, the Motif callback) passed to your application. The *string* parameter is a normal C string, for which you must allocate bytes to hold the ASCII result. XLookupString will *not* terminate this string, so you'll need to do this after the call. If the *event* parameter is not a KeyPress or KeyRelease event, you may have problems. Check the parameter first.

The value *max_length* specifies how many characters your code is willing to accept in the string (this value should be smaller than the number of bytes in the variable *string*, obviously). The *keysym* is a portable ID, which is useful for keys like function keys (**F1, F2** and so on) and special keys like **Page Up** and **Home**. The include files `<X11/keysym.h>` and `<X11/keysymdef.h>` define these keysyms and their families. The **F1** function key, for example, has a keysym defined as `XK_F1`. The **F2** key has a keysym of `XK_F2` and so on. The **Page Up** key, though, usually has a keysym of `XK_Prior`. You can look through the file `<X11/keysymdef.h>` for a larger list than you ever wanted to see. `XLookupString` returns the number of bytes actually placed into *string*. Remember, you need to terminate this character string.

The two important results from `XLookupString` are the *string* and the *keysym*. The *string* will contain an *a* when the user presses the **A** key (*A* for **Shift-A**) and so on. For those keys where there is no ASCII (ISO Latin-1) equivalent, like **F1**, the keysym will contain the proper result as a defined constant from the file `<X11/keysymdef.h>`.

If the key pressed is in the standard ASCII printable range, its value will be between 32 (ASCII space) and 126 (ASCII ~).

Officially, the encoding is ISO Latin-1, not ASCII. In European countries the values between 127 and 255 are probably in use for national symbols like umlauts.

N O T E

The key points here are that the keysym contains a standard constant for each character and that the *string* value may contain a printable string with the character's value.

`KeySyms` are generally portable, but some vendors, notably Hewlett-Packard, have defined extensions to the base `KeySym` set, extensions that make your code nonportable. And to make matters worse, you can run a program on a Hewlett-Packard workstation, but connect up to the display on an X terminal that has a different set of `KeySym` extensions. This is a very tough area of X, and there are not a lot of solutions. Anyway, use `XLookupString` to convert the nonportable keycode to something more portable.

Working With KeySyms

After you have a KeySym, you can deal with the key itself, or in our case, convert the KeySym to something we can print out to the screen. The Xlib function XKeysymToString returns the string *name* for a given KeySym:

```
char* XKeysymToString(KeySym keysym)
```

Don't free the returned string, as it comes from a static area. When you call XKeysymToString, you'll see results like those listed in Table 10.6.

Table 10.6 *Some strings returned by XKeysymToString.*

Returned String	Key on Keyboard
F4	**F4** function key
Next	**Page Down**, **PgDn**, or **Next**
Delete	**Del** or **Delete**
b	**B** key (not shifted)
B	**B** key (shifted)

Note that XKeysymToString doesn't return the *key*, but a symbolic *name* for the key.

Printing Keyboard-Event Information

Using XKeysymToString, we can print out some information on a given keyboard event:

```
void PrintKeyEvent(XKeyEvent* event)

{   /* PrintKeyEvent */
    KeySym          keysym;
    XComposeStatus  compose_status;
    int             length;
    char            string[10];

    switch(event->type) {
        case KeyPress:
            printf("KeyPress    "); break;
        case KeyRelease:
```

```
        printf("KeyRelease "); break;

    default:
        printf("Not a key event.\n");
        /* XLookupString fails on non-key event. */
        return;
}

/* Decode Key event. */
length = XLookupString(event,
        string,
        9,  /* max string size */
        &keysym,
        &compose_status);

if ((length > 0) && (length <= 9)) {
    string[length] = '\0';

    printf("Result of XLookupString [%s] ", string);
}

printf("KeySym [%s]\n", XKeysymToString(keysym) );

}   /* PrintKeyEvent */
```

We choose a 10-byte length for the string arbitrarily. This is generally large enough to hold any X character.

OSF KEYSYMS AND VIRTUAL KEYS

In addition to the X Window KeySyms, the Open Software Foundation, creators of the Motif toolkit, came up with their own set of *virtual keys* and *osfKeySyms*. KeySyms are intended to be portable across a number of systems, so it seems odd to add an extra layer of keyboard mapping, but that's what Motif does.

These osfKeySyms, as they are called, extend the X Window set of KeySyms with a number of Motif-specific key definitions, based on some idealized keyboard that simply no one has. The idea was to allow the designers of Motif to centralize the differences in keyboards.

Mostly, Motif binds a logical Motif key to an X KeySym. For example, the logical key osfHelp is normally bound to the XK_F1 KeySym (**F1** function key). Ideally, your keyboard should have an **osfHelp** key on it (at least, according to the OSF). Since most keyboards don't have a key labeled **osfHelp** (or even **Help** for that matter), the default is to bind the **F1** key to `osfHelp`.

That is, **F1** should call up help in most Motif applications. But some keyboards *do* provide a key labeled **Help**—Sun Type-5 and Type-4 keyboards, for example. In these cases, the proper binding for `osfHelp` would be the **Help** key. Each key may be mapped to an osfKeySym in a vendor-specific manner.

The bindings of the osfKeySyms to real (X Window) KeySyms occur in **.motifbind file**. You can place one of these in your home directory. Normally the Motif window manager, *mwm*, loads the **.motifbind** file, placing the data into a property on the root window. If you don't have a **.motifbind** file in your home directory, there may be a vendor file located inside of `/usr/lib/X11/XKeysymDB` (which usually contains other definitions as well). If that can't be found, Table 10.7 lists the fallback keys.

Table 10.7 *Fallback bindings for the osfKeySyms.*

osfKeySym	Default Key
`osfActivate`	Not bound (but usually is the **Enter** key)
`osfAddMode`	**Shift-F8**
`osfBackSpace`	**BackSpace**
`osfBeginLine`	**Home**
`osfCancel`	**Escape**
`osfClear`	**Clear**
`osfCopy`	Not bound
`osfCut`	Not bound
`osfDelete`	**Delete**
`osfDown`	**Down** (arrow)
`osfEndLine`	**End**
`osfHelp`	**F1**
`osfInsert`	**Insert**

continued

osfLeft	**Left** (arrow)
osfMenu	**F4**
osfMenuBar	**FIO**
osfPageDown	**Next**
osfPageLeft	Not bound
osfPageRight	Not bound
osfPageUp	**Prior**
osfPaste	Not bound
osfPrimaryPaste	Not bound
osfQuickPaste	not bound
osfRight	**Right** (arrow)
osfSelect	**Select**
osfUndo	**Undo**
osfUp	**Up** (arrow)

N O T E

With Solaris 2.2, Sun ships the Motif osfKeysyms in the /usr/openwin/lib/XKeysynDB file. You may have to copy that file to /usr/lib/X11 (or create a link), because many Motif applications are hard-coded to look in that directory.

In most cases, your keyboard will not have all the real keys listed. That's a problem with X Window software—you can never assume anything about the hardware.

To make matters worse, Motif layers on yet another binding for keys. Yes, we still find this hard to believe, but the osfKeySyms simply aren't enough. Motif adds in a set of virtual keys that act more like a logical event instead of an actual key press. These virtual key names begin with a *K* and most map directly to the osfKeySyms. For example, KCancel maps to osfCancel (which, in turn maps to **Escape**). KActivate maps to osfActivate, which is usually mapped to the **Return** key.

Why is this mess important? For a number of reasons, including the fact that all Motif keyboard translations use the virtual keys like KSelect, KHelp, and KCopy. In addition, all the documentation on Motif widgets uses the virtual keys as well.

Furthermore, the designers of Motif didn't stop with virtual keys. They went on to virtual mouse buttons, too, as listed in Table 10.8.

Table 10.8   *Motif virtual mouse buttons.*

Virtual Button	Real Mouse Button
BCustom	Button3
BTransfer	Button2
BExtend	**Shift**-Button1
BMenu	Button3
BSelect	Button1
BToggle	**Ctrl**-Button1

Luckily, you normally don't have to deal with this topic much. But it's important to at least be aware of these keyboard issues.

CREATING YOUR OWN EVENT-HANDLING FUNCTIONS

Most widgets provide a set of callback functions that are executed on certain pseudo-events, such as the activateCallback for XmPushButton widgets, that get executed when the user clicks the left mouse button inside the widget. There are quite a few built-in callback functions, which you can set up with XtAddCallback. If a widget callback is available, and you need notification of that event, then by all means use the widget's callback.

Sometimes, though, you need notification of other X events. For example, you may need to track the mouse motion over a XmDrawingArea widget (which we cover in the next chapter). If the widget doesn't provide a callback function for the event you're looking for, don't worry, you can always set up an Xt event-handling callback.

You can call XtAddEventHandler to set up a callback for additional events on a widget:

```
void XtAddEventHandler(Widget widget,
      EventMask eventmask,
      Boolean nonmaskable,
      XtEventHandler callback,
      XtPointer client_data)
```

The EventMask is an unsigned long int and holds the inclusive OR of the bit flags for the events you want. We provided the list of event flags in Table 10.9. XtPointer, as we've already covered, is a typedef for *char** or *void**, depending on your system.

Set the Boolean *nonmaskable* to True if you want the *callback* function called on one of the nonmaskable X events:

- ClientMessage
- GraphicsExpose
- MappingNotify
- NoExpose
- SelectionClear
- SelectionNotify
- SelectionRequest

The *client_data* parameter is a pointer to any extra data you want to pass to the callback function. The *callback* function should then take the following parameters:

```
void callback(Widget widget,
      XtPointer client_data,
      XEvent* event,
      Boolean* continue_to_dispatch)
```

In your callback function, don't mess with the *continue_to_dispatch* parameter. If you set the Boolean pointed at by *continue_to_dispatch* to False, none of the remaining callback functions will get executed. The *client_data* parameter points at the data you originally passed to XtAddEventHandler.

We cover an example event-handling callback function in the section titled "A Program to Examine X Events."

Event Masks

There are event masks to ask for just about every event type, as we show in Table 10.9.

Table 10.9   *Event masks.*

Mask Defined	Asks for Event Event Type
Button1MotionMask	MotionNotify
Button2MotionMask	MotionNotify
Button3MotionMask	MotionNotify
Button4MotionMask	MotionNotify
Button5MotionMask	MotionNotify
ButtonMotionMask	MotionNotify (any button)
ButtonPressMask	ButtonPress
ButtonReleaseMask	ButtonRelease
ColormapChangeMask	ColormapNotify
EnterWindowMask	EnterNotify
ExposureMask	Expose
FocusChangeMask	FocusIn, FocusOut
KeymapStateMask	KeymapNotify
KeyPressMask	KeyPress
KeyReleaseMask	KeyRelease
LeaveWindowMask	LeaveNotify
NoEventMask	None
OwnerGrabButtonMask	None
PointerMotionHintMask	None
PointerMotionMask	MotionNotify
PropertyChangeMask	PropertyNotify
ResizeRedirectMask	ResizeRequest

continued

StructureNotifyMask	CirculateNotify, ConfigureNotify,DestroyNotify, GravityNotify,MapNotify, ReparentNotify UnmapNotify
SubstructureNotifyMask	CirculateNotify, ConfigureNotify, CreateNotify, DestroyNotify, GravityNotify, MapNotify,ReparentNotify, UnmapNotify
SubstructureRedirectMask	CirculateRequest, ConfigureRequest, MapRequest
VisibilityChangeMask	VisibilityNotify

The event masks labeled *None* indicate that those masks don't correlate X events directly.

BUILDING YOUR OWN CUSTOM APPLICATION EVENT LOOP

So far we've covered two means for having your code execute on a certain event: widget callbacks and event-handling callbacks. These two methods are the preferred means for handling events with the Motif toolkit. Your applications, though, may need to go beyond what these two provide. In fact, you may need to create your own event loop itself.

We've found that the need to create a custom event loop usually occurs when converting legacy software to run under Motif. If you're developing a new Motif application from scratch, you shouldn't need your own event loop. But older software often assumed that it had total control over the system, and many older graphical programs poll the keyboard status, instead of having a central event loop. Other times you'll need to intercept a particular key, such as the **F3** key, to maintain compatibility with older software.

In such cases, you'll probably want to create a custom main event loop. That is, you'll need to replace XtAppMainLoop. Despite its seeming complexity, XtAppMainLoop looks surprisingly simple:

```
void XtAppMainLoop(XtAppContext app_context)

{
    XEvent      event;

    for (;;) {
        XtAppNextEvent(app_context, &event);

        /* You may want to intercept keys here... */

        XtDispatchEvent(&event);
    }
}
```

XtAppMainLoop loops forever. XtAppNextEvent blocks until the next event arrives from the X server (or another input source, such as a timer, generates an event). XtDispatchEvent then sends this event to the proper Motif widget. In between the two calls, you may want to write code that intercepts some of the events.

If you don't want a separate event loop and instead want to poll for events, you can call XtAppPending:

```
XtInputMask XtAppPending(XtAppContext app_context)
```

XtAppPending returns a nonzero status whenever events are available. If no events are available, XtAppPending flushes any pending X packets to the X server and then returns 0. XtAppPending shouldn't even block. The returned status, if nonzero, will include one or more of the bitmasks listed in Table 10.10, depending on what type of event is pending.

Table 10.10 *XtAppPending status values.*

Bit Flag	Reason
XtIMEvent	X event
XtIMTimer	Timer event, see Chapter 13 on timers
XtIMAlternateInput	Other event, such as from XtAppAddInput

You may get a combination of these bit flags if more than one type of X event is pending.

Adding Other Sources of Input

You can add other sources of input to the Xt main event loop
(XtAppMainLoop) with XtAppAddInput:

```
XtInputId XtAppAddInput(XtAppContext app_context,
    int source,
    XtPointer condition,
    XtInputCallbackProc callback,
    XtPointer client_data)
```

XtAppAddInput sets up a *callback* function to be called whenever a certain condition occurs on the *source* file descriptor. XtAppAddInput
returns an unsigned long integer ID, which can be used later on to remove
the *callback*.

The *source* parameter is specific to UNIX-like systems and indicates a
file descriptor to use for input, such as an open file, a TCP/IP socket, or a
pipe. On other operating systems, such as VMS or MS-DOS, these parameters may be defined differently.

The *condition* is again UNIX-specific and should be one of the conditions listed in Table 10.11.

Table 10.11 *XtAppAddInput conditions.*

Mask	Meaning
XtInputReadMask	Input ready
XtInputWriteMask	Output ready
XtInputExceptMask	Error condition

If you pass XtInputReadMask as the condition and the file
descriptor is always ready to read, your *callback* function will
get called all the time. Be careful about this.

N O T E

Your *callback* function should then look like:

```
typedef void (*XtInputCallbackProc)(XtPointer client_data,
```

```
        int* source,
    XtInputId* id)
```

In the callback, the *client_data* and *source* parameters are the values passed to XtAppAddInput. The *id* is the ID returned by XtAppAddInput.

The older XtAddInput function is considered obsolete:

```
XtInputId XtAddInput(int source,
    XtPointer condition,
    XtInputCallbackProc callback,
    XtPointer client_data)
```

If your code uses this function, you should upgrade to XtAppAddInput.

After you get the XtInputId returned from XtAppAddInput, you can remove a source of input with XtRemoveInput:

```
void XtRemoveInput(XtInputId id)
```

UPDATING THE DISPLAY

When one of your callback functions is executing, the main Motif event loop is not, at least on single-threaded systems (and Motif 1.2 is not ready for multithreaded applications). This fact is easy to forget, and you'll notice problems whenever you change the data in a widget but don't see it update on the screen.

For example, a common mistake is to have a "Search For" callback function that searches for a given entry. If you wanted a friendly interface, the first part of your callback should tell the user that the program is busy searching. To do this, you could set a new text string into an XmLabel widget or pop up a working dialog.

Unfortunately, if you just pop up the dialog and then continue processing, you'll notice that none of the widgets within the dialog get drawn. The window backgrounds do, but none of the widget insides get updated. That's because Motif is waiting for Expose events that tell it to draw into the newly managed windows. But, your application is still executing within the callback function. The main event loop never gets called, and the user never sees your friendly status message.

How do you get around this? Well, you could use Xt work procedures or timers (we cover both in Chapter 13). Or you can simply call XmUpdateDisplay to update the widgets in question:

```
void XmUpdateDisplay(Widget widget)
```

XmUpdateDisplay immediately handles any pending Expose events for the given *widget*.

A PROGRAM TO EXAMINE X EVENTS

We've put together a program that ties up the topics introduced in this chapter. This program creates a label widget and then sets up an event-handling callback function for Expose, mouse, and keyboard events. With this, we also add in a custom main-event loop.

The meat of the event-handling program follows:

```
/* evnthand.c */
#include <Xm/Xm.h>
#include <Xm/Label.h>
#include <stdio.h>

    /* Print info on events. */
extern void PrintEventInfo(XEvent* event);

    /*
     * Callback for Xt event handlers.
     * Note different parameters.
     */
static void event_handler(Widget widget,
    XtPointer client_data,
    XEvent* event,
    Boolean* continue_to_dispatch)

{   /* event_handler */

    PrintEventInfo(event);

}   /* event_handler */

    /* Custom main event-handling loop. */
void CustomAppMainLoop(XtAppContext app_context)

{   /* CustomAppMainLoop */
    XEvent  event;

    for (;;) {
        XtAppNextEvent(app_context, &event);
```

```
        /* You can intercept events here... */

        /*
         * Send nonintercepted
         * events to proper widgets.
         */
        XtDispatchEvent(&event);
    }

}   /* CustomAppMainLoop */

int main(int argc, char** argv)

{   /* main */
    Widget          parent;
    XtAppContext    app_context;
    Widget          label;
    Arg             args[20];
    Cardinal        n;

    /* Initialize the X Toolkit. */
    n = 0;
    parent = XtAppInitialize(&app_context,
            "Ppm",
            (XrmOptionDescList) NULL,
            0,
            (Cardinal*) &argc,
            argv,
            (String*) NULL,
            args, n);

    label = XtVaCreateManagedWidget("label",
            xmLabelWidgetClass, parent,
            NULL);

    /* Add in an event handler. */
    XtAddEventHandler(label,
        ButtonPressMask | ButtonReleaseMask |
        KeyPressMask    | KeyReleaseMask     |
        ExposureMask,
        False,
        (XtEventHandler) event_handler,
        (XtPointer) NULL);

    XtRealizeWidget(parent);

    /* Create our own event loop. */

    CustomAppMainLoop(app_context);

    return 0;

}   /* main */

/* end of file evnthand.c */
```

Printing General Event Information

The *evnthand* program calls the `PrintEventInfo` function to print out information on each event passed to our event-handling callback. `PrintEventInfo` then looks like:

```
    /* Print info on events. */
void PrintEventInfo(XEvent* event)

{   /* PrintEventInfo */

    switch(event->xany.type) {
        case Expose:
            printf("Expose event at ");
            printf("%d,%d size %d,%d count %d.\n",
                event->xexpose.x,
                event->xexpose.y,
                event->xexpose.width,
                event->xexpose.height,
                event->xexpose.count);
            break;
        case ButtonPress:
        case ButtonRelease:
            PrintButtonEvent((XButtonEvent*) event);
            break;
        case KeyPress:
        case KeyRelease:
            PrintKeyEvent((XKeyEvent*) event);
            break;
        default: ;
    }

}   /* PrintEventInfo */
```

This function calls the `PrintButtonEvent` and `PrintKeyEvent` functions presented above.

The results of the *evnthand* program are shown in Figure 10.1.

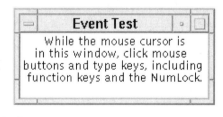

Figure 10.1 *The evnthand program.*

You'll also see a lot of data printed out to the terminal window from which you launched the *evnthand* program. For each key, mouse button, or Expose event, you'll see the primary data for that event, such as the following:

```
ButtonPress    at 133, 45 at 7327940 with Button1.
ButtonRelease at 133, 45 at 7328010 with Button1.
ButtonPress    at 134, 44 at 7328110 with Button1.
Double-click.
ButtonRelease at 134, 45 at 7328210 with Button1.
KeyPress    KeySym [Next]
KeyRelease KeySym [Next]
Expose event at 0,0 size 131,69 count 0.
```

Note how the program detects double-click events on the mouse buttons. You might also want to check how your X server handles the **NumLock** key. Oftentimes, X provides little support for the **NumLock** key.

SUMMARY

Motif programs, like all programs that sit on top of the X Window System, are driven by events arriving from the X server. These events include notification of keys pressed on the keyboard, mouse motions, and window movement. Motif handles these events in a central loop that reads the event and then dispatches it to the proper widget. In this way, Motif takes care of all X events coming from the server.

This central event loop, XtAppMainLoop, forever loops awaiting events. When an event arrives, XtAppMainLoop dispatches the event to the proper widget. Each widget then chooses how to best deal with the event. For example, an XmText widget takes incoming keys pressed on the keyboard as new text for the widget, while an XmPushButton looks for mouse-button events or a keystroke that represents a mnemonic.

Event-driven applications are powerful because the program essentially cedes control to the user. It's the user who drives the program by generating the majority of the events. The program is really still in control, but it gives the user the feeling that the user is running the show. This is very important if your applications support users who are new to computing. The big difference with event-driven programming is that events can come in at any time and in any order.

X events are messages generated by the X server and sent to your program. Sometimes other programs generate these events and then send them to your program through the X server. The user may create events by pressing keyboard keys, clicking mouse buttons, or moving the mouse pointer about the screen. Technically, the X server generates these events by monitoring the physical devices such as the keyboard, mouse, trackball, or box of dials. X even goes a step further than most windowing systems: A KeyPress is one event; the corresponding KeyRelease is another. Your applications can track mouse ButtonPress and ButtonRelease events as well.

You can also set which widget gets the initial keyboard focus for a container widget by setting the initialFocus resource and then place the value of the widget that you want to receive the initial keyboard focus. This widget must be a child of the container widget. You set this resource on the container widget, such as an XmForm or XmRowColumn widget.

An event in X is generated whenever the user presses a key on the keyboard—and whenever the user releases the key, too. Events are also generated by mouse-button clicks (press and release both generate events). In addition, the X server also generates events on its own. When a window changes size, the X server sends a ConfigureNotify event. When part of the window needs to be redrawn due to other windows moving out of the way, the X server sends an Expose event (or more likely, a number of Expose events).

Most widgets provide a set of callback functions that are executed on certain pseudo-events, such as the activateCallback for XmPushButton widgets, that get executed when the user clicks the left mouse inside the widget. There's quite a few built-in callback functions that you can set up with XtAddCallback. If a widget callback is available, and you need notification of that event, then by all means use the widget's callback.

Sometimes, though, you need notification of other X events. For example, you may need to track the mouse motion over an XmDrawingArea widget (which we cover in the next chapter). If the widget doesn't provide a callback function for the event you're looking for, don't worry, you can always set up an Xt event-handling callback.

You can call XtAddEventHandler to set up a callback for additional events on a widget.

When one of your callback functions is executing, the main Motif event loop is not, at least on single-threaded systems (and Motif 1.2 is not ready for multithreaded applications). This fact is easy to forget, and you'll notice problems whenever you change the data in a widget but don't see it update on the screen.

For example, a common mistake is to have a "Search For" callback function that searches for a given entry. If you wanted a friendly interface, the first part of your callback should tell the user that the program is busy searching. To do this, you could set a new text string into an `XmLabel` widget or pop up a working dialog.

How do you get around this? Well, you could use Xt work procedures or timers (we cover both in Chapter 13). Or you can simply call `XmUpdateDisplay` to update the widgets in question.

In the next chapter we cover the `XmDrawingArea` widget and down and dirty X drawing functions.

MOTIF FUNCTIONS AND MACROS INTRODUCED IN THIS CHAPTER

```
XmUpdateDisplay
```

X TOOLKIT INTRINSICS FUNCTIONS AND MACROS INTRODUCED IN THIS CHAPTER

```
XtAddEventHandler
XtAddInput
XtAppAddInput
XtAppPending
XtRemoveInput
```

X LIBRARY FUNCTIONS AND MACROS INTRODUCED IN THIS CHAPTER

```
XKeysymToString
XLookupString
```

CHAPTER 11

Down and Dirty with the Motif Drawing-Area Widget

This chapter covers:

- The Motif drawing-area widget
- The drawing-area callbacks
- Drawing with the low-level X library
- Xlib graphics contexts, or GCs
- The `XGCValues` Structure
- Drawing a variety of shapes
- Drawing lines, arcs, and rectangles
- Making the drawn-button widget act as a toggle
- Alternative uses for the drawn-button widget

405

USING X LIBRARY FUNCTIONS WITH THE MOTIF WIDGETS

Just about every commercial-grade Motif program we've developed required something that went beyond what the basic Motif toolkit offers. Most of these programs required some form of graphic output, be it scatter plots of data values, hypertext help, pictures of a factory assembly line, or three-dimensional CAD/CAM geometry.

Motif, by its very nature, concentrates on the user-interface portions of a program. But most programs go beyond the widgets supplied by Motif. Usually, what you need is the ability to draw some form of graphics in a window.

This chapter covers a very useful technique with Motif: the ability to use Xlib drawing functions with the Motif drawing-area and drawn-button widgets.

The drawing area widget comes in handy when you want the support a widget offers but find none of the Motif widget classes has the features you need. A common use of the drawing-area widget is for displaying scatter plots of data values, since Motif doesn't really offer a scatter-plot widget. (Of course, you can also write your own widgets. You can do this by inheriting the structure of the closest widget to what you want and then writing the proper code to integrate your widget into the Intrinsics. But writing widgets is a topic that's far too advanced for a beginning Motif book.)

SHORTCUT

Drawing with Ease

The two widget classes this chapter covers are the `XmDrawingArea` and `XmDrawnButton` classes.

A drawing area gives you a raw X window into which to draw. Create a drawing-area widget with `XmCreateDrawingArea`:

```
#include <Xm/DrawingA.h>

Widget XmCreateDrawingArea(Widget parent,
    char* widget_name,
    ArgList args
    Cardinal number_args)
```

The drawing area supports three main callbacks: exposeCallback, called on Expose events; inputCallback, called on user input; and resizeCallback, called when the window changes size. Use XtAddCallback to set up these callback functions. The drawn-button widget is like a combination of a drawing area and a push button. Create a drawn button with XmCreateDrawnButton:

```
#include <Xm/DrawnB.h>

Widget XmCreateDrawnButton(Widget parent,
     char* widget_name,
     ArgList args
     Cardinal number_args)
```

The drawn button supports five main callbacks: activateCallback, which gets called like the XmPushButton callback of the same name; armCallback, called when the pushbutton gets armed (gains the keyboard focus or the mouse enters the window); disarmCallback, called when the mouse leaves the window; exposeCallback, called when you need to redraw parts of the window; and resizeCallback, called when the window changes size.

THE DRAWING-AREA WIDGET

The drawing-area widget is essentially a widget that provides you with a blank drawing area, a rectangular area that your program can do with as it pleases using low-level X library calls. Even so, this widget is fully integrated into the Motif toolkit, so you can change resources and set up callbacks. You'll want to set up plenty of callbacks, because that's how you know when to draw into your drawing area.

Under the hood, the drawing-area widget is just a plain X window, but it's an X window that works with the Xt/Motif event loop, it's fully integrated into the Motif toolkit, and it supports X resources.

We summarize the XmDrawingArea widget class in Table 11.1.

Table 11.1   *The XmDrawingArea widget class.*

Widget class:	XmDrawingArea
Class pointer:	xmDrawingAreaWidgetClass
Include file:	<Xm/DrawingA.h>
Create with:	XmCreateDrawingArea

Create a drawing-area widget with XmCreateDrawingArea:

```
#include <Xm/DrawingA.h>

Widget XmCreateDrawingArea(Widget parent,
    char* widget_name,
    ArgList args
    Cardinal number_args)
```

Manage the widget with XtManageChild.

Drawing-Area Resources

In the code below (in the file **drawarea.c**), we create a drawing-area widget and arbitrarily set its width and height, using the width (XmNwidth in C programs) and height (XmNheight in C programs) resources. In our program, we hard-code the size for the drawing area, but you may want to place these values in a resource file or use a form widget or other container widget to control the layout and size of the drawing area.

N O T E   The drawing-area widget doesn't hold a size very well. We've found that in many versions of Motif, the drawing area tries to become as small as possible, which is very small. Hence, you'll see us hard-code the widget size in our program below.

Another resource you'll probably want to set is the resizePolicy resource (XmNresizePolicy in C programs). This resource controls whether the widget will grow or shrink. You can set it to one of the following values:

■   XmRESIZE_ANY

- ▪ XmRESIZE_GROW
- ▪ XmRESIZE_NONE

A value of XmRESIZE_NONE means that the drawing-area widget will maintain a fixed size. It will not grow or shrink, even if its surrounding parent form or other constraint widget changes size. A value of XmRESIZE_GROW means that the drawing-area widget may grow, but it won't ever shrink. A value of XmRESIZE_ANY (the default) means that the drawing-area widget will grow and shrink normally, as the user changes the size of the application's main window, for instance.

There's not really much to creating a drawing-area widget. You can treat a drawing-area widget as a widget in which you have to do everything manually. The main concern is drawing what you want into the widget. To do this, you need to set up the proper callback functions.

Drawing-Area Callbacks

The drawing-area widget offers three main types of callback functions: the expose callback, the input callback, and the resize callback. All three callbacks are tied intimately to the X Window System events that are generated on windows. The drawing-area widget gives you a raw window under X, and therefore, these callbacks are necessary if you want to draw into the window.

The callbacks are listed in Table 11.2.

Table 11.2   *Drawing-area callbacks.*

Callback	Name in C Programs	Meaning
exposeCallback	XmNexposeCallback	Redraw part of window
inputCallback	XmNinputCallback	User input arrived in window
resizeCallback	XmNresizeCallback	Window changed size

The expose callback function is called when the drawing-area widget's window gets an Expose event from the X server, or internally from Motif or the Xt Intrinsics. As we discussed in the last chapter, when your application gets an Expose event, it means that you need to redraw the portion of the window that was exposed.

The input callback is called whenever the user clicks a mouse button or presses a key inside your drawing-area widget's window. And, the resize callback is called whenever the drawing-area widget's window changes size.

All three callbacks get a pointer to an XmDrawingAreaCallbackStruct as the *call_data* parameter. The XmDrawingAreaCallbackStruct looks like:

```
typedef struct {
    int     reason;
    XEvent* event;
    Window  window;
} XmDrawingAreaCallbackStruct;
```

The *reason* field will be one of the following:

- ■ XmCR_EXPOSE for expose callbacks
- ■ XmCR_INPUT for input callbacks
- ■ XmCR_RESIZE for resize callbacks

We'll cover the easier callbacks first; then tackle the expose callback.

The Input Callback

The inputCallback gets called on KeyPress, KeyRelease, ButtonPress, and ButtonRelease events.

Some versions of Motif fail to call the inputCallback on KeyPress and KeyRelease events. This is a bug.

N O T E

We covered these input events in the last chapter, so in our *drawarea* program, we'll just print out the input events using the PrintEventInfo function provided in the last chapter.

The Resize Callback

The resizeCallback can cause a lot of grief. First, the callback may get called before a valid window exists for the widget, which is a problem for drawing functions (see the section entitled "Creating a Graphics Context," below). Second, the *event* field in the XmDrawingAreaCallbackStruct structure is NULL for the `resizeCallback`. If your code tries to access the *event* field, you'll likely experience a program crash.

Even with the NULL event, you can still get the widget's new width and height (the whole reason for the `resizeCallback` in the first place) by reading the `width` and `height` resources:

```
Widget      widget;
Dimension   width, height;

/* Get size of window. */
XtVaGetValues(widget,
    XmNwidth,  &width,
    XmNheight, &height,
    NULL);
```

The Expose Callback

The whole point of the `exposeCallback` is to alert your application that it needs to redraw part of the drawing-area's window.

When the `exposeCallback` gets called, the size of the exposed area is then in the *event* field of the `XmDrawingAreaCallbackStruct` pointer. This field points to an `XEvent`, which in this case is an `XExposeEvent`. From the last chapter, this looks like:

```
typedef struct {
    int           type;    /* Expose */
    unsigned long serial;
    Bool          send_event;
    Display*      display;
    Window        window;
    int           x, y;
    int           width, height;
    int           count;
} XExposeEvent;
```

The exposed area—the area that needs to be redrawn—will be held in the *x, y, width,* and *height* fields. (Remember that the origin is at the top left corner of a window.)

The *count* field counts down to 0, at which time the last Expose event in a batch has arrived. In the program below, we wait until the *count* field is 0 and then redraw the entire window. This is a lazy method for handling Expose events.

Redrawing the contents of the window, which you need to do on Expose events, requires a set of drawing functions.

DRAWING WITH THE LOW-LEVEL X LIBRARY

Luckily, the low-level X library provides a host of drawing functions, of which we'll just introduce the basics in this chapter. The drawing functions we cover include:

■ XDrawLine

■ XDrawRectangle

■ XFillRectangle

■ XDrawArc

■ XFillArc

Drawing Lines

The function XDrawLine is the X library line-drawing function (there are a few more, too, but this will suffice for now):

```
XDrawLine(Display* display,
     Drawable drawable,
     GC gc,
     int x1, int y1, /* starting point */
     int x2, int y2) /* ending point */
```

XDrawLine draws a line from (*x1,y1*) to (*x2,y2*) in the given window and using the given graphics context (GC). The GC controls the pen, or drawing, parameters. We cover more on GCs below. (Note that the *drawable* parameter can be a window or pixmap as well. We cover pixmaps in the next chapter.)

Remember that the X Window coordinate system places the origin in the upper left corner. Y values increase going down. Depending on what graphics systems you're used to, the origin location may fool you for awhile.

Drawing Rectangles

XDrawRectangle draws the outline of a rectangle:

```
XDrawRectangle(Display* display,
     Drawable drawable,
     GC gc,
     int x, int y,           /* 16-bit int */
```

```
unsigned int width,    /* 16-bit unsigned int */
unsigned int height)   /* 16-bit unsigned int */
```

You'll quickly note that all rectangular shapes in the X Window System are defined by a location (*x,y*) and a size (*width, height*). The location is the upper left corner.

Filling Rectangles

XFillRectangle fills in a rectangle:

```
XFillRectangle(Display* display,
    Drawable drawable,
    GC gc,
    int x, int y,          /* 16-bit int */
    unsigned int width,    /* 16-bit unsigned int */
    unsigned int height)   /* 16-bit unsigned int */
```

Drawing Arcs

Every graphics system seems to define arcs differently. In X, an *arc* is bounded by a rectangle, and the sweep of the arc is limited to the box formed by the rectangle. The arc begins at a *start angle* and draws an arc for a distance specified by a *path* or *sweep angle*. If that isn't confusing enough, the angle values are given in 64ths of a degree—meaning a full circular path is 360 degrees times 64—or 23,040.

XDrawArc, as the function name seems to imply, draws an arc:

```
XDrawArc(Display* display,
    Drawable drawable,
    GC gc,
    int x, y,                 /* 16-bit int */
    unsigned int width,       /* 16-bit unsigned int */
    unsigned int height,      /* 16-bit unsigned int */
    int start_angle,          /* 16-bit int, degrees * 64 */
    int sweep_angle)          /* 16-bit int, degrees * 64 */
```

XDrawArc draws an arc that fits in a rectangle, from *start_angle* to *sweep_angle*. Angles are in 64ths of a degree. That is, multiply the degrees by 64 to get the value to place into *start_angle* and *sweep_angle*.

The *width* and *height* parameters must be positive numbers, or you can get in trouble, especially with shared-library X servers. You may want to test the *width* and *height* parameters each time you try to draw or fill an arc:

```
if ( width < 1 ) {
```

```
        width = 1;
    }

    if ( height < 1 ) {
        height = 1;
    }
```

There's also a routine to fill in an arc. XFillArc fills in an arc:

```
XFillArc(Display* display,
    Drawable drawable,
    GC gc,
    int x, y,              /* 16-bit int */
    unsigned int width,    /* 16-bit unsigned int */
    unsigned int height,   /* 16-bit unsigned int */
    int start_angle,       /* 16-bit int, degrees * 64 */
    int sweep_angle)       /* 16-bit int, degrees * 64 */
```

XFillArc is based on the GC's current arc-filling mode (ArcChord or ArcPieSlice). ArcChord draws a line to connect the ends of the arcs and then fills in the inside area. ArcPieSlice, as the name implies, looks like it's filling a pie slice.

Setting the Arc-Filling Mode

You can change a GC's arc-filling mode with XSetArcMode:

```
XSetArcMode(Display* display,
    GC gc,
    int arc_mode)
```

XSetArcMode sets the mode for filling arcs in the graphics context to ArcChord (draw chords or circle segments) or ArcPieSlice (fill in slices of circles).

Flushing the Output Queue

When you're done drawing, call XFlush to send all the queued up drawing requests out to the X server (usually over a network link). XFlush flushes out the output queue and sends it to the X server:

```
XFlush(Display* display)
```

If you use Xlib functions, you should always call XFlush after drawing.

Because each batch you send to the X server may result in a network communication packet, judicious use of XFlush can make your programs work a lot better. If you call XFlush after every drawing function, you'll get your graphics out to the screen as soon as possible—remember the asynchronous delay imposed by X's distributed nature. Each time you call XFlush, though, your application incurs a network packet overhead. You probably don't want to call XFlush after every drawing function.

Instead, the best place to call XFlush is after you've drawn a logical grouping of items. For example, if you are drawing out a whole window of spreadsheet cells, call the Xlib drawing functions for the whole window and only then call XFlush to send out all the output. This way it looks like the whole window was updated at once. This generally looks better than drawing and flushing each cell one at a time—even if the total time for the drawing is the same.

CREATING A GRAPHICS CONTEXT

We mentioned a *graphics context*, or GC above. GCs are catch-all data structures that contain almost everything needed to specify pen parameters for drawing. The GC contains the foreground and background colors, the width of the pen for drawing lines, whether lines should be dashed or solid, and so on.

Before you can draw anything with the Xlib, you need to create a graphics context. A GC contains values like the current pen color and width of lines. Your application can have multiple GCs, but each one uses memory in the X server, so you don't want to create thousands of GCs, or you'll bog down the X server.

Use XCreateGC to create a new graphics context:

```
GC XCreateGC(Display* display,
     Drawable drawable,
     unsigned long mask,
     XGCValues* xgcvalues)
```

The *display* is the display connection pointer, and the *drawable* is the drawing-area widget's window (see "Getting the Display Pointer," below). Each GC is tied to a given *drawable*, usually to the drawing-area widget's window ID. (A drawable in X can be a window or a pixmap. We cover pixmaps in Chapter 12.)

There are a host of options for the *mask* and *xgcvalues* parameters, both of which are simply not needed for the simple graphics context we're going to create. In the code below, we create a GC for drawing:

```
Widget  drawa;
```

```
GC       gc;

gc = XCreateGC(XtDisplay(drawa),
         XtWindow(drawa),
         0L,  /* mask */
         (XGCValues*) NULL);
```

If you want to set up some GC parameters at creation, you'll need to fill in the fields you want in the XGCValues structure and then mark which fields you've filled in by setting in bit flags into the *mask*. The reason for the *mask* is that you don't have to fill in all the values into the XGCValues structure—just the values you want. The *mask* then contains a set of bit flags, indicating which fields of the XGCValues structure you filled in. The bit flags contain the inclusive OR of a set of predefined flags.

The XGCValues Structure

If you want to use different values than the defaults when you create a GC, you need to fill in the proper fields in the XGCValues structure:

```
typedef struct {
    int             function;      /* e.g. GXxor */
    unsigned long   plane_mask;
    unsigned long   foreground;
    unsigned long   background;
    int             line_width;    /* (in pixels) */
    int             line_style;
    int             cap_style;
    int             join_style;
    int             fill_style;
    int             fill_rule;
    int             arc_mode;
    Pixmap          tile;
    Pixmap          stipple;       /* 1 plane pixmap */
    int             ts_x_origin;
    int             ts_y_origin;
    Font            font;
    int             subwindow_mode;
    Bool            graphics_exposures;
    int             clip_x_origin;
    int             clip_y_origin;
    Pixmap          clip_mask;
    int             dash_offset;
    char            dashes;
} XGCValues;
```

If you create a GC and change some of the defaults in the XGCValues structure, you also need to set the proper bits in the *mask*. The *mask* holds the inclusive OR of the bit flags for the fields you fill in. In Table 11.3, we present the XGCValues field, the default value and the bit mask name.

Use the proper bit flags for the fields you fill in the XGCValues structure. In many cases, though, you can just stick with the default GC values.

Table 11.3 *GC default values and bitmasks.*

XGCValues Field	Default Value	Bitmask Name
arc_mode	ArcPieSlice	GCArcMode
background	1 (sometimes white)	GCBackground
cap_style	CapButt	GCCapStyle
clip_mask	None	GCClipMask
clip_x_origin	0	GCClipXOrigin
clip_y_origin	0	GCClipYOrigin
dashes	[4,4]	GCDashList
dash_offset	0	GCDashOffset
fill_rule	EvenOddRule	GCFillRule
fill_style	FillSolid	GCFillStyle
font	fixed	GCFont
foreground	0 (sometimes black)	GCForeground
function	GXcopy	GCFunction
graphics_exposures	True	GCGraphicsExposures
join_style	JoinMiter	GCJoinStyle
line_style	LineSolid	GCLineStyle
line_width	0	GCLineWidth
plane_mask	All planes (all 1s)	GCPlaneMask
stipple	Pixmap with all 1s	GCStipple
subwindow_mode	ClipByChildren	GCSubwindowMode
tile	pixmap with foreground	GCTile
ts_x_origin	0	GCTileStipXOrigin
ts_y_origin	0	GCTileStipYOrigin

N O T E

The default foreground and background colors (0 and 1, respectively) sometimes equate to white and black. But you cannot depend on this across computer systems. Always set the foreground and background color to values valid for your system. You can set the foreground and background colors with XSetForeground and XSetBackground, respectively:

```
XSetForeground(Display* display,
        GC gc,
        unsigned long foreground)

XSetBackground(Display* display,
        GC gc,
        unsigned long background)
```

The *foreground* and *background* parameters are the color indexes you want to draw with, such as the color index from the BlackPixel macro:

```
unsigned long
BlackPixel(Display* display, int
        screen_number)
```

BlackPixel returns the color index for black in the default colormap. (Actually, you're not guaranteed this color is black, but it usually is.) WhitePixel similarly returns the color index for white in the default colormap, with the same caveats:

```
unsigned long
WhitePixel(Display* display, int
        screen_number)
```

These options are too involved to get into in a book on Motif. See one of our other books, *Professional Graphics Programming in the X Window System* (Johnson and Reichard, MIS: Press, 1993), for more on the graphics context and drawing with the X library.

Getting the Display Pointer

To call just about any Xlib function, we need a display pointer and usually a window ID. This display pointer is first created when we set up a connection to an X server. In most Motif programs, the function XtAppInitialize hides the opening of a display connection, so we usually never see (and never have to deal with the hassles of) a display pointer.

(See `XtOpenDisplay` in Chapter 14, though.) In addition, since we're using Motif, we deal primarily with *widgets* instead of *windows*. To use the drawing functions introduced in this chapter, you must extract the display pointer and window ID for a given widget.

`XtDisplay` returns the display pointer for a given widget:

```
Display* XtDisplay(Widget widget)
```

If you have a gadget instead of a full-blown widget, use `XtDisplayOfObject`:

```
Display* XtDisplayOfObject(Widget widget)
```

`XtWindow` returns the window ID for a given widget:

```
Window XtWindow(Widget widget)
```

If you have a gadget, you need to use the `XtWindowOfObject` function to get the window ID:

```
Window XtWindowOfObject(Widget widget)
```

`XtWindowOfObject` returns the window ID of the parent widget, or the parent's parent widget, and so on if you have gadgets within gadgets.

N O T E Each widget normally has an associated window. None of these windows are created, though, until you call `XtRealizeWidget` to realize a widget hierarchy. Yet `XCreateGC` requires a valid window ID. Because of this, you'll want to call `XtRealizeWidget` *before* creating a graphics context.

Normally, when you call `XtRealizeWidget`, you also map the windows to the screen. This often makes your interface appear before you've created your graphic contexts (and performed other setup activity). If you don't like this, you can set the `mappedWhenManaged` resource to `False` before calling `XtAppInitialize`, as we do in the program below. This ensures that your top-level widget's window won't get mapped to the screen (and be made visible) until you later call `XtMapWidget`:

```
void XtMapWidget(Widget widget)
```

We usually call `XtMapWidget` just before calling `XtAppMainLoop`. Look in the **drawarea.c** code, presented below, to see how this all works together:

```
/* ... */

/* Don't map window with call to XtRealizeWidget. */
XtSetArg(args[n], XmNmappedWhenManaged, False); n++;

parent = XtAppInitialize(&app_context,
        "Ppm",
        (XrmOptionDescList) NULL,
        0,
        (Cardinal*) &argc,
        argv,
        (String*) NULL,
        args, n);

/* ... */

/* Must realize widgets before getting window ID. */
XtRealizeWidget(parent);

/* Create GC */
gc = XCreateGC(XtDisplay(drawa),
        XtWindow(drawa),
        0L,
        (XGCValues*) NULL);

/* ... */

/* Now, map widget. */
XtMapWidget(parent);

XtAppMainLoop(app_context);
```

Drawing Some Shapes

Before we get too involved in the *drawarea* example program, we should
cover drawing some shapes using the X library functions introduced above.
The following function, DrawShapes, uses these drawing functions to draw
a few shapes in the given *window*:

```
    /* Draw some shapes with Xlib. */
void DrawShapes(Display* display,
    Window window,
    GC gc,
    int width,
    int height)

{   /* DrawShapes */

    XDrawLine(display, window, gc,
        0, 0, width, height);

    XDrawLine(display, window, gc,
        0, height, width, 0);
```

```
XDrawRectangle(display, window, gc,
    width/4, height/4,
    width/2, height/2);

XFillRectangle(display, window, gc,
    width/2, height/2,
    width/4, height/4);

XFillArc(display, window, gc,
    width - 80, 20,
    80, 80,
    0, 270 * 64);

/* Send output to X server. */
XFlush(display);

}    /* DrawShapes */
```

This short primer won't make you an Xlib expert. There's so much material in the X library that you could write a book or three—which in fact we did (*Professional Graphics Programming in the X Window System, X Window Applications Programming*, and *Advanced X Window Applications Programming*; MIS: Press). There are a great many books on Xlib programming that you should read if you plan on using the drawing-area widget in your applications. There's just not enough space to cover Xlib and Motif programming at the same time. Try the example program in this chapter. If you have questions, start looking up some Xlib books.

THE DRAWING-AREA PROGRAM

The following program creates an `XmDrawingArea` widget and draws using Xlib calls into the widget's window (only when `Expose` events arrive, of course):

```
/* drawarea.c */
#include <Xm/Xm.h>
#include <Xm/DrawingA.h>
#include <stdio.h>

    /* Print info on events. */
extern void PrintEventInfo(XEvent* event);

    /* Draw some shapes with Xlib. */
void DrawShapes(Display* display,
    Window window,
    GC gc,
    int width,
```

```
            int height)

{       /* DrawShapes */

        XDrawLine(display, window, gc,
            0, 0, width, height);

        XDrawLine(display, window, gc,
            0, height, width, 0);

        XDrawRectangle(display, window, gc,
            width/4, height/4,
            width/2, height/2);

        XFillRectangle(display, window, gc,
            width/2, height/2,
            width/4, height/4);

        XFillArc(display, window, gc,
            width - 80, 20,
            80, 80,
            0, 270 * 64);

        /* Send output to X server. */
        XFlush(display);

}       /* DrawShapes */

void drawCB(Widget widget,
        XtPointer client_data,
        XtPointer call_data)

{       /* drawCB */
        XmDrawingAreaCallbackStruct*  ptr;
        GC*                           gc_ptr;
        Dimension                     width, height;

        /*
         * The Graphics Context is passed
         * as the client_data. Note pointer!
         */
        gc_ptr = (GC*) client_data;

        ptr = (XmDrawingAreaCallbackStruct*) call_data;

        if (ptr == NULL) {
            return;
        }

        switch(ptr->reason) {
            case XmCR_RESIZE:
                /* Get size of window. */
                XtVaGetValues(widget,
                    XmNwidth,  &width,
                    XmNheight, &height,
```

```
                    NULL);

            printf("New window size is %d by %d\n",
                width, height);
            break;
    case XmCR_EXPOSE:
        /*
         * We draw when all Expose
         * events are in.
         */
        if (ptr->event->xexpose.count == 0) {
            /* Get size of window. */
            XtVaGetValues(widget,
                XmNwidth,  &width,
                XmNheight, &height,
                NULL);

            DrawShapes(XtDisplay(widget),
                XtWindow(widget),
                *gc_ptr, (int) width, (int) height);
        }
        break;
    case XmCR_INPUT:
        PrintEventInfo(ptr->event);
        break;

    }

}   /* drawCB */

int main(int argc, char** argv)

{   /* main */
    Widget          parent;
    XtAppContext    app_context;
    Widget          drawa;
    Arg             args[20];
    Cardinal        n;
    GC              gc;
    int             screen;
    Display*        display;

    /* Initialize the X Toolkit. */
    n = 0;
    XtSetArg(args[n], XmNtitle, "Drawing Area"); n++;

    /* Don't map window with call to XtRealizeWidget. */
    XtSetArg(args[n], XmNmappedWhenManaged, False); n++;

    /* Hard-code a size. */
    XtSetArg(args[n], XmNwidth,  400); n++;
    XtSetArg(args[n], XmNheight, 350); n++;

    parent = XtAppInitialize(&app_context,
            "Ppm",
```

```
                    (XrmOptionDescList) NULL,
                    0,
                    (Cardinal*) &argc,
                    argv,
                    (String*) NULL,
                    args, n);

        /* Hard-code a size. */
        n = 0;
        XtSetArg(args[n], XmNresizePolicy, XmRESIZE_ANY); n++;

        drawa = XmCreateDrawingArea(parent,
                "drawa", args, n);

        /*
         * The graphics context isn't created yet, so
         * we pass a pointer to it as the client_data.
         */
        XtAddCallback(drawa,
            XmNexposeCallback,
            (XtCallbackProc) drawCB,
            (XtPointer) &gc);

        XtAddCallback(drawa,
            XmNinputCallback,
            (XtCallbackProc) drawCB,
            (XtPointer) &gc);

        XtAddCallback(drawa,
            XmNresizeCallback,
            (XtCallbackProc) drawCB,
            (XtPointer) &gc);

        XtManageChild(drawa);

        /* Must realize widgets before getting window ID. */
        XtRealizeWidget(parent);

        /* Create GC */
        display = XtDisplay(drawa);

        gc = XCreateGC(display,
                XtWindow(drawa),
                0L,
                (XGCValues*) NULL);

        screen = DefaultScreen(display);

        /* Set foreground and background colors. */
        XSetForeground(display, gc,
            BlackPixel(display, screen) );

        XSetBackground(display, gc,
            WhitePixel(display, screen) );

        /* Now, map widget. */
```

```
        XtMapWidget(parent);

        XtAppMainLoop(app_context);

        return 0;

    }    /* main */

    /* end of file drawarea.c */
```

One tricky part of the above program is how we pass a pointer to a GC as the client data to the drawing-area callback functions. Why pass a pointer to the GC? The GC is itself a pointer and XCreateGC allocates the memory for the GC structure. Since we set up the callbacks before creating the GC, we need to pass a pointer to the GC, instead of passing the GC itself. We could reverse the order of the calls and then pass just the plain GC and not a pointer to the GC. We wanted to point this out so that you're aware of these issues when passing data to your callback functions.

Running the Drawing-Area Program

When you run the *drawtest* program, you'll see a window like the one shown in Figure 11.1.

Figure 11.1   *The drawarea program.*

THE DRAWNBUTTON WIDGET CLASS

The XmDrawnButton widget is one of those widgets for which you don't really seem to have a use—at least at first glance. Like the XmDrawingArea widget, an XmDrawnButton widget provides an empty window in which to draw, but the XmDrawnButton widget adds a 3D border and the semantics of the pushbutton widget. The best way to view the XmDrawnButton widget is as a combination of the drawing area and the pushbutton. Like the XmDrawingArea, you can set up expose and resize callbacks. Like the pushbutton widget, you have an activate callback and can set the labelString resource to display a text string.

In most cases, a drawing-area or a pushbutton widget will be more appropriate than a drawn button (since both are easier to use than the drawn button). But the XmDrawnButton widget does some things very well. For instance, you can use an XmDrawnButton widget for a pushbutton that maintains its state, that is, a pushbutton that stays pushed (until you push it again). With this, you configure the XmDrawnButton to act much like a toggle button, but without the indicators. We cover how to do this below.

Table 11.4 *The XmDrawnButton widget class.*

Widget class:	XmDrawnButton
Class pointer:	xmDrawnButtonWidgetClass
Include file:	<Xm/DrawnB.h>
Create with:	XmCreateDrawnButton

Create an XmDrawnButton with XmCreateDrawnButton:

```
#include <Xm/DrawnB.h>

Widget XmCreateDrawnButton(Widget parent,
      char* widget_name,
      ArgList args
      Cardinal number_args)
```

Manage the widget with XtManageChild.

The resources listed in Table 11.5 are useful on the XmDrawnButton.

Table 11.5   *XmDrawnButton resources.*

Resource	Type	Default Value
labelString	XmString	NULL
pushButtonEnabled	Boolean	False
shadowType	unsigned char	XmSHADOW_ETCHED_IN

The shadowType can hold one of the following values:

■ XmSHADOW_ETCHED_IN

■ XmSHADOW_ETCHED_OUT

■ XmSHADOW_IN

■ XmSHADOW_OUT

The XmDrawnButton widget supports the callback functions listed in Table 11.6.

Table 11.6   *XmDrawnButton callback functions.*

Callback	Name in C Programs	Reason
activateCallback	XmNactivateCallback	XmCR_ACTIVATE
armCallback	XmNarmCallback	XmCR_ARM
disarmCallback	XmNdisarmCallback	XmCR_DISARM
exposeCallback	XmNexposeCallback	XmCR_EXPOSE
resizeCallback	XmNresizeCallback	XmCR_RESIZE

Each callback passes a pointer to an XmDrawnButtonCallbackStruct as the *call_data*. This structure looks like the following:

```
typedef struct {
    int     reason;
    XEvent* event;
    Window  window;
```

```
    int     click_count;
} XmDrawnButtonCallbackStruct;
```

As with the XmDrawingArea, the *event* field is NULL for the resize callback.

Making a Drawn Button Act as a Toggle

We can make an XmDrawnButton widget act as a toggle and maintain its state with a minimum amount of work. To do this, we need to configure the drawn button at creation time as well as set up an arm callback.

At creation time, set the pushButtonEnabled resource to False. This prevents the drawn button from changing the 3D bevel to follow the pushbutton semantics. If we leave the pushButtonEnabled resource alone, then the drawn button will look too much like a pushbutton. Instead, we want to control the 3D bevel. In fact, when the button is in its "in" state, we want to reverse the normal 3D bevel. That's why we need control over this feature.

We also must set up the initial shadowType to XmSHADOW_OUT. This will make the drawn button look like a pushbutton widget.

For the arm callback, we need to switch the 3D bevel each time the function is called. That is, on the first button press in the button (the first time the arm callback gets called), we want to change the drawn button to its "in" state. Then, the next time the user clicks the mouse over the button, we want to change it to its "out" state. The following callback function, set up as the armCallback, does just that.

```
        /* Switch "state" on arm callback. */
    void armCB(Widget widget,
        XtPointer client_data,
        XtPointer call_data)

    {   /* armCB */
        unsigned char   shadow;

        printf("XmCR_ARM\n");

        /* Get current shadow. */
        XtVaGetValues(widget,
            XmNshadowType, &shadow,
            NULL);

        /* Reverse shadow. */
        if (shadow == XmSHADOW_IN) {
```

```
        XtVaSetValues(widget,
            XmNshadowType, XmSHADOW_OUT,
            NULL);
    } else {
        XtVaSetValues(widget,
            XmNshadowType, XmSHADOW_IN,
            NULL);
    }

}   /* armCB */
```

A Program to Test the Drawn-Button Widget

The following short program shows how to use the XmDrawnButton widget in your code:

```
/* drawnb.c */
#include <Xm/Xm.h>
#include <Xm/DrawnB.h>
#include <Xm/RowColumn.h>
#include <stdio.h>

    /* Switch "state" on arm callback. */
void armCB(Widget widget,
    XtPointer client_data,
    XtPointer call_data)

{   /* armCB */
    unsigned char    shadow;

    printf("XmCR_ARM\n");

    /* Get current shadow. */
    XtVaGetValues(widget,
        XmNshadowType, &shadow,
        NULL);

    /* Reverse shadow. */
    if (shadow == XmSHADOW_IN) {
        XtVaSetValues(widget,
            XmNshadowType, XmSHADOW_OUT,
            NULL);
    } else {
        XtVaSetValues(widget,
            XmNshadowType, XmSHADOW_IN,
            NULL);
    }

}   /* armCB */
```

```
        /* Rest of callbacks for drawn button. */
void drawCB(Widget widget,
    XtPointer client_data,
    XtPointer call_data)

{   /* drawCB */
    XmDrawnButtonCallbackStruct* ptr;

    ptr = (XmDrawnButtonCallbackStruct*) call_data;

    switch(ptr->reason) {
        case XmCR_ACTIVATE:
            printf("\t XmCR_ACTIVATE\n");
            break;
        case XmCR_DISARM:
            printf("\t XmCR_DISARM\n");
            break;
        case XmCR_EXPOSE:
            printf("\t XmCR_EXPOSE\n");
            break;
        case XmCR_RESIZE:
            printf("\t XmCR_RESIZE\n");
            break;
        default: ;
    }

}   /* drawCB */

int main(int argc, char** argv)

{   /* main */
    Widget          parent;
    XtAppContext    app_context;
    Widget          row, drawnb;
    Arg             args[20];
    Cardinal        n;
    XmString        xmstring;

    /* Initialize the X Toolkit. */
    n = 0;
    XtSetArg(args[n], XmNtitle, "Drawn Button"); n++;

    parent = XtAppInitialize(&app_context,
            "Ppm",
            (XrmOptionDescList) NULL,
            0,
            (Cardinal*) &argc,
            argv,
            (String*) NULL,
            args, n);

    /* Use a row column container. */
    n = 0;
    row = XtVaCreateManagedWidget("row",
            xmRowColumnWidgetClass, parent,
```

```
                NULL);

    /* Create drawn button. */
    n = 0;
    XtSetArg(args[n], XmNpushButtonEnabled, False); n++;
    XtSetArg(args[n], XmNshadowType, XmSHADOW_OUT); n++;

    xmstring = XmStringCreateSimple("Drawn Button");

    XtSetArg(args[n], XmNlabelString, xmstring); n++;

    drawnb = XmCreateDrawnButton(row,
            "drawnb", args, n);

    XmStringFree(xmstring);

    /* Set up callbacks. */
    XtAddCallback(drawnb,
        XmNexposeCallback,
        (XtCallbackProc) drawCB,
        (XtPointer) NULL);

    XtAddCallback(drawnb,
        XmNarmCallback,
        (XtCallbackProc) armCB,
        (XtPointer) NULL);

    XtAddCallback(drawnb,
        XmNresizeCallback,
        (XtCallbackProc) drawCB,
        (XtPointer) NULL);

    XtAddCallback(drawnb,
        XmNactivateCallback,
        (XtCallbackProc) drawCB,
        (XtPointer) NULL);

    XtAddCallback(drawnb,
        XmNdisarmCallback,
        (XtCallbackProc) drawCB,
        (XtPointer) NULL);

    XtManageChild(drawnb);

    XtRealizeWidget(parent);
    XtAppMainLoop(app_context);

    return 0;

}   /* main */

/* end of file drawnb.c */
```

Other Uses for the Drawn-Button Widget

There are a number of other uses you can put the XmDrawnButton to. For instance, if you want to animate an image inside a pushbutton, the XmDrawnButton is perfect. This animation may help show the user what the pushbutton does. You use the armCallback to start the animation (after a short delay to allow the user to move the mouse around without starting a host of animations) and the disarmCallback to turn the animation off.

You may also want to change the picture inside the pushbutton while it's pressed, to present feedback to the user. For example, a pushbutton that takes a long time to execute could dynamically update its status by changing the picture inside the XmDrawnButton.

We suspect you can come up with a few more uses for the XmDrawnButton widget.

SUMMARY

When the Motif widget set doesn't offer what you need, you have three options. (1) You can dump Motif and get something else (but you wouldn't have read this far if that was a viable option, would you). (2) You can write your own widget, which may be necessary but is something newcomers to Motif want to avoid at all costs. (3) You can use the Motif drawing-area widget, a widget designed to meet those cases when a regular widget isn't enough.

If you use the drawing-area widget, you should learn about the X library (Xlib) and its set of function calls and events, because the drawing-area widget basically provides you a raw window in the X environment.

MOTIF FUNCTIONS AND MACROS INTRODUCED IN THIS CHAPTER

```
XmCreateDrawingArea
XmCreateDrawnButton
```

X TOOLKIT INTRINSICS FUNCTIONS AND MACROS INTRODUCED IN THIS CHAPTER

```
XtDisplay
XtDisplayOfObject
XtMapWidget
XtWindow
XtWindowOfObject
```

X LIBRARY FUNCTIONS AND MACROS INTRODUCED IN THIS CHAPTER

```
BlackPixel
WhitePixel
XCreateGC
XDrawArc
XDrawLine
XDrawRectangle
XFillArc
XFillRectangle
XFlush
XSetArcMode
XSetBackground
XSetForeground
```

CHAPTER 12

Bitmaps, Pixmaps, and Icons

This chapter covers:

- Using pixmaps for off-screen drawing
- Copying pixmaps to windows or other pixmaps
- Creating bitmaps, monochrome pixmaps
- Loading and saving ASCII bitmap files
- Editing bitmaps
- Setting pixmaps into XmLabel widgets
- Creating icons
- Setting the icon name as well as the icon bitmap

435

BITMAPS AND PIXMAPS

All our drawing so far has gone into widgets—windows on the display. But sometimes you want to draw into an off-screen area, later copying part (or all) of that area to a window on the screen. The X Window System provides pixmaps for this purpose. *Pixmaps* are X Window off-screen drawing areas. X uses the term *drawable* to denote a window or a pixmap. Both are things you can draw into, hence the term drawable. Because of this connection, you can use most Xlib drawing routines to draw into pixmaps as well as windows. To see anything in a pixmap, though, you must copy its contents to a window. Pixmaps work well for bitmap image files, icons, and backing store for complex drawings.

Pixmaps reside in the X server, and you can draw into them just like drawing into windows. Pixmaps have a width and height, but no x, y location on the screen.

SHORTCUT

Creating Pixmaps

You can create pixmaps with XCreatePixmap:

```
Pixmap XCreatePixmap(Display* display,
    Drawable drawable,
    unsigned int width,
    unsigned int height,
    unsigned int depth)
```

The *drawable* parameter is used to determine which screen to place the pixmap on. When you create a pixmap, you specify the desired *depth*. A large pixmap at a large *depth* obviously uses a lot of X server memory. A *depth* of 1 generates a monochrome pixmap, also called a *bitmap*. Bitmaps are very important, especially since program icons are bitmaps.

N O T E

If you intend to use a pixmap in a Motif widget, you must be careful to match the depths between the pixmap and the widget's window. We'll show how to do this later in this chapter.

Bitmaps: Single-Plane Pixmaps

Bitmaps are single-plane pixmaps. In fact, in X there is no bitmap data type. The term bitmap is just used as a convenience to signify a very common type of pixmap: a pixmap with a depth of 1.

Bitmaps are important when we discuss icons and bitmap files (see below). You can create a bitmap using `XCreatePixmap`, passing a *depth* of 1.

Freeing Pixmaps

Pixmaps tend to use a lot of memory in the X server, so whenever you are done with a pixmap, free it with `XFreePixmap`:

```
XFreePixmap(Display* display,
    Pixmap pixmap)
```

Clearing Pixmaps

When pixmaps are created, their contents are undefined. The memory used by a pixmap is not cleared, so if you try to copy a new pixmap to a window, you'll see some odd effects. Therefore, always clear any pixmaps you create.

You clear pixmaps by filling a rectangle the size of the pixmap, using whatever color you want, with `XFillRectangle`, which we covered in the last chapter.

Drawing into Bitmaps and Pixmaps

You can draw into pixmaps just like you draw into windows, as we covered in the last chapter. Pixmaps and windows are both drawables, so most drawing routines work on both windows and pixmaps. And yes, you do need a graphics context to draw into a pixmap. In fact, pixmaps act like windows in most respects.

You can draw into pixmaps just like drawing into windows, but since pixmaps are off-screen, you won't see the results of the drawing. To see the results, you need to copy data from the pixmap to a window.

Copying Areas

Two functions copy data from a pixmap to a window (or to another pixmap for that matter): XCopyArea and XCopyPlane.

XCopyArea copies a rectangular area—all the dots, or pixels—from one drawable to another. These drawables can be pixmaps or windows. Both drawables must have the same depth and the same root window (that is, be on the same screen):

```
XCopyArea(Display* display,
    Drawable src_drawable,
    Drawable dest_drawable,
    GC gc,
    int src_x,
    int  src_x,
    unsigned int width,
    unsigned int height,
    int dest_x,
    int dest_y)
```

XCopyPlane copies one-bit plane of one drawable to another, usually a pixmap to a window, but not always:

```
XCopyPlane(Display* display,
    Drawable src_drawable,
    Drawable dest_drawable,
    GC gc,
    int src_x,
    int src_y,
    unsigned int width,
    unsigned int height,
    int dest_x,
    int dest_y,
    unsigned long which_plane)
```

The bit plane to copy, *which_plane*, is normally 0x01, which copies the first (and only) plane of a one-plane bitmap to another drawable.

The nice thing about XCopyPlane is that the two drawables, the source and destination, don't need to have the same depth. You can then use XCopyPlane to copy between disparate drawables. In fact, we use XCopyPlane quite a lot for copying a bitmap (a single-plane pixmap) to a window, setting the *which_plane* parameter to 0x01.

Always make sure that you're copying data physically inside the window or pixmap. If you use a window like the *src_drawable*, make sure the window is visible.

NOTE

BITMAPS AND BITMAP FILES

X places a lot of emphasis on bitmaps. Bitmaps are used as icons and to create cursors. X fonts are described in terms of bitmaps. X even defines a portable means of storing bitmaps to disk. The X bitmap file format is an ASCII text format, used to avoid byte-ordering problems on many different architectures. This format doesn't store the pixmap per se, but instead stores the raw data used to generate the pixmap.

The odd thing about the X bitmap file format is that the format actually creates snippets of valid C code, as shown below:

```
#define mryuk_width 48
#define mryuk_height 48
static char mryuk_bits[] = {
   0x00, 0x00, 0xf0, 0x1f, 0x00, 0x00,
   0x00, 0x00, 0xff, 0xff, 0x01, 0x00,
   0x00, 0xc0, 0xff, 0xff, 0x07, 0x00,
   0x00, 0xf0, 0xff, 0xff, 0x1f, 0x00,
   0x00, 0xf8, 0xff, 0xff, 0x3f, 0x00,
   0x00, 0xfc, 0x0f, 0xe0, 0x7f, 0x00,
   0x00, 0xfe, 0x01, 0x00, 0xff, 0x00,
   0x00, 0x7f, 0x00, 0x00, 0xfc, 0x01,
   0x80, 0x3f, 0x00, 0x00, 0xf8, 0x03,
   0xc0, 0x0f, 0x00, 0x00, 0xe0, 0x07,
   0xe0, 0x07, 0x00, 0x00, 0xc0, 0x0f,
   0xe0, 0xc7, 0x00, 0x00, 0xc3, 0x0f,
   0xf0, 0xc3, 0x03, 0xc0, 0x83, 0x1f,
   0xf0, 0x01, 0x0f, 0xf0, 0x00, 0x1f,
   0xf8, 0x01, 0x3c, 0x3c, 0x00, 0x3f,
   0xf8, 0x00, 0x30, 0x0c, 0x00, 0x3e,
   0xf8, 0x00, 0x06, 0xc0, 0x00, 0x3e,
   0xf8, 0x80, 0x19, 0x20, 0x03, 0x3e,
   0x7c, 0x60, 0x20, 0x10, 0x0c, 0x7c,
   0x7c, 0x00, 0x00, 0x00, 0x00, 0x7c,
   0x7c, 0x00, 0x00, 0x00, 0x00, 0x7c,
   0x7c, 0x00, 0x00, 0x00, 0x00, 0x7c,
   0x7c, 0x00, 0x00, 0x00, 0x00, 0x7c,
   0x7c, 0x00, 0x00, 0x00, 0x00, 0x7c,
   0x7c, 0x00, 0xe0, 0x0f, 0x00, 0x7c,
   0x7c, 0x00, 0xfc, 0x7f, 0x00, 0x7c,
   0x7c, 0x00, 0x9f, 0xf3, 0x01, 0x7c,
   0xf8, 0x80, 0x9f, 0xf3, 0x03, 0x3e,
```

```
0xf8, 0xc0, 0x11, 0x11, 0x07, 0x3e,
0xf8, 0x60, 0x10, 0x11, 0x0c, 0x3e,
0xf8, 0x31, 0x10, 0x11, 0x18, 0x3f,
0xf0, 0x01, 0x10, 0x10, 0x30, 0x1f,
0xf0, 0x03, 0x10, 0x10, 0x80, 0x1f,
0xe0, 0x07, 0x10, 0x10, 0xc0, 0x0f,
0xe0, 0x07, 0x10, 0x10, 0xc0, 0x0f,
0xc0, 0x1f, 0x30, 0x18, 0xf0, 0x07,
0x80, 0x3f, 0x60, 0x0c, 0xf8, 0x03,
0x00, 0x7f, 0xc0, 0x07, 0xfc, 0x01,
0x00, 0xfe, 0x81, 0x03, 0xff, 0x00,
0x00, 0xfc, 0x0f, 0xe0, 0x7f, 0x00,
0x00, 0xf8, 0xff, 0xff, 0x3f, 0x00,
0x00, 0xf0, 0xff, 0xff, 0x1f, 0x00,
0x00, 0xe0, 0xff, 0xff, 0x0f, 0x00,
0x00, 0x00, 0xff, 0xff, 0x01, 0x00,
0x00, 0x00, 0xf0, 0x1f, 0x00, 0x00,
0x00, 0x00, 0x00, 0x00, 0x00, 0x00,
0x00, 0x00, 0x00, 0x00, 0x00, 0x00,
0x00, 0x00, 0x00, 0x00, 0x00, 0x00};
```

You can actually place the above structure in your C code. The resulting Mr. Yuk bitmap is shown in Figure 12.1.

Figure 12.1   *A sample bitmap.*

Loading Bitmap Files

You can read in an ASCII bitmap file from disk with XReadBitmapFile:

```
int XReadBitmapFile(Display* display,
    Drawable drawable,
    const char* filename,
    unsigned int* width,   /* RETURN */
    unsigned int* height,  /* RETURN */
    Pixmap* bitmap,        /* RETURN */
    int* x_hotspot         /* RETURN */
    int* y_hotspot)        /* RETURN */
```

XReadBitmapFile loads up the given *filename* and tries to convert the contents to an X bitmap. It is assumed that the file is actually an X bitmap file, or else XReadBitmapFile will return the status BitmapFileInvalid. XReadBitmapFile returns the *width* and *height* of the new bitmap. In addition, cursor bitmaps have hot spots. XReadBitmapFile also fills in these hot spots.

XReadBitmapFile returns a status of BitmapSuccess on success and BitmapOpenFailed, BitmapFileInvalid, or BitmapNoMemory on errors.

In many cases, you won't be concerned with the hot spot for the bitmap, since you normally won't be creating cursors. In addition, most bitmaps can be loaded from the root window, since XReadBitmapFile just uses the *drawable* parameter to get the screen. We put together a simple utility routine that eliminates the unnecessary parameters. The function ReadBitmapFile, below, reads in an X bitmap file and ignores the hot spots:

```
Pixmap ReadBitmapFile(Widget widget,
    char* filename,
    int* width,     /* RETURN */
    int* height)    /* RETURN */

{   /* ReadBitmapFile */
    Display*    display;
    Window      window;
    Pixmap      bitmap;
    int         x_hotspot, y_hotspot;
    int         status;

    display = XtDisplay(widget);

    window = RootWindow(display,
                DefaultScreen(display) );
```

```
status = XReadBitmapFile(display,
            window,
            filename,
            (unsigned int*) width,
            (unsigned int*) height,
            &bitmap,
            &x_hotspot, &y_hotspot);

if (status != BitmapSuccess) {
    return (Pixmap) None;
}

return bitmap;

}   /* ReadBitmapFile */
```

When you're done with the *bitmap*, be sure to free it with `XFreePixmap` (remember bitmaps are pixmaps).

Saving a Bitmap to Disk

You can save a bitmap to an ASCII file in the format described above using the `XWriteBitmapFile` function:

```
int XWriteBitmapFile(Display* display,
    const char* filename,
    Pixmap bitmap,
    unsigned int width,
    unsigned int height,
    int x_hotspot,
    int y_hotspot)
```

If the status returned is not `BitmapSuccess`, you have not saved the bitmap to a file. A status of `BitmapNoMemory` means that the routine failed in some way. The hot spots are for cursors, so if you have an icon (or other noncursor bitmap), simply set the *x_hotspot* and *y_hotspot* to –1.

Creating Pixmaps from Bitmap Data

Since the X bitmap file format is made up of C code fragments, you can include such a file in a C program with #include or simply use a text editor to stick the code into a C file. The data is a character pointer.

You can then call two X functions to create pixmaps from that raw character data. `XCreatePixmapFromBitmapData` creates a pixmap (one to many planes) from the raw bitmap data:

```
Pixmap XCreatePixmapFromBitmapData(Display* display,
    Drawable drawable,
    char* bitmap_data,
    unsigned int width,
    unsigned int height,
    unsigned long foreground,
    unsigned long background,
    unsigned int depth)
```

XCreateBitmapFromData creates a bitmap from the raw data:

```
Pixmap XCreateBitmapFromData(Display* display,
    Drawable drawable,
    char* bitmap_data,
    unsigned int width,
    unsigned int height)
```

This routine is often useful for converting raw bitmap data into a bitmap suitable for using as an icon.

Clearing Bitmaps

As we mentioned above, you need to clear all pixmaps at creation time. Bitmaps, as single-plane pixmaps, use special values for colors. All 1 bits within a bitmap indicate the foreground color, and all 0s indicate the background color, since bitmaps are monochrome. To clear a bitmap, use a foreground color of 0L, as shown in the following code:

```
Display*        display;
Pixmap          bitmap;
GC              gc;
unsigned int    width, height;

gc = XCreateGC(display, bitmap,
            0L,(XGCValues*) NULL);

/* Clear the pixmap. */
XSetForeground(display, gc, 0L);

XFillRectangle(display, bitmap, gc,
    0, 0, width, height);
```

When drawing into a bitmap, though, you normally want to use a color of 1L, to set 1s into the bitmap:

```
XSetForeground(display, pix_gc, 1L);
```

Creating Pixmaps from Bitmaps

When working with Motif label, pushbutton, and toggle-button widgets, you commonly have to convert a bitmap (a single-plane pixmap) into a true pixmap. Why? Because you want to display the bitmap in a window and you need to make the depths match between the bitmap and the window. Since you cannot make a bitmap deeper, you need to convert a single-plane pixmap (the bitmap) to a multiplane pixmap.

To do this, follow these steps:

1. Load in your bitmap file with XReadBitmapFile. This creates a bitmap.

2. Determine the depth of the window you need to match, by querying the depth resource.

3. Create a pixmap using the width and height of the bitmap and the depth of the window.

4. Create a GC for the pixmap.

5. Set the GC's foreground and background colors to the colors you want for the window. We usually use the foreground and background resources.

6. Call XCopyPlane to copy the bitmap data to the pixmap, using the new GC.

7. Free the GC, as it is no longer needed.

We can load the bitmap file with XReadBitmapFile or the ReadBitmapFile utility function introduced above. Steps 2 through 7 are performed by the utility function CreatePixmapFromBitmap, below:

```
Pixmap CreatePixmapFromBitmap(Widget widget,
    int width,
    int height,
    Pixmap bitmap)

{   /* CreatePixmapFromBitmap */
    Pixmap          pixmap;
    Display*        display;
    unsigned long   fore, back;
    GC              gc;
    int             depth;

    /* Get widget's colors and depth. */
```

```
XtVaGetValues(widget,
    XmNbackground, &back,
    XmNforeground, &fore,
    XmNdepth,      &depth,
    NULL);

display = XtDisplay(widget);

pixmap = XCreatePixmap(display, bitmap,
            width, height, depth);

if (pixmap == (Pixmap) None) {
    return pixmap;
}

/* Create GC for copying. */
gc = XCreateGC(display, pixmap,
        0L, (XGCValues*) NULL);

XSetForeground(display, gc, fore);
XSetBackground(display, gc, back);

/* Copy bitmap to pixmap. */
XCopyPlane(display,
    bitmap, /* source */
    pixmap, /* destination */
    gc,
    0, 0,   /* source x, y */
    width, height,
    0, 0,   /* destination x, y */
    0x01);  /* which plane */

/* Free GC */
XFreeGC(display, gc);

return pixmap;

}   /* CreatePixmapFromBitmap */
```

PIXMAPS AND LABEL WIDGETS

With Motif, you can set a label widget to hold either a pixmap or a text message in XmString format. The same goes for most widgets derived from XmLabel, including pushbuttons and toggle buttons. To do so, you need to set both the labelType and labelPixmap resources.

The labelType resource specifies what type of label widget we have, one that displays a pixmap (XmPIXMAP) or one that displays a string (XmSTRING). You can freely change a label widget from one type to another by setting the labelType resource.

If you set the `labelType` resource to `XmSTRING`, then the label widget will use the `labelString` resource, which holds the text message to display. (We've already covered the `labelString` resource in most of the example programs in this book.)

If you set the `labelType` resource to `XmPIXMAP`, then the label widget will use the `labelPixmap` resource. This resource needs to hold a valid X pixmap created to the proper depth.

To set a label widget (or a pushbutton or a toggle) to use a pixmap, you need the following code:

```
Widget      widget;
Pixmap      pixmap;

XtVaSetValues(widget,
    XmNlabelType,   XmPIXMAP,
    XmNlabelPixmap, pixmap,
    NULL);
```

You need to make sure that the pixmap has the same depth as the widget and uses the same colormap. The following utility function sets a pixmap into the `labelPixmap` resource for a widget:

```
void SetLabelPixmap(Widget widget,
    Pixmap pixmap)

{   /* SetLabelPixmap */

    XtVaSetValues(widget,
        XmNlabelType,   XmPIXMAP,
        XmNlabelPixmap, pixmap,
        NULL);

}   /* SetLabelPixmap */
```

The `SetLabelPixmap` function will work with most widgets that are derived from `XmLabel`, including `XmPushButton` and `XmToggleButton`.

To change widget back to displaying a text message, use the following code:

```
Widget      widget;
XmString    xmstring;

XtVaSetValues(widget,
    XmNlabelType,   XmSTRING,
    XmNlabelString, xmstring,
    NULL);
```

If we want to create a label widget that holds a pixmap, we need to make sure that the pixmap and the widget share the same depth, or else we'll see an X error. In addition, if we're starting with a monochrome bitmap, we probably want to draw the bitmap using the widget's foreground and background colors instead of plain old black and white.

To pull all this together, we've created a utility function that loads in an ASCII X bitmap file and places that bitmap into the `labelPixmap` resource for a label, pushbutton, or toggle-button widget.

Note that the `LoadBitmapLabel` function must also convert the single-plane bitmap to a pixmap of the proper depth.

The following code shows how to do this:

```
Boolean LoadBitmapLabel(Widget widget,
    char* filename)

{   /* LoadBitmapLabel */
    Pixmap      bitmap, pixmap;
    int         width, height;
    Display*    display;

    /* Load in bitmap file. */
    bitmap = ReadBitmapFile(widget, filename,
            &width, &height);

    if (bitmap == (Pixmap) None) {
        return False;
    }

    /* Create a pixmap from the bitmap. */
    pixmap = CreatePixmapFromBitmap(widget,
            width, height, bitmap);

    if (pixmap == (Pixmap) None) {
        return False;
    }

    /* Free bitmap. */
    display = XtDisplay(widget);

    XFreePixmap(display, bitmap);

    /* Set label to hold pixmap. */
    SetLabelPixmap(widget, pixmap);

    /* Don't free pixmap if we use it for a labelPixmap. */

    return True;

}   /* LoadBitmapLabel */
```

ICONS

Icons in X are small bitmaps that represent your program when the window manager iconifies (or minimizes, in Motif terminology) your window. (We discussed iconification in Chapter 1.) According to the official rules for well-behaved X programs, the *Inter-Client Communications Conventions Manual* or ICCCM, an icon must be a bitmap—so therefore icons are monochrome in X.

You can use a bitmap file or create your own pixmap (with a depth of 1) for use as a program icon.

After you create this icon pixmap (with a depth of 1, remember), you need to inform the window manager about your icon. To do this, set the iconPixmap resource on a top-level shell widget, such as the widget returned by XtAppInitialize. The icon-related resources appear in Table 12.1.

Table 12.1 *Icon-related resources.*

Resource	Type	Default Value
iconic	Boolean	False
iconMask	Pixmap	NULL
iconName	String	NULL
iconNameEncoding	Atom	STRING
iconPixmap	Pixmap	NULL
iconWindow	Window	NULL
iconX	int	-1
iconY	int	-1
initialState	int	NormalState

The iconic resource, if set to True, asks the window manager to start your program as an icon. The -iconic command-line parameter should also start your program as an icon.

The iconMask resource holds a bitmap that can be used as a mask for the icon, if the window manager supports icon masks. All 1 bits in the bitmap are the mask. This mask can be used to clip the iconPixmap.

The iconName resource holds the name to be used with the icon, if the window manager displays both icon bitmaps and icon names (most do). Since the amount of space for an icon name is typically small, you should use a short icon name. The real default is normally argv[0], the name of your program.

The iconNameEncoding resource specifies the text encoding for the iconName. Don't go near this resource, since it is used for internationalization.

The iconWindow is used if you want to create a colored icon. You do this by creating your own window and drawing into that window. This process is somewhat involved. See *Professional Graphics Programming in the X Window System* (Johnson and Reichard, MIS:Press, 1993), for more on this topic.

The iconX and iconY resources specify the location on the screen where you want the icon to appear. Many window managers restrict where icons can appear, and some place icons only within icon boxes. Because of this, you probably will have the least bit of luck with these resources.

The initialState resource is much like the iconic resource. The possible initialState settings are listed in Table 12.2.

Table 12.2   *Window states.*

State	Value	Meaning
WithdrawnState	0	Window is not visible.
NormalState	1	Window is visible.
IconicState	3	Window is replaced by an icon.

If you set the iconic resource to True, it will override the initialState resource.

N O T E

Everything to do with icons is the province of the window manager. Each icon-based resource you set is merely a *request* to the window manager, requests that the window manager can deny with impunity. Therefore, you cannot depend on this behavior. That said, we normally have no problems setting the icon or the icon name.

How Large Can You Make Icons?

The window manager controls the allowable sizes for icons. We find a good size for icons to be 48x48 pixels.

Creating Icons

The main way to create an icon is to create a pixmap with a depth of 1. You can then draw anything you like into the icon. Most program icons, though, are created using some form of bitmap editor, such as the *bitmap* program show in Figure 12.2.

This is because graphic artists want precise control over the look of most icons. In addition, it's a lot easier to use a bitmap-editing program than it is to hard-code all the commands to draw the dots above.

Normally, if you use *bitmap* or another bitmap-editing program, such as the OpenWindows *iconedit*, you'll write the bitmap out as an ASCII X bitmap file. You can then load this file with XReadBitmapFile or include the bitmap file directly in your code. It's usually better to include the icon directly in your code. Why? Icons are typically small, and every extra file that your program depends on is yet another file that can be installed in the wrong place or not installed at all.

If you place the icon bitmap in your code, you can use XCreateBitmapFromData to build a bitmap out of the raw ASCII data. You can then use this bitmap as an icon.

The following code creates a bitmap, from the Mr. Yuk bitmap shown in Figure 12.1, and then sets that bitmap as the program's icon:

```
Widget      parent;
Display*    display;
Pixmap      icon;

/* Call XtAppInitialize... */
```

```
/* Set up icon. */
display = XtDisplay(parent);

icon = XCreateBitmapFromData(display,
        RootWindow(display,
            DefaultScreen(display) ),
        mryuk_bits,
        mryuk_width, mryuk_height);

if (icon != (Pixmap) None) {
    XtVaSetValues(parent,
    XmNiconic,      True,    /* Start iconic. */
    XmNiconName,    "My Icon",
    XmNiconPixmap, icon,
    NULL);
}
```

Figure 12.2 *The bitmap program in action.*

A PROGRAM TO TEST BITMAPS AND ICONS

We've put together a program that tests out the concepts introduced in this chapter and shows how to use bitmaps in a program. We also create an icon and icon name.

To show off X bitmaps, we created a toolbar beneath the program's menu bar. A toolbar, very popular in word-processing and spreadsheet software, contains a number of pushbuttons with bitmap pictures. (We covered toolbars in Chapter 6 on container widgets.) In our program, the pictures aren't the best (it's obvious we're not graphic designers), but the concepts remain the same. Our toolbar program presents a window, which is shown in Figure 12.3.

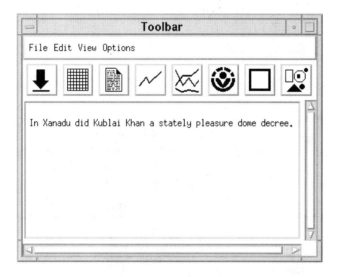

Figure 12.3 *The toolbar.*

You should pass this program a set of bitmap file names on the command line. For each bitmap, the program creates a pushbutton and loads the bitmap into the pushbutton using the LoadBitmapLabel function we developed in this chapter.

The subsequent icon and icon name (if your window manager supports these concepts, of course) are shown in Figure 12.4.

Figure 12.4   *Our custom icon.*

The source code for the *toolbar* program follows:

```
/* toolbar.c */
#include <Xm/Xm.h>
#include <Xm/Form.h>
#include <Xm/MainW.h>
#include <Xm/PushB.h>
#include <Xm/RowColumn.h>
#include <Xm/Separator.h>
#include <Xm/Text.h>
#include <stdio.h>

/* External functions */
extern Boolean LoadBitmapLabel(Widget widget,
        char* filename);

extern Widget CreatePushbutton(Widget parent,
    char* name, XtCallbackProc callback,
    XtPointer client_data);

extern Widget CreatePulldownMenu(Widget parent, char* name);

extern Widget CreateHelpMenu(Widget parent, char* name);

extern Widget CreateMenubar(Widget parent, char* name);

/* Icon bitmap. */
#define mryuk_width 48
#define mryuk_height 48
static char mryuk_bits[] = {
    0x00, 0x00, 0xf0, 0x1f, 0x00, 0x00,
    0x00, 0x00, 0xff, 0xff, 0x01, 0x00,
    0x00, 0xc0, 0xff, 0xff, 0x07, 0x00,
    0x00, 0xf0, 0xff, 0xff, 0x1f, 0x00,
    0x00, 0xf8, 0xff, 0xff, 0x3f, 0x00,
    0x00, 0xfc, 0x0f, 0xe0, 0x7f, 0x00,
    0x00, 0xfe, 0x01, 0x00, 0xff, 0x00,
    0x00, 0x7f, 0x00, 0x00, 0xfc, 0x01,
    0x80, 0x3f, 0x00, 0x00, 0xf8, 0x03,
    0xc0, 0x0f, 0x00, 0x00, 0xe0, 0x07,
    0xe0, 0x07, 0x00, 0x00, 0xc0, 0x0f,
```

```
    0xe0, 0xc7, 0x00, 0x00, 0xc3, 0x0f,
    0xf0, 0xc3, 0x03, 0xc0, 0x83, 0x1f,
    0xf0, 0x01, 0x0f, 0xf0, 0x00, 0x1f,
    0xf8, 0x01, 0x3c, 0x3c, 0x00, 0x3f,
    0xf8, 0x00, 0x30, 0x0c, 0x00, 0x3e,
    0xf8, 0x00, 0x06, 0xc0, 0x00, 0x3e,
    0xf8, 0x80, 0x19, 0x20, 0x03, 0x3e,
    0x7c, 0x60, 0x20, 0x10, 0x0c, 0x7c,
    0x7c, 0x00, 0x00, 0x00, 0x00, 0x7c,
    0x7c, 0x00, 0x00, 0x00, 0x00, 0x7c,
    0x7c, 0x00, 0x00, 0x00, 0x00, 0x7c,
    0x7c, 0x00, 0x00, 0x00, 0x00, 0x7c,
    0x7c, 0x00, 0x00, 0x00, 0x00, 0x7c,
    0x7c, 0x00, 0xe0, 0x0f, 0x00, 0x7c,
    0x7c, 0x00, 0xfc, 0x7f, 0x00, 0x7c,
    0x7c, 0x00, 0x9f, 0xf3, 0x01, 0x7c,
    0xf8, 0x80, 0x9f, 0xf3, 0x03, 0x3e,
    0xf8, 0xc0, 0x11, 0x11, 0x07, 0x3e,
    0xf8, 0x60, 0x10, 0x11, 0x0c, 0x3e,
    0xf8, 0x31, 0x10, 0x11, 0x18, 0x3f,
    0xf0, 0x01, 0x10, 0x10, 0x30, 0x1f,
    0xf0, 0x03, 0x10, 0x10, 0x80, 0x1f,
    0xe0, 0x07, 0x10, 0x10, 0xc0, 0x0f,
    0xe0, 0x07, 0x10, 0x10, 0xc0, 0x0f,
    0xc0, 0x1f, 0x30, 0x18, 0xf0, 0x07,
    0x80, 0x3f, 0x60, 0x0c, 0xf8, 0x03,
    0x00, 0x7f, 0xc0, 0x07, 0xfc, 0x01,
    0x00, 0xfe, 0x81, 0x03, 0xff, 0x00,
    0x00, 0xfc, 0x0f, 0xe0, 0x7f, 0x00,
    0x00, 0xf8, 0xff, 0xff, 0x3f, 0x00,
    0x00, 0xf0, 0xff, 0xff, 0x1f, 0x00,
    0x00, 0xe0, 0xff, 0xff, 0x0f, 0x00,
    0x00, 0x00, 0xff, 0xff, 0x01, 0x00,
    0x00, 0x00, 0xf0, 0x1f, 0x00, 0x00,
    0x00, 0x00, 0x00, 0x00, 0x00, 0x00,
    0x00, 0x00, 0x00, 0x00, 0x00, 0x00,
    0x00, 0x00, 0x00, 0x00, 0x00, 0x00};

void exitCB(Widget widget,
    XtPointer client_data,
    XtPointer call_data)

{   /* exitCB */

    exit(0);

}   /* exitCB */

void nullCB(Widget widget,
    XtPointer client_data,
    XtPointer call_data)

{   /* nullCB */
}   /* nullCB */
```

```
void CreateViewMenu(Widget menubar)

{   /* CreateViewMenu */
    Widget  menu;

    menu = CreatePulldownMenu(menubar, "View");

    (void) CreatePushbutton(menu, "All",
        (XtCallbackProc) nullCB, (XtPointer) NULL);

    (void) CreatePushbutton(menu, "Partial...",
        (XtCallbackProc) nullCB, (XtPointer) NULL);

    (void) XtVaCreateManagedWidget("sep",
        xmSeparatorWidgetClass, menu,
        XmNorientation, XmHORIZONTAL,
        NULL);

    (void) CreatePushbutton(menu, "By Date...",
        (XtCallbackProc) nullCB, (XtPointer) NULL);

    (void) CreatePushbutton(menu, "By Name...",
        (XtCallbackProc) nullCB, (XtPointer) NULL);

            (void) CreatePushbutton(menu, "By Other...",
        (XtCallbackProc) nullCB, (XtPointer) NULL);

}   /* CreateViewMenu */

void CreateOptionsMenu(Widget menubar)

{   /* CreateOptionsMenu */
    Widget  menu;

    menu = CreatePulldownMenu(menubar, "Options");

    (void) CreatePushbutton(menu, "Colors...",
        (XtCallbackProc) nullCB, (XtPointer) NULL);

}   /* CreateOptionsMenu */

int main(int argc, char** argv)

{   /* main */
    Widget          parent;
    XtAppContext    app_context;
    Widget          mainw, toolbar;
    Widget          menubar, menu;
    Widget          form, push, scrolled_text;
    Arg             args[20];
    Cardinal        n;
    Pixmap          icon;
    Display*        display;

    /* Initialize the X Toolkit. */
```

```
n = 0;
XtSetArg(args[n], XmNtitle, "Toolbar"); n++;

parent = XtAppInitialize(&app_context,
        "Ppm",
        (XrmOptionDescList) NULL,
        0,
        &argc,
        argv,
        (String*) NULL,
        args, n);

/* Set up icon. */
display = XtDisplay(parent);

icon = XCreateBitmapFromData(display,
        RootWindow(display,
            DefaultScreen(display) ),
        mryuk_bits,
        mryuk_width, mryuk_height);

if (icon != (Pixmap) None) {
    XtVaSetValues(parent,
        XmNiconic,      True,    /* Start iconic. */
        XmNiconName,    "My Icon",
        XmNiconPixmap, icon,
        NULL);
}

n = 0;
mainw = XmCreateMainWindow(parent, "mainw", args, n);

menubar = CreateMenubar(mainw, "menubar");

/* Create Menus. */
menu = CreatePulldownMenu(menubar, "File");

(void) CreatePushbutton(menu, "Exit",
    (XtCallbackProc) exitCB, (XtPointer) NULL);

menu = CreatePulldownMenu(menubar, "Edit");

(void) CreatePushbutton(menu, "Undo",
    (XtCallbackProc) nullCB, (XtPointer) NULL);

/* Dummy menus to show Motif Style Guide. */
CreateViewMenu(menubar);

CreateOptionsMenu(menubar);

/* Fill in work area. */
form = XtVaCreateWidget("form",
    xmFormWidgetClass, mainw,
    NULL);

toolbar = XtVaCreateManagedWidget("toolbar",
```

```
            xmRowColumnWidgetClass, form,
            XmNorientation,      XmHORIZONTAL,
            XmNtopAttachment,    XmATTACH_FORM,
            XmNleftAttachment,   XmATTACH_FORM,
            XmNrightAttachment,  XmATTACH_FORM,
            NULL);

    /* Create a scrolled multiline text widget. */
    n = 0;
    XtSetArg(args[n], XmNeditMode,
        XmMULTI_LINE_EDIT); n++;
    XtSetArg(args[n], XmNleftAttachment,
        XmATTACH_FORM); n++;
    XtSetArg(args[n], XmNrightAttachment,
        XmATTACH_FORM); n++;
    XtSetArg(args[n], XmNbottomAttachment,
        XmATTACH_FORM); n++;
    XtSetArg(args[n], XmNtopAttachment,
        XmATTACH_WIDGET); n++;
    XtSetArg(args[n], XmNtopWidget, toolbar); n++;

    scrolled_text = XmCreateScrolledText(form,
                        "text", args, n);

    XtManageChild(scrolled_text);

    /* Fill out toolbar. */
    for (n = 1; n < argc; n++) {
        push = CreatePushbutton(toolbar, argv[n],
                (XtCallbackProc) nullCB,
                (XtPointer) NULL);

        if (LoadBitmapLabel(push, argv[n]) == False) {
            printf("Error loading [%s]\n", argv[n]);
        }
    }

    XtManageChild(form);

    XmMainWindowSetAreas(mainw,
        menubar,
        (Widget) NULL, /* command window */
        (Widget) NULL, /* horiz scroll */
        (Widget) NULL, /* vert scroll */
        form);         /* work area */

    XtManageChild(mainw);

    XtRealizeWidget(parent);
    XtAppMainLoop(app_context);

    return 0;

}   /* main */

/* end of file toolbar.c */
```

In the program above, our toolbar is a row-column widget filled with push-buttons. Each pushbutton displays a `labelPixmap` instead of the normal `labelString`. Each command-line argument is read in as the name of a bitmap file. If you have the source-code diskette, you can call *toolbar* with the following command to load all the files ending with *.xbm*:

```
toolbar *.xbm
```

You can also create your own bitmaps with the *bitmap* program.

The row-column toolbar then fits into a form widget, which also holds a scrolled-text widget. We populate a menu bar with a set of Motif menus and create a menu from the built-in Mr. Yuk bitmap.

With all this, you should be ready to add bitmaps to your programs and create custom icons.

SUMMARY

This short chapter covered the creation and management of bitmaps, which are single-plane pixmaps. Bitmaps are used extensively in Motif for a variety of tasks, including icons (a task we illuminated through a sample program).

X LIBRARY FUNCTIONS AND MACROS INTRODUCED IN THIS CHAPTER

```
XCopyArea
XCopyPlane
XCreateBitmapFromData
XCreatePixmap
XCreatePixmapFromBitmapData
XFreePixmap
XReadBitmapFile
XWriteBitmapFile
```

CHAPTER 13

Background Processing and Timers with Xt

This chapter covers:

- Background processing with Xt
- Work procedures
- Timers
- Using timers to help detect mouse double-click events

459

FOREGROUND AND BACKGROUND PROCESSING

The last two chapters showed a set of X library functions that you can tie into Motif. This chapter goes one level higher and demonstrates the use of Xt Intrinsics functions for background processing. The Xt Intrinsics provides two main means for performing short tasks in the background, while the user interface remains responsive to incoming events. These two means are *timers* and work *procedures*.

As we've pointed out time and time again, Motif applications are essentially event-driven. That is, these applications await on events from the X server, generated by users or the server itself, and then act on these events. Event-driven applications tend to put the user in charge, as the application is always waiting to process a user command. Instead of the application controlling the user, the user controls the application.

Most event-driven programs have a central event loop somewhere—we're using the event loop in XtAppMainLoop. In this event loop, the application awaits a new event and then acts on it. Because of this fact, event-driven applications are potentially busy waiting a lot of the time—if events are coming in few and far between. If events are coming in with great frequency, then the application is very busy.

An application writer may want to use the potential dead time to good use. For example, a spreadsheet application could set up a work procedure to recalculate values based on modified cells. The key here is that if the user modifies a single cell in the spreadsheet, you don't want the user to wait a potentially long time while the spreadsheet recalculates all the cells that are linked to the modified cell. You could set up a work procedure to perform a gradual recalculation. This work procedure, for example, could update one cell every time it is called. After a short period of time, all the required cells would be updated. But the user interface still remains responsive during this entire time.

A LISP or Smalltalk programming system could reclaim unused memory, implementing garbage collection, using Xt work procedures. Since most of us aren't writing spreadsheets or LISP systems, a more common use is to create Xt widgets with work procedures. Many users complain of the long time it takes to get an X application started up. One reason for this time is that applications may be creating a number of widgets, and every widget creation involves at least one call to malloc—a routine not known for its speed. So you're left with a dilemma: Do you create all the dialog and other widgets at once, or do you create these widgets only when needed? Either way, you're just spreading around the time it takes to create these widgets. Users don't like waiting for a dialog to appear while your application creates and then manages the dialog widgets, and users don't want to wait a long time while the application first starts up. One potential solution is to set up a work procedure at start-up, when the work procedure gradually creates widgets—say one widget for each call to the work-procedure callback. This then makes the application start up faster, and it also provides better performance during execution.

The key here, though, is incremental. In order to provide interactive feedback with good performance, the application must respond quickly to any events that arrive.

The designers of the Xt Intrinsics added the concept of work procedures. You can register a procedure—really a C callback function—and have your function called when the system is idle. To maintain a good interactive performance, though, your work callback must execute all the way through very quickly, in well under a second. To make use of work procedures, you'll have to divide up any large tasks into very tiny blocks that can be executed in work callbacks.

SHORTCUT

Work Procedures and Timers

To set up a work procedure, call XtAppAddWorkProc:

```
XtWorkProcId
XtAppAddWorkProc(XtAppContext app_context,
    XtWorkProc callback,
    XtPointer client_data)
```

XtAppAddWorkProc sets up a work procedure and returns the work procedure ID. Any time you want to terminate the work procedure, you can pass this ID to XtRemoveWorkProc:

```
void  XtRemoveWorkProc(XtWorkProcId work_id)
```

To set up an Xt timer callback, use XtAppAddTimeOut:

```
XtIntervalId XtAppAddTimeOut(XtAppContext app_context,
    unsigned long interval,  /* milliseconds */
```

```
        XtTimerCallbackProc callback,
        XtPointer client_data)
```

XtAppAddTimeOut sets up a one-time timer callback. That is, sometime after *interval* milliseconds have elapsed, the Xt Intrinsics will call your *callback* function. If for some reason you don't want the timer to go off, you can remove the timer with XtRemoveTimeOut:

```
        void XtRemoveTimeOut(XtIntervalId timer_id)
```

WORK PROCEDURES

The work procedure should perform only a small amount of work and should return in a very short period of time, or your application will not be very responsive to the user. The whole idea of a work procedure is that of a cooperative background function. If your function doesn't cooperate, you can mess up the application's responsiveness. Sometimes this is necessary, but most times it isn't.

You pass a callback function to XtAppAddWorkProc. This is the function that gets executed when the main Xt event loop is idle. The formal type of this callback function is XtWorkProc, which has the following format:

```
typedef Boolean
(*XtWorkProc)(XtPointer client_data);
```

The *client_data* is the data that you passed to XtAppAddWorkProc.

Your work procedure, a C callback function, should then take the following format:

```
Boolean callback(XtPointer client_data)

{    /* callback */

    /* Perform a SMALL amount of work... */

    /* Make sure we get called again. */
    return False;

}    /* callback */
```

In your callback function, you return False if you want the callback to get executed again. If your work procedure is all done with its work, then return True. If the return value is True, the work procedure is automatically unregistered.

WARNING

There's a bug in X11R3 and X11R4 systems. If you are working with these libraries and your work procedure returns True, chances are you'll face a memory leak. This bug was fixed in Release 5.

Writing a Work-Procedure Callback

Even on a slow 25-MHz Intel 386-based machine, we were pleasantly surprised at how often our work callback got called. We created a very simple, dumb callback to demonstrate the use of XtAppAddWorkProc.

In the work_callback function, below, we print out a "Work" message every 1,000 times our function is called. After 100,000 times, the work_callback shuts itself off, by returning True. (Up to that time, it returns False to continue being called back.)

```
    /* Work procedure. */
Boolean work_callback(XtPointer client_data)

{   /* work_callback */
    int*    count;

    /* We assume the client_data has an int. */
    count = (int*) client_data;

    *count = *count + 1;

    if (( *count % 1000) == 0) {
        printf("Work %d\n", *count);
    }

    if (*count > 100000) {
        *count = 0;
        printf("Work procedure reset\n");

        return True;
    }

    return False;

}   /* work_callback */
```

The 100,000 returns end up being quicker than you'd expect. Thus work procedures are perfect for tasks like incrementally recalculating a spreadsheet.

N O T E

`XtAppAddWorkProc` replaces the older `XtAddWorkProc`. If you're still at Motif 1.0, you should use `XtAddWorkProc` instead of `XtAppAddWorkProc`. `XtAddWorkProc` takes the following parameters:

```
XtWorkProcId
XtAddWorkProc(XtWorkProc work_callback,
    XtPointer client_data)
```

`XtAddWorkProc` is obsolete, starting with Motif 1.1 and X11 Release 4. You should have at least these versions of Motif and X.

TIMERS

A timer sets up a function to be called when the timer times out. To set up an Xt timer callback, use `XtAppAddTimeOut`:

```
XtIntervalId XtAppAddTimeOut(XtAppContext app_context,
    unsigned long interval,  /* milliseconds */
    XtTimerCallbackProc callback,
    XtPointer client_data)
```

`XtAppAddTimeOut` sets up a *one-time timer callback*. That is, sometime after *interval* milliseconds have elapsed, the Xt Intrinsics will call your *callback* function. The Intrinsics make no guarantee that the timer will be exact, but normally the times are close to the desired *interval*. It all depends on what happens between the time you set up the timer and the time Xt notices your timer has expired. If a flurry of other events arrive during this interval, your timeout will most likely be late. Even with this imprecision, this is about the best you can get in a portable fashion.

    `XtAppAddTimeOut` returns a timer ID. If for some reason you don't want the timer to go off, you can remove the timer with `XtRemoveTimeOut`:

```
void XtRemoveTimeOut(XtIntervalId timer_id)
```

N O T E

Prior to X11 Release 4, the old method for creating an Xt timer was to call `XtAddTimeOut`. With Release 4 and higher, you should call the newer *XtApp* routines, such as `XtAppAddTimeOut`. `XtAddTimeOut` takes the following parameters:

```
XtIntervalId
XtAddTimeOut (unsigned long interval,
    XtTimerCallbackProc callback,
    XtPointer client_data)
```

Again, you should upgrade to `XtAppAddTimeOut` if possible.

Timer-Callback Functions

The timer-callback function type, `XtTimerCallbackProc`, is defined as:

```
typedef void (*XtTimerCallbackProc)
    (XtPointer client_data,
     XtIntervalId* timer_id);
```

Your callback function should look like the following code template:

```
void callback(XtPointer client_data,
    XtIntervalId* timer_id)

{    /* callback */
}    /* callback */
```

Since your callback is called from within the main Xt event loop, `XtAppMainLoop`, it should execute quickly. Your callback function should also refrain from calling its own event loop, as event loops within event callbacks (and a timer is, in a sense, an event) can confuse the Xt Intrinsics.

Two immediate uses for timers come to mind. First, timers are perfect for creating evenly spaced animation. To do this, each timer-callback function must set up the timer again and then draw one frame of the animation. Second, timers are perfect for helping to detect double-click events of the mouse.

Timing Out Mouse Clicks

Wait a second? Didn't we cover how to detect a double-click mouse-button press in Chapter 10 on events? Yes, we did. But, the method presented in Chapter 10 has one major limitation: It assumes that for a double-click event you can perform the single-click action on the first click and then add on the double-click action on the second click. The basic method for handling these events is as follows:

1. Get first click.

2. Perform a single-click action.

3. If a second click comes in, then you may have a double-click.

4. If you have a double-click, perform double-click action.

The *xterm* program works this way for selecting text. And, in fact, you'll have an easier time if you just use the method presented in Chapter 10.

If that method doesn't meet all your needs, you can add a timer. A timer is useful for those cases where the double-click action is distinct from the single-click action. In these cases, you *don't* want to perform the single-click action if you really have a double-click event. And since the X Window System doesn't really help you detect a double-click event, you're left on your own. You must register the single click and wait for a given period. If no further click (`ButtonPress`) arrives in that time, then you assume you have only a single click. If a second click arrives before the timer times out (and is within the distance constraint), then you have a double-click.

Timers are perfect for the task of detecting double (or triple, etc.) clicks on the mouse. Since X has no inherent ability to detect a double-click, the usual procedure is to set up a timer on the first click of a mouse with some arbitrary short time period. If you get a second click of the mouse before the timer times out, then you have a certified doubleclick. (You also need to check that the mouse hasn't moved out of a small area between the clicks, because the second click could be for some totally different purpose.) If the timer times out, then you have only a single click. (In addition, you have to worry about asynchronous network delays, but that's another matter.)

Using this method, then, every mouse click will engage a delay (for the amount of the timer interval) while your program determines if the event is a single click or a double click.

In the *backtest* program, below, we use a timer callback to detect a double click of the mouse (in a very primitive manner), to demonstrate the use of `XtAppAddTimeOut`. If a mouse click occurs (a `ButtonPress` event, just like we described in Chapter 10), then we set up a timer with `XtAppAddTimeOut`.

If a second click arrives, then we remove the timer with `XtRemoveTimeOut`.

To do this, we use an event-handler callback function to detect the mouse clicks. We also use the `DetectDoubleClick` function from Chapter 10 to ensure that our `ButtonPress` events actually occur within the proper small area:

```
/* Global application context. */
XtAppContext    app_context;
XtIntervalId    global_timer_id = 0;

    /* Event handler starts and stops timer. */
static void event_handler(Widget widget,
    XtPointer client_data,
    XEvent* event,
    Boolean* continue_to_dispatch)

{   /* event_handler */
    int status;

    /* We only look for Button1 presses. */
    if (event->type != ButtonPress) {
        return;
    }

    if (event->xbutton.button != Button1) {
        return;
    }

    /*
     * If timer is on, turn it off.
     * Otherwise, turn it on.
     */
    if (global_timer_id == 0) {
        printf("Timing.\n");

        global_timer_id =
            XtAppAddTimeOut(app_context,
                200,     /* interval */
                (XtTimerCallbackProc) timer_callback,
                (XtPointer) NULL);

        /* Store coordinates. */
        DetectDoubleClick((XButtonEvent*) event);
    } else {
        /*
         * Even though the user reacted in the
         * right amount of time, the user must
         * still click within the proper area.
         */
        status = DetectDoubleClick((XButtonEvent*) event);

        if (status == True) {
            printf("Double-click.\n");
        } else {
```

```
        printf("Not a double-click.\n");

        /* Call again to zero out. */
        DetectDoubleClick((XButtonEvent*) event);
    }

    XtRemoveTimeOut(global_timer_id);
    global_timer_id = 0;
    }

}   /* event_handler */
```

The `event_handler` function removes the timer if the user does indeed engage a double-click event. If the user doesn't, then the timer times out and calls our simple callback function:

```
    /* Timer callback called on time out. */
void timer_callback(XtPointer client_data,
    XtIntervalId* timer_id)

{   /* timer_callback */

    printf("Timed out! Not a double-click\n");

    /* Record that timer is off. */
    global_timer_id = 0;

}   /* timer_callback */
```

Obviously, you'll need to do more than print messages out in your code, but the above concepts should work.

THE BACKGROUND-PROCESSING TEST PROGRAM

We've put together a test program to test the two Xt methods for background processing. This program creates a pushbutton widget, which, if activated, starts a work-procedure callback. A label widget looks for `ButtonPress` events and then detects if the events are a single or double click of the mouse. Click on the **Quit** button, and the program will quit.

The code for the program follows:

```
/* backtest.c */
#include <Xm/Xm.h>
#include <Xm/Label.h>
#include <Xm/PushB.h>
#include <Xm/RowColumn.h>
#include <stdio.h>
```

```
extern Widget CreatePushbutton(Widget parent,
    char* name, XtCallbackProc callback,
    XtPointer client_data);

extern Boolean
    DetectDoubleClick(XButtonEvent* event);

/* Global application context. */
XtAppContext    app_context;
XtIntervalId    global_timer_id = 0;

    /* Timer callback called on timeout. */
void timer_callback(XtPointer client_data,
    XtIntervalId* timer_id)

{    /* timer_callback */

    printf("Timed out! Not a double-click\n");

    /* Record that timer is off. */
    global_timer_id = 0;

}    /* timer_callback */


    /* Event handler starts and stops timer. */
static void event_handler(Widget widget,
    XtPointer client_data,
    XEvent* event,
    Boolean* continue_to_dispatch)

{    /* event_handler */
    int status;

    /* We only look for Button1 presses. */
    if (event->type != ButtonPress) {
        return;
    }

    if (event->xbutton.button != Button1) {
        return;
    }

    /*
     * If timer is on, turn it off.
     * Otherwise, turn it on.
     */
    if (global_timer_id == 0) {
        printf("Timing.\n");

        global_timer_id =
            XtAppAddTimeOut(app_context,
                200,    /* interval */
                (XtTimerCallbackProc) timer_callback,
```

```
                    (XtPointer) NULL);

        /* Store coordinates. */
        DetectDoubleClick((XButtonEvent*) event);
    } else {
        /*
         * Even though the user reacted in the
         * right amount of time, the user must
         * still click within the proper area.
         */
        status = DetectDoubleClick((XButtonEvent*) event);

        if (status == True) {
            printf("Double-click.\n");
        } else {
            printf("Not a double-click.\n");

            /* Call again to zero out. */
            DetectDoubleClick((XButtonEvent*) event);
        }

        XtRemoveTimeOut(global_timer_id);
        global_timer_id = 0;
    }

}   /* event_handler */

    /* Callback quits program. */
void exitCB(Widget widget,
    XtPointer client_data,
    XtPointer call_data)

{   /* exitCB */

    exit(0);

}   /* exitCB */

    /* Work procedure. */
Boolean work_callback(XtPointer client_data)

{   /* work_callback */
    int*    count;

    /* We assume the client_data has an int. */
    count = (int*) client_data;

    *count = *count + 1;

    if (( *count % 1000) == 0) {
        printf("Work %d\n", *count);
    }

    if (*count > 100000) {
        *count = 0;
```

```
            printf("Work procedure reset\n");

            return True;
        }

        return False;

    }   /* work_callback */

        /* Callback starts up the work procedure. */
    void start_workCB(Widget widget,
        XtPointer client_data,
        XtPointer call_data)

    {   /* start_workCB */

        /*
         * app_context is global. You'll
         * often need this. client_data is
         * a pointer to work_count.
         */
        (void) XtAppAddWorkProc(app_context,
            (XtWorkProc) work_callback,
            client_data);

    }   /* start_workCB */

    int main(int argc, char** argv)

    {   /* main */
        Widget          parent;
        Widget          row, label;
        Arg             args[20];
        Cardinal        n;
        int             work_count;

        /* Initialize the X Toolkit. */
        n = 0;
        parent = XtAppInitialize(&app_context,
                "Ppm",
                (XrmOptionDescList) NULL,
                0,
                &argc,
                argv,
                (String*) NULL,
                args, n);

        row = XtVaCreateManagedWidget("row",
            xmRowColumnWidgetClass, parent,
            XmNorientation, XmHORIZONTAL,
            NULL);

        /* Pushbutton starts work procedure. */
        work_count = 0;
```

```
    (void) CreatePushbutton(row, "work",
        (XtCallbackProc) start_workCB,
        (XtPointer) &work_count);

    label = XtVaCreateManagedWidget("label",
            xmLabelWidgetClass, row,
            NULL);

    /* Set up event handler on the label widget. */
    XtAddEventHandler(label,
        ButtonPressMask,
        False,
        (XtEventHandler) event_handler,
        (XtPointer) NULL);

    (void) CreatePushbutton(row, "quit",
        (XtCallbackProc) exitCB, (XtPointer) NULL);

    XtRealizeWidget(parent);
    XtAppMainLoop(app_context);

    return 0;

}   /* main */

/* end of file backtest.c */
```

This program requires the following X resource file:

```
! Resource file for backtest.c in
! Chapter 13 of Power Programming Motif.
!
*fontList:      lucidasans-12
*background:    lightgrey

*title: Work Test

*label.labelString: Click Mouse and Start Timer
*quit.labelString:  Exit
*work.labelString:  Start Work Procedure

! end of resource file
```

Name this file **Ppm** and store it in your home directory.

When you run the program, you'll see something akin to what's shown in Figure 13.1.

The relevant double-click and work-procedure information is printed to your terminal.

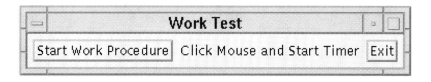

Figure 13.1   *The background-processing test program.*

PERFORMANCE

Most X programs block on input from the X server inside of
XtAppMainLoop. This allows your dormant program to use as few CPU
cycles as possible. If you use a timer or work procedure, though, the main-
event-handling loop needs to do a lot more work and can no longer block as
before. Because of this, adding timers or work procedures adds a significant
load. A work procedure, for example, essentially places Motif into a busy-
wait loop, where your work procedure is the busy part. Use timers and
work procedures where necessary, but skip them if you really don't need to
perform this kind of background processing.

SUMMARY

This chapter introduced background processing with work procedures and
timer callbacks, using Xt Intrinsics functions.

X TOOLKIT INTRINSICS FUNCTIONS AND MACROS INTRODUCED IN THIS CHAPTER

```
XtAppAddTimeOut
XtAppAddWorkProc
XtAddTimeOut
XtAddWorkProc
XtRemoveTimeOut
XtRemoveWorkProc
```

CHAPTER 14

Initializing the Xt Intrinsics Revisited

This chapter covers:

- Fallback resources
- Setting up your own command-line arguments
- The variable number of arguments function, `XtVaAppInitialize`
- The long method for initializing the Intrinsics

INITIALIZING THE XT INTRINSICS

For most of the programs in this book, we passed NULLs for a number of parameters to XtAppInitialize, our function to initialize the Xt Intrinsics. In this chapter, we expand on XtAppInitialize and go into a number of alternatives for more demanding applications.

SHORTCUT

XtAppInitialize

The basic parameters for XtAppInitialize follow:

```
Widget XtAppInitialize(
    XtAppContext* appcontext,   /* RETURN */
    String app_class_name,
    XrmOptionDescList xrm_options,
    Cardinal number_xrm_options,
    int* argc,       /* input/output */
    String* argv,    /* input/output */
    String* fallback_resources,
    ArgList args,     /* hard-coded resources */
    Cardinal number_args)
```

In this chapter, we'll go in depth into the fallback resources, which is a NULL-terminated array of resource commands, and the Xrm options, which allow you to set up your own command-line parameters and have the Xt Intrinsics set resource values based on the command line.

FALLBACK RESOURCES

Fallback resources are a compromise between hard-coded resources that cannot be overridden by the user and resource files that may—or may not— be installed properly. Fallback resources act as a safety valve in case the resource file can't be located. These fallback resources take effect only when the user does *not* set the same resource value in a resource file.

To use fallback resources, you need to build a NULL-terminated array of type String of resource-setting commands and pass these resources to XtAppInitialize:

```
/* Set up fallback resources. */
static String fallback_resources[] = {
```

```
         "*fontList:  lucidasans-24",
         "*background: dimgray",
         "*foreground: white",
         "*marginHeight: 54",
         "*quit.labelString: Push Me to Exit",
         "*Ppm.title: XtAppInitialize",
         NULL   /* end with a NULL */

}; /* fallback_resources */

int main(int argc, char** argv)

{    /* main */
     Widget         parent;
     XtAppContext   app_context;
     Arg            args[20];
     Cardinal       n;

     /* Initialize the X Toolkit Intrinsics. */
     n = 0;
     parent = XtAppInitialize(&app_context,
             "Ppm",
             xrm_options,
             XtNumber(xrm_options),
             &argc,
             argv,
             fallback_resources,
             args, n);

/* ... */

}
```

Using Fallback Resources

There's a lot of debate over the proper uses for fallback resources. Part of the debate centers around the use of the application defaults file, in our case, the X resource file named **Ppm**. Even though resources provide a great advantage for X programs, resource files are a disadvantage because the user or system administrator has to install both your application's executable *and* the resource file. Installing the resource file requires someone who is somewhat familiar with X.

Every application you ship should come with an application defaults file, or class resource file. System administrators should then install the defaults file in the proper systemwide location (usually /usr/lib/X11/app-defaults). When they install the defaults file, system administrators can also customize the file to use the preferred fonts and colors in use at their locations.

So the real purpose of the fallback resources is to provide a means to deal with the situation where this application defaults file can't be found. This is a common occurrence, since most X users have no idea as to what X resource files are anyway.

To deal with this situation, some Motif developers try placing their entire class-resource file into the fallback resources. This is generally not a good idea. These resources take up memory, and you're really abusing the intent of the fallback resources if you place your entire resource file into the fallback resources.

Some applications just use the fallback resources to pop up some kind of dialog box and then present an error message to the user. We generally don't term this friendly behavior. We recommend that your fallback resources provide enough information so that your program can work, although maybe not well, without an X resource file.

PARSING COMMAND-LINE OPTIONS

The Xt Intrinsics provides a handy means for automatically parsing command-line options, such as -iconic or -font. The drawback of this method is that Xt only sets X resource values based on the command-line options. Your application must then query these resources to determine what options were set. This usually isn't an onerous limitation.

To use Xt's method for parsing command-line options, you need to set up an array of XrmOptionDescRec structures and, of course, fill in the values properly.

Up to now, we've passed NULL to XtAppInitialize for the XrmOptionDescRec array. Now it's time to fill this out. The XrmOptionDescRec structure looks like:

```
typedef struct {
  char*         option;
  char*         specifier;
  XrmOptionKind argKind;
  XPointer      value;       /* Value if XrmoptionNoArg   */
} XrmOptionDescRec, *XrmOptionDescList;
```

The *option* field holds the command-line option, such as -foreground. The *specifier* field holds the resource specification to set if the command-line option is set. In our example, we'd probably use a resource *specifier* of *foreground (note the asterisk) to set the *foreground* resource if the user passed a command line with -foreground. The *argKind* field tells Xt what kind of command-line parameter we have. (We cover the choices in depth below.) Finally, the *value* field holds the value if the *argKind* is set to XrmoptionNoArg.

Determining the Type of Option

There are a number of choices for filling in the *argKind* field, based on XrmOptionKind:

```
typedef enum {
    XrmoptionNoArg,
    XrmoptionIsArg,
    XrmoptionStickyArg,
    XrmoptionSepArg,
    XrmoptionResArg,
    XrmoptionSkipArg,
    XrmoptionSkipLine,
    XrmoptionSkipNArgs
} XrmOptionKind;
```

If this seems confusing, Table 14.1 should help.

Table 14.1 *XrmOptionKind.*

Value	Meaning
XrmoptionIsArg	Flag itself, without -, is value
XrmoptionNoArg	Value field holds value
XrmoptionResArg	Full resource command is next argument
XrmoptionSepArg	Value follows flag with space between
XrmoptionSkipArg	Ignore and skip next argument
XrmoptionSkipLine	Ignore and skip rest of argv
XrmoptionSkipNArgs	Ignore and skip next *n* arguments
XrmoptionStickyArg	Value follows flag without space

With XrmoptionSkipNArgs, the value of *n* is held in the *value* field of XrmOptionDescRec.

With XrmoptionIsArg, the rest of the parameter holds the value. For example, if Xt looks for -x and you pass a -x9, then the value for the option will be 9.

Basically, the best rule of thumb is to remember that all Xt is doing for you is setting resource values. Therefore, the whole XrmOptionDescRec structure just tells Xt what resource and what value, based on the command-line parameter.

The best way to understand this is to try a few examples. We'll start with the following three-entry XrmOptionDescRec array:

```
/* Set up command-line parameters. */
static XrmOptionDescRec xrm_options[] = {
{ "-myoption", "*foreground", XrmoptionSepArg, NULL},
{ "-mybackcolor", "*background", XrmoptionNoArg,"orange"},
{ "-label", "*quit.labelString", XrmoptionSepArg, NULL}
};
```

We then assume that our program is named *xtinit*.

With this, the first entry in the XrmOptionDescRec array tells Xt to look for a command-line option of -myoption. If that option is found in the command line, then we assume that the command-line entry following this option holds a value (XrmoptionSepArg), in this case, a color value because of the resource we're setting. Xt then blithely assigns the *foreground resource to the string value of the commandline parameter. For example, to set the foreground color (the foreground resource), use the following syntax:

```
xtinit -myoption color
```

In this case the value *color* will be assigned to the *foreground resource, which sets the foreground color for all widgets, unless the widgets have a more detailed resource specification. For example, call *xtinit* with this command:

```
xtinit -myoption maroon
```

With the above command, you'll set the foreground resource to maroon. Note that the Xrm routines are rather blind. You could call the *xtinit* program with a command of:

```
xtinit -myoption fred
```

The Xrm routines would still try to set the *foreground resource, and you would see an error like the following:

```
Warning: Color name "fred" is not defined in server database.
```

The second entry in the XrmOptionDescRec array tells Xt that we have a single command-line option and that no data will follow it (XrmoptionNoArg). With the XrmoptionNoArg type, the XrmOptionDescRec structure's *value* field holds the value. That is, if Xt find the given command-line parameter, in this case -mybackcolor, then the resource (*background) is set to the value in the *value* field (orange). To set the background color (the background resource) to orange, you can call *xtinit* with the following command:

```
xtinit -mybackcolor
```

The third entry in the XrmOptionDescRec array tells Xt that we have another two-part option (XrmoptionSepArg). In this case, the parameter following -label on the command line holds the value that will be set into the *quit.labelString resource.

To set the labelString resource for the widget named *quit*, you can call *xtinit* with:

```
xtinit -label "This is my new message"
```

You can, of course, combine the three custom command-line options that we've set up:

```
xtinit -myoption purple -mybackcolor -label "Yow"
```

With the Xrm options, you can create your own command-line parameters and have the Xt Intrinsics parse these parameters for you. Note that you're setting only resource values. The setup isn't very involved and usually works quite well. In addition, the Intrinsics will also automatically parse all unique abbreviations of any of the command-line parameters you set up. For example, you can call *xtinit* with the following command:

```
xtinit -myb -myo red
```

Xt will parse both command-line parameters correctly.

It is this mechanism that allows you to pass -d for the -display command-line parameter.

A PROGRAM TO SHOW XRM OPTIONS

The *xtinit* program, below, shows how to use the Xrm options to have Xt handle the command-line options for you. The program also shows how to use fallback resources. The code follows:

```
/* xtinit.c */
#include  <Xm/Xm.h>
#include  <Xm/PushB.h>

/* Set up fallback resources. */
static String fallback_resources[] = {
  "*fontList:  lucidasans-24",
  "*background: dimgray",
  "*foreground: white",
  "*marginHeight: 54",
  "*quit.labelString: Push Me to Exit",
  "*Ppm.title: XtAppInitialize",
  NULL    /* end with a NULL */

}; /* fallback_resources */

/* Set up command-line parameters. */
static XrmOptionDescRec xrm_options[] = {
  { "-myoption",    "*foreground", XrmoptionSepArg, NULL},
  { "-mybackcolor", "*background", XrmoptionNoArg, "orange"},
  { "-label", "*quit.labelString", XrmoptionSepArg, NULL}
};

void exitCB(Widget widget,
    XtPointer client_data,
    XtPointer call_data)

{   /* exitCB */

    exit(0);

}   /* exitCB */

int main(int argc, char** argv)

{   /* main */
    Widget          parent;
    XtAppContext    app_context;
    Widget          push;
    Arg             args[20];
    Cardinal        n;

    /* Initialize the X Toolkit Intrinsics. */
    n = 0;
    parent = XtAppInitialize(&app_context,
            "Ppm",
```

```
                    xrm_options,
                    XtNumber(xrm_options),
                    &argc,
                    argv,
                    fallback_resources,
                    args, n);

        n = 0;
        push = XmCreatePushButton(parent, "quit", args, n);

        XtAddCallback(push,
            XmNactivateCallback,
            (XtCallbackProc) exitCB,
            (XtPointer) NULL);

        XtManageChild(push);

        XtRealizeWidget(parent);
        XtAppMainLoop(app_context);

        return 0;

    }   /* main */

/* end of file xtinit.c */
```

You should run this program without an X resource file to see how the fall-back resources work. To run the program without the resource file, you'll need to move the **Ppm** file in your home directory (or delete it). Then, run the *xtinit* program with an X resource file. In addition, run the program using the command-line parameters listed in the examples above. This will give you a good feel about how the Xrm options work.

XTVAAPPINITIALIZE

With later versions, the Xt Intrinsics offers a number of functions that take a variable number of parameters. These functions are generally easier to use, because you avoid the steps of calling XtSetArg to set up each resource value one at a time. Functions like XtVaCreateManagedWidget are much easier to use in your code than XtCreateManagedWidget. Similarly, we find XtVaAppInitialize easier to use than XtAppInitialize:

```
Widget XtVaAppInitialize(
    XtAppContext* app_context, /* RETURN */
    const String application_class,
    XrmOptionDescList xrm_options,
```

```
Cardinal number_options,
int* argc_ptr,    /* in/out */
String* argv,     /* in/out */
String* fallback_resources,
...)
```

Both functions perform essentially the same task, so use whichever you prefer. As you can see, the parameters to `XtVaAppInitialize` mimic those of `XtAppInitialize`, but you can skip the step for building up the `Arg` array.

In your code, you can use `XtVaAppInitialize` as follows:

```
XtAppContext  app_context;
Widget        parent;

/* Initialize X toolkit */
parent = XtVaAppInitialize(&app_context,
        "Ppm",
        (XrmOptionDescList) NULL,
        0,
        &argc,
        argv,
        (String*) NULL,
        XmNallowResize, True,
        NULL);
```

THE LONG METHOD FOR XtAppInitialize

Up to now, we have used `XtAppInitialize` or `XtVaAppInitialize` to handle all the tasks of setting up the connection to the X server, initializing the Xt Intrinsics, and creating a top-level shell widget. There are many cases, though, where you need information that you can get from an open display connection *before* you want to create the top-level shell widget. For example, if you want to use a nondefault visual, as is often the case with systems that support 24-bit planes of color, you need to open the display connection, find the proper visual, and only then create the top-level shell widget using this newly found visual. In such cases, you must be able to break out the component parts of `XtAppInitialize`.

You can break up `XtAppInitialize` and initialize the Xt Intrinsics using a longer method. As such, `XtAppInitialize` goes through six basic steps:

1. Calls `XtToolkitInitialize` to initialize the toolkit.

2. Calls `XtCreateApplicationContext` to create an application context.

3. Sets the fallback resources with `XtAppSetFallbackResources`.

4. Makes a copy of the command-line parameters in `argc` and `argv`, using `XtMalloc`, a front end to `malloc`.

5. Calls `XtOpenDisplay` to open a display connection to the X server.

6. Calls `XtAppCreateShell` to create a top-level shell widget.

Normally, `XtAppInitialize` calls each of these routines under the hood. To go through each of these steps in depth, we can start with `XtToolkitInitialize`:

```
void XtToolkitInitialize(void)
```

`XtToolkitInitialize` just initializes the data in the Xt Intrinsics. You need to call this routine first.

`XtCreateApplicationContext`, as you probably guessed, creates an application context:

```
XtAppContext XtCreateApplicationContext(void)
```

Set the fallback resources, which we discussed at the beginning of this chapter, with `XtAppSetFallbackResources`:

```
void XtAppSetFallbackResources(XtAppContext app_context,
        String* fallback_resources)
```

The next step is to copy the command-line parameters `argc` and `argv`. Why? Because various routines take these parameters and then modify the list. Since we need to pass the list to a number of Xt routines, we need a copy. The following code should make a copy of our application's command-line parameters:

```
#include <string.h>

int main(int argc, char** argv)

{
    int             copy_of_argc;
    char**          copy_of_argv;
    int             argv_size;

    /* Copy command-line parameters. */
    copy_of_argc = argc;
```

```
    argv_size = argc * (sizeof(char*));

    copy_of_argv = (char**) XtMalloc(argv_size);

    memcpy(copy_of_argv, argv, argv_size);

}
```

We use XtMalloc to allocate the memory. XtMalloc is typically a front end to the malloc function:

```
char* XtMalloc(Cardinal number_bytes)
```

For all intents and purposes, XtMalloc acts like malloc, as we stated in Chapter 5. Just be careful: If you allocate memory with XtMalloc, free the memory with XtFree:

```
void XtFree(char* ptr)
```

Once we have a copy of the command-line parameters, we use the parameters in the call to XtOpenDisplay. XtOpenDisplay opens a connection to the X server for a given application context.

```
Display* XtOpenDisplay(XtAppContext app_context,
    String display_name,
    String application_name,
    String application_class,
    XrmOptionDescRec* xrm_options,
    Cardinal number_options,
    int* argc_ptr,
    String* argv)
```

With XtOpenDisplay, you can pass NULL for a number of parameters. If you pass NULL for the *display_name* (the name of the X server to connect to), XtOpenDisplay will check the command-line parameters, argv, and also the DISPLAY environment variable. We almost always pass NULL for the *display_name*.

We can pass NULL for the *application_name*, too. In that case, XtOpenDisplay uses argv[0] for the application name. We normally pass "Ppm" for the *application_class*, at least for the example programs in this book. The rest of the parameters mimic those to XtAppInitialize.

In our code, we'll call XtOpenDisplay like the following:

```
display = XtOpenDisplay(app_context,
            NULL,   /* display name, use argv */
```

```
NULL,    /* app name, use arg[0] */
"Ppm",   /* class name */
(XrmOptionDescList) NULL,
0,
&argc, argv);
```

In most cases, an error opening the display connection is a fatal error. If XtOpenDisplay fails, it returns NULL for the display pointer.

After you establish the connection to the X server, you can query the X server, particularly if you're interested in using the full color hardware on a 24-bit color system. We'll cover how to find a 24-bit visual in the next chapter.

For now, the next step is to create our top-level application shell with XtAppCreateShell:

```
Widget XtAppCreateShell(String application_name,
    String application_class,
    WidgetClass widget_class,
    Display* display,
    ArgList args,
    Cardinal number_args)
```

XtAppCreateShell creates a top-level shell of the given *widget_class*. We normally use a class of applicationShellWidgetClass. As with XtOpenDisplay, you can pass NULL for the *application_name*, and XtAppCreateShell will use the name from XtOpenDisplay. You must place in the copy of the command-line parameters into the argc and argv resources for this first top-level shell.

In our code, we call XtAppCreateShell as follows:

```
/* Set in command-line parameters. */
n = 0;
XtSetArg(args[n], XmNargc, copy_of_argc); n++;
XtSetArg(args[n], XmNargv, copy_of_argv); n++;

XtSetArg(args[n], XmNallowResize, True); n++;

parent = XtAppCreateShell(NULL,
        "Ppm",
        applicationShellWidgetClass,
        display,
        args, n);
```

Putting this all together, we have a short program that uses the long method to initialize the Xt Intrinsics. The code follows:

```
/* xtlong.c */
```

```
#include <Xm/Xm.h>
#include <Xm/PushB.h>
#include <stdio.h>
#include <string.h>

/* Set up fallback resources. */
static String fallback_resources[] = {
  "*fontList:  lucidasans-24",
  "*background: dimgray",
  "*foreground: white",
  "*quit.labelString: Exit",
  "*Ppm.title: Long Xt Initialize",
  NULL    /* end with a NULL */

}; /* fallback_resources */

void exitCB(Widget widget,
    XtPointer client_data,
    XtPointer call_data)

{   /* exitCB */

    exit(0);

}   /* exitCB */

int main(int argc, char** argv)

{   /* main */
    Widget          parent;
    XtAppContext    app_context;
    Widget          push;
    Arg             args[20];
    Cardinal        n;
    Display*        display;
    int             copy_of_argc;
    char**          copy_of_argv;
    int             argv_size;

    /* Initialize X toolkit the long way. */
    XtToolkitInitialize();

    app_context = XtCreateApplicationContext();

    /* Set fallback resources. */
    XtAppSetFallbackResources(app_context,
        fallback_resources);

    /* Copy command-line parameters. */
    copy_of_argc = argc;

    argv_size = argc * (sizeof(char*));

    copy_of_argv = (char**) XtMalloc(argv_size);
```

```
        memcpy(copy_of_argv, argv, argv_size);

        /* Open display connection. */
        display = XtOpenDisplay(app_context,
                    NULL,   /* display name, use argv */
                    NULL,   /* app name, use arg[0] */
                    "Ppm",  /* class name */
                    (XrmOptionDescList) NULL,
                    0,      /* number options */
                    &argc, argv);

        /*
         * We assume an error opening
         * display is a fatal error.
         */
        if (display == (Display*) NULL) {
            fprintf(stderr, "Error opening X display.\n");
            exit(1);
        }

        /* In some programs, you may get a visual here. */

        /* Set in command-line parameters. */
        n = 0;
        XtSetArg(args[n], XmNargc, copy_of_argc); n++;
        XtSetArg(args[n], XmNargv, copy_of_argv); n++;

        XtSetArg(args[n], XmNallowResize, True); n++;

        parent = XtAppCreateShell(NULL, /* app name, use argv */
                "Ppm",
                applicationShellWidgetClass,
                display,
                args, n);

        /* Create child widget. */
        n = 0;
        push = XmCreatePushButton(parent, "quit", args, n);

        XtAddCallback(push,
            XmNactivateCallback,
            (XtCallbackProc) exitCB,
            (XtPointer) NULL);

        XtManageChild(push);

        XtRealizeWidget(parent);
        XtAppMainLoop(app_context);

        return 0;

}   /* main */

/* end of file xtlong.c */
```

Most sophisticated graphics applications need to use the long method for initializing the Xt Intrinsics. You'll need this if you intend to use a nondefault visual or use the PEXlib for 3D graphics. We cover these topics in the next two chapters.

SUMMARY

For most of the programs in this book, we passed NULLs for a number of parameters to XtAppInitialize, our function to initialize the Xt Intrinsics. In this chapter, we expanded on XtAppInitialize and went into a number of alternatives for more demanding applications.

X TOOLKIT INTRINSICS FUNCTIONS AND MACROS INTRODUCED IN THIS CHAPTER

```
XtAppCreateShell
XtCreateApplicationContext
XtOpenDisplay
XtToolkitInitialize
XtVaAppInitialize
```

CHAPTER 15

Colors, Colormaps, and Visuals

This chapter covers:

- More than you ever want to know about color in X
- Allocating sharable color cells
- Using Xt resource converters to convert names into color cells
- Read-only vs. read/write color cells
- Looking up color names
- Controlling how Motif allocates colors
- Setting color resources
- Visuals and colormaps
- Sharing standard colormaps between applications
- Creating standard colormaps
- Using the X miscellaneous utilities library

491

THE X COLOR MODEL

Color forms one of the most complicated topics in X. This chapter introduces color under the X Window System and shows how to customize how your Motif applications work with color.

Color is complex because graphics workstations use different means for controlling colors on the monitor. Some have color tables, some have color planes, and all seem to be different.

X, attempting to be device-independent, has to deal with all the many color implementations. Perhaps because of this, color in X appears overly complex. The seemingly simple task of drawing a line in red leads to all sorts of contortions in initializing colors and finding visuals.

Most of these different workstations are built on an *RGB color model:* red, green, and blue phosphors within each pixel are combined to form the different hues on the screen. Electron beams excite the phosphors, which in turn provide the color. Simultaneously exciting all phosphors produces a white pixel; when all are unexcited, you're left with a black pixel.

Color displays use multiple bits within a pixel, or dot on the screen, to further specify colors. These bits are also known as *planes*, and the most common color display contains eight planes (supporting 256 different colors). You have access to many more colors, even though only a limited number of them can actually be displayed at one time.

In contrast, monochrome displays have only one plane, and the phosphor is either on or off. Gray scales are simulated by making the red, green, and blue values equal.

At the other end of the spectrum, we're starting to see more and more workstations with up to 24 color planes, especially as costs dive ever downward. These are high-performance systems; you can see many more colors at a time at a greater resolution, but the trade-off is the overwhelming complexity of programming for these screens.

Color Cells

All color in X is based on the RGB model. Since most monitors work this way, using the RGB model makes sense. Each color takes up a color cell in a colormap. Some systems support only one colormap at a time, some allow for multiple colormaps, and some only allow you to read, but not write to, colormaps. These colormap options are based on the visual in use (see "Visuals and Colormaps," below). For now, we'll concentrate on the simplest visual class, `PseudoColor`.

To use color in X, you need to allocate a color cell in the colormap that your application is using. Actually, colormaps are tied to windows, so you could have a separate colormap for each window. Generally, this is not a good idea. First, it takes up precious system resources. Second, you're likely to see annoying flashing effects as the user moves the mouse about the screen, since most hardware supports only one active colormap at a time.

Each color cell in a colormap has its red, green, and blue values. The place in the colormap that the color cell occupies is called a *color index*. It is this index that you use to set the color. For example, in Chapter 11 we covered the `XSetForeground` function that sets the foreground color for a graphics context. The value you pass to `XSetForeground` is the color-index number. Color indexes are usually an unsigned long integer value (also defined as a `Pixel` type in Motif).

Each color cell is then represented by an index that, as you guessed, indexes into the colormap, either directly into one colormap or indirectly into decomposed red, green, and blue colormaps. Color index 42, for example, may have a red value of 0, a green value of 5125, and a blue value of 9104. (X RGB color values are defined on a scale that goes from 0 to 65535. Most graphics textbooks, though, use values from 0 to 255, because 256-color systems are so pervasive.)

SHORTCUT

Allocating Colors

Once you have a display pointer, you can start allocating color cells. The following code allocates a red color, by turning the red full on and the green and blue full off:

```
Widget    parent;
Display*  display;
XColor    xcolor;
Colormap  colormap;
int       status;

/* Call XtAppInitialize... */

display = XtDisplay(parent);
```

```
colormap = DefaultColormap(display,
             DefaultScreen(display) );

xcolor.flags = DoRed | DoGreen | DoBlue;
xcolor.red   = 65535;
xcolor.green = 0;
xcolor.blue  = 0;

/* Allocate color cell. */
status = XAllocColor(display,
         colormap,
         &xcolor);

/* Color cell is now in xcolor.pixel */
```

To get a colormap, you can use the default colormap for now. DefaultColormap returns the ID of the default colormap:

```
Colormap DefaultColormap(Display* display,
    int screen_number)
```

You can also query the colormap resource on a widget:

```
Widget    widget;
Colormap  colormap;

XtVaGetValues(widget,
    XmNcolormap, &colormap,
    NULL);
```

The colormap resource won't be valid unless you've called XtRealizeWidget for the widget's hierarchy.

We explain the XColor structure and XAllocColor below.

Allocating Color Cells

To use colors in X, you need to allocate color cells in a colormap. Color cells are normally defined by the fields in an XColor structure:

```
typedef struct {
    unsigned long  pixel;
    unsigned short red, green, blue;
    char           flags;
    char           pad;
} XColor;
```

The *pixel* field is the color index number in the colormap. The term *pixel* is a poor choice, because it has another common meaning: a dot on the screen. In X, each dot on the screen—pixel—has a pixel value, which is an index into a colormap.

The *red*, *green*, and *blue* fields contain the RGB values of the color, using a scale from 0 (off) to 65535 (full on). The X server scales these values to numbers acceptable to your graphics hardware. All colors in X are specified in terms of RGB. (The X Color Management System, or Xcms, allows for other color models, such as CIE and HVC. See *Professional Graphics Programming in the X Window System*, Johnson and Reichard, MIS:Press, 1993.)

With the *flags* field, you can specify whether all three RGB values should be used or not. Or together the flags you want from the list of DoRed, DoGreen, and DoBlue.

The XColor structure is used for a number of reasons. First, you can use the structure to hold an RGB definition of a color, even though that color has yet to be allocated from any colormap. In this case, the *pixel* field has no value. Only the *flags* and *red*, *green*, and *blue* fields are used.

Second, you can use the XColor structure to allocate a particular color from a colormap. In this case, the *pixel* field will be filled in from functions such as XAllocColor and XAllocNamedColor. The color is allocated with the RGB values in the *red*, *green*, and *blue* fields, based on the bit-flags in the *flags* field.

Sometimes this distinction can be confusing because of the multiple uses of the XColor structure.

Read-Only and Read/Write Color Cells

X provides two ways to allocate color cells: read-only and read/write. If you use a read-only color cell, you can allocate any RGB values, but you cannot later change the RGB values. That is, you can make a widget have a red background and later change the widget's background to blue, but you cannot change the *definition* of red with a read-only color cell. If you want to change the definition of your colors, you need to allocate read/write color cells. Most applications can use read-only colors.

The advantage of the read-only color cells is that with only a limited number of colors available, applications can share colors. For example, if two applications both allocate read-only color cells for red from the same colormap—typically the default colormap and with the same RGB values— then the X server will allocate only one color cell. This makes sense, as there's no need to have two color cells both with the same red color. Both applications can then share this same color. With only 256 colors available on most workstations, sharing colors becomes an effective technique to avoid filling up your colormap. This is one reason why you want to use the default colormap if possible.

Allocating Read-Only Color Cells

XAllocColor allocates a read-only color cell. It takes in a display, colormap, and an XColor structure:

```
Status XAllocColor(Display* display,
        Colormap colormap,
        XColor* xcolor)  /* input/output */
```

You must fill in the *red, green, blue* and *flags* fields of the structure. XAllocColor will attempt to allocate a color cell (or share an existing one) that holds the closest match the hardware supports to the RGB values passed to XAllocColor. If successful, XAllocColor will fill in the *pixel* field of the XColor structure. The *red, green,* and *blue* fields of the structure are filled in with the actual values used (if the color you requested couldn't be exactly matched by your workstation hardware). XAllocColor returns a nonzero value on success and a zero on failure.

After the call is successful, you have a pixel value (in the XColor structure) that is an entry into the colormap where the new color is located. The pixel value may be for a new color allocated by XAllocColor. If the same RGB values were already in use in another read-only (sharable) color cell, this pixel value is then the index for the shared color.

Color Names

X provides a database of color names and RGB values. This database contains familiar colors, like *red*, and some less common colors, like *lemon chiffon* and *mistyrose*. The colors are all listed with English names and their associated RGB values. A text version of this database is normally kept in **/usr/lib/X11/rgb.txt** (oftentimes, in **/usr/openwin/lib/X11/rgb.txt** on OpenWindows systems). This is compiled into **rgb.dir** and **rgb.pag** data files. An excerpt of the text file appears below:

```
240 255 240 honeydew
255 228 225 mistyrose
112 128 144 slategrey
176 196 222 light steel blue
```

```
255 160 122 light salmon
 69  69  69 gray27
255 250 205 lemon chiffon
245 245 220 beige
255 105 180 hot pink
176  48  96 maroon
245 255 250 mintcream
  0 255   0 green
255  99  71 tomato
255   0   0 red
255 165   0 orange
```

The *showrgb* program prints out the list of colors.

For each color, the red, green, and blue values, scaled from 0 to 255, appear first, then the color name. In X, RGB values are defined on a scale from 0 to 65,535. In the **rgb.txt** file, though, the values are scaled from 0 to 255. Under the hood, the X library performs the necessary conversion.

The case of the name doesn't matter. Nor does it matter if you separate words with spaces; *LightSalmon*, *light SALMON*, and *lIgHt SALmon* are all the same, as far as X is concerned. In Release 5 of the X Window System, there are over 730 color names in the default database.

You can use these values and have a program that uses red. This red may appear slightly different on each display, but generally this level of exactness is fine for Motif programs. X provides a set of convenience functions to allocate colors based on names looked up in the RGB database, such as *red*, *orange*, and *maroon*.

Looking Up Color Names

The nice thing about this RGB database is that you can look up a color, like *Red* or *LimeGreen*, on every X display and get back an RGB value for that color. XLookupColor does this:

```
Status XLookupColor(Display* display,
        Colormap colormap,
        const char* colorname,
        XColor* exactcolor)    /* RETURN */
        XColor* hardwarecolor) /* RETURN */
```

XLookupColor tries to find a match between the text name of the color, stored in *colorname*, and an entry in the system color database. If match is successful, XLookupColor will return a nonzero value. XLookupColor returns 0 on failure. When naming these colors, do not put any spaces in the names. Also, case does not matter, as *LimeGreen* and *LIMEGREEN* should resolve to the same color.

On return from XLookupColor, the *exactcolor* parameter holds the RGB components from the color database, exactly as they are in the RGB database. The *hardwarecolor* parameter holds the RGB components of the closest hardware match for the requested color using the visual for the given *colormap*. Sometimes this match may not be the best match.

After a color name has been looked up in the system color database, a particular color cell must be found or allocated in the application's colormap. You can use XAllocColor, as shown above, or XAllocNamedColor.

Allocating Named Colors

You can combine XLookupColor and XAllocColor in one X library call. XAllocNamedColor will look up the English color name and allocate a colormap cell for the color:

```
Status XAllocNamedColor(Display* display,
    Colormap colormap,
    const char* color_name,
    XColor* hardwarecolor, /* RETURN */
    XColor* exactcolor)    /* RETURN */
```

Note the strangely reversed order on the *hardwarecolor* and *exactcolor* from the XLookupColor function.

The following utility function, AllocNamedColor, calls XAllocNamedColor to allocate a read-only color cell. You can also pass a default color cell to AllocNamedColor, which the routine uses as a fallback if XAllocNamedColor fails to allocate the color cell. Your code then handles a lack of color cells in the given colormap. The code for AllocNamedColor follows:

```
/* xcolor.c */
#include  <Xm/Xm.h>

    /* Allocates a read-only color cell. */
unsigned long AllocNamedColor(Display* display,
    Colormap colormap,
    char* colorname,
    unsigned long default_color)

{   /* AllocNamedColor */
    XColor          hardwarecolor, exactcolor;
    unsigned long   color;
    int             status;

    status = XAllocNamedColor(display,
            colormap,
            colorname,
```

```
                    &hardwarecolor,
                    &exactcolor);

        if (status != 0) {
            color = hardwarecolor.pixel;
        } else {
            color = default_color;
        }

        return color;

    }   /* AllocNamedColor */

/* end of file xcolor.c */
```

Once you've allocated a color, the natural thing to do is use the new color with your Motif widgets.

Setting Color Resources

Once you've allocated a color cell, you can set any of the Motif color resources, such as foreground or background, to use that color. For example, to set the foreground resource within your application, you can call the following code:

```
Widget        widget;
unsigned long color;

/* Allocate color... */

/* Set color resource. */
XtVaSetValues(widget,
    XmNforeground, color,
    NULL);
```

You cannot set the foreground resource to a color name, you must use the proper unsigned long color index (also called a Pixel value in Motif). If you have only a color name, you can try using a resource converter.

Using Color-Resource Converters

In order to read in a resource file, Motif and the Xt Intrinsics must be able to convert the strings in the resource file to actual values of various data types. To do this, Xt calls a set of *resource converter* functions. You can also call one of these converters from your code (you can also write your own converters, but that's an advanced topic). To call a built-in converter, use the XtConvertAndStore function:

```
Boolean XtConvertAndStore(Widget widget,
    String from_type,
    XrmValue* from_value,
    String  to_type,
    XrmValue* to_value)  /* on/out */
```

XtConvertAndStore takes a structure that holds a resource value in some format (*from_type*) and converts it to a value of another type (*to_type*). Both the from and to values depend on the XrmValue structure. The XrmValue structure then looks like:

```
typedef struct {
    unsigned int   size;
    XPointer       addr;
} XrmValue, *XrmValuePtr;
```

In the structure, the *size* field holds the number of bytes pointed at by the *addr* field. The *addr* field holds the address of where the data are stored.

This probably seems confusing—and it is. The key is filling in the XrmValue structure and then choosing the proper converters.

Setting Up the From Data

In our case, the *from_type* will be XtRString, because it's a string type. (You can look in <X11/StringDefs.h> for a list of the resource converter strings.)

Setting Up the Return Data

You need to fill in the *to_value* XrmValue structure with the address information for the target data. Since we're dealing with an unsigned long, we should set the *size* field to the size of an unsigned long.

The *to_type* will be XtRPixel, since we want a Pixel (unsigned long) or color index value returned.

To put this together, the following utility function will convert a color name to an Xt Pixel value for use with a color resource like foreground or background:

```
/* cvtcolor.c */
#include  <Xm/Xm.h>
#include  <X11/StringDefs.h>
```

```
    /* Convert color name to color. */
Boolean CvtColor(Widget widget,
    char* color_name,
    unsigned long* color)   /* RETURN */

{   /* CvtColor */
    XrmValue        from_value, to_value;
    unsigned long   returned_color = 0;
    int             status;

    /* Set up our from value. */
    from_value.addr = color_name;
    from_value.size = strlen(from_value.addr);

    /* The to value holds the address of the result. */
    to_value.addr = (XtPointer) &returned_color;
    to_value.size = sizeof(unsigned long);

    status = XtConvertAndStore(widget,
            XtRString, &from_value,
            XtRPixel,  &to_value);

    *color = returned_color;

    return status;

}   /* CvtColor */

/* end of file cvtcolor.c */
```

With Motif 1.2, we had no problems with the definitions of
XtRString and XtRPixel. With Motif 1.1 and X11 Release 4,
though, we had to include the extra file <X11/StringDefs.h>
in order to compile *cvtcolor.c*.

N O T E

Other String Conversions

You can use Xt's built-in converters to convert a number of data types.
They are listed in Table 15.1.

Table 15.1   *Some of Xt's built-in converters.*

From Type	To Type	Meaning
XtRString	XtRBoolean	Converts on, off, true, false, yes, and no
XtRString	XtRFile	Opens file and returns file descriptor
XtRString	XtRFont	Loads font and returns font ID
XtRString	XtRPixel	Converts color name to Pixel

How Motif Selects Colors and How You Can Change This

Most Motif widgets that support user input provide some sort of 3D bevel. Pushbuttons, for example, have a 3D look that makes the buttons appear to stand out on the display. The Motif XmPrimitive widget class provides two resources for these 3D bevel colors, as listed in Table 15.2.

Table 15.2   *The 3D bevel resources.*

Resource	Type	Default Value
bottomShadowColor	Pixel	*dynamic*
bottomShadowPixmap	Pixmap	XmUNSPECIFIED_PIXMAP
topShadowColor	Pixel	*dynamic*
topShadowPixmap	Pixmap	XmUNSPECIFIED_PIXMAP

In most cases, Motif uses the color resources rather than the pixmaps.

The Motif library automatically generates what the toolkit thinks are good 3D bevel colors for any given background color. You'll note that all this hinges on choosing a background color in the first place. The Motif library does this by calling a *color-calculation function*. This function is called under the hood by the library routines that need to determine the 3D bevel colors for a widget. The color-calculation function also determines the selection and foreground colors for the widget, too.

The normal algorithm for choosing these colors is to use 85 percent% of the background color for the bottom shadow and 150 percent for the top shadow. (Treat this as a rule of thumb, as the actual algorithm is a little more involved than this.)

Background colors should be in the middle of the RGB scale. Ideally, the brightest (highest) value for red, green, or blue should be greater than 155 (on a 0 to 255 scale) and less than 175. The selection color (often the `armColor` resource, which is used, for example, when a pushbutton is armed) generally is a color between the background and the bottom shadow color.

If you start to think about it, Motif allocates a large number of colors: background, foreground, selection, top shadow, and bottom shadow. And that's just for one widget. If you use different colors on each widget, you'll soon use up all the colors available on a 256-color display.

If you don't like this algorithm, or you need tight control over the color cells used by Motif, you can customize the algorithm by changing the Motif color-calculation function. Motif allows you to pass your own function pointer to be used in place of the default function. Actually, the default color-calculation function uses a relatively good algorithm. In most cases, if you want to customize this, it's because you need to tightly control the colors used by Motif. For example, if you have a system that supports only 256 colors and you intend to display complex color image files, you want as many of those 256 colors as possible for your image files. By changing the color-calculation function, you have more accurate control over how many colors the Motif toolkit code actually allocates. Note that this color calculation function only affects your program. It does not change any other X or Motif program on the display.

You can change the default color-calculation function with `XmSetColorCalculation`:

```
#include <Xm/Xm.h>

XmColorProc
    XmSetColorCalculation(XmColorProc color_function)
```

`XmSetColorCalculation` takes your function pointer, *color_function*, and calls that, when necessary, to perform the color calculations. `XmSetColorCalculation` returns the previous color-calculation function.

The `XmColorProc` type is a function pointer for a color-calculation function. This function takes the following parameters:

```
void color_function(XColor* background_color, /* in */
    XColor* foreground_color,     /* RETURN */
    XColor* selection_color,      /* RETURN */
    XColor* top_shadow_color,     /* RETURN */
    XColor* bottom_shadow_color)  /* RETURN */
```

Your color-calculation function should fill in the *flags*, *red*, *green*, and *blue* fields of the returned `XColor` structures (for the foreground, selection, top shadow, and bottom shadow). Your function should *not* allocate the color cells for these colors. The Motif library will do this. You just get to choose the RGB values. But if you choose RGB values that are for color cells already allocated as read-only, Motif will use those same cells. Base your algorithm on the input data in the *background_color*.

You can retrieve the current color-calculation function with `XmGetColorCalculation`:

```
XmColorProc XmGetColorCalculation(void)
```

VISUALS AND COLORMAPS

To hide differences in color hardware, X supports *visuals*—abstractions for color hardware subsystems. Visuals are associated with *screens*, physical CRT monitors. The screen may support color or only scales of gray. (A monochrome screen is considered the degenerate case of a gray-scale screen). Each visual supports certain types of colormaps and these colormaps may be read-only or you may be able to write to them. The colormaps may also be decomposed into separate red, green, and blue spaces.

This leads to the six X visual classes:

- `DirectColor`
- `GrayScale`
- `PseudoColor`
- `StaticColor`
- `StaticGray`
- `TrueColor`

The static visual classes and `TrueColor` are read-only, whereas the others are writable and readable. By having read/write classes, you can create your own colors. Table 15.3 lists the six X visual classes and their attributes (color or gray-scale, decomposed, or undecomposed colormap), and whether you can write to colormaps under that visual.

Table 15.3 *X visual classes.*

Visual Class	Color/Gray	Colormap	Writable
DirectColor	Color	Decomposed	Yes
GrayScale	Gray-scale	Undecomposed	Yes
PseudoColor	Color	Undecomposed	Yes
StaticColor	Color	Undecomposed	No
StaticGray	Gray-scale	Undecomposed	No
TrueColor	Color	Decomposed	No

Under this model, a monochrome screen would be a degenerate `StaticGray` visual with a depth of 1 plane.

Most color workstations support 8 bit-planes of color with a `PseudoColor` visual. Other common color systems include 4 bit-planes of color (on standard VGA systems), 16 and 24 bit-planes.

`PseudoColor` is also the easiest visual to work with when programming color applications. The common 8 bit-plane color workstations support only 256 simultaneous colors. This limited number of displayable colors soon becomes a problem for image-processing, visualization, or 3D-rendering applications.

In most cases, your Motif applications will simply use the default visual and ignore all these issues. The problems arise when you move to systems with 24 bit-planes of color and want to take advantage of the complex color system provided by your hardware. For example, if you're writing a program that handles electronic mail, you won't need a lot of sophisticated color options. But if you later extend this program to allow users to mail 24-bit color images, then you'll need to come up with some way to view these images.

This may be necessary for complex graphics applications. In most cases, though, it is a lot easier to follow certain conventions and try to use the system defaults wherever possible, thereby making your applications work on any display monitor running X. We find that most color X servers under X11 Release 5 support multiple visuals of all six types on the same screen anyway, but generally `PseudoColor` visuals are the easiest to write code for.

The Default Visual

In many cases, the default visual will just be what is needed—usually a class of `PseudoColor`. Most X color systems, in fact, make a `PseudoColor` visual the default. If your application just needs a `PseudoColor` visual, check the default first and use it if possible. Again, color resources on the display are shared among all X applications, so the more defaults your application can use, the better-behaved X citizen it will be.

You can find the default visual with the `DefaultVisual` macro:

```
Visual* DefaultVisual(Display* display,
            int screen_number)
```

You can check which visuals are supported on your screen by using the *xdpyinfo* program. This program reports on many of the features supported by your X server. Visuals apply to screens, so a multiscreen display could support quite a few visuals. Each visual can support a number of colormaps.

Colormaps

A *colormap* is an index table used to look up colors. For example, color index 15 could be magenta and index 14, yellow. The colormap may be decomposed into separate red, green, and blue colormaps with the `DirectColor` and `TrueColor` visuals. All other visual types use undecomposed colormaps. That is, the colormap acts as a large array. For each element in the array, there are the red, green, and blue components for that color.

Each window on the X display has an associated colormap. You can create a new colormap and then change the colormap attributes for a given window, if you desire. Normally, though, you can use the default colormap and have each window use its parent's colormap.

Most workstations support just one hardware colormap. For a typical system with 8-bit planes of color, the hardware colormap will have 256 entries for 256 possible distinct colors.

In your applications, though, you may create a number of software colormaps. Each of these colormaps is associated with a given window. If the color hardware can support only one colormap at a time (which is the most common case), X must swap in and out these software colormaps. Each colormap becomes active in turn.

It is up to the window manager to perform colormap swapping. The *colormap focus* usually follows the mouse. That is, when the mouse pointer is in a window, the colormap focus follows the mouse and any colormaps for that window become active.

The problem with this colormap swapping is that it creates the Technicolor effects so disliked by users as the mouse moves about the screen. Consequently, it is generally a good idea to use the default colormap if at all possible.

Of course, workstation hardware isn't that simple. With the dropping costs of high-end graphics systems, more and more users will run workstations that support 24 bit-planes of color. With 24 bit-planes of color, you typically have more available color cells than pixels on your display. Right now, most monitors at most provide 1280x1024 pixels. Within a few years, though, we expect to see pixel resolutions in the range of 2000x2000 common.

Each colormap is made up of color cells or colormap entries. A 256-entry colormap obviously then has 256 color cells.

Using Visuals with X Toolkits

Using nondefault visuals with X toolkit programs can be a daunting task. There are a lot of things that can go wrong and not a lot of diagnostic information to help you out.

To use a nondefault visual in an X toolkit program, set the `visual` resource on a top-level shell widget before you create the widget. The first and most important thing to remember is that only Motif shell widgets support the visual resource. All other widgets are created using their parent's visual. The second thing to remember is that you need to set a number of resources all at once to be effective (and avoid nasty X errors, such as the `BadMatch` error on window creation). We list these resources in Table 15.4.

Table 15.4 *Resources to set when using nondefault visuals.*

Resource	Value
background	Background color
backgroundPixmap	A pixmap created for the visual
borderColor	Color for window border
borderPixmap	A pixmap created for the visual
colormap	A colormap created for the visual
depth	The depth of the visual
visual	The visual you want to use

You need to set only one of background or backgroundPixmap, as well as one of borderColor or borderPixmap. Usually the color resources are easier to code than the pixmaps.

To use a nondefault visual in an Xt-based program, follow these five steps:

1. Initialize the Xt Intrinsics the long way, using the method presented in Chapter 14.

2. Before creating the top-level shell widget, determine the proper visual you want to use.

3. Create a colormap for that visual.

4. Create a pixmap with the same depth as the visual. This pixmap will be used for the window border.

5. Set the colormap, depth, visual, background, and borderColor resources for the top-level shell widget and create the widget. You'll need to set those same resources on all other shell widgets you create.

N O T E

Be careful with the definition of shell widgets. Dialogs and menus use shell widgets (transient and override shells, respectively) under the hood. This part can often hit you unaware. If you get a BadMatch error on window creation (X_CreateWindow), chances are you messed up the visual resource on a shell widget.

Finding the Best Visual

To find the best visual, you first need to decide what the term *best* means. Usually, we look for a DirectColor visual with the greatest number of color planes and then fall back to the deepest StaticColor or PseudoColor visuals, but your definition may vary.

You can use XGetVisualInfo to track down those visuals that meet a given set of criteria.

```
#include <X11/Xutil.h>

XVisualInfo* XGetVisualInfo(Display* display,
    long visual_info_mask,
    XVisualInfo* visual_info_template,
    int* number_visuals)    /* RETURN */
```

You pass XGetVisualInfo a template that lists the information you're looking for. For example, you probably want to find the visuals on a certain screen and perhaps with a certain class. The *visual_info_mask* is a mask of bit-flags that tells XGetVisualInfo which fields in the *visual_info_template* your application filled in. See Table 15.5 for a list of these flags.

XGetVisualInfo provides an XVisualInfo structure that describes the visuals found. The XVisualInfo structure is defined in **<X11/Xutil.h>**:

```
typedef struct {
  Visual*      visual;
  VisualID     visualid;
  int          screen;
  int          depth;
#if defined(__cplusplus) || defined(c_plusplus)
  int          c_class;
#else  /* C, not C++ */
  int          class;
#endif
  unsigned long red_mask;
  unsigned long green_mask;
  unsigned long blue_mask;
  int          colormap_size;
  int          bits_per_rgb;
} XVisualInfo;
```

The *class* field is named *c_class* if you compile with C++.

Included in this structure is a pointer to the actual visual information. This pointer is usually what you're looking for.

The bitflags for XGetVisualInfo are listed in Table 15.5.

Table 15.5   *Mask bits for XGetVisualInfo.*

Mask Bits	XVisualInfo Field
VisualAllMask	*all fields*
VisualBitsPerRGBMask	bits_per_rgb
VisualBlueMaskMask	blue_mask
VisualClassMask	class
VisualColormapSizeMask	colormap_size
VisualDepthMask	depth
VisualGreenMaskMask	green_mask
VisualIDMask	visualid
VisualNoMask	*no fields*
VisualRedMaskMask	red_mask
VisualScreenMask	screen

Note that the *MaskMask* flags are indeed spelled correctly.

When done with the XVisualInfo array, free it with XFree.

The following code, for example, uses XGetVisualInfo to look for all the DirectColor visuals that reside on a given screen:

```
#include <X11/Xutil.h>

Display*    display;
long        visual_info_mask;
int         number_visuals;
XVisualInfo* visual_array;
XVisualInfo visual_info_template;

visual_info_template.class  = DirectColor;
visual_info_template.screen = DefaultScreen(display);

visual_info_mask = VisualClassMask |
                   VisualScreenMask;

visual_array = XGetVisualInfo(display,
                   visual_info_mask,
                   &visual_info_template,
                   &number_visuals);
```

Since we're not asking for very much with our very general query, we may get a lot of entries back. Your code should then go through the returned `XVisualInfo` array and find the visual that best matches your needs.

Getting a Colormap to Allocate Colors From

All the color-allocation routines use a colormap to allocate or lookup colors. You can use the default colormap in most cases, unless you find some need to create your own colormap (such as running out of color entries in the default colormap). Since we're working with Motif, though, we should use Motif's means to determine what colormap is used with your windows and allocate colors from that colormap.

For example, if you use an `XmDrawingArea` widget, you might want to set the colormap before creating the widget. (Normally, you want to set the colormap on all shell widgets you create.) After the colormap is created, you'll need to use the same colormap ID for allocating colors. Luckily, the Motif provides a `colormap` resource that you can query.

This resource will be valid after you've realized the widget tree using `XtRealizeWidget`. After that is done and your drawing widget created, you can query the colormap. This technique works whether you've created your own colormap or used the default—in either case the `colormap` resource will hold the proper ID.

WORKING WITH VISUALS AND COLORMAPS

In the last chapter, we covered how to use the long method for initializing the Xt Intrinsics. If you want to use a nondefault visual in your application, you need to use this long method. The program below extends this long method for initializing the Intrinsics and shows you where to place your code for finding visuals and creating colormaps. This program also uses the Xt resource converter to convert a color name into a `Pixel` value. The code follows:

```
/* xtvis.c */
#include <Xm/Xm.h>
#include <Xm/PushB.h>
#include <stdio.h>
#include <string.h>

    /* Convert color name to color. */
```

```
extern Boolean CvtColor(Widget widget,
    char* color_name,
    unsigned long* color);  /* RETURN */

void exitCB(Widget widget,
    XtPointer client_data,
    XtPointer call_data)

{   /* exitCB */

    exit(0);

}   /* exitCB */

int main(int argc, char** argv)

{   /* main */
    Widget          parent;
    XtAppContext    app_context;
    Widget          push;
    Arg             args[20];
    Cardinal        n;
    Display*        display;
    int             screen;
    Visual*         visual;
    Colormap        colormap;
    unsigned long   border, back;
    int             depth;
    int             copy_of_argc;
    char**          copy_of_argv;
    int             argv_size;
    unsigned long   color;

    /* Initialize X toolkit the long way. */
    XtToolkitInitialize();

    app_context = XtCreateApplicationContext();

    /* Copy command-line parameters. */
    copy_of_argc = argc;

    argv_size = argc * (sizeof(char*));

    copy_of_argv = (char**) XtMalloc(argv_size);

    memcpy(copy_of_argv, argv, argv_size);

    /* Open display connection. */
    display = XtOpenDisplay(app_context,
            NULL,
            NULL,
            "Ppm",
            (XrmOptionDescList) NULL,
            0,
            &argc, argv);
```

```
/*
 * We assume an error opening
 * display is a fatal error.
 */
if (display == (Display*) NULL) {
    fprintf(stderr, "Error opening X display.\n");
    exit(1);
}

/*
 * Get a visual. You may want
 * to find the best one available.
 * Here, we just use the default.
 */
screen   = DefaultScreen(display);

visual   = DefaultVisual(display, screen);

colormap = DefaultColormap(display, screen);

depth    = DefaultDepth(display, screen);

/*
 * If you change the visual,
 * always set up colors.
 */
border = BlackPixel(display, screen);
back   = BlackPixel(display, screen);

/*
 * If you use a nondefault
 * visual, set visual, colormap,
 * depth, background, and borderColor
 * resources.
 */
n = 0;
XtSetArg(args[n], XmNvisual,      visual); n++;
XtSetArg(args[n], XmNdepth,       depth); n++;
XtSetArg(args[n], XmNcolormap,    colormap); n++;
XtSetArg(args[n], XmNbackground,  back); n++;
XtSetArg(args[n], XmNborderColor, border); n++;

/* Set in command-line parameters. */
XtSetArg(args[n], XmNargc, copy_of_argc); n++;
XtSetArg(args[n], XmNargv, copy_of_argv); n++;

XtSetArg(args[n], XmNallowResize, True); n++;

/* We want to create windows without mapping. */
XtSetArg(args[n],
    XmNmappedWhenManaged, False); n++;

parent = XtAppCreateShell(NULL,
        "Ppm",
```

```
                applicationShellWidgetClass,
                display,
                args, n);

        /* Create child widget. */
        n = 0;
        push = XmCreatePushButton(parent, "quit", args, n);

        XtAddCallback(push,
            XmNactivateCallback,
            (XtCallbackProc) exitCB,
            (XtPointer) NULL);

        XtManageChild(push);

        /* Realize widget to get window IDs. */
        XtRealizeWidget(parent);

        /* Here, we can use the window IDs... */

        /* ... */

        /* Set the background color for the widget. */
        if (CvtColor(push, "LimeGreen", &color) == True) {
            XtVaSetValues(push,
                XmNbackground, color,
                NULL);
        }

        /* Map widget to screen. */
        XtMapWidget(parent);

        XtAppMainLoop(app_context);

        return 0;

    }   /* main */

/* end of file xtvis.c */
```

In the program above, we call the `DefaultDepth` macro to get the default depth of the default colormap:

```
int DefaultDepth(Display* display,
        int screen_number)
```

STANDARD COLORMAPS

Many X applications require most of, if not all, the available colors on a system. In addition, many image-processing applications need an easy way to convert an RGB value into a colormap index. Having such an easy conversion can improve the performance for processing images.

To aid these applications, the X Window System provides for the concept of a set of *standard colormaps*. These colormaps are sharable between applications and usually provide an evenly spaced color ramp. This evenly spaced color ramp allows your applications to convert RGB values to colormap indexes with a simple calculation formula.

Up to now, we've discussed how to share color cells in a colormap by allocating read-only cells, but not how to share colormaps themselves. Standard colormaps make such sharing easier. (You can also use other means to share X colormaps between applications. Just passing the colormap ID to another program usually suffices, although there are a number of associated issues to deal with.)

If you use standard colormaps, though, your application must follow a set of rules that well-behaved X programs use to ensure that these colormaps act as expected. You'll find these rules as part of the *Inter-Client Communications Conventions Manual*, or ICCCM.

To use a standard colormap, you must either create one or find one that another X application, such as xstdcmap, has created. In both cases, you'll end up with an XStandardColormap structure filled in with the proper values. The XStandardColormap structure, defined in <X11/Xutil.h>, looks like:

```
typedef struct {
    Colormap        colormap;
    unsigned long   red_max;
    unsigned long   red_mult;
    unsigned long   green_max;
    unsigned long   green_mult;
    unsigned long   blue_max;
    unsigned long   blue_mult;
    unsigned long   base_pixel;
    VisualID        visualid;
    XID             killid;
} XStandardColormap;
```

The *colormap* field holds the X colormap ID used by the standard colormap. The max fields—*red_max*, *green_max*, and *blue_max*—hold the maximum number of color cells for the red, green, and blue planes.

To use a common example, a frequently used standard colormap supplies three planes for red, three for green, and two for blue, using a notation of 3/3/2. In this example, *red_max* and *green_max* would both equal 7, whereas *blue_max* would equal 3. The basic idea is that with three planes, you have red values in the range of 0–7, hence a *red_max* of 7. With two planes, you have a range of blues of 0–3, hence a *blue_max* of 3.

The *visualid* field holds the ID number for the visual under which the colormap was created.

The multiplier fields *red_mult*, *green_mult*, and *blue_mult* are used for converting RGB values to pixels.

Standard Colormap Properties

The X Window System provides a means to store any named set of data associated with a window. This data is also typed, although the types are arbitrary. Such a collection of data associated with a window is called a *property*.

The property names are called *atoms* and start out as text strings. These text strings are converted to hash numbers by a process called *interning*. After an atom has been interned in the X server, your application (and any other X program) can use the atom ID number in place of the string. Each property has an atom for a name. The data types also start out as text strings and—you guessed it—are interned as atoms. (We cover atoms and properties in Chapter 18.) For now, we'll use the X server's built-in set of atoms for the standard colormaps.

For now, you need to know only that the standard colormaps are placed into properties, normally on the root window. Your application can then use these standard colormaps by reading the data from the property that holds the colormap you want. This is how applications share standard colormaps.

Properties Used by Standard Colormaps

The header file <X11/Xatom.h> defines the atoms that all X servers load up at start time. This file includes a number of predefined atoms for use with standard colormaps. You can use these atoms as the *property* parameter passed to XGetRGBColormaps, below.

The atoms below are numeric constants defined in <X11/Xatom.h>. The actual string interned for the atom is the constant without the *XA_* prefix. That is, the XA_RGB_BEST_MAP atom is the ID number for the interned string "RGB_BEST_MAP".

These atoms, which identify the types of standard colormaps, include:

- XA_RGB_BEST_MAP
- XA_RGB_BLUE_MAP
- XA_RGB_DEFAULT_MAP
- XA_RGB_GRAY_MAP
- XA_RGB_GREEN_MAP
- XA_RGB_RED_MAP

The Best Map

The best standard colormap tries to provide as many perceptually distinct colors as possible. The term *perceptually distinct* is a code phrase meaning that there are more green cells than red, and more red cells than blue. The intention is that the XA_RGB_BEST_MAP colormap be used for 3D applications and other programs that need as many distinct colors as possible. For workstations with 8 bit-planes of color, the allocation is probably 3/3/2. For 24 bit-planes of color, the allocation is likely 8/8/8.

The Default Map

XA_RGB_DEFAULT_MAP is a special standard colormap. It is intended to be a subset of the default colormap. Because of this, you have a better chance of avoiding the color flashing effects as the window manager swaps colormaps if you use the XA_RGB_DEFAULT_MAPcolormap. For this reason, we use the XA_RGB_DEFAULT_MAP standard colormap in the next chapter's program using PEXlib.

The default XA_RGB_DEFAULT_MAP provides a *red_max, green_max,* and *blue_max* of 5, using 216 uniformly distributed color cells and leaving 40 extra cells for other applications on a system with 256 color cells available.

The Red, Green, and Blue Maps

The XA_RGB_RED_MAP, XA_RGB_GREEN_MAP, and XA_RGB_BLUE_MAP standard colormaps all provide a colormap with shades of a single color: all-red, all-green, or all-blue, respectively. These colormaps are useful for generating color separations common with prepress applications.

The Gray Map

The XA_RGB_GRAY_MAP is a lot like the all-red, all-green, and all-blue colormaps described above. This property holds the best GrayScale colormap available on the screen.

Reading a Standard Colormap

Once a standard colormap is created, the official rules state that the properties describing these colormaps should be placed on the root window, since the root window is a window that is guaranteed to be always available. You can then read one of these properties to get an XStandardColormap structure for a standard colormap with the XGetRGBColormaps function:

```
#include <X11/Xutil.h>

Status XGetRGBColormaps(Display* display,
    Window window,
    XStandardColormap** std_colormaps, /* RETURN */
    int* number_colormaps,  /* RETURN */
    Atom property)
```

XGetRGBColormaps returns a nonzero value on success and 0 otherwise. Note that only the XA_RGB_DEFAULT_MAP standard colormap property (see below) should have more than one entry. All other properties should have only one entry. The *window* parameter should be the root window. You should call XFree to free the memory for the *std_colormaps*.

If you're lucky, some other application, such as a window manager or a special program named *xstdcmap*, will have already created the standard colormap you want. Of course, you cannot depend on this.If you want to use a standard colormap, you should always check first to see if the colormap you want is created, and then, if not, create it.

The process to do so is quite involved, but luckily there's a convenience function that takes care of this for you. XmuLookupStandardColormap checks for a given standard colormap and, if not found, will create it for you, providing you pass the proper parameters:

```
#include <X11/Xmu/StdCmap.h>

Status XmuLookupStandardColormap(Display* display,
    int screen_number,
    VisualID visualid,
    unsigned int depth,
    Atom property,
```

```
        Bool replace,
        Bool retain)
```

You can get the *visualid* from the `XVisualInfo` structure (if you called `XGetVisualInfo` to search for the best visual) or from `XVisualIDFromVisual`:

```
VisualID XVisualIDFromVisual(Visual* visual)
```

The *depth* should match the depth of the visual.

The *replace* parameter specifies whether or not to replace any existing standard colormap properties. The *retain* parameter specifies whether or not to retain the properties and colormaps for the duration of the X server session. `XmuLookupStandardColormap` creates a colormap if necessary (a *property* of `XA_RGB_DEFAULT_MAP` uses the default colormap, the rest require a new colormap).

`XmuLookupStandardColormap` is part of the X miscellaneous utilities library, or Xmu. This library contains a number of interesting routines, including a number that deal with standard colormaps. Unfortunately, Xmu is not considered an X Consortium standard, so these routines may not be available on your system. Xmu comes with the X releases from the X Consortium, but some vendors don't ship it.

Since in our examples we want to share the default colormap, the following routine gets the `XA_RGB_DEFAULT_MAP` standard colormap, creating it if necessary:

```
/* stdcmap.c */
#include  <Xm/Xm.h>
#include  <X11/Xatom.h>
#include  <X11/Xmu/StdCmap.h>

    /* Get a standard colormap. */
int GetStdColormap(Display* display,
    int screen,
    Visual* visual,
    int depth,
    XStandardColormap* std_colormap)

{   /* GetStdColormap */
    int                 status, i;
    int                 number_colormaps;
    XStandardColormap*  colormaps_returned;
    VisualID            visualid;

    /* Extract visual ID. */
```

```
    visualid = XVisualIDFromVisual(visual);

    /* Get a standard colormap. */
    status = XmuLookupStandardColormap(display,
            screen,
            visualid,
            depth,
            XA_RGB_DEFAULT_MAP,
            False,  /* Don't replace existing cmap. */
            True);  /* Keep this around. */

    if (status != 0) {
        status = XGetRGBColormaps(display,
            RootWindow(display, screen),
            &colormaps_returned,
            &number_colormaps,
            XA_RGB_DEFAULT_MAP);

        if (status != 0) {
            for (i = 0; i < number_colormaps; i++) {
                if (visualid ==
                    colormaps_returned[i].visualid) {

                    *std_colormap = colormaps_returned[i];

                    return True;
                }
            }

            /*
             * Note: we assume a failure is fatal,
             * so we don't free colormaps_returned.
             */
        }
    }

    return False;

}   /* GetStdColormap */

/* end of file stdcmap.c */
```

Compiling and Linking with the Xmu Library

To compile a Motif program and use the Xmu routines, you need the Xmu library, *libXmu.a*. Use the following template:

```
cc -o foo foo.c -lXm -lXmu -lXt -lX11
```

This finishes our initial coverage of color. There's a lot of complexity that we've avoided in this chapter, since most Motif applications simply don't need to mess with it.

SUMMARY

Color forms one of the most complicated topics in X. This chapter introduced color under the X Window System and showed how to customize how your Motif applications work with color. Color is complex because graphics workstations use different means for controlling colors on the monitor. Some have color tables, some have color planes, and all seem to be different. X, attempting to be device-independent, has to deal with all the many color implementations. Perhaps because of this, color in X appears overly complex. The seemingly simple task of drawing a line in red leads to all sorts of contortions in initializing colors and finding visuals. Most of these different workstations are built on an *RGB color model*: red, green, and blue phosphors within each pixel are combined to form the different hues on the screen. Electron beams excite the phosphors, which in turn provide the color. Simultaneously exciting all phosphors produces a white pixel; when all are unexcited you're left with a black pixel.

To use color in Motif, you need to allocate a color cell in the colormap that your application is using. Actually, colormaps are tied to windows, so you could have a separate colormap for each window. Generally, this is not a good idea. First, it takes up precious system resources. Second, you're likely to see annoying flashing effects as the user moves the mouse about the screen, since most hardware supports only one active colormap at a time. Each color cell in a colormap has its red, green, and blue values. The place in the colormap that the color cell occupies is called a color index. It is this index that you use to set the color. For example, in Chapter 11 we covered the XSetForeground function that sets the foreground color for a graphics context. The value you pass to XSetForeground is the color-index number. Color indexes are usually an unsigned long integer value (also defined as a Pixel type in Motif). Each color cell is then represented by an index that, as you guessed, indexes into the colormap, either directly into one colormap or indirectly into decomposed red, green, and blue colormaps. Color index 42, for example, may have a red value of 0, a green value of 5125, and a blue value of 9104. (X RGB color values are defined on a scale that goes from 0 to 65535. Most graphics text books, though, use values from 0 to 255, because 256-color systems are so pervasive.)

This is probably more about color than you need right now. After you get into sophisticated graphics programs, though, you'll need all this and more. In the next chapter we use visuals and standard colormaps as we show how to combine 3D graphics using PEXlib with Motif applications.

MOTIF FUNCTIONS AND MACROS INTRODUCED IN THIS CHAPTER

```
XmGetColorCalculation
XmSetColorCalculation
```

X MISCELLANEOUS UTILITIES FUNCTIONS AND MACROS INTRODUCED IN THIS CHAPTER

```
XmuLookupStandardColormap
```

X TOOLKIT INTRINSICS FUNCTIONS AND MACROS INTRODUCED IN THIS CHAPTER

```
XtConvertAndStore
```

X LIBRARY FUNCTIONS AND MACROS INTRODUCED IN THIS CHAPTER

```
DefaultColormap
DefaultDepth
DefaultVisual
XAllocColor
XAllocNamedColor
XGetRGBColormaps
XGetVisualInfo
XLookupColor
```

CHAPTER 16

3D Graphics with PEX and Motif

This chapter covers:

- PEXlib, a 3D library for X
- The PEX 3D extension to X
- Combining Motif with PEXlib
- Initializing PEXlib to run in a Motif drawing area
- Drawing with PEXlib
- PEX subset information
- Color-table approximations
- PEXlib color support
- Rendering images
- Problems with PEX
- Acquiring PEXlib

523

THREE-DIMENSIONAL GRAPHICS PROGRAMMING WITH X

The X Window System and Motif have brought a measure of standardization to graphics programming with UNIX—at least two-dimensional graphics programming. The problem for many years was the lack of standards in the three-dimensional arena. To compound this problem, few 3D graphics toolkits work at all with traditional two-dimensional X Window user-interface toolkits like Motif. This has led to some very sophisticated three-dimensional programs that sport terrible user interfaces, and somewhat sophisticated user interfaces that sport terrible 3D graphics.

Now, though, you can have the 3D graphics and a good-looking friendly user interface.

What makes all this possible is the combination of the Motif toolkit for the user interface and an X Window extension for three-dimensional programming, the PEX 3D extension to X. PEX, which became more important when adopted as part of the Common Open Software Environment, or COSE, is short for the PHIGS (and PHIGS-PLUS) Extension to X.

PHIGS, in turn, stands for Programmer's Hierarchical Interactive Graphics System and is one of many graphics standards, such as GKS, the Graphics Kernel System.

PEX provides added support in the X server—a lot of added support—for PHIGS graphics and includes a library for the C bindings to PHIGS. PEX is much more than PHIGS, though. PEX is really just an extension to the X server (a very large extension) and an extension of the X protocol. This PEX protocol is a lot like the low-level X protocol upon which all X programming libraries are built.

On top of the PEX protocol, you could layer any number of C programming libraries. The first such library was an implementation of the C binding to PHIGS. You could call the PHIGS routines to create PHIGS programs, which makes much of X transparent. This is all well and good, but we've found that for most real applications you need to jump down to the lower levels, just like you have to jump down beneath the Motif toolkit. PHIGS, in fact, doesn't work all that well with Motif applications, because PHIGS is built from the model that the 3D toolkit covers everything.

Even though PEX has PHIGS as its first name, PEXlib greatly divorces itself from PHIGS and instead provides you with a low-level access to the underlying PEX protocol. The PHIGS toolkit could then be layered on top of PEXlib, even though the original PHIGS toolkit with X11 Release 5 predates PEXlib. PEXlib acts much like the low-level X library, on top of which you can layer a number of wildly different X toolkits. Unfortunately, though, there's not a lot of PEXlib-based PEX toolkits out there, especially since PEXlib is still so new.

To best combine three-dimensional graphics with Motif, we use PEXlib.

SHORTCUT

Connecting PEXlib with Motif

The basic means for working with three-dimensional graphics and Motif is to use Motif for what it's good at—the user interface—and to use PEXlib for what it's good at—rendering 3D graphics.

To connect the two, you must create a Motif drawing-area widget and then pass this widget's window ID to PEXlib. With this drawing-area window, you create a PEXlib renderer and use this renderer to render PEX drawing commands. Use the Motif drawing-area callbacks to handle user input and to tell you when to draw when Expose events arrive.

PEXLIB

Unlike PHIGS, which provides a very high-level toolkit, the low-level library called PEXlib provides access to the low-level PEX protocol. Of course, by low level, we mean PEXlib lies closer to the PEX protocol. In reality, PEXlib provides a high-level view of 3D graphics.

Even at this high level, PEXlib uses a lot of complex X features like standard colormaps and nondefault visuals, covered in the last chapter. Like PHIGS, PEXlib is far too involved to cover in a book such as this. Instead, we'll go over some of the barest basics, concentrating on how to link up PEXlib and Motif. This is, after all, a book on Motif programming.

PEXlib supports a number of features such as structure mode or immediate mode graphics, internationalized text display, geometric transformations, different views of data, light sources, shading, double buffering, and picking. Some of these terms need explaining. *Structure mode* is where you store graphics primitives in a database for later rendering to the screen. *Immediate mode* is where you send the graphics primitives to PEX one by one and they are displayed immediately—or as quickly as your workstation supports. PEX does not support ray tracing, radiosity, or texture mapping.

COMBINING PEXLIB AND MOTIF

To combine PEXlib with Motif, you need to go through the following steps:

1. Determine if PEX is available.

2. Initialize Xt Intrinsics and set up a display connection to the X server. Usually you'll want to use the long method for initializing the toolkit, instead of calling `XtAppInitialize`, so that you can find the best visual.

3. Determine the best visual.

4. Set up a colormap for this visual. Using a standard colormap, such as `RGB_DEFAULT_MAP`, works best.

5. Initialize PEX with `PEXInitialize`.

6. Create a top-level shell widget using the visual you found and a colormap set up for that visual. Remember to set the proper resources for the shell, including `visual`, `colormap`, `background`, `borderColor`, and `depth`, if you don't use the default visual. You'll need to set these resources for each shell widget you create, including menus and dialogs.

7. Create Motif widgets for interface.

8. Create a drawing-area widget to hold the PEX geometry.

9. Map the drawing-area window to the screen.

10. Set up color approximation information for a PEX renderer. This step is necessary. (In fact, when we tried to skip it, we managed to knock out our X server.)

11. Create a PEX renderer. This acts much like the graphics context (or GC) for normal Xlib drawing routines.

12. Draw *(render* in PEX terminology) your 3D geometry from within the drawing area's Expose callback.

Determining if PEX Is Available

You can use the *xdpyinfo* program to determine if PEX is available, as all X extensions are optional add-ons to the core X protocol. Look in the output list of supported X extensions for the *X3D-PEX* extension.

```
number of extensions:      6
    XTestExtension1
    SHAPE
    MIT-SHM
    X3D-PEX
    Multi-Buffering
    MIT-SUNDRY-NONSTANDARD
```

If you see *X3D-PEX* in the output from *xdpyinfo*, you're doing fine.

Initializing the X Toolkit

Inside your program, you need to initialize the Xt Intrinsics and will most likely have to use the long method instead of the convenience method of using XtAppInitialize. In what should be old hat by now, the following code initializes the Xt Intrinsics:

```
/* Initialize X toolkit the long way */
XtToolkitInitialize();

app_context = XtCreateApplicationContext();

/* Copy command-line parameters. */
copy_of_argc = argc;

argv_size = argc * (sizeof(char*));

copy_of_argv = (char**) XtMalloc(argv_size);

memcpy(copy_of_argv, argv, argv_size);

/* Open display connection. */
display = XtOpenDisplay(app_context,
            NULL,   /* display name, use argv */
            NULL,   /* app name, use arg[0] */
            "Ppm",  /* class name */
            (XrmOptionDescList) NULL,
            0,      /* number options */
            &argc, argv);

/*
```

```
 * We assume an error opening
 * display is a fatal error.
 */
if (display == (Display*) NULL) {
    fprintf(stderr, "Error opening X display.\n");
    exit(1);
}
```

We stop before creating a top-level shell widget with `XtAppCreateShell`. Before creating a shell, we should set up a visual and colormap and then initialize PEX.

In most cases, your 3D programs will want to find the best visual on the display, by using the method described in the last chapter. You'll then want to get a standard colormap, because standard colormaps have the necessary information to set up a PEX color approximation table—a necessary task. If you do end up using the default visual and can use the default colormap, you may want to try to use the `RGB_DEFAULT_MAP` standard colormap.

The next step then is to initialize PEXlib.

Initializing PEXlib

As with all X extensions, PEX requires you to call a function to test if the extension is available. This function, `PEXInitialize`, also initializes the PEX extension code in the X server:

```
#include <X11/PEX5/PEXlib.h>

int PEXInitialize(Display* display,
    PEXExtensionInfo** pex_info,   /* RETURN */
    int message_length,
    char* error_message)           /* RETURN */
```

The *error_message* may contain a message if `PEXInitialize` fails. You must specify that maximum length of this message with the *message_length* parameter. A good *message_length* is `PEXErrorStringLength`, which is often 80 bytes.

All your PEXlib code must include the main PEXlib include file, `<X11/PEX5/PEXlib.h>`.

N O T E

The `PEX5` include directory was built to hold the include files for PEX versions 5 and 5.1. When PEX 6.0 arrives, this directory should change to `PEX6`. PEX 6.0 will not be fully compatible with PEX 5.1, so expect to make some changes updating your code.

`PEXInitialize` returns 0 on success or one of the following error codes on failure:

- `PEXBadExtension`
- `PEXBadFloatConversion`
- `PEXBadLocalAlloc`
- `PEXBadProtocolVersion`

`PEXBadExtension` means that the X server does not support PEX. There's not much you can do in this case.

`PEXBadFloatConversion` means your application and the X server cannot agree on a PEX floating-point format.

`PEXBadLocalAlloc` means that your application couldn't allocate space for all the PEX global variables and structures.

`PEXBadProtocolVersion` means that the PEX protocols don't match between your application and the X server. `PEXBadProtocolVersion` may become a common error as older PEX 5.1 programs run against a PEX 6.0 X server, or PEX 6.0 applications run against old vendor-supported PEX 5.1 X servers.

Extracting Information about PEX

The *pex_info* parameter passed to `PEXInitialize` contains information returned about the PEX code in the X server, stored in a `PEXExtensionInfo` structure. The `PEXExtensionInfo` structure looks like:

```
typedef struct {
    unsigned short    major_version;
    unsigned short    minor_version;
    unsigned long     release;
    unsigned long     subset_info;
    char*             vendor_name;
    int               major_opcode;
    int               first_event;
    int               first_error;
} PEXExtensionInfo;
```

For most X servers, the *major_version* will be 5 until PEX 6.0 comes out with X11 Release 6. If the *major_version* is 5, the *minor_version* will be 0 or 1, for PEX 5.0 or 5.1. The *release* is a number that the PEX server vendor can use. For the sample implementation that comes with X11 Release 5, the *release* number is 0.

The *vendor_name* can also be filled in by the PEX server vendor. A common *vendor_name* is "X3D-PEX Sample Implementation." This is what comes with the X server from the X Consortium. Note that the term *sample* is accurate—this version of the PEX extension is neither fast, complete, nor bug-free. We expect PEX to become much more robust and speedy in the next few years as X server vendors tune their versions of PEX. You can view PEX 5.1 much like the X server that came with X11 Release 2. In Release 3 the server was finally usable, and the Release 4 server improved the performance to a degree that it became worthwhile to use X. We expect PEX to require a few more versions before it becomes really workable. Even so, it's good to get in on the ground floor and learn PEXlib programming.

PEX Subset Information

Because PEX is so huge, many X servers, particularly X terminals, may have a hard time implementing the whole thing. So PEX supports the idea of subsets. The bottom line on subsets is that features you expect to be available may very well not be supported on any given X server. It's a good idea to check what's available.

Information on the supported subsets is stored in the *subset_info* field of the PEXExtensionInfo structure, which holds a set of bit-flags. This information is listed in Table 16.1.

Table 16.1   *PEX subset bit-flags.*

Flag	Value
PEXCompleteImplementation	0x0
PEXImmediateMode	0x1
PEXWorkstationOnly	0x2
PEXStructureMode	0x3

These bit-flags just refer to the lower 16 bits of the subset_info field. The upper 16 bits are reserved for the PEXlib vendor's use. You may want to mask the *subset_info* field with 0xFFFF to strip out the high bits.

These bit-flags indicate which subsets of PEX your X server supports. If you're lucky, you'll get a complete implementation (PEXCompleteImplementation). Otherwise, your X server may support immediate-mode graphics (PEXImmediateMode), the PEX structure mode (PEXStructureMode), PHIGS workstation resources (PEXWorkstationOnly), or any combination of the three.

Checking for Immediate-Mode Graphics

For simplicity, in this chapter we'll use the immediate-mode graphics only and leave structure-mode code as an exercise for the reader. (It is, after all, just a simple matter of programming).

Because we're using immediate-mode graphics, we need an easy way to test if the X server supports this option. To do this, we use the following code:

```
#include  <X11/PEX5/PEXlib.h>

int pex_check_immed_mode(PEXExtensionInfo* pex_info)

{    /* pex_check_immed_mode */

    /* Check if we support immediate-mode graphics. */
    if ((pex_info->subset_info & 0xFFFF) ==
        PEXCompleteImplementation) {
        return True;
    }

    if (pex_info->subset_info & PEXImmediateMode) {
        return True;
    }

    return False;

}    /* pex_check_immed_mode */
```

The utility function pex_check_immed_mode returns True if the PEX extension supports immediate-mode graphics; it returns False otherwise. We check only the lower 16 bits for PEXCompleteImplementation.

You may want to use this function in your code.

Calling PEXInitialize

Putting all this together, you can call PEXInitialize and check for support for immediate-mode graphics as shown in the utility code below:

```
#include  <X11/PEX5/PEXlib.h>
```

```
int pex_init(Display* display,
    PEXExtensionInfo** pex_info)  /* RETURN */

{   /* pex_init */
    int    status;
    char   error_message[PEXErrorStringLength+1];

    status = PEXInitialize(display,
            pex_info,
            PEXErrorStringLength,
            error_message);

    if (status != 0) {
        /* Switch on error status */
        switch(status) {
            case PEXBadExtension:
                printf("Bad Extension.\n");
                break;
            case PEXBadProtocolVersion:
                printf("Bad Protocol Version.\n");
                break;
            case PEXBadFloatConversion:
                printf("Bad Float Conversion.\n");
                break;
            case PEXBadLocalAlloc:
                printf("Bad Local Memory Alloc.\n");
                break;
        }

        return False;
    }

    if (pex_check_immed_mode(*pex_info) == False) {
        printf(
          "Error: PEX does not support immed. mode.\n");
        return False;
    }

    return True;

}   /* pex_init */
```

After you've initialized PEXlib, create a top-level shell widget using the visual you found and a colormap set up for that visual. Remember to set the proper resources for the shell, including visual, colormap, background, borderColor, and depth, if you don't use the default visual. You'll need to set these resources for each shell widget you create, including menus and dialogs.

Then create the Motif widgets for your interface, such as main windows, menu bars, menus, dialogs, and scrolled windows. This should be easy, as we've done this for a number of chapters now.

Chapter 11 covered how to create a drawing-area widget. To integrate PEXlib and Motif, we'll offer up a sacrificial drawing-area widget to PEXlib. Inside this widget, we'll only draw 3D graphics with PEXlib, but we'll do this drawing from within the Motif widget framework. This way, our program will provide a Motif interface, using widgets just like we've created in every chapter so far and also support complex three-dimensional graphics.

N O T E   This technique of using a drawing-area widget to support 3D graphics is common to a number of other 3D toolkits that run on X platforms, including Ithaca Software's HOOPS and Silicon Graphics' GL and OpenGL toolkits. All these toolkits work with Motif drawing-area widgets, although GL uses a subclass of the drawing area, a GLX drawing widget.

After we create the drawing-area widget, we need to ensure that it gets mapped to the screen, as PEXlib prefers to set up a renderer for a mapped window. In most cases (unless the parent is managed or mapped), managing a widget will map it to the screen.

Set Up Color Table Approximations

The hard part comes next. In order to do anything with PEX, you have to set up a color-approximation table. This color-approximation table is part of a great deal of work that you must do to get anything done with PEXlib. This step is absolutely necessary. (In fact, when we tried to skip it, we managed to knock out our X server.)

To set up a color-approximation table, you need to fill in a complex `PEXColorApproxEntry` structure:

```
typedef struct {
  PEXEnumTypeIndex   type;
  PEXEnumTypeIndex   model;
  unsigned short     max1;
  unsigned short     max2;
  unsigned short     max3;
  PEXSwitch          dither;
  unsigned char      reserved;
  unsigned long      mult1;
  unsigned long      mult2;
  unsigned long      mult3;
  float              weight1;
  float              weight2;
  float              weight3;
```

```
    unsigned long      base_pixel;
} PEXColorApproxEntry;
```

Luckily, most of the information you need to fill in this structure comes directly from the XStandardColormap structure that defines a standard colormap. This is why we tend to use standard colormaps with PEX applications. In addition, using a standard colormap lets us share the colormap with other PEX applications.

Filling in the PEXColorApproxEntry Structure

To fill in this structure, we make some assumptions about our use of PEX colors. For one thing, we really won't be exercising PEX much at all, so we're doing the minimum work necessary to get going with PEXlib. The idea is to test the PEXlib-to-Motif connection and not thoroughly get lost in the gory details of PEXlib. So we'll use the PEXlib RGB color-approximation model.

After you have a standard colormap, you can fill in the PEXColorApproxEntry structure mostly from the values in the XStandardColormap structure, as we show below:

```
#include <X11/PEX5/PEXlib.h>

XStandardColormap    std_colormap,
PEXColorApproxEntry  color_approx;

color_approx.weight1    = 0; /* Unused */
color_approx.weight2    = 0; /* Unused */
color_approx.weight3    = 0; /* Unused */

color_approx.type   = PEXColorSpace;
color_approx.model  = PEXColorApproxRGB;
color_approx.dither = PEXOn;

color_approx.base_pixel = std_colormap.base_pixel;

color_approx.max1    = std_colormap.red_max;
color_approx.max2    = std_colormap.green_max;
color_approx.max3    = std_colormap.blue_max;

color_approx.mult1   = std_colormap.red_mult;
color_approx.mult2   = std_colormap.green_mult;
color_approx.mult3   = std_colormap.blue_mult;
```

Most of the values come directly from the standard colormap. This helps to alleviate some of the overhead of PEXlib. Why are we filling this all in? We need to set up a color-approximation table before we can create a PEXlib renderer—the PEXlib equivalent to the Xlib graphics context.

We use a *type* of PEXColorSpace, because we're setting color. The *model* is PEXColorApproxRGB, but it could be one of:

- PEXColorApproxRGB
- PEXColorApproxCIE
- PEXColorApproxHSV
- PEXColorApproxHLS
- PEXColorApproxYIQ

We turn dithering on with PEXOn. We could have also turned it off with PEXOff.

After you fill in the PEXColorApproxEntry, you need to create a color-lookup table (or LUT) and fill in the LUT with the color-approximation table.

The first step is to create a generic PEXlib lookup table, in our case, a color-lookup table. To do so, we call PEXCreateLookupTable:

```
#include  <X11/PEX5/PEXlib.h>

PEXLookupTable
PEXCreateLookupTable(Display* display,
  Drawable drawable,
  int table_type)
```

We need to pass the display pointer and the drawing-area widget's window (which we can acquire with XtWindow). We also need to pass the table type, in our case, a PEXLUTColorApprox table. You can pick one of the table types listed in Table 16.2.

Table 16.2 *PEXlib table types.*

Table Type	Value
PEXLUTLineBundle	1
PEXLUTMarkerBundle	2
PEXLUTTextBundle	3
PEXLUTInteriorBundle	4
PEXLUTEdgeBundle	5
	continued

PEXLUTPattern	6
PEXLUTTextFont	7
PEXLUTColor	8
PEXLUTView	9
PEXLUTLight	10
PEXLUTDepthCue	11
PEXLUTColorApprox	12

PEXCreateLookupTable returns a PEXLookupTable ID, which is a standard XID:

```
typedef XID   PEXLookupTable;
```

An XID is the data type used for windows and pixmaps. Basically, it's a 32-bit long integer. Since the data value is an XID, this implies that the actual data is stored in the X server and that your application gets an ID or handle to this data.

This new PEX lookup table is created empty, so the next step is to fill in this new table with the color-approximation values. For this, we call PEXSetTableEntries:

```
#include  <X11/PEX5/PEXlib.h>

void PEXSetTableEntries(Display* display,
    PEXLookupTable table,
    unsigned int start_entry,
    unsigned int number_entries,
    int table_type,
    PEXPointer entries)
```

PEXSetTableEntries requires the display pointer, the table ID (which we just got back from PEXCreateLookupTable), the start entry (0 in our case, because we have a one-entry table), the number of entries (1 in our case), the table type (PEXLUTColorApprox), and a pointer to the actual entry data to set into the table. This pointer is cast to the PEXPointer type.

The PEXPointer data type works much like the XtPointer data type, which we use in Motif callbacks:

```
typedef void* PEXPointer;
```

The whole purpose of this exercise is to create a color-approximation table so that we can make PEXlib happy and create a PEXlib renderer without problems. Of course, in real PEXlib applications, you'll make much more use of this color table. For purposes of our example, we need to place this newly filled color lookup table into a `PEXRendererAttributes` structure. This `PEXRendererAttributes` structure holds the initial values when creating a PEX renderer.

The `PEXRendererAttributes` structure looks like:

```
typedef struct {
    PEXPipelineContext  pipeline_context;
    PEXStructurePath    current_path;
    PEXLookupTable      marker_bundle;
    PEXLookupTable      text_bundle;
    PEXLookupTable      line_bundle;
    PEXLookupTable      interior_bundle;
    PEXLookupTable      edge_bundle;
    PEXLookupTable      view_table;
    PEXLookupTable      color_table;
    PEXLookupTable      depth_cue_table;
    PEXLookupTable      light_table;
    PEXLookupTable      color_approx_table;
    PEXLookupTable      pattern_table;
    PEXLookupTable      text_font_table;
    PEXNameSet          highlight_incl;
    PEXNameSet          highlight_excl;
    PEXNameSet          invisibility_incl;
    PEXNameSet          invisibility_excl;
    int                 renderer_state;
    PEXEnumTypeIndex    hlhsr_mode;
    PEXNPCSubVolume     npc_subvolume;
    PEXViewport         viewport;
    PEXListOfClipRect   clip_list;
    PEXNameSet          pick_incl;
    PEXNameSet          pick_excl;
    PEXStructurePath    pick_start_path;
    PEXColorSpecifier   background_color;
    Bool                clear_image;
    Bool                clear_z;
    int                 echo_mode;
} PEXRendererAttributes;
```

As you can tell, there are a lot of values you can set into a PEXlib renderer. All we need to fill in, though, is the *color_approx_table* field.

Code to set up a color LUT and fill in the *color_approx_table* field follows:

```
#include  <X11/PEX5/PEXlib.h>
```

```
Display*                display;
Window                  drawing_window;
XStandardColormap       std_colormap;
PEXRendererAttributes   pex_attributes;
PEXColorApproxEntry     color_approx;

/*
 * Set up color approximations
 * into the PEXColorApproxEntry ...
 */

/* Create a color LUT. */
pex_attributes.color_approx_table =
    PEXCreateLookupTable(display,
        drawing_window,
        PEXLUTColorApprox);

/* Fill in the LUT. */
PEXSetTableEntries(display,
    pex_attributes.color_approx_table,
    0,  /* entry 0, default */
    1,
    PEXLUTColorApprox,
    &color_approx);
```

To put all this together, the pex_set_color_approx utility function provides the code to set up the color approximation table into the PEXRendererAttributes structure:

```
#include  <X11/PEX5/PEXlib.h>

    /* Set up color approximations. Necessary. */
void pex_set_color_approx(Display* display,
    Window drawing_window,
    XStandardColormap* std_colormap,
    PEXRendererAttributes* attributes) /* RETURN */

{   /* pex_set_color_approx */
    PEXColorApproxEntry color_approx;

    /* This routine assumes we have a color visual. */

    /* Set up color approximations. */
    color_approx.type   = PEXColorSpace;
    color_approx.model  = PEXColorApproxRGB;
    color_approx.dither = PEXOn;

    color_approx.base_pixel = std_colormap->base_pixel;

    color_approx.max1  = std_colormap->red_max;
    color_approx.max2  = std_colormap->green_max;
    color_approx.max3  = std_colormap->blue_max;
    color_approx.mult1 = std_colormap->red_mult;
    color_approx.mult2 = std_colormap->green_mult;
```

```
        color_approx.mult3 = std_colormap->blue_mult;

        color_approx.weight1 = 0; /* Unused */
        color_approx.weight2 = 0; /* Unused */
        color_approx.weight3 = 0; /* Unused */

        attributes->color_approx_table =
            PEXCreateLookupTable(display,
                drawing_window,
                PEXLUTColorApprox);

        PEXSetTableEntries(display,
            attributes->color_approx_table,
            0,  /* entry 0, default */
            1,
            PEXLUTColorApprox,
            &color_approx);

}    /* pex_set_color_approx */
```

Our utility function completely hides the intermediate step of filling in the `PEXColorApproxEntry` structure. We do this to avoid complexity in the calling code.

We're finally ready to create a PEX renderer, the last step before we can draw (render) with PEXlib into our Motif drawing-area window.

Create a PEX Renderer

A PEX renderer acts much like the graphics context used for normal Xlib drawing routines. Also, as is true of creating a GC, the function that creates a PEX renderer, `PEXCreateRenderer`, takes a bit-mask of flags that tells it which fields in the `PEXRendererAttributes` structure you've filled in. This concept of bit-flags should be old hat to anyone who programs with GCs.

To create a PEX renderer, call `PEXCreateRenderer`:

```
#include  <X11/PEX5/PEXlib.h>

PEXRenderer PEXCreateRenderer(Display* display,
    Drawable drawable,
    unsigned long mask,
    PEXRendererAttributes* pex_attributes)
```

A `PEXRenderer` data type is another one of those long integer IDs, much like `Window` and `Pixmap`:

```
typedef XID  PEXRenderer;
```

The code we use to create a renderer follows:

```
#include  <X11/PEX5/PEXlib.h>

Widget         drawing_area;
PEXRenderer    pexrenderer;
PEXRendererAttributes  pex_attributes;

/* Set up color-approx. table... */

pexrenderer =
    PEXCreateRenderer(XtDisplay(drawing_area),
        XtWindow(drawing_area),
        PEXRAColorApproxTable,  /* mask */
        &pex_attributes);
```

We pass only one bit-flag, the PEXRAColorApproxTable mask. You can choose from any and all of the following list of bit-flags listed in Table 16.3.

Table 16.3 *PEXRendererAttributes bit-flags.*

Bit flag	Field in **PEXRendererAttributes**
PEXRAPipelineContext	pipeline_context
PEXRACurrentPath	current_path
PEXRAMarkerBundle	marker_bundle
PEXRATextBundle	text_bundle
PEXRALineBundle	line_bundle
PEXRAInteriorBundle	interior_bundle
PEXRAEdgeBundle	edge_bundle
PEXRAViewTable	view_table
PEXRAColorTable	color_table
PEXRADepthCueTable	depth_cue_table
PEXRALightTable	light_table
PEXRAColorApproxTable	color_approx_table
PEXRAPatternTable	pattern_table
PEXRATextFontTable	text_font_table
PEXRAHighlightIncl	highlight_incl

continued

```
PEXRAHighlightExcl           highlight_excl
PEXRAInvisibilityIncl        invisibility_incl
PEXRAInvisibilityExcl        invisibility_excl
PEXRARendererState           renderer_state
PEXRAHLHSRMode               hlhsr_mode
PEXRANPCSubVolume            npc_subvolume
PEXRAViewport                viewport
PEXRAClipList                clip_list
PEXRAPickIncl                pick_incl
PEXRAPickExcl                pick_excl
PEXRAPickStartPath           pick_start_path
PEXRABackgroundColor         background_color
PEXRAClearImage              clear_image
PEXRAClearZ                  clear_z
PEXRAEchoMode                echo_mode
```

When you're all done with a PEX renderer, call `PEXFreeRenderer`:

```
#include  <X11/PEX5/PEXlib.h>

void PEXFreeRenderer(Display* display,
      PEXRenderer renderer)
```

Rendering with PEXlib

Finally we're ready to draw our 3D graphics with PEXlib. As with all Xlib drawing, we draw only from within the drawing area's Expose callback. Even though you're working with PEXlib, you still need to follow the standard X Window rules to never draw into a window until you receive an Expose event for that window. That's one of the good things about working with Motif and PEXlib: the basic rules don't change, although you add a new set of complex extensions to those rules.

You should bracket your PEX output primitives with `PEXBeginRendering` and `PEXEndRendering`:

```
#include  <X11/PEX5/PEXlib.h>
```

```
void PEXBeginRendering(Display* display,
    Drawable drawable,
    PEXRenderer renderer)

void PEXEndRendering(Display* display,
    PEXRenderer renderer,
    int flush)
```

These two functions set up the renderer to draw and then tell the X server that we're done drawing with that specific PEXRenderer. This allows the X server some freedom to shuffle things around, especially because typical PEXlib drawing requests are quite complex. You wouldn't use a complex 3D graphics library to draw just a few boxes would you?

The *flush* flag, if set to True, indicates that all undisplayed primitives should be displayed, not trashed.

We then call XFlush to send all the output immediately to the X server.

```
#include  <X11/PEX5/PEXlib.h>

Display*     display;
Window       window;
PEXRenderer pexrenderer;

PEXBeginRendering(display,
    window, pexrenderer);

/* Draw PEX primitives here... */

PEXEndRendering(display,
    pexrenderer, True);
XFlush(display);
```

With all this, you should be able to render PEX primitives, using functions like PEXPolyline, inside a Motif drawing-area widget and combine the best of both toolkits together in your applications.

Drawing Lines with PEXlib

The basic line-drawing function in PEXlib is PEXPolyline, which can draw a number of connected lines:

```
#include  <X11/PEX5/PEXlib.h>

void PEXPolyline(Display* display,
    XID resource_id,
    PEXOCRequestType request_type,
    unsigned int number_points,
    PEXCoord* points)
```

Even though it looks confusing, the *resource_id* is really the ID of the PEXRenderer we created above.

We pass a *request_type* of PEXOCRender, because we want immediate-mode graphics. You can pick from the request types listed in Table 16.4.

Table 16.4   *PEXlib request types.*

Request Type	Value
PEXOCRender	0
PEXOCStore	1
PEXOCRenderSingle	2
PEXOCStoreSingle	3

The PEXOCRenderSingle and PEXOCStoreSingle request types are useful for debugging.

You typically want to draw hundreds, if not thousands, of lines. A CAD drawing of an automobile door, for instance, may have thousands of lines, curves, splines, and other shapes. The lines you want to draw are stored in the PEXCoord array. You must provide PEXPolyline with a PEXCoord array as well as the number of points. PEXPolyline draws connected-line segments.

Each point looks like:

```
typedef struct {
  float  x;
  float  y;
  float  z;
} PEXCoord;
```

Each PEXCoord structure holds a single point in 3D space.

The PEX Origin

Unless you set up a transformation, the default coordinate system goes from 0.0 to 1.0. PEX also introduces an interesting quirk: the origin in PEX is the *lower* left corner.

The *Y* origin is the exact opposite of the X Window origin (the upper left corner). The default 3D coordinate system is right-handed in PEX.

In addition to drawing lines and other shapes, there are a number of routines you can call to control how the output line looks.

Setting the Line Width

To set the line width of the lines we draw, you can call PEXSetLineWidth:

```
#include  <X11/PEX5/PEXlib.h>

void PEXSetLineWidth(Display* display,
    XID resource_id,
    PEXOCRequestType request_type,
    double line_width)
```

Again, we pass the PEXRenderer as the *resource_id* and PEXOCRender as the *request_type*.

PEX Color

PEXlib provides a number of different ways to view color, mainly because high-end 3D visualization systems need to specify much more exacting colors. This introduction touches only briefly on the complexities of color in PEXlib.

We'll start with a concrete example—the task we want to complete: setting the color used for drawing lines. For this, we call the PEXSetLineColor function:

```
#include  <X11/PEX5/PEXlib.h>

void PEXSetLineColor(Display* display,
    XID resource_id,
    PEXOCRequestType request_type,
    int color_type,
    PEXColor* pexcolor)
```

Most of the parameters should be familiar by now except for the *color_type* and the PEXColor union. You can choose a *color_type* from those listed in Table 16.5.

Table 16.5 *PEXlib color types.*

Color Type	Value	Meaning
PEXColorTypeIndexed	0	Indexed color
PEXColorTypeRGB	1	RGB

continued

PEXColorTypeCIE	2	CIE LUV
PEXColorTypeHSV	3	Hue, saturation, value
PEXColorTypeHLS	4	Hue, lightness, saturation
PEXColorTypeRGB8	5	8-bit RGB
PEXColorTypeRGB16	6	16-bit RGB

We use a *color_type* of PEXColorTypeRGB, to keep to the simple RGB color space.

The PEXColor union holds the following different color types:

```
typedef union {
  PEXColorIndexed   indexed;
  PEXColorRGB       rgb;
  PEXColorHSV       hsv;
  PEXColorHLS       hls;
  PEXColorCIE       cie;
  PEXColorRGB8      rgb8;
  PEXColorRGB16     rgb16;
} PEXColor;
```

You can guess from the names that PEXlib supports CIE standard; hue, lightness, saturation (HLS); hue, saturation, value (HSV); and traditional red, green, blue (RGB) color spaces. For our simple introduction to PEXlib, we'll use the common RGB model and the PEXColorRGB portion of the union:

```
typedef struct {
  float   red;
  float   green;
  float   blue;
} PEXColorRGB;
```

To set up our PEXColor structure, then, we store values into the *red*, *green*, and *blue* fields of the PEXColorRGB structure, which is, in turn, held in the *rgb* field of the PEXColor union:

```
PEXColor     pexcolor;

pexcolor.rgb.red   = 0.0;
pexcolor.rgb.green = 1.0;
pexcolor.rgb.blue  = 0.0;
```

The RGB values are floating-point numbers and go from 0.0 (all off) to 1.0 (full on), which is far different from Xlib's use of integers in the range of 0 (all off) to 65535 (full on).

Putting PEXlib color together with `PEXSetLineColor` to set the line-drawing color, we can hide the messy details in the following utility function:

```
        /* Set line color via RGB. */
void pex_set_line_color(Display* display,
    PEXRenderer pexrenderer,
    float red,
    float green,
    float blue)

{   /* pex_set_line_color */
    PEXColor     pexcolor;

    pexcolor.rgb.red    = red;
    pexcolor.rgb.green  = green;
    pexcolor.rgb.blue   = blue;

    PEXSetLineColor(display, pexrenderer,
        PEXOCRender, PEXColorTypeRGB,
        &pexcolor);

}   /* pex_set_line_color */
```

Rendering in the Expose Callback

Now that we've performed all the necessary overhead imposed by PEXlib, the final step is to draw in our drawing-area's window, using PEXlib drawing commands. This completes the task of combining PEXlib and Motif.

You still must follow the basic X rule that you cannot draw into a window until an `Expose` event arrives. In our case, we get notified of `Expose` events in our drawing-area widget's `exposeCallback`.

In the drawing area's `exposeCallback`, we'll call a simple function to handle the rendering with PEXlib. In our case, we simply draw two lines, after setting the color and line width.

The code we'll use to draw two simple lines follows:

```
void RenderPEX(Display* display,
    Window window,
    PEXRenderer pexrenderer)

{   /* RenderPEX */
    PEXCoord     coords[10];

    printf("PEX rendering.\n");
```

```
PEXBeginRendering(display, window, pexrenderer);

/* First line. */
PEXSetLineWidth(display, pexrenderer,
    PEXOCRender, 8.4);

/* Set color. */
pex_set_line_color(display,
    pexrenderer, 0.5, 0.5, 1.0);

/* Draw lines. */
coords[0].x = 0.0;
coords[0].y = 0.0;
coords[0].z = 0.0;

coords[1].x = 1.0;
coords[1].y = 1.0;
coords[1].z = 1.0;

PEXPolyline(display, pexrenderer,
    PEXOCRender, 2, coords);

/* Second line. */
pex_set_line_color(display,
    pexrenderer, 1.0, 0.5, 0.75);

PEXSetLineWidth(display, pexrenderer,
    PEXOCRender, 4.2);

coords[0].x = 0.0;
coords[0].y = 1.0;
coords[0].z = 0.0;

coords[1].x = 1.0;
coords[1].y = 0.0;
coords[1].z = 0.0;

PEXPolyline(display, pexrenderer,
    PEXOCRender, 2, coords);

PEXEndRendering(display, pexrenderer, True);
XFlush(display);

}    /* RenderPEX */
```

In the PEXlib/Motif example program below, we call the `RenderPEX` routine whenever an `Expose` event arrives in the drawing area's window.

And that's it. To show how all this works in real life, we present a PEXlib/Motif program below.

A Program Combining PEXlib and Motif

The following program demonstrates the lessons in this chapter and combines PEXlib rendering with Motif. We use the standard colormap routine, GetStdColormap, from last chapter, as well as the menu routines from Chapter 4.

The code follows:

```
/* pexmotif.c */
#include <Xm/Xm.h>
#include <Xm/DrawingA.h>
#include <Xm/MainW.h>
#include <Xm/RowColumn.h>
#include <X11/PEX5/PEXlib.h>      /* PEX 5.1 */
#include <stdio.h>

    /* Print info on events. */
extern void PrintEventInfo(XEvent* event);

extern Widget CreatePushbutton(Widget parent,
    char* name,
    XtCallbackProc callback,
    XtPointer client_data);

    /* See chapter 4 on menus. */
extern Widget CreatePulldownMenu(Widget parent,
    char* name);

extern Widget CreateMenubar(Widget parent,
    char* name);

    /* Check if PEX supports immediate mode. */
extern int pex_check_immed_mode(PEXExtensionInfo* pex_info);

    /* Initializes PEX to immediate mode. */
extern int pex_init(Display* display,
    PEXExtensionInfo** pex_info);

    /* Set up color approximations. Necessary. */
extern void pex_set_color_approx(Display* display,
        Window drawing_window,
        XStandardColormap* std_colormap,
        PEXRendererAttributes* attributes); /* RETURN */

    /* Get a standard colormap. */
extern int GetStdColormap(Display* display,
    int screen, Visual* visual, int depth,
    XStandardColormap* std_colormap);

        /* Set line color via RGB. */
```

```
extern void pex_set_line_color(Display* display,
        PEXRenderer pexrenderer,
        float red, float green, float blue);

    /* Allocate X RGB color. */
extern
unsigned long AllocNamedColor(Display* display,
    Colormap colormap, char* colorname,
    unsigned long default_color);

void RenderPEX(Display* display,
    Window window,
    PEXRenderer pexrenderer)

{   /* RenderPEX */
    PEXCoord    coords[10];

    printf("PEX rendering.\n");

    PEXBeginRendering(display, window, pexrenderer);

    PEXSetLineWidth(display, pexrenderer,
        PEXOCRender, 8.4);

    /* Set color. */
    pex_set_line_color(display,
        pexrenderer, 0.5, 0.5, 1.0);

    /* Draw lines. */
    coords[0].x = 0.0;
    coords[0].y = 0.0;
    coords[0].z = 0.0;

    coords[1].x = 1.0;
    coords[1].y = 1.0;
    coords[1].z = 1.0;

    PEXPolyline(display, pexrenderer,
        PEXOCRender, 2, coords);

    pex_set_line_color(display,
        pexrenderer, 1.0, 0.5, 0.75);

    PEXSetLineWidth(display, pexrenderer,
        PEXOCRender, 4.2);

    coords[0].x = 0.0;
    coords[0].y = 1.0;
    coords[0].z = 0.0;

    coords[1].x = 1.0;
    coords[1].y = 0.0;
    coords[1].z = 0.0;

    PEXPolyline(display, pexrenderer,
```

```
            PEXOCRender, 2, coords);

    PEXEndRendering(display, pexrenderer, True);
    XFlush(display);

}   /* RenderPEX */

    /* Callback to exit program. */
void exitCB(Widget widget,
    XtPointer client_data,
    XtPointer call_data)

{   /* exitCB */

    exit(0);

}   /* exitCB */

void drawCB(Widget widget,
    XtPointer client_data,
    XtPointer call_data)

{   /* drawCB */
    XmDrawingAreaCallbackStruct*  ptr;
    Dimension                     width, height;
    PEXRenderer*                  pexrenderer;

    ptr = (XmDrawingAreaCallbackStruct*) call_data;

    if (ptr == NULL) {
        return;
    }

    switch(ptr->reason) {
        case XmCR_EXPOSE:
            /*
             * We draw when all Expose
             * events are in.
             */
            if (ptr->event->xexpose.count == 0) {

                /* We passed renderer ID as client_data. */
                pexrenderer = (PEXRenderer*) client_data;

                RenderPEX(XtDisplay(widget),
                    XtWindow(widget),
                    *pexrenderer);
            }
            break;
        case XmCR_INPUT:
            PrintEventInfo(ptr->event);
            break;

    }
```

```
}    /* drawCB */

int main(int argc, char** argv)

{    /* main */
    Widget              parent;
    XtAppContext        app_context;
    Widget              drawa, menubar, filemenu;
    Widget              mainw, exit_choice;
    Arg                 args[20];
    Cardinal            n;
    Display*            display;
    int                 status;
    PEXExtensionInfo*   pex_info;
    PEXRenderer         pexrenderer;
    int                 screen;
    Visual*             visual;
    Colormap            colormap;
    unsigned long       border, back;
    int                 depth;
    int                 copy_of_argc;
    char**              copy_of_argv;
    int                 argv_size;
    XStandardColormap   std_colormap;
    PEXRendererAttributes pex_attributes;

    /* Initialize X toolkit the long way. */
    XtToolkitInitialize();

    app_context = XtCreateApplicationContext();

    /* Copy command-line parameters. */
    copy_of_argc = argc;

    argv_size = argc * (sizeof(char*));

    copy_of_argv = (char**) XtMalloc(argv_size);

    memcpy(copy_of_argv, argv, argv_size);

    /* Open display connection. */
    display = XtOpenDisplay(app_context,
            NULL,
            NULL,
            "Ppm",
            (XrmOptionDescList) NULL,
            0,
            &argc, argv);

    /*
     * We assume an error opening
     * display is a fatal error.
     */
    if (display == (Display*) NULL) {
        fprintf(stderr, "Error opening X display.\n");
```

```
        exit(1);
}

/* Initialize PEX. */
status = pex_init(display, &pex_info);

if (status != True) {
    printf("PEX Error.\n");
    exit(-1);
}

/*
 * Get a visual. You may want
 * to find the best one available.
 * Here, we just use the default.
 */
screen = DefaultScreen(display);

visual = DefaultVisual(display, screen);

depth  = DefaultDepth(display, screen);

/* Get standard colormap. */
status = GetStdColormap(display, screen,
            visual, depth,
            &std_colormap);

if (status == True) {
    colormap = std_colormap.colormap;
}

/*
 * If you change the visual,
 * always allocate colors from
 * a colormap for the visual.
 */
border = AllocNamedColor(display, colormap,
        "white", 0L);

back   = AllocNamedColor(display, colormap,
        "black", 0L);

/*
 * If you use a nondefault
 * visual, set visual, colormap,
 * depth, background, and borderColor
 * resources.
 */
n = 0;
XtSetArg(args[n], XmNvisual,      visual); n++;
XtSetArg(args[n], XmNdepth,       depth); n++;
XtSetArg(args[n], XmNcolormap,    colormap); n++;
XtSetArg(args[n], XmNbackground,  back); n++;
XtSetArg(args[n], XmNborderColor, border); n++;
```

```
/* Set in command-line parameters. */
XtSetArg(args[n], XmNargc, copy_of_argc); n++;
XtSetArg(args[n], XmNargv, copy_of_argv); n++;

XtSetArg(args[n], XmNallowResize, True); n++;

/* We want to create windows without mapping. */
XtSetArg(args[n],
    XmNmappedWhenManaged, False); n++;

/* Hard-code a size. */
XtSetArg(args[n], XmNwidth,  350); n++;
XtSetArg(args[n], XmNheight, 350); n++;

parent = XtAppCreateShell(NULL, "Ppm",
            applicationShellWidgetClass,
            display, args, n);

/* Create menus and menu bar. */
n = 0;

mainw = XmCreateMainWindow(parent, "mainw", args, n);

menubar = CreateMenubar(mainw, "menubar");

/* Set resources on ALL shells. */
XtSetArg(args[n], XmNvisual,      visual); n++;
XtSetArg(args[n], XmNdepth,       depth); n++;
XtSetArg(args[n], XmNcolormap,    colormap); n++;
XtSetArg(args[n], XmNbackground,  back); n++;
XtSetArg(args[n], XmNborderColor, border); n++;

filemenu = CreatePulldownMenu(menubar, "file");

exit_choice = CreatePushbutton(filemenu, "quit",
        (XtCallbackProc) exitCB,
        (XtPointer) NULL);

/* Create drawing area. */
n = 0;
XtSetArg(args[n], XmNresizePolicy, XmRESIZE_ANY); n++;

XtSetArg(args[n], XmNbackground,  back); n++;
XtSetArg(args[n], XmNborderColor, border); n++;

drawa = XmCreateDrawingArea(mainw,
            "drawa", args, n);

/*
 * The graphics context isn't created yet, so
 * we pass a pointer to it as the client_data.
 */
XtAddCallback(drawa,
    XmNexposeCallback,
    (XtCallbackProc) drawCB,
```

```
        (XtPointer) &pexrenderer);

    XtAddCallback(drawa,
        XmNinputCallback,
        (XtCallbackProc) drawCB,
        (XtPointer) &pexrenderer);

    XtAddCallback(drawa,
        XmNresizeCallback,
        (XtCallbackProc) drawCB,
        (XtPointer) &pexrenderer);

    XtManageChild(drawa);

    XmMainWindowSetAreas(mainw,
        menubar,
        (Widget) NULL, /* command window */
        (Widget) NULL, /* horiz scroll */
        (Widget) NULL, /* vert scroll */
        drawa);

    XtManageChild(mainw);

    /* Must realize widgets before getting window ID. */
    XtRealizeWidget(parent);

    /* Set up color approximations. Necessary. */
    pex_set_color_approx(display, XtWindow(drawa),
        &std_colormap, &pex_attributes);

    /* Map widgets before creating PEX renderer. */
    XtMapWidget(parent);

    /* Set up PEX renderer. */
    pexrenderer = PEXCreateRenderer(XtDisplay(parent),
            XtWindow(drawa),
            PEXRAColorApproxTable,  /* mask */
            &pex_attributes);

    if (pexrenderer == 0) {
        printf("Bad PEX renderer.\n");
    }

    XtAppMainLoop(app_context);

    return 0;

}   /* main */

/* end of file pexmotif.c */
```

You'll need the following resource file for this program:

```
! Resource file for pexmotif.c in
! Chapter 16 of Power Programming Motif.
```

```
!
*fontList:       lucidasans-12
*background:     lightgrey

*title: PEXlib Test

*file.labelString: File
*file.mnemonic:    F
*quit.labelString: Exit
*quit.mnemonic:    x

! end of resource file
```

Name the file **Ppm** and place it in your home directory.

When you run this program, you'll see a window like the one shown in Figure 16.1.

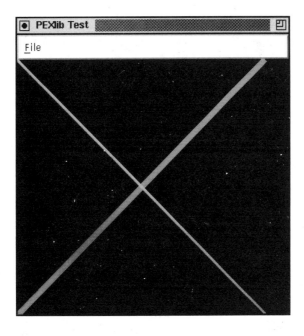

Figure 16.1 *The PEXlib/Motif example program.*

Compiling and Linking PEX Programs

PEXlib programs require the PEX5 library, **libPEX5.a**; the X library, **libX11.a**; and most likely the C math library, **libm.a**. For the standard colormap routines, we require the Xmu library, **libXmu.a**. And, of course, we need the Motif and Xt libraries.

Putting this all together, you can compile and link a Motif and PEXlib program using a command like the following:

```
cc -o pexmotif pexmotif.c -lXm -lXmu -lXt -lPEX5 -lX11 -lm
```

If you're missing any of these libraries, you'll have a hard time compiling the example program.

PEX Sample Implementation

You should see PEX support with most X servers that are at X11 Release 5 or higher. X11 R5 provided PEX version 5.0. The PEXlib and PEX 5.1 came as fixes to X11 R5. With Release 6, we should see PEX 6.0, which aims to correct many deficiencies with PEX 5.1. We'll all probably have to update our PEXlib programs with the advent of PEX 6.0.

Problems with PEX

The major problems with current PEX implementations are speed and size. PEX is a very complex protocol, especially with a PHIGS binding layered on top.

PEX comes only as an unoptimized sample implementation with X11 Release 5. It's up to individual vendors to optimize PEX for their hardware, much the same as the X server, although the base X server from the X Consortium often beats vendors at their own game. This sample implementation tends toward very slow program execution, and it doesn't support double buffering for animation. This PEX extension also works only on color screens.

In addition, most 3D applications generate very large amounts of data—this is the whole point of 3D applications. Somehow, all this data needs to travel over a network link to the PEX part of the X server. This is one of the rationales for direct-to-hardware libraries like Silicon Graphics' GL.

PEX programs, in fact, often generate flurries of X protocol requests. This leads to noticeable performance problems, especially since the X server—at least in most implementations—supports only a single thread of execution and must complete the entire—very large—PEX request before servicing other X applications. This tends to make your screen lock up while the X server handles the incoming storm of PEX requests.

These flurries of large packets tend to exceed the limits on the maximum size of X requests and provide the impetus for multithreaded X servers.

With multiple threads of execution, an X server could service other X applications at the same time it divides up a huge block of PEX requests into smaller chunks. This would change the appearance of your workstation from a single-tasking dead-in-the-water boat anchor back to a true multitasking workstation. The problem is that both the X server and the X programmer libraries weren't written with multiple threads in mind. X11 Release 6, though, should improve this situation for those who have operating system support for multiple threads. In fact, problems with PEX form one of the main driving forces behind the movement for a multithreaded X server.

Even with these limitations, there's been a lot of 3D momentum with X. After all, you no longer need special hardware to run portable 3D applications.

Acquiring PEXlib

PEXlib started out in the contributed code for X11 Release 5. The official PEXlib was first released as part of fix 19 for X11 Release 5. X11 Release 6 should include PEXlib as part of the standard system, along with PEX 6.0.

Because of this, you may have to go through some contortions to get PEXlib set up on your system. We acquired PEXlib from the X Consortium's electronic-mail server and compiled the library ourselves against a generic X11 Release 5 system.

Summary

The X Window System and Motif have brought a measure of standardization to graphics programming with UNIX—at least two-dimensional graphics programming. The problem for many years was the lack of standards in the three-dimensional arena. To compound this problem, few 3D graphics toolkits work at all with traditional two-dimensional X Window user-interface toolkits like Motif. This has led to some very sophisticated three-dimensional programs that sport terrible user interfaces and somewhat sophisticated user interfaces that sport terrible 3D graphics. Now, though, you can have the 3D graphics and a good-looking friendly user interface. What makes all this possible is the combination of the Motif toolkit for the user interface and an X Window extension for three-dimensional programming, the PEX 3D extension to X. PEX, which became more important when adopted as part of the Common Open Software Environment, or COSE, is short for the PHIGS (and PHIGS-PLUS) Extension to X.

This chapter covered the basics of PEXlib usage in Motif, including drawing lines and shapes and drawing into a window. Most of this information is basic, but it should give you a good start in the exploration of three-dimensional graphics within Motif.

PEX Library Functions and Macros Introduced in This Chapter

```
PEXBeginRendering
PEXCreateLookupTable
PEXCreateRenderer
PEXEndRendering
PEXFreeRenderer
PEXInitialize
PEXPolyline
PEXSetLineColor
PEXSetLineWidth
PEXSetTableEntries
```

CHAPTER 17

Multiple Top-Level Windows

This short chapter covers:

- Creating new top-level shells
- Making shell widgets appear and disappear from the screen
- The Close menu choice on the File menu

CREATING MULTIPLE TOP-LEVEL SHELLS

To this point, every Motif program we've created has used only one top-level window. That is, only one window was set up as an application main window under a top-level shell. In this chapter, we'll show how to add more top-level shell widgets, which will create more independent top-level windows.

Many sophisticated applications, like electronic-publishing systems, need a number of top-level shell windows on the screen at the same time. Some of these windows could be dialogs, but many will be top-level shells. In addition, there are other times when your application requires top-level windows that have more independence than typical dialogs. Online help, for example, is the perfect candidate for using a second top-level window.

We implement these secondary top-level windows as shell widgets.

Shell Widgets

Shell widgets exist to provide a layer between your program and the X Window System. A window manager in X, such as the Motif window manager *mwm*, requires that all top-level windows register certain information. This process of registering the proper information is rather complex, and the necessary information is defined in the *Inter-Client Communications Conventions Manual*—the ICCCM. In most cases, the Motif toolkit hides these messy details, except for presenting a few resources, such as the `title` resource that sets the window's title.

If we want to create more top-level windows, we need to create new top-level shell widgets.

SHORTCUT

Creating Shell Widgets

We can create a top-level application shell using the `applicationShellWidgetClass` with `XtAppCreateShell`, which we introduced in Chapter 14:

```
#include <X11/Shell.h>

Widget XtAppCreateShell(String application_name,
        String application_class,
```

```
    WidgetClass widget_class,
    Display* display,
    ArgList args,
    Cardinal number_args)
```

For secondary top-level shells, you should use a *widget_class* of `topLevelShellWidgetClass`.

In addition to `XtAppCreateShell`, there's a variable argument version called `XtVaAppCreateShell`:

```
#include <X11/Shell.h>

Widget XtVaAppCreateShell(String application_name,
    String application_class,
    WidgetClass widget_class,
    Display* display,
    ...)
```

TOP-LEVEL SHELLS

Each top-level shell widget has its own widget hierarchy, and this hierarchy must be realized with `XtRealizeWidget`, just like we've always done with the parent widget returned by `XtAppInitialize`.

Remember that when you realize a widget, all its managed children are realized, too.

Each of these top-level shells, when realized, can have only one child widget (usually a main window or a form or some widget that contains child widgets)—just like the top-level application shell widget created by `XtAppInitialize`.

Top-level shells are used for all permanent (or semipermanent) top-level windows, such as a help window.

The task before us now is to create another top-level shell widget. Putting this all together, we can then create a top-level shell using the following utility function:

```
#include  <Xm/Xm.h>
#include  <X11/Shell.h>

Widget CreateShell(Widget parent,
    char* app_class)

{   /* CreateShell */
```

```
Widget  widget;

widget = XtVaAppCreateShell(NULL,
            app_class,
            topLevelShellWidgetClass,
            XtDisplay(parent),
            XmNallowResize, True,
            NULL);

return widget;

}   /* CreateShell */
```

We use a widget class of `topLevelShellWidgetClass`.

NOTE Older systems that are still at X11 Release 3 and Motif 1.0 will need to use `XtCreateApplicationShell` instead of `XtAppCreateShell`. `XtCreateApplicationShell` takes the following parameters:

```
Widget XtCreateApplicationShell(String application_name,
        WidgetClass widget_class,
        ArgList args,
        Cardinal number_args)
```

If you've upgraded beyond Motif 1.0 and X11R3, you should use `XtAppCreateShell` instead.

POPUP SHELLS

If you'd rather not map and unmap these top-level shell widgets, you can use Xt popup shells. These are shell widgets that are popped up and down instead of managed and unmanaged.

Create a popup shell with `XtCreatePopupShell`:

```
Widget XtCreatePopupShell(String name,
    WidgetClass widget_class,
    Widget parent,
    ArgList args,
    Cardinal number_args)
```

You can also use the alternate variable-arguments form with `XtVaCreatePopupShell`:

```
Widget XtVaCreatePopupShell(String name,
    WidgetClass widget_class,
```

```
Widget parent,
...)
```

You can modify the `CreateShell` utility function to call `XtVaCreatePopupShell` by using the following code:

```
Widget CreateShell(Widget parent,
    char* app_class)

{   /* CreateShell */
    Widget  widget;

    widget = XtVaCreatePopupShell(app_class,
                topLevelShellWidgetClass,
                parent,
                XmNallowResize, True,
                NULL);

    return widget;

}   /* CreateShell */
```

After creating a popup shell, you need to realize the widget hierarchy with `XtRealizeWidget`. `XtRealizeWidget`, though, doesn't make a popup shell appear. Instead, you need to call `XtPopup`:

```
void XtPopup(Widget popup_shell,
    XtGrabKind grab_kind)
```

The *grab_kind* must then be one of the following:

```
typedef enum {
    XtGrabNone,
    XtGrabNonexclusive,
    XtGrabExclusive
} XtGrabKind;
```

Usually, we recommend you pass a *grab_kind* of `XtGrabNone`, which makes for a modeless top-level shell.

 In Chapter 7 on dialogs we mentioned that you shouldn't use `XtPopup` for Motif dialog widgets. That admonition remains in force. Only use `XtPopup` for top-level shell widgets that you create with `XtCreatePopupShell` or `XtVaCreatePopupShell`.

To make a popup shell disappear, which is much like unmanaging a dialog widget, call `XtPopdown`:

```
void XtPopdown(Widget popup_shell)
```

UTILITY FUNCTIONS FOR MULTIPLE TOP-LEVEL SHELLS

We've put together a set of utility functions for working with top-level shells. We put in code to allow you to choose between the popup-shell method and the XtVaAppCreateShell method. By defining POPUP_SHELL, you can compile the utility functions in **shell.c**, below, to work with popup shells. If you leave POPUP_SHELL commented out, the code will use the traditional mapping and unmapping to make the widgets appear.

We define three routines in **shell.c**: CreateShell, which creates a top-level shell; PopupShell, which makes a shell appear nonmodally; and PopdownShell, which makes a shell disappear. If you don't use popup shells, our utility CreateShell sets the shell widget to not be mapped when first managed (realized). This is to make the normal top-level shells act more like the popup shells, as the popup shells require an explicit function call (XtPopup) to make them appear.

The code for these three routines is in **shell.c**:

```
/* shell.c */
#include  <Xm/Xm.h>
#include  <X11/Shell.h>

/* Uncomment to use popup shells. */
/* #define POPUP_SHELL */

Widget CreateShell(Widget parent,
    char* app_class)

{   /* CreateShell */
    Widget  widget;

#ifdef POPUP_SHELL
    widget = XtVaCreatePopupShell(app_class,
            topLevelShellWidgetClass,
            parent,
            XmNallowResize, True,
            XmNmappedWhenManaged, False,
            NULL);

#else  /* !POPUP_SHELL */

    widget = XtVaAppCreateShell(NULL,
            app_class,
            topLevelShellWidgetClass,
            XtDisplay(parent),
```

```
                XmNallowResize, True,
                NULL);

#endif /* !POPUP_SHELL */

    return widget;

}   /* CreateShell */

    /* Show a shell. */
void PopupShell(Widget shell_widget)

{   /* PopupShell */

#ifdef POPUP_SHELL

    XtPopup(shell_widget, XtGrabNone);

#else   /* !POPUP_SHELL */

    XtMapWidget(shell_widget);

#endif  /* !POPUP_SHELL */

}   /* PopupShell */

    /* Hides a shell. */
void PopdownShell(Widget shell_widget)

{   /* PopdownShell */

#ifdef POPUP_SHELL

    XtPopdown(shell_widget);

#else /* !POPUP_SHELL */

    XtUnmapWidget(shell_widget);

#endif  /* !POPUP_SHELL */

}   /* PopdownShell */

/* end of file shell.c */
```

A PROGRAM TO TEST MULTIPLE TOP-LEVEL SHELLS

We've also put together a program to create and test multiple top-level shells. The program below creates three top-level shells, one normal shell returned from XtVaAppInitialize and two other top-level shells. To do so, we use the utility routines in **shell.c**, presented above.

The function `CreateWidgets`, below, creates a main window, menu bar, and File menu for each of the shells. The main top-level shell just has an Exit menu choice in the File menu. The two extra shells, though, sport a Close choice to allow you to close the extra shell window. `CreatePopmenu` creates a Pop menu that allows you to pop up those shells you've closed.

The callback functions then close or show a top-level shell using the `PopupShell` and `PopdownShell` utility functions.

The code for the **appshell.c** program follows:

```
/* appshell.c */
#include  <Xm/Xm.h>
#include  <Xm/Label.h>
#include  <Xm/MainW.h>
#include  <stdio.h>

/* Structure for our shell info. */
typedef struct {
    Widget  shell;
    char*   basename;
} ShellStruct;

/* External functions. */
extern Widget CreateShell(Widget parent,
    char* app_class);

        /* Show a shell. */
extern void PopupShell(Widget shell_widget);

        /* Hides a shell. */
extern void PopdownShell(Widget shell_widget);

extern Widget CreatePulldownMenu(Widget parent,
    char* name);

extern Widget CreateMenubar(Widget parent,
    char* name);

extern Widget CreatePushbutton(Widget parent,
    char* name,
    XtCallbackProc callback,
    XtPointer client_data);

void exitCB(Widget widget,
    XtPointer client_data,
    XtPointer call_data)

{   /* exitCB */
    ShellStruct*    shell_info;

    /* We assume ShellStruct is in client_data. */
    shell_info = (ShellStruct*) client_data;
```

```
    if (shell_info == NULL) {
        return;
    }

    printf("Exiting from %s.\n", shell_info->basename);

    exit(0);

}   /* exitCB */

void closeCB(Widget widget,
    XtPointer client_data,
    XtPointer call_data)

{   /* closeCB */
    ShellStruct*    shell_info;

    /* We assume ShellStruct is in client_data. */
    shell_info = (ShellStruct*) client_data;

    if (shell_info == NULL) {
        return;
    }

    printf("Closing %s.\n", shell_info->basename);

    PopdownShell(shell_info->shell);

}   /* closeCB */

    /* Make shell widget appear. */
void showCB(Widget widget,
    XtPointer client_data,
    XtPointer call_data)

{   /* showCB */
    ShellStruct*    shell_info;

    /* We assume ShellStruct is in client_data. */
    shell_info = (ShellStruct*) client_data;

    if (shell_info == NULL) {
        return;
    }

    PopupShell(shell_info->shell);

}   /* showCB */

    /* Creates menu bar and menus for a shell. */
Widget CreateWidgets(Widget parent,
    ShellStruct* shell_info,
    Boolean secondary_shell) /* is this one? */
```

```
{   /* CreateWidgets */
    char        name[100];
    Widget      mainw, menubar, label;
    Widget      exit_choice, filemenu;
    Arg         args[20];
    Cardinal    n;

    sprintf(name, "%s_mainw", shell_info->basename);

    n = 0;
    mainw = XmCreateMainWindow(parent,
            name, args, n);

    sprintf(name, "%s_menubar", shell_info->basename);

    menubar = CreateMenubar(mainw, name);

    filemenu = CreatePulldownMenu(menubar, "filemenu");

    /* If secondary shell, create a Close choice. */
    if (secondary_shell == True) {

        /* Pass ShellStruct to callback. */
        (void) CreatePushbutton(filemenu,
            "close", (XtCallbackProc) closeCB,
            (XtPointer) shell_info);
    }

        /* Pass ShellStruct to callback. */
    exit_choice = CreatePushbutton(filemenu,
            "quit", (XtCallbackProc) exitCB,
            (XtPointer) shell_info);

    sprintf(name, "%s_label", shell_info->basename);

    label = XtVaCreateManagedWidget(name,
            xmLabelWidgetClass, mainw,
            NULL);

    XmMainWindowSetAreas(mainw,
        menubar,
        (Widget) NULL, /* command window */
        (Widget) NULL, /* horiz scroll */
        (Widget) NULL, /* vert scroll */
        label);        /* work area */

    XtManageChild(mainw);

    /* Return menu-bar widget. */
    return menubar;

}   /* CreateWidgets */

    /* Creates menu to pop shells. */
void CreatePopmenu(Widget menubar,
```

```
        ShellStruct* shell_info_1,
        ShellStruct* shell_info_2)

{   /* CreatePopmenu */
    Widget  menu;

    menu = CreatePulldownMenu(menubar, "pop");

    /* Create popup menu choices. */
        (void) CreatePushbutton(menu,
            "pop1", (XtCallbackProc) showCB,
            (XtPointer) shell_info_1);

        (void) CreatePushbutton(menu,
            "pop2", (XtCallbackProc) showCB,
            (XtPointer) shell_info_2);

}   /* CreatePopmenu */

int main(int argc, char** argv)

{   /* main */
    Widget          parent;
    Widget          shell1, shell2;
    Widget          menubar;
    ShellStruct     parent_info;
    ShellStruct     shell_info_1;
    ShellStruct     shell_info_2;
    XtAppContext    app_context;

    /* Initialize Xt and create parent like normal. */
    parent = XtVaAppInitialize(&app_context,
            "Ppm",
            (XrmOptionDescList) NULL,
            0,
            &argc, argv,
            (String*) NULL,
            XmNallowResize, True
            NULL);

    /* Create widgets for this shell. */
    parent_info.shell  = parent;
    parent_info.basename = "main_app_shell";

    menubar = CreateWidgets(parent, &parent_info, False);

    CreatePopmenu(menubar,
        &shell_info_1, &shell_info_2);

    /* Create other shells. */
    shell1 = CreateShell(parent, "Ppm");
    shell2 = CreateShell(parent, "Ppm");

    /*
     * Create widgets for shells. Note
```

```
    * that these are secondary shells.
    */
   shell_info_1.shell   = shell1;
   shell_info_1.basename = "shell1";

   menubar = CreateWidgets(shell1, &shell_info_1, True);

   CreatePopmenu(menubar,
       &shell_info_1, &shell_info_2);

   shell_info_2.shell   = shell2;
   shell_info_2.basename = "shell2";

   menubar = CreateWidgets(shell2, &shell_info_2, True);

   CreatePopmenu(menubar,
       &shell_info_1, &shell_info_2);

   /* Realize shells. */
   XtRealizeWidget(parent);

   XtRealizeWidget(shell1);
   XtRealizeWidget(shell2);

   PopupShell(shell1);
   PopupShell(shell2);

   XtAppMainLoop(app_context);
   return 0;

}   /* main */

/* end of file appshell.c */
```

Running the Example Program

When you run this example program, you'll see three top-level shell widgets. You can close the extra shells with the Close menu choice on the File menu and pop them up with the two popup menu choices.

The program requires the following resource file:

```
! Resource file for Chapter 17
! of Power Programming Motif.
!
*fontList:       lucidasans-12
*background:      grey98

*title: Multiple Shell Test

*main_app_shell_label.labelString: \
Main application shell with its own menubar.
```

```
*shell1_label.labelString: \
Second shell with its own menubar.\n\
You can close this window with the \
Close menu choice.

*shell1_label.marginHeight: 24

*filemenu.labelString: File
*filemenu.mnemonic:    F

*shell2_label.labelString: \
Third shell with its own menubar.\n\
You can close this window with the \
Close menu choice.

*shell2_label.marginHeight: 24

*pop.labelString:    Pop
*pop1.labelString:   Pop Up Shell 2
*pop2.labelString:   Pop Up Shell 3

*quit.labelString:   Exit
*quit.mnemonic:      x

*close.labelString: Close

! end of resource file
```

Name this file **Ppm** and place it in your home directory.

SUMMARY

This chapter introduced a really simple concept in practice, but a hard one to figure out. Using multiple top-level shell widgets will be fairly common in your applications, especially if you tend to write very complex applications, like electronic-publishing systems.

X TOOLKIT INTRINSICS FUNCTIONS AND MACROS INTRODUCED IN THIS CHAPTER

```
XtCreatePopupShell
XtPopdown
XtPopup
XtVaAppCreateShell
XtVaCreatePopupShell
```

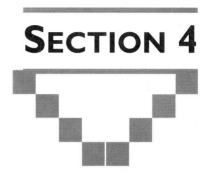

SECTION 4

Writing Well-Behaved Motif Applications

No application is an island unto itself, and that's especially true in the Motif environment. There's a whole set of rules your application must heed if it is to be considered a well-behaved Motif application.

Why should you care if your Motif application behaves well? Because users expect to be able to cut and paste data from one application to another. This application interoperability doesn't happen through magic; it happens because you set up your application to work with other applications. Most of these rules are contained in the *Inter-Client Communications Conventions Manual*, or ICCCM. The ICCCM is the Bible when it comes to application interoperability. It should be included in your X installation, and you may even want to take a look at it before attacking this section.

Being well-behaved involves a number of different methods. On one level, your application needs to work with window managers, separate applications that enforce the Motif look and feel. Chapter 18 covers how

573

your applications should work with *any* window manager, not necessarily the Motif window manager. This means setting resources sent to the window manager, including resource values on top-level shell widgets. Other topics covered in this chapter include an overview of other X-based window managers, such as the Open Look window manager.

On a more advanced level, well-behaved applications must be able to exchange data with other applications. There are a number of methods to do just that, and Chapters 19 and 20 describe each method in some depth.

Chapter 19 covers cut, copy, and paste operations using the Motif clipboard. A clipboard is a section of memory set aside to hold specific information. In this chapter, we explain how to cut or copy data to the clipboard in accepted formats and the process by which data are retrieved from the clipboard in the correct format.

However, there's one huge drawback to the Motif clipboard: It can be used only for exchanging data between Motif applications, not between Motif and non-Motif applications. Therefore, Chapter 20 covers the X Window methods for exchanging data between applications. This method involves creating active links between X selections. Although this method isn't as elegant as using the clipboard, it's the only way to have Motif applications communicate with non-Motif applications.

Finally, this section ends with a discussion of a feature new to Motif 1.2, drag and drop. The concept is simple: The user should be able to drag icons around the screen in order to perform basic functions. Some basic examples include dragging a file icon to a dumpster (but not a trash can, because Apple Computer claims to patented the metaphor of a trash can as a file-deletion device) to delete a file, or dragging a file icon to a printer icon to print that file. To the relief of programmers everywhere, the OSF made drag and drop rather easy to implement, with most of the work involving correct data formats. We show how to implement drag and drop in your code in Chapter 21.

CHAPTER 18

Working With Window Managers

This chapter covers:

- Window managers
- Rules for well-behaved applications
- Ways your program can influence the window manager
- Motif resources for working with the window manager
- Atoms and properties
- Window titles
- Window icons
- Window-manager menus
- The Motif window manager, *mwm*
- The Open Look window manager, *olwm*
- Working with other window managers

575

WHAT IS A WINDOW MANAGER?

A window manager is a separate X program that controls the layout and placement of windows on your screen. A window manager controls how much of the screen's real estate that any application can have and also allows you to resize, iconify, and move windows. You can run only one window manager per screen, and usually only one per X display.

As we described in Chapter 1, most window managers place a *titlebar* and other *decorations* around applications' main windows. This titlebar helps enhance the look and feel (or detract from it, depending on your perspective), and the decorations present a number of controls that allow users to manipulate the window.

You've probably been working most with *mwm*, the Motif window manager, but there are many other common window managers, as we list in Table 18.1.

Table 18.1   Common X Window window managers.

Program	Window Manager	Used Mainly with
dxwm	DECwindows window manager	DEC workstations
4Dwm	4D window manager	SGI workstations
mwm	Motif window manager	Motif-supported workstations
NCDwm	NCD Window manager	NCD X terminals
olvwm	Virtual Open Look window manager	X11R5
olwm	Open Look window manager	Sun workstations
twm	Tab window manager	X11R5, R4
tvtwm	Virtual tab window manager	X11R5
vtwm	Virtual tab window manager	X11R5
vuewm	HP VUE window manager	HP workstations
XDSwm	Visual window manager	Visual X terminals

There's a lot of fragmentation in window managers, but that should change for the better with the Common Open Software Environment, or COSE.

The main benefit of COSE, as far as the purposes of this book is concerned, is that Sun Microsystems, the number-one workstation and UNIX vendor, will adopt a window manager based on Motif and Hewlett-Packard's *vuewm* at the expense of Open Look.

WARNING
Even though Sun is migrating toward Motif, it will be years before most Sun installations upgrade fully to Motif. Sun is having problems getting users to upgrade to the Solaris operating system, and we expect the COSE/Motif upgrade to take years. Because of this and Sun's place in the workstation market, it's very important for your applications to work well under *olwm*, the window manager on Sun systems.

Most Motif-based workstations use *mwm* or a close variant like *vuewm* or *4Dwm*. Sun's OpenWindows uses *olwm* but will soon move the to COSE window manager.

In addition, many systems use the free window managers that come with X11R5 from the X Consortium, including *twm* and two virtual-window variants, *tvtwm* and *vtwm*.

Even with all this variance, most window managers follow the set of rules for well-behaved X programs, found in the *Inter-Client Communications Conventions Manual*, or ICCCM. We're going to cover a lot about the ICCCM in this chapter. We'll continue on with coverage of the ICCCM for the next three chapters.

The key, though, is that you cannot assume your programs will be running under *mwm*, so you must ensure that your applications can run under any window manager. This isn't very hard, but we'll provide a lot of tips in this chapter.

Key Window-Manager Features

There are a few key features you should know about window managers:

- The window manager is a separate X client in and of itself.
- You can change to a different window manager if you wish.
- The window manager controls the titlebar and other decorations placed on your application's windows. The window manager con-

trols the height of the titlebar, whether you can place a title in the titlebar, and all other window decorations.

■ The window manager is in charge. Period. Your applications may *request* the window manager do something, but the window manager may choose not to grant your requests.

■ Don't fight the window manager. You'll lose.

SHORTCUT

Window-Manager Resources

Since the window manager is a separate program, you must find a means to communicate your requests to the window manager. In Motif programs, with a few exceptions, you can communicate with the window manager by setting resource values on top-level shell widgets. The underlying toolkit code then sets the proper properties as expected by the window manager (we cover properties below).

Table 18.2 lists the following resources that can be set on top-level shell widgets.

Table 18.2 *Window-manager resources.*

Resource	Type	Default Value	Meaning
baseHeight	int	*dynamic*	Base size
baseWidth	int	*dynamic*	Base size
deleteResponse	unsigned char	XmDESTROY	See *WM_DELETE_WINDOW*
height	Dimension	*dynamic*	Widget height
heightInc	int	*dynamic*	Increment
iconic	Boolean	False	Start as icon?
iconMask	Pixmap	NULL	Mask for icon
iconName	String	NULL	Icon name
iconNameEncoding	Atom	STRING	Char set
iconPixmap	Pixmap	NULL	Icon bitmap
			continued

iconWindow	Window	NULL	Icon window
iconX	int	-1	Icon location
iconY	int	-1	Icon location
initialState	int	NormalState	Start as icon?
input	Boolean	True	Want keyboard input?
inputMethod	String	NULL	Locale modifier
keyboardFocusPolicy	unsigned char	XmEXPLICIT	Click to type
maxAspectX	int	*dynamic*	Max aspect ratio
maxAspectY	int	*dynamic*	Max aspect ratio
maxHeight	int	*dynamic*	Max height
maxWidth	int	*dynamic*	Max height
minAspectX	int	*dynamic*	Min aspect ratio
minAspectY	int	*dynamic*	Min aspect ratio
minHeight	int	*dynamic*	Min height
minWidth	int	*dynamic*	Min height
mwmDecorations	int	-1	*Mwm* window decorations
mwmFunctions	int	-1	Allowable functions
mwmInputMode	int	-1	Sets if modal
mwmMenu	String	NULL	Menu choices
overrideRedirect	Boolean	False	Override wm? (Menus)
preeditType	String	*dynamic*	*implementation dependent*
title	String	*dynamic*	Window title
titleEncoding	Atom	*dynamic*	Char set
transientFor	Widget	NULL	Holds parent
transient	Boolean	False	Transient?

continued

useAsyncGeometry	Boolean	False	Wait for wm on geometry?
waitForWm	Boolean	True	Wait on wm?
width	Dimension	*dynamic*	Widget width
widthInc	int	*dynamic*	Increment
windowGroup	Window	*dynamic*	Group leader
winGravity	int	*dynamic*	NorthWest-Gravity
wmTimeout	int	5000 ms	Timeout

The resource names that begin with *mwm* are specific to the Motif window manager. The rest should be generic, although sometimes different window managers interpret things differently.

The transient resource defaults to True for dialogs. Other resources also have different default values depending on whether you have a dialog, menu, or top-level shell widget.

FOLLOWING THE RULES FOR WELL-BEHAVED X PROGRAMS

As we're reminded every few minutes, X provides mechanism but not policy. X's designers work very hard at avoiding interface issues, merely providing the underlying facilities to create a user interface. The problem is, though, that users now expect programs to work together—in other words, to provide *interoperability* (a term that is almost as ridiculous as the acronym *GUI*).

From this desire for programs to work together, a set of conventions were created to specify how X applications should act together. It doesn't matter if you run your applications under Motif or Open Look or just plain X; all applications should follow these conventions, which are described in the ICCCM—the *Inter-Client Communications Conventions Manual*. Your applications can leverage a lot of power from following these conventions. Luckily, Motif takes care of most of the hard work. You will need to set some of the resources listed in Table 18.2, though. Under the hood, Motif converts these resource values into data called *properties*, which are used to communicate with other X programs, particularly the window manager.

The ICCCM covers a lot of ground and creates more confusion than any other topic in the X Window System. Included in the ICCCM are *mechanisms*—that word again—for applications to communicate with other applications and cooperate in dealing with shared resources, window managers, and session managers. The application-to-application communication will be covered in the following chapters. For now, we'll concentrate on what you need to do for your applications to be considered good citizens in the X world, and we'll reference sections of the ICCCM where you can look for more information.

If your application follows the rules in the ICCCM, it should be able to:

■ Run under any ICCCM-compliant window manager

■ Copy and paste data with other applications

■ Work with session managers so the applications can be restarted where they left off

■ Share colormaps between programs

In theory, the user should be able to choose a window manager that best meets the user's needs. The window manager then controls the screen layout (does it, for example, allow overlapping windows?) and provides a look and feel for the window decorations. Dialogs, for example, may receive special decorations, and so on. The basic rule in the ICCCM is that the window manager is in charge, and your application shouldn't care. Because of this, the ICCCM has many holes when it comes to getting information back from window managers—for example, determining the titlebar height or setting and getting window decorations.

The problem with this model is that most users simply don't know how or don't want to bother changing the default window manager, so users generally get stuck with the limitations of their current window manager. This lack of rules and standards in the ICCCM makes your job as an application designer tougher.

X Session Managers

Window managers aren't difficult to understand, but the idea of a session manager is an evolving concept. Basically, a session manager manages a *session*—a group of X applications doing some particular form of work.

Session managers are responsible for starting up the group of applications, saving the state of the applications (so that they can be restarted from where they left off), and closing down the programs.

Exactly what session managers do is fairly ambiguous, and many of the tough decisions (like how to save the state of an application) are left for applications to deal with—which means that most applications won't deal with it at all. The whole concept of session managers is still evolving, but you should expect to see more of them. Hewlett-Packard's *vuewm* merges a window and session manager into one program, and this forms the core of the COSE window/session manager.

SETTING RESOURCE VALUES FOR THE WINDOW MANAGER

The main way you interact with the window manager is by setting values to the resources in Table 18.2. One look at that huge list of resources is enough to scare anyone off, but don't worry. You need to set only the resources that you want to. Most Motif programs choose defaults that are workable, if not optimal.

In most applications, you should set at least the following resources on your top-level shell widgets:

- ■ deleteResponse
- ■ iconName
- ■ iconPixmap
- ■ title

The deleteResponse controls how an application reacts to a window-manager delete message, which we cover below in the section on "Window-Manager Protocols." We're already familiar with the icon resources and the title. The iconName and title resources often go into resource files.

Only when your application has special needs do you need to delve deeply into the rest of these resources. In the next few sections, we'll cover more of these resources in depth, so you can choose whether you want to set them or not.

Controlling Window Sizes

In your applications, the widgets naturally take care of their sizes. Furthermore, the widget sizes are highly dependent on the font selected by you—or the user. Japanese and Chinese fonts, for example, typically are a much larger size than Western-language fonts. All this affects the widget sizes, and Motif takes care of all this. Thus you often don't need to mess with any of the resources for setting the window sizes. But if you want tighter control over the window sizes, you can set a number of size resources, starting with the width and height. If you set these resources on a top-level shell widget, you control the whole application window.

If you want, you can set a shell widget's minimum size, by setting the minWidth and minHeight resources. This is useful if there's a size under which your application just doesn't make sense.

You can similarly set the maxWidth and maxHeight resources, which set a maximum size on your window.

If you want the window to size only in increments, you can set the widthInc and heightInc resources. These values are the width and height increments used by the window manager to control resizing. The window manager should only allow the window to be sized in increments of the baseWidth, and baseHeight resources plus multiples of the widthInc and heightInc resources, going from the minimum size to the maximum.

You can also set up an aspect ratio based on the minAspectX and minAspectY resources. The minimum aspect ratio is then minAspectX / minAspectY.

The maximum aspect ratio is set much the same using the maxAspectX and maxAspectY resources.

WINDOW TITLES

We've set the title resource for a number of chapters. With this resource, you can change the window's titlebar. X makes no guarantees that a window manager (assuming the user is even running a window manager) provides for titlebars. However, all major window managers provide for titlebars.

It's common for applications to place the program name as well as the name of the current file into the titlebar. For example, a word processor named *WunderWord* may set the titlebar to "WunderWord: chap18.doc" to indicate that the current file name is **chap18.doc**. With this, the user knows that the File menu's **Save** choice should save the current data to the file named **chap18.doc**. The titlebar is often a convenient place to store such information.

The titlebar itself is placed in a window controlled by the window manager. You're only allowed to suggest a text string to be placed in this titlebar. Yes, we'd like to place bitmaps in this titlebar, too, but that's not allowed by the ICCCM nor by any window manager we've seen.

The window manager reparents your top-level shell window. When your application creates a top-level shell window, the window manager intercedes by adding its own window around your application's window. This new window, owned and placed by the window manager, is slightly larger than your application's window. The extra space is used for the frame surrounding the application's window, including space for the titlebar.

When this new window appears, it changes your application's layout. Most window managers move your window down and slightly to the right. For example, if you start an application at 100,100, the window itself won't appear at 100,100. The window manager's titlebar will appear—at least with most window managers. In addition, since your window has a new parent, its origin will be a very low number, such as 8,32, instead of the original 100,100. That's because each window's location is relative to its parent. Since your application window gets a new parent window, its location changes in relation to this new parent window.

You should note that, after your window gets reparented, it is physically moved down and to the right. If the original coordinates for the window were 100,100, the new coordinates—global coordinates—may be 108,132.

This mode—or resource—in *mwm* is called positionIsFrame. If set to True, then the *x,y* position given is used to place the *mwm* frame. Your window is then moved down and to the right. If the positionIsFrame resource is False, then the *x,y* position given is used to place your application's window, and the *mwm* window frame is therefore higher and to the left of your window. Note that the positionIsFrame resource is an X resource for the *mwm* application. You can't set this from within your programs; you must instead configure *mwm*.

DIALOGS

Dialogs are considered special windows by most window managers. Dialogs usually get a different set of default decorations and may receive a special visual look to distinguish them.

Some window managers iconify all dialogs with a main application window, whereas others don't. Since this decision is technically up to the window manager, you're not supposed to interfere in this process—but sometimes you need to. In the section on icons, below, we discuss how to detect iconification, so you could unmanage all your dialogs when the parent top-level shell gets iconified.

There are a number of dialog-specific window manager resources. We list them in Table 18.3.

Table 18.3   *Dialog resources for window managers.*

Resource	Type	Meaning
`transientFor`	`Widget`	Holds parent top-level shell widget
`transient`	`Boolean`	`True` if dialog, `False` otherwise
`mwmInputMode`	`int`	Sets if modal

Modal Dialogs

Motif programs depend on the Motif window manager to support modal dialogs. Thus, if you run a non-Motif window manager, such as *twm* or *olwm*, chances are you'll lose this support. This problem impacts your Motif applications no matter on what platform you run. Since the user chooses which window manager to run, you always must be alert to this problem.

Personally, we strongly recommend against using any sort of modal dialogs ever. With the Motif and Xt Intrinsics callback mechanism, you can avoid most modal dialogs. For example, if you have a dialog that asks, "Do you really want to delete all your files?" you can have *that* dialog's **OK** button callback execute the delete command. The dialog callback will never be called unless the user presses the **OK** button in the dialog. The rest of the system can continue merrily on its way.

Setting Input Modes

You can set the `mwmInputMode` resource to one of the modes listed in Table 18.4.

Table 18.4 *Mwm input modes.*

Name	Value
MWM_INPUT_MODELESS	0
MWM_INPUT_PRIMARY_APPLICATION_MODAL	I
MWM_INPUT_SYSTEM_MODAL	2
MWM_INPUT_FULL_APPLICATION_MODAL	3

These modes, defined in the include file `<Xm/MwmUtil.h>`, correspond to the values of the `dialogStyle` resource presented in Chapter 7 on dialogs:

- ■ `XmDIALOG_SYSTEM_MODAL`
- ■ `XmDIALOG_PRIMARY_APPLICATION_MODAL`
- ■ `XmDIALOG_FULL_APPLICATION_MODAL`
- ■ `XmDIALOG_MODELESS`

You can set this resource only if the bulletin board is unmanaged.

If you set the `mwmInputMode` resource to `MWM_INPUT_SYSTEM_MODAL`, the user must respond to your dialog before doing *anything* with *any* other application or window. This can quickly lock up a system, especially if there are problems with the software. Use `MWM_INPUT_SYSTEM_MODAL` only if you're sure you know what you're doing. `MWM_INPUT_SYSTEM_MODAL` may be reasonable in a factory-automation application, but it doesn't make sense in a text editor.

NOTE

This mode depends on help from the Motif window manager, *mwm*. If *mwm* isn't the window manager in use, then `MWM_INPUT_SYSTEM_MODAL` won't work.

`MWM_INPUT_FULL_APPLICATION_MODAL` means that the user must respond to the dialog before doing anything else in the application.

`MWM_INPUT_PRIMARY_APPLICATION_MODAL` means that the user must respond to the dialog before interacting with the ancestor of the dialog widget, the parent widget used to create the dialog.

`MWM_INPUT_MODELESS,` of course, means that your dialogs place no such restrictions.

If you set the `dialogStyle` resource, there's no need to set the `mwmInputMode` resource. Remember that these modes are supported by *mwm* only and not by other window managers.

WINDOW DECORATIONS

If your application is running under *mwm*, you can set the `mwmDecorations` resource to control the window decorations. Actually, you're asking *mwm* to change the decorations, but usually *mwm* doesn't turn you down.

The `mwmDecorations` resource on a top-level shell holds a set of bit flags representing the decorations you wish to add or subtract from the window, as listed in Table 18.5.

Table 18.5 *Mwm decorations.*

Bit Flag	Meaning
`MWM_DECOR_ALL`	Turn off listed decorations
`MWM_DECOR_BORDER`	Window manager borders
`MWM_DECOR_MAXIMIZE`	**Maximize** (zoom) button
`MWM_DECOR_MENU`	Window menu (dash) button

continued

`MWM_DECOR_MINIMIZE`	**Minimize** (iconify) button
`MWM_DECOR_RESIZEH`	Resize handles
`MWM_DECOR_TITLE`	Actual titlebar

These decorations are defined in the include file `<Xm/MwmUtil.h>`.

Some decorations don't make sense without other ones. `MWM_DECOR_MAXIMIZE`, for example, won't work unless `MWM_DECOR_TITLE` is also enabled.

The default value of -1 for the `mwmDecorations` resource tells *mwm* to use the default decorations for that type of window (dialog or top-level shell). If you want to add to an existing set of decorations, you need to query the current value of the `mwmDecorations` resource and then OR that value with the bit flags for the decorations you want. If the `mwmDecorations` resource holds -1, then you should set the entire set of flags for the decorations you want.

The window manager controls the decorations—you're just asking for the decorations you want. The window manager, especially *mwm*, may allow only certain types of decorations on dialogs. Some versions of *mwm* prevent dialogs from holding the **Minimize** or **Maximize** button (`MWM_DECOR_MINIMIZE` and `MWM_DECOR_MAXIMIZE`). And, of course, this resource works only for *mwm* and close variants. (See the section on *olwm* below for how to set the decorations on windows under *olwm*.)

Removing Decorations

If `MWM_DECOR_ALL` (don't be fooled by this confusing name) is set, then the bit flags indicate decorations to *remove*, not decorations to *add*. Otherwise, the bit flags indicate decorations to add.

For example, to remove the **Maximize** button, you can set the `mwmDecorations` resource to (`MWM_DECOR_ALL` | `MWM_DECOR_MAXI-MIZE`), as shown in the following code:

```
Widget    shell;

XtVaSetValues(shell,
    XmNmwmDecorations,
        (MWM_DECOR_ALL | MWM_DECOR_MAXIMIZE),
    NULL);
```

The previous code asks *mwm* to remove the **Maximize** button.

ICONS

Most window managers allow you to iconify programs, although each window manager handles the process differently. Window managers are not required by the ICCCM to support iconification, but most do.

Window managers have the ultimate power to provide icons and to enforce rules for iconifying windows. Again, different window managers use different policies. Some window managers iconify all the windows in the same window group when you iconify a group leader (or even any of the group). Some window managers iconify all dialogs along with the main window of an application. Others, like some versions of *olwm* (unfortunately, there are many conflicting versions of *olwm*), allow for dialogs to be iconified independently of the application's main window.

The lesson: Don't depend on your application's windows to be iconified when the user turns one window into an icon. This means that you're depending on the window manager to perform a function that is not universally supported.

Controlling Window States

You can control your top-level shell window's initial state with the `iconic` or `initialState` resources. You can set the `iconic` resource to `True` to start a program as an icon. You could also set the `initialState` resource to `IconicState` to perform the same task. You can set the `initialState` to one of the states listed in Table 18.6.

Table 18.6 Window states.

State	Value	Meaning
WithdrawnState	0	Window is not visible
NormalState	I	Window is visible
IconicState	3	Window is replaced by an icon

If you set the iconic resource to True, it will override the initialState resource.

Iconifying Windows from Your Program

Normally, the user (via the window manager) chooses when to turn a window into an icon by some direct interaction with the window manager, such as clicking the mouse in the **Minimize** button. You can also initiate this action from within your programs. You can ask the window manager to iconify a window by calling XIconifyWindow from the low-level X library:

```
Status XIconifyWindow(Display* display,
    Window window,
    int screen_number)
```

XIconifyWindow returns a nonzero status if it managed to send the request properly. This tells you nothing about whether the request was received. The window manager may or may not iconify your window, but usually this action iconifies the window.

XIconifyWindow works with windows, not widgets. In your code, you'll use something like this:

```
Widget    shell;
int       status;

status = XIconifyWindow(XtDisplay(shell),
        XtWindow(shell),
        DefaultScreen(XtDisplay(shell) ) );
```

We use the XtDisplay, XtWindow, and DefaultScreen macros to get at the proper values.

N O T E
If you're working with a dialog created with one of the convenience routines like XmCreateInformationDialog, you'll need to use the parent (dialog shell) widget instead of the message box widget returned by XmCreateInformationDialog and similar functions:

```
Widget    dialog;
Widget    shell;

shell = XtParent(dialog);
```

You want to iconify the shell's window, not the message-box window.

You can also set the iconic resource to True to iconify a top-level widget.

Tracking Iconification

You can track when your window is iconified by setting up an event handler for UnmapNotify events. Use XtAddEventHandler to set this up and pass an event mask of StructureNotifyMask to ask for a host of event types, including UnmapNotify.

When an UnmapNotify event arrives for your window, you can assume it's been iconified.

SPLITTING ATOMS

We need to take a short digression here to explain in depth some X Window concepts that you'll need for more advanced interaction with window managers. The ICCCM and window managers use a lot of X atoms and properties to indicate values and store data. An atom, simply put, is a 32-bit hash number that represents a text string.

Atoms are 32-bit numbers used by X to speed string comparisons and avoid sending long strings over the network continuously. The X library function XInternAtom converts a string to an atom ID:

```
Atom XInternAtom(Display *display,
        String atom_name,
        Boolean only_if_exists)
```

If *only_if_exists* is False, the atom will be created if necessary. If *only_if_exists* is True, the atom will be returned only if it already existed. You almost always want to set *only_if_exists* to False. Here's how to convert the string "STRING" to an atom:

```
Atom   atom;
Display* display;

atom = XInternAtom(display,
        "STRING",
        False);
```

After you get an atom ID, you can exchange this value with other X programs, especially the window manager.

N O T E   Atom IDs are valid only for one session of the X server. Since the atoms are interned within the X server, you lose all atom IDs whenever the X server gets reset. If your application uses an atom, you must intern the atom each time your program runs. The only exceptions are those atoms that are built into the X server, which we cover below.

Motif provides its own function to intern an atom, `XmInternAtom`:

```
#include <Xm/MwmUtil.h>

Atom XmInternAtom(Display *display,
        String atom_name,
        Boolean only_if_exists)
```

`XmInternAtom` acts just like `XInternAtom`, but the Motif version also caches the atoms in the likely case your program calls `XmInternAtom` on a text string that the Motif toolkit already interned. This avoids network round-trips to the X server. You should call `XmInternAtom` in your programs to intern atoms.

Getting Atom Names

You can convert an atom ID back to a text string with `XGetAtomName` and `XmGetAtomName`:

```
String XGetAtomName(Display *display,
        Atom atom)

#include <Xm/MwmUtil.h>

String XmGetAtomName(Display *display,
        Atom atom)
```

With both functions, free the returned string with `XtFree`. Again, call the Motif version, `XmGetAtomName`.

What Are Atoms Used For?

An atom is essentially an ID for a text string, with the text string stored in the X server, so you can use atoms for anything you desire. In the X

Window world, though, atoms are usually used for data exchange between programs. Atoms are commonly used for:

- Data type IDs
- To name or identify properties on windows
- To set flags in data sent to the window or session manager

In order for this data exchange to work, both sides must agree to intern the same strings for their atoms. The ICCCM, for example, contains a number of strings that you should use for atoms if you want your application to remain well-behaved in the X environment.

Predefined Atoms

Atoms are heavily used for communication with window and session managers. Potentially, there is a performance pitfall every time an X application starts, as the startup would be bogged down as the application interned the same set of atoms as virtually every other X application. The designers of X nullified this potential problem by including a set of predefined atoms in the X server. These atoms are useful for communication with the window manager as well as data exchange between programs.

The atoms are actually stored in predefined slots in the X server's atom tables, so you're guaranteed that the same integer number refers to the same atom until the end of time (death, taxes, and atom tables). The numbers and definitions of these atoms are stored in `<X11/Xatom.h>`.

Unfortunately, the set of predefined atoms was locked in place far too early in X's design cycle. Because of this, you'll find that many atoms now common are not in this set. For example, the atom for `CLIPBOARD` (that is, the atom ID you get back from interning the string `"CLIPBOARD"`) is now used heavily by Motif applications for exchanging data. Yet `CLIPBOARD` isn't in the set of predefined atoms. Since the X protocol has been locked in place for at least six years (predating Motif), we're not going to see this situation change any time soon.

These predefined atoms fall into five main categories:

- Communications with the window and session managers
- Data types

- Data exchange
- Standard colormaps
- Fonts information

Window- and Session-Manager Atoms

The predefined atoms used for communicating with window and session managers are listed in Table 18.7.

Table 18.7   *X predefined window- and session-manager atoms.*

Text Name	Defined Macro in <X11/Xatom.h>
"WM_CLASS"	XA_WM_CLASS
"WM_CLIENT_MACHINE"	XA_WM_CLIENT_MACHINE
"WM_COMMAND"	XA_WM_COMMAND
"WM_HINTS"	XA_WM_HINTS
"WM_ICON_NAME"	XA_WM_ICON_NAME
"WM_ICON_SIZE"	XA_WM_ICON_SIZE
"WM_NAME"	XA_WM_NAME
"WM_NORMAL_HINTS"	XA_WM_NORMAL_HINTS
"WM_SIZE_HINTS"	XA_WM_SIZE_HINTS
"WM_TRANSIENT_FOR"	XA_WM_TRANSIENT_FOR
"WM_ZOOM_HINTS"	XA_WM_ZOOM_HINTS

Data-Type Atoms

The set of predefined data-type atoms is very useful, but incomplete, as we'll show in Chapter 20. These atoms are listed in Table 18.8.

Table 18.8   *X predefined atoms for data types.*

Text Name	Defined Macro in <X11/Xatom.h>
"ARC"	XA_ARC

continued

"ATOM"	XA_ATOM
"BITMAP"	XA_BITMAP
"CARDINAL"	XA_CARDINAL
"COLORMAP"	XA_COLORMAP
"CURSOR"	XA_CURSOR
"DRAWABLE"	XA_DRAWABLE
"FONT"	XA_FONT
"FULL_NAME"	XA_FULL_NAME
"INTEGER"	XA_INTEGER
"PIXMAP"	XA_PIXMAP
"POINT"	XA_POINT
"RECTANGLE"	XA_RECTANGLE
"STRING"	XA_STRING
"VISUALID"	XA_VISUALID
"WINDOW"	XA_WINDOW

Data-Exchange Atoms

The data-exchange atoms show a lot of wear. Not only is the essential CLIPBOARD missing, but you are no longer supposed to use the cut-buffer atoms, although the popular Andrew system still does.

The RESOURCE_MANAGER atom holds serverwide resource values. The PRIMARY and SECONDARY (along with the CLIPBOARD) are used in what X refers to as selections. Selections are really a form of active copy and paste—one of the most useful and productive features offered by X. We discuss selections in Chapter 20.

The predefined atoms for data exchange are listed in Table 18.9.

Table 18.9 *X predefined atoms for data exchange.*

Text Name	Defined Macro in <X11/Xatom.h>
"CUT_BUFFER0"	XA_CUT_BUFFER0
	continued

"CUT_BUFFER1"	XA_CUT_BUFFER1
"CUT_BUFFER2"	XA_CUT_BUFFER2
"CUT_BUFFER2"	XA_CUT_BUFFER3
"CUT_BUFFER3"	XA_CUT_BUFFER4
"CUT_BUFFER4"	XA_CUT_BUFFER5
"CUT_BUFFER5"	XA_CUT_BUFFER6
"CUT_BUFFER6"	XA_CUT_BUFFER7
"PRIMARY"	XA_PRIMARY
"RESOURCE_MANAGER"	XA_RESOURCE_MANAGER
"SECONDARY"	XA_SECONDARY

Standard Colormap Atoms

Chapter 15 delved into the mysteries of sharable (standard) colormaps. All these atoms are predefined in the X server and listed in Table 18.10.

Table 18.10   X predefined atoms for standard colormaps.

Text Name	Defined Macro in <X11/Xatom.h>
"RGB_COLOR_MAP"	XA_RGB_COLOR_MAP
"RGB_BEST_MAP"	XA_RGB_BEST_MAP
"RGB_BLUE_MAP"	XA_RGB_BLUE_MAP
"RGB_DEFAULT_MAP"	XA_RGB_DEFAULT_MAP
"RGB_GRAY_MAP"	XA_RGB_GRAY_MAP
"RGB_GREEN_MAP"	XA_RGB_GREEN_MAP
"RGB_RED_MAP"	XA_RGB_RED_MAP

Font-Information Atoms

The largest set of predefined atoms covers font information. You're not very likely to use these atoms directly in your code, although we'll list them in Table 18.11.

Table 18.11 *X predefined atoms for font information.*

Text Name	Defined Macro in <X11/Xatom.h>
"CAP_HEIGHT"	XA_CAP_HEIGHT
"COPYRIGHT"	XA_COPYRIGHT
"END_SPACE"	XA_END_SPACE
"FAMILY_NAME"	XA_FAMILY_NAME
"FONT_NAME"	XA_FONT_NAME
"ITALIC_ANGLE"	XA_ITALIC_ANGLE
"MAX_SPACE"	XA_MAX_SPACE
"MIN_SPACE"	XA_MIN_SPACE
"NORM_SPACE"	XA_NORM_SPACE
"NOTICE"	XA_NOTICE
"POINT_SIZE"	XA_POINT_SIZE
"QUAD_WIDTH"	XA_QUAD_WIDTH
"RESOLUTION"	XA_RESOLUTION
"STRIKEOUT_ASCENT"	XA_STRIKEOUT_ASCENT
"STRIKEOUT_DESCENT"	XA_STRIKEOUT_DESCENT
"SUBSCRIPT_X"	XA_SUBSCRIPT_X
"SUBSCRIPT_Y"	XA_SUBSCRIPT_Y
"SUPERSCRIPT_X"	XA_SUPERSCRIPT_X
"SUPERSCRIPT_Y"	XA_SUPERSCRIPT_Y
"UNDERLINE_POSITION"	XA_UNDERLINE_POSITION
"UNDERLINE_THICKNESS"	XA_UNDERLINE_THICKNESS
"WEIGHT"	XA_WEIGHT
"X_HEIGHT"	XA_X_HEIGHT

Now that we've covered atoms, the next step in our digression is to cover properties.

PROPERTIES

Properties are named, typed data, stored with a window in the X server. Any program with a window ID, a property name, and a data type can store data in a property. If two programs agree on the window, property, and data type, they can exchange data.

When exchanging data with window and session managers, the window ID comes from the top-level shell widgets. The property ID comes from a property name—a text string—and programs must agree on the name beforehand. The ICCCM provides a number of properties that you must agree to. Property names used by X are atoms, which you intern with XmInternAtom. The data type IDs are also atoms. The ICCCM provides a standard set of type ID atoms, such as STRING and INTEGER.

You write data to a property with XChangeProperty and read data with XGetWindowProperty.

Writing Data to Properties

You can change the data stored with a property on a window by calling XChangeProperty:

```
void XChangeProperty(Display* display,
    Window window,
    Atom property,
    Atom type,
    int format,  /* 8, 16 or 32 */
    int mode,
    unsigned char* data,
    int number_elements)
```

The *property* is the atom ID of the property to write to on the given *window*. The *mode* can be one of:

- PropModeAppend
- PropModePrepend
- PropModeReplace

To delete a property, you write out 0 bytes with a *mode* of PropModeReplace.

N O T E

The *type* is another atom and should identify the type of the data, such as STRING (the atoms interned for the text string "STRING").

The *format* tells XChangeProperty whether the data comes in 8-bit, 16-bit, or 32-bit items. You can store any data you want, but the X server just deals with it as an array of 8-, 16-, or 32-bit data elements. If you store a structure into a property, you must deal with issues like padding and byte alignment, although the X server handles byte-swapping issues.

The *number_elements* then tells how many of these data items are stored in the *data*. This is not necessarily the number of bytes held in *data*. That is, if the *format* is 32 (32 bits per item of data), the number of bytes will equal number_elements * 4.

When you write data to a property with XChangeProperty, the X server sends out a PropertyNotify event. If the window manager writes data to a known property on your application's top-level window, you can track PropertyNotify events on your window to know when to read the property data again.

Reading Data from Properties

To read data from a property on a window, call XGetWindowProperty:

```
int XGetWindowProperty(Display* display,
    Window window,
    Atom property,
    long long_offset,
    long long_length,
    Bool delete_flag,
    Atom request_type,
    Atom* actual_type,   /* RETURN */
    int* actual_format, /* RETURN, 8, 16 or 32 */
    unsigned long* number_items,  /* RETURN */
    unsigned long* bytes_after,   /* RETURN */
    unsigned char** data)  /* RETURN */
```

The *long_offset* is the offset in terms of 32-bit items. Normally, this is set to 0.

The *long_length* is how many 32-bit items to get. If you don't know the amount of data that was stored to the property, you can set the *long_length* to a magic value that signifies you want to read a good amount of data from the property. We use a magic value of 8192. In most cases, this allows us to read the entire property in one fell swoop. If not, you can use *bytes_after* to tell you how many bytes are left.

The act of reading a property may destroy the property data, if you wish. This is one reason why you usually want only one process to write to a property and one process to read from a property. If you set the *delete_flag* to True, the routine will delete the property after reading.

The *request_type* is an atom ID for the type of data you desire, such as WINDOW (XA_WINDOW) or STRING (XA_STRING). You can pass the constant AnyPropertyType if you don't care about the type.

XGetWindowProperty returns Success on success. If successful, XGetWindowProperty provides a lot of information about the property data it read in. This information includes:

- *actual_type*, the atom ID for the actual type that was stored with the property
- *actual_format*, the format for the data: 8, 16 or 32
- *number_items*, the number of 8-, 16-, or 32-bit items read
- *bytes_after*, the number of bytes remaining in the property after you read your data
- *data*, what you're really after: the data stored in the property

Don't consider any of these values valid if XGetWindowProperty doesn't return Success.

Use XFree to free the *data* when done.

WINDOW- AND SESSION-MANAGER PROPERTIES

Now we'll see why we made that digression into atoms and properties. In X, window and session managers should support a set of properties defined in the ICCCM.

These properties should be placed by your application on its top-level windows. The window or session manager may also write back properties on your windows. You should treat these properties, which we cover below, as read-only properties.

Table 18.12 lists the properties your application should set on its top-level windows.

Table 18.12 *Client-side window properties.*

Property	Purpose	ICCCM Section
WM_CLASS	Application name/class name	4.1.2.5
WM_CLIENT_MACHINE	Machine program is running on	5.1.1.2
WM_COLORMAP_WINDOWS	Windows that have special colormaps	4.1.2.8
WM_COMMAND	Command line to start program	5.1.1.1
WM_HINTS	Icon, input hint, etc.	4.1.2.4
WM_ICON_NAME	Icon name	4.1.2.2
WM_NAME	Window name	4.1.2.1
WM_NORMAL_HINTS	Size of window in normal state	4.1.2.3
WM_PROTOCOLS	Which wm protocols supported	4.1.2.7
WM_TRANSIENT_FOR	Which window a dialog works with	4.1.2.6

The ICCCM section listed comes from the ICCCM version 1.1, which coincided with Release 5. X11 Release 6 should dramatically expand the ICCCM, so some of the section numbers may change.

Luckily, Motif takes care of most of these properties for you. It's still helpful to know what the properties exist for, especially since you may need to read this information.

The WM_CLASS property holds two text strings: an instance (application) name, such as xterm, and a class-resource name, such as XTerm. You pass these values to XtAppInitialize.

The WM_CLIENT_MACHINE property should be the hostname of the machine (CPU) your application is running on—as seen from the machine the X server is running on. For example, if the application is running on machine *nicollet* but set up a connection to the X server at *nokomis:0.0* (on machine *nokomis*), then WM_CLIENT_MACHINE should be set to the string "nicollet", the name of the machine your application is running on.

WM_COLORMAP_WINDOWS holds a set of window IDs, using the atom for WINDOW as the type. Each window ID in this property is a window that has a private colormap. The window IDs are placed in order, and yes, you do need to end the list with your top-level shell's window, even if it uses the default colormap. You need to set this property only if you have some widgets, such as an XmDrawingArea, that use their own private colormaps. If you set the colormap on all shells (as we suggest in Chapter 15), then you won't have to bother with WM_COLORMAP_WINDOWS.

The WM_COMMAND property should contain the command necessary to start the application. That is (at least on UNIX-based systems), the command-line parameters, usually argv and argc (argv contains the parameters—a list of strings—and argc the number of parameters). Each application should place a WM_COMMAND property on one (and only one) top-level window. You may place a zero-length WM_COMMAND property on other top-level windows, but only one with a length greater than zero for your application.

The WM_HINTS property contains general window and icon information for the window manager. This is set from the following resources:

- ■ input
- ■ initialState
- ■ iconPixmap
- ■ iconWindow
- ■ iconX
- ■ iconY
- ■ iconMask
- ■ windowGroup

You can see how closely the window manager resources match the properties. The term *hints* comes from the fact that all your requests of the window manager are mere hints that the window manager may decline to heed.

As you probably guessed, the WM_ICON_NAME property identifies the icon name. You can set the iconName resource in your programs.

WM_NAME holds the window's name. Window managers should set this into your window's titlebar. You can set this with the title resource.

The WM_NORMAL_HINTS contains sizing hints for your application's window in its normal size, as opposed to the now-defunct zoomed size.

This property is set from the resources described above in the section on "Controlling Window Sizes," which include maxHeight and minWidth.

The WM_PROTOCOLS property holds a series of atoms. Each atom in WM_PROTOCOLS represents an application-to-window manager protocol that your application agrees to take part in. If you set one of these atoms, described in the section below on "Window-Manager Protocols," your application should faithfully maintain its side of the bargain. Usually you won't need much convincing, as the most common protocol, WM_DELETE_WINDOW, results in the destruction of your windows unless you follow the protocol.

WM_TRANSIENT_FOR represents the transientFor resource.

Properties Set By the Window Manager

The window manager sets a number of properties that you can read to gain information about top-level application windows. These properties include WM_STATE, which mirrors the initialState resource, and WM_ICON_SIZE, which contains a list of allowable icon sizes (see XGetIconSizes in the X library).

WINDOW-MANAGER PROTOCOLS

The ICCCM protocols all work in basically the same way. First, your application tells the window manager which protocols are supported. When the window manager wants to notify your application about the use of the protocols, i.e., when you should be doing something special, the window manager will send your application a ClientMessage event. When your application receives a ClientMessage event, your application is free to do its stuff. You can also set up a Motif callback instead of dealing with the low-level ClientMessage event.

Each atom in the WM_PROTOCOLS property represents an application-to-window manager protocol that your application agrees to take part in. If your application wants to participate in one of these protocols, it must tell the window manager by setting the proper atom into the WM_PROTOCOLS property or by calling XmAddWMProtocols:

```
#include <Xm/MwmUtil.h>

void XmAddWMProtocols(Widget shell,
```

```
Atom* protocols,
Cardinal number_protocols)
```

Use `XmAddWMProtocols` to add a number of protocol atoms to the `WM_PROTOCOLS` property and set up Motif to track events for this protocol. (There's no single-protocol version of `XmAddWMProtocol`.)

These protocols (and atoms) include:

■ `WM_DELETE_WINDOW`

■ `WM_SAVE_YOURSELF`

■ `WM_TAKE_FOCUS`

■ `_MOTIF_WM_MESSAGES`

`_MOTIF_WM_MESSAGES` is specific to Motif and is not part of the ICCCM rules. Even so, you may want to participate in this protocol (see "Extending the Window Manager Menu," below). Note that vendor-specific atoms should start with an underscore.

The `WM_DELETE_WINDOW` atom specifies that your application should be told when the user asks to delete your top-level window. If your application does not support `WM_DELETE_WINDOW`, the window manager may simply kill your window. For dialogs, the proper response to `WM_DELETE_WINDOW` is to unmanage the dialog. For the main application window, you should quit the application.

`WM_SAVE_YOURSELF` is closely related to X session managers. If your application supports `WM_SAVE_YOURSELF`, you will get a `ClientMessage` event when the window manager (or session manager) wants your application to save its "state"—whatever "state" is.

When your application receives a `WM_SAVE_YOURSELF` message, it should update the `WM_COMMAND` property on the given window to reflect the current state of the application so that it can be restarted. (This should imply that you may very well get this event just before the session manager shuts your application down.) That is, you should write out the command-line parameters required to restart the application to its current state. This is often used by session managers to store the command line to restart X applications where they left off. Do this by appending zero (no change) or more bytes to the `WM_COMMAND` property. You can write out the `WM_COMMAND` property by calling `XSetCommand`:

```
void XSetCommand(Display* display,
    Window window,
    char** argv,
    int argc)
```

If you pass 0 for *argc*, then XSetCommmand will append 0 bytes to the WM_COMMAND property on the given window.

The key, though, is passing the proper command-line parameters to restart your application in its current state. The state includes the current file loaded, the window's size and location, fonts, colors, and a host of other variables. Determining the proper state is usually not a trivial problem.

If the state hasn't changed, then just append zero bytes to the WM_COMMAND property. Your application is supposed to write to this property—even with zero bytes of additional data—because that signals your application has saved its state. (This generates a PropertyNotify event and also satisfies any session manager.)

After updating WM_COMMAND, your application's window may be terminated by *mwm* or *olwm*. Set this atom if your application supports this and will faithfully update WM_COMMAND.

Set the WM_TAKE_FOCUS atom in WM_PROTOCOLS if your application wants to mess with the keyboard focus in special ways, beyond the input hint in WM_HINTS. Motif already sets this protocol and takes care of the messy details of keyboard traversal for you. Normally, you don't want to mess with this protocol in your code.

XmAddWMProtocols acts as a macro over the function XmAddProtocols:

```
#include <Xm/MwmUtil.h>

void XmAddProtocols(Widget shell,
    Atom property,
    Atom* protocols,
    Cardinal number_protocols)
```

In this case, XmAddWMProtocols calls XmAddProtocols with a *property* of WM_PROTOCOLS.

You can remove protocols with XmRemoveWMProtocols and XmRemoveProtocols:

```
#include <Xm/MwmUtil.h>

void XmRemoveWMProtocols(Widget shell,
```

```
            Atom*    protocols,
            Cardinal number_protocols)

    void XmRemoveProtocols(Widget shell,
            Atom     property,
            Atom*    protocols,
            Cardinal number_protocols)
```

XmRemoveWMProtocols is a macro that calls XmRemoveProtocols with a *property* of WM_PROTOCOLS. You generally don't have occasion to remove any protocols, as the goal is to have these working during your application's entire session.

Receiving Messages for Window-Manager Protocols

After you set the proper protocols with XmAddWMProtocols, a window-manager protocol kicks in only when your application receives a special ClientMessage event. This event arrives if the window or session manager wants to initiate the protocol, so your code may never receive any ClientMessage events. Don't worry. If your program needs the message, the message will arrive.

ClientMessage events carry up to 20 bytes of data:

```
typedef struct {
int            type;    /* ClientMessage */
unsigned long  serial;
Bool           send_event;
Display*       display;
Window         window;
Atom           message_type; /* WM_PROTOCOLS */
int            format;
union {
    char  b[20];
    short s[10];
    long  l[5];  /* set to WM_DELETE_WINDOW, etc. */
    } data;
} XClientMessageEvent;
```

ClientMessage events are used in an arbitrary fashion for applications (don't forget that the window manager is really just another application) to communicate with each other. ClientMessage events can be used for any purpose, but with WM_PROTOCOLS there is a special format so you can identify these events from all other ClientMessage events.

There needs to be a way to distinguish the ClientMessage sent by the window manager indicating a WM_DELETE_WINDOW request from all other kinds of ClientMessage events.

If the *message_type* is the atom WM_PROTOCOLS, then you have received one of these window-manager protocol messages. In this case, the first data element (4 bytes) will contain an atom. That is, check the first long data element, data.l[0] . If that atom is WM_DELETE_WINDOW, then your application has just been asked to delete its window. The same principle applies for WM_TAKE_FOCUS, WM_SAVE_YOURSELF, and other window-manager protocols. The *format* should also be 32, for 32-bit data items (atoms are 32-bit values).

If all these conditions are met, then the user (through the intercession of the window manager) has asked to delete one of your application windows, with the proper window ID in the *window* field.

Dealing with ClientMessage events is usually handled by the low-level code called from XtAppMainLoop. If you want, you can set up a Motif callback function when one of these ClientMessage events arrives. This way, your application is spared the low-level details. It's still useful to know what's going on under the hood, though.

Protocol Callbacks

You can set up a callback to trap ClientMessage events related to one of the WM_PROTOCOLS protocols with XmAddWMProtocolCallback:

```
#include <Xm/MwmUtil.h>

void XmAddWMProtocolCallback(Widget shell,
        Atom protocol_atom,
        XtCallbackProc callback,
        XtPointer client_data)
```

You pass a *protocol_atom* that identifies the protocol you're interested in, such as WM_DELETE_WINDOW. You also need to provide a *callback* function and any *client_data*, if desired.

XmAddWMProtocolCallback is a macro that calls XmAddProtocolCallback and passes a property of WM_PROTOCOLS:

```
#include <Xm/MwmUtil.h>

void XmAddProtocolCallback(Widget shell,
        Atom property,
        Atom protocol_atom,
        XtCallbackProc callback,
        XtPointer client_data)
```

In the next sections, we describe how to put together all these diverse protocols and callbacks to actually trap the WM_DELETE_WINDOW messages, which usually indicate that the user has asked to close the window in question.

Handling WM_DELETE_WINDOW Messages

Some window managers may have a menu choice to delete a window. This can be nasty, since some window managers may just up and delete your application's top-level window out from under your program, generating lots of X protocol errors and terminating your program. No fun!

To confuse the issue further, different window managers use wildly different terminology to represent the same functions, as listed in Table 18.13.

Table 18.13 *Window-manager terminology.*

mwm	olwm	twm
Close	Quit	Delete
Minimize	Close	Iconify

To make this approach a bit nicer, the ICCCM has the WM_DELETE_WINDOW protocol. If your application supports this protocol, the window manager shouldn't up and delete your window. Instead, the window manager should ask nicely for your application to delete its own window. This should work with *mwm*, *olwm*, *twm*, and all other ICCCM-conforming window managers.

When the WM_DELETE_WINDOW message arrives, your application should save any work, perhaps prompting the user to save a file and then close down the window. If your application has only one top-level window, this probably means shutting down the whole program.

You may ask the user to confirm the delete-window choice. The user may cancel this. Don't delete the window if the user cancels the delete-window operation, obviously. WM_DELETE_WINDOW gives your application a little foreknowledge of impending doom.

There are five steps you need to go through in order to trap and handle WM_DELETE_WINDOW messages:

1. Set the deleteResponse on the top-level shell widget.
2. Intern the WM_DELETE_WINDOW atom with XmInternAtom.
3. Add the WM_DELETE_WINDOW protocol.
4. Set up a callback for the protocol.
5. Handle the event in the callback.

The deleteResponse resources are listed in Table 18.14.

Table 18.14 *The deleteResponse resource values.*

Value	Meaning
XmDESTROY	Destroy widget (main window)
XmUNMAP	Unmap widget (dialogs)
XmDO_NOTHING	Do nothing

For top-level shell widgets, set the deleteResponse resource to XmDO_NOTHING. You can set this when calling XtAppInitialize or XtVaAppInitialize:

```
/* ... */

/* Initialize toolkit. */
parent = XtVaAppInitialize(&app_context,
        "Ppm",
        (XrmOptionDescList) NULL,
        0,
        &argc, argv,
        (String*) NULL,
        XmNallowResize, True,
        XmNmappedWhenManaged, False,
        XmNdeleteResponse, XmDO_NOTHING,
        NULL);

/* ... */
```

For dialogs, set the deleteResponse resource to XmUNMAP, unless you want to unmap the dialog manually by calling XtUnmanageChild. In this case, use XmDO_NOTHING. This is useful if you need to perform some processing before unmanaging the dialog.

The next step is to intern the WM_DELETE_WINDOW atom with XmInternAtom, which we do in a special utility function, SetWMProtocols, to set the WM_DELETE_WINDOW protocol:

```
/* Global. */
Atom    wm_delete_window = (Atom) None;

    /* Set up WM_DELETE_WINDOW protocol. */
void SetWMProtocols(Widget shell,
    XtCallbackProc callback,
    XtPointer client_data)

{   /* SetWMProtocols */

    /* Intern atom if necessary. */
    if (wm_delete_window == (Atom) None) {
        wm_delete_window =
            XmInternAtom(XtDisplay(shell),
                "WM_DELETE_WINDOW",
                    False);
    }

    /* ... */
}   /* SetWMProtocols */
```

After we intern an atom for WM_DELETE_WINDOW, we need to add the WM_DELETE_WINDOW protocol with XmAddWMProtocols:

```
Atom    wm_delete_window;
Widget  shell;

XmAddWMProtocols(shell,
    &wm_delete_window,
    1);  /* One protocol. */
```

With the protocol added, we set up a callback for the protocol with XmAddWMProtocolCallback:

```
Atom    wm_delete_window = (Atom) None;

    /* Set up WM_DELETE_WINDOW protocol. */
void SetWMProtocols(Widget shell,
    XtCallbackProc callback,
    XtPointer client_data)

{   /* SetWMProtocols */

    /* ... */

    /* Set up protocol callback. */
    XmAddWMProtocolCallback(shell,
        wm_delete_window,
        callback,
```

```
        client_data);

}    /* SetWMProtocols */
```

We put all the `WM_DELETE_WINDOW` code presented so far into the
`SetWMProtocols` utility function:

```
/* protocol.c */
#include <Xm/Xm.h>
#include <Xm/AtomMgr.h>
#include <Xm/Protocols.h>

/* Global Atom. */
Atom    wm_delete_window = (Atom) None;

    /* Set up WM_DELETE_WINDOW protocol. */
void SetWMProtocols(Widget shell,
    XtCallbackProc callback,
    XtPointer client_data)

{    /* SetWMProtocols */

    /* Intern atom if necessary. */
    if (wm_delete_window == (Atom) None) {
        wm_delete_window =
            XmInternAtom(XtDisplay(shell),
                "WM_DELETE_WINDOW",
                False);
    }

    /* Check if interned. */
    if (wm_delete_window == (Atom) None) {
        return;
    }

    /* Set up protocol. */
    XmAddWMProtocols(shell,
        &wm_delete_window,
        1);  /* One protocol. */

    /* Set up protocol callback. */
    XmAddWMProtocolCallback(shell,
        wm_delete_window,
        callback,
        client_data);

}    /* SetWMProtocols */

/* end of file protocol.c */
```

With the protocol and callback function set up, we wait until the callback
gets called. This, of course, may never happen. The protocol gets activated
only on demand.

When your application receives the `WM_DELETE_WINDOW` request, it needs to decide how to proceed. Assume the user asked for the window to be deleted. Your program can pop up a dialog and ask the user to confirm or save any changes made to a document, but if the user wants to go ahead, then your program should remove the offending window.

In our example program at the end of this chapter, we set up a callback to exit the program on a `WM_DELETE_WINDOW` message.

WORKING WITH THE MOTIF WINDOW MANAGER

There are a number features specific to the Motif window manager that you may want to take advantage of. Since most Motif programs run under *mwm*, you usually don't have to worry much about window managers. Even so, your code should be able to deal with any ICCCM-compliant window manager. Users balk at running software that requires a certain window manager, especially if that window manager is not the default manager for the system. For example, on a Silicon Graphics workstation, your code should work with *4Dwm*, an *mwm* variant. We've seen some packages that require *mwm*, even though the two window managers are so close it's ridiculous. The fact of the matter is that *4Dwm* is the default window manager on Silicon Graphics workstations, for better or worse, and your programs should be able to live with that fact.

Is the Motif Window Manager Running?

The Motif window manager leaves a distinctive trail, which you can detect from inside your program. To check if *mwm* is the window manager, you can call `XmIsMotifWMRunning`:

```
Boolean XmIsMotifWMRunning(Widget shell)
```

`XmIsMotifWMRunning` returns `True` if it thinks *mwm* is running. This isn't that hard to spoof (see below). `XmIsMotifWMRunning` won't tell the difference between *mwm* and close variants. If you run under *vuewm* or *4Dwm*, `XmIsMotifWMRunning` will return `True` for both.

The Motif window manager places the `_MOTIF_WM_INFO` property on the root window to signify that *mwm* is running. The

`XmIsMotifWmRunning` function checks for this property. (You could write out a property like this to deceive the function.)

There are two 32-bit numbers in this property: a flags value of some bogus number and a window ID, which holds the ID of a window created by *mwm*.

The flags value should hold one of the flags listed in Table 18.15, but we find it often holds 0 instead, so don't depend on this number.

Table 18.15   *_MOTIF_WM_INFO flags.*

Flag	Value	Meaning
MWM_INFO_STARTUP_STANDARD	1	Standard start-up
MWM_INFO_STARTUP_CUSTOM	2	Customized start-up

Hewlett-Packard's *vuewm*, an *mwm* variant, indicates that it has a custom start-up by using the `MWM_INFO_STARTUP_CUSTOM` flag. Other *mwm* variants, though, just place 0 for the flags. These flags are defined in the include file `<Xm/MwmUtil.h>`.

Controlling the Window-Manager Menu

Most window managers under X provide some form of menu for all top-level windows—that is, for all applications. The Motif window manager, for example, provides a menu that allows users to move, size, iconify (called minimize in Motif lingo), and close (destroy) a window. This menu sits under the dash-shaped icon at the upper left corner of the window frame. The choices of this menu are listed in Table 18.16.

Table 18.16 *The default mwm window menu.*

Choice	Mnemonic	Accelerator
Restore	**R**	**Alt+F5**
Move	**M**	**Alt+F7**

continued

Size	S	Alt+F8
Minimize	n	Alt+F9
Maximize	x	Alt+F10
Lower	L	Alt+F3
Close	C	Alt+F4

If your program is running under *mwm*, you can control the functions listed in this window menu by setting the mwmFunctions resource. The mwmFunctions resource acts much like the mwmDecorations resource described above in the section on "Window Decorations." The mwmFunctions resource holds a set of bit flags, where each flag represents an *mwm* function you want to enable. If MWM_FUNC_ALL is set, then the bit flags indicate functions to *remove*, not functions to *allow*.

If you want to disable *mwm* functions, you need to include the MWM_FUNC_ALL flag.

The full set of flags are listed in Table 18.17.

Table 18.17   *Mwm functions.*

Bit Flag	Meaning
MWM_FUNC_ALL	Turn off listed functions
MWM_FUNC_CLOSE	Allow close
MWM_FUNC_MAXIMIZE	Allow maximize (zoom)
MWM_FUNC_MINIMIZE	Allow minimize (iconify)
MWM_FUNC_MOVE	Allow move
MWM_FUNC_RESIZE	Allow resize

These flags are defined in the include file <Xm/MwmUtil.h>.

Extending the Window-Manager Menu

In addition to controlling the predefined choices in the *mwm* window menu, you can also add new choices to this menu. The Motif window manager supports an f.send_msg function whereby any *mwm* menu choice can send a numeric "message" to an application. This forms a rather primitive means to send specialized (numeric) commands to an application. Your code can control the text of the menu choice and the number sent for the choice.

The *mwm*-specific _MOTIF_WM_MESSAGES protocol sets this up. _MOTIF_WM_MESSAGES acts a lot like the WM_DELETE_WINDOW protocol. Both are written to the WM_PROTOCOLS property on your application top-level windows.

You can set this up by using XmAddWMProtocols:

```
#include <Xm/MwmUtil.h>

Atom        protocol;
Widget      widget;

protocol = XmInternAtom(XtDisplay(widget),
            _XA_MWM_MESSAGES, False);

XmAddWMProtocols(widget, &protocol, 1);
```

The defined constant _XA_MWM_MESSAGES is the same as _XA_MOTIF_WM_MESSAGES, which is the string "_MOTIF_WM_MESSAGES". After setting up the protocol, you need to set up the menu choices and then add a callback for the new protocol.

The menu choices follow a rigid syntax:

```
Menu-choice  [mnemonic] [accelerator] mwm-function \n
```

The menu choice can be any text, like Choice1. This choice should *not* have any spaces in it. The mnemonic begins with an underscore, such as _h, to make the letter h in "Choice1" act as the mnemonic. Be careful not to conflict with the existing *mwm* window-menu choices listed in Table 18.16.

A valid menu choice follows:

```
Choice2 _h Alt<Key>F2 f.send_msg 1234 \n
```

This sets up a lowercase letter h as the mnemonic for Choice2 (note that the h is in the word Choice2), **Alt+F2** as the accelerator, and the *mwm* functions as f.send_msg. (You could also set up other *mwm* functions, such as f.beep, f.refresh, and f.quit_mwm. See your *mwm* documentation for a list of available functions. Only the f.send_msg function, though, sends a message to our application.) As in most X resources, errors are silently ignored. If you set up the same mnemonic or accelerator as another choice, you lose.

The f.send_msg function is what tells *mwm* to send a numeric message to our application. The message to be sent in our example is the number 1234.

The menu choice ends with a newline character, so you can add two or more window menu choices at the same time (end each choice with a newline character). To set up this string as a menu choice on the *mwm* menu, write the string to the mwmMenu resource on the top-level shell widget:

```
Widget    widget;

XtVaSetValues(widget,
    XmNmwmMenu,
       "Choice2 _h Alt<Key>F2 f.send_msg 1234\n",
    NULL);
```

This sets up a menu choice. It doesn't actually cause *mwm* to send a message. In addition, unless you set up the proper protocol, this menu choice will appear grayed out (insensitive to user input), and you won't be able to choose it from the menu.

To set up the protocol and add a callback function, we use XmInternAtom to intern both the _MOTIF_WM_MESSAGES atom and an atom for our messages, such as "_MY_MSG1". You then need to set up a protocol callback for WM_PROTOCOLS, using XmAddProtocolCallback.

There's a weird quirk here, however. We have to build up the number to send. Why? Because 1234 isn't a valid atom, and we have no way to specify the number used by an atom. So, we intern the string "_MY_MSG1" to get an atom, which is a number. We then ask *mwm* to send *this* number with our new menu choice. We build up the string for the mwmMenu resource with the following:

```
Atom      message1;
Display*  display;
char      string[256];

message1 = XmInternAtom(display,
           "_MY_MSG1", False);

sprintf(string,
    Choice2 _h Alt<Key>F2 f.send_msg %d\n",
    message1);
```

That's a lot of coding weirdness just to extend the *mwm* window menu. The code makes much more sense when put together, as we do in the function below, which adds two new menu choices to the *mwm* menu:

```
    /* Sets up extra mwm menu choices. */
void SetUpMwmMenu(Widget shell)

{   /* SetUpMwmMenu */
    Display*    display;
    Atom        motif_wm_messages;
    Atom        message1, message2;
    char        menu_items[1024];

    display = XtDisplay(shell);

    motif_wm_messages = XmInternAtom(display,
        _XA_MWM_MESSAGES, /* "_MOTIF_WM_MESSAGES" */
        False);

    message1 = XmInternAtom(display,
        "_MY_MSG1", False);

    message2 = XmInternAtom(display,
        "_MY_MSG2", False);

    /* Add mwm protocol. */
    XmAddWMProtocols(shell,
        &motif_wm_messages, /* Protocol */
        1);                 /* One protocol */

    /*
     * Create mwmMenu resource value. Each
     * menu choice ends with \n.
     */
    sprintf(menu_items,
        "%s %d\n %s %d\n",
        "Choice1 _h Alt<Key>F2 f.send_msg",
        message1,
        "Choice2 _e Ctrl<Key>F6 f.send_msg",
        message2);

    /* Insert menu item. */
    XtVaSetValues(shell,
        XmNmwmMenu, menu_items,
        NULL);

    /* Add protocol callbacks. */
    XmAddProtocolCallback(shell,
        motif_wm_messages, /* Property */
        message1,          /* Protocol */
        (XtCallbackProc) mwmMenuCB,
        (XtPointer) message1); /* client_data */

    XmAddProtocolCallback(shell,
```

```
            motif_wm_messages,    /* Property */
            message2,             /* Protocol */
            (XtCallbackProc) mwmMenuCB,
            (XtPointer) message2);  /* client_data */

    }    /* SetUpMwmMenu */
```

After calling this function, we'll see the default menu expanded in the manner shown in Figure 18.1.

Figure 18.1   *An extended mwm window menu.*

WORKING WITH OPEN LOOK AND OPENWINDOWS

The Open Look window manager, *olwm*, is common on Sun Microsystems workstations, as well as some versions of UNIX System V Release 4. Sun released the sources for *olwm* as part of the X contributed sources, so many free versions of UNIX, such as Linux and 386BSD, also make extensive use of *olwm*.

The key points of *olwm* include:

■ *Olwm* uses an entirely different set of window-manager conventions for controlling the decorations placed on your windows.

- In earlier versions of *olwm*, dialog windows do not get a titlebar at all. This feature appears in OpenWindows 2.0. The more common OpenWindows 3.0 and higher does support titlebars, by default, for dialogs.

- *Olwm* supports pushpins, which act much like Motif's tear-off menus. Pushpins work with dialogs and menus.

Open Look Window-Manager Properties in Depth

The Open Look window manager uses a completely different set of properties for controlling the decorations it places on your application's top-level windows. You can get around this problem with a little work, though. Both *mwm* and *olwm* use window properties to control the decorations, such as titlebars and iconified buttons the window manager should place on your application's windows. In true political fashion, both *olwm* and *mwm* use completely different mechanisms, instead of working toward some common standard. Luckily, with the COSE efforts, vendors are standardizing on one window manager, so these small battles shouldn't be large factors in the future.

To change the decorations for a window under *olwm*, we set the _OL_WIN_ATTR (window attributes) property. (*Olwm* properties all begin with an underscore, as do Motif-specific properties.)

This property, also of type _OL_WIN_ATTR, contains five 32-bit numbers: a flags field (which tells what of the other fields are filled in), a window-type field (which we're going to use), a menu-information field, a pushpin-state field, and a limited menu field. The flags field is a bitwise OR of the values listed in Table 18.18.

Table 18.18   _OL_WIN_ATTR: Olwm window attribute flags.

Value	Meaning
0x0001	Window-type information field is filled in
0x0002	Window-menu field
0x0004	Pushpin-state field
0x0008	Limited menu field

To change the window's decorations, we use a flags value of 0x0001, fill in the window-type field, and place zeros in the other fields. The window-type field tells *olwm* what type of window we have, but the choices, unfortunately, don't make a lot of sense. The window-type field can contain one of the atoms listed in Table 18.19.

Table 18.19   Olwm window types.

Atom	Meaning
_OL_WT_BASE	Base window
_OL_WT_CMD	Command window
_OL_WT_HELP	Help window
_OL_WT_NOTICE	Notice window
_OL_WT_OTHER	No default *olwm* decorations

The distinctions between these window types don't make a lot of sense. In most cases, we simply use the type of _OL_WT_OTHER. This tells *olwm* that we have an odd window and that by default *olwm* should place no decorations on our window. (We'll end up with decorations, but we must tell *olwm* all the decorations we want. See below.)

What happens when run under another window manager, such as *mwm*? Nothing. The Motif window manager simply doesn't look for *olwm*-specific window properties. You can set these properties in all your applications all the time. Or you can check for *mwm* and, if *mwm* isn't running, set these *olwm* properties.

You must set these properties before your windows are mapped. Many versions of *olwm* read these properties before mapping the window. If you change the properties while the window is visible, *olwm* may very well ignore your changes.

N O T E

Once we tell *olwm* that our window should have no default decorations using the _OL_WIN_ATTR property, above, we need to tell *olwm* that we do, indeed, want some window decorations, such as a titlebar.

Setting Olwm Decorations

The _OL_DECOR_ADD property tells *olwm* what decorations we want to add to our window. This property contains a list of atom IDs, each of which refers to a particular decoration. They are listed in Table 18.20.

Table 18.20 *Flags for adding or deleting olwm decorations.*

Atom	Meaning
_OL_DECOR_CLOSE	**Close** (iconify) button
_OL_DECOR_HEADER	Titlebar
_OL_DECOR_PIN	Pushpin
_OL_DECOR_RESIZE	Resize handles

Some of these decorations don't make sense without the others. For example, the _OL_DECOR_CLOSE requires the _OL_DECOR_HEADER. If you set _OL_DECOR_CLOSE without _OL_DECOR_HEADER, you're asking for trouble.

The simple method of merely setting the _OL_DECOR_ADD property with an atom of _OL_DECOR_HEADER does *not* give a Motif dialog a titlebar—at least under OpenWindows 2.0. (OpenWindows 3.0 and newer versions fix this problem.) For these older systems, we still have to set the _OL_WIN_ATTR property and tell *olwm* that we have a window type of _OL_WT_OTHER. If all your users have upgraded to the latest version of OpenWindows (3.2 as of this writing), this won't be a problem.

To set up the _OL_DECOR_ADD property, we need to intern atoms for "_OL_DECOR_ADD" and any decorations we choose to add, such as _OL_DECOR_HEADER. Then, we use XChangeProperty to set atoms into the _OL_DECOR_ADD property:

```
#include <X11/Xatom.h>  /* for XA_ATOM */

Display* display;
```

```
Window     window;
Atom       ol_decor_add;    /* "_OL_DECOR_ADD" */
Atom       ol_decor_header; /* "_OL_DECOR_HEADER" */
Atom       ol_decor_close;  /* "_OL_DECOR_CLOSE" */
Atom       atom_array[2];

/* Intern atoms... */

atom_array[0] = ol_decor_header;
atom_array[1] = ol_decor_close;

XChangeProperty(display,
    window,
    ol_decor_add, /* property. */
    XA_ATOM,      /* type. */
    32,           /* 32-bit data elements. */
    PropModeReplace,
    atom_array,
    2);           /* Two atoms. */
```

This is how you can deal with the problem of dialogs without titlebars.

Deleting Decorations

In addition to adding decorations, you can delete decorations. The _OL_DECOR_DEL property on application top-level windows tells *olwm* to delete or remove decorations to your window, beyond the decorations normally set up—acting the opposite of _OL_DECOR_ADD. _OL_DECOR_DEL supports the same atoms as shown in Table 18.20.

Fleshing Out the _OL_WIN_ATTR Property

The _OL_WIN_ATTR property on application top-level windows allows you to customize how *olwm* treats your window. Inside the property, you should set five 32-bit numbers, in order:

- ■ flags
- ■ window type
- ■ window-manager menu information
- ■ pushpin-state information
- ■ limited menu information

We covered the flags and window-type values above, under "Open Look Window Manager Properties in Depth."

Older versions of olwm, especially the version on the X11 Release 4 tapes, will not support all these flags and may in fact interpret the flags differently.

Menu Information

The menu-information value can hold a single atom that indicates what type of menu to provide for the window. Unlike *mwm*, which allows you to individually disable choices or add new choices, *olwm* is more restrictive. You can specify that you want one of two menus, or none at all, as listed in Table 18.21.

***Table 18.2**1* *_OL_WIN_ATTR menu-information atoms.*

Atom	Meaning
_OL_MENU_FULL	Full, standard window manager menu
_OL_MENU_LIMITED	Limited window manager menu
_OL_MENU_NONE	No window manager menu

This is not supported in older versions of *olwm*, such as the version on the X11 Release 4 tapes.

The traditional menus have the choices listed in Table 18.22.

Table 18.22 *The two menus.*

Full Menu	Limited Menu
Close	Dismiss or Cancel
Full Size	Back
Properties	Refresh
Back	Owner?
Refresh	
Quit	

See below to determine whether the limited menu has a **Dismiss** or **Cancel** choice.

Pushpin State

The pushpin-state field in the _OL_WIN_ATTR property sets the current value of the pushpin to out (0, the default) or pushed in (1). Normally this isn't used.

Limited Menu Dismiss/Cancel Option

This field in the _OL_WIN_ATTR property sets whether the limited menu has a **Dismiss** (0, the default) or a **Cancel** (1) choice.

Pushpins

One of the most striking features offered by *olwm* is a pushpin you can add to temporary windows like menus or dialogs. The closest Motif comes to push-pins are tear-off menus, which, of course, work only for menus, not dialogs.

With a pushpin, you can pin a dialog or menu to the screen. The window stays put, allowing you to continue and make choices in the window.

You can enable a pushpin by adding the _OL_DECOR_PIN atom to the _OL_DECOR_ADD property.

Tracking Pushpin State

After a pushpin is set up, *olwm* will write the current state of the pushpin to a property on your top-level window. If the pushpin state changes (pushed in or pulled out), *olwm* updates this property, the _OL_PIN_STATE property. Use this property to get information on the pushpin state. Do not write to this property—write to _OL_WIN_ATTR with its pin-state field.

_OL_PIN_STATE is a 32-bit integer set to 0 if the pushpin is out and 1 if the pushpin is pushed in.

To track the pushpin state, then, we need to call XtAddEventHandler with an event mask of PropertyChangeMask to track PropertyNotify events on our top-level window (the window with the pushpin). The fol-lowing function tracks the pushpin status when a PropertyNotify event arrives:

```
int GetPushpinState(Widget widget,
    XPropertyEvent* event)
```

```
{   /* GetPushpinState */
    int             status;
    Atom            actual_type;
    int             actual_format;
    int*            data;
    unsigned long   number_items;
    unsigned long   bytes_after;

    if ((event->state == PropertyNewValue) &&
        (event->atom == ol_pin_state)) {
        status = XGetWindowProperty(XtDisplay(widget),
                XtWindow(widget),
                ol_pin_state,
                0,      /* offset */
                1,      /* number items */
                False, /* don't delete */
                XA_INTEGER,
                &actual_type,
                &actual_format,
                &number_items,
                &bytes_after,
                (unsigned char**) &data);

        if (status == Success) {
            if (*data == 1) {
                return True;  /* pin is in. */
            } else {
                return False; /* pin is out. */
            }

            /* Free memory when done. */
            XFree((char*) data);
        }

    }

    /* If we get to here, it was not a pushpin event. */
    return -999;

}   /* GetPushpinState */
```

We again use some global atom values. Why? It is too expensive to intern atoms all the time, so we typically intern all the atoms we need when the application starts up.

Setting Up Pushpins

Putting this all together, the following code adds a pushpin to a top-level widget's window and sets up a callback routine to track the pushpin status:

```
/* Global atoms. */
Atom    ol_pin_state;
```

```
Atom    ol_decor_pin;
Atom    ol_decor_add;

    /* Sets up a pushpin. */
void SetOlwmPushpin(Widget widget,
    XtEventHandler callback,
    XtPointer client_data)

{   /* SetOlwmPushpin */

    /* Set up pin state for later queries. */
    ol_pin_state = XmInternAtom(XtDisplay(widget),
            "_OL_PIN_STATE", False);

    ol_decor_pin = XmInternAtom(XtDisplay(widget),
            "_OL_DECOR_PIN", False);

    ol_decor_add = XmInternAtom(XtDisplay(widget),
            "_OL_DECOR_ADD", False);

    /* Check on interning status. */
    if (ol_decor_pin == (Atom) None) {
        return;
    }

    /* Add this atom to the decorations. */
    XChangeProperty(XtDisplay(widget),
        XtWindow(widget),
        ol_decor_add,
        XA_ATOM,
        32, /* format */
        PropModeAppend, /* NOTE: append */
        (unsigned char*) &ol_decor_pin,
        1);

    /* Add event handler for property events. */
    XtAddEventHandler(widget,
        PropertyChangeMask,
        False,
        callback,
        client_data);

}   /* SetOlwmPushpin */
```

We pass a mode of PropModeAppend to XChangeProperty, so that we append data to the _OL_DECOR_ADD property. This is so we don't wipe out any other changes to the _OL_DECOR_ADD property.

Program Code for Working With Olwm

We provide a number of utility functions for working with *olwm* below: SetOlwmProperties allows us to control the window decorations placed on a window. `SetOlwmPushpin` sets up a pushpin, and `GetPushpinState` helps determine if a `PropertyNotify` event resulted in a change to the pushpin.

The code follows:

```
/* olwm.c */
#include  <Xm/Xm.h>
#include  <Xm/AtomMgr.h>
#include  <Xm/MwmUtil.h>      /* Window decorations, etc. */
#include  <X11/Xatom.h>

/* Global Atoms. */
Atom ol_win_attr     = (Atom) None; /* "_OL_WIN_ATTR" */
Atom ol_wt_other     = (Atom) None; /* "_OL_WT_OTHER" */
Atom ol_menu_none    = (Atom) None; /* "_OL_MENU_NONE" */
Atom ol_menu_full    = (Atom) None; /* "_OL_MENU_FULL" */
Atom ol_decor_add    = (Atom) None; /* "_OL_DECOR_ADD" */
Atom ol_decor_del    = (Atom) None; /* "_OL_DECOR_DEL" */
Atom ol_decor_close  = (Atom) None; /* "_OL_DECOR_CLOSE" */
Atom ol_decor_header = (Atom) None; /* "_OL_DECOR_HEADER" */
Atom ol_decor_resize = (Atom) None; /* "_OL_DECOR_RESIZE" */
Atom ol_decor_pin    = (Atom) None; /* "_OL_DECOR_PIN" */
Atom ol_pin_state    = (Atom) None; /* "_OL_PIN_STATE" */

    /* Sets olwm properties. */
void SetOlwmProperties(Widget shell,
    Boolean set_header,
    Boolean set_resize,
    Boolean set_close,
    Boolean menu)

{   /* SetOlwmProperties */
    Display*    display;
    Atom        atom_array[10];
    Window      window;
    int         atom_count;

    display = XtDisplay(shell);

    /* First, intern all the atoms. */
    if (ol_win_attr == (Atom) None) {
        ol_win_attr = XmInternAtom(display,
                "_OL_WIN_ATTR", False);

        ol_wt_other = XmInternAtom(display,
                "_OL_WT_OTHER", False);

        ol_menu_full = XmInternAtom(display,
                "_OL_MENU_FULL", False);

        ol_menu_none = XmInternAtom(display,
                "_OL_MENU_NONE", False);
```

```
    ol_decor_add = XmInternAtom(display,
            "_OL_DECOR_ADD", False);

    ol_decor_del = XmInternAtom(display,
            "_OL_DECOR_DEL", False);

    ol_decor_close = XmInternAtom(display,
            "_OL_DECOR_CLOSE", False);

    ol_decor_header = XmInternAtom(display,
            "_OL_DECOR_HEADER", False);

    ol_decor_resize = XmInternAtom(display,
            "_OL_DECOR_RESIZE", False);
}

/*
 * Check one Atom for errors. You
 * really should check them all.
 */
if (ol_win_attr == (Atom) None) {
    return;
}

/* Fill in _OL_WIN_ATTR data. */

/* The first element is the flags. */
atom_array[0] = 0x0001;  /* flag for window type. */

/* Tell olwm we're a different type of window. */
atom_array[1] = ol_wt_other; /* window type. */
atom_array[2] = 0x0; /* window manager menu. */
atom_array[3] = 0x0; /* pushpin state. */
atom_array[4] = 0x0; /* limited menu info. */

/* Check if we turn off window-menu button.  */
if (menu == False) {
    atom_array[0] = atom_array[0] | 0x0002;
    atom_array[2] = ol_menu_none;
} else {
    atom_array[0] = atom_array[0] | 0x0002;
    atom_array[2] = ol_menu_full;
}

/* Get window ID. */
window = XtWindow(shell);

/* Write _OL_WIN_ATTR data. */
XChangeProperty(display,
    window,
    ol_win_attr,
    ol_win_attr,    /* Type is same as Atom */
    32,      /* 32-bit entities */
    PropModeReplace,
    (unsigned char*)atom_array,
```

```
        5);

    /* Now, set decorations based on flags. */
    atom_count = 0;

    /* Resize handles. */
    if (set_resize == True) {
        atom_array[atom_count] = ol_decor_resize;
        atom_count = atom_count + 1;
    }

    /* Close (iconify) button. */
    if (set_close == True) {
        atom_array[atom_count] = ol_decor_close;
        atom_count = atom_count + 1;

        /* Can't ADD close without header. */
        atom_array[atom_count] = ol_decor_header;
        atom_count = atom_count + 1;
    } else {

        /* Can set header independently. */
        if (set_header == True) {
            atom_array[atom_count] = ol_decor_header;
            atom_count = atom_count + 1;
        }
    }

    if (atom_count > 0) {
        /* Change property. */
        XChangeProperty(display,
            window,
            ol_decor_add,  /* _OL_DECOR_ADD */
            XA_ATOM,
            32,
            PropModeReplace,
            (unsigned char*) atom_array,
            atom_count);
    }

}   /* SetOlwmProperties */

        /* Determines pushpin state. */
int GetPushpinState(Widget widget,
    XPropertyEvent* event)

{   /* GetPushpinState */
    int             status;
    Atom            actual_type;
    int             actual_format;
    int*            data;
    unsigned long   number_items;
    unsigned long   bytes_after;

    if ((event->state == PropertyNewValue) &&
```

```
        (event->atom == ol_pin_state)) {
        status = XGetWindowProperty(XtDisplay(widget),
                XtWindow(widget),
                ol_pin_state,
                0,      /* offset */
                1,      /* number items */
                False, /* don't delete */
                XA_INTEGER,
                &actual_type,
                &actual_format,
                &number_items,
                &bytes_after,
                (unsigned char**) &data);

        if (status == Success) {
            if (*data == 1) {
                return True;  /* pin is in. */
            } else {
                return False; /* pin is out. */
            }

            /* Free memory when done. */
            XFree((char*) data);
        }

    }

    /* If we get to here, it was not a pushpin event. */
    return -999;

}   /* GetPushpinState */

    /* Sets up a pushpin. */
void SetOlwmPushpin(Widget widget,
    XtEventHandler callback,
    XtPointer client_data)

{   /* SetOlwmPushpin */

    /* Set up pin state for later queries. */
    ol_pin_state = XmInternAtom(XtDisplay(widget),
            "_OL_PIN_STATE", False);

    ol_decor_pin = XmInternAtom(XtDisplay(widget),
            "_OL_DECOR_PIN", False);

    /* Check on interning status. */
    if (ol_decor_pin == (Atom) None) {
        return;
    }

    /* Add this atom to the decorations. */
    XChangeProperty(XtDisplay(widget),
        XtWindow(widget),
        ol_decor_add,
```

```
                    XA_ATOM,
                    32, /* format */
                    PropModeAppend, /* NOTE: append */
                    (unsigned char*) &ol_decor_pin,
                    1);

        /* Add event handler for property events. */
        XtAddEventHandler(widget,
            PropertyChangeMask,
            False,
            callback,
            client_data);

    }   /* SetOlwmPushpin */

/* end of file olwm.c */
```

A Program To Show How To Work With Window Managers

That about closes out our discussion of working with window managers. As with most complicated concepts associated with Motif, it's best to see for yourself how this all works through some code examples. We've put together an example program to help with that. The program below checks to see if *mwm* is running and sets the window decorations under *mwm* or *olwm* for a top-level shell widget and a dialog. It tracks the **Close** menu choice (based on the WM_DELETE_WINDOW window manager protocol), adds menu choices to the *mwm* window menu, and iconifies itself when asked.

Chances are you won't do all this in one program. We lumped it all together for the sake of convenience.

The *mwmtest* program code follows:

```
/* mwmtest.c */
#include  <Xm/Xm.h>
#include  <Xm/AtomMgr.h>
#include  <Xm/Label.h>
#include  <Xm/MessageB.h>
#include  <Xm/MwmUtil.h>      /* Window decorations, etc. */
#include  <Xm/Protocols.h>
#include  <Xm/RowColumn.h>
#include  <stdio.h>

extern Widget CreatePushbutton(Widget parent,
    char* name,
    XtCallbackProc callback,
    XtPointer client_data);
```

```
                    /* Set up WM_DELETE_WINDOW protocol. */
extern void SetWMProtocols(Widget shell,
        XtCallbackProc callback,
        XtPointer client_data);

    /* Sets olwm properties. */
extern void SetOlwmProperties(Widget shell,
    Boolean set_header,
    Boolean set_resize,
    Boolean set_close,
    Boolean menu);

                    /* Determines pushpin state. */
extern int GetPushpinState(Widget widget,
        XPropertyEvent* event);

                    /* Sets up a pushpin. */
extern void SetOlwmPushpin(Widget widget,
        XtEventHandler callback,
        XtPointer client_data);

    /* Event handler tracks olwm pushpin status. */
static void pin_event_handler(Widget widget,
    XtPointer client_data,
    XEvent* event,
    Boolean* continue_to_dispatch)

{   /* pin_event_handler */
    int status;

    /* Check if pushpin is out. */
    status = GetPushpinState(widget,
            (XPropertyEvent*) event);

    switch(status) {
        case False:
            printf("Pin is out.\n");
            /*
             * Note: newer versions of olwm
             * will also send WM_DELETE_WINDOW.
             */
            break;
        case True:
            printf("Pin is in.\n");
            break;
        default:
            printf("Not a pin event.\n");
    }

}   /* pin_event_handler */

    /* Asks window manager to iconify window. */
void iconifyCB(Widget widget,
    XtPointer client_data,
    XtPointer call_data)
```

```
{   /* iconifyCB */
    Widget*     shell;
    int         status;

    /* We assume shell widget is in client_data. */
    shell = (Widget*) client_data;

    if (shell != NULL) {
        status = XIconifyWindow(XtDisplay(*shell),
                XtWindow(*shell),
                DefaultScreen(XtDisplay(*shell) ) );

        if (status == 0) {
            printf("Failed in attempt to iconify.\n");
        } else {
            printf("Window should be iconified now.\n");
        }
    }

}   /* iconifyCB */

void exitCB(Widget widget,
    XtPointer client_data,
    XtPointer call_data)

{   /* exitCB */

    exit(0);

}   /* exitCB */

    /* Main shell should quit on Close. */
void close_exitCB(Widget widget,
    XtPointer client_data,
    XtPointer call_data)

{    /* close_exitCB */

    printf("Close choice on main window.\n");

    exit(0);

}    /* close_exitCB */

    /* Dialog shells should just be unmanaged on Close. */
void closeCB(Widget widget,
    XtPointer client_data,
    XtPointer call_data)

{   /* closeCB */
    Widget*  shell;

    /* Client_data has widget. */
    shell = (Widget*) client_data;
```

```
        printf("Close choice on window manager's menu.\n");

        XtUnmanageChild(*shell);

}    /* closeCB */

    /* Callback for EXTRA choices on mwm menu. */
void mwmMenuCB(Widget widget,
    XtPointer client_data,
    XtPointer call_data)

{    /* mwmMenuCB */
    Atom        message;
    Display*    display;
    char*       string;

    /* We passed the Atom as the client_data. */
    message = (Atom) client_data;

    /*
     * Due to the widget passed to this
     * routine, XtDisplay may fail, so call
     * XtDisplayOfObject instead.
     */
    display = XtDisplayOfObject(widget);

    string = XmGetAtomName(display, message);

    printf("Window menu choice for %s\n", string);

    /* Call XFree on the Atom name. */
    XFree(string);

}    /* mwmMenuCB */

    /* Sets up extra mwm menu choices. */
void SetUpMwmMenu(Widget shell)

{    /* SetUpMwmMenu */
    Display*    display;
    Atom        motif_wm_messages;
    Atom        message1, message2;
    char        menu_items[1024];

    display = XtDisplay(shell);

    motif_wm_messages = XmInternAtom(display,
        _XA_MWM_MESSAGES, /* "_MOTIF_WM_MESSAGES" */
        False);

    message1 = XmInternAtom(display,
        "_MY_MSG1", False);

    message2 = XmInternAtom(display,
```

```
            "_MY_MSG2", False);

    /* Add mwm protocol. */
    XmAddWMProtocols(shell,
        &motif_wm_messages,  /* Protocol */
        1);                   /* One protocol */

    /*
     * Create mwmMenu resource value. Each
     * menu choice ends with \n.
     */
    sprintf(menu_items,
        "%s %d\n %s %d\n",
        "Choice1 _h Alt<Key>F2 f.send_msg",
        message1,
        "Choice2 _e Ctrl<Key>F6 f.send_msg",
        message2);

    /* Insert menu item. */
    XtVaSetValues(shell,
        XmNmwmMenu, menu_items,
        NULL);

    /* Add protocol callbacks. */
    XmAddProtocolCallback(shell,
        motif_wm_messages,   /* Property */
        message1,             /* Protocol */
        (XtCallbackProc) mwmMenuCB,
        (XtPointer) message1);  /* client_data */

    XmAddProtocolCallback(shell,
        motif_wm_messages,   /* Property */
        message2,             /* Protocol */
        (XtCallbackProc) mwmMenuCB,
        (XtPointer) message2);  /* client_data */

}   /* SetUpMwmMenu */

int main(int argc, char** argv)

{   /* main */
    XtAppContext    app_context;
    Widget          parent;
    Widget          row;
    Widget          dialog;
    Widget          quit;
    Widget          mwm_label;
    Widget          dlg_label;
    Widget          iconify;
    Arg             args[20];
    Cardinal        n;
    XmString        xmstring;
    int             mwmFunctions;
    int             mwmDecorations;
```

```
/* Set up decorations. Turn off maximize. */
mwmDecorations = MWM_DECOR_ALL |
                MWM_DECOR_MAXIMIZE;

/* Turn off Move and Maximize function. */
mwmFunctions   = MWM_FUNC_ALL      |
                MWM_FUNC_MAXIMIZE |
                MWM_FUNC_MOVE;

/* Initialize toolkit. */
parent = XtVaAppInitialize(&app_context,
        "Ppm",
        (XrmOptionDescList) NULL,
        0,
        &argc, argv,
        (String*) NULL,
        XmNallowResize, True,
        XmNmappedWhenManaged, False,
        XmNdeleteResponse, XmDO_NOTHING,
        XmNmwmFunctions,   mwmFunctions,
        XmNmwmDecorations, mwmDecorations,
        NULL);

row = XtVaCreateManagedWidget("row",
        xmRowColumnWidgetClass, parent,
        XmNorientation, XmVERTICAL,
        NULL);

iconify = CreatePushbutton(row, "iconify",
        (XtCallbackProc) iconifyCB,
        (XtPointer) &parent);

(void) XtVaCreateManagedWidget("decorations",
        xmLabelWidgetClass, row,
        NULL);

mwm_label = XtVaCreateManagedWidget("mwm_label",
        xmLabelWidgetClass, row,
        NULL);

quit = CreatePushbutton(row, "quit",
        (XtCallbackProc) exitCB,
        (XtPointer) NULL);

/* Create dialog. */
xmstring = XmStringCreateSimple("Dialog Titlebar");

n = 0;
XtSetArg(args[n], XmNdialogTitle, xmstring); n++;

/* Since we have a callback, do nothing on close. */
XtSetArg(args[n], XmNdeleteResponse, XmDO_NOTHING); n++;

dialog = XmCreateInformationDialog(parent,
        "dialog", args, n);
```

```
XmStringFree(xmstring);

/*
 * Set up dialog window decorations
 * AFTER creating, so that we add to
 * existing set.
 */
XtVaGetValues(XtParent(dialog),
    XmNmwmDecorations, &mwmDecorations,
    XmNmwmFunctions,   &mwmFunctions,
    NULL);

/* Add resize handles to dialog. */
if (mwmDecorations == -1) {
    mwmDecorations = MWM_DECOR_BORDER |
                     MWM_DECOR_MENU   |
                     MWM_DECOR_TITLE  |
                     MWM_DECOR_RESIZEH;
} else {
    mwmDecorations =
        mwmDecorations | MWM_DECOR_RESIZEH;
}

mwmFunctions = mwmFunctions | MWM_FUNC_RESIZE;

XtVaSetValues(XtParent(dialog),
    XmNmwmDecorations, mwmDecorations,
    XmNmwmFunctions,   mwmFunctions,
    NULL);

/* Realize widgets to create window IDs. */
XtRealizeWidget(parent);

/* Check if mwm is running. */
if (XmIsMotifWMRunning(parent) == True) {

    /* Set up mwm window menu. */
    SetUpMwmMenu(parent);
    SetUpMwmMenu(XtParent(dialog) );

    /* Set up mwm_label. */
    xmstring =
      XmStringCreateSimple("Mwm is running.");

} else {
    /* Set up mwm_label. */
    xmstring =
      XmStringCreateSimple("Mwm is NOT running.");

    /* Set up olwm properties. */
    SetOlwmProperties(parent,
        True,   /* header. */
        True,   /* resize. */
        True,   /* close (iconify). */
```

```
                        True);   /* menu. */

                SetOlwmProperties(XtParent(dialog),
                        True,   /* header. */
                        False,  /* resize. */
                        False,  /* close (iconify). */
                        False); /* no menu. */

                /* Set up a pushpin on the dialog. */
            SetOlwmPushpin(XtParent(dialog),
                    (XtEventHandler) pin_event_handler,
                    (XtPointer) NULL);
            }

            XtVaSetValues(mwm_label,
                XmNlabelString, xmstring,
                NULL);

            XmStringFree(xmstring);

            /* Set up window protocols. */
            SetWMProtocols(parent,
                (XtCallbackProc) close_exitCB,
                (XtPointer) NULL);

            SetWMProtocols(XtParent(dialog),
                (XtCallbackProc) closeCB,    /* Unmanage. */
                (XtPointer) &dialog);

            /* Show widgets. */
            XtManageChild(dialog);
            XtMapWidget(parent);

            XtAppMainLoop(app_context);
            return 0;

        }   /* main */

        /* end of file mwmtest.c */
```

The *mwmtest* program uses the following resource file:

```
! Resource file for Chapter 18
! of Power Programming Motif.
!
*fontList:      lucidasans-12
*background:    grey98

*title: Window Manager Test

*quit.labelString:      Exit
*iconify.labelString:   Iconify
*decorations.labelString: Titlebar above should be\n\
missing maximize.
```

```
*dialog.messageString: Titlebar above should add\n\
resize handles.

! end of resource file
```

Name this file **Ppm** and store it in your home directory.

Summary

A window manager is a separate X program that controls the layout and placement of windows on your screen. A window manager controls how much of the screen's real estate that any application can have and also allows you to resize, iconify, and move windows. You can run only one window manager per screen, and usually only one per X display. Essentially, the window manager is the big Kahuna that your application must appease in order to run effectively. With Motif, it's the Motif window manager, or *mwm*.

The rules for interacting with the big Kahuna are laid out in the *Inter-Client Communications Conventions Manual*, or ICCCM. These rules ensure that your application will be a good Motif citizen and not cause any problems in cross-application communications. There are a lot of details to cover when looking at conformity with the ICCCM, as this rather long chapter indicates. However, there are a few things you can do right off the bat to make sure that your applications are good, conforming citizens.

For starters, don't depend on any window manager-specific features. It's just not realistic for you to demand that users run only the Motif window manager, for example. It's also not realistic for your programs to operate bizarrely under another window manager. So don't depend on the presence of pushpins on dialogs, an olwm-specific feature. Also note that Motif's modal dialogs, which demand user responses before allowing any other interaction, require *mwm*.

In fact, your applications should work with all compliant window managers. The majority of this chapter explains exactly how to do just that.

Even though you cannot demand that your users work under one particular window manager, you probably want to take advantage of the nice features offered by various window managers. Dialogs under *olwm* should take advantage of pushpins, even if you aren't using an Open Look toolkit.

Again, this topic is covered in this chapter, along with other methods of painlessly adapting Motif applications to work under virtually any window manager, including *olwm*.

MOTIF FUNCTIONS AND MACROS INTRODUCED IN THIS CHAPTER

```
XmAddProtocolCallback
XmAddProtocols
XmAddWMProtocolCallback
XmAddWMProtocols
XmGetAtomName
XmInternAtom
XmIsMotifWMRunning
XmRemoveProtocols
XmRemoveWMProtocols
```

X LIBRARY FUNCTIONS AND MACROS INTRODUCED IN THIS CHAPTER

```
XChangeProperty
XGetAtomName
XGetWindowProperty
XIconifyWindow
XInternAtom
XSetCommand
```

CHAPTER 19

Cut, Copy, and Paste with the Motif Clipboard

This chapter covers:

- The Motif clipboard
- `XmText` widget convenience routines for the clipboard
- Copying data to the clipboard
- Clipboard data formats
- Creating your own clipboard format
- Retrieving data from the clipboard
- Using the clipboard for undo functions
- Using the clipboard for redo functions
- Copying and pasting nontext data, such as pixmaps
- Copying data by name
- Two programs to test out the clipboard routines

CUT, COPY, AND PASTE OVERVIEW

As is common with most graphical interfaces, Motif provides a clipboard into which you can copy data for later pasting. This clipboard is very useful within your applications, especially text-editing programs, as well as for transferring data between applications. There's one main caveat, however: the Motif clipboard works only with Motif applications.

All hope is not lost, as the clipboard is just one means for exchanging data between X applications. We list the three methods of data exchange in Table 19.1.

Table 19.1   *Methods for data exchange.*

Method	Operations	Usage
Clipboard	Copy and paste	Motif programs only
Selections	Select and insert	All X programs
Drag and drop	Drag and drop	Motif 1.2 and higher programs only

We discuss the Motif clipboard in this chapter, X selections like the PRIMARY selection in Chapter 20 and drag and drop in Chapter 21.

Even if you choose not to use these Motif-supported means, you can also code a number of other forms for interprocess communication, or IPC, including writing data to X properties or sending ClientMessage events to applications.

And, of course, you can always use a number of non-X-related IPC schemes, including ToolTalk, TCP/IP network sockets, UNIX domain sockets, pipes, shared memory, and System V UNIX message queues. However, most of these plans are dependent on the operating system, and in theory your application should not rely on the operating system for anything. If you do venture into those areas, you're on your own. In this chapter, we'll stick to the Motif clipboard.

Using the Clipboard

The basic tasks we want to perform with the clipboard are completing the operations on the Motif Edit menu, especially the **Cut**, **Copy**, and **Paste** choices, as listed in Table 19.2.

Table 19.2   *The Edit menu.*

Menu Choice	Mnemonic	Purpose
Undo	**U**	Undoes the last thing the user did
Cut	**t**	Removes the selected material and puts it in the clipboard
Copy	**C**	Copies selected material to clipboard
Paste	**P**	Pastes contents of clipboard to current location
Clear	**l**	Clears selected material
Delete	**D**	Wipes out the selected material
Select All	**None**	Selects everything
Deselect All	**None**	Deselects all selected items

When the user selects data in a window, the user may want to copy that data to the clipboard and, of course, paste that data sometime later somewhere else—in the current application or in another application. All this can be done from the Motif clipboard.

There are two main ways to interact with the clipboard. Since the vast majority of all computer data is text (yes, even in a graphical interface, you're still mainly working with text), Motif provides a set of text clipboard convenience routines that dramatically simplify your interaction with the clipboard.

But not *all* data is text. And, in a graphical interface, users expect to be able to select bitmaps, colors, and other objects on the screen and then copy the data into the clipboard. You can do all this with the Motif clipboard, but be warned that few applications support arbitrary data types. In fact, you're lucky if an application even supports the clipboard's copy and paste of text. It's a sad tale, but many X programs skimp on interoperability. This should change in the future with the advent of more standardized file browsers and other applications where users will expect to copy and paste data. (Much of this will come from the COSE UNIX unification efforts.)

In the rest of this chapter, we'll start with the text-convenience routines and then cover how to interact with the Motif clipboard in depth.

SHORTCUT

Clipboard Text Routines

Since the vast majority of most application data is stored as text, Motif provides a set of handy utility routines for working with text and the clipboard. These routines mimic much of the Edit menu, so this makes it relatively easy to build a Motif text editor.

The following text routines work with the currently selected text inside a text widget:

- ◼ XmTextCopy
- ◼ XmTextCut
- ◼ XmTextPaste

To copy the selected text in a text widget to the clipboard, use XmTextCopy:

```
#include <Xm/Text.h>

Boolean XmTextCopy(Widget text_widget,
        Time timestamp)
```

XmTextCopy returns False if there is no selected text in the widget, if your application does not have ownership of the PRIMARY selection (see the next chapter for more on selections), or if the application could not assert ownership of the CLIPBOARD selection. XmTextCopy returns True otherwise, which means the routine worked.

You need to pass the text widget and a *timestamp*. This *timestamp* is used by X Window applications to synchronize between different network turnaround latencies. (Remember that X applications may actually compute anywhere on the network, which makes the task of synchronizing more difficult.) The basic problem the *timestamp* seeks to solve is to avoid messing up the order of the events: If a paste comes into the X server before the original copy, the *timestamp* can help mediate.

The problem is getting a proper *timestamp*. Motif callback routines pass an XEvent pointer, so you can use the *timestamp* from the event, if the event structure provides one. If not, call XtLastTimestampProcessed, which returns the *timestamp* for the last event processed:

```
Time XtLastTimestampProcessed(Display* display)
```

Since you're most likely to call XmTextCopy from within a callback function (probably a callback from a pushbutton widget on the Edit menu), the last event processed should have the valid *timestamp* (look in the *time* field). You can also use the constant CurrentTime, but be warned that this constant can mess up the synchronization between X programs. This problem occurs only if the user tries to paste, copy, and paste in quick succession. If you use the CurrentTime constant, the X server may think that your first paste is really the second, which is not likely to be useful to the user. We recommend against using CurrentTime if at all possible.

To cut the selected text and place it into the clipboard, call XmTextCut:

```
#include <Xm/Text.h>

Boolean XmTextCut(Widget text_widget,
        Time timestamp)
```

XmTextCut returns True on success; it returns False otherwise. See XmTextCopy above for the conditions.
To paste the text in the clipboard to the current insert position in the text widget, call XmTextPaste:

```
#include <Xm/Text.h>

Boolean XmTextPaste(Widget text_widget)
```

XmTextPaste returns True on success; it returns False otherwise. This routine does not require a timestamp, by the way.

XmTextField Functions

Motif provides a set of clipboard utility functions for working with the XmTextField widget. These functions mirror the XmText functions and are listed in Table 19.3.

Table 19.3 *XmTextField clipboard functions.*

XmText Function	XmTextField Function
XmTextCopy	XmTextFieldCopy
XmTextCut	XmTextFieldCut
XmTextPaste	XmTextFieldPaste
XmTextRemove	XmTextFieldRemove

Fleshing Out the Edit Menu for Text Widgets

For the **Delete** choice on the Edit menu, call XmTextRemove to remove the selected text:

```
#include <Xm/Text.h>

Boolean XmTextRemove(Widget text_widget)
```

XmTextRemove returns True if it succeeds; it returns False otherwise. XmTextRemove can fail if there is no selected text in the widget or if the application does not own the PRIMARY selection.

A Program To Test the Clipboard Text Routines

We've put together a program to test out the text-clipboard functions. The following program fills out much of the Edit menu (we still cheat and skip **Undo**, though).

This program implements a primitive text editor using the XmText widget. The Edit menu supports the following choices (with corresponding callback functions):

■ **Cut**, which calls XmTextCut

■ **Copy**, which calls XmTextCopy

- **Paste**, which calls `XmTextPaste`
- **Delete**, which calls `XmTextRemove`

We also flesh out much of the File menu, and include the following choices:

- **New**, which removes all the text in the text widget.
- **Open...**, which calls up a file-selection-box dialog to choose a file to load. This choice also changes the window's titlebar to reflect the new filename.
- **Save**, which saves the text into the current filename.
- **Save As...**, which saves the text to a different file. A file-selection dialog allows the user to choose this other file. This choice also changes the window's titlebar to reflect the new filename.
- **Exit**, which, as you might expect, quits the application.

This program uses the menu-creation utility routines presented in Chapter 4 and the text-widget file routines presented in Chapter 5.

The code for this text editor follows:

```
/* textclip.c */
#include   <Xm/Xm.h>
#include   <Xm/FileSB.h>
#include   <Xm/Label.h>
#include   <Xm/MainW.h>
#include   <Xm/MessageB.h>
#include   <Xm/Separator.h>
#include   <Xm/Text.h>
#include   <stdio.h>

/* Global data. */
Widget      topshell;
Widget      text;
Widget      open_dialog;
Widget      save_as_dialog;
Widget      error_dialog;
char        current_file[1024];

/* External functions. */
extern Widget CreatePushbutton(Widget parent,
    char* name,
    XtCallbackProc callback,
    XtPointer client_data);

extern Widget CreatePulldownMenu(Widget parent,
```

```
        char* name);

extern Widget CreateMenubar(Widget parent,
    char* name);

extern Boolean SaveFile(Widget widget,
    char* filename);

extern Boolean LoadFile(Widget widget,
    char* filename);

/* UTILITY FUNCTIONS. */

void DisplayError(char* message)

{   /* DisplayError */
    XmString    xmstring;

    /* Set dialog message. */
    xmstring = XmStringCreateSimple(message);

    XtVaSetValues(error_dialog,
        XmNmessageString, xmstring,
        NULL);

    XmStringFree(xmstring);

    /* Show dialog. */
    if ( !XtIsManaged(error_dialog) ) {
        XtManageChild(error_dialog);
    }

}   /* DisplayError */

void SetTitle(char* filename)

{   /* SetTitle */
    char    string[1024];

    sprintf(string, "Clipboard Test: %s", filename);

    XtVaSetValues(topshell,
        XmNtitle, string,
        NULL);

}   /* SetTitle */

void SaveToFile()

{   /* SaveToFile */
    int    status;
    char   message[1024];

    /* Save text to file. */
    status = SaveFile(text, current_file);
```

```
        if (status != True) {
            /* Display error dialog. */
            sprintf(message, "Failed to save data to %s.\n",
                current_file);

            DisplayError(message);
            return;
        }

        /*
         * By updating title bar, we
         * provide some feedback.
         */
        SetTitle(current_file);

    }   /* SaveToFile */

/*
 * EDIT MENU CALLBACKS.
 */

void cutCB(Widget widget,
    XtPointer client_data,
    XtPointer call_data)

{   /* cutCB */
    int status;

    status = XmTextCut(text,
        XtLastTimestampProcessed(XtDisplay(widget) ) );

    if (status == False) {
        /* Display error dialog. */
        DisplayError("Failed to cut any data.");
    }

}   /* cutCB */

void copyCB(Widget widget,
    XtPointer client_data,
    XtPointer call_data)

{   /* copyCB */
    int status;

    status = XmTextCopy(text,
        XtLastTimestampProcessed(XtDisplay(widget) ) );

    if (status == False) {
        /* Display error dialog. */
        DisplayError("Failed to copy any data.");
    }

}   /* copyCB */
```

```
void pasteCB(Widget widget,
    XtPointer client_data,
    XtPointer call_data)

{   /* pasteCB */
    int status;

    status = XmTextPaste(text);

    if (status == False) {
        /* Display error dialog. */
        DisplayError("Failed to paste any data.");
    }

}   /* pasteCB */

void deleteCB(Widget widget,
    XtPointer client_data,
    XtPointer call_data)

{   /* deleteCB */
    int status;

    status = XmTextRemove(text);

    if (status == False) {
        /* Display error dialog. */
        DisplayError("Failed to delete any data.");
    }

}   /* deleteCB */

void undoCB(Widget widget,
    XtPointer client_data,
    XtPointer call_data)

{   /* undoCB */

    printf("Undo.\n");

}   /* undoCB */

/*
 * FILE MENU CALLBACKS.
 */

    /* File menu New choice. */
void newCB(Widget widget,
    XtPointer client_data,
    XtPointer call_data)

{   /* newCB */

    /* This really should prompt user to save text. */
```

```
    XmTextReplace(text,
        (XmTextPosition) 0,
        XmTextGetLastPosition(text),
        " ");

    /* Clear out current file name. */
    strcpy(current_file, "NoName.txt");

    SetTitle(current_file);

}   /* newCB */

void openCB(Widget widget,
    XtPointer client_data,
    XtPointer call_data)

{   /* openCB */

    /* Call up load dialog. */
    if ( !XtIsManaged(open_dialog) ) {
        XtManageChild(open_dialog);
    }

}   /* openCB */

void saveCB(Widget widget,
    XtPointer client_data,
    XtPointer call_data)

{   /* saveCB */

    SaveToFile();

}   /* saveCB */

void save_asCB(Widget widget,
    XtPointer client_data,
    XtPointer call_data)

{   /* save_asCB */

    /* Show dialog. */
    if ( !XtIsManaged(save_as_dialog) ) {
        XtManageChild(save_as_dialog);
    }

}   /* save_asCB */

void exitCB(Widget widget,
    XtPointer client_data,
    XtPointer call_data)

{   /* exitCB */

    /* Should prompt to save here. */
```

```
        exit(0);

}    /* exitCB */

    /* Saves file to a new name. */
void save_as_fileCB(Widget widget,
    XtPointer client_data,
    XtPointer call_data)

{   /* save_as_fileCB */
    XmFileSelectionBoxCallbackStruct* ptr;
    char*    string;

    /* Extract file name */
    ptr =
        (XmFileSelectionBoxCallbackStruct*) call_data;

    XmStringGetLtoR(ptr->value,
        XmSTRING_DEFAULT_CHARSET,
        &string);

    strcpy(current_file, string);

    XtFree(string);

    XtUnmanageChild(save_as_dialog);

    SaveToFile();

}    /* save_as_fileCB */

    /* Loads file into text widget. */
void load_fileCB(Widget widget,
    XtPointer client_data,
    XtPointer call_data)

{   /* load_fileCB */
    XmFileSelectionBoxCallbackStruct* ptr;
    char*    string;
    char     message[1024];
    int      status;

    /* Extract file name */
    ptr =
        (XmFileSelectionBoxCallbackStruct*) call_data;

    XmStringGetLtoR(ptr->value,
        XmSTRING_DEFAULT_CHARSET,
        &string);

    strcpy(current_file, string);

    XtFree(string);
```

```
        XtUnmanageChild(open_dialog);

        status = LoadFile(text, current_file);

        if (status != True) {
            sprintf(message,
                "Error loading file [%s]\n",
                    current_file);

            DisplayError(message);
            return;
        }

        /* Set window title bar. */
        SetTitle(current_file);

}   /* load_fileCB */

int main(int argc, char** argv)

{   /* main */
    XtAppContext    app_context;
    Widget          mainw, menubar;
    Widget          filemenu, editmenu;
    Widget          undo;
    Arg             args[20];
    Cardinal        n;

    /* Initialize toolkit. */
    topshell = XtVaAppInitialize(&app_context,
                "Ppm",
                (XrmOptionDescList) NULL,
                0,
                &argc, argv,
                (String*) NULL,
                XmNallowResize, True,
                NULL);

    /* Create main window. */
    n = 0;
    mainw = XmCreateMainWindow(topshell,
                "mainw", args, n);

    /* Create menubar. */
    menubar = CreateMenubar(mainw, "menubar");

    filemenu = CreatePulldownMenu(menubar, "filemenu");

    (void) CreatePushbutton(filemenu, "new",
            (XtCallbackProc) newCB,
            (XtPointer) &text);

    (void) CreatePushbutton(filemenu, "open",
            (XtCallbackProc) openCB,
            (XtPointer) &text);
```

```
(void) CreatePushbutton(filemenu, "save",
        (XtCallbackProc) saveCB,
        (XtPointer) &text);

(void) CreatePushbutton(filemenu, "saveas",
        (XtCallbackProc) save_asCB,
        (XtPointer) &text);

(void) XtVaCreateManagedWidget("sep",
        xmSeparatorWidgetClass, filemenu,
        NULL);

(void) CreatePushbutton(filemenu, "exit",
        (XtCallbackProc) exitCB,
        (XtPointer) NULL);

/* Edit menu. */
editmenu = CreatePulldownMenu(menubar, "editmenu");

undo = CreatePushbutton(editmenu, "undo",
        (XtCallbackProc) undoCB,
        (XtPointer) NULL);

/* "Ghost" undo choice. */
XtSetSensitive(undo, False);

(void) CreatePushbutton(editmenu, "cut",
        (XtCallbackProc) cutCB,
        (XtPointer) NULL);

(void) CreatePushbutton(editmenu, "copy",
        (XtCallbackProc) copyCB,
        (XtPointer) NULL);

(void) CreatePushbutton(editmenu, "paste",
        (XtCallbackProc) pasteCB,
        (XtPointer) NULL);

/* Note how we put a separator before delete. */
(void) XtVaCreateManagedWidget("sep",
        xmSeparatorWidgetClass, editmenu,
        NULL);

(void) CreatePushbutton(editmenu, "delete",
        (XtCallbackProc) deleteCB,
        (XtPointer) NULL);

/* Create scrolled text. */
n = 0;
XtSetArg(args[n], XmNeditMode,
    XmMULTI_LINE_EDIT); n++;
XtSetArg(args[n], XmNscrollHorizontal, True); n++;
XtSetArg(args[n], XmNscrollVertical,   True); n++;
```

```
    text = XmCreateScrolledText(mainw, "text", args, n);

    XtManageChild(text);

    XmMainWindowSetAreas(mainw,
        menubar,
        (Widget) NULL,      /* command window */
        (Widget) NULL,      /* horiz scroll */
        (Widget) NULL,      /* vert scroll */
        XtParent(text) );   /* work area */

    XtManageChild(mainw);

    /* Clear out current file name. */
    strcpy(current_file, "NoName.txt");
    SetTitle(current_file);

    /* Create error dialog. */
    n = 0;
    XtSetArg(args[n], XmNdeleteResponse, XmUNMAP); n++;

    error_dialog = XmCreateErrorDialog(topshell,
            "error_dialog", args, n);

    /* Create file load dialog. */
    n = 0;
    XtSetArg(args[n], XmNdeleteResponse, XmUNMAP); n++;

    open_dialog = XmCreateFileSelectionDialog(topshell,
            "open_dialog", args, n);

    XtAddCallback(open_dialog, XmNokCallback,
        (XtCallbackProc) load_fileCB,
        (XtPointer) NULL);

    /* Create file save as dialog. */
    n = 0;
    XtSetArg(args[n], XmNdeleteResponse, XmUNMAP); n++;

    save_as_dialog =
        XmCreateFileSelectionDialog(topshell,
            "save_as_dialog", args, n);

    XtAddCallback(save_as_dialog, XmNokCallback,
        (XtCallbackProc) save_as_fileCB,
        (XtPointer) NULL);

    XtRealizeWidget(topshell);
    XtAppMainLoop(app_context);
    return 0;

}   /* main */

/* end of file textclip.c */
```

When we call XmMainWindowSetAreas, note how we call XtParent on the scrolled-text widget to attach the scrolled-window parent of the text widget to the main window.

Note also that in a real program, you should prompt the user to save the file on exiting, if the data were not saved. You should also, of course, provide online help and a working **Undo** choice on the Edit menu.

You'll need the following resource file for the program:

```
! Resource file for textclip.c in Chapter 19
! of Power Programming Motif.
!
*fontList:      lucidasans-12
*background:    grey92

*title:     Cut, Copy and Paste

! File menu
*filemenu.labelString: File
*filemenu.mnemonic:    F

*new.labelString:    New
*new.mnemonic:       N

*open.labelString:   Open...
*open.mnemonic:      O

*save.labelString:   Save
*save.mnemonic:      S

*saveas.labelString: Save As...
*saveas.mnemonic:    A

*exit.labelString:   Exit
*exit.mnemonic:      x

! Edit menu
*editmenu.labelString:  Edit
*editmenu.mnemonic:     E

*undo.labelString:      Undo
*undo.mnemonic:         U
*undo.accelerator:      Ctrl<Key>z
*undo.acceleratorText:  Ctrl-Z

*cut.labelString:       Cut
*cut.mnemonic:          t
*cut.accelerator:       Ctrl<Key>x
*cut.acceleratorText:   Ctrl-X

*copy.labelString:      Copy
*copy.mnemonic:         C
```

```
*copy.accelerator:       Ctrl<Key>c
*copy.acceleratorText:   Ctrl-C

*paste.labelString:      Paste
*paste.mnemonic:         P
*paste.accelerator:      Ctrl<Key>v
*paste.acceleratorText:  Ctrl-V

*delete.labelString:     Delete
*delete.mnemonic:        D

! Test resources, note monospaced font.
*text.fontList: \
 -*-lucidatypewriter-medium-r-*-*-12-120-*-*-m-*-*
*text.rows:      30
*text.columns:   80

! Dialogs
*error_dialog.dialogTitle: Cut, Copy and Paste: Error

*open_dialog.dialogTitle: Open New File

*save_as_dialog.dialogTitle: Save As A New File Name
*save_as_dialog.selectionLabelString:\
Specify new file name:

! end of resource file
```

Name this file **Ppm** and store it in your home directory.

Running the Text-Clipboard Program

When you run the *textclip* program, you'll be able to load text files, edit them, and then save them to disk. Select some text and then try out the Edit menu choices for **Cut**, **Copy**, **Paste**, and **Delete**.

We show the program's interface in Figure 19.1.

Of course, not all your data will be text, although the vast majority of all computer data is. Even so, you'll sometimes need to copy and paste bitmaps, color cells, and all sorts of other, perhaps arbitrary, data. The text-widget convenience routines—although very convenient—aren't enough. We need to delve deeper into the Motif clipboard.

```
┌──────────────────────────────────────────────────────────────┐
│ ─ │ Clipboard Test: /usr/spool/news/erc/books/ppm2nd/src/foo.txt │ ▫ │ □ │
├──────────────────────────────────────────────────────────────┤
│  File  Edit                                                    │
├──────────────────────────────────────────────────────────────┤
│  * Program to show XmText widget.                          ▲   │
│  *                                                             │
│  * Power Programming Motif, 2nd edition.                       │
│  * Copyright 1993 MIS: Press.                                  │
│  * E F Johnson                                                 │
│  */                                                            │
│  /* textprog.c */                                              │
│  #include <Xm/Xm.h>                                            │
│  #include <Xm/PushB.h>                                         │
│  #include <Xm/PanedW.h>                                        │
│  #include <Xm/Text.h>                                          │
│  #include <stdio.h>                                            │
│                                                                │
│                                                                │
│  /* Callback to extract XmText data and then exit program. */  │
│                                                                │
│  void exitCB(Widget widget,                                ▽   │
└──────────────────────────────────────────────────────────────┘
```

Figure 19.1   *The textclip program.*

THE MOTIF CLIPBOARD IN DEPTH

The Motif clipboard holds one data set at a time. That is, it holds the data from the last copy operation. If the user copies new data to the clipboard, the old data is removed.

The data ise stored in the X server in properties on the root window (all the clipboard property names start with _MOTIF_CLIP). Using this, your application can exchange data with other Motif applications. Unfortunately, the inner workings of the clipboard are proprietary to Motif, and you are stuck if you try to copy and paste data between an Open Look application and a Motif application. This is one of the more unfortunate aspects of the X Window *mechanism, not policy*, policy. (There's hope, though, because you can often use selections to exchange data, even between programs built with different toolkits. See the next chapter for more on this.)

Copying Data to the Clipboard

To copy data to the clipboard, you need to go through three steps:

1. Call XmClipboardStartCopy to begin the transfer of data to the clipboard.

2. Call XmClipboardCopy to copy your data into the clipboard. You may need to call this routine more than once.

3. Call XmClipboardEndCopy to complete the transaction.

Starting the Transaction

To begin a transfer of data to the clipboard, your application needs to lock the clipboard and allocate some temporary storage to hold the data while you're transferring it to the clipboard. (Using temporary storage also allows you to cancel a copy to the clipboard.) All of this is done by XmClipboardStartCopy:

```
#include <Xm/CutPaste.h>

int XmClipboardStartCopy(Display* display,
        Window window,
        XmString clipboard_label,
        Time timestamp,
        Widget by_name_widget,
        XmCutPasteProc by_name_callback,
        long* item_number) /* RETURN */
```

XmClipboardStartCopy returns XmClipboardSuccess or XmClipboardLocked on errors. You need to pass in the display pointer, the ID of a window in the application, usually the ID of a top-level shell window. You should consistently pass the same window ID and display pointer to the clipboard functions.

The *clipboard_label* is used to label the data. This is really a value used to identify the item in the clipboard, and the parameter is included in XmClipboardStartCopy to support a future clipboard-watching program (which you could write if you desire). For now, it's not used. We suggest placing your application's name in this parameter (as an XmString, remember).

The *timestamp* is used to synchronize requests to the X server.

The *by_name_widget* and *by_name_callback* are used only if you're copying data by name (or reference). Basically, in a copy by name, you're deferring the actual transfer of the data until requested later. This is useful if the user selects a very large amount of data, and copying the data (especially if it isn't used later) would be an expensive operation. We cover more on this below under "Copying Data by Name."

N O T E

The XmCutPasteProc typedef is new in Motif 1.2.

If you don't want to bother with the *timestamp* parameter, there's a convenience routine:

```
#include <Xm/CutPaste.h>

int XmClipboardBeginCopy(Display* display,
    Window window,
    XmString clipboard_label,
    Widget by_name_widget,
    XmCutPasteProc by_name_callback,
    long* item_number)  /* RETURN */
```

XmClipboardBeginCopy acts like XmClipboardStartCopy, but XmClipboardBeginCopy uses the constant CurrentTime for the timestamp. While this is easier on your part, we don't recommend using XmClipboardBeginCopy because of synchronization issues.

With either XmClipboardBeginCopy or XmClipboardStartCopy, use the returned *item_number* in calls to XmClipboardCopy.

Copying the Data

After you've successfully started a copy to the clipboard, you need to transfer your data. Use XmClipboardCopy:

```
#include <Xm/CutPaste.h>

int XmClipboardCopy(Display* display,
    Window window,
    long item_number,
    char* format_name,
    XtPointer buffer,
    unsigned long buffer_length,
    long private_number,
    long* by_name_data_number)  /* RETURN */
```

XmClipboardCopy copies *buffer_length* bytes of the data buffer to temporary storage allocated by XmClipboardStartCopy. It returns XmClipboardSuccess, XmClipboardLocked, or XmClipboardFail. You pass the same *item_number* as XmClipboardStartCopy returned. You should also pass the same window ID and display pointer.

Each call to XmClipboardCopy places data in the clipboard associated with a given target data type (the *format_name*). You can call XmClipboardCopy multiple times and store the same data under different targets or different data under the same or different targets.

You place the data to transfer into the buffer. If you pass a NULL buffer, this signals to XmClipboardCopy that your application will provide the data later, on request (the data will be provided by the *by_name_callback* passed to XmClipboardStartCopy, above).

The *by_name_data_number* is an ID returned by XmClipboardCopy. This ID will be passed to the *by_name_callback*, should your application defer the copy and agree to provide the data on request. Even if you're not deferring anything, you must provide this parameter.

The *private_number* is an ID your application can use.

Be sure to pass the same display pointer and window ID for all the clipboard calls.

NOTE

Finishing the Transaction

When you're all done copying data to the clipboard, call XmClipboardEndCopy to end the transaction:

```
#include <Xm/CutPaste.h>

int XmClipboardEndCopy(Display* display,
        Window window,
        long item_number)
```

XmClipboardEndCopy ends a copy to the clipboard and copies the data from temporary storage into the clipboard. The actual contents of the clipboard are stored in the X server. It returns XmClipboardSuccess, XmClipboardLocked, or XmClipboardFail. The *item_number* identifies the transaction and comes from XmClipboardStartCopy. Under the hood, XmClipboardEndCopy asserts ownership of the CLIPBOARD selection.

Instead of XmClipboardEndCopy, you could call XmClipboardCancelCopy to cancel the transaction:

```
#include <Xm/CutPaste.h>

int XmClipboardCancelCopy(Display* display,
        Window window,
        long item_number)
```

XmClipboardCancelCopy cancels an in-progress copy transaction to the clipboard, using the *item_number* to identify the transaction. It returns XmClipboardSuccess, XmClipboardLocked, or XmClipboardFail.

Motif Clipboard-Status Definitions

The Motif clipboard routines return a status value, which are listed in Table 19.4.

Table 19.4   Clipboard-status values.

Value	Meaning
XmClipboardFail	Operation failed, possibly on a lock or lack of one
XmClipboardSuccess	Operation worked
XmClipboardTruncate	Operation worked, but the data had to be truncated
XmClipboardLocked	Some other application already locked the clipboard
XmClipboardBadFormat	The format was NULL, or length not 8, 16, or 32
XmClipboardNoData	There are no data in the clipboard with the format

These status values are new in Motif 1.2. If you're using an older version of Motif, use Table 19.5 for compatibility.

NOTE

Table 19.5 *Compatibility definitions.*

Motif 1.2 Define	Motif 1.1 Define
XmClipboardFail	ClipboardFail
XmClipboardSuccess	ClipboardSuccess
XmClipboardTruncate	ClipboardTruncate
XmClipboardLocked	ClipboardLocked
XmClipboardBadFormat	ClipboardBadFormat
XmClipboardNoData	ClipboardNoData

Basically, the new definitions start with *Xm*, and the old ones don't. The integer values are the same.

Clipboard Formats

When you call `XmClipboardCopy`, you need to pass a format name, which should name a format registered with the Motif clipboard. Each format has an arbitrary name and a format length, which can be 8, 16, or 32. The format length identifies the size, in bits, of the integral data elements in the format. For example, the `"INTEGER"` format has data items that are each 32 bits long.

In order to exchange data with another application, both applications must agree on the same formats. Motif encourages the use of the preregistered built-in formats.

The Motif clipboard supports a number of built-in formats, including those listed in Table 19.6.

Table 19.6 *Some common built-in clipboard formats.*

Format Name	Defined Size	Size	Meaning
"BACKGROUND"	XM_PIXEL	32	Color index for background color
			continued

`"BITMAP"`	`XM_BITMAP`	32	Single-plane pixmap ID
`"CHARACTER_POSITION"`	`XM_SPAN`	32	Start and end of selection in bytes
`"CLASS"`	`XM_TEXT`	8	Application class name
`"CLIENT_WINDOW"`	`XM_WINDOW`	32	ID of window owning selection
`"COLORMAP"`	`XM_COLORMAP`	32	Colormap ID
`"COLUMN_NUMBER"`	`XM_SPAN`	32	Start and end column numbers
`"DRAWABLE"`	`XM_DRAWABLE`	32	Pixmap or window ID
`"FILE_NAME"`	`XM_TEXT`	8	Filename
`"FOREGROUND"`	`XM_PIXEL`	32	Color index for foreground color
`"HOST_NAME"`	`XM_TEXT`	8	Computer's network hostname
`"LENGTH"`	`XM_INTEGER`	32	Number of bytes in selection
`"LINE_NUMBER"`	`XM_SPAN`	32	Start and end line numbers
`"LIST_LENGTH"`	`XM_INTEGER`	32	Count of disjoint parts of selection
`"MODULE"`	`XM_TEXT`	8	Module name
`"MULTIPLE"`	`XM_ATOM_PAIR`	32	Used for multielement transactions
`"NAME"`	`XM_TEXT`	8	Window name
`"ODIF"`	`XM_TEXT`	8	ISO interchange format data
`"OWNER_OS"`	`XM_TEXT`	8	Owner's operating system name
`"PIXMAP"`	`XM_DRAWABLE`	32	Pixmap ID
`"PROCEDURE"`	`XM_TEXT`	8	Procedure name
`"PROCESS"`	`XM_INTEGER`	32	Process ID

continued

"STRING"	XM_STRING	8	ISO Latin-1 text string
"TARGETS"	XM_ATOM	32	Lists of data formats supported
"TASK"	XM_INTEGER	32	Task ID
"TIMESTAMP"	XM_INTEGER	32	Timestamp
"USER"	XM_TEXT	8	User name

These formats are the standard selection formats from the ICCCM. Some of the formats tend to the obscure. The "PROCEDURE" and "MODULE", for example, are very useful if you're writing a debugger or CASE (computer-aided software engineering) application. Note that the size is the size of elements. Most of the types support multiple data elements. For example, the "STRING" format most likely contains a number of 8-byte elements (characters in this case). We explain the most important formats in greater detail in the next chapter.

It's a good idea to use these formats so that other applications can interoperate with yours. In addition, using a built-in format saves you the effort of registering your format.

NOTE

The *XM* names above, like XM_TEXT, are defined as the size of the given data item, 8 in this case. These names also closely match that of the standard X atoms.

All the above formats should be preregistered. If you have problems on older systems, you may want to register these formats.

Registering New Clipboard Formats

You can register a format with XmClipboardRegisterFormat:

```
#include <Xm/CutPaste.h>

int XmClipboardRegisterFormat(Display* display,
        char* format_name,
        int format_length)
```

The *format_length* must be 8, 16, or 32. XmClipboardRegisterFormat returns a status of XmClipboardSuccess, XmClipboardLocked, XmClipboardFail, or XmClipboardBadFormat if *format_length* is not correct or *format_name* is NULL.

If you register your own format name, you should start your format name with an underscore. (This is from the ICCCM rules for atoms, but the concept still applies.)

Querying the Formats in the Clipboard Data

If you're working with different data formats, especially nontext formats, you may need to query the clipboard to see what kind of data is available. This is a two-step process.

First, you need to get a list of all the formats stored with the current data in the clipboard. (Remember, you can call XmClipboardCopy multiple times to store data in multiple formats.) To get a count of the number of formats currently in the clipboard data, call XmClipboardInquireCount:

```
#include <Xm/CutPaste.h>

int XmClipboardInquireCount(Display* display,
        Window window,
        int* number_formats, /* RETURN */
        unsigned long* format_name_max_length) /* RETURN */
```

XmClipboardInquireCount fills in the *number_formats* with the number of formats supported by the current data. That is, this is not a count of all the registered formats, but instead, it's a count of all the formats passed to XmClipboardCopy for the current set of data in the clipboard. (The clipboard maintains only one set of data at a time.)

XmClipboardInquireCount also provides the maximum length of the format names in the clipboard, so you know how large to allocate your text strings.

XmClipboardInquireCount returns XmClipboardSuccess, XmClipboardLocked, or XmClipboardNoData if there is no data in the clipboard.

After you have a count of the number of current formats, you call XmClipboardInquireFormat once for each format:

```
#include <Xm/CutPaste.h>

int XmClipboardInquireFormat(Display* display,
        Window window,
        int which_item,
        XtPointer format_name,          /* RETURN */
        unsigned long max_buffer_length,
        unsigned long* returned_length)  /* RETURN */
```

Call XmClipboardInquireFormat multiple times, passing a *which_item* from 1 to the number of formats returned by XmClipboardInquireCount. XmClipboardInquireFormat returns XmClipboardSuccess, XmClipboardLocked, XmClipboardNoData, or XmClipboardTruncate if the length of the *format_name* was longer than the allowed *max_buffer_length*.

After you know the formats, you can query how much data is stored for a given format by calling XmClipboardInquireLength:

```
#include <Xm/CutPaste.h>

int XmClipboardInquireLength(Display* display,
        Window window,
        char* format_name,
        unsigned long* returned_length)  /* RETURN */
```

These routines are mostly useful when copying and pasting nontext data.

Copying Data by Name

Users are fickle—and with the high price of UNIX software, they have a right to be. Users may copy data to the clipboard and then merrily go on with their work and—gasp—never paste that data anywhere. This may seem like a waste, but remember, with event-driven programming, the user is in charge. The user has every right to copy data to the clipboard and then never use that data.

With many selections, however, there's simply too much data to copy into the clipboard right away. Instead, you'll want to wait and see if the data is really used in a paste operation. Otherwise, there's no need to store the data into the clipboard if the copying operation is expensive.

A famous example, attributed to Mike Wexler (who helped create the ICCCM), is the case of an online encyclopedia program consisting of hundreds of megabytes, where the user chooses a **Select All** menu choice and then copies this data into the clipboard. In this case, you wouldn't want to transfer hundreds of megabytes into your X server, notwithstanding the fact that most X servers couldn't hold it all.

In another example, a graphical front-end to a relational database may provide the ability to select data, copy the data to the clipboard, and then later paste that data into another application or into other parts of the database. In this case, acquiring the data invokes time-consuming SQL queries. You'll want to avoid making the query unless the data is actually used.

All in all, the call is up to you. You can choose to copy the data directly to the clipboard with XmClipboardCopy or to defer the copy operation until later. To copy the data directly, pass a data buffer to XmClipboardCopy. To defer the copy operation until requested later, pass a NULL data buffer to XmClipboardCopy.

If you defer the operation, you must pass a by_name_callback function pointer to XmClipboardStartCopy. This should be a pointer to a function that will, indeed, serve up this data when requested.

The by_name_callback will be called with:

```
void (*by_name_callback)(Widget by_name_widget,
        int*    by_name_data_number,
        int*    private_number,
        int*    reason)
```

All the values, except for the reason, come from data passed to XmClipboardStartCopy or XmClipboardCopy. Treat all the integer pointers as read-only values. The reason will be XmCR_CLIPBOARD_DATA_DELETE (the data is no longer needed) or XmCR_CLIPBOARD_DATA_REQUEST (the deferred data is now requested).

If the reason is XmCR_CLIPBOARD_DATA_REQUEST, then your copy-call-back function now needs to serve up the data to the clipboard, since it are now requested. To serve up the data, call XmClipboardCopyByName, not XmClipboardCopy:

```
#include <Xm/CutPaste.h>

int XmClipboardCopyByName(Display* display,
        Window window,
        int by_name_data_number,
        char* buffer,
        unsigned long buffer_length,
        int private_number)
```

XmClipboardCopyByName copies the data in the buffer to the clipboard. In this case, you should *not* pass a buffer of NULL. You should pass the same display pointer and window ID given to all the clipboard functions. You'll need these values to determine what data to copy to the clipboard. And, yes, you're responsible for figuring this out. The buffer holds the data and the *buffer_length* the number of bytes in the buffer.

XmClipboardCopyByName returns XmClipboardSuccess or XmClipboardLocked.

N O T E After you pass the deferred data to the clipboard, Motif no longer expects your application to serve up the data, since it's been passed to the clipboard. You can free any memory allocated for this purpose.

If the reason is XmCR_CLIPBOARD_DATA_DELETE, then your application no longer needs to maintain the data. This reason is passed when another set of data is stored in the clipboard, overwriting the marker for your data.

If you use the deferred method with the clipboard, your application takes on the responsibility for the data. Your application must either store the data or be able to generate the data. In either case, your application is responsible for delivering the data on demand.

Retrieving Data from the Clipboard

There are two ways to retrieve data from the clipboard: a long way and a short way. The short way is easiest and just involves a single call to XmClipboardRetrieve:

```
#include <Xm/CutPaste.h>

int XmClipboardRetrieve(Display* display,
        Window window,
        char* format_name,
        XtPointer buffer,
        unsigned long max_length,      /* in bytes */
        unsigned long* return_length,  /* RETURN */
        long* private_number)          /* RETURN */
```

XmClipboardRetrieve returns XmClipboardSuccess, XmClipboardLocked, XmClipboardNoData, or XmClipboardTruncate if there are more data than could fit into the passed *max_length* of the buffer.

If you know exactly what data you want to retrieve, you can use the short method above. If you don't, you'll need to use the longer method for retrieving data from the clipboard.

Retrieving Data the Long Way

The long method still involves calling XmClipboardRetrieve, but you bracket the call (or calls) with XmClipboardStartRetrieve and XmClipboardEndRetrieve. That is, you call XmClipboardStartRetrieve to start an incremental retrieval and then call XmClipboardRetrieve as many times as necessary to get all the data. How do you know how much data is available? If XmClipboardRetrieve returns XmClipboardTruncate, more data is available. You may want to call XmClipboardInquireLength to determine the total length, or just keep calling XmClipboardRetrieve until you get all the data. (You may want to do both if the data count is very large.) Finally, call XmClipboardEndRetrieve to end the transaction.

XmClipboardStartRetrieve takes the following parameters:

```
#include <Xm/CutPaste.h>

int XmClipboardStartRetrieve(Display* display,
        Window window,
        Time timestamp)
```

XmClipboardStartRetrieve returns XmClipboardSuccess or XmClipboardLocked on errors.

XmClipboardEndRetrieve ends the transaction and takes just two parameters:

```
#include <Xm/CutPaste.h>

int XmClipboardEndRetrieve(Display* display,
        Window window)
```

XmClipboardEndRetrieve returns XmClipboardSuccess or XmClipboardLocked.

If you don't know much about the data in the clipboard, which is a likely case, chances are you'll need to use the long method to retrieve the clipboard data.

Undoing Clipboard Operations

To enable your application to undo operations, you can call XmClipboardUndoCopy:

```
#include <Xm/CutPaste.h>

int XmClipboardUndoCopy(Display* display,
        Window window)
```

If the display and window parameters match the last data copied to the clipboard, then this data are removed. The previous data in the clipboard—that is, the data that was in the clipboard before the last copy operation—is restored.

XmClipboardUndoCopy returns XmClipboardSuccess or XmClipboardLocked on errors.

NOTE XmClipboardUndoCopy swaps the two items in the clipboard buffer. Therefore, if you call XmClipboardUndoCopy twice, you are performing a *redo* operation—you're undoing the undo and restoring the clipboard to its original state.

This feature of Motif is undocumented, though, so it may be changed in later versions of the toolkit. Don't depend on this information.

A PROGRAM TO COPY PIXMAP DATA

To test the clipboard routines with a data type that is *not* text, we've put together an example program that copies pixmaps to the clipboard and then pastes them. You can run two copies of this program, using different pixmaps for each, and then see how the Motif clipboard routines work for pasting nontext data.

The program shows a row of pushbuttons with pixmaps. You can select any pushbutton to copy that pixmap into the clipboard. If you select the **Paste** button, the pixmap in the clipboard will be pasted into a label widget.

Copying Pixmap Data to the Clipboard

We set up a pushbutton activateCallback function to handle the copy routine. When any of the pushbuttons are pushed, the button copies its pixmap ID into the Motif clipboard.

When we call XmClipboardCopy, we pass a format name of "PIXMAP"and a private number of 42 (the answer to the ultimate question of life, the universe, and everything). The length is 4 bytes, since we have one 32-bit value (the pixmap ID).

```
    /* Copy pixmap to clipboard. */
void copyCB(Widget widget,
    XtPointer client_data,
    XtPointer call_data)

{   /* copyCB */
```

```
Time        timestamp;
long        item_number;
Display*    display;
long        bynameid;
Pixmap      pixmaps[5];

display   = XtDisplay(topshell);

timestamp = XtLastTimestampProcessed(display);

/* ... */

/* We assume client_data has a pixmap ID. */
pixmaps[0] = (Pixmap) client_data;

/* Copy data. */
status = XmClipboardCopy(display,
        XtWindow(topshell),
        item_number,    /* from XmClipboardStartCopy */
        "PIXMAP",       /* format name */
        (XtPointer) pixmaps,  /* data buffer */
        (unsigned long) 4,    /* buffer length */
        42L,            /* private number */
        &bynameid);     /* by name ID. */

        /* ... */
}   /* copyCB */
```

Retrieving Pixmap Data

When the user presses the **Paste** button, the program tries to paste a pixmap from the clipboard. If no pixmap is available, the pasteCB callback routine returns:

```
/* Paste clipboard pixmap to global pixlabel. */
void pasteCB(Widget widget,
    XtPointer client_data,
    XtPointer call_data)

{   /* pasteCB */
    int         status;
    Pixmap      pixmaps[5];
    unsigned long return_length;
    long        private_number;

    status = XmClipboardRetrieve(XtDisplay(topshell),
        XtWindow(topshell),
        "PIXMAP", /* format name */
        (XtPointer) pixmaps,  /* buffer */
        4L,       /* max length */
        &return_length,
        &private_number);
```

```
    if (status != ClipboardSuccess) {
        printf("Failed in XmClipboardRetrieve: %d.\n",
            status);
        return;
    }

    if (pixmaps[0] == (Pixmap) None) {
        printf("Error: bad pixmap.\n");
        return;
    }

    /* Verify depths. */
    status = CompareDepths(pixlabel, pixmaps[0]);

    /* Set retrieved pixmap into label widget. */
    if (status == True) {
        /* Set pushbutton to display pixmap. */
        SetLabelPixmap(pixlabel, pixmaps[0]);
    }

}   /* pasteCB */
```

Again, we use 4 bytes of data. If the routine does find a pixmap in the clipboard, it verifies that the pixmap's depth matches that of a label widget. If the depths match, the label widget displays a new pixmap.

Comparing Depths

Before we set a label or pushbutton widget's labelPixmap resource to a pixmap that we acquired from the Motif clipboard, we need to verify that the depth of the pixmap matches that of the widget we intend to place the pixmap in. We simply have no idea where this pixmap came from or what sort of irresponsible software created it. Therefore, we must ensure that the depths match or we'll most likely generate an X error.

To check the depth of a drawable—a window or pixmap—call XGetGeometry:

```
Status XGetGeometry(Display* display,
    Drawable drawable,
    Window*  root,              /* RETURN */
    int*     x,                 /* RETURN */
    int*     y,                 /* RETURN */
    unsigned int* width,        /* RETURN */
    unsigned int* height,       /* RETURN */
    unsigned int* border_width, /* RETURN */
    unsigned int* depth)        /* RETURN */
```

XGetGeometry returns a nonzero value on success and 0 on failure.

Why do we do this? In case the application that put the pixmap in the clipboard created the pixmap to a different depth. With the X Window System, defensive programming is a must. We could also check for the size, to see if the pixmap is rather huge, but in our sample program we don't check this.

Here's a utility routine to compare the depths of a drawable—a window or pixmap—with a widget:

```
/* Compares depth of window or pixmap with widget. */
Boolean CompareDepths(Widget widget,
    Drawable drawable)

{   /* CompareDepths */
    Window       root;
    int          x, y;
    unsigned int width, height, border_width;
    unsigned int widget_depth, drawable_depth;
    int          status;

    /* Verify depths. */
    status = XGetGeometry(XtDisplay(widget),
        drawable,
        &root,
        &x, &y,
        &width, &height,
        &border_width,
        &drawable_depth);

    if (status == 0) {
        printf("Error: could not get depth of 0x%x\n",
            drawable);
        return False;
    }

    /* Get widget's depth. */
    XtVaGetValues(widget,
        XmNdepth, &widget_depth,
        NULL);

    if (drawable_depth == widget_depth) {
        return True;
    } else {
        return False;
    }

}   /* CompareDepths */
```

Example Code for Copying Pixmap Data

The code for the *pixclip* program follows:

```c
/* pixclip.c */
#include  <Xm/Xm.h>
#include  <Xm/CutPaste.h>
#include  <Xm/Label.h>
#include  <Xm/PanedW.h>
#include  <Xm/RowColumn.h>
#include  <stdio.h>

/* Global data. */
Widget    topshell;
Widget    pixlabel;

/* External functions. */

extern Widget CreatePushbutton(Widget parent,
    char* name,
    XtCallbackProc callback,
    XtPointer client_data);

extern Pixmap ReadBitmapFile(Widget widget,
    char* filename,
    int* width,   /* RETURN */
    int* height); /* RETURN */

extern Pixmap CreatePixmapFromBitmap(Widget widget,
    int width,
    int height,
    Pixmap bitmap);

extern void SetLabelPixmap(Widget widget,
    Pixmap pixmap);

    /* Compares depth of window or pixmap with widget. */
Boolean CompareDepths(Widget widget,
    Drawable drawable)

{   /* CompareDepths */
    Window       root;
    int          x, y;
    unsigned int width, height, border_width;
    unsigned int widget_depth, drawable_depth;
    int          status;

    /* Verify depths. */
    status = XGetGeometry(XtDisplay(widget),
        drawable,
        &root,
        &x, &y,
        &width, &height,
```

```
            &border_width,
            &drawable_depth);

    if (status == 0) {
        printf("Error: could not get depth of 0x%x\n",
            drawable);
        return False;
    }

    /* Get widget's depth. */
    XtVaGetValues(widget,
        XmNdepth, &widget_depth,
        NULL);

    if (drawable_depth == widget_depth) {
        return True;
    } else {
        return False;
    }

}   /* CompareDepths */

    /* Copy pixmap to clipboard. */
void copyCB(Widget widget,
    XtPointer client_data,
    XtPointer call_data)

{   /* copyCB */
    int         status;
    Time        timestamp;
    long        item_number;
    Display*    display;
    XmString    xmstring;
    long        bynameid;
    Pixmap      pixmaps[5];

    display = XtDisplay(topshell);

    timestamp = XtLastTimestampProcessed(display);

    xmstring = XmStringCreateSimple("pixclip");

    status = XmClipboardStartCopy(display,
            XtWindow(topshell),
            xmstring,
            timestamp,
            (Widget) NULL,
            NULL,
            &item_number);

    XmStringFree(xmstring);

    if (status != ClipboardSuccess) {
        printf("Failed in XmClipboardStartCopy: %d.\n",
            status);
```

```
        return;
    }

    /* We assume client_data has a pixmap ID. */
    if (client_data == NULL) {
        return;
    }

    pixmaps[0] = (Pixmap) client_data;

    if (pixmaps[0] == (Pixmap) None) {
        printf("Error: bad pixmap.\n");
        return;
    }

    /* Copy data. */
    status = XmClipboardCopy(display,
            XtWindow(topshell),
            item_number,  /* from XmClipboardStartCopy */
            "PIXMAP",      /* format name */
            (XtPointer) pixmaps,  /* data buffer */
            (unsigned long) 4,    /* # buffer bytes */
            42L,            /* private number */
            &bynameid);     /* by name ID. */

    if (status != ClipboardSuccess) {
        printf("Failed in XmClipboardCopy: %d.\n",
            status);
        return;
    }

    /* End transaction. */
    status = XmClipboardEndCopy(display,
            XtWindow(topshell),
            item_number);

    if (status != ClipboardSuccess) {
        printf("Failed in XmClipboardEndCopy: %d.\n",
            status);
        return;
    }

}   /* copyCB */

    /* Paste clipboard pixmap to global pixlabel. */
void pasteCB(Widget widget,
    XtPointer client_data,
    XtPointer call_data)

{   /* pasteCB */
    int           status;
    Pixmap        pixmaps[5];
    unsigned long return_length;
    long          private_number;
```

```
        status = XmClipboardRetrieve(XtDisplay(topshell),
                XtWindow(topshell),
                "PIXMAP", /* format name */
                (XtPointer) pixmaps,  /* buffer */
                4L,          /* max length */
                &return_length,
                &private_number);

        if (status != ClipboardSuccess) {
            printf("Failed in XmClipboardRetrieve: %d.\n",
                status);
            return;
        }

        if (pixmaps[0] == (Pixmap) None) {
            printf("Error: bad pixmap.\n");
            return;
        }

        /* Verify depths. */
        status = CompareDepths(pixlabel, pixmaps[0]);

        /* Set retrieved pixmap into label widget. */
        if (status == True) {
            /* Set pushbutton to display pixmap. */
            SetLabelPixmap(pixlabel, pixmaps[0]);
        }

}   /* pasteCB */

void exitCB(Widget widget,
    XtPointer client_data,
    XtPointer call_data)

{   /* exitCB */

    exit(0);

}   /* exitCB */

int main(int argc, char** argv)

{   /* main */
    XtAppContext    app_context;
    Widget          pane, toprow;
    Widget          push, paste, quit;
    Arg             args[20];
    Cardinal        n;
    Pixmap          bitmap, pixmap;
    int             width, height;

    /* Initialize toolkit with global topshell. */
    topshell = XtVaAppInitialize(&app_context,
                "Ppm",
                (XrmOptionDescList) NULL,
```

```
                    0,
                    &argc, argv,
                    (String*) NULL,
                    XmNallowResize, True,
                    NULL);

/* Create a paned window. */
n = 0;
pane = XmCreatePanedWindow(topshell,
        "pane", args, n);

/* Create a row column for the top pixmaps. */
toprow = XtVaCreateWidget("toprow",
        xmRowColumnWidgetClass, pane,
        XmNorientation, XmHORIZONTAL,
        NULL);

/* Create pixmaps for pushbuttons. We assume
   all of argv remaining are bitmap file names.
 */
for (n = 1; n < argc; n++) {
    /* Load bitmap file. */

    bitmap = ReadBitmapFile(toprow, argv[n],
            &width, &height);

    if (bitmap == (Pixmap) None) {
        continue;
    }

    /* Create pixmap from bitmap. */
    pixmap = CreatePixmapFromBitmap(toprow,
            width, height, bitmap);

    if (pixmap == (Pixmap) None) {
        continue;
    }

    /* Free bitmap. */
    XFreePixmap(XtDisplay(toprow), bitmap);

    /* Create pushbutton widget, pass pixmap ID. */
    push = CreatePushbutton(toprow, argv[n],
            (XtCallbackProc) copyCB,
            (XtPointer) pixmap);

    /* Set pushbutton to display pixmap. */
    SetLabelPixmap(push, pixmap);
}

/* Create pushbuttons to control program. */
paste = CreatePushbutton(pane, "paste",
        (XtCallbackProc) pasteCB,
        (XtPointer) NULL);
```

```
/* Global label widget to hold the pasted data. */
/* Uses size of last-loaded bitmap. */
pixlabel = XtVaCreateManagedWidget("pixlabel",
        xmLabelWidgetClass, pane,
        XmNwidth,  width,
        XmNheight, height,
        NULL);

quit = CreatePushbutton(pane, "exit",
        (XtCallbackProc) exitCB,
        (XtPointer) NULL);

XtManageChild(toprow);
XtManageChild(pane);

XtRealizeWidget(topshell);
XtAppMainLoop(app_context);
return 0;

}   /* main */

/* end of file pixclip.c */
```

The resource file for this program follows:

```
! Resource file for pixclip.c in Chapter 19
! of Power Programming Motif.
!
*fontList:      lucidasans-12
*background:    grey92

*title:    Pixmap Clipboard

*exit.labelString:     Exit
*paste.labelString:    Paste
*pixlabel.labelString: Retrieved Data

! end of resource file
```

Name this file **Ppm** and place it in your home directory.

Running the Pixmap Clipboard Program

To fully test the *pixclip* program, we advise running two copies. That way, you'll see how the Motif clipboard works in transferring pixmap data between applications.

The *pixclip* program takes all command-line parameters as the names of bitmap files to load. We use the same bitmap file-loading routines that we introduced in Chapter 12.

Each of these command-line parameters should be the name of a bitmap file. The *pixclip* program then converts the bitmaps into pixmaps of the proper depth and sets the pixmaps into a set of Motif pushbuttons. When pressed, each pushbutton will copy its pixmap into the clipboard.

If you press the **Paste** pushbutton, the program will try to retrieve a pixmap ID from the clipboard. If this succeeds, the program then places the pixmap into the target label widget, so you can see which pixmap was pasted.

Therefore, this works best when you run more than one copy of the program, so that you can paste different pixmaps between the applications, as we show in Figure 19.2.

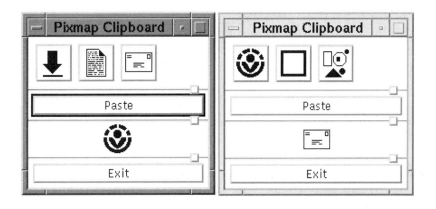

Figure 19.2 *Running two copies of the pixclip program.*

If you try to paste without first copying something to the clipboard, you'll see an error message printed by the *pixclip* program. If you similarly try to paste text when the program expects a pixmap, you'll also see a printed error message.

SUMMARY

As is common with most graphical interfaces, Motif provides a clipboard into which you can copy data for later pasting. This clipboard is very useful within your applications, especially text-editing programs, as well as for transferring data between applications. In addition to the Motif clipboard, there are other X Window-based methods of transferring data between applications. This chapter covered only the Motif clipboard; the next two chapters cover the X-based methods for transferring data. Your applications must follow the mechanisms described in these three chapters if they are to function as good Motif citizens.

The idea behind a clipboard is rather simple: It serves as a storage area for data cut or copied from an application window. When the user selects data in a window, the user may want to copy that data to the clipboard and, of course, paste that data sometime later somewhere else—in the current application or in another application. All this can be done from the Motif clipboard.

There are two main ways to interact with the clipboard. Since the vast majority of all computer data is text (yes, even in a graphical interface, you're still mainly working with text), Motif provides a set of text-clipboard convenience routines that dramatically simplify your interaction with the clipboard. But not *all* data is text. And, in a graphical interface, users expect to be able to select bitmaps, colors, and other objects on the screen and then copy the data into the clipboard. You can do all this with the Motif clipboard, but be warned that few applications support arbitrary data types. In fact, you're lucky if an application even supports the clipboard's copy and paste of text. It's a sad tale, but many X programs skimp on interoperability. This should change in the future with the advent of more standardized file browsers and other applications where users will expect to copy and paste data. (Much of this will come from the COSE UNIX unification efforts.)

This chapter covered the text-convenience routines and then covered how to interact with the Motif clipboard in depth. These steps, while appearing to be rather boring, are very important for your applications.

In the next chapter, we extend our discussion of data exchange by going over the X selection mechanism for active selecting and inserting.

MOTIF INTRINSICS FUNCTIONS AND MACROS INTRODUCED IN THIS CHAPTER

```
XmClipboardBeginCopy
XmClipboardCancelCopy
```

```
XmClipboardCopy
XmClipboardCopyByName
XmClipboardEndCopy
XmClipboardEndRetrieve
XmClipboardInquireCount
XmClipboardInquireFormat
XmClipboardInquireLength
XmClipboardRegisterFormat
XmClipboardRetrieve
XmClipboardStartCopy
XmClipboardStartRetrieve
XmClipboardUndoCopy
XmTextCopy
XmTextCut
XmTextPaste
XmTextRemove
XmTextFieldCopy
XmTextFieldCut
XmTextFieldPaste
XmTextFieldRemove
```

X TOOLKIT INTRINSICS FUNCTIONS AND MACROS INTRODUCED IN THIS CHAPTER

```
XtLastTimestampProcessed
```

X LIBRARY FUNCTIONS AND MACROS INTRODUCED IN THIS CHAPTER

```
XGetGeometry
```

CHAPTER 20

X Selections for Active Data Exchange

This chapter covers:

- ▓ Active data exchange with X selections
- ▓ Standards for selections
- ▓ Selection data types, or targets
- ▓ Requesting the value of a current selection
- ▓ Acquiring selection ownership
- ▓ Converting the selection data on request
- ▓ XmText widget convenience routines for selections

X SELECTIONS

Selections are the X Window System's means for providing an active select-and-insert mechanism. They also provide a generalized query-reply inter-process communication (IPC) mechanism. The name *selection* comes from the fact that selection data usually is generated by the user selecting something on the screen. For example, the user can select text in a text widget. This text then appears highlighted, and the application asserts ownership of a selection.

We consider selections an active means of data exchange, because the data is never copied to some neutral location, like the Motif clipboard. Instead, the receiving application merely asks the owning application to send over the data. The clipboard described in the last chapter is more passive, unless you copy values by name.

Selections are powerful and confusing, and most explanations of the X selection mechanism are buried in the back of the text, covered with the most confusing language possible, or both. Each selection-related function is described, but few books describe how to put these calls together, which, of course, is a shame, since selections provide one of the most powerful features of X.

Don't panic. Selections are easy. Really. The Xt Intrinsics provide a number of utility routines that dramatically cut the complexity of coding for selections. Even so, the task is involved. This chapter covers that task and explains X selections from the Xt Intrinsics, showing how you can use these in your code.

It took us a long time to be convinced that selections are really good. But if you look at how selections work, you'll see that selections help provide a very productive environment under the X Window System. Selections provide for an active selection and insertion. That is, you don't need to copy the data into a neutral clipboard in the X server. Instead, the inserting (consumer) application asks the selection owner (producer) for the data. The consumer can ask for the data in a number of formats. It's up to the producer to convert the data. To help mediate this, the producer must provide on demand a list of data types, called *targets*, that the producer supports.

Some uses for selections include the following:

■ The user selects text in one application, say *xterm*, and then pastes the text into another application, say our text editor (the *textclip* program) from the previous chapter. Usually, the user can do this with simple mouse actions (the leftmost button selects and the middle button inserts the selected data in most default cases) instead of calling up a clipboard menu.

■ A text editor asks a debugger for the line number and file name in which an error occurred. The editor then displays that file at that line, so the user can correct the error.

■ The user selects two pieces of text and asks for them to be exchanged.

User's View of Selections

From the user's point of view, here's how selections work.

1. The user selects something, usually text.

2. In another application window, at a later time, the user tries to insert the current selection, usually by clicking the middle mouse button. This application asks the owning application for the selection data.

3. When the owning application sends over the selected data, the data appears in the window where the user clicked the mouse button.

Note that there's no intermediate step of going to a clipboard. This makes selections quicker from a user's perspective, but it is also dependent on state: There can be only one owner of a given selection (usually the PRIMARY selection) at a time.

Programmer's View of Selections

Programming selections isn't as easy as the user's view suggests. The basic mechanism seems overly complex, and the X Consortium plans to make this even more complex with X11 Release 6, so fasten your seat belts—you're in for a bumpy ride. However, the Xt Intrinsics provide a number of utility functions to ease the chore of coding for selections.

The Xt Intrinsics hide the underlying communication and negotiation protocols. Instead of coding this, your application provides a callback function that is called when the data arrives.

The programmer's view of selections then follows this model:

1. The user selects something, usually text.

2. The application asserts ownership of a selection. By convention, this is usually the PRIMARY selection.

3. Another application at a later time asks the X server for the value of the selection. The requesting application also requests that the data be converted to an arbitrary format.

4. The X server notifies the owning application via an X event.

5. The owning application writes the data out in the requested format onto a property on a window. When done, the owning application sends a SelectionNotify event to the requesting application. (Xt hides this event from the requesting program and instead executes a callback).

6. The requesting application then reads the property from the window and inserts the data into the current work area.

SHORTCUT

Programming Selections

To get the current value of a given *selection* converted to the *target* data format, call XtGetSelectionValue:

```
void XtGetSelectionValue(Widget widget,
    Atom selection,
    Atom target,
    XtSelectionCallbackProc callback,
    XtPointer client_data,
    Time timestamp)
```

XtGetSelectionValue requests that the X server notify the selection owner; the selection owner is then expected to deliver the data at some later time. But the data isn't here yet. Instead, you must wait until some time later when your *callback* gets executed. The Xt Intrinsics hide the messy communication details and simply call your *callback* function when the data arrives.

The *callback* should take the following read-only parameters:

```
typedef void (*XtSelectionCallbackProc)(
    Widget widget,
    XtPointer client_data,
    Atom* selection,
    Atom* type,
    XtPointer value,
    unsigned long* value_length,
    int* format);
```

In order for selections or any other program-to-program communication method to work, all the programs must agree on a set of rules for how the communication takes place. These conventions appear in the *Inter-Client Communications Conventions Manual*, the ICCCM. Because these conventions are in the ICCCM, you should be able to use selections to exchange data between applications created with a number of X toolkits—unlike the Motif clipboard, which is proprietary to Motif applications.

ICCCM Selections

Selections are the X Window System's means for implementing quick selection and insertion between applications. Under the hood, selections are atoms that you pass around asking for data—usually the data the user selected in a window with the mouse, but not always.

Selections are global to the X server. Only one application at a time may own a given selection.

If you wish, though, you can use any atom you desire for a selection. The only caveat is that the X server rigidly enforces the rule that only one application may own a given selection atom at a time. Ownership in this case is the means used to control access to the data. The owning application owns the selected data. Any other application may request copies of the data (in a number of formats), but only one application owns the data.

When another application asserts ownership of a selection, the original owner loses the selection.

The Three Little Selections

Each selection is an atom. In order for selections to work, therefore, applications have to agree beforehand on what strings to intern to use these atoms. Whether you agree or not, the ICCCM defines three atoms to use for selections:

- ■ PRIMARY
- ■ SECONDARY
- ■ CLIPBOARD

Under the hood, Motif asserts ownership of the PRIMARY and CLIPBOARD selections when needed. For example, if you select text inside an XmText widget, Motif will automatically assert ownership of the PRIMARY selection. It's only when you have some custom data or special need that you will want to assert ownership of a selection. For example, if you're writing a debugging application that is closely tied to an editor, you may want to write some code for handling selections.

The following paragraphs describe the three common selections.

The PRIMARY Selection

The main selection is the PRIMARY selection, which uses a built-in atom ID of XA_PRIMARY, from <X11/Xatom.h>. When the user selects data in an *xterm* window or in a Motif XmText widget, the application asserts ownership of the PRIMARY selection.

See section 2.6.1.1 in the ICCCM for more information on the PRIMARY selection.

The SECONDARY Selection

The SECONDARY selection is an extra selection, often used when the user wants to exchange the PRIMARY and SECONDARY selections (allowing some form of backtracking or undoing) or make another selection without disturbing the PRIMARY selection. Rarely used, XA_SECONDARY is defined in <X11/Xatom.h>. You don't need to worry so much about SECONDARY, though, as PRIMARY is the primary concern.

The CLIPBOARD Selection

This selection is used for a clipboard-style application like *xclipboard*. Motif uses the CLIPBOARD selection to control access to the Motif clipboard, as described in the last chapter. Open Look applications often use the CLIPBOARD selection where other applications use PRIMARY.

There is no predefined atom for CLIPBOARD, so you must intern the string "CLIPBOARD" with XmInternAtom..

NOTE

It's easiest to start looking at selections from the point of view of the data requester.

Asking for Selection Data

With the Motif clipboard, an application stores data in the clipboard in a given format. The application can store data in a number of formats into the clipboard. The retrieving application, then, is limited to one of these formats.

Unlike the Motif clipboard, X selections allow a broad range of data formats. The idea is that the requesting application asks the application that owns the selection to convert the data to a given format. The basic underlying concept of selections is that you ask the owner of a selection for "the data" and you ask the owner to put "the data" into the type of data—called the *target* type—you want. For example, if the user selects text in a window, the obvious data format to ask for is text. In addition, though, other attributes of this selection may be important to your application. You may need to know how long the selected text is. You may want to get the font the text is in, the foreground color, or the starting and ending character positions in the text window. You may want the window ID of where the text appears so that you can highlight the window. There are a lot of different attributes about selected data that your application may need. Luckily, with X selections, you can ask the selected owner for all this by using different target types.

The idea, though, is that you can ask the selection owner to give you the selected data in any target type you want, provided the owning program supports that data target type. We could call this formatting the data, but X selections use the term *format* to refer to how big each basic element is: 8, 16, or 32 bits. We'll stick to *target* type to refer to the type of data you want.

For example, if the user selected some text with a mouse, another application could ask the owning program for the selected text. In this case, you ask for the selection with a target type of XA_STRING. Another program, perhaps an editor, could ask the owning program for the name of the file in which the selected text is to be found, the line numbers where the selected text starts and ends, and so on.

We've been assuming that the base type of the selected data is text. This, of course, isn't always so. Therein lies the beauty of the selection mechanism. A bitmap editor could allow users to cut and paste bitmaps between applications. A color chooser could allow the user to select a color (perhaps using a Pantone method like real printers use). Other applications could ask for that color from the owning application. With interoperable applications, you can concentrate each application on what it does best. You no longer have to make each application into a be-all, end-all program. An Internet news reader doesn't have to have an electronic-mail program built in; the news reader and the mail program could communicate through selections.

Requesting the Selection

You request the selected data by calling XtGetSelectionValue:

```
void XtGetSelectionValue(Widget widget,
    Atom selection,
    Atom target,
    XtSelectionCallbackProc callback,
    XtPointer client_data,
    Time timestamp)
```

XtGetSelectionValue returns no status and in fact returns immediately. This is one of the most confusing aspects to X selections. XtGetSelectionValue requests that the X server notify the selection owner; the selection owner is then expected to deliver the data at some later time. But the data isn't here yet. Instead, you must wait until sometime later when your *callback* gets executed. The Xt Intrinsics hide the messy communication details and simply call you *callback* function when the data arrives.

There's always the possibility that the data won't arrive, and Xt takes care of this, too. It calls your *callback* and passes a special error value, which we cover below.

With XtGetSelectionValue, you pass a *widget*, the *selection* atom you're looking for (most likely XA_PRIMARY for the PRIMARY selection), a *target* data type (we cover the common targets in Table 20.1), and a *timestamp* to help mediate synchronization issues on slow networks. You also pass a *client_data* pointer, which is passed in turn to your *callback* function.

The *callback* function gets called when the selection data arrives and takes the following parameters:

```
typedef void (*XtSelectionCallbackProc)(
    Widget widget,
    XtPointer client_data,
    Atom* selection,
    Atom* type,
    XtPointer value,
    unsigned long* value_length,
    int* format);
```

Even though most of the values are pointers, treat these values as read-only. The *selection* points at the selection atom, most likely having a value of XA_PRIMARY. If the data never arrived, Xt provides an error value for the *selection* to indicate a conversion failure, XT_CONVERT_FAIL:

```
#define XT_CONVERT_FAIL (Atom)0x80000001
```

The *type* atom holds the ID of the data type, such as XA_STRING (another built-in atom) for text string data. The *value* points at the actual data. The *value_length* holds the number of elements, which is often *not* the number of bytes. The *format* tells you how large each individual value element is: 8, 16, or 32 bits. By combining the *value_length* with the *format*, you can determine how to extract the data from the value.

Inside your *callback* function, you should program defensively and check the *selection* atom for XT_CONVERT_FAIL and also see if it's less than or equal to 0. All other atoms should also be checked to ensure that the value is greater than 0. Check the *value_length* to ensure that you actually have some data with the *value* pointer.

Requesting Multiple Data Formats Simultaneously

You can also acquire a number of values at one time, using XtGetSelectionValues:

```
void XtGetSelectionValues(Widget widget,
    Atom selection,
    Atom* targets,
    int number_targets,
    XtSelectionCallbackProc callback,
    XtPointer* set_of_client_data,
    Time timestamp)
```

There are a few quirks to XtGetSelectionValues, but otherwise it acts like XtGetSelectionValue. XtGetSelectionValues takes an array of target atoms, *targets*, and a count of the number of target atoms in the array, *number_targets*. When each target type of data arrives, your *callback* function will get called. The *client_data* passed to this callback is one element in the *set_of_client_data* array: the element that corresponds to the target. That is, if you provide an array of five *targets*, you also need to provide an array of five `client_data` pointers in *set_of_client_data*. The second element in the targets array will get the data from the second element in the *set_of_client_data* array.

To help ease the confusion, we'll use `XtGetSelectionValues` in our example program below.

Selection Targets

In order for data exchange to work, both sides must agree on the same selections as well as the same data types, or targets. The ICCCM defines a number of standard data target types that fit many needs. Your applications are also free to define your own types, but remember, you'll need applications that understand these types to exchange data with.

We list the common ICCCM target types in Table 20.1.

Table 20.1   *Target types.*

Target	Base Type	Built-In Atom	Element Size
BACKGROUND	PIXEL	*None*	32
BITMAP	BITMAP	XA_BITMAP	32
CHARACTER_POSITION	SPAN	XA_INTEGER	32
CLASS	TEXT	*None*	8
CLIENT_WINDOW	WINDOW	XA_WINDOW	32
COLORMAP	COLORMAP	XA_COLORMAP	32
COLUMN_NUMBER	SPAN	XA_INTEGER	32
COMPOUND_TEXT	COMPOUND_TEXT	*None*	8
DELETE	NULL	*None*	32
DRAWABLE	DRAWABLE	XA_DRAWABLE	32

continued

FILE_NAME	TEXT	*None*	8
FOREGROUND	PIXEL	*None*	32
HOST_NAME	TEXT	*None*	8
INSERT_PROPERTY	NULL	*None*	32
INSERT_SELECTION	NULL	*None*	32
LENGTH	INTEGER	XA_INTEGER	32
LINE_NUMBER	SPAN	XA_INTEGER	32
LIST_LENGTH	INTEGER	XA_INTEGER	32
MODULE	TEXT	*None*	8
MULTIPLE	ATOM_PAIR	XA_ATOM_PAIR	32
NAME	TEXT	*None*	8
ODIF	TEXT	*None*	8
OWNER_OS	TEXT	*None*	8
PIXMAP	DRAWABLE	XA_PIXMAP	32
PROCEDURE	TEXT	*None*	8
PROCESS	INTEGER	XA_INTEGER	32
STRING	STRING	XA_STRING	8
TARGETS	ATOM	XA_ATOM	32
TASK	INTEGER	XA_INTEGER	32
TIMESTAMP	INTEGER	XA_INTEGER	32
USER	TEXT	*None*	8

These targets are very similar to the clipboard formats listed in Chapter 19 in Table 19.6.

N O T E

Each of the targets listed in Table 20.1 may indicate more than one data element. For example, STRING data should be expected to have more than one 8-bit character.

We cover some of the more interesting and obscure target types below.

Targets like CHARACTER_POSITION, which have a SPAN base type, hold two integers: usually the start and end values. Asking for the CHARACTER_POSITION target, then, is a request to get the starting and ending character position where the selected data lies.

The CLASS target contains the data from the WM_CLASS window manager property. See Chapter 18 for details.

The CLIENT_WINDOW target holds the application's window, that is, the window in which the selected data appear.

The FILE_NAME target requests the full path name of the current file your application is working on or wants to work on.

The LENGTH target requests the size, in bytes of the selected data.

Requesting the NAME target asks for the owning application's name.

The STRING target is for ISO Latin-1 text. The TEXT target is for text in the owning application's preferred format, which is usually the STRING format, but may be in a wildly different format in Asian countries. COMPOUND_TEXT is textual data encoded in the X Consortium compound text format. This is very useful for exchanging international text.

The PROCESS and TASK targets may also support a TEXT data type.

Diverging Opinions: HOST_NAME

Asking for the HOST_NAME target requests the network hostname of the machine the owning application is computing on. This is useful information with the X Window System's network transparency—even though we don't mention this regularly, you must always keep in mind that not all X applications run on the same machine.

Usually your application sets this information on the WM_CLIENT_MACHINE property on your top-level window. The diverging opinion is that many applications built with the Athena widget set, including *xterm*, use the name HOSTNAME without an underscore. This, of course, generates a different atom. Which is correct? The ICCCM lists HOST_NAME, with the underscore, as being correct. We normally choose to support both spellings.

The Target of Evil: OWNER_OS

If the HOST_NAME divergence isn't enough, the OWNER_OS target is evil. We found that if we selected text in an *xterm* window and then asked for the

PRIMARY selection with a target type of OWNER_OS, we managed to knock out the *xterm* application. This is obviously a bug in the *xterm* sources (and will probably be fixed in the official sources by the time you read this), but we mention it because there are a lot of older versions of X out there.

In an ideal world, asking for the OWNER_OS target would get you the text name of the operating system that the selection owner application is running under. (Again, remember that X applications may compute on any machine on the network.)

Required Targets

Table 20.1 lists target types your application may want to support and may want to ask other applications to provide. The ICCCM requires all applications support the MULTIPLE, TARGETS, and TIMESTAMP targets (read more about this in section 2.6.2 of the ICCCM). It's a good idea to support more targets than these three, though, because of their limited usefulness.

The MULTIPLE Target

If an application wants to ask your program to provide the current selection data in a number of formats (perhaps the text data and the file name the data came from, as well as the position in the file where the text was selected and so on), that application will use the MULTIPLE target type. This means there are multiple targets you need to respond to.

In the property with the MULTIPLE data lies a set of ATOM_PAIR data. These pairs are each a target type and a property ID, and both are X atoms.

The first item in the property is the target type (one of the types discussed here, probably) your code needs to convert the selected data to. The second item is the property on which you should write the data for the given target type. In each ATOM_PAIR, the first item is a target type (one of many) and the second item is a property ID. Your application should then convert the selection data to the asked-for target type and write that data to the paired property ID (all on the same given window ID). Repeat this process for every ATOM_PAIR stored in the original property. Confusing? You bet.

The TARGETS Target

It's hard for another application to guess what kind of data types your application supports, so the ICCCM designers came up with the TARGETS target.

TARGETS is a list of the target data types your application supports for export—the list of what target types other applications can ask of your application. Since each target type is an atom, the TARGETS response is a list of atoms. Your application should respond with the list of target types (atoms) that your application supports.

The TIMESTAMP Target

The TIMESTAMP target is the timestamp (in X server terms) of when your application became the given selection's owner. If you call XtOwnSelection on the PRIMARY selection, your application should be able to return the timestamp passed to XtOwnSelection.

The proper response to a TIMESTAMP request is to format the time-stamp as a 32-bit integer (real type XA_INTEGER) and write that value into the requested property on the requested window.

Targets with Side Effects

The DELETE target asks the owning application to delete the selected data. Whether the owning application accedes to this request or not is up to the application. The INSERT_PROPERTY target asks that the owning application insert the data in the passed property into the selection. The INSERT_SELECTION target provides an ATOM_PAIR with a selection and a target. The owning application should read the property and then acquire the selection data in the proper target type. When all this is done, the returned data should be inserted into the selection. As you'd expect, these targets tend to be rarely used.

The returned data from these types will be an atom of type NULL.

What To Do When You Get the Data

When the data finally arrives, your application receives a raw pointer. It's up to your code to convert this pointer to data into meaningful information. The format and type information should help in converting the data. We show a number of examples for this in the convert_ATOM, convert_INTEGER, convert_WINDOW, and sel_dataCB functions in **primary.c**, later in this chapter.

Controlling Timeouts

If you ask for selection data, Xt will wait only so long and then assume that an error took place. You can control this timeout with XtAppSetSelectionTimeout:

```
void XtAppSetSelectionTimeout(XtAppContext app_context,
    unsigned long timeout) /* milliseconds */
```

The default timeout is 5000 milliseconds (5 seconds) and comes from the selectionTimeout resource.

You can query the selection timeout value by calling XtAppGetSelectionTimeout:

```
unsigned long
    XtAppGetSelectionTimeout(XtAppContext app_context)
```

Don't call the obsolete functions XtSetSelectionTimeout and XtGetSelectionTimeout. Call the newer application context routines shown above.

N O T E

Acquiring Selection Ownership

Each selection in use is owned by a window. This ownership is global to the display. The selection is just an atom, but an atom with an owner. To assert ownership of a selection, call XtOwnSelection:

```
Boolean XtOwnSelection(Widget widget
    Atom selection,
    Time timestamp,
    XtConvertSelectionProc convert_callback,
    XtLoseSelectionProc lose_callback,
    XtSelectionDoneProc done_callback)
```

If XtOwnSelection returns True, the *widget* now owns the *selection*. You should pass a valid *timestamp* to XtOwnSelection, not the constant CurrentTime.

To use XtOwnSelection, you need to set up three callback functions:

■ The *convert_callback*, which is called when another application requests that your application convert the data to a given target type

■ The *lose_callback*, which lets you know you've lost the selection ownership

■ The *done_callback*, which is executed after the requesting application has picked up the data

You can pass NULL for both the *done_callback* and *lose_callback*, but not the *convert_callback*. Note that if the *done_callback* is NULL, the *convert_callback* must allocate memory only with an Xt memory-allocation routine (like XtMalloc), because Xt will automatically free the data. If the *done_callback* is not NULL, then your code is responsible for freeing the data.

The Data-Conversion Callback

As a selection owner, your application is responsible for delivering the selection data, on demand, to any X application (including your own application). When any program requests the selection value, Xt will call your *convert_callback*, which takes the following parameters:

```
typedef Boolean (*XtConvertSelectionProc)(
    Widget widget,
    Atom* selection,
    Atom* target,
    Atom* actual_type,          /* RETURN */
    XtPointer* value,           /* RETURN */
    unsigned long* value_length, /* RETURN, in elements */
    int* format);               /* RETURN */
```

The first check to make is if your function can convert the data to the requested target type. If not, the function should return False.

The function should convert the data for the *selection* into the given *target*, and then supply the *actual_type*, often not the same as the *target*. For example, the CLIENT_WINDOW *target* has an actual type of XA_WINDOW (the built-in atom for WINDOW).

You also need to provide the *format* (8, 16, or 32) and of course the *value*. Set the *value_length* to the number of data elements in the *value* data. It's most likely that your code will allocate memory for the value with XtMalloc. This step is necessary if you don't provide a *done_callback* to XtOwnSelection.

The Done-With-Conversion Callback

The done callback gets executed when the requesting application gets around to picking up the data delivered by the convert callback. On a slow network, this may take some time.

The done callback should free any memory allocated by the convert callback, and it takes the following parameters:

```
typedef void (*XtSelectionDoneProc)(
    Widget widget,
    Atom* selection,
    Atom* target);
```

In many ways, the done callback exists to prevent Xt from calling XtFree on your *value* data.

The Losing-Selection Callback

When you lose the selection, your lose callback gets executed with the following parameters:

```
typedef void (*XtLoseSelectionProc)(
    Widget widget,
    Atom* selection);
```

It is normally considered bad form to try to reacquire a selection just because you lost it. Selections exist for the convenience of the user, not your program. An exception to this rule is a clipboard application like *xclipboard*, which reasserts ownership of the CLIPBOARD selection each time another application grabs it. This is so *xclipboard* can display the current clipboard value. (Note that *xclipboard* and the Motif clipboard don't always work well together.)

Incremental Selections

The Xt Intrinsics also provide for the case where your data is simply too large to transfer in one call. If this condition fits your data, you can use a set of incremental selection functions and callbacks, where each call to a callback generates part of the data.

This topic is far too involved for a Motif programming book, but the concepts are essentially the same as for selections where you transfer all the data at once—except, of course, you're transferring only part of the data at a time.

Disowning Selections

If your application no longer wishes to uphold the responsibilities of selection ownership, it can give up the selection by disowning it with XtDisownSelection:

```
void XtDisownSelection(Widget widget,
    Atom selection,
    Time timestamp)
```

A PROGRAM TO TEST SELECTIONS

We've put together a program to test out selection code. The primary program, shown below, queries the owner of a selection for a number of targets and then prints this data into a scrolled XmText widget. We found that such a program helped us to better understand the game of 20 questions, which you ask the owner of the selection data. Therefore, the primary program asks the selection owner to provide the selection data in the following target data types, in order:

- TARGETS
- STRING
- TEXT
- NAME
- HOST_NAME
- HOSTNAME (without underscore)
- USER
- FILE_NAME
- CLIENT_WINDOW
- LIST_LENGTH
- LENGTH
- TIMESTAMP
- CHARACTER_POSITION

Obviously, some of the targets are more interesting than others. The caching abilities of XmInternAtom comes in handy here, because Motif has already interned a number of these atoms.

When the data arrives, our sel_dataCB function converts the various data types to text, for display in the XmText widget.

The program code follows:

```
/* primary.c */
#include  <Xm/Xm.h>
#include  <Xm/AtomMgr.h>
#include  <Xm/PanedW.h>
#include  <Xm/RowColumn.h>
#include  <Xm/Text.h>
#include  <Xm/ToggleB.h>
#include  <X11/Xatom.h>
#include  <stdio.h>

/* Global widgets. */
Widget    topshell;
Widget    text;

/* Global atoms. */
Atom      selCLIPBOARD;
Atom      selSPAN;
Atom      selTEXT;
Atom      selTARGETS;
Atom      current_selection;

/* Global list of requested targets. */
#define MAX_ATOM_LIST    100

Atom      target_list[MAX_ATOM_LIST+1];
int       target_count = 0;

/* External function. */
extern Widget CreatePushbutton(Widget parent,
    char* name,
    XtCallbackProc callback,
    XtPointer client_data);

    /* Appends text to end of text widget. */
void AppendText(Widget widget,
  char* string)

{   /* AppendText */

    XmTextInsert(widget,
        XmTextGetLastPosition(widget),
        string);

}   /* AppendText */

    /* Creates toggle as a radio button, from chap. 6. */
Widget CreateRadioButton(Widget parent,
    char* name,
    XtCallbackProc callback,
    XtPointer client_data)

{   /* CreateRadioButton */
    Widget  toggle;

    toggle = XtVaCreateManagedWidget(name,
```

```
                    xmToggleButtonWidgetClass, parent,
                    XmNindicatorType, XmONE_OF_MANY,
                    NULL);

        XtAddCallback(toggle,
            XmNvalueChangedCallback,
            callback,
            client_data);

        return toggle;

    }   /* CreateRadioButton */

/*
Interns or uses built-in atoms for
use with selections:
    CHARACTER_POSITION
    CLASS
    CLIENT_WINDOW
    FILE_NAME
    HOST_NAME
    LENGTH
    LIST_LENGTH
    NAME
    OWNER_OS
    STRING
    TARGETS
    TEXT
    TIMESTAMP
    USER

Uses global target_list and target_count.
*/

void InternSelAtoms(Widget widget)

{   /* InternSelAtoms */
    Display*    display;

    display = XtDisplay(widget);

    /* Get three main selection atoms. */
    /* XA_PRIMARY   is built in. */
    /* XA_SECONDARY is built in. */
    selCLIPBOARD = XmInternAtom(display,
                    "CLIPBOARD", False);

    /* PRIMARY is default. */
    current_selection = XA_PRIMARY;

    /* Get some basic types. */
    selSPAN    = XmInternAtom(display,
                    "SPAN", False);
    selTEXT    = XmInternAtom(display,
                    "TEXT", False);
```

```
    selTARGETS = XmInternAtom(display,
              "TARGETS", False);

    /* Build list of targets to ask for. */
    target_count = 0;
    target_list[target_count++] = selTARGETS;
    target_list[target_count++] = XA_STRING;
    target_list[target_count++] = selTEXT;

    target_list[target_count++] =
        XmInternAtom(display, "NAME", False);

    target_list[target_count++] =
        XmInternAtom(display, "HOST_NAME", False);

    /* ICCCM says HOST_NAME, xterm says HOSTNAME. */
    target_list[target_count++] =
        XmInternAtom(display, "HOSTNAME", False);

    target_list[target_count++] =
        XmInternAtom(display, "USER", False);
    target_list[target_count++] =
        XmInternAtom(display, "FILE_NAME", False);
    target_list[target_count++] =
        XmInternAtom(display, "CLIENT_WINDOW", False);
    target_list[target_count++] =
        XmInternAtom(display, "LIST_LENGTH", False);
    target_list[target_count++] =
        XmInternAtom(display, "LENGTH", False);
    target_list[target_count++] =
        XmInternAtom(display, "TIMESTAMP", False);
    target_list[target_count++] =
        XmInternAtom(display,
          "CHARACTER_POSITION", False);
    target_list[target_count++] =
        XmInternAtom(display, "CLASS", False);

    /* The selection of evil: crashes R5 xterm. */
    /*
    target_list[target_count++] =
        XmInternAtom(display, "OWNER_OS", False);
    */

}    /* InternSelAtoms */

    /* Converts a list of atoms to text. */
convert_ATOM(Widget widget,
    Atom* atom_array,
    int number_atoms)

{    /* convert_ATOM */
    int i;
    char*   name;

    for (i = 0; i < number_atoms; i++) {
```

```
            name = XmGetAtomName(XtDisplay(widget),
                atom_array[i] );

            if (name != NULL) {
                AppendText(widget, "\n      ");
                AppendText(widget, name);

                XtFree(name);
            }
        }

    }    /* convert_ATOM */

    /* Converts integer values to text. */
void convert_INTEGER(Widget widget,
    int* int_array,
    int number_ints)

{    /* convert_INTEGER */
    int  i;
    char    string[1024];

    /* Convert first int. */
    sprintf(string, "\n      %d", int_array[0] );

    AppendText(widget, string);

    /* Convert rest. */
    for (i = 1; i < number_ints; i++) {
        sprintf(string, ", %d", int_array[i] );
        AppendText(widget, string);
    }

}    /* convert_INTEGER */

    /* Converts window IDs to text. */
void convert_WINDOW(Widget widget,
    Window* window_array,
    int number_windows)

{    /* convert_WINDOW */
    int  i;
    char    string[1024];

    /* Convert first window. */
    sprintf(string,
        "\n      0x%x", window_array[0] );

    AppendText(widget, string);

    /* Convert rest. */
    for (i = 1; i < number_windows; i++) {
        sprintf(string, ", %x", window_array[i] );
        AppendText(widget, string);
    }
```

```
}   /* convert_WINDOW */

    /* Callback to convert each target data. */
void sel_dataCB(Widget widget,
    XtPointer client_data,
    Atom* selection,
    Atom* type,
    XtPointer value,
    unsigned long* value_length,
    int* format)

{   /* sel_dataCB */
    Display*    display;
    char*       type_name;
    char*       target_name;
    Atom        target;
    char        string[1024];

    /* Check for errors. */
    if (( *selection == XT_CONVERT_FAIL) ||
        ( *selection <= 0)) {
        AppendText(text,
            "\n Selection callback: No response.\n");
        return;
    }

    /* Get selection name */
    switch( *selection) {
        case XA_PRIMARY:
            AppendText(text, "\n PRIMARY selection:");
            break;
        case XA_SECONDARY:
            AppendText(text, "\n SECONDARY selection:");
            break;
        default :
            if ( *selection == selCLIPBOARD) {
                AppendText(text,
                    "\n CLIPBOARD selection:");
            }
    }

    display = XtDisplay(widget);

    /* We passed target as client_data. */
    target = (Atom) client_data;

    if (target <= 0) {
        AppendText(text, "\n Bad target.\n");
        return;
    }

    target_name = XmGetAtomName(display, target);

    AppendText(text, " Target is: ");
```

```
AppendText(text, target_name);

XtFree(target_name);

/* Show length. */
if ( *value_length <= 0) {
    AppendText(text, "\n No length.\n");
    return;
}

sprintf(string,
    "\n Number items is %d.", *value_length);
AppendText(text, string);

/* Get type name. */
if ( *type <= 0) {
    AppendText(text, "\n Bad type.\n");
    return;
}

type_name = XmGetAtomName(display, *type);

AppendText(text, "\n Type is: ");
AppendText(text, type_name);

XtFree(type_name);

/* Show format. */
switch( *format) {
    case 8:
        AppendText(text, "\n Format is 8.");
        break;
    case 16:
        AppendText(text, "\n Format is 16.");
        break;
    case 32:
        AppendText(text, "\n Format is 32.");
        break;
    default: ;
}

/* Now, convert data. */
switch( *type) {
    case XA_ATOM:
        convert_ATOM(text, (Atom *) value,
            *value_length);
        break;
    case XA_STRING:
        AppendText(text, "\n Value: ");
        AppendText(text, (char*) value);
        break;
    case XA_INTEGER:
        convert_INTEGER(text, (int*) value,
            *value_length);
        break;
```

```
        case XA_WINDOW:
            convert_WINDOW(text, (Window*) value,
                *value_length);
            break;
        default: /* Non-constant cases. */

            /* May be internationalized! */
            if ( *type == selTEXT) {
                AppendText(text, "\n Value: ");
                AppendText(text, (char*) value);
            }

            /* A span is two ints. */
            if ( *type == selSPAN) {
                convert_INTEGER(text, (int*) value,
                    *value_length);
            }

            /* Motif often returns TARGETS with
             * a type of TARGETS instead of the
             * official ICCCM type of ATOM.
             */
            if ( *type == selTARGETS) {
                convert_ATOM(text, (Atom *) value,
                    *value_length);
            }
    }

    AppendText(text, "\n");

} /* sel_dataCB */

    /* Queries active selection. */
void requestCB(Widget widget,
    XtPointer client_data,
    XtPointer call_data)

{   /* requestCB */
    int        status;
    Time       timestamp;
    Display*   display;

    display = XtDisplay(topshell);

    timestamp =
        XtLastTimestampProcessed(display);

    /* Request current selection data. */
    XtGetSelectionValues(topshell,
        current_selection,
        target_list,
        target_count,
        (XtSelectionCallbackProc) sel_dataCB,
        (XtPointer*) target_list, /* client_data list */
        timestamp);
```

```
    /* Clear text. */
    XmTextReplace(text,
        (XmTextPosition) 0,
        XmTextGetLastPosition(text),
        " ");

}   /* requestCB */

    /* Toggles active selection to query. */
void toggleCB(Widget widget,
    XtPointer client_data,
    XtPointer call_data)

{   /* toggleCB */
    char*   ptr;

    ptr = (char*) client_data;

    switch(ptr[0]) {
        case 'S':  /* SECONDARY */
            XtVaSetValues(topshell,
                XmNtitle, "SECONDARY Selection",
                NULL);

            current_selection = XA_SECONDARY;
            break;
        case 'C':  /* CLIPBOARD */
            XtVaSetValues(topshell,
                XmNtitle, "CLIPBOARD Selection",
                NULL);

            current_selection = selCLIPBOARD;
            break;
        case 'P':  /* PRIMARY */
            XtVaSetValues(topshell,
                XmNtitle, "PRIMARY Selection",
                NULL);

            current_selection = XA_PRIMARY;
        default : ;
    }

    /* Clear text widget. */
    XmTextReplace(text,
        (XmTextPosition) 0,
        XmTextGetLastPosition(text),
        " ");

}   /* toggleCB */

void exitCB(Widget widget,
    XtPointer client_data,
    XtPointer call_data)
```

```
{   /* exitCB */

    exit(0);

}   /* exitCB */

int main(int argc, char** argv)

{   /* main */
    XtAppContext    app_context;
    Widget          pane, selrow, prim_toggle;
    Widget          pushrow;
    Arg             args[20];
    Cardinal        n;

    /* Initialize toolkit with global topshell. */
    topshell = XtVaAppInitialize(&app_context,
            "Ppm",
            (XrmOptionDescList) NULL,
            0,
            &argc, argv,
            (String*) NULL,
            XmNallowResize, True,
            NULL);

    /* Create a paned window. */
    n = 0;
    pane = XmCreatePanedWindow(topshell,
            "pane", args, n);

    /* Create row column for selections. */
    selrow = XtVaCreateWidget("selrow",
            xmRowColumnWidgetClass, pane,
            XmNorientation, XmVERTICAL,
            XmNradioBehavior,  True,
            XmNradioAlwaysOne, True,
            NULL);

    /* Create toggles for the selections. */
    prim_toggle = CreateRadioButton(selrow,
        "primary",
        (XtCallbackProc) toggleCB,
        (XtPointer) "PRIMARY");

    /* Set first toggle to on. */
    XmToggleButtonSetState(prim_toggle, True,
        False); /* Don't notify yet. */

    (void) CreateRadioButton(selrow,
        "secondary",
        (XtCallbackProc) toggleCB,
        (XtPointer) "SECONDARY");

    (void) CreateRadioButton(selrow,
        "clipboard",
```

```
            (XtCallbackProc) toggleCB,
            (XtPointer) "CLIPBOARD");

    /* Create row column for pushbuttons. */
    pushrow = XtVaCreateWidget("pushrow",
                xmRowColumnWidgetClass, pane,
                XmNorientation, XmHORIZONTAL,
                NULL);

    (void) CreatePushbutton(pushrow, "request",
            (XtCallbackProc) requestCB,
            (XtPointer) NULL);

    (void) CreatePushbutton(pushrow, "exit",
            (XtCallbackProc) exitCB,
            (XtPointer) NULL);

    /* Create scrolled text to hold selection data. */
    n = 0;
    XtSetArg(args[n], XmNeditMode,
        XmMULTI_LINE_EDIT); n++;
    XtSetArg(args[n], XmNscrollHorizontal, True); n++;
    XtSetArg(args[n], XmNscrollVertical,   True); n++;

    text = XmCreateScrolledText(pane,
                "text", args, n);

    XtManageChild(text);

    XtManageChild(selrow);
    XtManageChild(pushrow);
    XtManageChild(pane);

    /* Intern all the necessary atoms. */
    InternSelAtoms(topshell);

    XtRealizeWidget(topshell);
    XtAppMainLoop(app_context);
    return 0;

}   /* main */

/* end of file primary.c */
```

The resource file for the *primary* program follows:

```
! Resource file for primary.c in Chapter 20
! of Power Programming Motif.
!
*fontList:      lucidasans-12
*background:    grey92

*title: PRIMARY Selection

*exit.labelString:    Exit
```

```
*request.labelString: Request Selection Data

*primary.labelString:   PRIMARY
*secondary.labelString: SECONDARY
*clipboard.labelString: CLIPBOARD

! Test resources, note monospaced font.
*text.fontList: \
  -*-lucidatypewriter-medium-r-*-*-12-*-*-*-m-*-*
*text.rows:    30
*text.columns: 80

! end of resource file
```

Name this file **Ppm** and store it in your home directory.

When you run the *primary* program, you'll see widgets like those shown in Figure 20.1.

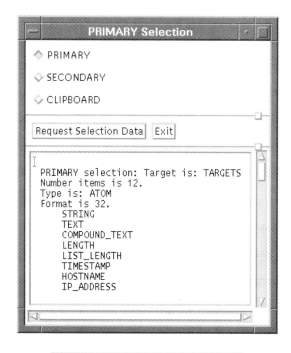

Figure 20.1   *The primary program.*

Select data somewhere on the screen and press the button marked **Request Selection Data** to acquire the current data for the PRIMARY, SECONDARY, or

CLIPBOARD selection. If you try this with two Motif applications (such as the *textclip* program from the last chapter) and *xterm*, you'll see some differences in how the underlying toolkit handles selections.

XmTEXT CONVENIENCE ROUTINES

As with the Motif clipboard, the XmText and XmTextField widgets provide a number of utility convenience routines to speed your work with text widgets.

To get the selected text in a text widget, call XmTextGetSelection:

```
#include <Xm/Text.h>

char*  XmTextGetSelection(Widget text_widget)
```

Call XtFree to free the returned text.

To get the position of the selected text, call XmTextGetSelectionPosition:

```
#include <Xm/Text.h>

Boolean XmTextGetSelectionPosition(Widget text_widget,
        XmTextPosition* left,  /* RETURN */
        XmTextPosition* right) /* RETURN */
```

If XmTextGetSelectionPosition returns True, then the *left* parameter will hold the text position (starting from 0) of the left boundary of the PRIMARY selection in the text widget. The *right* parameter will hold the text position of the right boundary. XmTextGetSelectionPosition returns False if the widget doesn't own the PRIMARY selection.

To clear the PRIMARY selection in a text widget, call XmTextClearSelection:

```
#include <Xm/Text.h>

void XmTextClearSelection(Widget text_widget,
        Time timestamp)
```

You can programmatically set the PRIMARY selection in the text widget by calling XmTextSetSelection:

```
#include <Xm/Text.h>
```

```
void XmTextSetSelection(Widget text_widget,
        XmTextPosition start_position,
        XmTextPosition end_position,
        Time timestamp)
```

`XmTextSetSelection` selects all the text starting with the *start_position* up to and including the *end_position*. Text positions start counting at 0.

The `XmTextField` widget, listed in Table 20.2, provides similar functions.

Table 20.2 *XmTextField selection functions.*

XmText	XmTextField
XmTextClearSelection	XmTextFieldClearSelection
XmTextGetSelection	XmTextFieldGetSelection
XmTextGetSelectionPosition	XmTextFieldGetSelectionPosition
XmTextSetSelection	XmTextFieldSetSelection

Summary

Selections are X's means for providing a generalized query-reply inter-process communication mechanism. Selections are powerful and confusing. You'll earn your stripes as an advanced Motif programmer if you master selections.

Each selection is an atom. You need to convert the selection name to an atom, using `XmInternAtom`. After a program claims the selection, other programs, if they know about the selection, may ask the selection owner questions about the selection. These questions usually cover the data associated with a selection in a string format with a target type of `XA_STRING` (where `XA_STRING` is a predefined atom). The owner of the selection then converts the selection data into the proper target type, puts the data in a property on the asking program's window, and then sends a `SelectionNotify` event to the asking program. Ideally, the selection owner provides data in any target type, provided the owning program supports that data target type.

The selection named PRIMARY is the main selection in the ICCCM for typical cut-and-paste operations using the built-in atom called XA_PRIMARY. PRIMARY is the selection used when a user selects some text in an *xterm* window, probably by far the most common use of cut and paste in X.

There are three required target types—TIMESTAMP, MULTIPLE, and TARGETS—and a host of common types your application should support. The MULTIPLE type has the name of a property and a window ID. In that property lie many items of type ATOM_PAIR (really just two atoms, or pairs of XA_ATOM types). In each ATOM_PAIR, the first item is a target type (one of many) and the second item is a property ID. Your application should then convert the selection data to the asked-for target type and write that data to the paired property ID (all on the same given window ID). The TIMESTAMP target is the timestamp (in X server terms) of when your application became the given selection's owner. The TARGETS target is the list of data types (targets) your application supports. Since each target type is an atom, the TARGETS response is a list of atoms (atoms are 32-bit values).

The CHARACTER_POSITION target type has a base type of SPAN. A SPAN is two integers (that is, two of the built-in atom XA_INTEGER). The CHARACTER_POSITION target type should be the start and end position of the selected data, in bytes. The LENGTH target type should be the length of the selection—the number of bytes—stored as an INTEGER.

With each type of target, you can usually store more than one item. For example, SPAN is really two INTEGERS. When you write out the property data, use a target type of XA_INTEGER and a number of items of 2 (with enough bytes of data filled in, of course). That way, the TARGETS target is really just an XA_ATOM type, with many atoms stored in the list. That's what the *number_items* variable is about in the calls XGetWindowProperty and XChangeProperty.

When your application owns the PRIMARY selection, it needs to respond to SelectionRequest events. GetTargetData() is the main function used to collect the different types of data and prepare the raw data bytes, which will be later written to the requesting program's window.

Just about every application wishing to use selections should support the PRIMARY selection. PRIMARY is the main means for cut-and-paste operations between applications. From the user's point of view, selected text should be easily pasted into any other application.

Selections are rather confusing. You may want to look up Chapter 19 in one of our other books, *Advanced X Window Applications Programming* (Johnson and Reichard, MIS: Press, 1990), for a lengthy tutorial on selections.

In the next chapter, we finish our discussion of program-to-program data exchange and cover a new feature in Motif: drag and drop.

MOTIF INTRINSICS FUNCTIONS AND MACROS INTRODUCED IN THIS CHAPTER

```
XmTextClearSelection
XmTextFieldClearSelection
XmTextFieldGetSelection
XmTextFieldGetSelectionPosition
XmTextFieldSetSelection
XmTextGetSelection
XmTextGetSelectionPosition
XmTextSetSelection
```

X TOOLKIT INTRINSICS FUNCTIONS AND MACROS INTRODUCED IN THIS CHAPTER

```
XtAppSetSelectionTimeout
XtDisownSelection
XtGetSelectionValue
XtGetSelectionValues
XtOwnSelection
```

CHAPTER 21

Drag and Drop

This chapter covers:

- Drag and drop in Motif
- User views of drag and drop
- Configuring a drop site to accept data
- Setting up a drag source to start a drag operation
- Setting drag-and-drop preferences
- Setting up a data-transfer callback
- A program to test drag sites
- Creating a data-conversion callback
- A program for testing drag and drop
- Drag-and-drop protocols
- Problems with drag and drop

719

DRAG-AND-DROP OVERVIEW

Drag and drop is an interface style where users select objects on the screen, drag these objects around the screen, and then drop the objects in a new location. For example, a file-browser application should allow users to drag icons representing files on top of directory icons, thereby copying the file to a new location, or onto printer icons, thereby printing the files. Other uses include a file trash can: the files dropped into the trash can icon are deleted.

Drag and drop then become components in *direct-manipulation interfaces*, where the user can directly manipulate objects displayed on the screen. There are many different implementations of drag and drop in the computer world, with no two operating in exactly the same fashion. However, the consensus is that drag and drop make an operating environment easy to use, and so Motif 1.2 adds support for drag and drop in applications.

Drag-and-drop support is new in Motif 1.2. If you don't have a version of the Motif libraries at 1.2 or higher, you won't have much luck running the programs in this chapter.

NOTE

We're skipping our shortcut in this chapter for one simple reason: Drag and drop is incredibly easy to implement. Read on for the simple explanation of drag and drop.

SHORTCUT

Built-In Widget Support

How much code do you have to write to support drag and drop? None. In fact, you could probably jump ahead to the next chapter, unless you want to add new data types or customize anything.

The best thing about Motif's implementation of drag and drop is that most built-in widgets already support it, without any extra coding on your part. The `XmLabel`, `XmList`, `XmPushButton`, and `XmText` widgets are drag sources, as shown in Table 21.1.

Table 21.1 *Built-in widget support for drag and drop.*

Widget	Drag Source	Drop Site	Target Types
XmLabel	Yes	No	COMPOUND_TEXT
XmList	Yes	No	COMPOUND_TEXT
XmPushButton	Yes	No	COMPOUND_TEXT
XmText	Yes	Yes	COMPOUND_TEXT
XmTextField	No	Yes	COMPOUND_TEXT

You can select and drag data (as compound text) from these widgets and drop them into any drop site. The XmText and XmTextField widgets are built-in drop sites that can accept dragged objects as compound text.

In addition to the widgets listed in Table 21.1, you can program other widgets to act as drag sources and drop sites. You can support any arbitrary data types, although it's best to stick to common data types. The compound-text exchange format, COMPOUND_TEXT, is the lingua franca for most Motif widgets.

The rest of this chapter builds on our discussions of atoms, properties, and selections, introducing drag-and-drop programming in Motif applications.

USING DRAG AND DROP

A drag starts when the user holds down the middle mouse button (technically, the virtual button BTransfer—and remember that users can change the button definitions) over data in a widget. This widget is then known as the *drag source*, the source of the drag operation. The cursor shape changes to a *drag icon*, which tells the user that a drag operation is in process. (Technically, the new shape is called an icon, even though it's usually implemented as a different cursor.)

The user moves the mouse pointer about the screen while holding down the middle mouse button before releasing the mouse button over some other widget. The release of the mouse button *drops* the data on the target widget. The dragged item can be dropped over any area of the screen. although only certain areas, called *drop sites*, are coded to accept a drop operation. When the object is dropped over a drop site, you may see a set of visual effects (you can use the default effects or program your own). If you drop the object over some place that is not a drop site, or over a drop site that is coded to accept a different type of data, you'll usually see some effects that show the data scurrying back to the original drag source. Again, you can customize this in your code, but the existing effects look pretty good, so we usually save ourselves the effort and stick to the defaults.

After a drop begins, code in the drop site and drag source negotiate over what data formats (such as text or bitmaps) and what operation (copy, move, or link) should occur. Usually, some form of data from the drag source gets transferred to the drop site. What happens next is up to the application. If the user drags a file icon on top of a printer icon, then the user would normally expect the application to print the file.

The default operation is to copy the data from the drag source to the drop site, but Motif applications are free to change this default. If you desire a different operation, such as a move, you can force the issue with a number of mouse and keyboard combinations.

Mouse Button/Key Combinations

When you drag an object about the screen, are you copying it, moving it, or doing something else? The Motif drag and drop allows for applications to choose the default operations, based on what is natural to support. (Do you really want to copy the contents of a file to the trash? Instead, you'd rather trash the file itself.)

To allow the user some control, though, you can use a set of key combinations in association with the middle mouse button to force a copy, move, or link operation. Table 21.2 lists the common key and mouse combinations for forcing drag-and-drop operations.

Table 21.2 *Default drag-and-drop operations.*

Mouse Button	Key Modifier	Operation
Button2	None	Default (usually copy)

continued

Button2	**Shift**	Force move
Button2	**Control**	Force copy
Button2	**Shift-Control**	Force link
Button2	**F1**	Ask for help on drop site

As with most aspects of Motif, the user may customize this. In addition, you can probably tell that these operations were built with a specific application in mind—a graphical file and directory browser. Not all operations make sense for all applications. You may have trouble performing a link operation with colormaps, for example. As usual, use Table 21.1 as a guideline and do what makes sense in your applications.

SETTING UP DRAG AND DROP

To set up drag and drop, there are responsibilities on the part of both the dragging application (the drag source) and on the receiving application (the drop site). Of course, both applications may be the same. It just makes sense to divide up the responsibilities—and the code—along these logical divisions.

Much like the X concept of selections, covered in the last chapter, each drop source can support a number of data formats called targets. The data formats are identified by target atoms, such as COMPOUND_TEXT, TIMESTAMP, and FILE_NAME.

COMPOUND_TEXT is very important because that's the default format used for exchanging text between applications.

Converting to and from Compound Strings

The X Consortium defined a format for storing text in multiple encodings, which allows for international text. This format is known as *compound text* and is intended by the ICCCM for use in exchanging text between applications. (The compound text format is described in the X Consortium document *Compound Text Encoding*.)

There's even an atom defined for the data target of compound text: COMPOUND_TEXT. (Note that you must intern this atom yourself.)

Unfortunately, this compound text format overlaps with the purposes for Motif's XmString data. Because of this, you'll need to convert compound text data to and from Motif XmString data.

To do this, XmCvtCTToXmString converts data in COMPOUND_TEXT format to a Motif XmString:

```
XmString XmCvtCTToXmString(char* compound_text)
```

To convert an XmString into COMPOUND_TEXT format, use XmCvtXmStringToCT:

```
char* XmCvtXmStringToCT(XmString xmstring)
```

Coordinating Drags and Drops

In order for drag and drop to work, the drag source and the drop site must support at least one matching target atom and at least one common operation (copy, move, or link). The drag source's exportTargets resource is compared with the drop site's importTargets resource. Both resources contain a list of selection atoms. (See Table 20.1 in Chapter 20 for a list of selection atoms.) You can use any atoms you'd like (including proprietary ones), but the more obscure atoms you pick, the fewer applications will support your atoms. As you can guess, many more applications will support COMPOUND_TEXT than _ERIC_AND_KEVIN_FORMAT. (Their loss.)

While the drag is taking place, you can use the default visual animated effects or create your own. The XmDragIcon widget defines the graphical effects when the mouse pointer is dragged over certain areas. In most cases, though, you can use the default visual effects.

There are two main parts to setting up drag and drop. First, you must set up the drop site, so that it accepts data from a drag operation. Second, you must set up the drag source to initiate a drag operation and provide the data to transfer.

Setting Up a Drop Site

To make a widget a drop site, you must register it with the XmDropSite registry. The XmDropSite registry holds a list of widgets that are preregistered as drop sites. You add a widget to the drop site registry with XmDropSiteRegister:

```
#include <Xm/DragDrop.h>

void XmDropSiteRegister(Widget widget,
        ArgList args,
        Cardinal number_args)
```

XmDropSiteRegister registers the given widget, such as an XmPushButton widget, as a drop site ready and willing to accept data from drag operations.

You'll need the include file <Xm/DragDrop.h> for all your drag-and-drop code.

N   O   T   E

When you call XmDropSiteRegister, you'll pass along a set of resources that tells Motif how your drop site should act. You should set the following resources as listed in Table 21.3.

Table 21.3   *XmDropSite resources.*

Resource	Type	Default Value
dropSiteOperations	unsigned char	XmDROP_MOVE | XmDROP_COPY
importTargets	Atom*	NULL
numImportTargets	Cardinal	0

The dropSiteOperations resource contains a set of bit flags that indicates what operations you widget supports. These operations are listed in Table 21.4.

Table 21.4   *Drag-and-drop operations.*

Operation	Meaning
XmDROP_COPY	Copy
XmDROP_LINK	Link
XmDROP_MOVE	Move

You should set in the inclusive OR of all the bit flags your widget supports. The default is the value (XmDROP_MOVE | XmDROP_COPY), which supports both the move and copy operations.

The importTargets resource contains a list of atoms that identifies all the targets this drop site supports. The most common target is the COM-POUND_TEXT atom.

The numImportTargets resource tells XmDropSiteRegister how many target atoms are in the importTargets resource.

You must also set up a drop callback that gets called when a drop operation begins, as listed in Table 21.5.

Table 21.5 *The XmDropSite drop callback.*

Callback	Structure	Reason
dropProc	XtCallbackProc	XmCR_DROP_MESSAGE

We cover the drop callback under the section "Drop-Site Callbacks," below.

In your code, you can call XmDropSiteRegister as follows:

```
Widget          widget;
Arg             args[20];
Cardinal        n;
Atom            targets[10];
XtCallbackProc  callback;

/* Support copy and move; not link */
n = 0;
XtSetArg(args[n],
    XmNdropSiteOperations,
    XmDROP_COPY | XmDROP_MOVE); n++;

/* Set up callback function. */
XtSetArg(args[n],
    XmNdropProc, callback); n++;

/* Set up target Atom for COMPOUND_TEXT */
targets[0] =
    XmInternAtom(XtDisplay(widget),
    "COMPOUND_TEXT", False);

XtSetArg(args[n],
```

```
    XmNimportTargets, targets); n++;
XtSetArg(args[n],
    XmNnumImportTargets, 1); n++;

XmDropSiteRegister(widget, args, n);
```

You can unregister a drop site with `XmDropSiteUnregister`:

```
#include <Xm/DragDrop.h>

void XmDropSiteUnregister(Widget widget)
```

In most cases, you'll never need to unregister a drop site. Instead, call `XmDropSiteRegister` and maintain a widget as a drop site throughout your program session.

Once you call `XmDropSiteRegister`, your widget is now a potential drop site. You must provide at least two callback functions.

Drop-Site Callbacks

The drop site is responsible for setting up two callback functions: a drop callback to initiate or cancel the drop, and a data-transfer callback to extract the data.

The drop callback is passed to `XmDropSiteRegister` and controls the start of a drop operation. Inside this drop callback, you'll set up the data-transfer callback. We cover both in depth in the next sections.

The Drop Callback

When you register a widget as a drop site with `XmDropSiteRegister`, you must place a drop callback in the `dropProc` resource. Motif calls this callback function when a drop operation just starts. This callback is responsible for verifying the data target formats and ensuring that the operation (`XmDROP_COPY`, `XmDROP_LINK`, or `XmDROP_MOVE`) is supported. The drop callback must also set up the proper resources and call `XmDropTransferStart`, which we cover in the section on "Calling `XmDropTransferStart`," below.

The drop callback takes the standard Motif callback parameters:

```
void DropCB(Widget widget,
    XtPointer client_data,
    XtPointer call_data)
```

```
{     /* DropCB */
}     /* DropCB */
```

The *call_data* parameter is a pointer to an `XmDropProcCallbackStruct`:

```
typedef struct _XmDropProcCallbackStruct {
    int           reason;
    XEvent*       event;
    Time          timeStamp;
    Widget        dragContext;
    Position      x, y;
    unsigned char dropSiteStatus;
    unsigned char operation;
    unsigned char operations;
    unsigned char dropAction;
} XmDropProcCallbackStruct, *XmDropProcCallback;
```

The most important field is the *operation* field. This field contains the current requested operation, one of

■ `XmDROP_COPY`

■ `XmDROP_LINK`

■ `XmDROP_MOVE`

■ `XmDROP_NOOP`

`XmDROP_NOOP` stands for no operation.

Your drop callback function can change the *operation* field if necessary.

Don't confuse the *operation* field with the *operations* field. The *operation* field holds the current operation. The *operations* field (with an *s*) holds the list of all supported operations (the inclusive OR of the above bit flags).

N O T E

If your drop callback detects a problem, it may change the `dropSiteStatus` field. This field can hold a value of `XmDROP_SITE_INVALID` or `XmDROP_SITE_VALID`.

The `dropAction` field will hold one of `XmDROP` or `XmDROP_HELP`. This tells you whether the user asked for help on the drop site.

The `dragContext` field holds the widget ID of an `XmDragContext`. You'll need this for calling `XmDropTransferStart`.

Calling XmDropTransferStart

In the drop procedure, you *must* call `XmDropTransferStart`:

```
#include <Xm/DragDrop.h>

Widget XmDropTransferStart(Widget widget,
        ArgList args,
        Cardinal number_args)
```

`XmDropTransferStart` initiates the transfer of data to the drop site. It creates and returns an `XmDropTransfer` pseudo-widget. You must fill in the proper resources that allow the drop operation to terminate or continue successfully.

`XmDropTransferStart` returns a newly created `XmDropTransfer` widget. Do not create an `XmDropTransfer` widget by any other means, as this will mess up the toolkit's internal data structures. This is part of the problem of trying to back-fit drag and drop onto a pseudo-widget structure. (The whole idea of these pseudo-widgets is to allow you to set the data values with resources, as you can with real widgets.)

Even if you don't intend to transfer any data, you must call `XmDropTransferStart`. You should set the `transferStatus` resource to `XmTRANSFER_FAILURE` if you want to terminate the drop.

XmDropTransfer Resources

The `XmDropTransfer` widget supports a number of resources, listed in Table 21.6.

Table 21.6   *XmDropTransfer resources.*

Resource	Type	Default Value
dropTransfers	XmDropTransferEntryRec*	NULL
incremental	Boolean	False
numDropTransfers	Cardinal	0
transferStatus	unsigned char	XmTRANSFER_SUCCESS

You need to set up these resources before calling `XmDropTransferStart`.

The transferStatus resource can be set to XmTRANSFER_SUCCESS or XmTRANSFER_FAILURE. If your drop callback detects a problem, then set the transferStatus resource to XmTRANSFER_FAILURE. Otherwise, you should leave the default value of XmTRANSFER_SUCCESS. For example, the following code shows how to terminate a bad drop:

```
void DropCB(Widget widget,
    XtPointer client_data,
    XtPointer call_data)

{   /* DropCB */
    XmDropProcCallbackStruct*   ptr;
    Arg                         args[20];
    Cardinal                    n;

    ptr =
        (XmDropProcCallbackStruct*) call_data;

    /* We support only one operation. */
    if (ptr->operation != XmDROP_COPY) {

        XtSetArg(args[n], XmNtransferStatus,
            XmTRANSFER_FAILURE); n++;

        XmDropTransferStart(ptr->dragContext, args, n);
        return;
    }

    /* ... */

}   /* DropCB */
```

The dropTransfers resource provides a list of transactions. Each transaction in the list needs to be processed before the drop terminates. Motif will automatically try each transfer in turn. Normally, you choose which data type and set up only one transfer.

To set up one or more transfers, you need to fill in an XmDropTransferEntryRec structure for each transfer. The XmDropTransferEntryRec structure looks like:

```
typedef struct _XmDropTransferEntryRec {
    XtPointer   client_data;
    Atom        target;
} XmDropTransferEntryRec, *XmDropTransferEntry;
```

For each transaction, you need to fill in the *target* atom. For example, if you're coding a callback to accept COMPOUND_TEXT data, you'd set the atom for COMPOUND_TEXT into the *target* field. You may also pass any *client_data* your routine needs.

The numDropTransfers resource specifies how many XmDropTransferEntryRec structures (how many transactions) are set in the array in the dropTransfers resource.

If you intend to go through with the drop operation, the most important resource to set is the transferProc. This resource contains the function to call to actually transfer the data and has the same type as the XtSelectionCallbackProc.

Finishing the Drop Callback

Putting this all together, we end up with the following example drop callback:

```
/* Global for "COMPOUND_TEXT" Atom. */
Atom    compound_text = (Atom) None;

void DropCB(Widget widget,
    XtPointer client_data,
    XtPointer call_data)

{   /* DropCB */
    XmDropProcCallbackStruct*   ptr;
    XmDropTransferEntryRec      entries[2];
    Arg                         args[20];
    Cardinal                    n;

    ptr =
        (XmDropProcCallbackStruct*) call_data;

    /* We support only one operation. */
    if (ptr->operation != XmDROP_COPY) {
        XtSetArg(args[n], XmNtransferStatus,
            XmTRANSFER_FAILURE); n++;

        XmDropTransferStart(ptr->dragContext, args, n);
        return;
    }

    n = 0;
    entries[0].target = compound_text;

    /* Pass widget as client data */
    entries[0].client_data = (XtPointer) widget;

    XtSetArg(args[n], XmNdropTransfers, entries); n++;
    XtSetArg(args[n], XmNnumDropTransfers, 1); n++;
    XtSetArg(args[n], XmNtransferProc, TransferCB); n++;

    XmDropTransferStart(ptr->dragContext, args, n);

}   /* DropCB */
```

The above callback function passes the target of the COMPOUND_TEXT atom and the *client_data* of our widget ID. This allows the transfer callback to work for a number of widgets.

The Data-Transfer Callback

The data-transfer callback is responsible for actually providing the data for transfer from the drag source to the drop site. This callback takes the same parameters as an XtSelectionCallbackProc, described in the last chapter:

```
typedef void (*XtSelectionCallbackProc)(Widget widget,
    XtPointer client_data,
    Atom*  selection,
    Atom*  type,
    XtPointer value,
    unsigned long* value_length,
    int*  format);
```

In your code, you need to take the passed *value* and do whatever needs to be done. For example, when transferring COMPOUND_TEXT to a label widget, the obvious thing to do is place that text in the labelString resource for the widget. An example data-transfer callback below that does just this.

```
/* Global for "COMPOUND_TEXT" Atom. */
Atom    compound_text = (Atom) None;

void TransferCB(Widget widget,
    XtPointer client_data,
    Atom* selection,
    Atom* type,
    XtPointer value,
    unsigned long value_length,
    int format)

{   /* TransferCB */
    XmString    xmstring;
    Widget      label;

    /* We assume client data has label widget ID. */
    label = (Widget) client_data;

    /* Motif mostly uses COMPOUND_TEXT format. */
    if (*type == compound_text) {

        xmstring = XmCvtCTToXmString(value);

        XtVaSetValues(label,
            XmNlabelString, xmstring,
            XmNlabelType,   XmSTRING,
            NULL);
```

```
        XmStringFree(xmstring);
    }
}   /* TransferCB */
```

In the above data-transfer callback function, we call XmCvtCTToXmString
to convert the *value*, which is assumed to be in COMPOUND_TEXT format, to
an XmString. The routine then sets the labelString resource for the
label widget (the widget was passed as *client_data*).

In addition, the callback checks the actual target type to ensure that it
is COMPOUND_TEXT.

In the callback, the *selection* parameter will be the atom for
_MOTIF_DROP.

Example Program Testing Drop Sites

We've put together a program to test creating a drop site. We've found
through painful experience that it's easiest to start with the drop site and
then add the drag-source code later, which is how we organized this chapter.

The program below creates two XmText and two XmPushButton widgets. We register one of the pushbutton widgets (already a built-in drag
source) as a drop site by calling XmDropSiteRegister.

Since the XmText and XmPushButton widgets already act as drag
sources, we don't need to provide any code for that task in this program.

The drop program follows:

```
/* drop.c */
#include  <Xm/Xm.h>
#include  <Xm/Label.h>
#include  <Xm/PanedW.h>
#include  <Xm/RowColumn.h>
#include  <Xm/Text.h>
#include  <Xm/AtomMgr.h>
#include  <Xm/DragDrop.h>
#include  <stdio.h>

/* Global for "COMPOUND_TEXT" Atom. */
Atom    compound_text = (Atom) None;

/* External functions. */
extern Widget CreatePushbutton(Widget parent,
    char* name,
    XtCallbackProc callback,
    XtPointer client_data);
```

```
void exitCB(Widget widget, XtPointer client_data,
    XtPointer call_data)

{   /* exitCB */

    exit(0);

}   /* exitCB */

void TransferCB(Widget widget,
    XtPointer client_data,
    Atom* selection,
    Atom* type,
    XtPointer value,
    unsigned long value_length,
    int format)

{   /* TransferCB */
    XmString    xmstring;
    Widget      label;

    /* We assume client data has label widget ID. */
    label = (Widget) client_data;

    /* Motif mostly uses COMPOUND_TEXT format. */
    if (*type == compound_text) {

        xmstring = XmCvtCTToXmString(value);

        XtVaSetValues(label,
            XmNlabelString, xmstring,
            XmNlabelType,   XmSTRING,
            NULL);

        XmStringFree(xmstring);
    }

}   /* TransferCB */

void DropCB(Widget widget,
    XtPointer client_data,
    XtPointer call_data)

{   /* DropCB */
    XmDropProcCallbackStruct*   ptr;
    XmDropTransferEntryRec      entries[2];
    Arg                         args[20];
    Cardinal                    n;

    ptr =
        (XmDropProcCallbackStruct*) call_data;

    /* We support only one operation. */
    if (ptr->operation != XmDROP_COPY) {
```

```
            XtSetArg(args[n], XmNtransferStatus,
                XmTRANSFER_FAILURE); n++;

            XmDropTransferStart(ptr->dragContext,
                args, n);
            return;
        }

        n = 0;
        entries[0].target = compound_text;

        /* Pass widget as client data */
        entries[0].client_data = (XtPointer) widget;

        XtSetArg(args[n], XmNdropTransfers, entries); n++;
        XtSetArg(args[n], XmNnumDropTransfers, 1); n++;
        XtSetArg(args[n], XmNtransferProc,
            TransferCB); n++;

        XmDropTransferStart(ptr->dragContext,
            args, n);

    }    /* DropCB */

Widget CreateTextEntry(Widget parent,
    char* name)

{    /* CreateTextEntry */
    Widget  widget;
    Arg args[10];
    int n;

    n = 0;
    XtSetArg(args[n], XmNeditMode,
        XmSINGLE_LINE_EDIT); n++;

    widget = XmCreateText(parent, name, args, n);

    XtManageChild(widget);

    return widget;

}    /* CreateTextEntry */

/* Registers the given widget as a drop site. */
/* We use global atom for the target. */
void RegisterDropSite(Widget widget,
    XtCallbackProc callback)

{    /* RegisterDropSite */
    Arg         args[20];
    Cardinal    n;
    Atom        targets[10];

    n = 0;
```

```
        XtSetArg(args[n], XmNdropSiteOperations,
            XmDROP_COPY); n++;

        /* Set up callback function. */
        XtSetArg(args[n], XmNdropProc, callback); n++;

        /* Set up target Atoms. */
        targets[0] = compound_text;

        XtSetArg(args[n], XmNimportTargets,
            targets); n++;
        XtSetArg(args[n], XmNnumImportTargets,
            1); n++;

        XmDropSiteRegister(widget, args, n);

    }   /* RegisterDropSite */

int main(int argc, char** argv)

{   /* main */
    Widget          parent;
    XtAppContext    app_context;
    Arg             args[20];
    int             n;
    Widget          pane, text1, text2, push1;
    Widget          push2;

    parent = XtVaAppInitialize(&app_context,
                "Ppm",
                (XrmOptionDescList) NULL,
                0,
                &argc, argv,
                (String*) NULL,
                XmNallowResize, True,
                NULL);

    /* Create a paned window. */
    n = 0;
    pane = XmCreatePanedWindow(parent,
                "pane", args, n);

    /* Create text areas. */
    text1 = CreateTextEntry(pane, "text1");
    text2 = CreateTextEntry(pane, "text2");

    /* Create a pushbutton as a drop site. */
    push1 = CreatePushbutton(pane, "push1",
                (XtCallbackProc) exitCB,
                (XtPointer) NULL);

    /* Create a second pushbutton as a drag source. */
    push2 = CreatePushbutton(pane, "push2",
                (XtCallbackProc) exitCB,
                (XtPointer) NULL);
```

```
        XtManageChild(pane);

        /* Intern Atoms. */
        compound_text = XmInternAtom(XtDisplay(parent),
                "COMPOUND_TEXT", False);

        /* Register drop sites. */
        RegisterDropSite(push1,
            (XtCallbackProc) DropCB);

        XtRealizeWidget(parent);
        XtAppMainLoop(app_context);

        return 0;

    }   /* main */

/* end of file drop.c */
```

The program in **drop.c** (as well as the **dragdrop.c** program later in this chapter) both use the following resource file:

```
! Resource file for Chapter 21
! of Power Programming Motif.
!
*fontList:       lucidasans-12
*background:     grey92

*title: Drag and Drop

*exit.labelString:  Exit

*push1.labelString: Drop Site
*push2.labelString: Built-In Drag Source

! end of resource file
```

Name this file **Ppm** and store it in your home directory.

Running the Drop-Site Program

When you run the *drop* program, you'll see widgets like those shown in Figure 21.1.

If you hold down the middle mouse button over the lower pushbutton (labeled **Built-In Drag Source**), you can drag its text to the other pushbutton or to one of the XmText widgets, as shown in Figure 21.2.

Figure 21.1 *The drop program.*

Figure 21.2 *The drop program after dragging and dropping text.*

This should provide a good background to the intricacies of the drop site. The next task is to tackle the more difficult drag source.

SETTING UP A WIDGET AS A DRAG SOURCE

A drag source must initiate a drag operation and must also provide the data when dropped. Each of these tasks is performed by a callback function. The odd part is that the callback starting a drag operation must be set up from a translation, which is a resource that customizes how a widget responds to events.

In brief, to set up a widget as a drag source, you need to:

1. Add actions to connect a text string to your function that starts a drag operation.

2. Set up a translation that overrides a `ButtonPress` on `Button2` to call the drag-start function.

3. Pass this translation to the translations resource for each widget that you wish to make into a drag source. You must pass this resource during widget creation.

4. Inside the drag-start function, you need to configure the drag context to call a conversion callback. This callback is expected to convert the data to the desired target type.

5. The conversion callback then converts the data to the requested format and supplies the bytes to Motif, which, in turn, negotiates with the drop-site application to transfer the data.

Adding Drag Actions

An *action* is a means to connect a text string that names a function to actually execute that C function. This may seem strange, but Xt actions are really a great idea.

The underlying concept is that the user can configure a key or mouse button with a translation resource to execute a certain function in your code. Since the resource file is a text file, there needs to be some way to connect the text string in the resource file to the actual C function. Xt does this by using `XtActionsRec` structures:

```
typedef struct _XtActionsRec{
    String       string;
    XtActionProc proc;
} XtActionsRec;
```

The *string* field holds a text string name, such as `"StartDragOperation"`. This is the name that appears in the X resource file. The *proc* field then holds a pointer to a function. This is the C function to be called. By convention, the *string* name and the function name should match. That is, if the *string* field holds `"StartDragOperation"`, the *proc* field should hold `StartDragOperation`, where `StartDragOperation` is a valid C function.

The function should also take the following parameters:

```
typedef void (*XtActionProc)(Widget widget,
```

```
XEvent* event,
String* params,
Cardinal* number_params);
```

Usually you'll see arrays of XtActionsRec structures, which allow for connecting a number of text strings to a number of C functions (the connection is one-to-one). For this, Xt defines a data type for an array of these structures, XtActionList:

```
typedef struct _XtActionsRec *XtActionList;
```

You then fill in an array of these structures as globals in your program. For example, if we create a function named StartDragOperation, we could set up an XtActionsRec array as follows:

```
static XtActionsRec drag_actions[] = {
{ "StartDragOperation",
    (XtActionProc) StartDragOperation}
};
```

Usually, you'll have more than one element in the array of XtActionsRec structures, but to keep our example simple, we'll just use one.

After you've set up an array of XtActionsRec structures, you can pass this to XtAppAddActions:

```
void XtAppAddActions(XtAppContext app_context,
    XtActionList actions,
    Cardinal number_actions)
```

XtAppAddActions adds the XtActionList array to the list of actions used by the X translation manager.

To get the *number_actions*, the preferred style is to use XtNumber, a quaint Xt macro that returns the number of items filled in a given structure. This macro is defined as:

```
#define XtNumber(array) \
    ((Cardinal) (sizeof(array) / sizeof(array[0])))
```

Don't worry about how XtNumber works. Just use it.

Putting this all together, we set up our one-record action table with the following code:

```
static XtActionsRec drag_actions[] = {
{ "StartDragOperation",
    (XtActionProc) StartDragOperation}
};
```

```
XtAppContext     app_context;

/* ... */

XtAppAddActions(app_context,
   drag_actions,
   XtNumber(drag_actions) );
```

We cover actions in greater depth in Chapter 23. For now, the above code sets up our action so that we can call the StartDragOperation function from a translation table.

Setting Up a Translation Table

A translation table is a resource that maps keys or buttons to actions, using the definition of actions from above. The key task here is to override any mapping of the mouse Button2 presses. To conform with the Motif style, we want a Button2 press to start a drag operation. This all seems odd, but it's necessary to override any previous mapping for Button2 events.

We set up a single-element translation table that overrides any previous mapping:

```
#override <Btn2Down>: StartDragOperation()"
```

This tells the Xt translation manager that when the user presses the mouse Button2 down, Xt should call the function StartDragOperation. (It assumes you have set up an action for the text string "StartDragOperation".)

In a C program, we set up a translation table like the following:

```
/* Global Translation table entry. */
static char dnd_translations[] =
    "#override <Btn2Down>: StartDragOperation()";
```

The #override overrides any previous definitions. Be careful with this option. You usually don't want to override all the translations on a widget.

You must then parse the translation table with XtParseTranslationTable:

```
XtTranslations XtParseTranslationTable(String table)
```

XtParseTranslationTable parses the translation table text into an internal Xt representation. The only concern here is the value of type

XtTranslations to set a widget's translations resource. In our drag-and-drop program, below, we'll set up the translations as follows:

```
/* Global Translation table entry. */
static char dnd_translations[] =
    "#override <Btn2Down>: StartDragOperation()";

XtTranslations  translations;

    /* ... */

translations =
        XtParseTranslationTable(dnd_translations);
```

Once we have the translations, we pass these to a newly created widget. This makes that widget a drag source.

Creating a Widget with Translations

To make a widget act as a source for drag operations, set up the translation for mouse Button2 presses. This translation is passed to the translations resource for each widget that we wish to make into a drag source. You must pass this resource during widget creation.

For example, to create a pushbutton widget that acts as a drag source, use the following code:

```
Widget          parent;
Widget          drag_source;
Arg             args[10];
Cardinal        n;
XtTranslations  translations;

n = 0;
XtSetArg(args[n], XmNtranslations,
    translations); n++;

drag_source = XmCreatePushButton(parent,
                "drag_source", args, n);
```

With the above code, we've set up Xt to call the function StartDragOperation on button presses with the middle mouse button (Button2).

The Drag-Start Function

Inside the StartDragOperation function, you need to create and configure a drag context to start the drag operation. Call XmDragStart:

```
#include <Xm/DragDrop.h>

Widget XmDragStart(Widget widget,
        XEvent* event,
        ArgList args,
        Cardinal number_args)
```

XmDragStart returns an XmDragContext widget, another pseudowidget that requires some care. Any deviation from the standard procedure and you'll most likely face problems. XmDragStart also begins the drag operation.

Your drag start function must perform the following tasks:

1. Advertise the target data types that your application supports for dragging.

2. Set up the allowable drag operations (XmDROP_COPY, XmDROP_LINK, and XmDROP_MOVE).

3. Register a data-conversion procedure that will convert and supply the data on demand.

The Drag Context

Before calling XmDragStart, you should set up a number of XmDragContext resources, from among those listed in Table 21.7.

Table 21.7 *XmDragContext resources.*

Resource	Type	Default Value
clientData	XtPointer	NULL
dragOperations	unsigned char	XmDROP_MOVE | XmDROP_COPY
exportTargets	Atom*	NULL
incremental	Boolean	False
numExportTargets	Cardinal	0

The clientData resource is passed to the conversion callback as the *client_data* parameter.

The dragOperations resource is a bit mask of the various bit flags that represent the operations your application supports. This value should be the inclusive OR of the bit flags that represent supported operations. You can choose from XmDROP_COPY, XmDROP_LINK, and XmDROP_MOVE.

The exportTargets resource holds an array of atoms. Each atom in the array signifies a target data type that your application advertises it supports for drag and drop. The numExportTargets resource then holds a count of the number of data items.

The incremental resource is a flag that indicates whether or not the data will be passed incrementally. (Dragging data incrementally is an advanced topic; it is too advanced for this book.)

The XmDragContext supports a host of other resources, all oriented around the visual effects and animation used when dragging. Look up XmDragContext in the *OSF/Motif Programmer's Reference* for more on this.

In addition to setting resources, you must also set up a conversion callback into the convertProc resource. The convertProc resource should hold a pointer to a function that takes the following parameters:

```
typedef Boolean (*XtConvertSelectionIncrProc)(
    Widget widget,
    Atom*   selection,
    Atom*   target,
    Atom*   type,                 /* RETURN */
    XtPointer* value,             /* RETURN */
    unsigned long* value_length,  /* RETURN */
    int* format,                  /* RETURN */
    unsigned long* max_length,
    XtPointer client_data,
    XtRequestId* request_id)
```

As with selections, described in the last chapter, the important return values to set are the *type, value, value_length,* and *format.*

The Drag-Start-Action Callback

Putting this all together, create a drag-start function like the following one:

```
/* Called by action routine in translation table. */
void StartDragOperation(Widget widget,
    XEvent* event,
    String* params,
    Cardinal* number_params)

{   /* StartDragOperation */
    Arg         args[40];
    Cardinal    n;
    Atom        targets[10];
```

```
            /* Fill up array of targets. */
            targets[0] = XA_PIXMAP;

            n = 0;
            XtSetArg(args[n], XmNexportTargets, targets); n++;
            XtSetArg(args[n], XmNnumExportTargets, 1); n++;

            XtSetArg(args[n], XmNdragOperations,
                XmDROP_COPY); n++;

            XtSetArg(args[n], XmNconvertProc,
                PixmapConvertProc); n++;

            XmDragStart(widget, event, args, n);

     }   /* StartDragOperation */
```

With the above call to XmDragStart, we're off into a drag operation. Instead of using COMPOUND_TEXT, we advertise support for dragging pixmaps. You can use any arbitrary data types for the exportTargets resource. It's a good idea to stick to the standard target types, though.

Just before the call to XmDragStart, above, we set up a convertProc callback. This is the data-conversion callback.

Creating the Data-Conversion Callback

The data-conversion callback function is responsible for converting the data to the proper type and returning the data so that Motif can transfer it to the drop site.

The convertProc should return True if it succeeds in converting the data and False otherwise.

In addition, you must allocate the memory for the value parameter by calling XtMalloc. Why? Because Xt will automatically free this memory later with XtFree.

Our sample convertProc, PixmapConvertProc, converts the data to the PIXMAP target, by extracting the labelPixmap resource from a known pushbutton widget (drag_source). The code follows:

```
Widget   drag_source;

Boolean PixmapConvertProc(Widget widget,
    Atom* selection,
    Atom* target,
    Atom* type,                    /* RETURN */
```

```
            XtPointer* value,            /* RETURN */
            unsigned long* value_length, /* RETURN */
            int* format,                 /* RETURN */
            unsigned long* max_length,
            XtPointer client_data,
            XtRequestId* request_id)

    {   /* PixmapConvertProc */
        Pixmap      pixmap;
        Pixmap*     pixmap_ptr;

        if (*target == XA_PIXMAP) {
            XtVaGetValues(drag_source,
                XmNlabelPixmap, &pixmap,
                NULL);

            *type = XA_PIXMAP;
            pixmap_ptr = (Pixmap*) XtMalloc(sizeof(Pixmap) );

            memcpy(pixmap_ptr, &pixmap, 4);

            *value = (XtPointer) pixmap_ptr;
            *value_length = 1;
            *format = 32;

            return True;
        }

        /* If we get to here, we have an unknown target. */
        return False;

    }   /* PixmapConvertProc */
```

EXAMPLE PROGRAM TESTING DRAG AND DROP

To clarify all these confusing drag-and-drop options, we put together a program that provides both the drag source and the drop-site code. To further extend our discussion, we exchange PIXMAP data instead of exchanging text. This, combined with the text example in **drop.c**, above, should show that you can drag and drop any arbitrary data types.

The **dragdrop.c** program, below, copies the drop-site code from the **drop.c** program, above. However, the **dragdrop.c** program handles PIXMAP data in the drop site, not COMPOUND_TEXT. Look in the TransferCB and DropCB functions for more on this.

To get pixmap data, this program uses the LoadBitmapLabel function from Chapter 12. We load an arbitrary bitmap. You can change the file name to fit an X bitmap file on your system.

The code for **dragdrop.c** follows:

```
/* dragdrop.c */
#include  <Xm/Xm.h>
#include  <Xm/PanedW.h>
#include  <Xm/PushB.h>
#include  <Xm/RowColumn.h>
#include  <Xm/AtomMgr.h>
#include  <Xm/DragDrop.h>
#include  <X11/Xatom.h>
#include  <stdio.h>
#include  <string.h>

/* Global for "COMPOUND_TEXT" Atom. */
Atom    compound_text = (Atom) None;
Widget  drag_source;

/* External functions. */
extern Widget CreatePushbutton(Widget parent,
    char* name,
    XtCallbackProc callback,
    XtPointer client_data);

    /* Loads a bitmap file into a widget's label. */
extern Boolean LoadBitmapLabel(Widget widget,
    char* filename);

void exitCB(Widget widget,
    XtPointer client_data,
    XtPointer call_data)

{   /* exitCB */

    exit(0);

}   /* exitCB */

void pushCB(Widget widget,
    XtPointer client_data,
    XtPointer call_data)

{   /* pushCB */
    XmString    xmstring;

    /* Change widget back to text. */
    xmstring = XmStringCreateSimple((char*) client_data);

    XtVaSetValues(widget,
        XmNlabelString, xmstring,
        XmNlabelType,   XmSTRING,
        NULL);

    XmStringFree(xmstring);

}   /* pushCB */
```

```
void TransferCB(Widget widget,
    XtPointer client_data,
    Atom* seltype,
    Atom* type,
    XtPointer value,
    unsigned long length,
    int format)

{   /* TransferCB */
    Widget      label;
    Pixmap*     pixmap;

    /* We assume client data has label widget ID. */
    label = (Widget) client_data;

    if (*type == XA_PIXMAP) {
        pixmap = (Pixmap*) value;

        XtVaSetValues(label,
            XmNlabelPixmap, *pixmap,
            XmNlabelType,   XmPIXMAP,
            NULL);
    }

}   /* TransferCB */

void DropCB(Widget widget,
    XtPointer client_data,
    XtPointer call_data)

{   /* DropCB */
    XmDropProcCallbackStruct*   ptr;
    XmDropTransferEntryRec      entries[2];
    Arg                         args[20];
    Cardinal                    n;

    ptr =
        (XmDropProcCallbackStruct*) call_data;

    n = 0;
    entries[0].target = XA_PIXMAP;

    /* Pass widget as client data */
    entries[0].client_data = (XtPointer) widget;

    XtSetArg(args[n], XmNdropTransfers, entries); n++;
    XtSetArg(args[n], XmNnumDropTransfers, 1); n++;
    XtSetArg(args[n], XmNtransferProc,
        TransferCB); n++;

    XmDropTransferStart(ptr->dragContext,
        args, n);

}   /* DropCB */
```

```
/* Registers the given widget as a drop site. */
/* We use global atoms for the targets. */

void RegisterDropSite(Widget widget,
    XtCallbackProc callback)

{   /* RegisterDropSite */
    Arg         args[20];
    Cardinal    n;
    Atom        targets[10];

    n = 0;
    XtSetArg(args[n], XmNdropSiteOperations,
        XmDROP_COPY | XmDROP_MOVE); n++;

    /* Set up callback function. */
    XtSetArg(args[n], XmNdropProc, callback); n++;

    /* Set up target Atoms. */
    targets[0] = XA_PIXMAP;

    XtSetArg(args[n], XmNimportTargets,
        targets); n++;
    XtSetArg(args[n], XmNnumImportTargets, 1); n++;

    XmDropSiteRegister(widget, args, n);

}   /* RegisterDropSite */

Boolean PixmapConvertProc(Widget widget,
    Atom* selection,
    Atom* target,
    Atom* type,                  /* RETURN */
    XtPointer* value,            /* RETURN */
    unsigned long* value_length, /* RETURN */
    int* format,                 /* RETURN */
    unsigned long* max_length,
    XtPointer client_data,
    XtRequestId* request_id)

{   /* PixmapConvertProc */
    Pixmap      pixmap;
    Pixmap*     pixmap_ptr;

    if (*target == XA_PIXMAP) {
        XtVaGetValues(drag_source,
            XmNlabelPixmap, &pixmap,
            NULL);

        *type = XA_PIXMAP;
        pixmap_ptr = (Pixmap*) XtMalloc(sizeof(Pixmap) );

        memcpy(pixmap_ptr, &pixmap, 4);
```

```
                    *value = (XtPointer) pixmap_ptr;
                    *value_length = 1;
                    *format = 32;

                    return True;
            }

            /* If we get to here, we have an unknown target. */
            return False;

    }   /* PixmapConvertProc */

            /* Called by action routine in translation table. */
    void StartDragOperation(Widget widget,
            XEvent* event,
            String* params,
            Cardinal* number_params)

    {   /* StartDragOperation */
            Arg         args[40];
            Cardinal    n;
            Atom        targets[10];

            /* Fill up array of targets. */
            targets[0] = XA_PIXMAP;

            n = 0;
            XtSetArg(args[n], XmNexportTargets,
                targets); n++;
            XtSetArg(args[n], XmNnumExportTargets, 1); n++;

            XtSetArg(args[n], XmNdragOperations,
                XmDROP_COPY); n++;

            XtSetArg(args[n], XmNconvertProc,
                PixmapConvertProc); n++;

            XmDragStart(widget, event, args, n);

    }   /* StartDragOperation */

    /* Global Translation table entry. */
    static char dnd_translations[] =
        "#override <Btn2Down>: StartDragOperation()";

    /* Global action entry. */
    static XtActionsRec drag_actions[] = {
     { "StartDragOperation",
          (XtActionProc) StartDragOperation}
    };

    int main(int argc, char** argv)

    {   /* main */
            Widget          parent;
```

```
XtAppContext    app_context;
Arg             args[20];
Cardinal        n;
Widget          pane, push1;
XtTranslations  translations;

parent = XtVaAppInitialize(&app_context,
            "Ppm",
            (XrmOptionDescList) NULL,
            0,
            &argc, argv,
            (String*) NULL,
            XmNallowResize, True,
            NULL);

/* Add action table. */
XtAppAddActions(app_context,
    drag_actions,
    XtNumber(drag_actions) );

/* Create a paned window. */
n = 0;
pane = XmCreatePanedWindow(parent,
        "pane", args, n);

/* Create a pushbutton as a drop site. */
push1 = CreatePushbutton(pane, "push1",
            (XtCallbackProc) pushCB,
            (XtPointer) "Text");

/* Add in our translation table. */
translations =
    XtParseTranslationTable(dnd_translations);

n = 0;
XtSetArg(args[n], XmNtranslations,
    translations); n++;

/* Create a second pushbutton as a drag source. */
drag_source = XmCreatePushButton(pane,
                "drag_source", args, n);

XtAddCallback(drag_source,
    XmNactivateCallback,
    (XtCallbackProc) exitCB,
    (XtPointer) NULL);

LoadBitmapLabel(drag_source, "radura1.xbm");

XtManageChild(drag_source);

XtManageChild(pane);

/* Intern Atoms. */
compound_text = XmInternAtom(XtDisplay(parent),
```

```
                "COMPOUND_TEXT", False);

    /* Register drop sites. */
    RegisterDropSite(push1,
        (XtCallbackProc) DropCB);

    XtRealizeWidget(parent);
    XtAppMainLoop(app_context);
    return 0;

}   /* main */

/* end of file dragdrop.c */
```

This program uses the same resource file as the *drop* program above.

The results of the *dragdrop* program are shown in Figure 21.3.

Figure 21.3   *The dragdrop program.*

When running this program, you can drag the pixmap over the top pushbutton. The results of this action are shown in Figure 21.4.

Figure 21.4   *The dragdrop program after dragging.*

Pressing on the top pushbutton should reset it to display text, so that you can try dragging again. The results of this action are shown in Figure 21.5.

Figure 21.5   *The dragdrop program after resetting.*

DRAG-AND-DROP PROTOCOLS

Motif 1.2 offers two main drag-and-drop protocols: *dynamic* and *preregister*. The preregister protocol requires that drop-site widgets must preregister to be used. A database of this preregister information is stored so that any Motif application can get at the information. The dynamic protocol determines valid drop sites on the fly. This, obviously, requires quite a bit of message passing between applications.

The Motif toolkit handles both protocols with the same functions. In normal circumstances, your applications shouldn't care which protocol is in use. (In fact, the protocol can change during a drag operation.)

Determining the Preferred Drag-and-Drop Styles

The XmDisplay object, a pseudowidget new in Motif 1.2, holds information about drag-and-drop styles, in the form of resources. The resource dragInitiatorProtocolStyle has a default value of XmDRAG_PREFER_RECEIVER, while the dragReceiverProtocolStyle resource has a default value of XmDRAG_PREFER_PREREGISTER.

The dragInitiatorProtocolStyle resource specifies the protocol when widgets act as drag sources. This potential values of this resource are listed in Table 21.8.

Table 21.8 *DragInitiatorProtocolStyle values.*

Constant	Meaning
XmDRAG_NONE	Does not support drag and drop
XmDRAG_DROP_ONLY	Supports drop only, no animation
XmDRAG_PREREGISTER	Supports preregister protocol
XmDRAG_DYNAMIC	Supports only dynamic protocol
XmDRAG_PREFER_PREREGISTER	Prefers preregister protocol
XmDRAG_PREFER_DYNAMIC	Prefers dynamic protocol
XmDRAG_PREFER_RECEIVER	Defers to drop-site preference

The dragReceiverProtocolStyle resource specifies the protocol when widgets act as drop sites. The resource values are listed in Table 21.9.

Table 21.9 *DragReceiverProtocolStyle values.*

Constant	Meaning
XmDRAG_NONE	Does not support drag and drop
XmDRAG_DROP_ONLY	Supports drop only, no animation
XmDRAG_PREREGISTER	Supports preregister protocol
XmDRAG_DYNAMIC	Supports only dynamic protocol
XmDRAG_PREFER_PREREGISTER	Prefers preregister protocol
XmDRAG_PREFER_DYNAMIC	Prefers dynamic protocol

N O T E

XmDRAG_PREFER_RECEIVER is not allowed for the dragReceiverProtocolStyle resource.

To access the XmDisplay pseudowidget for a given display connection, call XmGetXmDisplay:

```
#include <Xm/Display.h>

Widget XmGetXmDisplay(Display* display)
```

XmGetXmDisplay returns the XmDisplay object for a given display connection. Note that the function is named *XmGetXmDisplay*, not *XmGetDisplay*.

PROBLEMS WITH DRAG AND DROP

The main problems with Motif's drag and drop include:

■ Interoperability with other programs

■ Lack of standardization

■ Slow performance

■ Server grabs make debugging difficult

The Motif 1.2 drag-and-drop protocol works among all Motif 1.2 applications, but not with applications created using any other toolkit. That is, you can drag and drop data between Motif toolkit programs, but not between Motif programs and OLIT programs, or XView programs, or any other non-Motif program. This, of course, defeats the whole purpose of drag and drop.

As of this writing, there are at least five competing drag-and-drop protocols. Luckily, the *Inter-Client Communications Conventions Manual* should include a standardized drag-and-drop protocol in X11 Release 6. Most of the standard will be based on part of the Motif protocol (the dynamic protocol, most likely), so your Motif applications should still work under X11R6.

Motif's drag and drop is not known for its performance. If you build a drag-and-drop file manager, for example, expect slow performance on the drags and drops. At version 1.2, Motif is still new to drag and drop, so further versions should improve the performance.

To help on performance, Motif's drag and drop grabs the X server while the drag operation takes place. This allows for faster animation effects but makes debugging more difficult. If your program locks up in the midst of an X server grab, none of the other programs on your display will be able to receive any mouse or keyboard input. You'll be forced to log in from a different terminal and kill your X processes. This, obviously, makes it tougher to debug errant drag or drop callbacks.

SUMMARY

In this chapter, we provided a brief glance at Motif's drag and drop. We focused on introducing the basic concepts of drag and drop and showing you how to use this technique in working programs. Even so, there's a lot more to the subject. If you think that what we covered is confusing, just wait until you delve into the animation effects.

By now, you should be ready to tackle the Motif reference manual to further customize your drags and drops.

MOTIF INTRINSICS FUNCTIONS AND MACROS INTRODUCED IN THIS CHAPTER

```
XmCvtCTToXmString
XmCvtXmStringToCT
XmDragStart
XmDropSiteRegister
XmDropSiteUnregister
XmDragStart
XmDropTransferStart
```

X TOOLKIT INTRINSICS FUNCTIONS AND MACROS INTRODUCED IN THIS CHAPTER

```
XtAppAddActions
XtParseTranslationTable
```

SECTION 5

Advanced Motif Topics

There are certain things that every Motif application must support if it's going to be taken seriously in the marketplace. This section covers a few of those topics.

Chapter 22 begins the section with a discussion of option and pop-up menus, which are considered advanced menus in the Motif universe. They are used in situations where the standard pull-down menu isn't applicable.

A grab bag of sorts is presented in Chapter 23, all relating to X resources. While we covered resources early in the text, Chapter 23 returns to the topics and covers advanced subjects like translation tables, actions, floating-point resources, and resource converters.

Chapter 24 discusses error-handling in Motif. Personally, we feel that a professional approach to error-handling (that is, handling errors with grace and dignity, always keeping the user well-informed as to what is happening) is one of the best ways your software can interact with the end user–which, of course, it is designed to do.

The other way to please end users is to include a professional online-help system, as covered in Chapter 25. Help is one of the most neglected areas in the Motif world, as users lucky to get *any* online help at all—never mind a well-thought-out system that's actually of use to the user. While online-help support is difficult to implement and maintain, your software will greatly benefit in the long run.

CHAPTER 22

Advanced Menus

This chapter covers:

- Using option menus for exclusive choices
- Creating and configuring option menus
- Problems with option menus
- Option-menu child widgets
- A program for creating option menus
- Creating pop-up menus
- Making pop-up menus appear
- Tracking the mouse location for pop-up menus
- A program for creating pop-up menus
- Information that should be placed in pop-up menus

OPTION AND POP-UP MENUS

In addition to the pull-down menus covered in Chapter 4, Motif offers two other types of menus: option and pop-up menus. *Option menus* present a list of exclusive choices, and the user can pick one at a time. *Pop-up menus* act much like pull-down menus, only they usually pop up when the user presses the rightmost mouse button (`Button3`).

This chapter covers these advanced menu techniques.

SHORTCUT

Creating Option and Pop-Up Menus

Create an option menu with `XmCreateOptionMenu`:

```
#include <Xm/RowColumn.h>

Widget XmCreateOptionMenu(Widget parent,
        char* name,
        ArgList args,
        Cardinal number_args)
```

You should first create a pull-down menu and then set the option's `subMenuId` resource to hold the pull-down menu widget.

Create a pop-up menu with `XmCreatePopupMenu`:

```
#include <Xm/RowColumn.h>

Widget XmCreatePopupMenu(Widget parent,
        char* widget_name,
        ArgList args
        Cardinal number_args)
```

You then must manage the pop-up menu manually to make it appear. If you do this from an event-handling function or Motif widget callback, you can make the pop-up menu appear at the current mouse cursor location by calling `XmMenuPosition` before calling `XtManageChild`:

```
#include <Xm/RowColumn.h>

void XmMenuPosition(Widget popup,
        XButtonPressedEvent* event)
```

OPTION MENUS

An option menu combines a label, a pushbutton, and a menu. The current active choice appears in the pushbutton, as shown in Figure 22.1.

Figure 22.1   *An option menu at rest.*

When you press the leftmost mouse button (Button1) over the pushbutton part of the option menu, the menu itself appears, as shown in Figure 22.2.

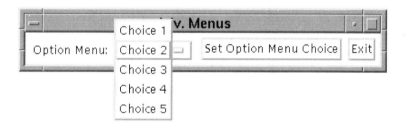

Figure 22.2   *An option menu in action.*

The current choice always appears in the pushbutton part of the option menu.

Creating Option Menus

Creating option menus is a two-step process, mirroring the process for creating a pull-down menu: you created the pull-down menu and then a cascade button (which controls the menu's visibility), linking the cascade to the menu.

You create option menus similarly. First, you create a normal pull-down menu with `XmCreatePulldownMenu`. Then you create an option menu with `XmCreateOptionMenu`, setting the `subMenuId` resource to connect the option part to the pull-down menu.

`XmCreateOptionMenu` takes the following parameters:

```
#include <Xm/RowColumn.h>

Widget XmCreateOptionMenu(Widget parent,
        char* name,
        ArgList args,
        Cardinal number_args)
```

Manage the option menu with `XtManageChild`.

As you can see, an option menu is really an `XmRowColumn` widget, specially configured. In addition, the term *option menu* is a bit of a misnomer. An option menu really holds two gadgets: a label to display a message and a specially configured pushbutton to call up the pull-down menu. Thus the menu created by `XmCreateOptionMenu` really isn't a menu at all.

You should always set the `subMenuId` resource before creating an option menu.

N O T E

The pull-down menu is a normal pull-down menu, so you can configure it as described in Chapter 4. In addition, you can set the `tearOffModel` resource (new in Motif 1.2) to `XmTEAR_OFF_ENABLED`. This will allow the user to tear off the pull-down menu, just like the user can tear off menus on the menu bar.

Putting this all together, you can create a pull-down menu and an option with the following code:

```
#include <Xm/RowColumn.h>

Widget      parent;
Widget      pulldown;
Widget      option;
Arg         args[20];
Cardinal    n;

/* Create pulldown menu for option. */
n = 0;
```

```
pulldown = XmCreatePulldownMenu(parent,
          "pulldown", args, n);

/* Create option menu. */
n = 0;
XtSetArg(args[n], XmNsubMenuId, pulldown); n++;

option = XmCreateOptionMenu(parent,
          "option", args, n);

/* Manage option, not menu. */
XtManageChild(option);
```

When you add menu choices to the option menu, you create them as push-button widgets, just like you did for pull-down menus.

NOTE

When you create these pushbutton widgets, be sure to use the pull-down menu as the parent, *not* the option.

Configuring Option Menus

Since an option menu is really an XmRowColumn widget, you can set a number of row-column resources. When you read the reference information on the row-column widget, you'll need to sort out all resources that don't apply to row columns configured as option menus. After they are sorted out, a smaller set remains. Of these resources, the most essential ones appear in Table 22.1.

Table 22.1 *Useful option menu resources.*

Resource	Type	Default Value
labelString	XmString	NULL
menuHistory	Widget	NULL
subMenuId	Widget	NULL

The labelString resource applies only to option menus. It holds the text message to display to the left of the option pushbutton.

The `subMenuId` resource holds the ID of the pull-down menu widget. This connects the option part to the menu part. You need to set this resource before creating an option menu.

The `menuHistory` resource is used to change and query the current active choice.

Setting the Current Choice

You can set the current active choice in an option menu by changing the value of the `menuHistory` resource:

```
Widget    option;
Widget    menu_choice;

XtVaSetValues(option,
    XmNmenuHistory, menu_choice,
    NULL);
```

Unfortunately, you must do this by widget ID, not by item number. Because of this, you may want to keep track the child pushbutton widgets so that you can change the option menu.

Option-Menu Child Widgets

When you call `XmCreateOptionMenu`, you get back a row-column widget that manages two child gadgets. The first gadget holds the `labelString` text message. The second is the pushbutton that calls up the menu when pressed.

You may need to set resources on these gadgets to change their behavior. Because of this, Motif provides two functions to query these widget IDs.

`XmOptionLabelGadget` returns the label gadget:

```
#include <Xm/RowColumn.h>

Widget XmOptionLabelGadget(Widget option)
```

`XmOptionButtonGadget` returns the pushbutton gadget:

```
#include <Xm/RowColumn.h>

Widget XmOptionButtonGadget(Widget option)
```

Problems with Option Menus

We've faced a number of problems with option menus. The most annoying is lining up option menus in data-entry forms. Because the option menu contains a label tied to a pushbutton, you'll have a hard time lining an option menu up with other label-text field or label-pushbutton combinations. Why? Because you have little control over the separation between the option menu's elements. You can control the placement of the whole set, but not of the parts.

Because of this, we often disable the option menu's label gadget. Instead, we use a regular label widget, and then we can place the label widget in column one and the option menu in column two of an arbitrary data-entry form.

To disable the label gadget, we merely unmanage it:

```
#include <Xm/RowColumn.h>

Widget label;
Widget option;

label = XmOptionLabelGadget(option);

XtUnmanageChild(label_widget);
```

The other main problem with option menus occurs if you try to delete some of the child widgets inside the pull-down menu. If you do this, you'll have problems if the option's `menuHistory` resource points at a now-deleted widget. In this case, set the `menuHistory` resource to a valid widget before deleting.

A Program To Test Option Menus

Option menus aren't that hard to work with. Even so, we've put together an example program to let you test the option menu's dynamics and see one in a working program.

In the code below, we create an option menu and a separate pushbutton that sets the option to display the first choice in the menu.

The code for this program follows:

```
/* optmenu.c */
#include  <Xm/Xm.h>
```

```
#include  <Xm/RowColumn.h>
#include  <stdio.h>

/* Global widgets. */
Widget   option;

/* External function. */
extern Widget CreatePushbutton(Widget parent,
    char* name,
    XtCallbackProc callback,
    XtPointer client_data);

    /* Called on menu choices. */
void menuCB(Widget widget,
    XtPointer client_data,
    XtPointer call_data)

{   /* menuCB */

    /* Client data is text. */
    printf("Menu choice [%s]\n",
        (char*) client_data);

}   /* menuCB */

    /* Sets current option menu choice. */
void set_optionCB(Widget widget,
    XtPointer client_data,
    XtPointer call_data)

{   /* set_optionCB */
    Widget  menu_choice;

    menu_choice = (Widget) client_data;

    /* Option menu is global. */
    XtVaSetValues(option,
        XmNmenuHistory, menu_choice,
        NULL);

}   /* set_optionCB */

void exitCB(Widget widget,
    XtPointer client_data,
    XtPointer call_data)

{   /* exitCB */

    exit(0);

}   /* exitCB */

int main(int argc, char** argv)

{   /* main */
```

```
XtAppContext    app_context;
Widget          row, set_menu, quit;
Widget          parent;
Widget          opt_menu, opt_child;
Arg             args[20];
Cardinal        n;

parent = XtVaAppInitialize(&app_context,
            "Ppm",
            (XrmOptionDescList) NULL,
            0,
            &argc, argv,
            (String*) NULL,
            XmNallowResize, True,
            NULL);

row = XtVaCreateWidget("row",
            xmRowColumnWidgetClass, parent,
            XmNorientation, XmHORIZONTAL,
            NULL);

/* Create pulldown menu for option. */
n = 0;
opt_menu = XmCreatePulldownMenu(row,
            "opt_menu", args, n);

/* Create option menu. */
n = 0;
XtSetArg(args[n], XmNsubMenuId, opt_menu); n++;

option = XmCreateOptionMenu(row,
            "option", args, n);

/* Menu choice parent is
 * pulldown menu not option.
 */
opt_child = CreatePushbutton(opt_menu, "opt_child1",
        (XtCallbackProc) menuCB,
        (XtPointer) "opt_child1");

(void) CreatePushbutton(opt_menu, "opt_child2",
        (XtCallbackProc) menuCB,
        (XtPointer) "opt_child2");

(void) CreatePushbutton(opt_menu, "opt_child3",
        (XtCallbackProc) menuCB,
        (XtPointer) "opt_child3");

(void) CreatePushbutton(opt_menu, "opt_child4",
        (XtCallbackProc) menuCB,
        (XtPointer) "opt_child4");

(void) CreatePushbutton(opt_menu, "opt_child5",
        (XtCallbackProc) menuCB,
        (XtPointer) "opt_child5");
```

```
        /* Manage option, not menu. */
        XtManageChild(option);

        /* Create pushbutton to change option. */
        set_menu = CreatePushbutton(row, "set_menu",
                (XtCallbackProc) set_optionCB,
                (XtPointer) opt_child);

        quit = CreatePushbutton(row, "exit",
                (XtCallbackProc) exitCB,
                (XtPointer) NULL);

        XtManageChild(row);

        XtRealizeWidget(parent);
        XtAppMainLoop(app_context);
        return 0;

}    /* main */

/* end of file optmenu.c */
```

The resource file for the example program follows:

```
! Resource file for Chapter 22
! of Power Programming Motif.
!
*fontList:      lucidasans-12
*background:    grey92

*title: Adv. Menus

*exit.labelString:      Exit
*set_menu.labelString: Set Option Menu Choice

*option.labelString: Option Menu:

! Menu choices.
*opt_child1.labelString: Choice 1
*opt_child2.labelString: Choice 2
*opt_child3.labelString: Choice 3
*opt_child4.labelString: Choice 4
*opt_child5.labelString: Choice 5

! end of resource file
```

Copy this file to your home directory and name it **Ppm**.

POP-UP MENUS

Pop-up menus exist as an expert-user feature. For experts, a pop-up menu provides a set of common choices at the touch of a mouse button—the rightmost mouse button (Button3), according to the Motif style guide. In most cases, the pop-up menu should appear at the current mouse location, which saves the user from traveling to the menu bar. (On a large monitor, you must move the mouse a great distance to go from the bottom of the screen to the top—assuming the menu bar is on top). The choices in the pop-up menu should be shortcuts for commonly used options.

Pop-up menus act a lot like pull-down menus, except that pop-up menus appear at the current mouse location. In addition, you usually must manage a pop-up menu yourself, while pull-down menus have cascade buttons to do the dirty work.

Typically you use an incoming mouse ButtonPress event (on the rightmost mouse button) to trigger a pop-up menu. Because of this, you'll need to track these events so you can manage the pop-up menu at the proper time.

Creating Pop-Up Menus

Create a pop-up menu by calling XmCreatePopupMenu:

```
#include <Xm/RowColumn.h>

Widget XmCreatePopupMenu(Widget parent,
    char* widget_name,
    ArgList args,
    Cardinal number_args)
```

For the parent widget, you can use the widget from which you'll pop up the menu. For example, in our program below, we create a label widget and then set up an event handler to track ButtonPress events. We use this label widget as the parent for the pop-up menu.

N O T E

In all other menu code, we've created the actual menu with XmCreatePulldownMenu. In this case, though, be sure to use XmCreatePopupMenu.

Once you've created a pop-up menu, you can fill it in with menu choices just like you do for pull-down or option menus. This remains constant, so create XmPushButton widgets for the menu choices as you've done since Chapter 4.

Making Pop-Up Menus Appear

When you want a pop-up menu to appear, call XtManageChild on the widget returned by XmCreatePopupMenu. In other words, don't call XtManageChild until you're ready to have the menu appear on the screen. Call XmCreatePopupMenu to create the menu, and then call XtManageChild later, when you're ready to pop up the menu.

The key to popping up the menu is to locate it at the current mouse position. There's a number of low-level X routines to get the current mouse position, but the easiest step is to use the Motif convenience function XmMenuPosition:

```
#include <Xm/RowColumn.h>

void XmMenuPosition(Widget popup,
        XButtonPressedEvent* event)
```

You pass XmMenuPosition the pop-up menu widget and an XButtonPressedEvent pointer. This event should come from an Xt event handler or a drawing-area widget input callback function. XmMenuPosition ensures that the next time you manage the pop-up widget it will appear on the screen near the location of the mouse when the ButtonPress event occurred.

In your code, you can call XmMenuPosition as follows:

```
XEvent*     event;
Widget      popup;

/* We're only interested in Button3. */
if (event->xbutton.button == Button3) {

    /* Locate menu to mouse. */
    XmMenuPosition(popup,
        (XButtonPressedEvent*) event);

    /* Popup menu. */
    XtManageChild(popup);
}
```

The pop-up menu will automatically pop down—unmanage itself—when the user makes a menu choice or cancels the menu.

A Program To Test Pop-Up Menus

We've created a program to test pop-up menus. The following program creates a label widget and sets up an event handler on the label to track ButtonPress events. In the event-handler callback function, we pop up the pop-up menu if the user pressed Button3, the rightmost mouse button.

Using the code below as a guide, you should be able to create and manipulate pop-up menus:

```
/* popup.c */
#include   <Xm/Xm.h>
#include   <Xm/Label.h>
#include   <Xm/RowColumn.h>
#include   <stdio.h>

/* External function. */
extern Widget CreatePushbutton(Widget parent,
    char* name,
    XtCallbackProc callback,
    XtPointer client_data);

    /* Event handler to popup menu. */
static void event_handler(Widget widget,
    XtPointer client_data,
    XEvent* event,
    Boolean* continue_to_dispatch)

{   /* event_handler */
    Widget    popup;

    /* We passed menu as client_data. */
    popup = (Widget) client_data;

    if (popup == NULL) {
        return;
    }

    /* We're only interested in Button3. */
    if (event->xbutton.button == Button3) {

        /* Locate menu to mouse. */
        XmMenuPosition(popup,
            (XButtonPressedEvent*) event);

        /* Popup menu. */
        XtManageChild(popup);
    }
```

```
}    /* event_handler */

    /* Called on menu choices. */
void menuCB(Widget widget,
    XtPointer client_data,
    XtPointer call_data)

{    /* menuCB */

    /* Client data is text. */
    printf("Menu choice [%s]\n",
        (char*) client_data);

}    /* menuCB */

void exitCB(Widget widget,
    XtPointer client_data,
    XtPointer call_data)

{    /* exitCB */

    exit(0);

}    /* exitCB */

int main(int argc, char** argv)

{    /* main */
    XtAppContext    app_context;
    Widget          row, quit;
    Widget          parent;
    Widget          popup;
    Widget          label;
    Arg             args[20];
    Cardinal        n;

    parent = XtVaAppInitialize(&app_context,
            "Ppm",
            (XrmOptionDescList) NULL,
            0,
            &argc, argv,
            (String*) NULL,
            XmNallowResize, True,
            NULL);

    row = XtVaCreateWidget("row",
            xmRowColumnWidgetClass, parent,
            XmNorientation, XmHORIZONTAL,
            NULL);

    /* Create label widget to popup menu. */
    label = XtVaCreateManagedWidget("label",
            xmLabelWidgetClass, row,
            NULL);
```

```
        quit = CreatePushbutton(row, "exit",
                (XtCallbackProc) exitCB,
                (XtPointer) NULL);

        XtManageChild(row);

        /* Create popup menu. */
        n = 0;
        popup = XmCreatePopupMenu(label,
                    "popup", args, n);

        /* Menu choice parent is popup menu.
         */
        (void) CreatePushbutton(popup, "pop_child1",
                (XtCallbackProc) menuCB,
                (XtPointer) "pop_child1");

        (void) CreatePushbutton(popup, "pop_child2",
                (XtCallbackProc) menuCB,
                (XtPointer) "pop_child2");

        (void) CreatePushbutton(popup, "pop_child3",
                (XtCallbackProc) menuCB,
                (XtPointer) "pop_child3");

        (void) CreatePushbutton(popup, "pop_child4",
                (XtCallbackProc) menuCB,
                (XtPointer) "pop_child4");

        (void) CreatePushbutton(popup, "pop_child5",
                (XtCallbackProc) menuCB,
                (XtPointer) "pop_child5");

        /* Set mouse button event handler on label. */
        XtAddEventHandler(label,
            ButtonPressMask,
            False,
            (XtEventHandler) event_handler,
            (XtPointer) popup);

        XtRealizeWidget(parent);
        XtAppMainLoop(app_context);
        return 0;

    }   /* main */

/* end of file popup.c */
```

The *popup* program uses the following X resource file:

```
! Resource file for popup.c in Chapter 22
! of Power Programming Motif.
!
*fontList:      lucidasans-12
```

```
*background:      grey92

*title: Popup Menus

*exit.labelString:      Exit

*label.labelString: Press the rightmost mouse\n\
button over this widget to\n\
pop up a popup menu.

*label.background:  grey
*label.foreground:  white

! Menu choices.
*pop_child1.labelString: Choice 1
*pop_child2.labelString: Choice 2
*pop_child3.labelString: Choice 3
*pop_child4.labelString: Choice 4
*pop_child5.labelString: Choice 5

! end of resource file
```

Name this file **Ppm** and store it in your home directory.

The results of this program are shown in Figure 22.3.

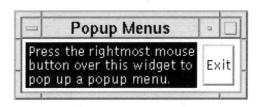

Figure 22.3 *The popup program.*

If you hold down the rightmost mouse button, you'll see the pop-up menu shown in Figure 22.4.

The menu should appear near your mouse cursor.

Using Pop-Up Menus

Since the pop-up menu remains invisible most of the time, you should place items in a pop-up menu only if they appear somewhere else in the interface. Why? Because new users will have no idea that a pop-up menu even exists. Remember that pop-up menus are expert-user features.

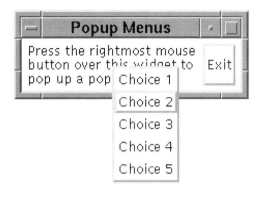

Figure 22.4 *The pop-up menu.*

SUMMARY

Motif offers two other types of menus: option and pop-up menus. Option menus present a list of exclusive choices, and the user can pick one at a time. Pop-up menus act much like pull-down menus, only they usually pop up when the user presses the rightmost mouse button (Button3).

The process for creating an option menu is similar to the process for creating a pull-down menu. First, you create a normal pull-down menu with XmCreatePulldownMenu. Then you create an option menu with XmCreateOptionMenu, setting the subMenuId resource to connect the option part to the pull-down menu.

Pop-up menus exist as an expert-user feature. For experts, a pop-up menu provides a set of common choices at the touch of a mouse button—the rightmost mouse button (Button3), according to the Motif style guide. In most cases, the pop-up menu should appear at the current mouse location, which saves the user from traveling to the menu bar. (On a large monitor, you must move the mouse a great distance to go from the bottom of the screen to the top—assuming the menu bar is on top.) The choices in the pop-up menu should be shortcuts for commonly used options.

MOTIF FUNCTIONS AND MACROS INTRODUCED IN THIS CHAPTER

```
XmCreateOptionMenu
XmCreatePopupMenu
XmOptionButtonGadget
XmOptionLabelGadget
```

CHAPTER 23

Translation Tables, Actions, and Advanced Resources

This chapter covers:

- Translation tables
- Translation directives
- Discarding translations
- Modifier keys
- Actions
- Using floating-point resources
- Advanced resource converters
- Cheating with resource converters
- Application-created resource values
- Setting up an XtResource array
- A program to test resources, translations, and actions

777

ADVANCED RESOURCE HANDLING

This chapter glories in obscure trivialities. (Of course, all of X and Motif seems to do that.) Unfortunately for all of us, you need to know these obscurities because they impact your programs. In this chapter we flesh out our discussion of X resources and cover a number of advanced topics, including translation tables, actions, floating-point resources, and resource converters.

SHORTCUT

Overriding Translation Values

You can use XtOverrideTranslations in your code to override individual translation values for a resource, as show below:

```
/* Global Translation table entry. */
static char text_translations[] =
  "#override \
     <Key>F2: beep() \n\
     <Key>F3: beginning-of-file() \n";

    /* ... */

Widget         parent;
Widget         text;
Arg            args[20];
Cardinal       n;
XtTranslations translations;

    /* ... */

n = 0;
text = XmCreateScrolledText(parent,
        "text", args, n);

/* Parse translations. */
translations =
    XtParseTranslationTable(text_translations);

/* Modify translations. */
XtOverrideTranslations(text, translations);
```

You can ask Xt to convert a resource value inside a call to XtVaSetValues, as shown in the code below:

```
XtVaSetValues(widget,
    XtVaTypedArg,
        XmNbackground, XmRString,
            "bisque", (strlen("bisque") + 1),
    NULL);
```

TRANSLATING TRANSLATION TABLES

Translations in X are a means to customize the way keystrokes and mouse actions interact with your Motif programs, using resource-setting commands.

Each widget, such as a scroll bar or pushbutton, has an internal *translation table* that defines how that widget handles input events like keystrokes and mouse clicks. The translation table maps input events to internal functions, called *actions*. All Motif widgets have a set of built-in supported actions. You can also add your own, since the translation table makes no distinction between your actions and the built-in ones.

All translations for a given widget are grouped together in a table, and this table is set with one X resource command. The basic syntax for each entry in the translation table is:

```
<Event> : action()
```

The event appears between angle brackets, followed by a colon, and then the name of the action (function) to execute. The open and close parentheses indicate that the action is sent no parameters. (You always need the parentheses.)

Some action routines may also accept parameters, such as the key-select(right).

Keyboard keys, like letters of the alphabet or function keys, use the following syntax:

```
<Key> F1 : action() \n\
<Key> E : action()  \n\
<Key> 6 : action()  \n
```

Every line uses a \n (newline) to end the translation for a given key, and all but the last have a \ to allow the resource command to extend over multiple lines. The whole translation table is a single resource-setting command.

The #override command tells the X translation manager to use your commands to override any previous commands for the same events.

To put this all together, the following translation resource overrides the definition of two keys, **F2** and **F3**, for an XmText widget named *text*. **F2** will ring the bell using the *beep* action. **F3** will jump to the beginning of the text widget with the *beginning-of-file* action. The whole resource-setting command appears below:

```
*text.translations:\
#override \n\
   <Key>F2: beep() \n\
   <Key>F3: beginning-of-file() \n
```

Both actions, *beep* and *beginning-of-file*, are built in to the XmText widget and documented in the *OSF/Motif Programmer's Reference*.

Translation Directives

The #override acts as a directive to tell the translation manager how to deal with the new translations and what to do about any old translations— you must assume that every Motif widget already has a set of translations installed for it. The allowable directives are listed in Table 23.1.

Table 23.1   *Translation directives.*

Directive	Meaning
#augment	Old translation takes priority in conflicts.
#override	New translation takes priority in conflicts.
#replace	Replace *all* previous translations, even if there is no conflict.

Modifier Keys

You can set up translations to work only when certain modifier keys are held down, such as the **Shift** key, **Control** key (often abbreviated **Ctrl**), or *Meta* key (often labeled **Alt** on your keyboard). The syntax for this follows:

```
Shift Ctrl Meta <Btn2Up> : action()
```

In the above example, the **Shift**, **Control**, and *Meta* keys all must be held down when the event—the middle mouse button—is released. (Btn2Up is an abbreviation for a ButtonRelease event on Button2.) You can mix and match modifier keys.

N O T E Be careful when trying to set up translations that use the *Meta* key combined with function keys. The Motif window manager already takes over most *Meta* functions, such as *Meta*-**F4**. See Table 18.16 in Chapter 18 for a listing.

If you *don't* want a modifier key, you can use the tilde (~) character, which, of course, means "not" to C programmers:

```
~Shift <Key> F5 : Help()
```

The above example means that if the user presses the **F5** function key while the **Shift** key is not held down, the translation manager will call the Help action routine.

The translation manager executes only the *first* action that matches an event. This means that general rules should go at the end, and specific rules at the beginning, of a translation table. The second action below will not be called, since the first translation will trap all **F8** key presses.

```
<Key> F8 : action_a()
Ctrl <Key> F8 : action_never_called()
```

Instead of the above example, place the second translation *before* the first:

```
Ctrl <Key> F8 : action_will_get_called()
<Key> F8 : action_a()
```

In translations, you can use the official X event name, like ButtonPress, or one of the abbreviations for buttons, keys, and modifiers listed in Table 23.2.

Table 23.2 *Translation event, mouse, and key abbreviations.*

Abbreviation	**Event or Modifier**
Ctrl	Control modifier
Meta	Meta modifier
	continued

Shift	Shift modifier
BtnDown	ButtonPress
BtnUp	ButtonRelease
Btn1Down	Button1 ButtonPress
Btn1Up	Button1 ButtonRelease
Btn2Down	Button2 ButtonPress
Btn2Up	Button2 ButtonRelease
Btn3Down	Button3 ButtonPress
Btn3Up	Button3 ButtonRelease
Btn4Down	Button4 ButtonPress
Btn4Up	Button4 ButtonRelease
Btn5Down	Button5 ButtonPress
Btn5Up	Button5 ButtonRelease
BtnMotion	MotionNotify with any button pressed
Btn1Motion	MotionNotify with Button1 pressed
Btn2Motion	MotionNotify with Button2 pressed
Btn3Motion	MotionNotify with Button3 pressed
Btn4Motion	MotionNotify with Button4 pressed
Btn5Motion	MotionNotify with Button5 pressed
Circ	CirculateNotify
CircReq	CirculateRequest
Clrmap	ColormapNotify
Configure	ConfigureNotify
ConfigureReq	ConfigureRequest
Create	CreateNotify
Destroy	DestroyNotify
Enter	EnterNotify
EnterWindow	EnterNotify
Expose	Expose
FocusIn	FocusIn

continued

FocusOut	FocusOut
Grav	GravityNotify
GrExp	GraphicsExpose
Key	KeyPress
KeyDown	KeyPress
KeyUp	KeyRelease
Keymap	KeymapNotify
Leave	LeaveNotify
LeaveWindow	LeaveNotify
Map	MapNotify
Mapping	MappingNotify
MapReq	MapRequest
Message	ClientMessage
Motion	MotionNotify
MouseMoved	MotionNotify
NoExp	NoExpose
Prop	PropertyNotify
PtrMoved	MotionNotify
Reparent	ReparentNotify
ResReq	ResizeRequest
SelClr	SelectionClear
Select	SelectionNotify
SelReq	SelectionRequest
Unmap	UnmapNotify
Visible	VisibilityNotify

Setting Up a Translation Table

As we discussed in Chapter 21, you can hard-code translations into your C programs by placing the translation settings inside a global text string, much like the following:

```
/* Global Translation table entry. */
static char text_translations[] =
    "#override <Key>F2: beep()\n\
                <Key>F3: beginning-of-file()";
```

Before you can use these translations for a widget, you must parse the translation table with XtParseTranslationTable:

```
XtTranslations XtParseTranslationTable(String table)
```

XtParseTranslationTable parses the translation-table text into an internal Xt representation. We don't have to worry about this representation, except that we need a value of type XtTranslations to set a widget's translations resource. Once we have the translations, we pass these to a newly created widget.

A better method, though, is to use XtOverrideTranslations or XtAugmentTranslations. XtOverrideTranslations takes a translation table and merges it in with a widget's existing translation table, overriding the old values with the new where conflicts occur:

```
void XtOverrideTranslations(Widget widget,
        XtTranslations translations)
```

XtOverrideTranslations pointedly ignores any of the directives like #augment or #replace. It treats all new translations as having the #override directive.

You need to call XtOverrideTranslations after you've created the widget. In your code, you can call XtOverrideTranslations as follows:

```
/* Global Translation table entry. */
static char text_translations[] =
  "#augment \
      <Key>F2: beep() \n\
      <Key>F3: beginning-of-file() \n";

  /* ... */

Widget          parent;
Widget          text;
Arg             args[20];
Cardinal        n;
XtTranslations  translations;

  /* ... */

n = 0;
text = XmCreateScrolledText(parent,
```

```
            "text", args, n);

    /* Parse translations. */
    translations =
        XtParseTranslationTable(text_translations);

    /* Modify translations. */
    XtOverrideTranslations(text, translations);
```

N O T E

In the code example above, XtOverrideTranslations ignores the #augment directive.

XtAugmentTranslations acts much like XtOverrideTranslations, but XtAugmentTranslations merges in the new translations nondestructively: Where conflicts occur, the old translation value remains, and the new one is discarded. XtAugmentTranslations takes the same parameters as XtOverrideTranslations:

```
    void XtAugmentTranslations(Widget widget,
            XtTranslations translations)
```

In your code, you can call XtAugmentTranslations as follows:

```
    /* Global Translation table entry. */
    static char text_translations[] =
        "#override \
            <Key>F2: beep() \n\
            <Key>F3: beginning-of-file() \n";

        /* ... */

    Widget          parent;
    Widget          text;
    Arg             args[20];
    Cardinal        n;
    XtTranslations  translations;

        /* ... */

    n = 0;
    text = XmCreateScrolledText(parent,
            "text", args, n);

    /* Parse translations. */
    translations =
        XtParseTranslationTable(text_translations);
```

```
/* Modify translations. */
XtAugmentTranslations(text, translations);
```

In the code example above, XtAugmentTranslations ignores the #override directive. Be careful—in many cases, the Motif widget will already have translations for a given key combination. The XmText widget, in particular, has over 74 built-in translations in Motif 1.2.

Getting Rid of Translations

If you decide to remove all the translations for a widget, you can call XtUninstallTranslations:

```
void XtUninstallTranslations(Widget widget)
```

This removes all translations for a given widget.

WARNING Most Motif widgets require translations to handle any sort of mouse and keyboard input. If you call XtUninstallTranslations, you may make your widget completely nonfunctional.

Formal Translation-Table Syntax

The formal syntax for translation tables are listed in Table 23.3.

Table 23.3 *Translation-table syntax.*

translationTable	= [directive] { production }
directive	= ("#replace" | "#override" | "#augment") "\n"
production	= lhs ":" rhs "\n"
lhs	= (event | keyseq) { "," (event | keyseq) }
keyseq	= """ keychar {keychar} """
keychar	["^" | "$" | "\"] <ISO Latin 1 character>
event	= [modifier_list] "<"event_type ">" ["(" count["+"] ")"] {detail}
modifier_list	= (["!"] [":"] {modifier}) | "None"

continued

modifier	= ["~"] modifier_name
count	= ("I" | "2" | "3" | "4" | ...)
modifier_name	= "@" \<keysym> | \<see Table 23.2>
event_type	= \<see Table 23.2>
detail	= \<event specific details>
rhs	{ name "(" [params] ")" }
name	namechar { namechar }
namechar	{ "a"-"z" | "A"-"Z" | "0"-"9" | "_" | "-" }
params	= string {"," string}
string	= quoted_string | unquoted_string
quoted_string	= "" {\<Latin I character> | escape_char} ["\\"] ""
escape_char	= "\"
unquoted_string	= {\<Latin I character except space, tab, ",", "\n", ")">}

Everything in quotation marks in the above table is literal characters that should be used as is. The triple sets of quotation marks, (""") mean that you place a quotation mark in the translation.

The *params* are a list of parameters that will be passed to the given action procedure. If you want to embed a quotation mark (") in a quoted string, use C's escape character: \".

Documenting Actions and Translations

Your Motif applications should document the list of default actions, which shows what actions will be accepted by a given application. Only power users will ever care to tackle translations, but since Xt and Motif already support translations, you can provide this powerful feature to your users for only a limited amount of effort.

After you set up translations, the next step is to set up actions.

ACTIONS SPEAK LOUDER THAN WORDS

As we stated in Chapter 21, an action is a means to connect a text string that names a function to actually execute that C function. Actions are referenced in translation tables, as the translation table just ties a key combination with an action.

To recap Chapter 21, in your code, you combine a text name, such as "MyAction", with a function pointer, MyAction. The idea is that when the translation table determines that the widget should call the "MyAction" action, the actual function MyAction gets called. To set up this connection between text strings and function pointers, you need to fill in an array of XtActionsRec structures and then pass this array to XtAppAddActions:

```
/* Global action entry. */
static XtActionsRec my_actions[] = {
 { "MyAction", (XtActionProc) MyAction}
};

/* ... */

int main(int argc, char** argv)

{    /* main */
XtAppContext     app_context;
Widget           parent;

/* ... */

    parent = XtVaAppInitialize(&app_context,
            "Ppm",
            (XrmOptionDescList) NULL,
            0,
            &argc, argv,
            (String*) NULL,
            XmNallowResize, True,
            XmNtitle, "Translation Test",
            NULL);

    /* Add in custom action. */
    XtAppAddActions(app_context,
        my_actions,
        XtNumber(my_actions) );

/* ... */

}     /* main */
```

The XtActionsRec structure looks like:

```
typedef struct _XtActionsRec{
    String        string;
    XtActionProc proc;
} XtActionsRec;
```

Once you set up an array of XtActionsRec structures, you can pass this array to XtAppAddActions, which takes the following parameters:

```
void XtAppAddActions(XtAppContext app_context,
    XtActionList actions,
    Cardinal number_actions)
```

Passing Parameters to Action Routines

You can pass parameters to an action by filling in data between the open and close parenthesis in the translation table. In the following translation table, the MyAction action will get parameters passed to it:

```
/* Global Translation table entry. */
static char text_translations[] =
  "#override \
      Shift<Key>F2: MyAction(p1,p2,p3,p4) \n\
      <Key>F2: beep() \n\
      <Key>F3: beginning-of-file() \n";
```

Each of the parameters, separated by commas, will be passed to your action routine. Unfortunately, each parameter is passed as a string, so you're responsible for converting the data to the proper types. In the translation table above, the MyAction action will get the following parameters:

```
"p1", "p2", "p3", "p4"
```

You can then code the action routine like the following, which prints out each of the parameters passed to it:

```
        /* Called by action routine in translation table. */
void MyAction(Widget widget,
    XEvent* event,
    String* params,
    Cardinal* number_params)

{   /* MyAction */
    int i;

    printf("MyAction\n");

    if (params == (String*) NULL) {
       return;
    }

    if (*number_params > 0) {
        printf("\t parameters: ");
    }

    /* This action just prints parameters. */
```

```
for (i = 0; i < *number_params; i++) {
    printf("%s ", params[i] );
}

printf("\n");

}    /* MyAction */
```

NOTE

The `Cardinal` value *number_params* is passed as a pointer, so be sure to treat the data type properly, as we do in the above code. Failure to do so will probably result in a core dump with your program crashing.

If you use the translation table from above, then the `MyAction` function should print out the following data:

```
MyAction
          parameters: p1 p2 p3 p4
```

Calling Actions Directly

In your code, you don't have to wait for the user to invoke a translation by pressing the correct key combination. If you want, you can call actions directly from your code. To do so, call `XtCallActionProc`:

```
void XtCallActionProc(Widget widget,
    String action,
    XEvent* event,
    String* params,
    Cardinal* number_params)
```

`XtCallActionProc` looks up the given *action* and then, if found, calls the action's function with the given parameters. If the *action* isn't found, Xt prints out a warning message. Remember that action names are indeed case-sensitive.

As is usual with the X Window System and Motif, it's up to you to set up all the parameters correctly. Thus, you'll need to fill in the proper *event* and parameters (*params*) to pass to the action.

Looking Up Actions

The *OSF/Motif Programmer's Reference* lists all the actions with each widget's entry, along with the translations that tie the actions to key combinations. There are many built-in actions that you may be able to take advantage of and save yourself a lot of time writing code.

ADVANCED RESOURCES

We end this chapter with a miscellaneous set of useful techniques for more advanced resource handling. These include floating-point resource values, more on resource converters, and application-created resources.

Floating-Point Resource Values

If you try to mix floating-point values and X resources or *client_data* callback parameters, you're asking for trouble. For one thing, the size of a float value is not always the same size as an XtPointer. Even if the two sizes are the same, you'll generally have problems. What can you do?

The simplest solution is to use a pointer to a float value and pass that pointer as the *client_data*. This ensures that Xt and Motif will pass the proper value to your callback. The drawback is that this pointer has to point somewhere, and you're responsible for maintaining that memory.

Cheating With Resource Converters

In Chapter 15, we discussed how to use resource converters in your code with XtConvertAndStore to convert a color name to a valid pixel value. In this chapter, we introduce another technique to take advantage of Xt's resource converter in calls to XtVaSetValues.

You can ask Xt to convert a resource value inside a call to XtVaSetValues, as shown in the code below:

```
XtVaSetValues(widget,
    XtVaTypedArg,
        XmNbackground, XmRString,
            "bisque", (strlen("bisque") + 1),
    NULL);
```

The code above asks Xt to convert a color name, "bisque", to a pixel data type for use as a background color resource value.

Normally, each pair of arguments you pass to XtVaSetValues has a resource name and a value. The code above extends this idea by making the two values stretch out to five.

XtVaTypedArg is a special value that tells Xt that the next four arguments consist of a resource that must be converted. These four arguments combined then become the resource value (once converted).

The first argument determines the target resource, in this case XmNbackground. The second determines the source data type. In virtually all cases, this will be XmRString, because we're taking advantage of Xt's ability to convert a text string into a value of the proper type. The third argument points at the data, usually in string format. The fourth argument tells Xt how many bytes are in the data. With string data, we can simply use the C function strlen to get this value.

We've had good luck converting color names this way, but not font names—at least with X11 Release 4 and Motif 1.1.

N O T E

Application-Created Resources

Application-created or application-specific resources are essentially variables in your program that the user can set externally from X resource files. These variables don't need to have anything to do with Motif. Even so, the user can set values to these variables from resource files, which you're already likely to be using for user customization anyway. Thus you can extend resource files to allow the user to customize the part of your application that has nothing to do with X or Motif—most likely the majority of your application.

For example, if you're writing an electronic-mail application, you may want to allow the user to configure the location of the mail spool file, the file to look for new mail messages. Why do you need to do this? Because many versions of UNIX place these messages in different locations. You need some way for the user or system administrator to tell your program this location.

We're *not* recommending that you make your users edit resource files. We feel strongly that your application should have a graphical means to configure it. However, you may want to store this configuration on disk as an X resource file, since this format is so convenient because of all the built-in support for X resources.

N O T E

To set up these application-specific resources, you need to perform four steps:

1. Determine the name, purpose, data type, and default value for each resource.

2. Create a structure to hold your data for these resources.

3. Set up an `XtResource` array that describes your resources in a format that the Xt resource manager will understand.

4. Call `XtVaGetApplicationResources`, which will acquire the resource values or place in the default values you specified.

In the next few sections, we'll go through the four steps outlined above, using an example program that acts as a front end to UNIX electronic mail.

In our mail program, we'll need to figure out the default location for the user's mail file. This mail file holds incoming messages. In many versions of UNIX, this location is **/usr/spool/mqueue/user-name**, where **user-name** is the name of the user. For example, with user *erc*, the default mail file will be **/usr/spool/mqueue/erc**.

We can query the user name from within a C program, although we're not sure exactly where the operating system places the mail file. Usually, though, the mail file directory will remain constant for the whole system. Therefore, we can ask the system administrator to specify the mail directory, as the system administrator should know it. We want to avoid asking the user questions, because users often don't know the answer to esoteric system configuration questions.

For starters, we'll set up a resource in which the administrator can set up the mail file. We'll call this resource `mailSpoolFile` and require that it be of type `String`. (This data type is obvious for the name of a file, but other resources may be harder to type.) The default value will be `"/usr/spool/mqueue/"`.

The next resource we'll need for our hypothetical mail program is a command to invoke the printer. This is another area where many systems diverge. We again pick a `String` resource type and name this one `printerCommand`. The default value will be `"lp -c"`, for the System V UNIX `lp` command. (Real workstations use `lpr`, of course.)

Finally, for our simple example, we want a non-`String` resource. So we'll add a `Boolean` resource to determine whether our mail program should use the default mail-transport agent or not. We'll name this resource useMailAgent and give a default value of False. (If you don't know about mail-transport agents, don't worry, as we're just using this for a non-String resource.)

Creating a Structure To Hold the Values

After we determine the data types, names, and default values, we need to define a C structure to hold *all* our custom resources. For our example, we can use a structure as follows:

```
typedef struct {
    String  mail_spool_file;
    String  printer_command;
    Boolean use_mail_agent;
} MailResources;
```

Note that all resource values are contiguous in the structure. (The Xt macro XtOffsetOf, which we cover below, handles the magic necessary to deal with structure-padding issues.)

We then need to declare a structure of this new type, so we can actually store our values:

```
MailResources MyMailResources;
```

Setting Up the XtResource Array

The next step involves a lot of code but is really simple after you notice the symmetry. We'll provide a little background and then show the code, which is simpler to follow than the background. Don't worry if you get confused.

We must describe each of our new resources to the Xt resource manager in a way that Xt can understand. Xt requires us to fill in an XtResource structure for each of our custom resources. This structure looks like:

```
typedef struct _XtResource {
  String     resource_name;
  String     resource_class;
  String     resource_type;
  Cardinal   resource_size;
  Cardinal   resource_offset;
  String     default_type;
  XtPointer  default_addr;
} XtResource, *XtResourceList;
```

The *resource_name* field contains the name of the resource, such as `mailSpoolFile`. The *resource_class* is the class name for the resource. By convention, this is the resource name with the first letter capitalized, e.g., `MailSpoolFile`. The *resource_type* should be a built-in type that Xt understands. We'll use `XmRString` and `XmRBoolean` for our resources.

You can fill in the *resource_size* field by using the `sizeof` operator. For example, to get the size of the `String` data type, use `sizeof(String)`.

The *resource_offset* field is tricky. This is the offset in our `MailResources` structure where the data should be placed. To get the *resource_offset* field, *always* call the `XtOffsetOf` macro:

```
Cardinal XtOffsetOf(structure-type, field-name)
```

In your code, you'll call `XtOffsetOf` as follows:

```
XtOffsetOf(MailResources, mail_spool_file)
```

where `MailResources` is the structure type and *mail_spool_file* is the field.

The above code gets the proper value for the *resource_offset* field for the first of our custom resources.

The *default_type* field holds a value that tells Xt where the default value comes from. In all our code, we'll present the default value directly in the *default_addr* field, so we fill in the *default_type* field with `XmRImmediate`. We strongly advise you to follow this route.

This is all very confusing The following code should make all this much clearer:

```
/* Custom resource definitions.
 * Note how each second entry
 * starts with an uppercase letter.
 */
#define XmNmailSpoolFile      "mailSpoolFile"
#define XmCMailSpoolFile      "MailSpoolFile"
#define XmNprinterCommand     "printerCommand"
#define XmCPrinterCommand     "PrinterCommand"
#define XmNuseMailAgent       "useMailAgent"
#define XmCUseMailAgent       "UseMailAgent"

static XtResource my_resources[] = {
    {
        XmNmailSpoolFile,
        XmCMailSpoolFile,
        XmRString,
```

```
               sizeof(String),
               XtOffsetOf(MailResources, mail_spool_file),
               XmRImmediate,
               (XtPointer) "/usr/spool/mqueue/"
          },
          {
               XmNprinterCommand,
               XmCPrinterCommand,
               XmRString,
               sizeof(String),
               XtOffsetOf(MailResources, printer_command),
               XmRImmediate,
               (XtPointer) "lp -c"
          },
          {
               XmNuseMailAgent,
               XmCUseMailAgent,
               XmRBoolean,
               sizeof(Boolean),
               XtOffsetOf(MailResources, use_mail_agent),
               XmRImmediate,
               (XtPointer) False
          },
     };
```

The code above follows the convention of defining symbols for the resource names, such as `XmNmailSpoolFile` for the resource name and `XmCMailSpoolFile` for the resource class name.

Acquiring the Custom Resource Values

The final step in all this is to call `XtVaGetApplicationResources`:

```
void XtVaGetApplicationResources(Widget widget,
     XtPointer  user_data_structure,  /* in/out */
     XtResourceList resources,
     Cardinal number_resources,
     ...)
```

`XtVaGetApplicationResources` looks in all the configured locations for resources for the resources described in the *resources* parameter. The *widget* supplies the top-level base from which to acquire the resources. In virtually all cases, we'll pass the top-level widget returned by `XtAppInitialize` or `XtVaAppInitialize`.

`XtVaGetApplicationResources` uses the special magic in `XtOffsetOf` to place the resource values into your structure.

Usually you don't pass any extra parameters, so you can call `XtVaGetApplicationResources` in your code as we show below:

```
XtVaGetApplicationResources(parent,
    &MyMailResources,
    my_resources,
    XtNumber(my_resources),
    NULL);
```

After you're done calling `XtVaGetApplicationResources`, your `MyMailResources` structure will hold either the user-given resource values or the default values we set up for the resources. Thus you can access fields of this structure to get at the values. For example, `MyMailResources.mail_spool_file` will hold the `mailSpoolFile` resource value.

A PROGRAM TO TEST RESOURCES, TRANSLATIONS, AND ACTIONS

We've put together a very short program to provide examples of a number of the techniques introduced in this chapter. Try running this program and testing out the translations for the **F2**, **Shift-F2**, and **F3** keys.

The code follows:

```
/* translat.c */
#include   <Xm/Xm.h>
#include   <Xm/Text.h>
#include   <stdio.h>

/* Global resource data for custom resources. */
typedef struct {
    String  mail_spool_file;
    String  printer_command;
    Boolean use_mail_agent;
} MailResources;

MailResources MyMailResources;

/* Custom resource definitions.
 * Note how each second entry
 * starts with an uppercase letter.
 */
#define XmNmailSpoolFile    "mailSpoolFile"
#define XmCMailSpoolFile    "MailSpoolFile"
#define XmNprinterCommand   "printerCommand"
#define XmCPrinterCommand   "PrinterCommand"
#define XmNuseMailAgent     "useMailAgent"
#define XmCUseMailAgent     "UseMailAgent"

/* Tell Xt about our resources.
```

```
 * Note the symmetry.
 */
static XtResource my_resources[] = {
    {
        XmNmailSpoolFile,
        XmCMailSpoolFile,
        XmRString,
        sizeof(String),
        XtOffsetOf(MailResources, mail_spool_file),
        XmRImmediate,
        (XtPointer) "/usr/spool/mqueue/"
    },
    {
        XmNprinterCommand,
        XmCPrinterCommand,
        XmRString,
        sizeof(String),
        XtOffsetOf(MailResources, printer_command),
        XmRImmediate,
        (XtPointer) "lp -c"
    },
    {
        XmNuseMailAgent,
        XmCUseMailAgent,
        XmRBoolean,
        sizeof(Boolean),
        XtOffsetOf(MailResources, use_mail_agent),
        XmRImmediate,
        (XtPointer) False
    },
};

/* Global Translation table entry. */
static char text_translations[] =
  "#override \
        Shift<Key>F2: MyAction(p1,p2,p3,p4) \n\
        <Key>F2: beep() \n\
        <Key>F3: beginning-of-file() \n";

    /* Called by action routine in translation table. */
void MyAction(Widget widget,
    XEvent* event,
    String* params,
    Cardinal* number_params)

{   /* MyAction */
    int i;

    printf("MyAction\n");

    if (params == (String*) NULL) {
        return;
    }

    if (*number_params > 0) {
```

```
        printf("\t parameters: ");
    }

    /* This action just prints parameters. */
    for (i = 0; i < *number_params; i++) {
        printf("%s ", params[i] );
    }

    printf("\n");

}   /* MyAction */

/* Global action entry. */
static XtActionsRec my_actions[] = {
 { "MyAction", (XtActionProc) MyAction}
};

int main(int argc, char** argv)

{   /* main */
    XtAppContext    app_context;
    Widget          text;
    Widget          parent;
    Arg             args[20];
    Cardinal        n;
    XtTranslations  translations;

    parent = XtVaAppInitialize(&app_context,
                "Ppm",
                (XrmOptionDescList) NULL,
                0,
                &argc, argv,
                (String*) NULL,
                XmNallowResize, True,
                XmNtitle, "Translation Test",
                NULL);

    /* Set up our custom resources. */
    XtVaGetApplicationResources(parent,
        &MyMailResources,
        my_resources,
        XtNumber(my_resources),
        NULL);

    /* Print out our custom resources. */
    printf("My custom mail resources include:\n");
    printf("\t Mail spool file: [%s]\n",
        MyMailResources.mail_spool_file);
    printf("\t Printer command: [%s]\n",
        MyMailResources.printer_command);

    if (MyMailResources.use_mail_agent == True) {
        printf("\t Use mail agent.\n");
    } else {
        printf("\t Don't use mail agent.\n");
```

```
        }

        /* Add in custom action. */
        XtAppAddActions(app_context,
            my_actions,
            XtNumber(my_actions) );

        /* Create scrolled text for work area. */
        n = 0;
        XtSetArg(args[n], XmNeditMode,
            XmMULTI_LINE_EDIT); n++;
        XtSetArg(args[n], XmNrows, 10); n++;
        XtSetArg(args[n], XmNcolumns, 30); n++;

        text = XmCreateScrolledText(parent, "text", args, n);

        /* Parse translations. */
        translations =
            XtParseTranslationTable(text_translations);

        /* Modify translations. */
        XtOverrideTranslations(text, translations);

        /* Use XtVaTypedArg type converter. */
        XtVaSetValues(text,
            XtVaTypedArg, XmNbackground, XmRString,
                "bisque", (strlen("bisque")+1),
            NULL);

        XtManageChild(text);

        XtRealizeWidget(parent);
        XtAppMainLoop(app_context);
        return 0;

    }   /* main */

    /* end of file translat.c */
```

This program also uses the following resource file with custom application-specific resources:

```
! Resource file for Chapter 23
! of Power Programming Motif.
!
! Motif resources.

*background:     grey92

! Application-created resources.

*mailSpoolFile: /usr/spool/mqueue/
*printerCommand: lp -c -d myprinter
*useMailAgent:   True
```

```
! end of resource file
```

Name this file **Ppm** and store it in your home directory. You may want to change some of the values above to see how the program can detect the values.

When you run this program, it will print out the values acquired from the application-specific resources.

SUMMARY

In this chapter we fleshed out our discussion of X resources and covered a number of advanced topics, including translation tables, actions, floating-point resources, and resource converters.

Translations in X are a means to customize the way keystrokes and mouse actions interact with your Motif programs, using resource-setting commands. Each widget, such as a scroll bar or pushbutton, has an internal translation table that defines how that widget handles input events like keystrokes and mouse clicks. The translation table maps input events to internal functions, called actions. All Motif widgets have a set of built-in supported actions. You can also add your own, since the translation table makes no distinction between your actions and the built-in ones. All translations for a given widget are grouped together in a table, and this table is set with one X resource command.

You can set up translations to work only when certain modifier keys are held down, such as the **Shift** key, **Control** key (often abbreviated **Ctrl**), or *Meta* key (often labeled **Alt** on your keyboard).

Your Motif applications should document the list of default actions, which shows what actions will be accepted by a given application. Only power users will ever care to tackle translations, but since Xt and Motif already support translations, you can provide this powerful feature to your users for only a limited amount of effort.

An action is a means to connect a text string that names a function so that it actuallys execute that C function. Actions are referenced in translation tables, as the translation table just ties a key combination with an action. However, you don't have to wait for the user to invoke a translation by pressing the correct key combination. If you want, you can call actions directly from your code.

The chapter ended with a discussion of floating-point resource values, resource converters, and application-created resources, as well as a program that illustrates the features discussed in the chapter.

X Toolkit Intrinsics Functions and Macros Introduced in This Chapter

```
XtAugmentTranslations
XtCallActionProc
XtOffsetOf
XtOverrideTranslations
XtUninstallTranslations
XtVaGetApplicationResources
```

CHAPTER 24

Handling Errors

This chapter covers:

- Displaying Xt errors and warning messages
- The four kinds of Motif errors
- Looking up error messages
- Low-level error routines
- Overriding the default Xt error and warning functions
- Fatal error messages
- Handling Xlib errors
- Trapping Xlib errors
- X error events
- Fatal I/O errors

HANDLING ERRORS IN MOTIF PROGRAMS

To develop robust applications, you need to intercept and handle most errors. The standard answer of just printing a message and terminating the application is simply not acceptable to most users. Surprisingly enough, this is the default behavior for all programs based on the Xt Intrinsics—a terrible method of error handling. Therefore, your applications must do *something* to deal with errors.

The best approach toward errors, of course, is to stop them from ever happening. Because of this, you should always check the return value from all Motif, Xt, and Xlib function calls. You should also attempt to verify all parameters. For example, the scale widget, XmScale, requires that the minimum resource hold a value less than or equal to the maximum resource. Before setting the minimum, your application should check the new value against the maximum.

Unfortunately, you cannot prevent all errors in this way. Motif programs tend to allocate large amounts of RAM using dynamic memory-allocation functions like malloc (technically, it's XtMalloc, but generally this calls malloc under the hood). On any dynamic system, you may indeed run out of memory at any time, so you cannot prevent this type of error from occurring. Instead, you must deal with the error somehow, although memory-allocation errors tend to be tough to handle.

In addition, you may detect errors in your code and want to display the error in the same manner as Xt errors. Xt provides plenty of functions to do this.

A Motif Spin on Errors

Motif presents four views of errors:

- Xt fatal error, such as a memory-allocation error
- Xt nonfatal warning, such as a bad resource value
- Xlib fatal error, such as loss of connection to X server
- Xlib nonfatal error, such as bad window ID

Your code must deal with all four types.

This chapter covers Xt and Xlib methods for presenting and dealing with errors.

A QUICK ERROR PRIMER

SHORTCUT To display a fatal Xt error message and exit, call `XtAppError`:

```
void XtAppError(XtAppContext app_context,
   String message)
```

To display a nonfatal Xt warning message, call `XtAppWarning`:

```
void XtAppWarning(XtAppContext app_context,
   String message)
```

To trap low-level nonfatal Xlib errors, set up an error-handling function with `XSetErrorHandler`:

```
XErrorHandler XSetErrorHandler(
   XErrorHandler handler)
```

To trap fatal Xlib I/O errors, set up the fatal error-handling function with `XSetIOErrorHandler`:

```
XIOErrorHandler XSetIOErrorHandler(
   XIOErrorHandler handler)
```

XT ERROR HANDLING

The Xt Intrinsics provides two views of the error-handling system: a high-level view that will build up messages for you, and a low-level view that actually displays the messages.

Your applications can call either level to report errors. You can also override both sets of error-handling functions should you desire some custom processing. We find the low-level routines much easier to use than the high-level functions, if only because of the number of parameters and all the formatting issues.

We'll start with the high-level routines, though, and then delve down into the low-level routines.

High-Level Xt Routines

To display a fatal error with the high-level routines, use `XtAppErrorMsg`:

```
void XtAppErrorMsg(XtAppContext app_context,
    String name,
    String type,
    String class,
    String default,
    String* params,
    Cardinal* number_params)
```

The *name* holds the name of the error, such as `"allocError"`, the *type* something like `"malloc"`. For Xt, the class is `"XtToolkitError"`.

If no message can be found in the error database, the *default* message is used instead.

The *params* are a set of strings that should be inserted into the message to be displayed. There's no standard means for setting up the *params*. The *number_params* points at the number of parameters. Note that *number_params* is a pointer.

`XtAppErrorMsg` calls the current high-level fatal error-handling function, passing along all the parameters. This function should call `XtAppGetErrorDatabaseText` to get the text message associated with the error.

To display a nonfatal warning message, call `XtAppWarningMsg`:

```
void XtAppWarningMsg(XtAppContext app_context,
    String name,
    String type,
    String class,
    String default,
    String* params,
    Cardinal* number_params)
```

`XtAppWarningMsg` takes the same parameters as `XtAppErrorMsg`.

Formatting the Xt Error Messages

To look up an Xt error or warning message, call `XtAppGetErrorDatabaseText`:

```
void XtAppGetErrorDatabaseText(XtAppContext app_context,
    String name,
    String type,
    String class,
```

```
String default,
String buffer, /* RETURN */
int number_bytes,
XrmDatabase database)
```

XtAppGetErrorDatabaseText looks up the given error in the error *database* and fills that error *message* into the *buffer*. If XtAppGetErrorDatabaseText can find no message, it copies the *default* message into the *buffer*.

With many errors, the returned buffer will have C-style sprintf formatting commands, so the error or warning message function can use sprintf to fill in the parameters. For example, the *Cannot allocate colormap entry for "%s"* message (see the list of error messages below) has a %s so that the erroneous value can be inserted into the string. The erroneous value would then be one of the *params* passed to XtAppWarningMsg.

In the default case, both XtAppErrorMsg and XtAppWarningMsg call XtAppGetErrorDatabaseText to look up the error message.

To get the error database to pass to XtAppGetErrorDatabaseText, call XtAppGetErrorDatabase:

```
XrmDatabase* XtAppGetErrorDatabase(
    XtAppContext app_context)
```

Overriding the High-Level Xt Error Handlers

You can override the default fatal-error message handler by installing your own with XtAppSetErrorMsgHandler:

```
XtErrorMsgHandler XtAppSetErrorMsgHandler(
    XtAppContext app_context,
    XtErrorMsgHandler handler)
```

XtAppSetErrorMsgHandler returns the old error-message handler.

Your error-message function must take the following parameters:

```
typedef void (*XtErrorMsgHandler)(
    String name,
    String type,
    String class,
    String default,
    String* params,
    Cardinal* number_params);
```

These are the same parameters passed to XtAppErrorMsg and XtAppWarningMsg, above.

The fatal error handler is called, obviously enough, only when a fatal error occurs. In your error-handling functions you must be very careful about calling any Motif or Xt functions. A fatal error already occurred, so you're not likely to have full access to creating dialog boxes and widgets, especially if the fatal error involved lack of memory.

You can set the nonfatal message handler, called the *warning message handler*, with `XtAppSetWarningMsgHandler`:

```
XtErrorMsgHandler XtAppSetWarningMsgHandler(
   XtAppContext app_context,
   XtErrorMsgHandler handler)
```

`XtAppSetWarningMsgHandler` returns the old warning message handler.

Your warning-handling function takes the same parameters as the fatal error-handling function above.

The high-level error and warning message handlers are responsible for formatting a message and then pass that message on to `XtAppError` and `XtAppWarning`, the low-level routines. You'll find that these low-level routines are easier to code for than the high-level routines. Furthermore, you're more likely to override the low-level routines than the high-level ones.

Low-Level Xt Error Routines

Even though the low-level routines are more convenient, they're considered holdovers from previous versions and so may be obsoleted one day. Consider yourself warned.

The high-level Xt error routines call two low-level functions to actually display the messages the high-level routines build up. To display a fatal error message, call `XtAppError`:

```
void XtAppError(XtAppContext app_context,
   String message)
```

`XtAppError` calls the current low-level error-handling function to display the message. The default error-handling function prints out the message to `stderr` (for UNIX systems, at least) and then exits. That's right. A fatal error is considered *fatal*. If you override this, you may want to save your files and perform any needed emergency rescue operations on your data before exiting.

To display a warning message, call `XtAppWarning`:

```
void XtAppWarning(XtAppContext app_context,
  String message)
```

`XtAppWarning` calls the current low-level warning message handler function. The default function just prints the message to `stderr`. The default routine does not exit your program.

Overriding the Low-Level Xt Error-Handling Functions

Like with the high-level routines, you can also override the low-level error-handling functions. `XtAppSetErrorHandler` overrides the current low-level fatal error-handling function:

```
XtErrorHandler XtAppSetErrorHandler(
    XtAppContext app_context,
    XtErrorHandler handler)
```

`XtAppSetErrorHandler` returns the previous error-handling function.

`XtAppSetWarningHandler` sets the low-level warning message handling function:

```
XtErrorHandler XtAppSetWarningHandler(
    XtAppContext app_context,
    XtErrorHandler handler)
```

`XtAppSetWarningHandler` returns the current low-level warning function.

Both low-level error-handling routines then take the following `message` parameter:

```
typedef void (*XtErrorHandler)(String message);
```

Xt Error and Warning Messages

The Xt Intrinsics provide a set of error messages that you may experience. We present them here to help you debug your Motif applications. For each error and warning message, we present the message, its name, and its type. The type is useful to track the error message back to a function. A type of *xtUnmanageChildren* points you to the function `XtUnmanageChildren`. In a number of cases, more than one function can generate the same error.

Xt Fatal-Error Messages

For each entry, the default error message is listed first. This is what the X toolkit will print out on an error. The type of error is listed following the error message. Our favorite name is *ambiguousParent*.

Application shell is not a windowed widget?
```
        invalidParent          realize
```

Argument count > 0 on NULL argument list in XtGetValues
```
        invalidArgCount        xtGetValues
```

Argument count > 0 on NULL argument list in XtSetValues
```
        invalidArgCount        xtSetValues
```

Attempt to manage a child when parent is not Composite
```
        invalidParent          xtManageChildren
```

Attempt to unmanage a child when parent is not Composite
```
        invalidParent          xtUnmanageChildren
```

Cannot perform calloc
```
        allocError             calloc
```

Cannot perform malloc
```
        allocError             malloc
```

Cannot perform realloc
```
        allocError             realloc
```

Can't Open Display
```
        invalidDisplay         xtInitialize
```

Can't find popup in _XtMenuPopup
```
        invalidPopup           xtMenuPopup
```

Couldn't find ancestor with display information
```
        noAppContext           widgetToApplicationContext
```

Couldn't find per display information
```
        noPerDisplay           closeDisplay
        noPerDisplay           getPerDisplay
```

Events are disappearing from under Shell
```
        missingEvent           shell
```

Event with wrong window
```
        invalidWindow          eventHandler
```

internal error: no selection property context for display
```
        noSelectionProperties  freeSelectionProperty
```

invalid condition passed to XtAddInput
```
        invalidParameter       xtAddInput
```

MenuPopup wants exactly one argument
```
        invalidParameters      xtMenuPopupAction
```

No realize class procedure defined
        invalidProcedure   realizeProc

NULL insert_child procedure
        nullProc   insertChild

Pixel to color conversion needs screen and colormap arguments
        wrongParameters   cvtIntOrPixelToXColor

RemovePopupFromParent requires non-NULL popuplist
        invalidParameter   removePopupFromParent

Select failed
        communicationError   select

Shell widget *widget name* has zero width and/or height
        invalidDimension   shellRealize

Shell's window manager interaction is broken
        internalError   shell

String to cursor conversion needs screen argument
        wrongParameters   cvtStringToCursor

String to font conversion needs screen argument
        wrongParameters   cvtStringToFont
        wrongParameters   cvtStringToFontStruct

String to pixel conversion needs screen and colormap arguments
        wrongParameters   cvtStringToPixel

Subclass of Constraint CallConstraintSetValues
        invalidClass   constraintSetValue

Trying to merge translation tables with cycles, and can't resolve this cycle.
        translationError   mergingTablesWithCycles

Unresolved inheritance operation
        invalidProcedure   inheritanceProc

Widget class *class name* found when subclass of *class name* expected: %s
        subclassMismatch   xtCheckSubclass

Widget *widget name* has zero width and/or height
        invalidDimension   xtCreateWindow

XtAppCreateShell requires non-NULL widget class
        invalidClass   xtAppCreateShell

XtCreatePopupShell requires non-NULL parent
        invalidParent   xtCreatePopupShell

XtCreatePopupShell requires non-NULL widget class
        invalidClass   xtCreatePopupShell

XtCreateWidget requires non-NULL parent
        invalidParent   xtCreateWidget

XtCreateWidget requires non-NULL widget class

```
invalidClass            xtCreateWidget
```

XtMakeGeometryRequest - NULL parent. Use SetValues instead
```
invalidParent           xtMakeGeometryRequest
```

XtMakeGeometryRequest - parent has no geometry manager
```
invalidGeometryManager xtMakeGeometryRequest
```

XtMakeGeometryRequest - parent not composite
```
invalidParent           xtMakeGeometryRequest
```

XtMenuPopdown called with num_params != 0 or 1
```
invalidParameters       xtmenuPopdown
```

XtPopdown requires a subclass of shellWidgetClass
```
invalidClass            xtPopdown
```

XtPopup requires a subclass of shellWidgetClass
```
invalidClass            xtPopup
```

Xt Nonfatal-Warning Messages

Warnings are less serious than errors. These messages typically don't cause your program to exit.

... found while parsing '%s'
```
translationParseError        showLine
```

Actions not found: %s
```
translationError             unboundActions
```

argument count > 0 on NULL argument list
```
invalidArgCount              getResources
```

Attempt to change already registered window.
```
registerWindowError          xtRegisterWindow
```

Attempt to unregister invalid window.
```
registerWindowError          xtUnregisterWindow
```

Cannot allocate colormap entry for "%s"
```
noColormap                   cvtStringToPixel
```

Cannot convert string "%s" to type "%s"
```
conversionError              string
```

Cannot find callback list in XtAddCallbacks
```
invalidCallbackList          xtAddCallbacks
```

Cannot find callback list in XtCallCallback
```
invalidCallbackList          xtCallCallback
```

Cannot find callback list in XtOverrideCallbacks
```
invalidCallbackList          xtOverrideCallback
```

Cannot find callback list in XtRemoveAllCallbacks
```
invalidCallbackList          xtRemoveAllCallbacks
```

Cannot find callback list in XtRemoveCallbacks
`invalidCallbackList`   `xtRemoveCallbacks`

Cannot find resource name *resource name* **as argument to conversion**
`invalidResourceName`   `computeArgs`

Can't change widget depth
`invalidDepth`   `setValues`

Can't find display structure
`displayError`   `invalidDisplay`

Can't remove accelerators from NULL table
`translationerror`   `nullTable`

Can't translate event through NULL table
`translationError`   `nullTable`

Color to Pixel conversion needs no extra arguments
`wrongParameters`   `cvtXColorToPixel`

CopyFromParent must have non-NULL parent
`invalidParent`   `xtCopyFromParent`

Initializing Resource Lists twice
`initializationError`   `xtInitialize`

Intializing Translation manager twice
`translationError`   `xtTranslateInitialize`

Integer to Bool conversion needs no extra arguments
`wrongParameters`   `cvtIntToBool`

Integer to Boolean conversion needs no extra arguments
`wrongParameters`   `cvtIntToBoolean`

Integer to Font conversion needs no extra arguments
`wrongParameters`   `cvtIntToFont`

Integer to Pixel conversion needs no extra arguments
`wrongParameters`   `cvtIntToPixel`

Integer to Pixmap conversion needs no extra arguments
`wrongParameters`   `cvtIntToPixmap`

Integer to Short conversion needs no extra arguments
`wrongParameters`   `cvtIntToShort`

MergeTM to TranslationTable needs no extra arguments
`invalidParameters`   `mergeTranslations`

Missing ".
`translationParseError` `parseString`

No type converter registered for '%s' to '%s' conversion.
`typeConversionError`   `noConverter`

Not all children have same parent in XtManageChildren
`ambigiousParent`   `xtManageChildren`

Not all children have same parent in XtUnmanageChildren
ambigiousParent   xtUnmanageChildren

Null child passed to XtManageChildren
invalidChild   xtManageChildren

Null child passed to XtUnmanageChildren
invalidChild   xtUnmanageChildren

null delete_child procedure in XtDestroy
invalidProcedure   deleteChild

Old translation table was null, cannot modify.
translationError   mergingNullTable

Overriding earlier translation manager actions.
translationError   ambiguousActions

Pop-up menu creation is only supported on ButtonPress or EnterNotify events.
invalidPopup   unsupportedOperation

RemovePopupFromParent, widget not on parent list
invalidWidget   removePopupFromParent

Representation size %d must match superclass's to over ride %s
invalidSizeOverride   xtDependencies

Representation type %s must match superclass's to over ride %s
invalidTypeOverride   xtDependencies

resource count > 0 on NULL resource list
invalidResourceCount   getResources

set_values_almost procedure shouldn't be NULL
invalidProcedure   set_values_almost

Shell subclass did not take care of geometry in XtSetValues
invalidGeometry   xtMakeGeometryRequest

String to AcceleratorTable needs no extra arguments
invalidParameters   compileAccelerators

String to Bool conversion needs no extra arguments
wrongParameters   cvtStringToBool

String to Boolean conversion needs no extra arguments
wrongParameters   cvtStringToBoolean

String to Display conversion needs no extra arguments
wrongParameters   cvtStringToDisplay

String to File conversion needs no extra arguments
wrongParameters   cvtStringToFile

String to Integer conversion needs no extra arguments
wrongParameters   cvtStringToInt
wrongParameters   cvtStringToShort
wrongParameters   cvtStringToUnsignedChar

String to TranslationTable needs no extra arguments
        invalidParameters   compileTranslations

translation table syntax error: %s
        translationParseError   parseError

Tried to remove non-existant accelerators
        translation error   nullTable

Widget class %s version mismatch: widget %d vs. intrinsics %d.
        versionMismatch   widget

Widget has no shell ancestor
        invalidShell   xtTranslateCoords

Window Manager is confused
        communicationError   windowManager

XtAddGrab requires exclusive grab if spring_loaded is TRUE
        grabError   grabDestroyCallback

XtRemoveInput: Input handler not found
        invalidProcedure   inputHandler

XtRemoveGrab asked to remove a widget not on the grab list
        grabError   xtRemoveGrab

XLIB ERRORS

Surprisingly enough, these Xt functions just handle Xt errors. Xt ignores errors in the low-level X library. Since the default Xlib error-handling functions terminate your application, you probably want to override these functions as well to build a robust Motif application. You'll know you've hit an Xlib error when you see a message like the one below:

```
X Error of failed request: BadDrawable (invalid Pixmap or Window
parameter)
 Major opcode of failed request: 76 (X_ImageText8)
 Minor opcode of failed request: 0
 Resource id in failed request: 0x1
 Serial number of failed request: 12
 Current serial number in output stream: 13
```

The BadDrawable error tells us that the error involved a bad drawable ID: a bad window or pixmap. In addition, we can guess from the opcode of 76 (X_ImageText8) that the error had to do with a call to XDrawImageString or some similar function that outputs text. Finally, the resource ID of the failed request is 0x1, which is normally a bad value. Later, when drawing to this nonexistent, bad window (or pixmap), the application faulted. The serial numbers and minor opcodes don't do you a lot of good.

Common errors include:

- ▤ `BadFont`, an invalid font
- ▤ `BadName`, when the application attempts to load a nonexistent font
- ▤ `BadMatch`, usually involving attempts to copy data between drawables with different depths
- ▤ `BadAlloc`, the dreaded out-of-memory error

Trapping Xlib Errors in Your Code

Like the Xt Intrinsics, which separates problems into fatal errors and nonfatal warnings, the X library provides two error-trapping functions, `XSetErrorHandler` and `XSetIOErrorHandler`.

`XSetErrorHandler` traps normal nonfatal errors, such as out-of-memory and bad window ID errors.

`XSetIOErrorHandler` traps fatal I/O errors, such as losing the network connection to the X server. Your application generally cannot recover from a fatal I/O error.

NOTE The Xt Intrinsics calls a fatal problem an *error*. The low-level X library calls this an *I/O error*. The Xt Intrinsics call a nonfatal problem a *warning*. The low-level X library calls this an *error*. This divergence of terminology tends to confuse. We use the terms *nonfatal* and *fatal* to help you sort out the terminology.

You pass `XSetErrorHandler` a nonfatal error-handling function to be called back when error events arrive:

```
XErrorHandler XSetErrorHandler(
    XErrorHandler handler)
```

`XSetErrorHandler` returns a pointer to the old error-handling function. Your error-handler function will be passed the `Display` pointer and a pointer to the error event:

```
typedef int (*XErrorHandler)(
    Display* display,
    XErrorEvent* error_event);
```

In your code, you can create an error-handling function like we present below:

```
int ErrorHandler(Display* display,
  XErrorEvent* event)

{  /* ErrorHandler */
  char  string[130];

  XGetErrorText(display,
    event->error_code,
    string,
    120);

  fprintf(stderr,
    "\n\n X Error:\n\t %s\n", string);

  fprintf(stderr,
    "\t Serial number of request: %ld\n",
    event->serial);

  fprintf(stderr,
    "\t Op Code: %d.%d %s\n\tError Code: %d\n",
    event->request_code,
    event->minor_code,
    ErrorCodes[event->request_code],
    event->error_code);

  fprintf(stderr,
    "\t Resource ID of failed request: %ld\n",
    event->resourceid);

  fprintf(stderr, "\t on display %s.\n",
    DisplayString(display) );

  return 0; /* unused. */

}  /* ErrorHandler */
```

This error handler does nothing more than merely report the error to stderr. It calls XGetErrorText to get the default text message for the error:

```
XGetErrorText(Display* display,
  int error_code,
  char* buffer, /* RETURN */
  int buffer_length)
```

XGetErrorText looks up the message corresponding to the given *error_code* and then fills in the *buffer* with up to *buffer_length* characters from the Xlib error database.

X defines no return type for XGetErrorText. It was written in pre-ANSI C, so you must assume that it has a default int return type.

N O T E

X Error Events

Your error-handling function gets passed an `XErrorEvent` that describes the error returned from the X server. This event looks like the following:

```
typedef struct {
  int         type;
  Display*    display;
  unsigned long  serial;
  unsigned char  error_code;
  unsigned char  request_code;
  unsigned char  minor_code;
  XID         resourceid;
} XErrorEvent;
```

The X library delivers `XErrorEvent` structures to the error-handling function set up with `XSetErrorHandler`. If you set up an error handler with `XSetErrorHandler` and an X library error occurs, your error handler will be called sometime after the error occurred. Why? Because the error events actually come from the X server, and the X server may get the offending request long after your code has returned from whatever function generated the error. These error events arrive asynchronously, which makes it hard to associate the error with the offending routine. You can pull some useful information from the `XErrorEvent` structure, though.

The *error_code* tells what type of error happened. The `XGetErrorText` Xlib function, described above, returns the text message for a given error code. We list the error codes in Table 24.1.

Table 24.1   *X error codes.*

Error Code	Value	Meaning
Success	0	No error
BadRequest	1	Bad request code
BadValue	2	Integer parameter out of range
BadWindow	3	Parameter not a valid `Window`
BadPixmap	4	Parameter not a valid `Pixmap`
BadAtom	5	Parameter not a valid `Atom`
BadCursor	6	Parameter not a valid `Cursor`

continued

BadFont	7	Parameter not a valid Font
BadMatch	8	Parameter mismatch
BadDrawable	9	Parameter not a valid Pixmap or Window
BadAccess	10	Attempt to perform an illegal operation
BadAlloc	11	Insufficient resources or memory
BadColor	12	No such colormap
BadGC	13	Parameter not a valid GC
BadIDChoice	14	Choice not in range or already used
BadName	15	Font or color name doesn't exist
BadLength	16	Request length incorrect
BadImplementation	17	Server is defective

The *request_code* in the XErrorEvent structure is the X protocol request number for the routine that actually caused the error. This can help when associating the error to the offending part of your code. The *minor_code* is, appropriately enough, the minor op-code of the failed X request.

The *resourceid*, an XID, is the ID of the offending resource, such as a window or pixmap. It is defined as an unsigned long.

The *type*, *display*, and *serial* fields are usually next to worthless. The *type* tells Xlib we have an error event. The *display* identifies the display connection, but 99.99 percent of all X programs connect to only one display anyway, making this of limited use. And the *serial* field is the serial number of the request, which usually isn't very helpful unless you are debugging an X server.

Handling Fatal Input/Output Errors

XSetErrorHandler sets up a function called for any nonfatal X error, such as when a bad window ID is passed to a drawing function. Other X errors, though, are fatal to an X program, especially errors involving loss of the server connection. This type of error could happen if the X server program itself tipped over, or if the network communication went down.

X calls these fatal errors *I/O errors*. If one occurs, Xlib will terminate your program, whether you like it or not. You can, however, set up a fatal-error-handler function, much like the regular nonfatal-error-handler function. This fatal-error handler, though, will be the last routine that your program executes. Therefore, it is a good idea to save files or generally clean up the system as much as possible in the little time remaining. (You can use the C routines `setjmp` and `longjmp` to jump out of the function and avoid the termination, if you wish.)

From a fatal-error handler, you cannot use any Xlib or Xt or Motif routines that would generate a request of the X server (an I/O error means that the link to the X server is severed). You can register your fatal-error-handler function with X by calling the `XSetIOErrorHandler` function and passing the address of your fatal-error-handler routine.

```
XIOErrorHandler XSetIOErrorHandler(
    XIOErrorHandler handler)
```

Like `XSetErrorHandler`, `XSetIOErrorHandler` returns the old error-handling function starting. Your fatal-error-handler function is passed the (now bad) display pointer:

```
typedef int (*XIOErrorHandler)(
    Display* display);
```

The default fatal-error function just prints the message to `stderr` and exits. In a computer-aided design (CAD) program or an industrial process-control program, though, the story would probably be different. It seems rather arrogant for X to decide that it will terminate your program on a fatal I/O error, since it might be better if you could try to reopen a display connection at a later time, but that's what you have to live with.

In any case, most commercial-grade X applications will want to create error-handling routines like those described above.

SUMMARY

To develop robust applications, you need to intercept and handle most errors. The standard answer of just printing a message and terminating the application is simply not acceptable to most users. Surprisingly enough, this is the default behavior for all programs based on the Xt Intrinsics—a terrible method of error handling. Therefore, your applications must do *something* to deal with errors.

This chapter showed the various methods of dealing with X and Motif errors and listed all the possible error messages and what generates them.

X TOOLKIT INTRINSICS FUNCTIONS AND MACROS INTRODUCED IN THIS CHAPTER

```
XtAppError
XtAppErrorMsg
XtAppGetErrorDatabase
XtAppGetErrorDatabaseText
XtAppSetErrorMsgHandler
XtAppSetWarningMsgHandler
XtAppWarning
XtAppWarningMsg
```

X LIBRARY FUNCTIONS AND MACROS INTRODUCED IN THIS CHAPTER

```
XGetErrorText
XSetErrorHandler
XSetIOErrorHandler
```

CHAPTER 25

Online Help

This chapter covers:

- Calling help with the **F1** or **Help** keys
- Help menu choices
- Creating a help menu
- Creating the help dialog
- The Motif `helpCallback`
- Creating context-sensitive help
- Context-sensitive help for menu bars
- Context-sensitive help for scrolled widgets
- Creating a help cursor
- Creating product-information help

How To Earn Popularity From Your Users

Help forms one of the most neglected features for Motif applications. Even so, users expect any application to provide online help. The Motif style guide, as well, encourages online help with the Help menu. After users see windows and pull-down menus, their expectations on user-friendliness go way up. Adding in a good online help system is an effective way to improve productivity with software you create.

Unfortunately, there are few standards for Motif help. Motif provides nothing as nice as the help system that comes with Microsoft Windows. In fact, Motif provides little help for developers building online help.

Because of this, help is one area where most Motif applications fail miserably. Few provide really good help. Why? Because it's difficult.

This chapter should provide you with a set of tools for implementing online help. We build on our coverage of the Help menu in Chapter 4 and add in context-sensitive help and product-information help, as well as provide an example help dialog. What we won't do, though, is create a multifont whiz-bang graphics hypertext help system. That small exercise is left to the reader.

Help Keys and Functions

SHORTCUT

In Motif programs, the user has three means to call up help:

- The **F1** or **Help** keys
- The Help menu
- Context-sensitive help

The Help action is usually tied to the **F1** or **Help** keys. This action calls the helpCallback set up for a widget. Motif supports the helpCallback for all widgets.

To get context-sensitive help, you can call XmTrackingLocate or XmTrackingEvent to switch into a modal mode while the user moves the mouse about the screen and finally clicks the leftmost mouse button over a widget.

`XmTrackingLocate` or `XmTrackingEvent` will then return this widget ID:

```
Widget XmTrackingLocate(Widget widget,
    Cursor cursor,
    Boolean confine_to)

Widget XmTrackingEvent(Widget widget,
    Cursor cursor,
    Boolean confine_to,
    XEvent* event)   /* RETURN */
```

`XmTrackingEvent` is new in Motif 1.2.

HELP AND THE HELP MENU

Every Motif application should have a menu bar with a Help menu. Since the menu bar generally remains visible, the Help menu lets the user know that online help is available at the simple click of a mouse.

The Help menu choices are listed in Table 25.1.

Table 25.1   *Help menu choices.*

Traditional Choice	Mnemonic	New Style Choice	Mnemonic
On Context...	C	Context-Sensitive Help...	C
On Help...	H	Using Help...	H
On Window...	W	Overview...	O
On Keys...	K	Keyboard...	K
Index...	I	Index...	I
Tutorial...	T	Tutorial...	T
On Version...	V	Product Information...	P

You can use the terminology from the traditional or new style choices, but you cannot mix and match. We find that the new style seems more natural.

If your application doesn't provide a certain type of help, such as an online tutorial, then you should skip that menu choice, obviously. Note that few Motif programs provide an online tutorial. Also note that since every Help menu choice has an ellipses, each choice should bring up a help dialog.

Using the traditional terminology, the **On Context...** choice should provide help on the current context—that is on what the user is currently trying to do. The idea is to provide context-sensitive help, which we cover below.

The **On Help...** choice shows how to use the help system. We really hope your help system isn't very tough to learn; otherwise, it won't be much help.

On Window... describes the window from which help was requested, including the standard ways to interact with that window.

On Keys... provides help on the special keys used in the application, especially on the mnemonics. Motif uses quite a few keyboard accelerators and allows the user to customize quite a bit more.

The **Index...** choice should provide an index to help topics.

You'll really be lucky if you ever see a **Tutorial...** choice in an application. If you create a quality online tutorial, your users will love you.

The **On Version...** choice should display information including the name of the application and any version numbers associated with the application. Usually copyright messages are part of this help choice.

Creating a Help Menu

You create the Help menu just like you create any other Motif pull-down menus on the menu bar. The only thing special about this **Help** cascade button is that we want the button to be on the far right, as the Motif Help menu is supposed to be. To do this, we have to set up the resource menuHelpWidget (XmNmenuHelpWidget in your C programs). This resource needs to be set on the parent menu bar (not on the **Help** cascade button) and needs to specify a widget—in this case, the help cascade button widget.

For example, after you create the **Help** cascade button, you can call XtVaSetValues on the menu bar as follows:

```
Widget    menubar;
Widget    help_cascade;
/* … */

XtVaSetValues(menubar,
```

```
XmNmenuHelpWidget, help_cascade,
NULL);
```

Always create the Help menu last. When the user uses the keyboard shortcuts to traverse the menu bar, the Help menu will be traversed in the proper order. Otherwise, all bets are off.

N O T E

Calling Up Help

In Motif applications, the user has three means to call up help:

- Pressing the **F1** or **Help** keys
- Calling for context-sensitive help on a widget from the Help menu
- Choosing any of the other options on the Help menu, which should call up help on the given subject.

The Motif style guide specifies that the **F1** key should call up help, unless the keyboard provides a key labeled **Help** (common on Sun Microsystems workstations). By default, most widgets have this wired into an action named Help. The Help action, in turn, tries to call the helpCallback for the widget that currently has the keyboard focus.

Sometimes you'll be surprised which widget get its helpCallback called when you press **F1**. If you have a pull-down menu, usually the menu bar, not the menu or the currently armed menu choice, will get the helpCallback. It's important to set up a helpCallback for widgets like menu bars, where you would normally not expect the user to ask for help.

N O T E

This helpCallback should, obviously enough, display some form of help. If you really get fancy, you can create an SGML (Standard Generalized Markup Language) online hypertext help system. We're a little more modest. Instead, we create a simple, but workable, help dialog.

Creating the Help Dialog

When the user asks for help, we provide a dialog like the one shown in Figure 25.1.

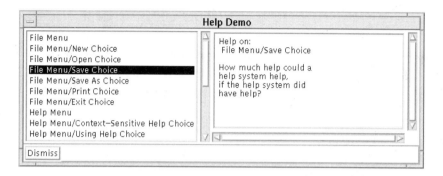

Figure 25.1 *The Help dialog.*

On the left side, we have a scrolled list of all the available help topics. The right side holds the actual help text in a scrolled XmText widget. Isn't our help text helpful?

Commercial-grade applications require much more extensive help. You'll probably want to add hypertext links, searching, and backtracking, but that's far beyond the scope of this book.

For our modest online help system, we create a single instance of a help dialog. The programmer can fill in a scrolled list of help topics, and for each topic, you can specify the text. Our basic help dialog interface uses the following functions, which we create below:

- HelpDlgShow, which manages the help dialog to make it visible
- HelpDlgCreate, which you call once to create all the help widgets
- HelpDlgSetText, which you call to set the help text into the scrolled XmText widget
- HelpDlgAddTopic, which adds a help topic to the scrolled list of topics
- HelpDlgDeleteAllTopics, which allows you to delete all the list topics

With these functions, we make the callbacks visible, so that you can determine when to make the help dialog appear and what text it should display. The help program, below, fills in one list of help topics, but you can switch lists at any time. You specify the function you want for the list callback when you call HelpDlgCreate.

HelpDlgCreate creates a form dialog, a row column, scrolled list, scrolled text, separator, and pushbutton to dismiss the dialog.

When you call the HelpDlgCreate function, you need to pass a *parent* widget, usually the top-level shell returned by XtAppInitialize or XtVaAppInitialize, and a *topic_callback*, which is set up as the scrolled-list widget's singleSelectCallback. You pass the *client_data* for this list callback in the *topic_data* parameter. Thus, when the user selects a topic to get help on, your *topic_callback* will get called. You can then choose to fill in the scrolled text with any help text you desire, by calling HelpDlgSetText. Your code is always in charge.

The *help_callback* is the function to set up for the helpCallback. This parameter ensures that users can call for help on help, something that's easy to forget about. The *help_text_data* is the helpCallback *client_data* for the scrolled-text widget. The *help_topic_data* is similarly the helpCallback *client_data* for the scrolled-list widget.

The code for HelpDlgCreate appears in the **helpdlg.c** file, in the "Code for the Help-Dialog Routines" section, below.

The HelpDlgAddTopic function just calls XmListAddItemUnselected to append a list item. HelpDlgDeleteAllTopics similarly calls XmListDeleteAllItems to delete all the items in the list.

When you use these routines, you'll need to call HelpDlgCreate first to create all the widgets. Call HelpDlgAddTopic to fill in the scrolled list of help topics. Whenever you want to display help, call HelpDlgSetText to fill in the text. Finally, call HelpDlgShow to make the help dialog appear.

Code for the Help-Dialog Routines

The code for all our help-dialog utility functions appears in the file **helpdlg.c**.

```
/* helpdlg.c */
#include <Xm/Xm.h>
#include <Xm/Form.h>
#include <Xm/Label.h>
#include <Xm/List.h>
#include <Xm/PushB.h>
#include <Xm/RowColumn.h>
#include <Xm/Separator.h>
#include <Xm/Text.h>
```

```c
#include <stdio.h>

/* Globals for on helpdlg dialog. */
static Widget   help_dialog = (Widget) NULL;
static Widget   help_topic  = (Widget) NULL;
static Widget   help_text   = (Widget) NULL;

    /* Callback to unmanage dialog. */
static void unmanage_helpdialogCB(Widget widget,
    XtPointer client_data,
    XtPointer call_data)

{   /* unmanage_helpdialogCB */
    Widget  dialog;

    dialog = (Widget) client_data;

    if (dialog != (Widget) NULL) {
        if (XtIsManaged(dialog) ) {
            XtUnmanageChild(dialog);
        }
    }

}   /* unmanage_helpdialogCB */

    /* Show help dialog. */
void HelpDlgShow()

{   /* HelpDlgShow */

    /* Show help dialog. */
    if (! XtIsManaged(help_dialog) ) {
        XtManageChild(help_dialog);
    }

}   /* HelpDlgShow */

    /* Create help dialog. */
void HelpDlgCreate(Widget parent,
    XtCallbackProc topic_callback,
    XtPointer topic_data,
    XtCallbackProc help_callback,
    XtPointer help_text_data,
    XtPointer help_topic_data)

{   /* HelpDlgCreate */
    Arg         args[20];
    Cardinal    n;
    Widget      row, sep, dismiss;

    n = 0;
    XtSetArg(args[n], XmNallowResize, True); n++;
    help_dialog = XmCreateFormDialog(parent,
            "help_dialog", args, n);
```

```
row = XtVaCreateWidget("row",
    xmRowColumnWidgetClass, help_dialog,
    XmNorientation, XmHORIZONTAL,
    NULL);

/* Create Scrolled list of help topics. */
n = 0;
XtSetArg(args[n], XmNselectionPolicy,
    XmSINGLE_SELECT); n++;

help_topic = XmCreateScrolledList(row,
        "help_topic", args, n);

XtAddCallback(help_topic,
    XmNsingleSelectionCallback,
    topic_callback,
    topic_data);

XtAddCallback(help_topic,
    XmNhelpCallback,
    help_callback,
    help_topic_data);

XtAddCallback(XtParent(help_topic),
    XmNhelpCallback,
    help_callback,
    help_topic_data);

/* Create text widget to display help. */
n = 0;
XtSetArg(args[n], XmNeditMode,
        XmMULTI_LINE_EDIT); n++;

help_text = XmCreateScrolledText(row,
        "help_text", args, n);

XtAddCallback(help_text,
    XmNhelpCallback,
    help_callback,
    help_text_data);

XtAddCallback(XtParent(help_text),
    XmNhelpCallback,
    help_callback,
    help_text_data);

/* Create button area at bottom. */
sep = XtVaCreateManagedWidget("sep",
    xmSeparatorWidgetClass, help_dialog,
    XmNtopAttachment,    XmATTACH_WIDGET,
    XmNtopWidget,        row,
    XmNleftAttachment,   XmATTACH_FORM,
    XmNrightAttachment,  XmATTACH_FORM,
    NULL);
```

```
    dismiss = XtVaCreateManagedWidget("dismiss",
        xmPushButtonWidgetClass, help_dialog,
        XmNtopAttachment,     XmATTACH_WIDGET,
        XmNtopWidget,         sep,
        XmNbottomAttachment, XmATTACH_FORM,
        XmNleftAttachment,   XmATTACH_FORM,
        NULL);

    XtAddCallback(dismiss,
        XmNactivateCallback,
        (XtCallbackProc) unmanage_helpdialogCB,
        (XtPointer) NULL);

    /* Set up scrolled area attachments. */
    XtVaSetValues(row,
        XmNtopAttachment,     XmATTACH_FORM,
        XmNleftAttachment,    XmATTACH_FORM,
        XmNrightAttachment,   XmATTACH_FORM,
        NULL);

    XtManageChild(help_topic);

    XtManageChild(help_text);
    XtManageChild(row);

}   /* HelpDlgCreate */

    /* Sets help text in dialog. */
void HelpDlgSetText(char* text)

{   /* HelpDlgSetText */

    if (help_text == (Widget) NULL) {
        return;
    }

    XmTextReplace(help_text,
        (XmTextPosition) 0,
        XmTextGetLastPosition(help_text),
        text);

}   /* HelpDlgSetText */

    /* Adds topic to list of topics. */
void HelpDlgAddTopic(char* topic)

{   /* HelpDlgAddTopic */
    XmString    xmstring;

    if (help_topic == (Widget) NULL) {
        return;
    }

    xmstring = XmStringCreateSimple(topic);
```

```
        XmListAddItemUnselected(help_topic,
            xmstring,
            0); /* position 0 means append. */

        XmStringFree(xmstring);

}   /* HelpDlgAddTopic */

    /* Delete all help topics. */
void HelpDlgDeleteAllTopics()

{   /* HelpDlgDeleteAllTopics */

    if (help_topic == (Widget) NULL) {
        return;
    }

    XmListDeselectAllItems(help_topic);

    XmListDeleteAllItems(help_topic);

}   /* HelpDlgDeleteAllTopics */

/* end of file helpdlg.c */
```

Even with the help dialog presented above, you're still responsible for creating the original `helpCallback` that actually calls up this help dialog. We do this to allow you to store help in any files or create any help organization you want.

Organizing Help

Whether you use a fancy hypertext system with links, graphics, and multiple fonts or the more modest system shown in this chapter, we find that organizing the help to display around the concept of topics is the most effective means to deal with help messages. We also usually use a hierarchical topic organization. For example, the File menu topic will present an overview of the topics for the choices in the File menu, such as **Save** or **Exit**. Each of these choices also has its own topic, a subtopic of the File menu topic.

In any case, all the help techniques presented in this chapter are based on the idea that every help message is indexed by a textual help topic.

On our sample program, we just hard-code the help information, which really isn't all that helpful. What we're trying to show is not the text of the help messages, but instead how to create an online help system that reacts to the user asking for help.

Once we have the help dialog down, we need to come up with ways to call up the help. You should set up a `helpCallback` on every widget that accepts user input (and a few others as well). You should also fill in the Help menu, which we cover in the next few sections.

Context-Sensitive Help

The **On Context...** or **Context-Sensitive Help...** menu choice in the Help menu should provide help on any widget the user picks. There's some special code you need to do for this, but it's not that difficult.

When the user chooses the **On Context...** menu choice, the cursor should change shape to a question mark and then your program should present help on the first widget the user clicks in. This may seem difficult, but luckily Motif provides a utility function, `XmTrackingLocate`, that takes care of most of the dirty work.

With Motif 1.1, you can call `XmTrackingLocate` to have the user locate a widget to get help on:

```
Widget XmTrackingLocate(Widget widget,
    Cursor cursor,
    Boolean confine_to)
```

`XmTrackingLocate` grabs exclusive control of the mouse pointer and waits for the user to click (press and release) the leftmost mouse button or press and release a key. `XmTrackingLocate` returns the widget that the user selected, or `NULL` if the user did not select a widget in your application.

Essentially, `XmTrackingLocate` places your application into a modal state until the user selects a widget. This modal state should last only a short while. When this happens, your application is locked up awaiting the user to press a key or click the leftmost mouse button.

You should normally pass a top-level shell as the *widget*, but you don't have to.

The *cursor* is a standard X cursor shape. We usually use the question cursor. The mouse cursor will change to this shape for the duration of the call to `XmTrackingLocate` and then switch back to the normal cursor on each window.

If you set *confine_to* to `True`, then the mouse cursor will be confined to the window that underlies the *widget*. If you pass a pushbutton widget, then this will probably be a very small area. Because of the fact that an application may have a number of top-level windows on the screen, we usually pass `False`.

XmTrackingEvent

In Motif 1.2, you should call `XmTrackingEvent` instead of `XmTrackingLocate`. Both functions act similarly, but `XmTrackingEvent` also returns the `ButtonRelease` or `KeyRelease` event that it used to choose the widget:

```
Widget XmTrackingEvent(Widget widget,
    Cursor cursor,
    Boolean confine_to,
    XEvent* event)   /* RETURN */
```

`XmTrackingEvent` replaces `XmTrackingLocate`, but `XmTrackingEvent` isn't available until Motif 1.2. We use the following code, which automatically configures itself at compile time based on the value of the `XmVersion` macro (1001 in Motif 1.1, 1002 in Motif 1.2, etc.):

```
Widget   toplevel, selected_widget;
Cursor   context_cursor;
XEvent   returned_event;

    /* … */

#if XmVersion > 1001

    /* Locate widget to get help on. */
    selected_widget = XmTrackingEvent(toplevel,
                    context_cursor,
                    False,  /* Confine to. */
                    &returned_event);

#else   /* Motif 1.1 */

    /* Locate widget to get help on. */
    selected_widget = XmTrackingLocate(toplevel,
                    context_cursor,
                    False); /* Confine to. */
#endif /* Motif 1.1 */
```

Creating a Cursor

Both `XmTrackingLocate` and `XmTrackingEvent` require a cursor ID, which you can create with the X library routine `XCreateFontCursor`:

```
#include  <X11/cursorfont.h>

Cursor XCreateFontCursor(Display* display,
    unsigned int cursor_shape)
```

XCreateFontCursor creates and returns a cursor from a bitmap and a mask located in the *cursor* font (an actual font named *cursor*). The *cursor_shape* is the ID of one of these cursors in the *cursor* font. You can find the IDs in the X library include file <X11/cursorfont.h>. For help, we usually use XC_question_arrow for the shape, but there's also XC_gumby, XC_trek, and XC_pirate, in case you're daring.

When you're done with a cursor, free it by calling XFreeCursor:

```
XFreeCursor(Display* display,
    Cursor cursor)
```

XFreeCursor has no defined return type, so assume it uses the default return type of int, although the routine returns nothing.

N O T E

Once you've called XFreeCursor, you can no longer use the cursor ID.

Presenting Help on the Widget

After we've located a widget with either XmTrackingLocate or XmTrackingEvent, what next? We need to somehow display help on that particular widget. The easiest way to do this is to call the helpCallback for that widget.

Motif supports a helpCallback for every widget. We want to call the selected widget's helpCallback and let our helpCallback take care of the rest. This allows you to write less code, since you already need to create a helpCallback to handle the **F1** or **Help** keys. We need a way to call a widget's callback. To do this, we call the Xt function XtCallCallbacks:

```
void XtCallCallbacks(Widget widget,
    String callback_name,
    XtPointer call_data)
```

In our case, we need a *callback_name* of XmNhelpCallback. For the *call_data*, we're not sure what to pass. Since we're writing the function that will actually be called, we can agree on conventions for the *call_data*.

PUTTING TOGETHER CONTEXT-SENSITIVE HELP

To put together our work on context-sensitive help, we have the following function that you can use as a callback for the **Context-Sensitive Help...** menu choice on the Help menu:

```
/* context.c */
#include  <Xm/Xm.h>
#include  <X11/cursorfont.h>  /* Cursor defines. */
#include  <stdio.h>

/* Global for cursor. */
Cursor  context_cursor = (Cursor) None;

    /* Callback for context-sensitive help. */
void contextCB(Widget widget,
    XtPointer client_data,
    XtPointer call_data)

{   /* contextCB */
    Display*              display;
    Widget                selected_widget;
    Widget                toplevel;
    XEvent                returned_event;
    XmAnyCallbackStruct*  new_call_data;

    /* We assume client_data has shell widget. */
    toplevel = (Widget) client_data;

    if (toplevel == (Widget) NULL) {
        return;
    }
    new_call_data =
        (XmAnyCallbackStruct*) call_data;

    /* Create Cursor, if necessary. */
    if (context_cursor == (Cursor) None) {

        display = XtDisplay(widget);
        context_cursor =
            XCreateFontCursor(display,
                    XC_question_arrow);
    }

    /* Motif 1.2 Adds XmTrackingEvent. */
#if XmVersion > 1001

    /* Locate widget to get help on. */
    selected_widget = XmTrackingEvent(toplevel,
                    context_cursor,
                    False,  /* Confine to. */
```

```
                         &returned_event);
#else  /* Motif 1.1 */

    /* Locate widget to get help on. */
    selected_widget = XmTrackingLocate(toplevel,
                          context_cursor,
                          False); /* Confine to. */
#endif /* Motif 1.1 */

    /* Call that widget's helpCallback. */
    if (selected_widget != (Widget) NULL) {

        /* Set reason to help. */
        new_call_data->reason = XmCR_HELP;

        XtCallCallbacks(selected_widget,
            XmNhelpCallback,
            new_call_data);
    }

}    /* contextCB */

/* end of file context.c */
```

Context-Sensitive Help for Menus

There's one big problem with both XmTrackingEvent and XmTrackingLocate: You cannot click on a widget that isn't visible. You especially cannot pull down a menu to get help on a particular menu choice—which is dumb because that's most likely what you want help on anyway. (If you have tear-off menus with Motif 1.2, you can first tear off the menu and then ask for context-sensitive help on the menu choice.)

You can set up a helpCallback on the cascade button that sits on the menu bar. For example, the user can ask for context-sensitive help on the File menu's cascade button. This should then present help on the whole File menu.

In addition to the problems with XmTrackingEvent and XmTrackingLocate, you'll find that we need a new utility function to create a pushbutton widget with a helpCallback. The code for this follows:

```
    /* Creates pushbutton and sets up help CB. */
Widget CreatePushbuttonWithHelp(Widget parent,
    char* name,
    XtCallbackProc callback,
    XtPointer client_data,
    XtCallbackProc help_callback,
```

```
                XtPointer help_data)

    {   /* CreatePushbuttonWithHelp */
        Widget    push;
        Arg       args[20];
        Cardinal  n;

        n = 0;
        push = XmCreatePushButton(parent,
                name, args, n);

        /* Set up callback. */
        XtAddCallback(push,
            XmNactivateCallback,
            callback,
            client_data);

        /* Set up help callback. */
        XtAddCallback(push,
            XmNhelpCallback,
            help_callback,
            help_data);

        XtManageChild(push);

        return push;

    }   /* CreatePushbuttonWithHelp */
```

Context-Sensitive Help for Menu Bars

With XmTrackingEvent and XmTrackingLocate, the user can pick a menu bar, too, so we should set up a helpCallback on the menu bar. The help that this brings up should aim at covering the entire menu bar and all its pull-down menus.

Context-Sensitive Help for Scrolled Widgets

With a scrolled-text widget, you can get either the text widget and the parent scrolled window back from XmTrackingEvent (and XmTrackingLocate, too). Because of this, you should set up a helpCallback on the parent of scrolled-text and scrolled-list widgets.

On-Version Help

The **On Version...** or **Product Information...** help message should contain information about the version of the program, such as the version number, the date the program was created, the authors, and any copyright information you want to place in the box. If this sounds dry and boring, you should look at some PC software with the **About...** box equivalent. PC applications have a lot of fun with this and include things like fireworks and animated dogs to liven up this help dialog.

Even though we don't have any barking dogs, we can create the *On Version...* help message by using a message box dialog similar to the ones introduced in Chapter 7.

Creating the On-Version Help Dialog

We use an XmMessageBox dialog for our product information. This really only allows us to present a text message. In your applications, though, you probably want to create a custom dialog and show something spiffy to make your program look better.

Because we're using a message-box dialog, the message to display should be placed into the messageString resource for the dialog. (We do this with the resource file at the end of the chapter.)

The code for our product information or on-version dialog appears below.

```
/* version.c */
#include <Xm/Xm.h>
#include <Xm/MessageB.h>
#include <stdio.h>

/* Global for on version dialog. */
static Widget   on_version_dialog = (Widget) NULL;

    /* Callback to unmanage dialog. */
static void unmanage_versionCB(Widget widget,
    XtPointer client_data,
    XtPointer call_data)

{   /* unmanage_versionCB */
    Widget  dialog;

    dialog = (Widget) client_data;

    if (dialog != (Widget) NULL) {
        if (XtIsManaged(dialog) ) {
            XtUnmanageChild(dialog);
        }
    }

}   /* unmanage_versionCB */

    /* Callback for On Version help. */
```

```
void on_versionCB(Widget widget,
    XtPointer client_data,
    XtPointer call_data)

{   /* on_versionCB */
    Widget      toplevel;
    Arg         args[20];
    Cardinal    n;

    /* We assume client_data has top-level shell. */
    toplevel = (Widget) client_data;

    /* Create dialog if necessary. */
    if (on_version_dialog == (Widget) NULL) {
        if (toplevel == (Widget) NULL) {
            return;
        }

        n = 0;
        on_version_dialog =
            XmCreateMessageDialog(toplevel,
                "on_version_dialog",
                args, n);

        XtAddCallback(on_version_dialog,
            XmNokCallback,
            (XtCallbackProc) unmanage_versionCB,
            (XtPointer) on_version_dialog);

        /* get rid of Cancel and Help. */
        XtUnmanageChild(
            XmMessageBoxGetChild(on_version_dialog,
                XmDIALOG_CANCEL_BUTTON) );
        XtUnmanageChild(
            XmMessageBoxGetChild(on_version_dialog,
                XmDIALOG_HELP_BUTTON) );
    }

    /* Check for errors. */
    if (on_version_dialog == (Widget) NULL) {
        return;
    }

    /* Show On Version dialog. */
    if (! XtIsManaged(on_version_dialog) ) {
        XtManageChild(on_version_dialog);
    }

}   /* on_versionCB */

/* end of file version.c */
```

The on_versionCB function creates the message-box dialog only if necessary and then unmanages the **Cancel** and **Help** buttons. In this dialog, we allow only the **OK** button.

A Program To Show On-Context Help

We've put together a program to allow you to test the dynamics of online help. The basic idea is that the user has three means to call up help: The **F1** or **Help** keys, the Help menu, and context-sensitive help.

In our program, below, the helpCB is where you should place whatever code you need to call up help on a given subject. By convention, we pass the help topic name as the *client_data*, so you can search on this in a help file or files. The topicCB, which is passed to the HelpDlgCreate help dialog utility routine in **helpdlg.c**, simply extracts the scrolled-list item as text and then calls the helpCB to display the help on the given topic. Since all forms of help are so similar, you might want to code your help in a similar fashion.

The code for the help application appears below.

```c
/* help.c */
#include   <Xm/Xm.h>
#include   <Xm/CascadeB.h>
#include   <Xm/List.h>
#include   <Xm/MainW.h>
#include   <Xm/RowColumn.h>
#include   <Xm/PushB.h>
#include   <Xm/Separator.h>
#include   <Xm/Text.h>
#include   <stdio.h>

    /* Callback for context-sensitive help. */
extern void contextCB(Widget widget,
    XtPointer client_data,
    XtPointer call_data);

    /* Callback for On Version help. */
extern void on_versionCB(Widget widget,
    XtPointer client_data,
    XtPointer call_data);

    /* Create help dialog. */
extern void HelpDlgCreate(Widget parent,
        XtCallbackProc topic_callback,
        XtPointer topic_data,
        XtCallbackProc help_callback,
        XtPointer help_text_data,
        XtPointer help_topic_data);

    /* Show help dialog. */
extern void HelpDlgShow();
```

```
      /* Sets help text in dialog. */
extern void HelpDlgSetText(char* text);

      /* Adds topic to list of topics. */
extern void HelpDlgAddTopic(char* topic);

      /* Delete all help topics. */
extern void HelpDlgDeleteAllTopics();

      /* Creates pushbutton and sets up help CB. */
Widget CreatePushbuttonWithHelp(Widget parent,
      char* name,
      XtCallbackProc callback,
      XtPointer client_data,
      XtCallbackProc help_callback,
      XtPointer help_data)

{     /* CreatePushbuttonWithHelp */
      Widget    push;
      Arg       args[20];
      Cardinal  n;

      n = 0;
      push = XmCreatePushButton(parent,
                name, args, n);

      /* Set up callback. */
      XtAddCallback(push,
          XmNactivateCallback,
          callback,
          client_data);

      /* Set up help callback. */
      XtAddCallback(push,
          XmNhelpCallback,
          help_callback,
          help_data);

      XtManageChild(push);

      return push;

}     /* CreatePushbuttonWithHelp */

      /* Called to present help. */
void helpCB(Widget widget,
      XtPointer client_data,
      XtPointer call_data)

{     /* helpCB */
      char    text_for_help[1024];

      /* This function really should call
       * up a file on the given help topic,
       * which we pass as the client_data.
```

```
        */

        /* Client data is text. */
        sprintf(text_for_help,
            "Help on:\n %s\n\n",
            (char*) client_data);

        strcat(text_for_help,
            "How much help could a\n");
        strcat(text_for_help,
            "help system help,\n");
        strcat(text_for_help,
            "if the help system did\n");
        strcat(text_for_help,
            "have help?\n\n\n");

        HelpDlgSetText(text_for_help);

        printf("Help callback [%s]\n",
            (char*) client_data);

        HelpDlgShow();

}    /* helpCB */

        /* Called from help topic list. */
void topicCB(Widget widget,
    XtPointer client_data,
    XtPointer call_data)

{    /* topicCB */
    XmListCallbackStruct* ptr;
    char*                 string;

    ptr = (XmListCallbackStruct*) call_data;

    XmStringGetLtoR(ptr->item,
        XmSTRING_DEFAULT_CHARSET,
        &string);

    /* Call helpCB to display help. */
    helpCB(widget, (XtPointer) string,
        call_data);

    /* Free text string. */
    XtFree(string);

}    /* topicCB */

        /* Called on menu choices. */
void menuCB(Widget widget,
    XtPointer client_data,
    XtPointer call_data)

{    /* menuCB */
```

```
    /* Client data is text. */
    printf("Menu choice [%s]\n",
        (char*) client_data);

}   /* menuCB */

void exitCB(Widget widget,
    XtPointer client_data,
    XtPointer call_data)

{   /* exitCB */

    exit(0);

}   /* exitCB */

int main(int argc, char** argv)

{   /* main */
    XtAppContext    app_context;
    Widget          mainw, menubar;
    Widget          filemenu, helpmenu;
    Widget          fcascade, hcascade;
    Widget          text;
    Widget          parent;
    Arg             args[20];
    Cardinal        n;

    parent = XtVaAppInitialize(&app_context,
                "Ppm",
                (XrmOptionDescList) NULL,
                0,
                &argc, argv,
                (String*) NULL,
                XmNallowResize, True,
                NULL);

    n = 0;
    mainw = XmCreateMainWindow(parent,
                "mainw", args, n);

    n = 0;
    menubar = XmCreateMenuBar(mainw,
                "menubar", args, n);

    XtAddCallback(menubar,
        XmNhelpCallback,
        (XtCallbackProc) helpCB,
        (XtPointer) "menubar");

    XtManageChild(menubar);

    /* Create file menu the long way. */
    n = 0;
```

```
#ifdef XmNtearOffModel

    XtSetArg(args[n], XmNtearOffModel,
        XmTEAR_OFF_ENABLED); n++;

#endif  /* XmNtearOffModel */

    filemenu = XmCreatePulldownMenu(menubar,
        "filemenu", args, n);

    /* Create cascade. */
    n = 0;
    XtSetArg(args[n], XmNsubMenuId, filemenu); n++;

    fcascade = XmCreateCascadeButton(menubar,
                "filemenu", args, n);

    /* Add help to cascade. */
    XtAddCallback(fcascade,
        XmNhelpCallback,
        (XtCallbackProc) helpCB,
        (XtPointer) "File Menu");

    XtManageChild(fcascade);

    /* Create menu choices for file menu. */
    (void) CreatePushbuttonWithHelp(filemenu, "new",
            (XtCallbackProc) menuCB,
            (XtPointer) "new",
            (XtCallbackProc) helpCB,
            (XtPointer) "File Menu/New Choice");

    (void) CreatePushbuttonWithHelp(filemenu, "open",
            (XtCallbackProc) menuCB,
            (XtPointer) "open",
            (XtCallbackProc) helpCB,
            (XtPointer) "File Menu/Open Choice");

    /* Separator. */
    (void) XtVaCreateManagedWidget("sep",
            xmSeparatorWidgetClass, filemenu,
            XmNorientation, XmHORIZONTAL,
            NULL);

    (void) CreatePushbuttonWithHelp(filemenu, "save",
            (XtCallbackProc) menuCB,
            (XtPointer) "save",
            (XtCallbackProc) helpCB,
            (XtPointer) "File Menu/Save Choice");

    (void) CreatePushbuttonWithHelp(filemenu, "saveas",
            (XtCallbackProc) menuCB,
            (XtPointer) "saveas",
            (XtCallbackProc) helpCB,
```

```
                        (XtPointer) "File Menu/Save As Choice");

        /* Separator. */
        (void) XtVaCreateManagedWidget("sep",
                xmSeparatorWidgetClass, filemenu,
                XmNorientation, XmHORIZONTAL,
                NULL);

        (void) CreatePushbuttonWithHelp(filemenu, "print",
                (XtCallbackProc) menuCB,
                (XtPointer) "print",
                (XtCallbackProc) helpCB,
                (XtPointer) "File Menu/Print Choice");

        /* Separator. */
        (void) XtVaCreateManagedWidget("sep",
                xmSeparatorWidgetClass, filemenu,
                XmNorientation, XmHORIZONTAL,
                NULL);

        (void) CreatePushbuttonWithHelp(filemenu, "exit",
                (XtCallbackProc) exitCB,
                (XtPointer) NULL,
                (XtCallbackProc) helpCB,
                (XtPointer) "File Menu/Exit Choice");

        /* Create help menu the long way. */
        n = 0;

#ifdef XmNtearOffModel

        XtSetArg(args[n], XmNtearOffModel,
            XmTEAR_OFF_ENABLED); n++;

#endif   /* XmNtearOffModel */

        helpmenu = XmCreatePulldownMenu(menubar,
            "helpmenu", args, n);

        /* Create cascade. */
        n = 0;
        XtSetArg(args[n], XmNsubMenuId, helpmenu); n++;

        hcascade = XmCreateCascadeButton(menubar,
                    "helpmenu", args, n);

        /* Add help to cascade. */
        XtAddCallback(hcascade,
            XmNhelpCallback,
            (XtCallbackProc) helpCB,
            (XtPointer) "Help Menu");

        /* Tell menu bar this is help menu. */
        XtVaSetValues(menubar,
            XmNmenuHelpWidget, hcascade,
```

```
            NULL);

    XtManageChild(hcascade);

    /* Pass top-level widget as client_data. */
    (void) CreatePushbuttonWithHelp(helpmenu, "context",
            (XtCallbackProc) contextCB,
            (XtPointer) parent,
            (XtCallbackProc) helpCB,
            (XtPointer)
                "Help Menu/Context-Sensitive Help Choice");

    /* Rest of Help choices call helCB on activate. */
    (void) CreatePushbuttonWithHelp(helpmenu, "onhelp",
            (XtCallbackProc) helpCB,
            (XtPointer) "Help Menu/Using Help Choice",
            (XtCallbackProc) helpCB,
            (XtPointer) "Help Menu/Using Help Choice");

    (void) CreatePushbuttonWithHelp(helpmenu,
            "helpoverview",
            (XtCallbackProc) helpCB,
            (XtPointer) "Help Menu/Overview Choice",
            (XtCallbackProc) helpCB,
            (XtPointer) "Help Menu/Overview Choice");

    (void) CreatePushbuttonWithHelp(helpmenu, "onkeyboard",
            (XtCallbackProc) helpCB,
            (XtPointer) "Help Menu/Keyboard Choice",
            (XtCallbackProc) helpCB,
            (XtPointer) "Help Menu/Keyboard Choice");

    (void) CreatePushbuttonWithHelp(helpmenu, "index",
            (XtCallbackProc) helpCB,
            (XtPointer) "Help Menu/Index Choice",
            (XtCallbackProc) helpCB,
            (XtPointer) "Help Menu/Index Choice");

    (void) CreatePushbuttonWithHelp(helpmenu, "tutorial",
            (XtCallbackProc) helpCB,
            (XtPointer) "Help Menu/Tutorial Choice",
            (XtCallbackProc) helpCB,
            (XtPointer) "Help Menu/Tutorial Choice");

    /* Call special on_versionCB. */
    (void) CreatePushbuttonWithHelp(helpmenu, "onversion",
            (XtCallbackProc) on_versionCB,
            (XtPointer) parent, /* client_data */
            (XtCallbackProc) helpCB,
            (XtPointer)
                "Help Menu/Product Information Choice");

    /* Create scrolled text for work area. */
    n = 0;
    XtSetArg(args[n], XmNeditMode,
```

```
            XmMULTI_LINE_EDIT); n++;

text = XmCreateScrolledText(mainw,
        "text", args, n);

XtAddCallback(text,
    XmNhelpCallback,
    (XtCallbackProc) helpCB,
    (XtPointer) "Scrolled Text");

/* Add same help to scrolled window parent. */
XtAddCallback(XtParent(text),
    XmNhelpCallback,
    (XtCallbackProc) helpCB,
    (XtPointer) "Scrolled Parent of XmText");

XtManageChild(text);

XmMainWindowSetAreas(mainw,
    menubar,
    (Widget) NULL,    /* command window */
    (Widget) NULL,    /* horiz scroll */
    (Widget) NULL,    /* vert scroll */
    XtParent(text));  /* work area */

XtManageChild(mainw);

/* Create Help dialog and fill in topics. */
HelpDlgCreate(parent,
    (XtCallbackProc) topicCB,
    (XtPointer) NULL,
    (XtCallbackProc) helpCB,
    (XtPointer) "Help Dialog/Help Text",
    (XtPointer) "Help Dialog/Help Topics");

HelpDlgAddTopic("File Menu");
HelpDlgAddTopic("File Menu/New Choice");
HelpDlgAddTopic("File Menu/Open Choice");
HelpDlgAddTopic("File Menu/Save Choice");
HelpDlgAddTopic("File Menu/Save As Choice");
HelpDlgAddTopic("File Menu/Print Choice");
HelpDlgAddTopic("File Menu/Exit Choice");
HelpDlgAddTopic("Help Menu");
HelpDlgAddTopic(
    "Help Menu/Context-Sensitive Help Choice");
HelpDlgAddTopic("Help Menu/Using Help Choice");
HelpDlgAddTopic("Help Menu/Overview Choice");
HelpDlgAddTopic("Help Menu/Keyboard Choice");
HelpDlgAddTopic("Help Menu/Index Choice");
HelpDlgAddTopic("Help Menu/Tutorial Choice");
HelpDlgAddTopic("Help Menu/Product Information Choice");
HelpDlgAddTopic("Help Dialog/Help Text");
HelpDlgAddTopic("Help Dialog/Help Topics");
HelpDlgAddTopic("Menubar");
HelpDlgAddTopic("Scrolled Text");
```

```
        HelpDlgAddTopic("Help Menu/Choice");

        XtRealizeWidget(parent);
        XtAppMainLoop(app_context);
        return 0;

}     /* main */

/* end of file help.c */
```

The *help* program uses the following resource file:

```
! Resource file for Chapter 25
! of Power Programming Motif.
!
*fontList:       lucidasans-12
*background:     lightgrey

*title:      Help Demo

*text.rows:     14
*text.columns:  40

! File menu
*filemenu.labelString: File
*filemenu.mnemonic:    F

*new.labelString:    New
*new.mnemonic:       N

*open.labelString:   Open…
*open.mnemonic:      O

*save.labelString:   Save
*save.mnemonic:      S

*saveas.labelString: Save As…
*saveas.mnemonic:    A

*print.labelString:  Print…
*print.mnemonic:     P

*exit.labelString:   Exit
*exit.mnemonic:      x

! Help menu
*helpmenu.labelString: Help
*helpmenu.mnemonic:    H

*context.labelString: Context-Sensitive Help…
*context.mnemonic:    C

*onhelp.labelString: Using Help…
*onhelp.mnemonic:    H
```

```
*helpoverview.labelString: Overview…
*helpoverview.mnemonic:    O

*onkeyboard.labelString: Keyboard…
*onkeyboard.mnemonic:    K

*index.labelString:   Index…
*index.mnemonic:      I

*tutorial.labelString: Tutorial…
*tutorial.mnemonic:    T

*onversion.labelString: Product Information…
*onversion.mnemonic:    P

! On Version Dialog
*on_version_dialog.dialogTitle: Product Information
*on_version_dialog.messageString: \
Help Demo \n\
Version 1.0\n\n\
Pretend we have an animated dog barking.\n\n\
Copyright 1993, MIS: Press,\n\
All rights reserved.

! Help Dialog
*help_dialog.title:    Help Dialog
*help_text.rows:       10
*help_text.columns:    40

*help_topic.visibleItems: 10

!*text_label.labelString:  Help Text
!*topic_label.labelString: Help Topics
*dismiss.labelString:     Dismiss
! end of resource file
```

Name this file **Ppm** and store it in your home directory.

When you run this program, you'll see a main application window like the one shown in Figure 25.2.

Try pressing **F1** to get help. You probably also want to try the context-sensitive help, which is easier to understand in use than it is to describe.

If you ask for product-information help, you'll see the message-box dialog from **version.c**, as shown in Figure 25.3.

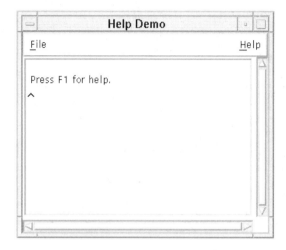

Figure 25.2   *The Help program.*

Figure 25.3   *The product-information dialog.*

COSE Help

The Common Open Software Environment, which we've mentioned frequently in this book, plans to provide a number of features to aid online help. If you run your applications only on COSE systems, then you should be able to use these help widgets when available.

Unfortunately, some vendors, notably Silicon Graphics, have so far remained at arm's length from the COSE efforts. If you choose to take advantage of any of the COSE widgets, you may well have a lot of work to do to port your code to other, non-COSE platforms.

SUMMARY

Help forms one of the most neglected features for Motif applications. Even so, users expect any application to provide online help. The Motif style guide, as well, encourages online help with the Help menu. Once users see windows and pull-down menus, their expectations on user-friendliness go way up. Adding a good online help system is an effective way to improve productivity with the software you create.

However, Motif doesn't make online help a very simple proposition, so it's up to you to do the dirty work yourself. This chapter guided you through that process.

MOTIF FUNCTIONS AND MACROS INTRODUCED IN THIS CHAPTER

```
XmTrackingEvent
XmTrackingLocate
```

X TOOLKIT INTRINSICS FUNCTIONS AND MACROS INTRODUCED IN THIS CHAPTER

```
XtCallCallbacks
```

X LIBRARY FUNCTIONS AND MACROS INTRODUCED IN THIS CHAPTER

```
XCreateFontCursor
XFreeCursor
```

SECTION 6

Cutting-Edge Motif

Programming in Motif is an ever-changing landscape, and it's important that you be aware of the trends coming down the pike, so you can better plan for them in the present. This section covers such trends, as well as other important topics that tend to be ignored in other Motif texts.

We begin the section in Chapter 26 with a discussion of Motif optimization, which tends to somewhat of a limited topic. Why? Because much of Motif simply can't be optimized–the underlying operating system controls a certain portion of the action, as well as the Xt Intrinsics. Still, there are things to look at to speed up your Motif applications somewhat.

Chapter 27 cover an extremely important topic: Internationalization of Motif clients. The world is entering the age of a global economy, and even if your applications aren't planned for foreign consumption at the moment, there's the pretty good chance they will be in the future. With Motif, it's easier to plan for internationalization at the present than retrofitting existing code down the road.

Chapter 28 discussing C++ and its future within Motif. There will be a few things to watch for when migrating to C++ in the future–and we all know that is inevitable–so this chapter points the way.

Finally, we end the book with Chapter 29, which covers how to move Open Look applications to Motif. This isn't as daunting a subject as you might think–after all, both Motif and Open Look are based on the Xt Intrinsics, so a certain amount of core functionality remains in common–but there are certainly a number of things to watch for when migrating code. With the emergence of COSE and Sun's announcement that OLIT is a dead-end product, we think that many Open Look programmers will benefit greatly from this chapter.

CHAPTER 26

Optimizing Motif

This chapter covers:

- Performance bottlenecks in Motif applications
- Whether to use gadgets or widgets
- Whether to use the `XmTextField` or `XmText` widget
- Warnings against stealing cycles
- Tips to improve your application's performance

857

IMPROVING PERFORMANCE OF MOTIF APPLICATIONS

Over the years, we've identified a number of techniques to improve the performance of Motif applications. These are not quantifiable performance enhancements, unfortunately. Not only is performance hard to measure, but the performance of Motif applications also depends a lot on which version of Motif you're using. In addition, since the X Window System allows for applications to run on one machine and display on another, you introduce all sorts of complexities into such an environment, especially if you use X terminals. Networking dynamics are tough to get a handle on and even tougher to improve.

Even so, in this chapter we present our best advice on improving your Motif applications. Before doing a lot of work, you should measure the current performance of your applications with a tool such as *prof* or *gprof*. Then, you should determine the major performance bottlenecks and only then spend a lot of time optimizing. If you don't do this, you'll spend a lot of time gaining only a few compute cycles while the main bottlenecks go unresolved.

SHORTCUT

Some Basic Performance Tips

To achieve maximum performance, you should buy lots of RAM and CPU power, which is the hardware solution to most software problems. This may even be cheaper than trying to optimize your code, depending on how cheaply you can acquire hardware or who is actually footing the bill. Software development is, after all, a very labor-intensive, expensive task.

In your software, though, you can:

■ Get a fast `malloc` library. Motif applications are `malloc` pigs, allocating dynamic memory at the drop of a hat.

■ Upgrade to at least X11 Release 5. Each version of the X server has gotten better and better. The low-level X library and the Xt Intrinsics have also improved with each release.

■ Avoid gadgets.

■ Try to use the dynamic drag-and-drop protocol, not the preregister protocol.

■ Use shared libraries if possible.

■ Manage child widgets together with `XtManageChildren`.

DROPPING THE BALL ON DRAG AND DROP

Many users of Motif's drag and drop (new in Motif 1.2) are dismayed by the lack of performance. In Motif 1.2, drag and drop supports two protocols: preregister and dynamic. The preregister protocol requires that drop site widgets must preregister to be used. A database of this preregister information is stored so that any Motif application can get at the information. The dynamic protocol determines valid drop sites on the fly.

We advise you to use the dynamic protocol. The dynamic protocol simply works better and faster. There's another nice bonus to using the dynamic protocol, as the *Inter-Client Communications Conventions Manual*, or ICCCM, will standardize on the dynamic protocol but not the preregister protocol—at least that's the word as of this writing.

The preregister protocol sports a number of problems. One, it must maintain a drop-site database, which slows down your application and all others that use the preregister protocol. In addition, there are some quirks and bugs that afflict the preregister protocol, including the not-so-nice tendency to draw into the drop site's window. If the drop site uses a different visual than the drag source, you're asking for problems with Motif 1.2. (We hope this is corrected soon.)

To set the protocol, you can set the `dragInitiatorProtocolStyle` and `dragReceiverProtocolStyle` resources on the XmDisplay object. The default is the preregister protocol (`XmDRAG_PREFER_PREREGISTER`). Try setting both resources to `XmDRAG_DYNAMIC`. If you have problems, fall back by just requesting this change by setting both to `XmDRAG_PREFER_DYNAMIC`.

If you don't use drag and drop at all, you can disable the feature by setting the `dragInitiatorProtocolStyle` and `dragReceiverProtocolStyle` resources both to `XmDRAG_NONE`. This means that your applications won't interact with other Motif programs in as friendly a manner—but it will speed things up.

To get the XmDisplay object, call `XmGetXmDisplay`:

```
#include <Xm/Display.h>

Widget XmGetXmDisplay(Display* display)
```

Making a List

If you make heavy use of XmList widgets, you'll note that XmListAddItems is not very efficient. If you face a performance issue with the list, you may want to look into writing your list data into an XmStringTable and setting the items and icomCount resources yourself with XtSetValues or XtVaSetValues.

Be warned that messing with an XmStringTable is not for the faint of heart.

DISPUTES IN PERFORMANCE

In addition to the points listed above, there are a few topics that stir great debate, such as the old gadgets vs. widgets slug fest.

Gadgets vs. Widgets: Widgets Win

Gadgets, or windowless widgets, were developed for Motif 1.0 in an era (circa X11 Release 3) when a window was a very expensive construct. Because of that, the designers of Motif tried to share windows when possible to save on the enormous overhead (in the X server) mandated by windows. Motif applications, by and large, create hundreds of windows (usually one per widget), so the potential savings were looked on as quite valuable.

Since that time, X11 Releases 4 and 5 both dramatically optimized the X server, reducing the window overhead in terms of memory and performance. In more modern systems, gadgets don't provide anywhere near the same improvements as they did in Motif 1.0. Therefore, gadgets are of mixed value.

Gadgets save memory in the X server at the expense of greater computing resources needed to track MotionNotify events. The MotionNotify events come from the fact that the most commonly used gadgets, pushbuttons, need to react when the mouse pointer enters the widget. If the widget has an underlying window, the toolkit can ask for EnterNotify and

`LeaveNotify` events. Gadgets, being windowless, must track the slightest motion of the mouse by using `MotionNotify` events. Since there are a lot less `EnterNotify` and `LeaveNotify` events than `MotionNotify` events, gadgets incur a penalty on performance.

In addition to the greater number of events that gadgets or their parents must track, in some versions of Motif gadgets use more memory in your application than do widgets.

Gadgets are useful if your X server is memory challenged, but you have a lot of performance in the machine your applications compute on. For example, if you have an X terminal with a low amount of memory (under 8MB of RAM), then you may want to off-load some memory from the X server into your application, which runs on another machine.

But, in general, the current wisdom is to avoid gadgets.

XmTextField vs. XmText: XmText Wins

There's a similar debate between the `XmTextField` and the `XmText` widgets. The `XmTextField` was designed to be a lightweight, single-line text-editing widget that would save on the `XmText` widget's overhead for managing multiple lines of text.

Unfortunately, this simply isn't so. At least through Motif 1.1, the `XmText` widget worked better, had fewer problems, and was more efficient than the `XmTextField`.

Chances are you're already using a scrolled `XmText` widget anyway, so you're already linking in Motif's `XmText` code. You might as well keep on using the `XmText` instead of linking in the `XmTextField` code as well. Also, the duplicated functions for everything that `XmText` provides, such as `XmTextGetString` and `XmTextFieldGetString`, increases your code's size and complexity.

TIPS TO IMPROVE PERFORMANCE

Our final section on optimization lists a number of tips you can use to take an active stance toward improving performance.

Allocating Memory

Motif applications are `malloc` pigs, allocating dynamic memory at the drop of a hat. Get a fast `malloc` library.

Motif applications allocate about 50K of RAM at startup and then every single widget creation also allocates more RAM. In addition, just about every `XmString` function allocates memory under the hood, especially any function that creates an `XmString`. Many calls to `XtSetValues` or `XtGetValues` also allocate dynamic memory, especially anything to do with text strings.

To allocate memory, Motif officially uses `XtMalloc`, which normally just sits on top of the normal C library `malloc`. If your system provides a faster `malloc` library, sometimes named **libXmalloc.a**, then try that library. Always verify that these libraries, advertised as being faster, really do increase performance for your applications, though.

Use Shared Libraries Where Possible

You're probably running a number of X applications at a time. Most users run a window manager, at least two terminal emulators (which includes programs such as *xterm*, *winterm*, *hpterm*, or *aixterm*), a clock program, and any other applications you need. All these programs use the low-level X library. Most also use the Xt Intrinsics. Therefore, if you can get shared versions of **libX11.a** and **libXt.a**, use them.

Motif applications use these libraries as well as the Motif library, **libXm.a**. With the advent of COSE and the corresponding death of Open Look, you'll be running a lot more Motif applications, so it would help to use a shared library.

On a side note, if you use a Sun workstation, you're probably running a lot of XView and OLIT programs, because it will take some time for users to migrate to COSE/Motif versions of their Open Look software. The XView library, in particular, isn't known for its slender applications. Luckily, Sun's SunOS and Solaris operating systems both provide shared versions of these and most other X libraries. Look for shared versions of **libxview.a**, **libolgx.a**, and **libXol.a**.

Managing Multiple Widgets at Once

Ironically, with Motif 1.2, managing widgets—always expensive in terms of performance—became even more expensive. Because of this, you should be careful when you manage child widgets.

A good tip is to try to set as many resource values as possible on the widget and manage only when complete. This is because some resource values are more expensive to set once managed.

If you need to manage a number of widgets at once, `XtManageChildren` is much more efficient than multiple calls to `XtManageChild`. `XtManageChildren` takes the following parameters:

```
void XtManageChildren(WidgetList children,
    Cardinal number_children)
```

The *children* are an array of widgets:

```
typedef Widget *WidgetList;
```

You gain performance with `XtManageChildren` if all the widgets in the children array all descend from the same managed and realized parent widget. You don't gain much if you call `XtManageChildren` on an array of widgets whose parent widgets are unrealized or unmanaged.

There's also an `XtUnmanageChildren`:

```
void XtUnmanageChildren(WidgetList children,
    Cardinal number_children)
```

`XtUnmanageChildren` is more efficient than multiple calls to `XtUnmanageChild`.

Creating Widgets

The main technique to improving the creation time for widgets is to set as many resources as possible when creating, rather than after the widget is managed. This is generally much more efficient, especially for resources that impact the widget's size. For example, the `labelString` resource of an `XmLabel` widget determines its initial size—at least the size it asks its parent for. If you call `XtSetValues` to set the size after managing the label widget, this will be more expensive than passing the `labelString` resource to `XmCreateLabel` or `XtVaCreateManagedWidget`.

If you create as many widgets as possible before realizing the widget hierarchy, you then can speed things up a lot. (Realizing a widget creates the window in the X server.) After the top-level parent is realized with `XtRealizeWidget`, all child widgets are normally realized when they are managed. Because of this quirk, if you can delay realizing the top-level shell widget, you should get greater performance.

Once a widget is realized, any size changes (called *geometry negotiation* in Xt terminology) require network requests to the X server to change the size of the window. Before realizing, all such geometry negotiation can take place solely within your application.

Buy RAM

X applications eat RAM, more RAM than you'd ever believe. If you develop software, your workstation should have at least 32MB of RAM.

Also, don't use a fancy color image file for a screen background. If you have an 8-bit image that is the size of a 1280x1024 pixel screen, then the amount of RAM used just for the image is *at least* 1280x1024x8, or 10,485,760 bytes. (Remember that there will always be some image overhead).

Get a Faster CPU

No, we're not paid anything by the workstation vendors that want your upgrade money—not yet, anyway. But there is a hardware solution to many software problems. The X Window System and Motif are very demanding on system performance. The faster the machine you have, the better things will be.

Steal CPU Cycles from Someone Else

If your neighbor got the upgrade and you didn't, remember that X allows you to run the applications on your neighbor's machine, stealing CPU cycles, and then display the applications at your desk on your machine. You can offload a lot of tasks this way.

If you get into trouble doing this, you can trot out a number of excuses, such as "I was testing networking dynamics and how they impact performance for our software" or "Your workstation is running a different version of the low-level X library, so I need to ensure that our applications don't have any problems on that platform." If these excuses don't work, don't blame us—they worked for us.

Destroying Widgets

Don't destroy widgets. There are a lot of memory leaks in both Motif and the Xt Intrinsics. X11 Release 5 solves many of these, but not all. Avoid calling XtDestoyWidget:

```
void XtDestoyWidget(Widget widget)
```

XtDestoyWidget destroys a widget in a two-step process. It becomes an issue if you call XtDestoyWidget in a callback routine. In that case, XtDestoyWidget just marks the widget for destruction. The widget will not be really destroyed until you return control to the main event loop.

Speeding Application Startup

Motif programs tend to take a long time to start up. Because of this, you may want to do a number of things to speed the startup phase, even if it means deferring processing until later.

Skip Those Environment Variables

If you use the X resource environment variables, such as XUSERFILE-SEARCHPATH or XFILESEARCHPATH (described in Chapter 3), you're dramatically increasing the number of disk directories that Xt looks in for X resource files. Xt already looks in a number of locations on disk, so that each extra directory involves another file access, in the worst case. Avoid setting these environment variables if possible.

No one really understands these environment variables, anyway.

Don't Match the Resource Class Name to the Executable Name

The class name you pass to XtAppInitialize or XtVaAppInitialize, such as "Ppm" in this book, is used to look up class resource files. For example, with a class name of "Ppm", Xt will look for a file named **Ppm** (located in your home directory or **/usr/lib/X11/app-defaults.**).

The key problem is if you use a class name that is the same as you program's executable name. In this case, if your executable is in the same X resource path, Xt will merrily read in your executable file and search it for X resources. (This often happens if you place the X resource file in the same directory as the executable program and then use an X environment variable to point at the directory.)

Since most Motif executables are at least 1 or 2MB in size, this can dramatically increase the time it takes to start up the application. For example, a popular freeware calendar program named *plan*, passes "plan" to XtAppInitialize as the class name—the same name as the executable.

Using Timers or Work Procedures to Create Widgets

Most Motif programs go through a boring, if similar, sequence: Call XtAppInitialize or XtVaAppInitialize and then start creating widgets. When all the widgets are created, call XtRealizeWidget. The problem with this method is that most real applications have hundreds of widgets. Creating this many widgets at once results in a noticeable slowdown.

We advise creating a smaller set of widgets up front and then using a timer (set up with XtAppAddTimeOut) or a background work procedure (set up with XtAppAddWorkProc) to create more widgets. In each callback, create one or two widgets.

The idea is to use idle time after the application starts up to gradually create the widgets. Since the task is spread out, it no doubt takes more time to execute. But the key is that the user may never notice this. The user should see the application start up faster and then may never notice the slight degradation due to the background processing. See Chapter 13 for more on timers and background work procedures.

If you plan your start-up phase correctly, you can optimize this. For example, an application that deals with files is most likely to need the Open file dialog long before it needs a Save As dialog, because users normally load in a file first before saving it under a different name. Whether you create widgets all at once or gradually later on (or on demand, as some applications do), having a strategy that determines the best order can help speed things up.

Use Fonts Sparingly

Fonts use a lot of resources in the X server. In addition, the X server typically loads fonts from files on disk (disk operations are usually expensive and slower compared to memory accesses) or from a font server (new in X11 Release 5). In either case, each additional font your application uses involves more overhead on the part of the X server and a greater time to start up your application.

Use fonts sparingly. Use what you need, but don't go wild with different type sizes, styles, and fonts.

SUMMARY

There are many ways to enhance Motif performance, and they are listed in this chapter.

X TOOLKIT INTRINSICS FUNCTIONS AND MACROS INTRODUCED IN THIS CHAPTER

```
XtDestoyWidget
XtManageChildren
XtUnmanageChildren
```

CHAPTER 27

Writing International Applications

This chapter covers:

- An overview of internationalization
- Terminology
- ANSI C locales
- Support for internationalization in X11 Release 5
- Coding your Motif applications for internationalization
- Manipulating multibyte- and wide-character data
- Supporting Asian languages in Motif programs
- Input methods
- Internationalization faux pas

INTERNATIONALIZATION OVERVIEW

The purpose of internationalization is to have one application that can run any place in the world and yet interact with the user in the user's native language. That is, if you run your application in Korea, it shows all text messages in Korean and accepts Korean input. If you run your application in Sweden, it shows all text messages in Swedish and accepts Swedish input.

The major goal of internationalization is not changing the binary application to run in a different country. The same executable program reconfigures itself under different languages, called *locales*. To do this, you must separate out all text messages (and most likely bitmaps as well). For this, you need a separate set of *localizations* for each target market. In most cases, the separate localization data is stored in a file or files external to your programs. For instance, there would be a set of localization files supporting the German language, a set of localization files supporting the Swedish language, and so on.

Since most new UNIX software uses an X Window front end for the user interface, the key to developing internationalized applications is developing internationalized X applications. This task, always difficult, becomes a lot easier with facilities added in X11 Release 5 and Motif 1.2.

N O T E
You'll need at least X11 Release 5 or higher and Motif 1.2 or higher to take advantage of the programs in this chapter. In addition to the versions of X and Motif, you'll also need an operating system that supports different locales. For Asian languages, you'll need an input method server, as well, such as xwnmo. As of this writing, few operating systems support Asian locales.

This chapter briefly introduces the arcane art of internationalizing your software and covers how to write Motif programs to support a number of languages.

SHORTCUT

Turning Japanese

To enable your applications for international text processing, you should call `XtSetLanguageProc` before calling `XtAppInitialize` or `XtVaAppInitialize`:

```
#if XtSpecificationRelease > 4

    /* Set up locale. */
    XtSetLanguageProc(NULL, NULL, NULL);

#endif /* X11R5 or higher. */

    parent = XtVaAppInitialize(&app_context,
            "Ppm",
            (XrmOptionDescList) NULL,
            0,
            &argc, argv,
            (String*) NULL,
            XmNallowResize, True,
            NULL);
```

`XtSetLanguageProc` officially takes the following parameters:

```
XtLanguageProc XtSetLanguageProc(
    XtAppContext app_context,
    XtLanguageProc language_proc,
    XtPointer client_data)
```

You typically pass `NULL` for all three parameters.

That's about all to internationalizing your Motif applications, ignoring for the moment the massive amount of work necessary to localize your applications.

WHY INTERNATIONALIZE?

The global—that is, countries apart from the United States—market is one of the fastest-growing markets for computer software. This alone should be a good incentive to internationalize your applications. In addition, users worldwide are beginning to expect that software they buy support their local languages. Users in Japan want Japanese versions of their software. This then becomes yet another hurdle you must jump over to successfully market your wares.

Few companies in this day and age can concentrate on the market in just one country. Even if it's not a hot issue today, you'll eventually need to support other languages in your software. To do this, it's best to design for internationalization right away. Trying to backfit internationalization on a noninternationalized program is not easy and usually much harder than just doing it right the first time.

Terminology

Before we delve too deeply into internationalization arcana, we should cover some of the terminology. Like many areas of computer science, internationalization seems to have its own language.

Locale

A *locale* encapsulates the character set, language, language dialect, currency information, and formatting preferences of a given group. Locales include English as used in the United States, English as used in the United Kingdom, French as used in Canada, French as used in Switzerland, and French as used in France. As you can tell, the locale is more than just the country. Canada, for instance, has two official languages: English and French. In Europe, multiculturalism is the norm: Any software producer wanting to sell into Switzerland must support French, German, and English, at the very least.

The locale is actually made up of three parts:

■ the language, such as French

■ the country, such as Canada

■ the character encoding, such as Latin-1 (ISO 8859-1)

The locale includes currency symbols (such as the *$* or *DM*, which stands for Deutsch Mark), the decimal point (the period [.] in the United States, but the comma [,] in much of Western Europe), and text-collation orders (A comes before B and so on).

Character Set

A *character set* is a set of all the characters, alphabetic and otherwise, necessary to construct words and sentences in a given language. For example,

ASCII, the American Standard Code for Information Interchange, is a 7-bit character set in use in the United States. Since ASCII is a 7-bit character set, it has only 128 code points.

ISO 8859-1, also called Latin-1, is an 8-bit character set that represents most Western European languages (except Greek), including French, German, and English. ISO 8859-1 maintains compatibility with ASCII for the first 128 code points; the code points above 128 represent national characters, such as an umlaut in German (e.g., *ü*). The separation of the characters means that ISO 8859-1 data doesn't sort easily.

The X Window System makes extensive use of ISO 8859-1, and most X fonts support this character set.

Internationalization

Internationalization is the process of making your software operable under a number of different locales. Your programs should have no dependency on a given language, custom, time, date and money formats, and character encoding. This usually involves three main steps:

1. Separate out all locale-specific information from your program. This includes all text messages your program displays. Often these messages are then stored in message catalogs or X resource files.

2. Ensure that your program doesn't depend on a given locale. You'd be surprised at how many assumptions your code makes about the current locale.

3. Enable your program to dynamically check the locale and reconfigure itself to run under the current locale.

Based on these steps, the process of internationalizing is a lot like that of making your code portable between machine architectures, only harder.

Internationalization is often abbreviated to *I18N*, as there are 18 letters between the *I* and the *N* in Internationalization.

Localization

Once you've internationalized your software, you need to *localize* it for a specific locale. For example, localizing for Japanese involves translating all text messages to Japanese, handling Japanese input, and ensuring that all the code is internationalized.

Localization includes the process of translating all text messages into another language, observing local customs in software, and making sure none of the bitmaps are designed to offend the local population.

If you truly separate out all locale-specific information from your software, you can localize without modifying the application's binary executable. Usually this process isn't that neat, especially when supporting Asian languages. After you do it the first time, though, it becomes much easier.

Some computer geeks abbreviate localization as *L10N*.

Message Catalog

A *message catalog* is a compiled database of text messages that your application accesses at runtime. The messages for each language reside in separate message catalogs. The ideal is that message catalogs should hold all locale-specific text.

Unfortunately, there are two main de facto standards for message catalogs: XPG and MNLS.

XPG stands for the X/Open Portability Guide, a document published by X/Open. XPG message catalogs use functions like `catopen` and `catgets`.

MNLS stands for UNIX System Laboratories' Multi-National Language Support and is common in UNIX System V Release 4. MNLS uses routines like `gettxt` or `pfmt`.

Motif programs may also use X resource files instead of message catalogs for storing text messages.

Input Method

An *input method* is a means—usually software—to convert the user's keyboard input into text in the local language. Those of us reading this in the United States probably take input methods for granted. Most Asian languages like Chinese support thousands of characters. Since making a keyboard with this many keys is impractical, users in China take advantage of an input method to convert their keystrokes into Chinese. Usually, the user has to type a number of keystrokes to equal one character in the language. Sometimes, users make use of modifier keys, like a compose key. Other times, the input method is phonetically based.

Multibyte and Wide Characters

Asian text requires many more data points than the 256 allowed in one-byte character sets like Latin-1. Because of this, Asian characters usually require more than a single byte per character. You must dissuade yourself of the notion that a logical "character" in a language is stored in an 8-bit `char` data type. ANSI/ISO C doesn't require that a `char` be 8 bits, but it almost always is, and a host of applications depend on this behavior.

NOTE

One of the major—false—assumptions in noninternationalized code is that one byte equals one logical character in the language. This is also the toughest assumption to correct.

There are two main methods for creating characters that take up more than one byte each. *Wide characters* keep the idea that each character is a single size. Wide characters require more than one byte per character, however, so most wide-character encodings use two or four bytes per character (a short or long int for each character). ISO-10646 and the 16-bit Unicode subset are the two most popular wide-character formats.

Multibyte characters are variable length. That is, one logical character in a multibyte-character encoding may have one, two, three, or up to six bytes, whatever is necessary and most efficient. Because of this, your code cannot easily iterate through a text string, because you cannot index into a given position and assume it starts a new character. This is the main disadvantage of multibyte-character encodings.

The main advantage for multibyte-character encodings is that you can still use `char*` pointers for text strings. In addition, the ANSI C library provides much more support for multibyte-character encodings than it does for wide characters. For example, the `printf` function supports multibyte characters if your locale is set up properly.

Another advantage is that wide-character encodings force all characters to a larger size, whether they need it or not. English text files in a wide encoding usually double or quadruple in size, while a multibyte-character encoding of the same data may actually result in a file the same size as an equivalent ASCII file. EUC, JIS, and Shift-JIS are popular multibyte-character encodings.

Currently most of the UNIX industry uses multibyte-character encodings, such as EUC or JIS for Asian languages, while Microsoft Windows NT uses Unicode wide characters. The future points to Unicode, but widespread adoption of Unicode is still a few years away.

If you use ANSI/ISO C, you can determine the maximum number of bytes in a logical multibyte character in the current locale with MB_CUR_MAX, defined in the include file <stdlib.h>.

LOCALES AND STANDARD C

The locale encapsulates the character set, language, dialect, and formatting preferences for a given group. Your application is responsible for setting the locale to the proper value. Once the standard C library changes its behavior based on the current locale. For example, when formatting numbers, the decimal point may change to a comma (,) instead of the period (.).

For locales, ANSI C recognizes a number of categories, shown in Table 27.1.

Table 27.1   Locale categories.

Category	Meaning
LC_ALL	All categories
LC_COLLATE	Collation (sorting) with strcoll and strxfrm.
LC_CTYPE	Character classification: islower, and multibyte characters
LC_MONETARY	Currency symbol and monetary formatting information returned by localeconv
LC_NUMERIC	Decimal-point character, numeric formatting
LC_TIME	Time and date formatting with ascftime, cftime, getdate, and strftime

UNIX System V Release 4 and other versions of UNIX also add the LC_MESSAGES category, used with message catalogs.

If you're particularly cruel, you could set each category of the locale to something different. For example, you may want to have all times and dates formatted in Chinese, money in Italian, and sort in the order of French Canadian. For most programs, though, you'll simply use LC_ALL when you set the locale.

Setting the Locale

Set the locale with the ANSI C function setlocale:

```
#include <locale.h>
char* setlocale (int category,
        const char* locale)
```

The default locale is the "C" locale, named for ANSI C, but really meaning U.S. English. You need to pass the *category*, listed in Table 27.1, and the actual value of the *locale*, such as *de* or *ja_JP*. These values are determined by what your operating system supports.

There are also a few special, though commonly used, values listed in Table 27.2.

Table 27.2   *Special setlocale values.*

Locale Value	Meaning
""	(Not NULL) Set to default
NULL	Don't set locale, but return current

Just about every program that calls setlocale calls it as follows:

```
setlocale(LC_ALL, "");
```

This sets up all categories to their defaults. Usually, the LANG environment variable sets the default for all categories, but you can also set other environment variables to specify the values for different categories.

Although they may differ on some systems, these environment variables are listed in Table 27.3.

Table 27.3 *Locale category environment variables.*

Category	Environment Variable
LC_COLLATE	LC_COLLATE
LC_CTYPE	LC_CTYPE
LC_MESSAGES	LC_MESSAGES
LC_MONETARY	LC_MONETARY
LC_NUMERIC	LC_NUMERIC
LC_TIME	LC_TIME

LC_MESSAGES is not standardized.

N O T E

In all cases, if the environment variable listed above isn't set, setlocale uses the LANG environment variable.

The assumption is that a user in Denmark has the system set up in the proper locale for Denmark, whatever the name is (usually "da," but that's beside the point). The goal is for your application to not need to know or care what the locale setting is.

On return, setlocale returns the new locale. If it fails, the routine returns NULL.

If you pass NULL for the *locale*, setlocale returns the current locale but does not set anything. This is how you query the locale.

On many systems, setlocale and the C library use a set of locale databases, normally stored in **/usr/lib/locale/locale-name**, such as **/usr/lib/locale/C** and **/usr/lib/locale/de**.

N O T E

On some systems, this information may be located under **/usr/lib/nls**. Consult your system documentation for more information.

Testing Locales

You can test `setlocale` with the short program given below. When you run the program below, you'll see a number printed out:

```
#include <stdio.h>
#include <locale.h>

int main(int argc, char** argv)

{
    setlocale(LC_ALL, "");

    printf("%f\n", 1234567.890);
}
```

In the default "C" locale, you'll see output like the following:

```
1234567.890000
```

We can change the locale and try the program again. The following command sets the LANG environment variable to German:

```
setenv LANG de
```

N O T E

Check your system documentation for a list of supported locales.

If you set your LANG environment variable to "de" (for Deutch—German to the rest of us), you'll see output like the following:

```
1234567,890000
```

The LANG Environment Variable and Locale Names

Usually you set the LANG environment variable to the same value you pass to `setlocale`. Most versions of UNIX (Hewlett-Packard is a glaring exception) use the following format:

```
language[_territory[.codeset][@modifier]
```

The *language*, for example, may be *fr* for French or *de* for German. The *territory* identifies places where the language may be used but is used differently, such as in the collating order. For example, fr_CA identifies French in Canada.

The *codeset* is mainly important in Asian countries where you have a number of codesets to choose from, although your system will generally support only one codeset per language. For example, ja_JP.EUC identifies Japanese in Japan using the EUC (Extended UNIX Code) codeset.

The *modifier* is also mostly used with Asian languages. A common use for the modifier is to specify the X Window input method. For example, a common input method is called *Xsi*, and the modifiers to specify this are @im=_XWMNO, which could make a full locale name of:

    ja_JP.EUC@im=_XWMNO

The modifiers are not standardized.

Some common locale names appear in Table 27.4.

Table 27.4 *Some locale names.*

Locale	Meaning
fr_FR	French in France
fr_CA	French in Canada
en_AU	English in Australia
en_US	English in the United States
C	Default (English) ANSI C locale
ja_JP.EUC	Japanese in Japan with EUC encoding
ja_JP.ujis	Japanese in Japan with UJIS encoding
ko_KR	Korean in Korea
zh_CN	Chinese
zh_TW	Chinese (Traditional)

N O T E

Hewlett-Packard uses the LANG environment variable differently than most other systems. On an HP system, you set LANG to *german* instead of *de* (short for Deutsch). Other HP values include *dutch* and *italian*.

Effects of Locales on C Functions

Once you set the locale, a number of C library functions, like `printf` and `strcoll`, act differently. The `printf` family (`fprintf`, `sprintf`, etc.), for example, will use the current locale for printing the decimal point for numeric values.

If you run in a multibyte-character locale, you can still use `printf` and the like, because multibyte-character data still uses `char*` pointers to represent text strings. Remember that the text is *not* formatted the same, though, and you'll need to use special functions to iterate through a multibyte-character text string (see "Manipulating International Text," below).

N O T E With international applications, you should use `strcoll` to collate strings in place of `strcmp`. The locale impacts `strcoll` but not `strcmp`, so `strcmp` always uses the default US ASCII ordering.

You can find out many of the current locale settings, such as the decimal point, by calling `localeconv`:

```
#include <locale.h>

struct lconv* localeconv (void)
```

When you call `localeconv`, you get back a pointer to an `lconv` structure, which you should treat as a read-only data structure. This structure has the following elements:

```
struct lconv  {
    char* decimal_point;
    char* thousands_sep;
    char* grouping;
    char* int_curr_symbol;
    char* currency_symbol;
    char* mon_decimal_point;
    char* mon_thousands_sep;
    char* mon_grouping;
    char* positive_sign;
    char* negative_sign;
    char int_frac_digits;
    char frac_digits;
    char p_cs_precedes;
    char p_sep_by_space;
    char n_cs_precedes;
```

```
    char n_sep_by_space;
    char p_sign_posn;
    char n_sign_posn;
};
```

The *decimal_point* is the decimal point string for nonmonetary values. The *thousands_sep* is also used for nonmonetary values to separate groups of digits, usually thousands. Many of these values are character strings and may hold more than one character.

FORMATTING CURRENCY

For currency, the *int_curr_symbol* is the international currency symbol, which should start with the three letters defined by ISO-4217, such as *USD* for United States Dollars. The *currency_symbol* is the local currency symbol, such as *$*. The *mon_decimal_point* is the decimal point used to format money. The *mon_thousands_sep* separates groups of digits in money values.

The *mon_grouping* holds a set of numbers. Each number shows the grouping used for thousands in monetary values.

The *frac_digits* hold the number of fractional digits to display for money, such as 2 for the United States (cents). The *int_frac_digits* applies to internationally formatted money.

Formatting Positive Monetary Values

The *positive_sign* holds a sign, if any, that is used for positive monetary values. In the United States, there is no such sign.

The *p_cs_precedes* is set to 1 if the *currency_symbol* precedes the money value, or 0 if the *currency_symbol* follows the money value. The *p_sep_by_space* is set to 1 if the *currency_symbol* has a space to separate it from the monetary value; 0 if there is no space. Both of these apply for positive values.

The *p_sign_posn field* tells where to position the *positive_sign* for non-negative money values. The field is explained in Table 27.5.

Table 27.5   *The p_sign_posn field.*

Value	Meaning
0	Parentheses surround the quantity and `currency_symbol`
I	The sign string precedes the quantity and `currency_symbol`
2	The sign string succeeds the quantity and `currency_symbol`
3	The sign string immediately precedes the `currency_symbol`
4	The sign string immediately succeeds the `currency_symbol`

Formatting Negative Monetary Values

The *negative_sign* provides a sign to use if negative monetary values require one, such as "*-*" in the United States.

The *n_cs_precedes* is set to 1 if the *currency_symbol* precedes the money value or 0 if the *currency_symbol* follows the money value.

The *n_sep_by_space* is set to 1 if the *currency_symbol* has a space to separate it from the monetary value; 0 if there is no space, for negative values.

The *n_sign_posn* field tells where to position the *negative_sign* for nonnegative money values and uses the same codes as shown in Table 27.5.

Table 27.6 shows some of the `lconv` values for various countries from the ANSI C standard.

Table 27.6   *Locale information for various countries.*

lconv field	Italy	Netherlands	Norway	Switzerland
`int_curr_symbol`	"ITL."	"NLG "	"NOK "	"CHF "
`currency_symbol`	"L."	"F"	"kr"	"SFrs."
`mon_decimal_point`	""	","	","	"."
`mon_thousands_sep`	"."	"."	"."	","
`mon_grouping`	"\3"	"\3"	"\3"	"\3"

continued

positive_sign	""	""	""	""
negative_sign	"-"	"-"	"-"	"C"
int_frac_digits	0	2	2	2
frac_digits	0	2	2	2
p_cs_precedes	1	1	1	1
p_sep_by_space	0	1	0	0
n_cs_precedes	1	1	1	1
n_sep_by_space	0	1	0	0
p_sign_posn	1	1	1	1
n_sign_posn	1	4	2	2

XII RELEASE 5 AND INTERNATIONALIZATION

X11 R5 adds a lot of support for international applications, including:

- Support for ANSI C locales
- Support for wide and multibyte characters
- Input methods that allow for Asian text input

X11R5 does not support vertical text or do much of anything for right-to-left text, which is required for Arabic and Hebrew.

Although imperfect, you can go a long ways toward worldwide software with X11R5 and Motif 1.2. One of the major new components in X11 Release 5 is the concept of an input method.

Input Methods

An input method converts the user's keyboard input into text in the local language. Users in Japan, for example, usually input text phonetically. X11R5 adds support for input-method software. You run the input method server, such as xwmno, and then tell your program to connect up to this server. This is where the locale modifiers come in.

With X11R5, though, there's a major problem in that there's no standards for input methods. X11R6 should standardize on this. Until then, your applications will most likely get compiled for one and only one input method, so you must ensure that your users run the same input method software. Since there are so few methods available, this often isn't a big deal.

Internationalization Resources

You can set the `xnlLanguage` resource to specify a given language, much as you can with the `LANG` environment variable. You can also set the `xnlLanguage` resource with the `-xlnLanguage` command-line parameter.

In most cases, you should use the current locale rather than setting the `xnlLanguage` resource.

Location of International Resource Files

We covered the location of X resource files in Chapter 3. Basically, the locale is used as a directory name. For example, if you place your class resource file in your home directory, then you place the German class resource file in a subdirectory named **de**. This should be a subdirectory of your home directory.

In the case of the example programs in this book, we use a class name of `Ppm` and therefore name our class resource files **Ppm**. By default, you place the resource file in your home directory, say **/u/erc/Ppm**. The German class resource file would then go into **/u/erc/de/Ppm** (assuming the locale is **de**). In both cases, the resource file, **Ppm**, has the same name, just a different location.

Xt looks for the proper resource file for the given locale. Calling `XtSetLanguageProc` with three `NULL` parameters will set your locale.

This feature of the X toolkit then makes it easy to store all your text messages inside X resource files. You can create a French resource file with all the French messages, a Swahili resource file with all the Swahili messages, and an Albanian resource file with all the Albanian messages.

If the locale-specific resource file can't be found, Xt defaults to the original resource file (**/u/erc/Ppm** in our example).

Coding Toolkit Applications for Internationalization

The basic step you need to make in your code to enable Xt's internationalization features is to add in one call before calling XtAppInitialize. You
need to call XtSetLanguageProc first:

```
#if XtSpecificationRelease > 4

    /* Set up locale. */
    XtSetLanguageProc(NULL, NULL, NULL);

#endif /* X11R5 or higher. */

    parent = XtVaAppInitialize(&app_context,
            "Ppm",
            (XrmOptionDescList) NULL,
            0,
            &argc, argv,
            (String*) NULL,
            XmNallowResize, True,
            NULL);
```

XtSetLanguageProc takes the following parameters:

```
XtLanguageProc XtSetLanguageProc(XtAppContext  app_context,
    XtLanguageProc language_proc,
    XtPointer client_data)
```

In most cases, you pass NULL, NULL, and NULL for the parameters, which
tells XtSetLanguageProc to use the default language procedure:

```
XtSetLanguageProc(NULL, NULL, NULL);
```

You can set up your own language procedure, which will take the following
parameters:

```
typedef String (*XtLanguageProc)(Display* display,
    String language,
    XtPointer client_data);
```

The language procedure should set up and verify the locale. With ANSI C,
this callback should call setlocale as follows:

```
setlocale(LC_ALL, language);
```

In the default language procedure, any errors from calling setlocale will
be displayed with XtWarning. Next, the default language procedure calls
XSupportsLocale to verify the locale and check that X has support for

this locale. If this locale is not supported, the language procedure again calls XtWarning and resets the locale to "C" with:

```
setlocale(LC_ALL, "C");
```

XSupportsLocale takes no parameters:

```
Bool XSupportsLocale(void)
```

XSupportsLocale returns True if the X environment supports the current locale; it returns False otherwise.

The default language procedure then calls XSetLocaleModifiers with an empty string:

```
if (! XSetLocaleModifiers("")) {
    /* ... */
}
```

XSetLocaleModifiers takes the following parameter:

```
char* XSetLocaleModifiers(char* modifier_list)
```

The *modifier_list* is any extra modifiers that can be used with the locale. Usually you pass NULL. You can also set the XMODIFIERS environment variable to the same values you pass to XSetLocaleModifiers:

```
setenv XMODIFIERS @im=_XWNMO
```

Finally, the default language procedure returns the value of the current locale, which it obtains by calling setlocale yet again, but with a locale of NULL:

```
char* returned_local;
returned_local = setlocale(LC_ALL, NULL);

return returned_local;
```

In X11 Release 5, the default language procedure looks like the following:

```
static String _XtDefaultLanguageProc(
    Display*    display;    /* unused */
    String      language;
    XtPointer   client_data; /* unused */
{
    if (! setlocale(LC_ALL, language))
        XtWarning(
     "locale not supported by C library, locale unchanged");
    if (! XSupportsLocale()) {
```

```
        XtWarning(
          "locale not supported by Xlib, locale set to C");
        setlocale(LC_ALL, "C");
    }
    if (! XSetLocaleModifiers(""))
        XtWarning(
        "X locale modifiers not supported, using default");

    /* re-query in case overwritten */
    return setlocale(LC_ALL, NULL);
}
```

MANIPULATING INTERNATIONAL TEXT

When you start internationalizing, you must treat text differently than the old standby of using `char*` pointers for text where each char (byte) in the text equals one logical character. Instead, you must switch your code to use either multibyte-character data or wide characters.

There are problems with both approaches, and it's generally considered wasteful and slow to convert back and forth inside your programs. For now, multibyte-characters are the norm for UNIX systems, but wide characters, particularly Unicode characters, will be the norm in the future.

In the next sections, we examine some of the issues you must face with both multibyte and wide characters. This material strays from our focus on Motif but is important background for Motif's support for international text.

Working With Multibyte-Character Data

Most applications require some form of text processing. In fact, it's exceedingly rare to see applications that don't do anything with text. This leads us to the real problem with multibyte-character encodings: You lose the one-to-one match between characters and data elements in your array of text. The fifth data element (byte or short int) is no longer necessarily the fifth character.

This has its greatest impact when you need to access a single character. You must go through extra effort because you have to iterate through the text string to track down the character. To do this, you can use the `mblen` function, which returns the number of bytes that forms the next character:

```
#include <stdlib.h>

int mblen(const char* mb_string,
    size_t number_bytes)
```

If *mb_string* is non-NULL, `mblen` returns the number of bytes that forms the next logical character, if that logical character requires no more than *number_bytes* bytes.

Using the information returned by `mblen`, you can then iterate through all the logical characters in a multibyte data string and process each one in turn. Normally, you pass `MB_CUR_MAX` as the number of bytes in an individual character, as the example below shows:

```
char*   mb_string;
int     number_bytes;

number_bytes = mblen(mb_string,
                MB_CUR_MAX);
```

The main disadvantage of multibyte characters is that you cannot easily iterate through the characters in a text string, as you can with traditional 8-bit character strings. This is where wide characters come in.

Working With Wide Characters

Wide characters use single-size characters, only the size is larger than 8 bits. Common sizes include 16 and 32 bits. The up-and-coming Unicode encoding makes all characters 16 bits long. With that size, the Unicode Consortium covers most known modern languages and is working on less commonly used languages (from a computing standpoint), including Burmese, Ethiopic, Khmer, and ancient Egyptian hieroglyphs.

The full-blown international standards that work under ISO-10646 use a 32-bit character size. The scaled back 16-bit Basic Multilingual Plane (BMP), also called UCS2 (for universal character set—two-byte form), uses Unicode as its base. Unicode definitely has the momentum behind it.

The advantages of wide characters are that all characters have the same size and you can easily iterate through all the characters in a text string. The main disadvantages include the facts that you need a whole new set of functions to manipulate wide-character strings and that your text files double in size (assuming a 16-bit wide-character size).

To use wide characters, ANSI/ISO C introduces a new data type, wchar_t. This type is defined to be large enough to hold wide-character text in all encodings supported by your system and is typically 16 or 32 bits long, depending on your system. From a programmer's point of view, though, you're not supposed to worry how large wchar_t really is, although we know in real life that this information is essential. The wchar_t data type is defined in both <stddef.h> and <stdlib.h>.

In your C programs, a wide-character literal is defined with an L prefix, as follows:

```
L'e'
```

A wide-character string also uses an L prefix:

```
L"wide  char string"
```

In addition to mblen, the include file <stdlib.h> also declares a number of other functions that help convert between wide-character and multibyte-character data, such as mbtowc and wctomb.

The mbtowc function converts a multibyte character to a single wide character:

```
#include <stdlib.h>

int mbtowc(wchar_t* wide_char,
    const char* mb_string,
    size_t number_bytes)
```

If *wide_char* is not a NULL pointer, mbtowc determines how many bytes are in the given multibyte character, up to *number_bytes* bytes, and then converts that multibyte character to a single wide character. This seems a lot like what mblen does, only you get a conversion to a wide character as a side effect, if the *wide_char* is not NULL. In fact, the two calls below are equivalent:

```
#include <stdlib.h>

char*    mb_string;
int      number_bytes;

number_bytes = mblen(mb_string,
            MB_CUR_MAX);

number_bytes = mbtowc((wchar_t *)0,
            mb_string, MB_CUR_MAX);
```

Note that mbtowc is not known for speed.

To reverse the process and convert from a wide character to a multibyte character, use `wctomb`:

```
#include <stdlib.h>

int wctomb(char* mb_string,
    wchar_t wide_char)
```

The `wctomb` function converts the given wide character, *wide_char*, to a multibyte character, writing at most MB_CUR_MAX bytes into *mb_string*.

Similar functions `mbstowsc` and `wsctombs` convert multibyte- and wide-character strings.

Motif and Multibyte Characters

For now, Motif and X default to using multibyte characters, but you can use whichever scheme you want, assuming your system provides support for the text encodings and that you have X Window fonts as well for the character set.

Motif's string format, `XmString`, has always supported local language text, at least to a limited degree. This string format is used in all but the `XmText` and `XmTextField` widgets.

The problem so far has been that these text widgets, `XmText` and `XmTextField`, accepted only 8-bit Latin-1 text. Motif 1.2 allows you to store multibyte- and wide-character data in Motif 1.2 text widgets. Even so, the Motif toolkit punts on the issue of character encoding. Basically, if you set up the current locale to support the Shift-JIS multibyte-character encoding, then Motif will work with that, so long as your `fontList` resources are set up properly. This is one of the most confusing aspects to writing international applications. How can you tell what character encodings are supported? From within a program, this is nearly impossible.

With the Motif text widgets, though, when you write a character array into the `value` resource, or use a convenience function like `XmTextReplace`, the toolkit assumes you're writing in text in the current encoding supported by the current locale.

You can also use traditional Latin-1 8-bit text, using the same resources (`value`) and functions you're used to. If you store multibyte character data into a text widget, you'll also use these old functions, such as `XmTextInsert` and `XmTextSetString`.

That's the nice part about using multibyte-character data: You normally don't have to worry much about the data, as the same functions work for reading and writing multibyte-character data to and from text widgets as they do for traditional Latin-1 or ASCII 8-bit text. (Yes, ASCII is a 7-bit standard, but virtually all implementations we've seen use 8-bit characters for ASCII data.)

If you stick with the default multibyte-character encodings, you won't have to change much of your code that uses the XmText and XmTextField widgets.

If you have wide-character data, though, you need to use the new functions that come with Motif 1.2. Most of these function names end with *Wcs*, such as XmTextInsertWcs and XmTextSetStringWcs. These closely mimic the non-wide-character functions.

If you prefer to set a resource instead of calling one of the Motif convenience functions, the wide-character string resource is valueWcs. The default value resource is value, which holds multibyte-character data or traditional Latin-1 text. If you set the valueWcs resource, it overrides the value resource, which may make it more difficult to switch between multibyte- and wide-character encodings.

The value resource uses data of type String, while valueWcs uses data of type wchar_t*.

The Motif XmText and XmTextField widgets support a number of convenience functions for working with wide-character-string data.

XmText Wide-Character Functions

To set wide-character data into an XmText widget, set the valueWcs resource or use the XmTextSetStringWcs convenience function:

```
#include <Xm/Text.h>

void XmTextSetStringWcs(Widget widget,
        wchar_t* wc_text)
```

To retrieve a wide-character string from an XmText widget, use XmTextGetStringWcs:

```
#include <Xm/Text.h>

wchar_t* XmTextGetStringWcs(Widget widget)
```

The XmText widget supports wide-character functions that mimic most old-style character functions. They are listed in Table 27.7.

Table 27.7 *XmText wide-character functions.*

Multibyte	Wide Character
XmTextFindString	XmTextFindStringWcs
XmTextGetSelection	XmTextGetSelectionWcs
XmTextGetString	XmTextGetStringWcs
XmTextGetSubstring	XmTextGetSubstringWcs
XmTextInsert	XmTextInsertWcs
XmTextReplace	XmTextReplaceWcs
XmTextSetString	XmTextSetStringWcs

These functions act like their non-wide-character counterparts, only the wide-character functions take wchar_t* data rather than char* data.

The XmTextField widget also supports a number of wide-character functions, as listed in Table 27.8.

Table 27.8 *XmTextField wide-character functions.*

Multibyte	Wide Character
XmTextFieldGetSelection	XmTextFieldGetSelectionWcs
XmTextFieldGetString	XmTextFieldGetStringWcs
XmTextFieldGetSubstring	XmTextFieldGetSubstringWcs
XmTextFieldInsert	XmTextFieldInsertWcs
XmTextFieldReplace	XmTextFieldReplaceWcs
XmTextFieldSetString	XmTextFieldSetStringWcs

These functions take the same parameters and return the same results as the XmText routines, only these functions work with the XmTextField widget, not XmText.

Wide-Character Data Callbacks

If you use wide-character data in text widgets, you'll also need to pay close attention to the callback functions, especially the modifyVerifyCallback, which is called before text is inserted or deleted into an XmText widget. This callback allows your code to check modifications to the text data and ensure correctness, if you need to do so. We used this callback in Chapter 5 to implement a password-entry program.

Motif 1.2 introduces a new callback, the modifyVerifyCallbackWcs. This callback acts much like the traditional modifyVerifyCallback, but modifyVerifyCallbackWcs passes wide-character data in the callback structure, the new XmTextVerifyCallbackStructWcs:

```
typedef struct {
    int       reason;
    XEvent*   event;
    Boolean   doit;
    long      currInsert, newInsert;
    long      startPos, endPos;
    XmTextBlockWcs text;
} XmTextVerifyCallbackStructWcs, *XmTextVerifyPtrWcs;
```

The XmTextBlockWcs structure then looks like:

```
typedef struct {
    wchar_t* wcsptr;
    int      length;
} XmTextBlockRecWcs, *XmTextBlockWcs;
```

For comparision, the old-style callback structure, XmTextVerifyCallbackStruct, looks like:

```
typedef struct {
    int          reason;
    XEvent*      event;
    Boolean      doit;
    long         currInsert, newInsert;
    long         startPos, endPos;
    XmTextBlock  text;
} XmTextVerifyCallbackStruct, *XmTextVerifyPtr;
```

If you set up callbacks for both modifyVerifyCallback and modifyVerifyCallbackWcs, then the modifyVerifyCallback callbacks are executed first, followed by the modifyVerifyCallbackWcs callbacks. Note that the first set of routines may modify the data before the modifyVerifyCallbackWcs routines get called.

SUPPORTING ASIAN LANGUAGES

The key to supporting Asian languages is getting an operating system that provides the Asian locales and input method software. If you don't have this, you're lost.

Unfortunately, as of this writing, few vendors ship support for Asian locales—at least to customers in the United States. This is starting to change, though.

If you're lucky, your operating system will ship with support for Asian languages. Among them, Japanese is the most commonly supported language. You'll often have to load this up as a special option when you upgrade or install a new operating system version. Be warned that the Japanese support takes up around 40MB of disk space.

Asian Input Methods

To test out your programs under an Asian locale, you need to have both locale support and an input method server. One of the most common input method servers is called `xwnmo`. You need to start this input method on your system (see your system manuals for more information) and then set your locale to an Asian locale, such as `ja_JP.EUC@im=_XWNMO`.

In many cases, you won't even be able to get the `xwnmo` input method started. See your system administrator, who'll probably be as confused as you.

How Input Methods Work

To show how input methods work, we'll present an example with Japanese.

Japanese uses four main alphabets:

- *Kanji*, the ideographic character set based on Chinese. There are roughly 50,000 ideograms in a Kanji codeset, each of which stands for a word, idea, or phrase.

- *Katakana*, a phonetic alphabet with 64 characters, including punctuation. Since Katakana is phonetic, it is closer to Western European languages, like English—in concept, at least. Katakana is often used for presenting foreign words in Japanese.

■ *Hirgana*, an alphabet of phonetic symbols (also called a *syllabary*) used mainly in conjunction with Kanji and in printed media.

■ *Romanji*, what we in the United States would call the English alphabet.

With four alphabets, you can imagine that text processing is not easy in Japan.

There are two common methods for inputting text in Japan. One method uses a form of **Compose** key—in effect a Kanji key (turn on the Kanji shift state to enter Kanji). The other, more popular method uses phonetic input. With this phonetic input, the user enters a syllable in Romanji, using the traditional QWERTY keys on the keyboard. A syllable, such as *ha*, is entered *h a* into the preedit area. The input method software then converts the syllable to the proper Hirgana or Katakana character. Once enough of these characters are entered, the input method software determines the proper Kanji ideogram. In many cases, the software cannot determine the proper Kanji ideogram and so presents a menu or list of choices for the user to select from.

Preedit Areas

The preedit area is a window or set of windows owned by the input method software and presents an area for the user to type in whatever keystrokes are necessary to compose the characters in the target language, such as Chinese or Korean.

There are four main styles of preedit areas:

■ Root window
■ Off the spot
■ Over the spot
■ On the spot

The *root-window* style places the input method window over the root window. This makes the input method look like any other normal X application. It is illustrated in Figure 27.1.

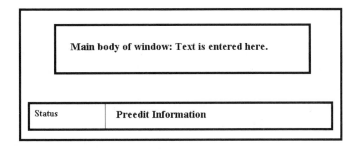

Figure 27.1 *The root-window style.*

In the *off-the-spot* style, the input method window insinuates itself into your application. Often this area goes beneath the main part of your application's window. Because this input method window appears inside your application, your program and the input method need to cooperate on things like screen space, colors, and fonts. Luckily, Motif takes care of most of this for you.

This style is called off-the-spot because the input method window still is offset from where the actual text is displayed. Figure 27.2 illustrates this method.

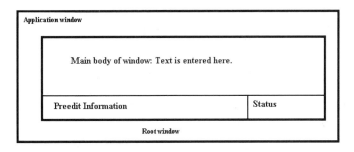

Figure 27.2 *The off-the-spot style.*

With the *over-the-spot* style, the input method displays a very small window over the actual data area where the user is entering text. In many cases, the over-the-spot window has no borders and appears invisible to the user because it looks like there is no special input method window at all. This style requires even more cooperation with the application.

The *on-the-spot* style is even more complex. Instead of doing much of anything, the input method just invokes your application's callbacks to do all the dirty work itself. Your application must perform the editing in place, which tends to get complex when you add in multiple alphabets and the effects of delete keys.

Even though it's the most complex style, a properly implemented on-the-spot style is the most intuitive style. However, the point is moot. Motif, as of version 1.2.1, does not support this style. Later versions may, though.

Choosing the Preferred Style

To register a preference for a preedit style, you can set the `preeditType` resource on a top-level shell. Of course, just to make life a joy, there are no standards for this resource. All the Motif documentation claims the values for this resource are implementation dependent. You can also set the `inputMethod` resource, which should hold the input method modifiers to the locale, such as `@im=_XWNMO`. Again, this is implementation dependent.

Character Sets

There are a number of common character sets used in Asian countries, listed in Table 27.9.

Table 27.9 *Character sets in Asia.*

Language	Standards	Character Sets
Chinese (PRC)	GB2312-80	Chinese
Chinese (Taiwan)	CNS11643	Chinese
Japanese	JIS X 0201	Katakana
	JIS X 0208	Kanji, Kana, Latin, Greek, Cyrillic, and much more
	JIS X 0212	Supplemental Kanji
Korean	KSC5601.1987-0	Hangul

Font Lists

You'll need to set up a valid `fontList` resource for any Asian text. For Japanese, you'll need a number of fonts, such as the following:

```
*fontList: \
-jis-fixed-medium-r-normal--16-150-75-75-c-160-jisx0208.1983-0, \
-sony-fixed-medium-r-normal--16-150-75-75-c-80-iso8859-1,\
-sony-fixed-medium-r-normal--16-150-75-75-c-80-jisx0201.1976-0
```

These fonts should be valid on most X servers. Use the `xlsfonts` program to list the available fonts.

N O T E

WRITING INTERNATIONALIZED APPLICATIONS

We've put together a program to test out locales. Be warned that this program doesn't do anything interesting unless your operating system supports a number of locales. You'd be surprised at how little operating-system support there is.

This program should be run under different locales. If you've set up the resource files properly, the program should load up the proper language-specific text. The magic that takes care of this is the call to `XtSetLanguageProc`.

Other than that, the program below just shows a Motif File menu. We provide an X resource file for a German file menu after the program. The program code follows:

```
/* language.c */
#include  <Xm/Xm.h>
#include  <Xm/MainW.h>
#include  <Xm/RowColumn.h>
#include  <Xm/Separator.h>
#include  <Xm/Text.h>
#include  <stdio.h>
#include  <locale.h>

/* External functions. */
extern Widget CreatePushbutton(Widget parent,
    char* name, XtCallbackProc callback,
    XtPointer client_data);

extern Widget CreatePulldownMenu(Widget parent,
```

```
    char* name);

extern Widget CreateMenubar(Widget parent,
    char* name);

    /* Called on menu choices. */
void menuCB(Widget widget,
    XtPointer client_data,
    XtPointer call_data)

{   /* menuCB */

    /* Client data is text. */
    printf("Menu choice [%s]\n",
        (char*) client_data);

}   /* menuCB */

void exitCB(Widget widget,
    XtPointer client_data,
    XtPointer call_data)

{   /* exitCB */

    exit(0);

}   /* exitCB */

int main(int argc, char** argv)

{   /* main */
    XtAppContext    app_context;
    Widget          mainw, menubar;
    Widget          filemenu;
    Widget          text;
    Widget          parent;
    Arg             args[20];
    Cardinal        n;
    char*           locale;

#if XtSpecificationRelease > 4

    /* Set up locale. */
    XtSetLanguageProc(NULL, NULL, NULL);

#endif /* X11R5 or higher. */

    parent = XtVaAppInitialize(&app_context,
                "Ppm",
                (XrmOptionDescList) NULL,
                0,
                &argc, argv,
                (String*) NULL,
                XmNallowResize, True,
                NULL);
```

```
/* Now, let's query our locale. */
locale = setlocale(LC_ALL, NULL);

printf("Locale is [%s]\n", locale);

n = 0;
mainw = XmCreateMainWindow(parent,
        "mainw", args, n);

menubar = CreateMenubar(mainw, "menubar");

filemenu = CreatePulldownMenu(menubar, "filemenu");

(void) CreatePushbutton(filemenu, "new",
        (XtCallbackProc) menuCB,
        (XtPointer) "new");

(void) CreatePushbutton(filemenu, "open",
        (XtCallbackProc) menuCB,
        (XtPointer) "open");

/* Separator. */
(void) XtVaCreateManagedWidget("sep",
        xmSeparatorWidgetClass, filemenu,
        XmNorientation, XmHORIZONTAL,
        NULL);

(void) CreatePushbutton(filemenu, "save",
        (XtCallbackProc) menuCB,
        (XtPointer) "save");

(void) CreatePushbutton(filemenu, "saveas",
        (XtCallbackProc) menuCB,
        (XtPointer) "saveas");

/* Separator. */
(void) XtVaCreateManagedWidget("sep",
        xmSeparatorWidgetClass, filemenu,
        XmNorientation, XmHORIZONTAL,
        NULL);

(void) CreatePushbutton(filemenu, "print",
        (XtCallbackProc) menuCB,
        (XtPointer) "print");

/* Separator. */
(void) XtVaCreateManagedWidget("sep",
        xmSeparatorWidgetClass, filemenu,
        XmNorientation, XmHORIZONTAL,
        NULL);

(void) CreatePushbutton(filemenu, "exit",
        (XtCallbackProc) exitCB,
        (XtPointer) NULL);
```

```
    /* Create scrolled text for work area. */
    n = 0;
    XtSetArg(args[n], XmNeditMode,
        XmMULTI_LINE_EDIT); n++;

    text = XmCreateScrolledText(mainw,
            "text", args, n);

    XtManageChild(text);

    XmMainWindowSetAreas(mainw,
        menubar,
        (Widget) NULL,    /* command window */
        (Widget) NULL,    /* horiz scroll */
        (Widget) NULL,    /* vert scroll */
        XtParent(text));  /* work area */

    XtManageChild(mainw);

    XtRealizeWidget(parent);
    XtAppMainLoop(app_context);
    return 0;

}   /* main */

/* end of file language.c */
```

The English resource file for the program follows:

```
! ENGLISH Resource file for Chapter 27
! of Power Programming Motif.
!
*fontList:     lucidasans-12
*background:   lightgrey

*title:     English (American, at least)

*text.rows:     24
*text.columns:  40

! File menu
*filemenu.labelString: File
*filemenu.mnemonic:    F

*new.labelString:     New
*new.mnemonic:        N

*open.labelString:    Open...
*open.mnemonic:       O

*save.labelString:    Save
*save.mnemonic:       S

*saveas.labelString: Save As...
```

```
*saveas.mnemonic:     A

*print.labelString:   Print...
*print.mnemonic:      P

*exit.labelString:    Exit
*exit.mnemonic:       x

! end of resource file
```

Name this file **Ppm** and store it in your home directory. The program just shows a File menu (in English), as we show in Figure 27.3.

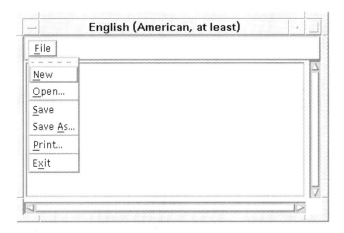

Figure 27.3   *The File menu.*

Storing text messages in resource files is a good thing, at least where internationalization is concerned, because of Xt's ability to read in the proper file. For example, we can create a German resource file and then store it in the **de** directory (a subdirectory of your home directory). The German resource file for the above program follows:

```
! German (Deutsch) Resource file for Chapter 27
! of Power Programming Motif.
!
*fontList:      lucidasans-12
*background:    lightgrey
*title: Deutsch

*text.rows:     24
*text.columns:  40
```

```
! File menu
*filemenu.labelString: Datei
*filemenu.mnemonic:    D

*new.labelString:      Neu
*new.mnemonic:         N

! Oeffnen has an umlaut
!*open.labelString:    Oeffnen...
! The trigraph \326 should be O umlaut
*open.labelString:     \326ffnen...
*open.mnemonic:        f

*save.labelString:     Speichern
*save.mnemonic:        p

*saveas.labelString: Speichern unter...
*saveas.mnemonic:      u

*print.labelString:  Drucken...
!*print.mnemonic:       D

*exit.labelString:   Beenden
*exit.mnemonic:        B

! end of resource file
```

The German resource file fills in the Datei (or File) menu. You should place this file in a directory named **de** off your home directory. As usual, name the file **Ppm**. That is, store this file in **$HOME/de/Ppm**.

If you've stored the file in the right place, then Xt will automatically read it in, assuming you're running under the German locale (usually de).

When you do this, you'll see the program display a German Datei menu instead of the English File menu, as shown in Figure 27.4.

Note the *Ö* in *Öffnen*. We used the Latin-1 trigraph, \326, to set up this character. You can easily add trigraphs to your X resource files.

Practical Internationalization Issues

Internationalization isn't easy. The hardest task we find now is just trying to test things out. We faced a lot of problems just trying to get a Japanese input method started, let alone testing anything.

Here are some tips we suggest to aid your efforts:

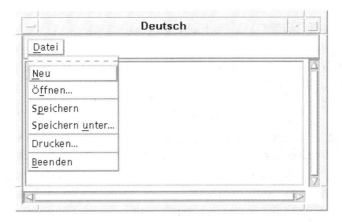

Figure 27.4   *The German Datei menu.*

■ Decide right away where you text messages will go. Will you place them in a message catalog and then set the labelString and other text resources dynamically? Or will you store your text messages in an X resource file, letting Xt take care of the work?

■ If you use a resource file, you'll need to enter trigraphs for national characters like umlauts. The xfd (X font displayer) program can help determine the numbers, as can a calculator that handles different base numbers, like octal. Be sure to load up a Latin-1 font (or whatever codeset you're working under). Hewlett-Packard systems, for example, ship with a number of HP-Roman-8 fonts, so don't confuse the two codesets.

■ Testing Asian input is amusing, but difficult.

■ Get local help on your translation efforts. You don't want to confuse, bemuse, amuse, or offend your customers inadvertently.

In many cases, choosing the right terminology is tough. To help figure out the official terminology for the Motif menus, you can look in *The GUI Guide: International Terminology for the Windows Interface* (European Edition, Microsoft, Microsoft Press, 1993). Although aimed at Windows 3.1, the Windows interface is so close to Motif's that you'll be able to use the same terminology in your applications.

INTERNATIONALIZATION FAUX PAS

Internationalization isn't easy, and it comes with its own set of pitfalls, problems, and tribulations. Your best bet is always to work with a person or organization that has experience in your target market.

You need to be careful in all aspects of your user interface, as well as your product's name and advertisements. You'd be surprised how much of what we do assumes a certain cultural outlook.

The UNIX operating system, for example, is full of violent imagery, such as daemons and zombies. You *kill* a process to stop it—which isn't as bad as the HP-1000's operating system, where you *off* a process to kill it.

Product Names and Packaging

Be careful with product names and packaging. To get an example of how easy it is to make a cultural faux pas, the following are some names of products in Japan. As in the United States, where French-sounding names add a cachet of elegance, many countries use English-sounding names for the same purpose.

Table 27.10 lists some interesting products in Japan.

Table 27.10   *Some English names used by Japanese products.*

Product Name	Explanation
Calpis	Beverage
Creap	Artificial coffee creamer
Green Piles	Lawn fertilizer
Hand Job	Portable computer
Pocari Sweat	Beverage
Trim Pecker	Trousers

In certain parts of Africa, the cultural tradition is to display a picture of the package contents on the outside packaging. This helps in areas where many different languages are used. Therefore, Africans viewing the picture of a cute baby on the packaging of Gerber baby food were definitely surprised. Their expectations of the product's contents were not what the vendor had in mind.

(Some of these anecdotes and products come from Dave Taylor's excellent *Global Software*. See Appendix A for more information.)

Icons

In many ways, using icons eases your translation efforts. If you can use a picture and avoid words, then you shouldn't have to translate as much. Unfortunately, you'll likely have to translate a number of icons to make them understandable to users in other countries.

Avoid puns and word games in icons. It's hard enough to connect some obscure picture to a program function without the designer of the interface adding yet another layer of translation, making you figure out all the puns and word games. Although an icon of an insect may mean computer fault (bug) to people in the United States, it may bring up no such connotation in another country. In another example, an iconic picture of a ship's window, a porthole, may be somewhat related to a viewport for English speakers (view*port*/*port*hole), the connotation is lost in Japan and other countries. In fact, even if you don't internationalize your software, porthole isn't all that intuitive to English speakers either.

It's also odd how some symbols may make a comeback—even incorrectly. The U.S. country mailbox, so commonly pictured in electronic-mail software, actually has the flag placed *down* after the mail carrier arrives. The flag was placed *up* to tell the mail carrier that there was mail waiting to be picked up. Most software, though, reverses this. (As you can tell, we were raised in a rural environment where people actually do these things.) The cylindrical trash can icon may look a lot like a British mailbox, and confusing these two tasks is not a good thing.

The bottom line is that when localizing you must be able to localize any bitmap imagery in your application as well as the text.

SUMMARY

The purpose of internationalization is to have one application that can run any place in the world and yet interact with the user in the user's native language. That is, if you run your application in Korea, it shows all text messages in Korean and accepts Korean input. If you run your application in Sweden, it shows all text messages in Swedish and accepts Swedish input.

This chapter covered the rather straightforward method of internationalizing applications under Motif and the X Window System.

MOTIF FUNCTIONS AND MACROS INTRODUCED IN THIS CHAPTER

```
XmTextFindStringWcs
XmTextFieldGetSelectionWcs
XmTextFieldGetStringWcs
XmTextFieldGetSubstringWcs
XmTextFieldInsertWcs
XmTextFieldReplaceWcs
XmTextFieldSetStringWcs
XmTextGetSelectionWcs
XmTextGetStringWcs
XmTextGetSubstringWcs
XmTextInsertWcs
XmTextReplaceWcs
XmTextSetStringWcs
```

X TOOLKIT INTRINSICS FUNCTIONS AND MACROS INTRODUCED IN THIS CHAPTER

```
XtSetLanguageProc
```

X LIBRARY FUNCTIONS AND MACROS INTRODUCED IN THIS CHAPTER

```
XSetLocaleModifiers
XSupportsLocale
```

CHAPTER 28

C++ and Motif

This chapter covers:

- Combining C++ with Motif
- Motif callback functions from C++
- Strategies for working with C++ object classes and Motif
- Encapsulating Motif's widget classes in C++ objects
- Encapsulating high-level user interface constructs in C++
- C++ developments in future versions of Motif

PROGRAMMING WITH C++ AND MOTIF

As more and more developers migrate from C to C++, they want to take advantage of C++'s object-oriented technology with their X Window toolkits. This seems natural enough, but as with all aspects of Motif, it's harder than it should be.

The major problem is simple: The X Toolkit Intrinsics, upon which Motif is based; is built with a form of C-based pseudo-object orientation. Getting this pseudo-object orientation to work with the C++ object model is no trivial task. If you attempt this, you'll end with an inelegant solution to what should be a prime candidate for C++ object-oriented programming.

As we've used in every chapter so far, the basic data type in Motif is the widget. Under the hood, the `Widget` data type is really a pointer to a complex structure. This structure makes extensive use of C function pointers to allow for a form of inheritance. In addition, the Xt Intrinsics provide for a class object (called the *class pointer*), which is even more useful for inheritance. The `XmPushButton` widget class pointer, for example, inherits much of the behavior from the `XmLabel` class pointer. Thus widgets act very much like C++ objects but enforce their own inheritance style, which is radically different from the C++ model for inheritance.

But widgets and C++ objects don't really mix. And that's the main problem. Basically, what you end up with is a C++ class hierarchy that sits over Motif and the Xt Intrinsics. You can encapsulate each Motif widget class with a C++ class, or you can combine a number of Motif widgets into C++ classes, or you can do both.

SHORTCUT

Like Oil and Water

The most common problem programmers face when trying to merge C++ and Motif is that you cannot use a C++ member function as a Motif callback, unless the member function is declared `static`. This is because of the hidden *this* pointer that C++ adds to non-`static` member functions.

In addition, you should pass the C++ object *this* pointer as the *client_data* to Motif callbacks. This way you'll be able to pass the proper object to the `static` member function that's used as a Motif callback.

COMPILING WITH MOTIF HEADERS

When C++ code gets compiled, the C++ compiler mangles the names of your functions, structures, and classes. This name mangling may convert a function named `activateCB` to `activateCB__12MyPushButtonFv`. These mangled names are actually used in the object modules generated by the C++ compiled and used by the linker. You normally never worry about these mangled names so long as you have a debugger that supports C++, but you need to remember that name mangling takes place.

With C code, though, if compiled under a C compiler, as most of your system libraries are, no name mangling takes place. To work with C code, your C++ code must turn off this mangling.

Since Motif, Xt, and the low-level X library are all written in C, you need to ensure that your C++ code includes any Motif or X function and structure definitions in C scope, not C++ scope.

C++ provides a simple `extern "C"` construct that allows you to declare that everything within the curly braces is considered C scope, not C++.

If you want to declare C functions in C++ code, you should wrap the C code in the `extern "C"` construct:

```
extern "C" {
    /* C code goes here. */
}
```

Of course, the `extern "C"` construct is not valid C, so you must place only the `extern "C"` statement in C++ code. Isn't that ironic?

To help with this (and other problems), most C++ compilers define a symbol, `__cplusplus` or `c_plusplus`, that tells you if you're compiling under C++ or C.

For example, you can place the following code in the beginning and end of a C header file, so that the file will be compiled in the proper scope (C) under C *and* C++:

```
#if defined(__cplusplus) || defined(c_plusplus)
```

```
extern "C" {
#endif

    /* Regular C definitions go here
     * in between...
     */

#if defined(__cplusplus) || defined(c_plusplus)
}
#endif
```

The above code looks ugly, but it works. Since Motif was written in C and you'll have libraries in C scope, you need to ensure that something like the above appears in your header files. Luckily, the Motif header files as of Motif 1.2 should include the code shown above in every header file. This should save you a lot of effort and grief.

Once you get the header files to compile properly, you have to deal with Xt callback functions.

Motif Callback Functions and C++

Motif uses callback functions extensively. Since the majority of your application rests inside the XtAppMainLoop event-handling loop, you need to set up callback functions to get anything done.

To set up a callback function, you register the address of a C function with XtAddCallback. At the appropriate moment, your callback gets executed.

Most Motif callbacks are of the type XtCallbackProc and take the following parameters:

```
typedef void (*XtCallbackProc)(
    Widget widget,
    XtPointer client_data,
    XtPointer call_data);
```

This is old hat. We've been using these callbacks since Chapter 2. Callbacks form an effective technique with C programs, but their effectiveness tends to decrease with C++. Why? Because what you'd like to do is use C++ member functions for objects, instead of registering callback functions.

C++ makes this especially difficult because non-static member functions have a hidden first parameter, the infamous *this* pointer, which points at the object's memory. Of course, the Xt library knows nothing of the *this* pointer. Xt callbacks and C++ member functions don't mix, so you have to invent some other technique to merge C callback functions with C++ objects.

The most common solution is to create a `static` member function for you object's class. This function is passed as the C callback.

N O T E This is the most common problem programmers face when trying to merge C++ and Motif. You cannot use a C++ member function as a Motif callback, unless the member function is declared `static`.

Client Data

Most Motif callback functions allow you to pass a `void` pointer (`XtPointer`) that points at any extra data you need in the callback. We've made extensive use of the *client_data* parameter in our examples in this book, as you most likely do in your code as well.

With C++, though, you tend to lose this extra parameter. Why? Because you need to pass the *this* pointer, which points at the C++ object's memory, as the *client_data*. If you pass the *this* pointer as the *client_data*, then you can get full access to the C++ object in the callback. If you use this technique, you then must store any extra data inside the C++ object that you want to access in the callback function.

Passing the *this* pointer as the *client_data* is another essential technique when mixing C++ and Motif.

For example, say we created a C++ class that sits on top of the Motif `XmPushButton` widget. Such a class should offer some form of function that could be called on the `XmPushButton` widget's `activateCallback`. After creating the underlying `XmPushButton` widget, this class would need to set up an `activateCallback` using a `static` member function, as follows:

```
Widget    widget;

XtAddCallback(widget,
    XmNactivateCallback,
    &MyPushButton::motifCB,
    (XtPointer) this);
```

The *this* pointer is passed as the client data. You could define your pushbutton wrapper class something like the code below:

```
class MyPushButton : public MyWidget {
public:
        // Object's function that
        // is executed on a callback.
    virtual void activateCB(void);

    // ...
protected:
        // Static Motif callback function.
    static void motifCB(Widget widget,
        XtPointer client_data,
        XtPointer call_data);

    // ...
};
```

The activateCB member function is called by the static motifCB function. Since the activateCB member function is declared virtual, derived classes can provide their own activateCB member functions.

Then, in the static motifCB function, your code calls the activateCB member function for the object passed as the *client_data*:

```
void MyPushButton::motifCB(Widget widget,
    XtPointer client_data,
    XtPointer call_data)

{       /* motifCB */
        MyPushButton*   obj;

        obj = (MyPushButton*) client_data;

        if (obj != NULL) {
                obj->activateCB();
        }

}       /* motifCB */
```

Remember to always check that the *call_data* parameter is not NULL, or your program will most likely crash with a core dump when you try to execute the activateCB member function from the (NULL) pointer.

STRATEGIES FOR MOTIF AND C++

There seem to be two main strategies for mixing C++ and Motif, which we summarize briefly:

■ Create a set of C++ classes that encapsulate the Motif widget classes to provide an object-oriented interface wrapper on top of Motif.

■ Diverge from Motif and create a set of user-interface C++ classes that encapsulate higher-level constructs (like a menu bar complete with menus or a label/text field combination) in C++ objects. In the private data, the C++ objects then access Motif widgets. With this strategy, you don't even try to match up the Motif widget class hierarchy with the C++ class hierarchy.

Encapsulating Motif Widget Classes in C++

Because the Xt Intrinsics provide their own C-based pseudo-object-oriented layer, and this layer is not very accessible from C++ unless you want to delve deep into the inner workings of the Xt Intrinsics, the common approach is to use C++ to provide wrappers around the existing widget classes, such as Motif's pushbutton class, we used in the example above. The idea of a wrapper library has merit in that you get to use the C++ object syntax and inheritance. You also get C++'s strong type checking. What you don't get, unfortunately, is a true object-oriented graphical interface library.

You can, though, use C++ to take care of a lot of the tedious aspects to writing Motif programs. Here's an example of a primitive attempt at wrapping Motif widgets inside of C++ classes. The MyWidget class is at the top of the class tree, and it holds a Motif widget ID:

```
/* mywidget.h */
#ifndef mywidget_h_
#define mywidget_h_ 1

#include  <Xm/Xm.h>

// This simple class encapsulates a Motif widget.
class MyWidget {
public:
    MyWidget()  { setwidget(NULL); }

        // Destructor destroys Motif widget
    ~MyWidget()
        { if (_widget != NULL) {
           XtDestroyWidget(_widget);
           }
        }

    void setwidget(Widget widget)
        { _widget = widget; }
```

```
        Widget getwidget()
            { return _widget; }

        void manage()
            { if (! XtIsManaged(_widget)) {
              XtManageChild(_widget);
              }
            }

        void unmanage()
            { if (XtIsManaged(_widget)) {
              XtUnmanageChild(_widget);
              }
            }

    private:
            // Motif's Widget ID.
        Widget  _widget;
    };

    #endif   /* ! mywidget_h_ */
    /* end of file mywidget.h */
```

You can then derive a pushbutton class from `MyWidget`:

```
    /* mybutton.h */
    #ifndef mybutton_h_
    #define mybutton_h_ 1

    #include  "mywidget.h"

    // The MyPushButton class encapsulates a pushbutton.
    class MyPushButton : public MyWidget {
    public:
            // Object's function that
            // is executed on a callback.
        virtual void activateCB(void);

        MyPushButton(MyWidget& parent, char* name);

        virtual ~MyPushButton() { }

    protected:
            // Ensures you must call
            // constructor with parameters.
        MyPushButton() { }

            // Static Motif callback function.
        static void motifCB(Widget widget,
            XtPointer client_data,
            XtPointer call_data);
    };

    #endif   /* ! mybutton_h_ */
```

```
/* end of file mybutton.h */
```

You can specialize the pushbutton behavior to create new classes, such as a very simple exit pushbutton class:

```
/* myexit.h */
#ifndef myexit_h_
#define myexit_h_      1

#include  "mybutton.h"

extern "C" {
void exit(int);
}

// MyExitButton quits the application.
class MyExitButton : public MyPushButton {
public:
    virtual void activateCB(void)
        { exit(0); }

    MyExitButton(MyWidget& parent,
            char* name) :
        MyPushButton(parent, name) { }

    virtual ~MyExitButton() { }

protected:
    // Ensures you must call
    // constructor with parameters.
    MyExitButton() { }
};

#endif /* ! myexit_h_ */

/* end of file myexit.h */
```

This exit button class defines its own `activateCB` member function, which quits the application. Note that we create the `MyExitButton` by just passing the parameters passed to the constructor on to the `MyPushButton` class constructor.

To flesh out the code, we have the following C++ code file for the `MyPushButton` class:

```
/* mybutton.cc */
#include "mybutton.h"
#include <Xm/PushB.h>
#include <stdio.h>

// static activateCallback for widget.
void MyPushButton::motifCB(Widget widget,
```

```
        XtPointer client_data,
        XtPointer call_data)

{    /* motifCB */
    MyPushButton*    obj;

    obj = (MyPushButton*) client_data;

    if (obj != NULL) {
        obj->activateCB();
    }

}    /* motifCB */

    // You should override this.
void MyPushButton::activateCB(void)

{    /* activateCB */

    printf("activateCB\n");

}    /* activateCB */

    // Constructor creates widget.
MyPushButton::MyPushButton(MyWidget& parent,
    char* name)

{    /* MyPushButton */
    Widget        widget;
    Widget        parentwidget;
    Arg           args[20];
    Cardinal      n;

    parentwidget = parent.getwidget();

    // Create Motif widget
    n = 0;
    widget = XmCreatePushButton(parentwidget,
                name, args, n);

    XtAddCallback(widget,
        XmNactivateCallback,
        &MyPushButton::motifCB,
        (XtPointer) this);

    // Store widget ID in object.
    setwidget(widget);

    if (widget != NULL) {
        manage();
    }

}    /* MyPushButton */

/* end of file mybutton.cc */
```

Every widget under this scheme has a name and a `MyWidget` parent.

Fleshing Out Our C++ Library

Pushbuttons alone aren't much fun. We need a container class, such as a paned window. We can derive such a class from the `MyWidget` class and create the `MyPanedWindow` class:

```
/* mypane.h */
#ifndef mypane_h_
#define mypane_h_    1

#include  "mywidget.h"

//  MyPanedWindow encapsulates an
//  XmPanedWindow widget.
class MyPanedWindow : public MyWidget {
public:
    MyPanedWindow(MyWidget& parent,
            char* name);

    virtual ~MyPanedWindow() { }

protected:
        // Ensures you must call
        // constructor with parameters.
    MyPanedWindow() { }
};

#endif  /* ! mypane_h_ */
/* end of file mypane.h */
```

We list the code for this class below:

```
/* mypane.cc */
#include  "mypane.h"
#include  <Xm/PanedW.h>

MyPanedWindow::MyPanedWindow(MyWidget& parent,
        char* name)

{   /* MyPanedWindow */
    Arg         args[20];
    Cardinal    n;
    Widget      widget;

    n = 0;
    widget = XmCreatePanedWindow(parent.getwidget(),
            name, args, n);

    setwidget(widget);

    // Don't manage until filled.
```

```
}    /* MyPanedWindow */

/* end of file mypane.cc */
```

You can easily create other container widgets using this code as a model.

We not only need container widgets, we need shell widgets as well, at least the top-level shell widget returned by XtAppInitialize. To do so, we can still derive this class from MyWidget:

```
/* myshell.h */
#ifndef myshell_h_
#define myshell_h_  1

#include  "mywidget.h"

class MyTopShell : public MyWidget {
public:
    MyTopShell(int* argc,
        char** argv,
        char* appclass,
        String* fallbacks);

    void realize()
        { XtRealizeWidget(getwidget()); }

    void mainloop()
        { XtAppMainLoop(_appcontext); }

    virtual ~MyTopShell() { };

private:
        // Ensures you must call
        // constructor with parameters.
    MyTopShell() { }

    XtAppContext    _appcontext;
};

#endif  /* ! myshell_h_ */
/* end of file myshell.h */
```

We also need to initialize the Xt Intrinsics. We present the code for this below:

```
/* myshell.cc */
#include "myshell.h"

MyTopShell::MyTopShell(int* argc,
    char** argv,
    char* appclass,
    String* fallbacks)
```

```
{    /* MyTopShell */
     Widget    widget;
     Arg       args[20];
     Cardinal  n;

     n = 0;
     XtSetArg(args[n], XmNallowShellResize, True); n++;

     widget = XtAppInitialize(&_appcontext,
                 appclass,
                 NULL, 0,
                 argc, argv,
                 fallbacks,
                 args, n);

     setwidget(widget);

}    /* MyTopShell */

/* end of file myshell.cc */
```

SAMPLE PROGRAM TO ENCAPSULATE WIDGETS

We now have a very minimalist C++ widget library that sits on top of Motif. Obviously, this is not a complete library by any means, but it has enough functions and classes that we can create a simple program demonstrating one way to mix C++ with Motif. The code for this short program follows:

```
/* mycpp.cc */
#include "mybutton.h"
#include "myexit.h"
#include "mypane.h"
#include "myshell.h"

//  Set up Xt fallback resources.
static String fallback_resources[] = {
  "*quit.labelString: Exit",
  "*push.labelString: Push me, please.",
  "*title:           Motif C++ Test",
  NULL
};

int main(int argc, char** argv)

{    /* main */

     MyTopShell   parent(&argc, argv,
             (char*) "Ppm",
```

```
        fallback_resources);

    // Create paned window
MyPanedWindow   pane(parent, "pane");

    // Note the constructors create
    // the Motif widgets.
MyPushButton    push(pane, "push");
MyExitButton    quit(pane, "quit");

    // Containers aren't managed.
    pane.manage();

    // Realize widget and handle events.
    parent.realize();
    parent.mainloop();

    return 0;

}   /* main */

/* end of file motifcpp.cc */
```

The above program uses the following resource file:

```
! Resource file for Chapter 28
! of Power Programming Motif.
!
*background:    grey92

*quit.labelString: Exit
*push.labelString: Push me, or else!
*title:         Motif C++ Test

! end of resource file
```

Name this file **Ppm** and store it in your home directory.

When you run this program, you'll see a simple paned window with two pushbuttons. The idea isn't to show a fancy program but instead to give you a brief glimpse of what C++ has to offer for interface-related code and to offer one way you can meld C++ with Motif.

How you work with C++ and Motf is largely a mtter of taste. In the examples above, we made two decisions that probably won't sit well with many of you. First, instead of using C callbacks, our examples imply that you must derive your own class for each type of pushbutton. Taken to an extreme, this could mean a separate class for every pushbutton and menu choice in your program—probably not a good idea in anything but a simple example program.

Secondly, our constructors create the actual Motif widget. This has some odd implications. We must initialize the Xt Intrinsics with `XtAppInitialize` before we declare any objects of the `MyPushButton` class. This raises a question of differing styles. Do you place code that actually creates the underlying Motif widgets in the constructor, or should you avoid any processing that can fail in the constructor? The ParcPlace OI toolkit (a non-Motif X toolkit), for example, has functions that specifically create C++ objects that represent user-interface elements. Although this may seem to violate the object-oriented approach, it does provide for safer code. Remember that under the hood, you're calling Motif, Xt, or X library calls, and many of these calls can fail.

And thirdly, we just encapsulated the low-level Motif widgets with C++ classes. In real applications you'll need to do this, and you'll also want to create your own interface classes built from multiple low-level Motif widgets. For example, your pull-down menu class may hold all the menu choices (in Motif, each menu choice is a separate pushbutton widget or gadget). You might want to build a radio box class to hold exclusive choices instead of building such a box from low-level `XmToggleButton` widgets.

When building your own C++ classes from multiple Motif widgets, it seems to make sense to place low-level Motif widgets, such as toggle buttons and single-line text widgets, inside of Motif container widgets. You could combine the toggle button with a text field and place the resulting combination inside a row-column widget. All three Motif widgets could make a logical class in C++. The problem you'll face, though, is when you have many of these C++ objects and you try to line up the text fields. This is a common drawback for placing each logical C++ object inside a Motif container widget.

The Great Debate: Use Callbacks or Subclass

There seems to be two main approaches to setting up your own code with C++. Chances are you're creating a C++ library of user-interface objects, whether they encapsulate Motif widgets directly or use higher-level constructs. If this is the case, then how do you allow callers of the C++ library to insert their own code?

One answer, used in the program above, requires programmers to subclass the base objects to insert their own code. For example, we built the `MyExitButton` class above by subclassing the `MyPushButton` class.

The only specialization added by the MyExitButton class is to override the default activateCB virtual member function. Other C++ libraries, like Microsoft's Foundation Class library for windows, use this technique.

This solution seems elegant at first glance, but it tends to become tedious in the long run. Programmers often balk at subclassing just to customize a single small function. After all, you have to set up the constructors and destructors, as well as the class definition for each unique object. This becomes a problem in any commercial-grade application, where you're likely to have hundreds of menu choices and up to a thousand pushbutton widgets. Subclassing for each separate pushbutton is not fun.

In Motif with C, you just pass separate callback functions. This leads to a second common approach: allowing your own form of callback functions. You can go to all sorts of lengths to place an object-oriented wrapper over callbacks, but they mostly boil down to something similar to C callback functions.

Use whatever approach fits your needs.

Using Higher-Level Constructs

The C++ code we've shown so far just places a small wrapper around the facilities provided by Motif. An alternate strategy is to divorce the C++ class library from the Motif widget class hierarchy and instead concentrate on creating object-oriented user-interface classes that encapsulate higher-level constructs.

For example, you may want to create an RGB (red, green, blue) color editor class that includes three Motif XmScale widgets (along, perhaps, with an XmPushButton to show the color and a few XmLabels to explain the interface). All these widgets together may become one logical user-interface element.

Another good example is the prompted text entry. In most programs, you combine an XmLabel widget, the prompt, with an XmText widget, the entry, to make one logically combined element. In fact, you'll find that for most user-input widgets, you'll match up a label with the input widget (XmPushButton, XmText, XmTextField, and so on). These logical combinations are prime candidates for C++ classes.

N O T E

If you do create widget classes using this strategy, be careful with Motif's container widget classes. It's tempting to place each combination of widgets into a container, such as the XmRowColumn widget. The drawback to this approach is that you'll experience untold grief trying to get all your widgets to line up. So, we advise you to look into ways to treat a number of Motif widgets inside one C++ object as one unit but still place them inside a container widget that is shared among a number of these C++ objects. This way, you'll have a better chance creating business data-entry forms that actually line up.

For example, if you create a prompted text entry C++ class that holds an XmLabel and an XmText widget, you'll often want to place a number of these C++ objects (each with two Motif widgets) into one container widget, such as an XmForm.

Use the strategy you feel works best, whether it be one of the two presented in this chapter or one you invent on your own.

DERIVING YOUR OWN WIDGET CLASSES

Because Motif is based on the Xt Intrinsics, you'll have a hard time deriving your own widget classes. Even though it's easy to specialize the behavior of classes somewhat, you'll have a hard time if you need to mess with the Motif widget internals. For example, the Motif text widget supports a resource, wordWrap, that controls whether the widget wraps words at the right margin. You can encapsulate the basic text widget in a C++ class, then derive a new, more specialized, C++ class that turns on word wrap. This is easy because Motif supports a word wrap resource. But if you then want to derive your text-widget class to create a hypertext class, you're out of luck. You must deal with the Xt Intrinsics layer of pseudo-object orientation, which is not really available to the programmer who uses the Motif libraries. If you have the Motif sources, you can create, in a process called subclassing, your own widgets, but you cannot use the simple C++ mechanism for inheritance. You must instead use the complex Xt mechanism for inheritance.

What it boils down to is that you can put together two or more primitive Motif widgets to create your own multiwidget classes, or you can create classes that merely set up different default Motif resources, but you lose the benefits of C++'s class system when you must write your own widgets at the Xt level. None of these approaches are truly satisfactory, but we've found the benefits of C++ far outweigh the drawbacks.

In most of our work, we don't encapsulate Motif so much as create user interface objects and then place the necessary Motif widget or widgets inside the class structure.

FUTURES: MERGING C++ AND THE XT INTRINSICS

The Open Software Foundation, makers of Motif, are working on a future C++ extension to Motif. This extension will encapsulate the Xt `Widget` data structure with a C++ class, allowing you to derive your own classes.

While this may sound encouraging, one look at the `Widget` data structure is enough to send shivers down anyone's back. In addition, the C++ object that encapsulates a Widget depends on having the C++ object share the exact same memory layout as the C structure, which also sounds scary from a portability point of view.

In any case, the next version of Motif should offer much more support for C++.

OTHER C++ AND MOTIF IMPLEMENTATIONS

Back to the real world of here and now, there are a number of available C++ libraries that encapsulate Motif.

- ■ View.h++ and MouseWrapper.h++ from Rogue Wave encapsulate all of Motif, including `XmStrings`. The library also provides a Model-View-Controller (MVC) paradigm (commonly found in Smalltalk software). The MouseWrapper.h++ adds a library of rubber-banding widgets, a canvas, a tree display, and a number of graphic types. View.h++ and MouseWrapper.h++ are commercial products.

- ■ Motif++ is a freely available wrapper library for Motif. Contact the Motif++ mailing list (motif++-request@cv.ruu.nl to get on the list, motif++@cv.ruu.nl for the actual list) for more information.

■ Xm++ is another wrapper library, also freely available, from the Vienna User Interface Group. Contact xmplus@ani.univie.ac.at for more information. Xm++ supports both the Motif and Athena widget sets.

■ InterViews, from Stanford University, is a freely available C++ library that supports a Motif-like look and feel. InterViews is not based on any Motif code, but it is the base for the X Consortium's Fresco toolkit. InterViews is available for anonymous FTP from interviews.stanford.edu in the pub directory. Look for 3.1.tar.Z or a later version, if available.

■ Another non-Motif C++ toolkit that provides a Motif look and feel is ParcPlace's OI toolkit. Contact ParcPlace for more information.

CHAPTER 29

Migrating from Open Look to Motif

This chapter covers:

- Strategies for porting to Motif
- Utility functions to hide differences between OLIT and Motif
- Converting widget types in creation functions
- Converting resource names and values
- Working with a different window manager
- Supporting the Motif Style Guide
- Creating menus and menu choices in OLIT
- Comparing OLIT and Motif widgets
- Comparing resources and resource values

929

PORTING TO MOTIF

With the emergence of the Common Open Software Environment and agreement between major UNIX vendors on the level of standardization needed in future development, a major casualty that affects most Motif programmers is the demise of SunSoft's Open Look interface and the Open Look Intrinsics Toolkit, or OLIT. Now that SunSoft endorsed Motif over Open Look, you must begin planning the migration to Motif if you have been using OLIT. Yes, SunSoft will continue to fix bugs in OLIT, but all new development has stopped.

This would include migrating Open Look applications to Motif, but this isn't as complicated a move as you might think. Since both Motif and OLIT are based on the Xt Intrinsics, you gain a number of advantages for porting:

■ Both toolkits make extensive use of the `Widget` data type. The parameters to your functions may remain the same while you port the code inside the functions.

■ Much of your code will readily convert to Motif. In many cases, all you have to do is change the resource names and a few function calls.

■ Both toolkits use `XtVaSetValues` and `XtCreateManagedWidget`.

This chapter goes over our main strategies for porting OLIT code to Motif.

SHORTCUT

Strategies for Porting to Motif

Our strategy for porting to Motif uses the following steps:

1. Use utility functions; then port the utilities to Motif.
2. Convert widget types in creation functions (use `XtVaCreateManagedWidget` where appropriate).
3. Convert resource names and values.
4. Don't depend on the window manager, *olwm*.
5. Convert all remaining code.
6. Break down and support the Motif Style Guide.

Use Utility Functions

You probably have a library of utility functions that eases your programming task with OLIT. Our first step is to port these functions to Motif. The trick is to make the function parameters and return types, the API, as generic as possible so that you can just slip in the Motif implementations of the preexisting utility functions.

Of course, this never works out as easily as it sounds. If your code uses utility functions, such as a routine to create a pull-down menu, you can then convert the utility functions to Motif. After you do so, all of a sudden large sections of your code automatically migrate. For example, both Motif and OLIT traditionally use a widget for each menu choice. Both widgets are pushbuttons: XmPushButton in Motif and OblongButton in OLIT. (Even though both widgets are pushbuttons, you need to perform special processing to get the parent widget in OLIT, so we cannot just use a generic pushbutton function.)

Menu Choices

You can create a utility function to create a menu choice. Choose a set of parameters, such as the ones shown below:

```
Widget CreateMenuChoice(Widget parent_menu,
    char* name,
    XtCallbackProc callback,
    XtPointer client_data)
```

The CreateMenuChoice choice should, as you guessed, create a menu choice, hiding the internal details of this task. Once we decide on the API, we can then create an OLIT version:

```
#include <X11/Intrinsic.h>
#include <X11/StringDefs.h>
#include <Xol/OpenLook.h>
#include <Xol/OblongButt.h>

Widget CreateMenuChoice(Widget parent_menu,
    char* name,
    XtCallbackProc callback,
    XtPointer client_data)

{    /* CreateMenuChoice */
    Widget        menupane;
    Widget        widget;
```

```
/* We need to get a new parent,
 * from the actual menu.
 */
XtVaGetValues(parent_menu,
    XtNmenuPane, &menupane,
    NULL);

/* Create a pushbutton using this new parent. */
widget = XtVaCreateManagedWidget(name,
            oblongButtonWidgetClass, menupane,
            NULL);

/* Set up callback. */
XtAddCallback(widget,
    XtNselect,
    callback,
    client_data);

return widget;

}   /* CreateMenuChoice */
```

This function just takes in and returns parameters that are generic to both Motif and OLIT.

We create the OLIT version first so that you can port your existing OLIT code to use this function. With Motif, you use an XmPushButton widget, with a class of xmPushButtonWidgetClass. With OLIT, use an OblongButton, with a class of oblongButtonWidgetClass.

OLIT oblong buttons use the select callback, while Motif pushbuttons use the activateCallback. The callback information structures that are passed by the toolkit to your application's callback function are different, too. In the case of pushbuttons, we usually ignore this data, making the issue moot.

N O T E

Motif functions usually begin with *Xm* and OLIT functions, with *Ol*. With resource names, you use the *XtN* prefix in OLIT code and *XmN* in Motif code. For example, the background resource will be coded as XtNbackground in OLIT and XmNbackground in Motif.

Once your OLIT code uses the CreateMenuChoice function, we can port the insides of the function to Motif, as shown:

```
#include <Xm/Xm.h>
#include <Xm/PushB.h>
```

```
    /* Same as pushbutton in Motif. */
Widget CreateMenuChoice(Widget parent_menu,
    char* name,
    XtCallbackProc callback,
    XtPointer client_data)

{   /* CreateMenuChoice */
    Widget      widget;

    widget = XtVaCreateManagedWidget(name,
            xmPushButtonWidgetClass, parent_menu,
            NULL);

    /* Set up callback. */
    XtAddCallback(widget,
        XmNactivateCallback,
        callback,
        client_data);

    return widget;

}   /* CreateMenuChoice */
```

Pull-Down Menus

The next step is to create the pull-down menu itself. Again, Motif and OLIT are surprisingly similar, but they have a few differences.

With OLIT, all you have to do is create a `MenuButton` widget to get the pull-down menu and the Motif cascade button, as the `MenuButton` actually corresponds to the Motif `XmCascadeButton`. When you create the `MenuButton`, OLIT automatically creates a hidden menu pane, which corresponds to the `XmRowColumn` widget in Motif that actually is the menu.

With Motif, you have to create each of these widgets separately.

That said, we can determine a utility function that takes just two parameters:

```
Widget CreatePulldownMenu(Widget parent,
    char* name)
```

The following code creates a pull-down menu in OLIT:

```
#include <X11/Intrinsic.h>
#include <X11/StringDefs.h>
#include <Xol/OpenLook.h>

#include <Xol/MenuButton.h>

Widget CreatePulldownMenu(Widget parent,
    char* name)
```

```
{   /* CreatePulldownMenu */
    Widget    menu;

    /* Create pulldown menu. */
    menu = XtVaCreateManagedWidget(name,
              menuButtonWidgetClass,
              parent,
              XtNlabelJustify,  OL_LEFT,
              XtNrecomputeSize, TRUE,
              NULL);

    return menu;

}   /* CreatePulldownMenu */
```

The following code, from Chapter 4, creates a pull-down menu in Motif:

```
#include <Xm/Xm.h>
#include <Xm/CascadeB.h>
#include <Xm/RowColumn.h>

Widget CreatePulldownMenu(Widget parent,
    char* name)

{   /* CreatePulldownMenu */
    Widget    menu;
    Widget    cascade;
    Arg       args[20];
    Cardinal  n;

    /* Engage tear-off menu if supported. */
    n = 0;

#ifdef XmNtearOffModel

    XtSetArg(args[n], XmNtearOffModel,
        XmTEAR_OFF_ENABLED); n++;

#endif  /* XmNtearOffModel */

    menu = XmCreatePulldownMenu(parent,
            name, args, n);

    /* Create cascade button and connect to menu. */
    n = 0;
    XtSetArg(args[n], XmNsubMenuId, menu); n++;

    cascade = XmCreateCascadeButton(parent,
                name, args, n);

    XtManageChild(cascade);

    return menu;

}   /* CreatePulldownMenu */
```

NOTE

There are a few differences in how the widgets act. In OLIT, you pull down the menu with the rightmost mouse button. In Motif, you use the leftmost mouse button. In OLIT, clicking the leftmost mouse button over the `MenuButton` widget executes the default menu choice.

In addition, both toolkits use the `mnemonic` resource, but in OLIT, when the user types the menu's mnemonic, the menu default choice gets activated. In Motif, the menu just pulls down.

For text labels, you can port the OLIT `StaticText` widget to Motif's `XmLabel`. We can then specify a `CreateLabel` function as follows:

```
Widget CreateLabel(Widget parent,
    char* name)
```

The OLIT `CreateLabel` function follows:

```
#include <X11/Intrinsic.h>
#include <X11/StringDefs.h>
#include <Xol/OpenLook.h>
#include <Xol/StaticText.h>

Widget CreateLabel(Widget parent,
    char* name)

{   /* CreateLabel */
    Widget  label;

    label = XtVaCreateManagedWidget(name,
            staticTextWidgetClass, parent,
            NULL);

    return label;

}   /* CreateLabel */
```

The Motif `CreateLabel` function follows:

```
#include <Xm/Xm.h>
#include <Xm/Label.h>

Widget CreateLabel(Widget parent,
    char* name)

{   /* CreateLabel */
    Widget  label;

    label = XtVaCreateManagedWidget(name,
```

```
                   xmLabelWidgetClass, parent,
                   NULL);

      return label;

   }   /* CreateLabel */
```

Motif XmLabel widgets use the XmString data type for its labelString resource. Prior to OLIT 3.2, the StaticText widget uses a String data type for its string resource. We cover more on this below in the section on "Motif Strings."

Relating Widget Types

Many of the Motif widgets have direct analogs in OLIT, so that much of what you have to do is to change the widget creation to use the resources and widget classes from the other toolkit.

Table 29.1 lists the widget types in OLIT and some reasonable comparisons to Motif. Note that these widgets don't always port one-to-one to Motif.

Table 29.1   *Comparing OLIT widgets to Motif*

OLIT	Motif
AbbrevMenuButton	XmCascade, XmRowColumn as pull-down menu
BulletinBoard	XmBulletinBoard
Caption	1.2 XmFrame with label
CheckBox	XmToggleButton
ControlArea	XmRowColumn
DrawArea	XmDrawingArea
DropTarget	See Chapter 21 on drag and drop
Exclusives	XmRowColumn as radio box
FileChooser	XmFileSectionDialog
FontChooser	*None*
FooterPanel	XmLabel as message area for XmMainWindow
Form	XmForm

continued

Gauge	XmScale; future Motif thermometer widget
MenuButton	XmCascade, XmRowColumn as pull-down menu
MenuShell	XmMenuShell
NonExclusives	XmRowColumn
NoticeShell	XmDialogShell, or warning dialog
NumericField	XmTextField with XmLabel and XmArrowButtons
OblongButton	XmPushButton
PopupWindowShell	XmDialogShell
RectButton	XmToggleButton
RubberTile	XmForm, perhaps
Scrollbar	XmScrollBar
ScrolledWindow	XmScrolledWindow
ScrollingList	XmList, with scroll bars
Slider	XmScale
StaticText	XmLabel
Stub	XmDrawingArea
TextEdit	XmText
TextField	XmTextField
TextLine	XmTextField with XmLabel

For some entries in Table 29.1, like the FooterPanel, the Motif equivalent doesn't really do justice to the OLIT widget. In this case, we're just outlining a possible strategy to help ease your port. This is not necessarily the best solution.

There's also nothing in Motif that really matches the OLIT Caption widget. You can use an XmFrame with a frame title (new in Motif 1.2), but this does not provide anywhere near all the formatting options of the Caption widget.

For OLIT's Gauge widget, you can try to get away with using the Motif XmScale widget. You'll probably want to make the XmScale insensitive to user input. In the future version, Motif should provide a thermometer widget that more closely matches the OLIT Gauge.

Creating Widgets

Motif provides a host of convenience functions for creating widgets. OLIT tends more to using the Xt functions like `XtCreateManagedWidget` and `XtVaCreateManagedWidget`. These Xt functions also work with Motif. If you know you'll have to port between the two toolkits, you may want to use the Xt creation functions where possible in your Motif code.

For example, to create a form widget, `XmForm`, in Motif, use the following code:

```
#include <Xm/Xm.h>
#include <Xm/Form.h>

Widget   form, parent;
String   name;

form = XtVaCreateManagedWidget(name,
        xmFormWidgetClass,
        parent,
        NULL);
```

In OLIT, the corresponding `Form` widget class is `formWidgetClass`:

```
#include <Xol/OpenLook.h>
#include <Xol/Form.h>

Widget   form, parent;
String   name;

form = XtVaCreateManagedWidget(name,
        formWidgetClass,
        parent,
        NULL);
```

The code looks remarkably similar. Of course, the placement resources are entirely different, so you'll need to do some work to properly place the form's child widgets.

Menu Bars

Unlike Motif, OLIT really doesn't support the concept of a menu bar. Most Motif applications sport a menu bar atop the main application window, per the Motif style. This menu bar is a Motif `XmRowColumn` widget that you can create with the `XmCreateMenuBar` convenience function:

```
#include <Xm/Xm.h>
#include <Xm/RowColumn.h>

Widget XmCreateMenuBar(Widget parent,
```

```
char* name,
ArgList args,
Cardinal number_args)
```

The cascade buttons, mentioned above, are then placed as child widgets of the menu bar.

OLIT programs often have a set of menu-button widgets across the top of the application's main window. You can simulate a Motif menu bar in OLIT by using the `ControlArea` widget, as the following code shows:

```
#include <Xol/OpenLook.h>
#include <Xol/ControlAre.h>

Widget  menubar, parent;
char*   name;

menubar = XtVaCreateManagedWidget(name,
        controlAreaWidgetClass,
        parent,
        XtNlayoutType, OL_FIXEDROWS,
        XtNalignCaptions, TRUE,
        NULL);
```

We set the `layoutType` resource to `OL_FIXEDROWS`, instead of `OL_FIXED-COLS`. This makes the `ControlArea` widget lay out horizontally. We also specify that we want the captions aligned (`alignCaptions`). Use the menu-bar widget, then, as the parent for the `MenuButtons` you create.

Drawing Areas

With OLIT 3.0, you have a `DrawArea` widget that more closely matches the Motif `XmDrawingArea` widget than the older OLIT `Stub` widget. If at all possible, you should update any OLIT code that uses the `Stub` widget. The `DrawArea` widget ports better to Motif and provides better support in OLIT, as well. Both the `DrawArea` and `XmDrawingArea` widgets support a similar set of callback functions, as listed in Table 29.2.

Table 29.2 *Drawing-area callbacks.*

Motif	OLIT
`exposeCallback`	`exposeCallback`
`inputCallback`	*not applicable*

continued

resizeCallback	resizeCallback
not applicable	graphicsExposeCallback

The Motif callback structure for the XmDrawingArea widget follows:

```
typedef struct {
    int     reason;
    XEvent* event;
    Window  window;
} XmDrawingAreaCallbackStruct;
```

The *reason* field is set to XmCR_EXPOSE, XmCR_RESIZE, or XmCR_INPUT, depending on the event that caused the callback. The *event* field points at an XExposeEvent structure on Expose events, an XConfigureEvent structure on ConfigureNotify events (for resizing), and a mouse (XButtonEvent) or keyboard (XKeyEvent) event structure for input events.

The OLIT callback structure for the DrawArea widget looks like the following:

```
typedef struct {
    int         reason;
    XEvent*     event;
    Position    x;
    Position    y;
    Dimension   width;
    Dimension   height;
} OlDrawAreaCallbackStruct;
```

The *reason* field will be OL_REASON_EXPOSE for Expose events, OL_REASON_GRAPHICS_EXPOSE for GraphicsExpose events, and OL_REASON_RESIZE for resize (ConfigureNotify) events.

Resolving Conflicting Resources

Even though both toolkits share similar core and shell resources, the toolkits diverge greatly on the resources supported by individual widgets. You'll have to look up the needed widgets in the proper OLIT or Motif reference manual.

Even so, some resource closely match. Table 29.3 lists some resources.

Table 29.3 *Comparing OLIT and Motif resources.*

OLIT Resource	Type	Motif Resource	Type
background	Pixel	background	Pixel
backgroundPixmap	Pixmap	backgroundPixmap	Pixmap
borderColor	Pixel	borderColor	Pixel
borderPixmap	Pixmap	borderPixmap	Pixmap
font	XFontStruct*	fontList	XmFontList
foreground	Pixel	foreground	Pixel
height	Dimension	height	Dimension
string	String	labelString	XmString
width	Dimension	width	Dimension
x	Position	x	Position
y	Position	y	Position

Not all resources map one-to-one. The font and string resources, in particular, diverge. Therefore, you'll need to look up each widget's resources in both the OLIT and Motif references.

Motif Strings

Motif provides a complex set of XmString creation and manipulation functions. Just about every Motif widget, except for XmText and XmTextField, requires XmStrings.

A Motif XmLabel widget requires you to convert a C string into an XmString and then set the XmString as the value of the labelString resource.

With OLIT, on the other hand, you can just set the string or label resources, depending on the widget, to the C string.

OLIT 3.2 introduces internationalized text strings into OLIT. You can use the new OlFont and OlStr data types along with the textFormat resource to control how text is formatted.

N O T E

The OLIT `StaticText` widget displays the text set into the `string` resource.

To hide some of these differences, we can define a function that sets the label into a widget (`XmLabel` or `StaticText`). Our `SetLabel` function takes the following parameters:

```
void SetLabel(Widget widget,
    char* message)
```

The OLIT `SetLabel` function follows:

```
void SetLabel(Widget widget,
    char* message)

{   /* SetLabel */

    XtVaSetValues(widget,
        XtNstring, message,
        NULL);

}   /* SetLabel */
```

The more complex Motif `SetLabel` function follows:

```
#include <Xm/Xm.h>

void SetLabel(Widget widget,
    char* message)

{   /* SetLabel */
    XmString    xmstring;

    xmstring = XmStringCreateSimple(message);

    XtVaSetValues(widget,
        XmNlabelString, xmstring,
        NULL);

    XmStringFree(xmstring);

}   /* SetLabel */
```

Font Lists

Motif applications use font lists to define the fonts used by any widget that displays text. The Motif `fontList` resource takes an `XmFontList` (pointer to a font-list structure).

Up to OLIT 3.2, OLIT applications used the simpler font resource which uses a pointer to a single font structure, an XFontStruct. With OLIT 3.2, you can use the OlFont data type to hold either an XFontSet or an XFontStruct*.

Don't Depend on Window Manager

Since even SunSoft plans to move to Motif, you'll see the Open Look window manager, *olwm*, fading away in a few years. Even if you don't port to Motif, you'll need to break any dependence on the *olwm* window manager.

Two areas where OLIT applications depend on *olwm* include using the window manager menu to quit the application and using *olwm* pushpins to dismiss dialogs.

Many Open Look applications have no means to quit. Instead, you're supposed to use the **Quit** menu choice from *olwm's* window menu. Every Motif application should have a means to quit. The standard for Motif programs is to use the **Exit** choice on the File menu.

Many Open Look dialogs are even worse. The traditional means to dismiss the dialogs is to use an *olwm* pushpin. Don't depend on pushpins any more. Every Motif dialog should have a **Cancel**, **Done**, or **Dismiss** pushbutton.

Open Look Pushpins and Motif Tear-Off Menus

Olwm supports the concept of pushpins on menus. You can configure a pushpin by setting the pushpin resource to OL_OUT. Setting the pushpin resource to OL_NONE, the default, disables a pushpin.

```
#include <Xol/OpenLook.h>
#include <Xol/MenuButton.h>

Widget  menubtn, parent;

menubtn = XtVaCreateManagedWidget("menubutton",
        menuButtonWidgetClass,
        parent,
        XtNlabelJustify,  OL_LEFT,
        XtNrecomputeSize, TRUE,
        XtNpushpin, OL_OUT,
        NULL);
```

The Motif toolkit doesn't support pushpins, but you can make your Motif program set the proper window-manager properties if your program runs under *olwm*. If you do this, your Motif programs can sport pushpins just like OLIT programs—under *olwm*, of course. We described how to do this in Chapter 18 on window managers.

Port the Rest of the Code

In the next step, you simply port the rest of your code to Motif. It's certainly easier said than done, but there are a few techniques that can help. In the sections below, we cover some odds and ends that can help your port, including:

- Comparing OLIT and Motif include files
- Initializing the toolkits
- Updating the display
- Online help
- Drag and drop
- Compiling and linking

OLIT Include Files

OLIT include files are stored in the **Xol** subdirectory, usually **/usr/open-win/include/Xol** under OpenWindows. The Motif include files are stored in the **Xm** subdirectory, usually **/usr/include/Xm**.

The basic OLIT include file, necessary for all OLIT programs, is `<Xol/OpenLook.h>`. The basic Motif include file, again necessary, is `<Xm/Xm.h>`. Like Motif, each OLIT widget has a separate include file.

After you get the include files down pat, you need to initialize the toolkit.

Initializing The Toolkit

To initialize OLIT programs, you need to call `OlToolkitInitialize`, before calling the standard Xt initializer, `XtAppInitialize`, as shown:

```
int main(int argc, char** argv)

{
XtAppContext  app_context;
Widget        parent;
Cardinal      n;
```

```
Arg            args[20];

OlToolkitInitialize( (XtPointer) NULL);

n = 0;
parent = XtAppInitialize(&app_context,
            "Ppm",
            (XrmOptionDescList) NULL,
            0,
            &argc, argv,
            (String*) NULL,
            args, n);

    /* ... */
}
```

The parameter to `OlToolkitInitialize` is reserved for future use, so we pass `NULL`.

With Motif, you only need to call `XtAppInitialize` (with the same parameters).

Updating the Display

In a few cases in this book, we've needed to update the display of a given widget inside a callback function (that is, without returning to the main event loop). For this, Motif provides the `XmUpdateDisplay` function:

```
#include <Xm/Xm.h>

void XmUpdateDisplay(Widget widget)
```

OLIT similarly provides `OlUpdateDisplay`, which takes the same parameter:

```
#include <Xol/OpenLook.h>

void OlUpdateDisplay(Widget widget)
```

Online Help

Although the Motif Style Guide requires online help and a Help menu, Motif does little more than list the Help menu choices. OLIT, on the other hand, provides quite an extensive set of facilities supporting online help. This is one of the first things you'll miss in moving to Motif. (The COSE efforts may add help to Motif in the future, though.)

There's simply no Motif counterpart for `OlRegisterHelp`, nor the OLIT help mechanism. You're on your own.

Drag and Drop

Both OLIT and Motif implement different drag-and-drop styles. OLIT makes extensive use of the `DropTarget` widget to facilitate drag and drop. Motif, on the other hand, has you register widgets as drop sites. You'll find that the convert selection procedures look a lot alike between OLIT and Motif, though, as both drag-and-drop implementations do use the X selection mechanism.

Even so, since drag and drop is so different, we refer you to Chapter 21 for a thorough discussion of Motif's implementation.

Compiling and Linking

When you compile OLIT programs, you typically have to specify where the include files are located, such as **-I/usr/openwin/include**. You may have to do this for Motif as well, depending on where your Motif header files are located.

With linking, you basically need to swap the `Xol` library for the `Xm` library.

Motif programs need the Motif, Xt, and X libraries. You can compile and link a Motif program stored in **foo.c** with the following command:

```
cc -o foo foo.c -lXm -lXt -lX11
```

OLIT programs require the OLIT, Xt, and X libraries. To compile and link OLIT programs, use the following command as a template:

```
cc -I/usr/openwin/include \
    -o foo foo.c -lXol -lXt -lX11
```

Support the Motif Style Guide

As long as you're going to the hassle to create a Motif program, you might as well bite the bullet and follow the whole Motif Style Guide. One of the main benefits of Motif is consistency with other Motif applications. To achieve this consistency, you must follow the Style Guide.

SOURCE CODE FOR THE OLIT PROGRAM

In this chapter, we've presented a number of techniques to help you port your OLIT applications to Motif. To help show some of these techniques, we present the following OLIT program and its Motif analog. Notice how similar the two programs look. Except for the utility functions and setting up the main window, the programs are virtually identical.

The code for the OLIT program follows. The Motif program appears after the OLIT program.

```
/* olit.c */
#include <X11/Intrinsic.h>
#include <X11/StringDefs.h>
#include <Xol/OpenLook.h>

#include <Xol/ControlAre.h>
#include <Xol/MenuButton.h>
#include <Xol/OblongButt.h>
#include <Xol/StaticText.h>

Widget CreateMenuChoice(Widget parent_menu,
    char* name,
    XtCallbackProc callback,
    XtPointer client_data)

{   /* CreateMenuChoice */
    Widget      menupane;
    Widget      widget;

    /* We need to get a new parent,
     * from the actual menu.
     */
    XtVaGetValues(parent_menu,
        XtNmenuPane, &menupane,
        NULL);

    /* Create a pushbutton using this new parent. */
    widget = XtVaCreateManagedWidget(name,
            oblongButtonWidgetClass, menupane,
            NULL);

    /* Set up callback. */
    XtAddCallback(widget,
        XtNselect,
        callback,
        client_data);

    return widget;

}   /* CreateMenuChoice */

Widget CreatePulldownMenu(Widget parent,
    char* name)

{   /* CreatePulldownMenu */
    Widget      menu;
```

```
        /* Create pulldown menu. */
        menu = XtVaCreateManagedWidget(name,
                menuButtonWidgetClass,
                parent,
                XtNlabelJustify,   OL_LEFT,
                XtNrecomputeSize, TRUE,
                NULL);

    return menu;

}   /* CreatePulldownMenu */

Widget CreateLabel(Widget parent,
    char* name)

{   /* CreateLabel */
    Widget  label;

    label = XtVaCreateManagedWidget(name,
            staticTextWidgetClass, parent,
            NULL);

    return label;

}   /* CreateLabel */

void SetLabel(Widget widget,
    char* message)

{   /* SetLabel */

    XtVaSetValues(widget,
        XtNstring, message,
        NULL);

}   /* SetLabel */

void exitCB(Widget widget,
    XtPointer client_data,
    XtPointer call_data)

{   /* exitCB */

    exit(0);

}   /* exitCB */

int main(int argc, char** argv)

{   /* main */
    XtAppContext  app_context;
    Display*      display;
    Widget        parent;
    Widget        mainw;
    Widget        menubar;
    Widget        filemenu;
    Widget        exitchoice;
```

```
Widget        label;

/* Initialize X toolkit */
OlToolkitInitialize( (XtPointer) NULL);

parent = XtVaAppInitialize(&app_context,
        "Ppm",
        (XrmOptionDescList) NULL,
        0,
        &argc, argv,
        (String*) NULL,
        NULL);

/* Create main window. */
mainw = XtVaCreateManagedWidget("main",
        controlAreaWidgetClass, parent,
        XtNmappedWhenManaged, True,
        XtNlayoutType, OL_FIXEDCOLS,
        XtNalignCaptions, TRUE,
        NULL);

/* Create "menubar". */
menubar = XtVaCreateManagedWidget("menubar",
        controlAreaWidgetClass, mainw,
        XtNlayoutType, OL_FIXEDROWS,
        XtNalignCaptions, TRUE,
        NULL);

/* Create File menu. */
filemenu = CreatePulldownMenu(menubar, "filemenu");

/* Create menu choice. */
exitchoice = CreateMenuChoice(filemenu, "exit",
            (XtCallbackProc) exitCB,
            (XtPointer) NULL);

/* Create label in main window. */
label = CreateLabel(mainw, "label");

SetLabel(label, "My Label Message");

XtRealizeWidget(parent);
XtAppMainLoop(app_context);
return 0;

}    /* main */

/* end of file olit.c */
```

SOURCE CODE FOR THE MOTIF PROGRAM

Our Motif program mimics the OLIT application. None of this code should
be new. The program follows:

```c
/* motif.c */
#include <Xm/Xm.h>
#include <Xm/CascadeB.h>
#include <Xm/Label.h>
#include <Xm/MainW.h>
#include <Xm/PushB.h>
#include <Xm/RowColumn.h>

    /* Same as pushbutton in Motif. */
Widget CreateMenuChoice(Widget parent_menu,
    char* name,
    XtCallbackProc callback,
    XtPointer client_data)

{   /* CreateMenuChoice */
    Widget      widget;

    widget = XtVaCreateManagedWidget(name,
                xmPushButtonWidgetClass, parent_menu,
                NULL);

    /* Set up callback. */
    XtAddCallback(widget,
        XmNactivateCallback,
        callback,
        client_data);

    return widget;

}   /* CreateMenuChoice */

Widget CreatePulldownMenu(Widget parent,
    char* name)

{   /* CreatePulldownMenu */
    Widget  menu;
    Widget  cascade;
    Arg     args[20];
    int     n;

    /* Engage tear-off menu if supported. */
    n = 0;

#ifdef XmNtearOffModel

    XtSetArg(args[n], XmNtearOffModel,
        XmTEAR_OFF_ENABLED); n++;

#endif  /* XmNtearOffModel */

    menu = XmCreatePulldownMenu(parent,
            name, args, n);

    /* Create cascade button and connect to menu. */
    n = 0;
```

```
        XtSetArg(args[n], XmNsubMenuId, menu); n++;

        cascade = XmCreateCascadeButton(parent,
                    name, args, n);

        XtManageChild(cascade);

        return menu;

}    /* CreatePulldownMenu */

Widget CreateLabel(Widget parent,
    char* name)

{    /* CreateLabel */
    Widget  label;

        label = XtVaCreateManagedWidget(name,
                xmLabelWidgetClass, parent,
                NULL);

        return label;

}    /* CreateLabel */

void SetLabel(Widget widget,
    char* message)

{    /* SetLabel */
    XmString    xmstring;

        xmstring = XmStringCreateSimple(message);

        XtVaSetValues(widget,
            XmNlabelString, xmstring,
            NULL);

        XmStringFree(xmstring);

}    /* SetLabel */

void exitCB(Widget widget,
    XtPointer client_data,
    XtPointer call_data)

{    /* exitCB */

        exit(0);

}    /* exitCB */

int main(int argc, char** argv)

{    /* main */
    XtAppContext  app_context;
```

```
Display*      display;
Widget        parent;
Widget        mainw;
Widget        menubar;
Widget        filemenu;
Widget        exitchoice;
Widget        label;
Arg           args[20];
Cardinal      n;

parent = XtVaAppInitialize(&app_context,
          "Ppm",
          (XrmOptionDescList) NULL,
          0,
          &argc, argv,
          (String*) NULL,
          NULL);

/* Create main window. */
n = 0;
mainw = XmCreateMainWindow(parent,
          "mainw", args, n);

/* Create "menubar". */
n = 0;
menubar = XmCreateMenuBar(mainw,
              "menubar", args, n);

XtManageChild(menubar);

/* Create File menu. */
filemenu = CreatePulldownMenu(menubar, "filemenu");

/* Create menu choice. */
exitchoice = CreateMenuChoice(filemenu, "exit",
              (XtCallbackProc) exitCB,
              (XtPointer) NULL);

/* Create label in main window. */
label = CreateLabel(mainw, "label");

SetLabel(label, "My Label Message");

XmMainWindowSetAreas(mainw,
    menubar,
    (Widget) NULL,    /* command window */
    (Widget) NULL,    /* horiz scroll */
    (Widget) NULL,    /* vert scroll */
    label);           /* work area */

XtManageChild(mainw);

XtRealizeWidget(parent);
XtAppMainLoop(app_context);
return 0;
```

```
}    /* main */

/* end of file motif.c */
```

When you run the OLIT program, you'll see a pull-down menu like the one shown in Figure 29.1.

Figure 29.1 *The OLIT program.*

The Motif program looks quite similar, as you can see by looking at Figure 29.2.

Figure 29.2 *The Motif program.*

Both programs use the following combined resource file:

```
! Resource file for Chapter 29
! of Power Programming Motif.
!
! Generic
*background: grey92
*title:      OLIT to Motif
```

```
*filemenu.mnemonic:      F

! Motif
*exit.labelString:      Exit
*filemenu.labelString: File

! OLIT
*exit.label:      Exit
*filemenu.label: File

! end of resource file
```

Name this file **Ppm** and place it in your home directory.

Is porting between Motif and OLIT all this easy? No, but it's remarkable how similar the toolkits are. The techniques presented in this chapter should help you in your efforts.

For more practical examples in similarities between OLIT and Motif, see our book *Professional Graphics Programming in the X Window System* (Johnson and Reichard, MIS: Press, 1993). This book covers a number of graphics topics with example programs in both OLIT and Motif.

SUMMARY

Porting applications from OLIT to Motif isn't that difficult, but it requires attention to detail. It's a matter of following these steps:

1. Use utility functions; then port the utilities to Motif.

2. Convert widget types in creation functions (use `XtVaCreateManagedWidget` where appropriate).

3. Convert resource names and values.

4. Don't depend on the window manager, *olwm*.

5. Convert all remaining code.

6. Break down and support the Motif Style Guide.

OLIT INTRINSICS FUNCTIONS AND MACROS INTRODUCED IN THIS CHAPTER

```
OlToolkitInitialize
OlUpdateDisplay
```

APPENDIX A

Where to Go From Here

Now that you're ready to conquer the world as the mighty Motif programmer, it's time for us to point out several avenues containing further information: namely, the Open Software Foundation, the X Consortium, and a bibliography of essential books.

THE OPEN SOFTWARE FOUNDATION

The OSF offers a score of services past the core Motif functionality explained in the book. Some of the services include:

- **Software Support.** A Motif support license from the OSF comes in two forms: full service and technology-update service. Full service includes all source code and updates for one year, participation in electronic discussion groups, phone support, and more. Technology-update service includes only source code, updates, and bug reports.

- **Training.** The OSF offers regular training in Motif programming in Santa Clara, Calif., and Tyngsboro, Mass. Contact the OSF for dates and prices.

955

■ **Certification.** The Open Software Foundation certifies applications on three levels:

Level 1: These applications are certified by the OSF to comply with the *OSF/Motif Style Guide.*

Level 2 and Level 3: These applications must pass the OSF/Motif Validation Test Suite and comply with all OSF style guidelines. Level 2 applications are designated as "validated," while Level 3 certification allows the developer to use the trademarked OSF/Motif as part of the product name.

This certification policy will remain in place for the near future. However, in the future certification will be taken over by X/Open, the standards group.

■ **Testing Services.** The OSF offers a Quality Assurance Test Suite for testing Motif applications. This includes automated test driver libraries, which simulate user actions via a scripting language to ensure conformity with the *OSF/Motif Style Guide;* memory-monitoring tests; and a performance measurement.

The Open Software Foundation also offers a number of services unrelated to Motif. For instance, the OSF has released a set of specifications regarding open systems, called Distributed Computing Environment (DCE), which forms part of the COSE specifications. Pursuant to that, the OSF offers training, consultation, and documentation regarding DCE and open systems.

The address is:

Open Software Foundation
11 Cambridge Center
Cambridge, MA 02142
617/621-8700
info@osf.org

THE X WINDOW SYSTEM

To do anything with this book, you'll need Motif as well as the X Window System. X is amazingly easy to acquire: The X Consortium gives it away (charging for the cost of the media, such as tapes) and doesn't require royalty payments on X applications. You don't need to license X, as the philosophy is to make X as widespread a programming tool as possible.

The X Consortium sells X, along with printed manuals and *X Window System: The Complete Reference to Xlib, X Protocol, ICCCM, XLFD*, third edition (also discussed later in this appendix). X is shipped on a set of 1600dpi or QIC-24 tapes in UNIX tar format. Call or write:

> ***X Consortium, Inc.***
> ***One Memorial Drive***
> ***P.O. Box 546***
> ***Cambridge, MA 02142-0004***
> ***617/374-1000***

During the course of this book we've referred to several documents from the X Consortium, such as the *Inter-Client Communications Conventions Manual or Compound Text Encoding*. These documents are included in the X distribution.

You can also pick up the latest X11 release from a number of archive sites on the Internet or via UUCP via USENET. It is generally easier on everyone concerned if you pick up X from the nearest archive site.

There are many, many commercial firms offering X in one form or another; a quick glance through the ads of a UNIX magazine will yield many possibilities.

BOOKS

There are a number of books that will add to your working knowledge of Motif. We've divided them into four categories: Motif books, internationalization books, PEX books, and X Window books.

Motif

Kobara, Shiz, *Visual Design with OSF/Motif*, Addison-Wesley, 1991. This excellent book shows how to create good-looking Motif displays. It doesn't cover programming but instead goes over the various resources that impact each widget's visual look. Kobara describes how to make your Motif application look much better than the defaults. Essentially a book for programmers, it is also useful for interface designers.

Sherlock, Margie, *Using DECwindows Motif for Open VMS*, Margie Sherlock, 1993. This book is a niche product, to be sure, but it is also a good intro to Motif for DEC users.

Young, Douglas A., *Object-Oriented Programming with C++ and OSF/Motif*, Prentice Hall, 1992.

Young, Douglas A., *The X Window System: Programming and Applications with Xt, OSF/Motif edition*, Prentice Hall, 1990.

Internationalization

Digital Equipment Corp., *Digital Guide to Developing International Software*, Digital Press, 1991.

Jones, Scott, *et al.*, *Digital Guide to Developing International User Information*, Digital Press, 1992.

Microsoft Corp., *The GUI Guide: International Terminology for the Windows Interface*, Microsoft Press, 1993. Although technically written for Microsoft Windows 3.x, this book is very useful for translating the File menu and other elements into 14 different European languages. Since the Windows interface closely matches Motif, we found this to be one of the most helpful books to aid translation.

Plauger, P. J. and Jim Brodie, *ANSI and ISO Standard C Programmer's Reference*, Microsoft Press, 1992. This book covers standard C and is useful for locale-related information.

Taylor, Dave, *Global Software*, Springer-Verlag, 1992. This is a very interesting, very informative book on internationalization. It won't give you a lot of code you can use, but it does cover many issues in internationalization.

PEX, PHIGS, and PEXlib

Gaskins, Tom, *PEXlib Programming Manual*, O'Reilly & Associates, 1992.

Gaskins, Tom, *PHIGS Programming Manual*, O'Reilly & Associates, 1992.

Howard, Toby, Terry Hewitt, R.J. Hubbold, and K.M. Wyrwas, *A Practical Introduction to PHIGS and PHIGS PLUS*, Addison-Wesley, 1991.

X Window

Asente, Paul J. and Ralph R. Swick, *X Window System Toolkit*, Digital Press, 1990. This book is the bible of the Xt Intrinsics.

Johnson, Eric F. and Kevin Reichard, *Advanced X Window Applications Programming*, MIS:Press, 1990. Hey, we're biased, OK?

Johnson and Reichard, *Professional Graphics Programming in the X Window System*, MIS:Press, 1993. Thick enough to stun an ox, this tome covers professional-level programming using X, Motif, and Open Look. For many users, this will be the logical successor to the book you're now reading.

Johnson and Reichard, *Using X*, MIS:Press, 1992. This book covers X resources and how to work with, troubleshoot, and conquer the X Window System.

Johnson and Reichard, *X Window Applications Programming*, second edition, MIS:Press, 1992. This book introduces X library programming.

Open Software Foundation, *OSF/Motif Programmer's Reference, Revision 1.2*; *OSF/Motif Style Guide, Revision 1.2*; and *OSF/Motif Programmer's Guide, Revision 1.2*, all Prentice Hall, 1993. These are the official Motif manuals.

Scheifler, Robert W. and James Gettys, with Jim Flowers, Ron Newman, and David Rosenthal, *X Window System: The Complete Reference to Xlib, X Protocol, ICCCM, XLFD*, third edition, Digital Press, 1992. The title says it all.

APPENDIX B

System-Specific Issues

APPLYING SYSTEM-SPECIFIC INFORMATION TO THIS BOOK

Although Motif and the X Window System provide for a lot of portability for your applications, there are still a number of issues to address on various platforms. This appendix discusses some of these issues.

We thought about this appendix for a long time, wondering whether we should document problems that may well be fixed by the time you read this. We decided to include the information anyway, because we realize that many sites are slow to upgrade—with good reason—to the latest versions of vendor operating systems. In this appendix we're very careful about version numbers, so you'll know about a problem that may effect you.

We certainly hope that vendors fix the problems listed here, and indeed many of the problems are solved in the latest vendor releases.

Sun Microsystems Issues

Sun Microsystems uses the brand name OpenWindows to describe their graphical-interface implementation, which is mostly built around the X Window System. Besides X, OpenWindows also adds the Sun NeWS (Network extensible Windowing System) protocol and layers the Open Look interface on top—for now. In future versions, Sun plans to drop NeWS and Open Look in favor of a generic X Window release and Motif.

There are some quirks to the OpenWindows installation that may cause you some problems if you're going after totally portable code. Most of the quirks relate to the location of files.

Location of Files under OpenWindows

While the rest of the world (or most of it anyway) places X files in **/usr/lib/X11** and executables in **/usr/bin/X11**, Sun chose **/usr/openwin/lib** and **/usr/openwin/bin**. Not only is this confusing, but it can cause great problems with interpreting keys pressed on the keyboard.

Motif adds a number of virtual keysyms to the generic X keysym file, normally stored in **/usr/lib/X11/XKeysymDB** (see Chapter 10).

Of course, the **/usr/lib/X11** directory doesn't exist on Suns, which can lead to the all-too-frequent problem of seeing literally thousands of Xt translation manager errors when you run a Motif program on a Sun. The answer is to install the **XKeysymDB** file in the proper location and place the Motif virtual keysym commands in that file. (Installing such a file isn't easy on users. Often these directories require *root* access.)

The location of XKeysymDB is unfortunately compiled into many versions of the low-level X library. If you face this problem (or want to prevent it), you can find out where your applications expect to find XKeysymDB by using the following command:

```
strings your_app | grep XKeysymDB
```

In the above example, *your_app* is the name of the executable program for your application. When you run this command, you'll see something like:

```
/usr/lib/X11/XKeysymDB
```

N O T E

Sun's Solaris 2.1 operating system has many of the Motif keysyms in a **XKeysymDB** file, in **/usr/openwin/lib**.

Compiling and Linking on Suns

Since most X libraries on a Sun are stored in **/usr/openwin/lib**, you'll need to add this to your search path when compiling. Include files are also in **/usr/openwin/include**. So, you can compile and link with the following command:

```
cc -o foo foo.c -I/usr/openwin/include \
    -L/usr/openwin/lib -lXm -lXt -lX11
```

As of Solaris 2.2, Sun systems don't ship with the Motif libraries or include files. The next version of Solaris should, though, as Sun moves to COSE compliance.

Hewlett-Packard Issues

Hewlett-Packard, as we write this, is the number-two workstation vendor after Sun Microsystems. It seems that being in the top requires some form of odd configuration, as HP systems, like Sun systems, show their quirks.

Much to our dismay, for example, when you compile and run a Motif application on an HP system under the Visual User Environment (VUE) interface, you'll notice that your application's widgets, especially the menu bar, seem to act of their own volition. The menu bar's background color changes from your setting to some color that VUE decided is right. VUE also changes the top and bottom shadow colors, to make proper-looking 3D bevels. You can try to set the background resource to another color, to no avail.

HP customized its Motif libraries so that the VUE can enforce its colors under the hood, beyond normal program control. Since VUE forms the basis of the COSE user interface, many non-HP users may soon experience this joy as well.

VUE uses HP's Broadcast Message Server (a technology rejected by COSE in favor of Sun's ToolTalk) to dynamically change application colors. Users can call up VUE's Style Manager and change the current color palette, or "set" in VUE terminology. When users do this, application colors also change, along with the colors of all VUE-compatible applications. It's neat to watch this happen dynamically.

But VUE enforces this color scheme on an application whether the program likes it or not. HP's position is that VUE *is* the interface, so your Motif applications should conform to VUE, and not the other way around. There's precedent for this in that all X applications must conform to the desires of the window manager, as documented in the official rules for well-behaved X applications, the *Inter-Client Communications Conventions Manual*.

In most cases, it really doesn't matter what color is used for your application's menu bar, as most applications allow the user to modify this via X resource files anyway.

The problem arises when you attempt to control exactly which colors your application uses. For example, you may wish to enforce your own conformity between platforms. You may very well want your Sun Motif applications to act exactly like your HP Motif applications. Most workstation users work at multivendor sites. It seems natural for users at such sites to expect similar software to look and act the same on various UNIX platforms, whether the systems come from Sun, HP, IBM, Silicon Graphics, or DEC. Plus, if you write color-intensive applications, such as anything that views image files, complex data, or 3D geometry, you also need to control every color your application uses.

Most color UNIX systems sold today support only 256 simultaneous colors (with 8-bit planes of color). If you have a 24-bit color system, the menu-bar background color isn't as important. But if you have only 256 colors, you need more control over how your application uses colors.

What can you do? The HP documentation is rather coy in this regard. After a lot of digging, we came up with a possible solution, but one to watch out for.

If you set the useColorObj resource to False, this should stop VUE from messing with your application's colors. For example, you can place the following command in your class resource file (we've used a file name of **Ppm** for a class name of "Ppm" throughout this book):

```
*useColorObj:  False
```

Unfortunately, this will cause your program to crash if you run under the HP-UX 8.07 operating system. HP-UX 9.01 solves this problem. You can also get a patch to HP-UX (really it's just an X patch) for 8.07. The patch is PHSS_1657. Contact your HP representative for more information.

Other VUE Extensions

VUE also sets up default resources for fonts, especially for XmText and XmTextField widgets. An example configuration follows:

```
*Font:      -*-prestige-medium-r-normal-*-120-*
*FontList: -*-swiss*742-bold-r-normal-*-120-*

*XmText*FontList: \
 -*-prestige-medium-r-normal-*-120-*
*XmTextField*FontList: \
 -*-prestige-medium-r-normal-*-120-*
```

You can override this, though, with your own font resources.

ANSI C Issues

On older versions of the HP-UX operating system, particularly version 8.07, you'll have a lot of problems using ANSI C with function prototypes and X include files. HP-UX 8.07 doesn't handle the caddr_t data type very well. (Later versions of X replace caddr_t with XtPointer.) The error you'll get is that caddr_t is not defined.

To handle this, we often define our own macro, HPUX_FIX, when we compile under HP-UX 8.07. Before you include any of the Motif include files, insert this code:

```
           /* Bug fix for HP-UX 8.0x. */
#ifdef HPUX_FIX
typedef char*   caddr_t;
#endif  /* HPUX_FIX */

#include <Xm/Xm.h>
```

By now, most users should have upgraded to HP-UX 9.01 or higher. We mention the caddr_t problem just in case you have yet to upgrade. This problem does *not* occur under the 9.01 operating system.

N O T E

Include Files

Hewlett-Packard systems place the X include files in nonstandard locations. For HP-UX 9.01, you'll find the X11 Release 5 include files in

/usr/include/X11R5. The Release 4 include files are located in **/usr/include/X11R4**.

The Motif include files are stored in **/usr/include/Motif1.2** and **/usr/include/Motif1.1**, depending on the version of Motif you're using. You must also link with the proper libraries.

Library Files and Linking

HP's libraries are also found in nonstandard locations. The X libraries can be found in **/usr/lib/X11R5** and **/usr/lib/X11R4**. The Motif libraries have a home in **/usr/lib/Motif1.2** and **/usr/lib/Motif1.1**.

Compiling and Linking on HP Systems

Under HP-UX 9.01, you can compile and link with the following command:

```
cc -I/usr/include/X11R5 -I/usr/include/Motif1.2 \
    -o foo foo.c \
    -L/usr/lib/Motif1.2 -lXm   \
    -L/usr/lib/X11R5 -lXt -lX11
```

Under HP-UX 8.07, you can compile and link with the following command:

```
cc -I/usr/include/X11R4 -I/usr/include/Motif1.1 \
    -o foo foo.c \
    -L/usr/lib/Motif1.1 -lXm   \
    -L/usr/lib/X11R4 -lXt -lX11
```

Issues with 386/486/Pentium Systems

Most 386/486/Pentium systems, particularly Intel-based UNIX systems, require a number of other libraries, usually because networking is considered an option on those systems. SCO OpenDesktop, for example, requires:

```
cc -Di386 -DLAI_TCP -DSYSV -o foo foo.c \
    -lXm -lXt -lX11 -ltlisock -lsocket -lnsl_s
```

Interactive (SunSoft) SVR3.2 requires:

```
cc -o foo foo.c -lXm -lXt -lX11 -lnsl_s
```

APPENDIX C

Motif Application Builders

Beginning programmers assume that an application builder will make their lives simpler—after all, if the application does the dirty work, the programmer is free to do the creative stuff, like design interfaces and eat pizza.

In our experiences, though, the application builder does a lot of the basic work for you, which makes them useful in prototyping situations. However, when it comes to creating well-performing applications, we find that Motif application builders leave a little to be desired. The resulting code is frequently on the sluggish side, and by the time you master the complex application builder, you could have mastered basic Motif programming and more.

Still, many people are intrigued by the notion of application builders, so we present this list. These are commercial application builders that focus on X and Motif development for a number of UNIX workstation platforms. In addition, there are a slew of cross-platform development packages, like XVT, concentrating on code generation for a number of platforms, including DOS, Windows, and the Macintosh.

Builder Xcessory, Integrated Computer Solutions
201 Broadway, Cambridge, MA 02139. 617/621-0060. info@ics.com

ExoCODE, EXOC
7250 Cicero Av., Suite 201, Lincolnwood, IL 60646. 708/676-5555

Teleuse, Telesoft
5959 Cornerstone Court W., San Diego, CA 92121. 619/457-2700.

UIM/X, Visual Edge Software
101 1st St., Suite 443, Los Altos, CA 94022. 415/948-0753.

X-Designer, DataViews
800/732-3200.

INDEX

Obtaining the Example Source Code For This Book

We've put together a companion source-code diskette for *Power Programming Motif*, containing all the example programs in the book. This diskette is an MS-DOS-formatted disk containing the C sources in ASCII files.

All files on the source-code diskette should be straight ASCII files. All examples are in standard ANSI/ISO C, except for Chapter 28, which uses C++. When you transfer these files to a UNIX machine, you'll probably want to convert the file names to lower-case (except for the Makefile). There are no special subdirectories. All files should be in the root directory on the floppy disk—place the files in any directory you like in your user account.

To use the source-code diskette, you will need some way to transfer these files from the DOS-formatted diskette to your X development system. You can look at Kermit, Ethernet FTP, or NFS, or you can read the DOS diskette directly on your UNIX box. (Many UNIX workstations, such as the Sun SPARC-10, come with a disk drive and software that can read DOS-formatted diskettes.)

We tested our code on a number of platforms, as listed in Table D.1.

Table D.1   *Tested platforms.*

Hardware	O.S.	X version	Motif/OLIT version
HP 705	HP-UX 8.07	R4	Motif 1.1
HP 720	HP-UX 9.01	R5	Motif 1.2
IBM R2/6000	AIX 3.2	R4	Motif 1.1
SGI	Irix 4.0.5	R4	Motif 1.1
SGI	Irix 5.1	R5	Motif 1.2
486	ISC SVR3.2 3.0	R4	Motif 1.1
486	ISC SVR3.2 3.0	R5	Motif 1.1
Sun SPARC	Solaris 2.1	R4	Motif 1.1

In this book, we focus on writing portable code, so the example programs should work on most configurations. Many of the examples require Motif 1.2—for example, Chapter 21 on drag and drop—but these instances are clearly marked in the text. Others require certain extensions to X (PEX in Chapter 16) or extra libraries (the Xmu library used in Chapter 15 ships with many—but not all—X platforms), or even an extra compiler, as is the case with Chapter 28 (C++). In the text, we documented a number of problems on the various platforms. Due to configuration differences, you may experience problems on your system.

- -

MIS:PRESS
4375 West 1980 South
Salt Lake City, Utah 84104
(810) 972-2221

MIS:
PRESS

_____
NAME (PLEASE PRINT OR TYPE)

_____
ADDRESS

_____
CITY   STATE   ZIP

Call toll-free
1-800-488-5233 • 1-800-628-9658

Power Programming...Motif
ISBN: 1-55828-323-4   Only $29.95
Add $2.00 for shipping & handling (Foreign $6.00)
Check one:
❑ VISA   ❑ Mastercard
❑ American Express
❑ Check enclosed $ _____

_____
ACCOUNT NO.

_____
EXP. DATE

_____
SIGNATURE

Warning 709: In compatible pointer type assignment
get_text 7. edit [0]).

方法
將 get_text方 捕到 呼叫程式之後
程式